Historical Linguistics

An Introduction

Historical Linguistics

An Introduction

THIRD EDITION

Lyle Campbell

The MIT Press
Cambridge, Massachusetts

© Lyle Campbell, 1998, 2004, 2013

Published in the United States and Canada
by the MIT Press 2013

First edition published 1998
Second edition published 2004
Third edition first published in Great Britain
by Edinburgh University Press 2013

Typeset in Times
by Servis Filmsetting Ltd, Stockport, UK, and
printed and bound in Malta by
Gutenberg Press

Library of Congress Cataloging-in-Publication Data

Campbell, Lyle.
Historical linguistics : an introduction / Lyle Campbell. — Third edition.
   p.   cm
Includes bibliographical references and indexes.
ISBN 978-0-262-51849-9 (pbk. : alk. paper)
1. Historical linguistics. I. Title.
P140.C36   2013
417'.7—dc23   2012038044

10 9 8 7 6 5 4 3 2

Contents

⌐⌐

List of Tables

———

List of Figures and Maps

⌐⌐

Preface

A number of historical linguistics textbooks exist, but this one is different. Most others talk *about* historical linguistics; they may illustrate concepts and describe methods, and perhaps discuss theoretical issues, but they do not focus on how *to do* historical linguistics. A major goal of this book is to present an accessible, hands-on introduction to historical linguistics which does not just talk about the topics, but shows how to apply the procedures, how to think about the issues and, in general, how to do what historical linguists do. To this end, this text contains abundant examples and exercises to which students can apply the principles and procedures in order to learn for themselves how to 'do' historical linguistics. This text differs also by integrating topics now generally considered important to the field but which are often lacking in other historical linguistics textbooks; these include syntactic change, grammaticalization, sociolinguistic contributions to linguistic change, distant genetic relationships (how to show that languages are related), areal linguistics and linguistic prehistory. Also, the range of examples is greater and the number of languages from which examples are presented is much broader. Many examples are selected from the history of English, French, German and Spanish to make the concepts which they illustrate more accessible, since these are languages with which more students have some acquaintance, but examples from many non-Indo-European languages are also presented; these show the depth and richness of the various concepts and methods, and sometimes provide clearer cases than those available in the better-known Indo-European languages. In short, this text differs in its emphasis on accessibility, its 'how-to' orientation, its range of languages and examples, and its inclusion of certain essential but neglected topics.

This book is intended as an introductory textbook for historical linguistics courses, and assumes only that readers will have had an introduction to linguistics. It is hoped that linguists in general and others interested in language-related matters will also find things of interest to them in this book, though it is primarily intended for students of historical linguistics who have little background.

Historical linguistic practice today is linked with theories of general linguistics, particularly with regard to attempts to explain 'why' language changes. In this book, an attempt is made to keep to a minimum the complications for understanding and applying historical linguistics that diverse current theories often occasion. At the same time, however, basic linguistic terminology is employed with little explanation. Readers who have had some prior introduction to linguistics will fare better; in particular, some familiarity with phonetic symbols may be useful. (The symbols of the International Phonetic Alphabet are used in this text; see Chart 1 for a list of these and other symbols utilized in this book.) However, even without getting bogged down in theoretical details, phonetic notation or the mass of general linguistic terms utilized in talking about language, one can understand much of historical linguistics. For more detail on the topics covered here, the references cited throughout the book and the sources given in the general bibliography at the end, which contains references to most of the general works on historical linguistics, can be consulted.

Readers will perhaps notice a recurring struggle in the text. I believe it is important for students to have some sense of the general thinking concerning the various topics discussed, and to this end I occasionally mention how matters are typically presented in other textbooks or how they are generally seen by practicing historical linguists. At the same time, I personally do not necessarily accept everything that is talked about and so feel some obligation to argue for what (I hope) is a better understanding of some topics. In such instances, I have attempted to present a reasonably unbiased account of opposing opinions. It is important for students to understand how historical linguists think and the sorts of arguments and evidence that would be necessary to resolve such issues. Ultimately, most of these involve areas where the differences of opinion can be decided only on the basis of substantive evidence which is not currently available but is hoped for from future research. Seeing the various sides of these issues should provide a basis for students to reach their own conclusions when the evidence becomes available, although it is not appropriate or possible in an introductory text to go into intricate detail concerning controversies and unresolved issues of the field.

A second struggle concerns the question of how to present complex notions. Definition and description without examples is usually not clear, but examples with no prior understanding of the concepts involved are also not clear. So, what should be presented first, contextless definitions or contextless examples? I have chosen to present first the concepts and then the examples to illustrate them. In several cases in the text, it will prove most valuable for clarity's sake to read the definitions, description and discussion, then the examples, and then to reread the general description and discussion – this may be true of anything, but is especially relevant in some contexts here.

Acknowledgements

⌇

I thank Alice C. Harris, Brian Joseph and Roger Lass for extremely helpful comments on a manuscript version of this book, and Raimo Anttila, William Bright, Una Canger, Antony Deverson, Adrienne Lehrer, Heidi Quinn, Seija Tiisala and Sarah Thomason for their help and answers to questions pertaining to specific sections. Special acknowledgement and thanks go to Michael Weiss for the Indo-European section of Chapter 16. I thank the several scholars who answered questions or offered helpful information, comments or corrections which helped in the preparation of this second edition, especially Rich Alderson, Cynthia Allen, Andrew Carstairs-McCarthy, Tony Deverson, Jaan Terje Faarlund, Andrew Garrett, Russell Gray, Verónica Grondona, Laszlo Honti, Jay Jasanoff, Johanna Laakso, Yaron Matras, Elisabeth Norcliffe, Victor Parker, Heidi Quinn, Don Ringe, Malcolm Ross, Tapani Salminen, Pekka Sammallahti, and Brent Vine, among several others. With respect to matters specific to this third edition, I am grateful to Robert Blust, Claire Bowern, Matthias Brenzinger, Mark Donohue, Nicholas Evans, Harald Hammarström, Sharon L. Hargus, Bernd Heine, John Huehnergard, John Justeson, Harold Koch, Terence M. Neary, Timothy J. Pulju, and Marc Zender for helpful comments, information, and corrections, and for answering specific questions. It goes without saying that none of these friends and scholars is responsible for any misuse or disregard of some of their comments and information. (Not all their recommendations could be implemented, due in part to limitations of space, sometimes to competing recommendations they made, and at times to my own difference of opinion.) I am extremely grateful to these scholars for their input. I also thank several students who volunteered their solutions to some of the exercises in the book, Haowen Jiang in particular.

I thank Kevin Cowan, cartographer of the Department of Geography, Australian National University, for making the maps. I am especially grateful to Marc Zender for the figures (illustrations) in Chapter 15 and for the cover illustration, and to Simon J. Greenhill for the figures in Chapter 17.

Also, two basic references have been employed extensively in examples cited in this book. For Indo-European forms, I have relied primarily on Calvert Watkins' *The American Heritage Dictionary of Indo-European Roots* (2000). This has the advantage of being consistent and a readily available basic reference, for comparison. It does not, however, represent the Indo-European laryngeals directly in the main entries. (Mallory and Adams *Encyclopedia of Indo-European* (1997) can be consulted to see the forms with the laryngeals present.) For the history of words in English, I have used the *Oxford English Dictionary* (Oxford University Press, 1991) extensively.

Phonetic Symbols and Conventions

The conventions for presenting examples used in this book are widely utilized in linguistics, but it will be helpful to state the more important of these for readers unfamiliar with them.

Most linguistic examples are given in italics and their glosses (translations into English) are presented in single quotes, for example: Finnish *rengas* 'ring'.

In instances where it is necessary to make the phonetic form clear, the phonetic representation is presented in square brackets ([ ]), for example: [sĩŋ] 'sing'. In instances where it is relevant to specify the phonemic representation, this is given between slashed lines (//), for example: German *Bett* /bɛt/ 'bed'. The convention of angled brackets (< >) is utilized to show that the form is given just as it was written in the original source from which it is cited, for example: German <Bett> 'bed'.

A hyphen (-) is used to show the separation of morphemes in a word, as in *jump-ing* for English *jumping*. Occasionally, a plus sign (+) is used to show a morpheme boundary in a context where it is necessary to show more explicitly the pieces which some example is composed of.

It is standard practice to use an asterisk (*) to represent reconstructed forms, as for example Proto-Indo-European *penkʷe* 'five'.

A convention in this text (not a general one in linguistics) is the use of ✗ to represent ungrammatical or non-occurring forms. Outside of historical linguistics, an asterisk is used to indicate ungrammatical and non-occurring forms; but since in historical linguistic contexts an asterisk signals reconstructed forms, to avoid confusion ✗ is used for ungrammatical or non-occurring forms.

It is standard in historical linguistics to use > to mean 'changed into', for example: *p > b (original p changed into b), and < to mean 'changed from, comes from', for example: b < *p (b comes from original p).

To show an environment where something occurs, the notation of / __ is used, where __ indicates the location of the material that changes, much as in the idea of 'fill in the blank'. Thus, a change in which *p* became *b* between vowels is represented as: p > b / V__V. A change conditioned by something in the context before the segment which changes is represented as, for example, in: k > č / __i (meaning *k* became *č* [IPA [tʃ]] in the environment before *i*). A change conditioned by something in the environment after the segment which changes is represented as, for example, in: k > č / i __ (meaning *k* became *č* in the environment after *i*). The symbol # means 'word boundary', so that /__ # means 'word-finally' and / # __ means 'word-initially'.

To avoid notational (and theoretical) complications, when whole classes of sounds change or when only a single phonetic feature of a sound or class of sounds changes, sometimes just individual phonetic attributes are mentioned, for example: *stops > voiced*, meaning 'all the stop consonants change by becoming voiced'. Distinctive feature notation and other theoretical apparatus are not used in this text, in order to make the examples more accessible to readers who have less background.

Finally, there are traditions of scholarship in the study of different languages and language families which differ significantly from one another with respect to the phonetic notation that they use. For example, vowel length is represented by a 'macron' over the vowel in some (as for example, [ā]), as a colon (or raised dot) after the vowel in others (as [a:]), and as a repetition of the vowel in still others (as [aa]). In this book, for the presentation of some of the examples cited, some of these different notational conventions commonly used for the various languages involved have been kept, though in cases where difficulty of interpretation might result, forms are also given in IPA symbols.

Phonetic Symbols Chart

	Bilabial	Labiodental	Dental	Alveolar	Palato-alveolar	Retroflex	Palatal	Velar	Uvular	Pharyngeal	Glottal
Voiceless stops	p			t		ʈ		k	q		ʔ
Voiced stops	b			d				g	ɢ		
Voiceless affricates				ts	č						
Voiced affricates				dz	ǰ						
Voiceless fricatives	ɸ	f	θ	s	ʃ	ṣ	ç	x	χ	ħ	h
Voiced fricatives	β	v	ð	z	ʒ	ẓ		ɣ	ʁ	ʕ	
Nasals	m			n		ɳ	ɲ	ŋ	N		
Approximants	w			ɹ			j		ʀ		
Laterals				l							

	Front		Central		Back
High					
close (tense)	i	y	ɨ	ʉ	u
open (lax)	ɪ	ʏ			ʊ
Mid					
close (tense)	e	ø	ə		o
open (lax)	ɛ	œ			ɔ
Low	æ		a		ɑ

C^h	aspirated consonant
C̪	dental consonant
C'	glottalized consonant
C^w	labialized consonant
C^j, C^y	palatalized consonant

Phonetic Symbols Chart

V̥, C̥	voiceless sound
tl	voiceless lateral affricate
ɫ	velarized or pharyngealized lateral approximant
l̥	voiceless lateral approximant (sometimes symbolized as ɫ)
ɓ	voiced imploded bilabial stop
ṣ	voiceless apical alveolar fricative
ṣ̌	voiceless laminal retroflex fricative
č̣	voiceless laminal retroflex affricate
ć	voiceless prepalatal affricate (IPA [tɕ])
ç	voiceless prepalatal (alveolo-palatal) fricative
r (or r̃)	voiced alveolar trill
ɾ	voiced alveolar flap (tap)
lʲ, lʸ	voiced palatalized alveolar lateral approximant, palatal "l" (IPA [ʎ])
ḥ	voiceless pharyngeal fricative (used in Arabic sources)
ḍ, ṭ, ṣ	pharyngealized consonants (as in Arabic)
Ç	retroflex consonants as represented in Sanskrit, South Asian and Native American sources
i̯	voiced high front semivowel (second vowel in some diphthongs, not the nucleus of the syllable)
ʍ	voiceless rounded labiovelar approximant (devoiced w)
Ṽ, V̨	nasalized vowel
V:, V̄	long vowel (vowel length)
C:	long consonant (geminate consonant)
ñ, nʲ, nʸ	palatalized alveolar nasal, palatal nasal (IPA [ɲ])
x̣	fronted velar fricative
ṇ	symbol for retroflex nasal used in Sanskrit sources
ń	palato-alveolar nasal (Sanskrit)
ś	voiceless palato-alveolar fricative (used in Sanskrit sources) (IPA [ʃ]); also:
ś	voiceless prepalatal fricative (IPA [ç])
*k̂, *ĝ, *ĝh	'palatal' stops in Indo-European

Note that usually no distinction is made between [a] and [ɑ], and *a* is often used to symbolize both.

1

Introduction

3e [ye] knowe ek [also] that in (the) fourme [form] of speche [speech] is
  chaunge [change],
With-inne [within] a thousand 3eer [years], and wordes tho [then]
That hadden [had] pris [value], now wonder [wonderfully] nyce [stupid] and
  straunge [strange, foreign]
Us thenketh hem [we think them/they seem to us]; and 3et [yet] thei [they]
  spake [spoke] hem [them] so,
And spedde [succeeded] as wel [well] in loue [love] as men now do.

(Geoffrey Chaucer [1340–1400],
Troilus and Criseyde, book II, lines 22–6)

1.1 Introduction

What is historical linguistics? Historical linguists study language change. If you
were to ask practicing historical linguists why they study change in language,
they would give you lots of different reasons, but certainly included in their
answers would be that it is fun, exciting and intellectually engaging, that it
involves some of the hottest topics in linguistics, and that it has important contributions to make to linguistic theory and to the understanding of human nature.
There are many reasons why historical linguists feel this way about their field.
For one, a grasp of the ways in which languages can change provides the student
with a much better understanding of language in general, of how languages work,
how their pieces fit together, and in general what makes them tick. For another,
historical linguistic methods have been looked to for models of rigour and excel-
lence in other fields. Historical linguistic findings have been utilized to solve
historical problems of concern to society which extend far beyond linguistics (see
Chapter 16). Those dedicated to the humanistic study of individual languages
would find their fields much impoverished without the richness provided by
historical insights into the development of these languages – just imagine the
study of any area of non-modern literature in French, German, Italian, Spanish
or other languages without insights into how these languages have changed. A
very important reason why historical linguists study language change and are
excited about their field is because historical linguistics contributes significantly

to other sub-areas of linguistics and to linguistic theory. For example, human cognition and the human capacity for language learning are central research interests in linguistics, and historical linguistics contributes significantly to this goal. As we determine more accurately what can change and what cannot change in a language, and what the permitted versus impossible ways are in which languages can change, we contribute significantly to the understanding of universal grammar, language typology and human cognition in general – fundamental to understanding our very humanity.

More linguists list historical linguistics as one of their areas of specialization (not necessarily their first or primary area of expertise) than any other subfield of linguistics (with the possible exception of sociolinguistics). That is, it is clear that there are many practicing historical linguists, though this may seem to be in contrast to the perception one might get from a look at the lists of required courses in linguistics programmes, from the titles of papers at many professional linguistic conferences, and from the tables of contents of most linguistics journals; nevertheless, historical linguistics is a major, thriving area of linguistics, as well it should be, given the role it has played and continues to play in contributing towards the primary goals of linguistics in general.

1.1.1   What historical linguistics isn't

Let's begin by clearing away some possible misconceptions, by considering a few things that historical linguistics is *not* about, though sometimes some non-linguists think it is. Historical linguistics is not concerned with the *history of linguistics*, though historical linguistics has played an important role in the development of linguistics – being the main kind of linguistics practiced in the nineteenth century – and indeed historical linguistic notions had a monumental impact in the humanities and social sciences, far beyond just linguistics. For example, the development of the comparative method (see Chapter 5) is heralded as one of the major intellectual achievements of the nineteenth century.

Another topic not generally considered to be properly part of historical linguistics is the ultimate *origin of human language* and how it may have evolved from non-human primate call systems, gestures, or whatever, to have the properties we now associate with human languages in general. Many hypotheses abound, but it is very difficult to gain solid footing in this area. Historical linguistic theory and methods are very relevant for research here, and can provide checks and balances in this field where speculation often far exceeds substantive findings, but this is not a primary concern of historical linguistics itself.

Finally, historical linguistics is also not about determining or preserving pure, 'correct' forms of language or attempting to prevent change. The popular attitude towards change in language is resoundingly negative. The changes are often seen as corruption, decay, degeneration, deterioration, as due to laziness or slovenliness, as a threat to education, morality and even to national security. We read laments in letters to newspapers stating that our language is being destroyed, deformed and reduced to an almost unrecognizable remnant of its former and rightful glory. These are of course not new sentiments, but laments like this are found throughout history. For example, even from Jakob and Wilhelm Grimm

(1854: iii), of fairytale fame and founding figures in historical linguistics, we read:

> The farther back in time one can climb, the more beautiful and more perfect he finds the form of language, [while] the closer he comes to its present form, the more painful it is to him to find the power and adroitness of the language in decline and decay.

The complaint has even spawned poetry:

> Coin brassy words at will, debase the coinage;
> We're in an if-you-cannot-lick-them-join age,
> A slovenliness provides its own excuse age,
> Where usage overnight condones misusage,
> Farewell, farewell to my beloved language,
> Once English, now a vile orangutanguage.
> (Ogden Nash, *Laments for a Dying Language*, 1962)

However, change in language is inevitable, and this makes complaints against language change both futile and silly. All languages change all the time (except dead ones). Language change is just a fact of life; it cannot be prevented or avoided. All the worries and fears notwithstanding, life always goes on with no obvious ill-effects in spite of linguistic change. Indeed, the changes going on today which so distress some in our society are exactly the same in kind and character as many past changes about which there was much complaint and worry as they were taking place but the results of which today are considered enriching aspects of the modern language. The beauty (or lack thereof) that comes from linguistic change may be in the eye (better said, in the ear) of the beholder, but language change is not really good or bad; mostly it just is. Since it is always taking place, those who oppose ongoing changes would do their stress-levels well just to make peace with the inevitability of language change. Of course, society can assign negative or positive value to things in language (be they new changing ones or old ones), and this can have an impact on how or whether these things change. This sociolinguistic conditioning of change is an important part of historical linguistics (see Chapters 7 and 13).

1.2 What is Historical Linguistics About?

As already mentioned, historical linguistics deals with language change. Historical linguistics is sometimes called *diachronic* linguistics (from Greek *dia-* 'through' + *chronos* 'time' + *-ic*), since historical linguists are concerned with change in language or languages over time. This is contrasted with *synchronic* linguistics, which deals with a language at a single point in time; for example, linguists may attempt to write a grammar of present-day English as spoken in some particular speech community, and that would be a synchronic grammar. Similarly, a grammar written of Old English intended to represent a single point in time would also be a synchronic grammar. There are various ways to study language *diachronically*. For example, historical linguists may study changes in the history of a single language, for instance the changes from Old English to Modern English, or between Old French and Modern French, to mention just two examples. Modern English is very different from Old English, as is Modern French from Old French. Often the study of the history of a single language is called *philology*, for example English philology, French philology, Hispanic philology and so on. (The term *philology* has several other senses as well; see Chapter 15.)

The historical linguist may also study changes revealed in the comparison of related languages, often called *comparative* linguistics. We say that languages are related to one another when they descend from (are derived from) a single original language, a common ancestor: for example, the modern Romance languages (which include Italian, French, Spanish, Portuguese and others) descend from earlier Latin (see Chapters 5 and 6).

In the past, many had thought that the principal domain of historical linguistics was the study of 'how' languages change, believing that answers to the question of 'why' they change were too inaccessible. However, since the 1960s or so, great strides have been achieved also in understanding 'why' languages change (see Chapter 13). Today, we can say that historical linguistics is dedicated to the study of 'how' and 'why' languages change, both to the methods of investigating linguistic change and to the theories designed to explain these changes.

Some people imagine that historical linguists mostly just study the history of individual words – and many people are fascinated by word histories, as shown by the number of popular books, newspaper columns and radio broadcasts dedicated to the topic, more properly called *etymology* (derived from Greek *etumon* 'true' [neuter form], that is, 'true or original meaning of a word'). The primary goal of historical linguistics is *not* etymologies, but accurate etymology is an important product of historical linguistic work. Let us, for illustration's sake, consider a couple of examples and then see what the real role of etymology in historical linguistics is. Since word histories have a certain glamour about them for many people, let's check out the history of the word *glamour* itself. Surprisingly, it connects with a main concern of modern linguistics, namely *grammar*. (The example of *glamour* is also considered in Hock and Joseph 1996 and by Pinker 1994.)

Glamour is a changed form of the word *grammar*, originally in use in Scots English; it meant 'magic, enchantment, spell', found especially in the phrase 'to cast the glamour over one'. It did not acquire its sense of 'a magical or fictitious beauty or alluring charm' until the mid-1800s. *Grammar* has its own interesting history. It was borrowed from Old French *grammaire*, itself from Latin *grammatica*, ultimately derived from Greek *gramma* 'letter, written mark'. In Classical Latin, *grammatica* meant the methodical study of literature broadly. In the Middle Ages, it came to mean chiefly the study of or knowledge of Latin and hence came also to be synonymous with learning in general, the knowledge peculiar to the learned class. Since this was popularly believed to include also magic and astrology, French *grammaire* came to be used sometimes for the name of these occult 'sciences'. It is in this sense that it survived in *glamour*, and also in English *gramarye*, as well as in French *grimoire* 'conjuring book, unintelligible book or writing'. English *gramarye*, *grammary* means 'grammar, learning in general, occult learning, magic, necromancy', a word revived in literary usage by later writers; it is clearly archaic and related to the cases of vocabulary loss discussed in Chapter 9.

What is of greater concern to historical linguists is not the etymology of these words per se, but the kinds of changes they have undergone and the techniques or methods we have at our disposal to recover this history. Thus, in the history of the words *glamour* and *grammar* we notice various kinds of change: borrowing from Greek to Latin and ultimately from French (a descendant of Latin) to English, shifts in meaning, and the sporadic change in sound (*r* to *l*) in the derived word *glamour*. Changes of this sort are what historical linguistics is about, not just the individual word histories. These kinds of changes that languages can and do undergo and the techniques that have been developed in historical linguistics to recover them are what the chapters of this book are concerned with.

Let's take *goodbye* as a second example. This everyday word has undergone several changes in its history. It began life in the late 1500s as *god be with you* (or *ye*), spelled variously as *god be wy ye*, *god b'uy*, and so on. The first part changed to *good* either on analogy with such other greetings as *good day*, *good morning* and *good night*, or as a euphemistic deformation to avoid the blasphemy of saying *god* (taboo avoidance) – or due to a combination of the two. The various independent words in *god be with you* were amalgamated into one, *goodbye*, and ultimately even this was shortened (clipped) to *bye*.

In large part, then, a word's etymology is the history of the linguistic changes it has undergone. Therefore, when we understand the various kinds of linguistic change dealt with in the chapters of this book, the stuff that etymologies are made of and based on becomes clear. Historical linguists are concerned with all these things broadly and not merely with the history behind individual words. For that reason, etymology is not the primary purpose of historical linguistics, but rather the goal is to understand language change in general; and when we understand this, then etymology, one area of historical linguistics, is a by-product of that understanding. For an explanation of the notions of borrowing, analogy, amalgamation, clipping and sound change mentioned in these examples, see Chapters 2, 3, 4 and 9.

1.3 Kinds of Linguistic Changes: An English Example

As seen in these sample etymologies, there are many kinds of linguistic change. A glance at the chapter titles of this book reveals the major ones. In effect, any aspect of a language's structure can change, and therefore we are concerned with learning to apply accurately the techniques that have been developed for dealing with these kinds of changes, with sound change, grammatical change, semantic change, borrowing, analogy and so on, and with understanding and evaluating the basic assumptions upon which these historical linguistic methods are based.

We can begin to get an appreciation for the various sorts of changes that are possible in language by comparing a small sample from various stages of English. This exercise compares Matthew 26:73 from translations of the Bible at different time periods, starting with the present and working back to Old English.

This particular example was selected in part because it talks about language and in part because in translations of the Bible we have comparable texts from the various time periods which can reveal changes that have taken place:

1. Modern English (*The New English Bible*, 1961):
   Shortly afterwards the bystanders came up and said to Peter, 'Surely you are another of them; your accent gives you away!'
2. Early Modern English (*The King James Bible*, 1611):
   And after a while came vnto him they that stood by, and saide to Peter, Surely thou also art one of them, for thy speech bewrayeth thee.
3. Middle English (*The Wycliff Bible*, fourteenth century):
   And a litil aftir, thei that stooden camen, and seiden to Petir, treuli thou art of hem; for thi speche makith thee knowun.
4. Old English (*The West-Saxon Gospels*, c. 1050):
   þa æfter lytlum fyrste genēalǣton þa ðe þær stodon, cwǣdon to petre. Soðlice þu eart of hym, þyn sprǣc þe gesweotolað.
   [Literally: then after little first approached they that there stood, said to Peter. Truly thou art of them, thy speech thee makes clear.]

In comparing the Modern English with the Early Modern English (1476–1700) versions, we note several kinds of changes. (1) *Lexical*: in Early Modern English *bewrayeth* we have an example of lexical replacement. This word was archaic already in the seventeenth century and has been replaced by other words. It meant 'to malign, speak evil of, to expose (a deception)'. In this context, it means that Peter's way of speaking, his accent, gives him away. (2) *Grammatical* (syntactic and morphological) change: from *came vnto* [unto] *him they* to the Modern English equivalent, *they came to him*, there has been a syntactic change. In earlier times, English, like other Germanic languages, had a rule which essentially inverted the subject and verb when preceded by other material (though this rule was not obligatory in English as it is in German), so that because *and after a while* comes first in the sentence, *they came* is inverted to *came they*. This rule has for the most part been lost in Modern English. Another grammatical change (syntactic and morphological) is seen in the difference between *thou . . . art* and *you are*. Formerly, *thou* was 'you (singular familiar)' and contrasted with *ye/you* 'you (plural or singular formal)', but this distinction was lost. The *-eth* of *bewrayeth* was the 'third person singular' verb agreement suffix; it was replaced in time by *-(e)s* (*giveth* > *gives*). (3) *Sound change*: Early Modern English was not pronounced in exactly the same way as Modern English, but it will be easier to show examples of sound changes in the earlier texts (below). (4) *Borrowing*: the word *accent* in Modern English is a loanword from Old French *accent* 'accent, pronunciation' (see Chapter 3 on borrowing). (5) *Changes in orthography* (spelling conventions): while mostly differences in orthography (spelling conventions) are not of central concern in historical linguistics, we do have to be able to interpret what the texts represent phonetically in order to utilize them successfully (this is part of philology; see Chapter 15). In *vnto* for modern *unto* we see a minor change in orthographic convention. Earlier in many European languages, there was in effect no distinction between the letters *v* and *u* (the Latin alphabet, upon which most European writing systems are based, had no such difference); both could be used to represent either the vowel /u/ or the consonant /v/ or in other cases /w/, though for both /v/ and /u/ usually *v* was used initially (<vnder> 'under') and *u* medially (<haue> 'have'). One could tell whether the vowel or consonant value was intended only in context – a *v* between consonants, for example, would most probably represent /u/. More revealing examples of changes in orthography are seen (below) in the Old English text. In *thou* (formerly pronounced /θu:/) we see the influence of the French scribes – French had a monumental influence on English after the Norman French conquest of England in 1066. The *ou* was the French way of spelling /u/, as in French *nous* /nu/ 'we'; later, English underwent the Great Vowel Shift (a sound change, mentioned below) in which /u:/ became /au/, which explains why words such as *thou*, *house* and *loud* (formerly /θu:/, /hu:s/ and /lu:d/ respectively) no longer have the sound /u:/ that the French orthographic *ou* originally represented.

Examples of kinds of changes seen in the comparison of the Middle English (1066–1476) text with later versions include, among others, (1) *Sound change*: final -*n* was lost by regular sound change under certain conditions, as seen in the comparison of Middle English *stooden, camen* and *seiden* with their modern equivalents *stood, came* and *said*. (2) *Grammatical change* (morphological and syntactic): the forms *stooden, camen* and *seiden* ('stood', 'came' and 'said') each contain the final -*n* which marked agreement with the third person plural subject ('they', spelled *thei*). When final -*n* was lost by sound change, the grammatical change was brought about that verbs no longer had this agreement marker (-*n*) for the plural persons. (3) *Borrowing*: the *hem* is the original third person plural object pronoun, which was replaced by *them*, a borrowing from Scandinavian, which had great influence on English.

Between Old English (c. 450–1066) and Modern English we see many changes. Some of the kinds of change represented in this text include (1) *Lexical change*: there are instances of loss of vocabulary items represented by the words in this short verse, namely *genēalǣton* 'approached', *cwǣdon* 'said' (compare archaic *quoth*), *soðlice* 'truly' (*soothly*, compare *soothsayer* 'one who speaks the truth') and *gesweotolað* 'shows, reveals'. (2) *Sound change*: English has undergone many changes in pronunciation since Old English times. For example, the loss of final -*n* in certain circumstances mentioned above is also illustrated in *þyn* 'thy' (modern 'your') (in *þyn sprǣc* 'thy speech' [modern 'your accent']). A sporadic change is seen in the loss of *r* from *sprǣc* 'speech' (compare German *Sprache* 'language, speech', where the *r* is retained). English vowels underwent a number of changes. One is called the Great Vowel Shift (mentioned above), in which essentially long vowels raised (and long high vowels /i:/ and /u:/ became diphthongs, /ai/ and /au/, respectively). This is seen in the comparison of some of the Old English words with their Modern English equivalents:

soðlice /so:θ-/	soothly /suθ-/ ('soothly, truly')
þu /θu:/	thou /ðau/
þyn /θi:n/	thy /ðai/
þe /θe:/	thee /ði/

(3) *Grammatical*: the change mentioned above, the loss of the subject–verb inversion when other material preceded in the clause, is seen in a comparison

of *genēalǣton þa* 'approached they' with the modern counterpart for 'they approached'. The loss of case endings is seen in *æfter lytlum*, where the *-um* 'dative plural' is lost and no longer required after prepositions such as *after*. The same change which was already mentioned above in the Middle English text is seen again in the loss of the *-n* 'third person plural' verbal agreement marker, in *genēalǣton* '(they) approached', *stodon* '(they) stood' and *cwǣdon* '(they) said'. Another change is the loss of the prefix *ge-* of *genēalǣton* 'approached' and *geswe- otolað* 'shows'. This was reduced in time from [je] to [j] to [i] and finally lost, so that many perfect forms ('has done', 'had done') were no longer distinct from the simple past ('did'); that is, in the case of *sing/sang/have sung*, these remain distinct, but in the case of *bring/ brought/have brought* they are not distinct, though formerly the *have brought* form would have borne the *ge-* prefix, distinguishing it from the *brought* ('past') without the prefix, which is now lost from the language. (4) *Orthographic*: there are many differences in how sounds are represented. Old English *þ* 'thorn' and *ð* 'eth' have been dropped and are spelled today with *th* for both the voiceless (θ) and voiced (ð) dental fricatives. The *æ* (called 'ash', from Old English *æsc*, its name in the runic alphabet) is also no longer used.

The various sorts of changes illustrated in this short text are the subject matter of the chapters of this book.

1.4 Exercises

Exercise 1.1

This exercise is about attitudes towards language change.

1. Try to find letters to newspapers or columns in newspapers or magazines, or on blogs, which express opinions on the quality of English in use today and about changes that are taking place. What do you think they reveal about attitudes towards language change?
2. Ask your friends, family and associates what they think about language today; do they think it is changing, and if so, is it getting better or worse?
3. Find books or articles on 'proper' English (prescriptive grammar); do they reveal any attitude towards changes that are going on in today's language?
4. Consider the many things that schoolteachers or school grammar books warn you against as being 'wrong' or 'bad grammar'. Do any of these involve changes in the language?
5. Compare books on etiquette written recently with some written thirty years ago or more; find the sections which deal with appropriate ways of speaking and use of the language. What changes have taken place in the recommendations made then and now? Do these reveal anything about change in the language or in language use?

Exercise 1.2

Observe the language you hear around you, and think about any changes that are going on now or have taken place in your lifetime. For example, if you are old enough, you might observe that *gay* has changed its basic meaning: today it mostly means 'homosexual' although until recently it did not have this meaning, but rather meant only 'happy, cheerful'. Slang changes at a rather fast rate; what observations might you make about recent slang versus earlier slang? Can you find examples of ongoing change in other areas of the language besides just vocabulary?

Exercise 1.3

Changes in spelling and occasional misspellings have been used to make inferences about changes in pronunciation. This can, of course, be misleading, since spelling conventions are sometimes used for other purposes than just to represent pronunciation. Try to find examples of recent differences in spelling or of misspellings and then try to imagine what they might mean, say, to future linguists looking back trying to determine what changed and when it changed. For example, you might compare the spelling *lite* with *light*, *gonna* with *going to*, *wannabee* with *want to be*, or *alright* and *alot* with *all right* and *a lot* respectively. In particular, variations in spellings can be very revealing; see if you can find examples which may suggest something about language change.

Exercise 1.4

A number of examples from Shakespeare's plays, written in the Early Modern English period, are presented here which illustrate differences from how the same thing would be said today. Think about each example and attempt to state what changes have taken place in the language that would account for the differences you see in the constructions mentioned in the headings, the negatives, auxiliary verbs and so on. For example, in the first one we see: *Saw you the weird sisters?* The Modern English equivalent would be *Did you see the weird sisters?* Had the heading directed your attention to yes–no questions, you would attempt to state what change had taken place, from former *saw you* (with inversion from *you saw*) to the modern version which no longer involves inversion but requires a form of *do* (*did you see*) which was not utilized in Shakespeare's version.

Treatment of negatives:

1. Saw you the weird sisters? . . . Came they not by you? (*Macbeth* IV, i)
2. I love thee not, therefore pursue me not (*A Midsummer Night's Dream* II, 1, 188)
3. I know thee not, old man: fall to thy prayers (*Henry V* V, v)
4. Let not thy mother lose her prayers, Hamlet: I pray thee, stay with us; go not to Wittenberg (*Hamlet* I, ii)
5. But yet you draw not iron (*A Midsummer Night's Dream* II, i, 196)
6. Tempt not too much the hatred of my spirit (*A Midsummer Night's Dream* II, i, 211)
7. And I am sick when I look not on you (*A Midsummer Night's Dream* II, i, 213)
8. I will not budge for no man's pleasure (*Romeo and Juliet* III, i)
9. I cannot weep, nor answer have I none (*Othello* IV, ii)
10. I am not sorry neither (*Othello* V, ii)

Treatment of auxiliary verbs:

1. Macduff is fled to England (*Macbeth* IV, i) = 'has fled'
2. The king himself is rode to view their battle (*Henry V* IV, iii) = 'has ridden'
3. Thou told'st me they were stolen into this wood (*A Midsummer Night's Dream* II, i, 191) = 'had stolen away/hidden'

Treatment of comparatives and superlatives:

1. She comes more nearer earth than she was wont (*Othello* 5, 2)
2. This was the most unkindest cut of all (*Julius Caesar* 3, 2)
3. What worser place can I beg in your love (*A Midsummer Night's Dream* II, i, 208)

Differences in verb agreement inflections (endings on the verbs which agree with the subject):

1. The quality of mercy is not strain'd
   It droppeth as the gentle rain from heaven
   Upon the place beneath: it is twice blessed;
   It blesseth him that gives and him that takes

   (*The Merchant of Venice* IV, i)

2. The one I'll slay, the other slayeth me

   (*A Midsummer Night's Dream* II, i, 190)

3. O, it offends me to the soul to
   Hear a robostious periwig-pated fellow tear
   A passion to tatters

   (*Hamlet* III, i, 9–11)

4. And could of men distinguish, her election
   Hath seal'd thee for herself: for thou hast been
   As one, in suffering all, that suffers nothing

   (*Hamlet* III, i, 68–71)

Exercise 1.5

The following is a sample text of Middle English, from Chaucer c. 1380. It is presented three lines at a time: the first is from Chaucer's text; the second is a word-by-word translation, with some of the relevant grammatical morphemes indicated; the third is a modern translation. Compare these lines and report the main changes you observe in morphology, syntax, semantics and lexical items. (Do not concern yourself with the changes in spelling or pronunciation.)

The Tale of Melibee, Geoffrey Chaucer (c. 1380)

Upon a day bifel that he for his desport is went into the feeldes hym to pleye.
on one day befell that he for his pleasure is gone to the fields him to play.
'One day it happened that for his pleasure he went to the fields to amuse himself.'

[NOTE: *is went* = Modern English 'has gone'; with verbs of motion the auxiliary used was a form of the verb 'to be', where today it is with 'to have']

His wif and eek his doghter hath he laft inwith his hous,
his wife and also his daughter has he left within his house,
'His wife and his daughter also he left inside his house,'
    [NOTE: *wif* = 'wife, woman']

of which the dores wer-en faste y-shette.
of which the doors were-Plural fast Past.Participle-shut
'whose doors were shut fast.'

Thre of his old foos ha-n it espied, and sett-en laddres to the walles of
    his hous,
three of his old foes have-Plural it spied, and set-Plural ladders to the
    walls of his house,
'Three of his old enemies saw this, and set ladders to the walls of his house,'

and by wyndowes ben entred, and betten his wyf,
and by windows had entered, and beaten his wife,
'and entered by the windows, and beat his wife,'
    [NOTE: *ben entred* = 'have entered', a verb of motion taking 'to be'
    as the auxiliary]

and wounded his doghter with fyve mortal woundes in fyve sondry
    places –
and wounded his daughter with five mortal wounds in five sundry
    places –
'and wounded his daughter with five mortal wounds in five different
    places –'

this is to sey-n, in hir feet, in hir handes, in hir erys, in hir nose, and in
    hir mouth, –
this is to say-Infinitive, in her feet, in her hands, in her ears, in her nose,
    and in her mouth, –
'that is to say, in her feet, in her hands, in her ears, in her nose, and in her
    mouth –'

and left-en hir for deed, and went-en awey.
and left-Plural her for dead, and went-Plural away.
'and left her for dead, and went away.'

(Lass 1992: 25–6)

Exercise 1.6

The text in this exercise is a sample of Early Modern English, from William Caxton, *Eneydos* (c. 1491). As in Exercise 1.5, three lines are presented: the first is from Caxton's text; the second is a word-by-word translation, with some of the relevant grammatical morphemes indicated; the third is a more colloquial modern translation. Compare these lines and report the main changes you observe in morphology, syntax, semantics and lexical items. (Again, do not concern yourself with the changes in spelling or pronunciation beyond the most obvious ones.)

And that commyn englysshe that is spoken in one shyre varyeth from a
    nother. In so moche
and that common English that is spoken in one shire varies from another.
    In so much
'And the common English that is spoken in one county varies so much
    from [that spoken in] another. In so much'

that in my days happened that certayn marchauntes were in a ship in
    tamyse
that in my days happened that certain merchants were in a ship in
    Thames
'that in my time it happened that some merchants were in a ship on the
    Thames'

for to haue sayled ouer the see to zelande/ and for lacke of wynde thei
    taryed atte forlond;
for to have sailed over the sea to Zeeland. And for lack of wind they
    tarried at.the coast;
'to sail over the sea to Zeeland. And because there was no wind, they
    stayed at the coast'
    [NOTE: Zeeland = a province in the Netherlands]

and wente to land for to refreshe them And one of theym, named shef-
    felde a mercer
and went to land for to refresh them. And one of them, named Sheffield,
    a mercer,
'and they went on land to refresh themselves. And one of them, named
    Sheffield, a fabric-dealer,'

cam in to an hows and axed [aksed] for mete, and specyally he axyd
    after eggys.
came into a house and asked for meat, and especially he asked after eggs.
'came into a house and asked for food, and specifically he asked for
    "eggs".'

And the goode wyf answerede. that she coude no frenshe.
and the good woman answered that she could no French.
'And the good woman answered that she knew no French.'

And the marchaunt was angry. for he also coude speke no frenshe.
and the merchant was angry, for he also could speak no French,
'And the merchant was angry, because he couldn't speak any French
either.'
[NOTE: *coude* = 'was able to, knew (how to)']

but wolde haue hadde egges/ and she vnderstode hym not/
but would have had eggs; and she understood him not.
'but he wanted to have eggs; and she did not understand him.'
[NOTE: *wolde* = 'wanted', the source of Modern English *would*]

And thenne at laste a nother sayd that he wolde haue eyren/
and then at last an other said that he would have eggs.
'and then finally somebody else said that he wanted to have eggs.'

then the good wyf said that she understod him wel/
then the good woman said that she understood him well.
'Then the good woman said that she understood him well.'

(Source of Caxton's text: Fisher and Bornstein 1974: 186–7)

2

Sound Change

From one point of view the sound shift seems to me to be a barbarous aberration from which other quieter nations refrained, but which has to do with the violent progress and yearning for liberty as found in Germany in the early Middle Ages, and which started the transformation of Europe.

(Jakob Grimm, 1848)

2.1 Introduction

Perhaps the most thoroughly studied area of historical linguistics is sound change. Over time, the sounds of languages tend to change. The study of sound change has yielded very significant results, and important assumptions that underlie historical linguistic methods, especially the comparative method, are based on these findings. An understanding of sound change is truly important for historical linguistics in general, and this needs to be stressed – it plays an extremely important role in the comparative method and hence also in linguistic reconstruction, in internal reconstruction, in detecting loanwords, and in determining whether languages are related to one another. These topics and the methods for dealing with them are the subject of later chapters. This chapter is about how sounds change.

Sound change is a major concern of historical linguistics; it is often the main feature of books on the history of individual languages. Typically, sound changes are classified, often in long lists of many different kinds of sound changes, each with its own traditional name (some with more than one name). To be at home with sound change, it is necessary to know the most frequently used of these names. The most commonly recurring kinds of sound changes in the world's languages are listed and exemplified in this chapter. They are organized in a representative classification of sound changes, but there is nothing special about this particular arrangement, and different textbooks present a variety of other classifications.

2.2 Kinds of Sound Change

Regular sound changes are accorded great amounts of attention in historical linguistics, and rightly so – they are extremely important to the methods and theories about language change. In fact, the most important basic assumption in historical linguistics is that sound change is regular, a fundamental principle with far-reaching implications for the methods that will be considered in later chapters. *Regular* changes recur generally and take place uniformly wherever the phonetic circumstances in which the change happens are encountered. To say that a sound change is regular means that the change takes place whenever the sound or sounds which undergo the change are found in the circumstances or environments that condition the change. For example, original *p* regularly became *b* between vowels in Spanish (p > b/V__V); this means that in this context between vowels, every original *p* became a *b*; it is not the case that some original intervocalic *p*'s became *b* in some words, but became, say, *ʃ* in some other words and *ø* in still other words, in unpredictable ways. If a sound could change in such arbitrary and unpredictable ways, the change would not be regular; but sound change is regular (though as we will see in other chapters, some other kinds of change can also affect sounds, so that the results do not appear regular but are subject to other kinds of explanations).

This is called 'the *regularity principle*' or 'the *Neogrammarian hypothesis*'. The Neogrammarians, beginning in about 1876 in Germany, became extremely influential in general thinking about language change, and about sound change in particular. The Neogrammarians were a group of younger scholars who antagonized the leaders of the field at that time by attacking older thinking and loudly proclaiming their own views. The early Neogrammarians included Karl Brugmann, Berthold Delbrück, August Leskien, Hermann Osthoff, Hermann Paul and others. They were called *Junggrammatiker* 'young grammarians' in German, where *jung-* 'young' had the sense of 'young Turks', originally intended as a humorous nickname for the rebellious circle of young scholars, although they adopted the term as their own name. English *Neogrammarian* is not a very precise translation. Their slogan was: *sound laws suffer no exceptions* (Osthoff and Brugmann 1878). The notion of the 'regularity of the sound laws' became fundamental to the comparative method (see Chapter 5). By 'sound laws' they meant merely 'sound changes', but they referred to them as 'laws' because they linked linguistics with the rigorous sciences which dealt in laws and law-like statements. We will return to the regularity principle in more detail in Chapter 5.

Sound changes are also typically classified according to whether they are *unconditioned* or *conditioned*. To understand these categories, it will be helpful to read the description of them here, then look at the examples, and then reread these definitions again. When a sound change occurs generally and is not dependent on the phonetic context in which it occurs, that is, not dependent on or restricted in any way by neighbouring sounds, it is *unconditioned*. Unconditioned sound changes modify the sound in all contexts in which it occurs, regardless of what other sounds may be found in words containing the changing sound: that is, the change happens irrespective of the phonological context in which the sound that changes may be found. When a change takes place only in certain contexts (when it is dependent upon neighbouring sounds, upon the sound's position within words, or on other aspects of the grammar), it is *conditioned*. Conditioned changes are more restricted and affect only some of the sound's occurrences, those in particular contexts, but not other occurrences which happen to be found in environments outside the restricted situations in which the change takes effect. For example, the Spanish change of *p* to *b* intervocalically (mentioned above) is conditioned; only those *p*'s which are between vowels become *b*, while *p*'s in other positions (for example, at the beginning of words) do not change. On the other hand, most varieties of Latin American Spanish have changed palatalized *l* to *y*, that is, *lʸ* > *y* (IPA *ʎ* > *j*) unconditionally, as for example in *calle* 'street' /kalʸe/ > /kaye/ – every instance of an original *lʸ* has changed to *y* regardless of the context in which the *lʸ* occurred.

The distinction between *phonemic* and *non-phonemic* changes is present in some fashion in most treatments of sound change. It has to do with the recognition of distinct levels of phonological analysis in linguistic theory – the phonetic level and the phonemic level. There is sometimes disagreement about how the second level is to be understood, that is, about how abstract phonemes may be (how different or distant they can be from the phonetic form) and how they are to be represented. Naturally, if there were full agreement in phonological theory about the 'phonemic' level, there would be more of a consensus in historical linguistics on how to talk about the aspects of sound change which relate to it. However, for our purposes, a definitive characterization is not crucial, so long as we recognize that talk about sound change makes reference to two distinct levels. In general, it is helpful to think of phonetics as representing the actually occurring physical sounds, and of phonemes as representing the speakers' knowledge or mental organization of the sounds of their language. A non-phonemic change (also called *allophonic* change) does not alter the total number of phonemes in the language or change one phoneme into another phoneme. Some call the non-phonemic changes *shifts*, referring to the shift in pronunciation (at the phonetic level), with no change in the number of distinctive sounds. A *phonemic* change is defined as one which does affect the inventory of phonemes (the basic sounds that native speakers hold to be distinct) by adding to or deleting from the number of phonemes/basic sounds of the language, or one in which one phoneme changes into another phoneme.

2.3   Non-phonemic (Allophonic) Changes

Non-phonemic changes have not been considered as important as phonemic changes (below), perhaps because they do not change the structural organization of the inventory of sounds.

2.3.1   Non-phonemic unconditioned changes

(1) In varieties of English, *u* > *ʉ* (central rounded vowel), and in some dialects even on to *y*, as in 'shoe' [ʃu] > [ʃʉ], and in some even [ʃy].

(2) Pipil (a Uto-Aztecan language of El Salvador): *o* > *u*. Proto-Nahua, Pipil's immediate ancestor, had the vowel inventory /i, e, a, o/. When Pipil changed *o* to *u*, this did not change the number of distinctive vowels, and therefore it is a non-phonemic change. Since the change affected all instances of *o*, turning them all into *u* regardless of other sounds in the context, it is an unconditioned change.

(3) Guatemalan Spanish: *r* > *š*. The 'trilled' *r* found in most Spanish dialects has become the so-called 'assibilated' *r* (phonetically a voiceless laminal retroflex fricative) in rural Guatemalan Spanish. Since *r* becomes *š* in all contexts, without restrictions which depend upon neighbouring sounds, this is an unconditioned change. In this change, one sound, *š*, is switched for another, for *r*, but the number of distinctive sounds (phonemes) in the language is not changed; therefore, it is a non-phonemic change.

2.3.2 Non-phonemic conditioned changes

(1) Many English dialects have undergone a change in which a vowel is phonetically lengthened before voiced stops, for example, /bɛd/ > [bɛ·d] 'bed'.

(2) Spanish dialects: n > ŋ /__ #. In many dialects of Spanish, final *n* has changed so that it is no longer pronounced as [n], but rather as a velar nasal [ŋ], as in *son* 'they are' [son] > [soŋ], *bien* 'well, very' [bjen] > [bjeŋ]. This is a conditioned change, since *n* did not change in all its occurrences, but only where it was at the end of words. It is non-phonemic, since the change results in no change at the phonemic level. Before the change, the phoneme /n/ had one phonetic form (allophone), [n]; after the change, /n/ came to have two non-contrastive variants (allophones), predictable from context, with [ŋ] word-finally and [n] when not in final position.

2.4 Phonemic Changes

Two principal kinds of phonemic changes are *mergers* and *splits*.

2.4.1 Merger (A, B > B, or A, B > C)

Mergers are changes in which, as the name suggests, two (or more) distinct sounds merge into one, leaving fewer distinct sounds (fewer phonemes) in the phonological inventory than there were before the change.

(1) Most varieties of Latin American Spanish: *ľ* (spelled '*ll*') and *y* merge, *ľ,y* > *y* (IPA *ʎ, j* > *j*; the *ľ* is also often written [ʎ]) in IPA). Spanish used to contrast the two sounds and this contrast is still maintained in some dialects of Spain and in the Andes and adjacent regions of South America; however, in most of Latin America and in many dialects of Peninsular Spanish (as the Spanish of Spain is called), these two sounds have merged into one, to *y* (IPA [j]), as in *calle* /kalʸe/ > /kaye/ 'street' and *llamar* /lʸamar/ > /yamar/ 'to call'. As a consequence, both *halla* 'find' and *haya* 'have (subjunctive)', for example, have merged (/alʸa/ and /aya/ > /aya/), resulting in the two words being homophonous. Another pair is *rallo* /ralʸo/ 'I grate' and *rayo* /rayo/ 'ray', both now homophonous, /rayo/.

(2) Latin American Spanish: θ, ṣ > ṣ. Peninsular Spanish contrasts the two sounds, dental fricative *θ* and apical alveolar fricative *ṣ*, which merged to *ṣ* in Latin American and some Peninsular dialects. For example, *caza* /kaθa/ 'hunt, chase' and *casa* /kaṣa/ 'house' are both /kaṣa/ throughout most of Latin America. This change illustrates the rarer kind of merger where the two original sounds

merge into some third sound which was not formerly present in the language (symbolized above as A, B > C).

(3) Sanskrit: *e, o, a > a* (in most contexts; the *o > a* part is conditioned in some instances) (*e, o > a*; that is, *e* and *o* merging with existing *a*). Some words which illustrate this merger are seen in Table 2.1 where the Sanskrit examples (which have undergone the merger) are compared with Latin cognates (which preserve the original vowel); the original vowel before the Sanskrit change is also seen in the Proto-Indo-European forms listed, from which both the Sanskrit and Latin words derive.

TABLE 2.1: Sanskrit–Latin cognates showing Sanskrit merger of *e, o, a > a*

Sanskrit	Latin	Proto-Indo-European	
ad-	ed-	*ed-	'to eat'
danta	dent-	*dent-	'tooth'
avi-	ovi-	*owi-	'sheep'
dva-	duo	*dwo-	'two'
ajra-	ager	*aĝro-	'field' (compare *acre*)
apa	ab	*apo	'away, from'

(NOTE: the asterisk (*) is used to symbolize forms that are unattested but reconstructed by linguists; see Chapter 5.)

(4) Proto-Indo-European (PIE) *o, *ə, *a > Proto-Germanic *a. Some examples which illustrate this change in Germanic but not in other branches of Indo-European are as follows (only the first syllable is relevant here).

PIE		Greek	Latin	Gothic	OHG	English
*o	*oktố(u)-	oktố	octo	ahtau [axtau]	ahto	'eight'
*ə	*pətḗr (<*ph₂tḗr)	patḗr	pater	fadar	fater	'father'
*a	*aĝro-	agrós	ager	akrs	ackar	'field' (acre)

(5) Proto-Indo-European (PIE) *ō, *ā > Proto-Germanic *ō. For example: PIE *plō-tu- > Proto-Germanic *flōduz 'flowing water, deluge' (Old English *flōd* 'flood'); PIE *bhrāter- > Proto-Germanic *brōðar- 'brother' (Old English *brōðor* 'brother'; compare Sanskrit *bhrā́tar*, Latin *frāter*).

An important *axiom* concerning mergers is: *mergers are irreversible*. This means that when sounds have completely merged, a subsequent change, say some generations later, will not be able to restore the original distinctions. Thus, for example, in the Sanskrit case in paragraph (3) above, after the merger, children would learn all the words in Table 2.1 with the vowel *a*, and there would be no basis left in the language for determining which of these words with *a* may have originally had *e* or which had *o* that became *a*, or which had retained original *a* unchanged. A language learner arriving upon the scene long after the merger was completed would find no evidence in these words which would permit him or her successfully to change the vowel back to *e* where it had once been an *e* in *danta* 'tooth', and not to *e* but rather back to *o* in *dva-* 'two'.

Occasionally we encounter examples of what at first might appear to be instances of reversal of merger, but these never turn out to be real instances of the reversal of a merger in the same dialect or in the speech of all the speakers of the language or variety involved. An example which illustrates this is the merger of /v/ and /w/ in dialects of southern England, especially in Cockney, East Anglia, and the southeast, with examples such as *walley* for *valley*, *willage* for *village*, also with cases of hypercorrection (see Chapter 4) such as *voif* for *wife* – Sam Weller in Charles Dickens' *Pickwick Papers* calls himself *Veller*. This merger disappeared towards the end of the nineteenth century. It was stigmatized in local speech, where both merged and non-merged pronunciations persisted as variants determined by sociolinguistic factors. The greater prestige of the non-merged pronunciations in the broader speech community – where the merger did not take place – won out, making it appear that the merger was reversed, when in fact no complete merger had taken place so no reversal took place. Rather, the merger was simply lost with the adoption of the more prestigious non-merged pronunciation that had always been extant in the speech community and which characterized the more prestigious dialect from which it was borrowed. (Cf. Ihalainen 1994: 227.) Other cases of seeming reversal of mergers include the merger of /ɔr/ (as in *cord, born*) and /ar/ (as in *card, barn*) in St Louis, Missouri, and the merger of /ir/ (as in *fear*) and /ɛr/ (as in *fair*) in Charleston, South Carolina (Labov 2010: 123–30). Seeming reversal of these mergers did not involve completely merged sounds in the particular phonological systems in question being split into two distinct sounds which previously existed in that system. Rather, these seeming reversals involved situations where some speakers in the community still maintained the contrast or where forms with the contrast were borrowed from a different system which was more prestigious and had not undergone the merger, or where whole dialects were replaced by other dialects. There are no known cases of seeming reversals of merger in languages where the merger was completed and no tokens of the non-merged forms were heard anywhere in the environment. As Labov (2010: 138) says, 'the reversal of the *card/cord* merger is part and parcel of the general replacement of the traditional St. Louis dialect by an approximation of the Northern Cities Shift of the Inland North . . . Similarly, the reversal of the *fear/fair* merger is an integral component of the replacement of the traditional Charleston dialect by the regional Southeastern pattern.'

2.4.2   Split (A > B, C)

To comprehend splits, we need to understand another axiom: *splits follow mergers*. That is, in splits, the sounds in question do not themselves change in any physical way, but phonetically they stay as they were; rather it is the merger of other sounds in their environment which causes the phonemic status of the sounds involved in the splits to change from being predictable conditioned variants of sounds (allophonic) to unpredictable, contrastive, distinctive sounds (phonemic). This is illustrated well by the history of 'umlaut' in English.

(1) Split in English connected with umlaut. 'Umlaut' is a kind of sound change in which a back vowel is fronted when followed by a front vowel (or *j*) (usually in the next syllable). Umlaut initially created front-vowel allophones of back vowels, which became phonemic when the front vowel of the umlaut environment was lost. Note that for the purposes of splits and mergers, loss is considered to be merger with 'zero'. We'll trace this in stages to see the developments and the split as a consequence of the merger.

STAGE 1 (Proto-Germanic), just phonemic /u/ and /o/, each with only one form (allophone):

mūs- 'mouse', *mūs-iz* 'mice'; *fōt-* 'foot', *fōt-iz* 'feet'

STAGE 2 (umlaut), /u/ and /o/ develop allophones, [ȳ] and [ø̄], respectively, when followed by /i, j/ in the next syllable:

mūs-i > mȳsi 'mice'; *fōt-i > fø̄ti* 'feet'; *mūs* 'mouse', *fōt* 'foot'

STAGE 3 (loss of final *i*):

mȳsi > mȳs 'mice'; *fø̄ti > fø̄t* 'feet'; *mūs* 'mouse', *fōt-* 'foot'

At this stage, since the final *-i* which had conditioned the variants (allophones) was no longer present, but had been lost (merged with 'zero'), the result was that *ū* contrasted with *ȳ* and *ō* contrasted with *ø̄*, all four now as distinct phonemes. At this stage, we see the split as a consequence of the merger, but let's complete the story. Next, the front rounded vowels lost their rounding (*ȳ > ī*; *ø̄ > ē*), an unconditioned change in which the rounded front vowels merged with their unrounded counterparts: *mȳs > mīs* 'mice'; *fø̄t > fēt* 'feet'. Finally, these underwent the Great Vowel Shift, in which long vowels raised (for example, *ē > ī*) and long high vowels diphthongized (for example, *ī > ai*), with Modern English as a result: *mīs > /*mais/ 'mice' and *fēt > /*fit/ 'feet'. This series of changes is shown graphically in Table 2.2, where // represents the phonemic status of these forms, and [ ] shows the phonetic status.

TABLE 2.2: Historical derivation of 'mouse', 'mice', 'foot', 'feet'

	mouse	*mice*	*foot*	*feet*
Stage 1 (no changes)	/mu:s/	/mu:s-i/	/fo:t/	/fo:t-i/
	[mu:s]	[mu:s-i]	[fo:t]	[fo:t-i]
Umlaut	/mu:s/	/mu:s-i/	/fo:t/	/fo:t-i/
	[mu:s]	[my:s-i]	[fo:t]	[fø̄:t-i]
Loss of *-i* (= split after merger)	/mu:s/	/my:s/	/fo:t/	/fø̄:t/
	[mu:s]	[my:s]	[fo:t]	[fø̄:t]
Unrounding	/mu:s/	/mi:s/	/fo:t/	/fe:t/
	[mu:s]	[mi:s]	[fo:t]	[fe:t]
Great Vowel Shift	/maus/	/mais/	/fu:t/	/fi:t/

(2) Palatalization in Russian. In Old Russian, palatalization of consonants was predictable (allophonic), conditioned by a following front vowel, as in *krovĭ* [krovʲĭ] 'blood' in comparison with *krovŭ* [krovŭ] 'shelter'. Later, however, the short/lax final vowels ĭ and ŭ were lost (ĭ, ŭ > Ø / __#), a merger with Ø ('zero'). So, ĭ and ŭ merged with Ø ('zero'), leaving /vʲ/ and /v/ in contrast and therefore as distinct phonemes, as shown by new minimal pairs such as *krovʲ* 'blood' and *krov* 'shelter' which come about as a result of the merger with Ø (actually loss) of the final vowels, one of which (the front one) had originally conditioned the allophonic palatalization so that the palatalized and non-palatalized versions of the sound were merely variants of a single basic sound (that is, they were allophones of the same phoneme). Thus, in this example, *vʲ* and *v* split as a result of the merger with Ø which affected these final vowels.

(3) English /n/ had the predictable (allophonic) variant [ŋ] which occurred only before *k* and *g*. Later, final *g* was lost in these forms (g > Ø / ŋ__#); that is, final *g* merged with Ø in this context, leaving /n/ and /ŋ/ in contrast, since now both nasals came to occur at the end of words where formerly the *ŋ* had depended on the presence of the following *g* which is no longer there, as in /sɪn/ 'sin' and /sɪŋ/ 'sing' (from earlier [sɪŋg] before the *g* was lost). Thus /n/ split into /n/ and /ŋ/ when the merger of another sound (*g* with Ø in this case) left the two in contrast.

(4) Split and merger in Nahuatl. The axiom that splits follow mergers is illustrated well by a merger in Nahuatl that caused the split which resulted in /ʃ/ contrasting phonemically with /s/. In Nahuatl (Uto-Aztecan family), *s* originally had two variants (allophones), [ʃ] before *i* and [s] everywhere else, as in:

Phonemic:	/sima/ 'to shave'	/sɨma/ 'to prepare plant leaves for extracting fibres'
Phonetic:	[ʃima]	[sɨma]

Then Nahuatl underwent the merger, *i, ɨ > i* (that is, *ɨ > i*, resulting in former *ɨ* being merged with *i*): *sɨma* > [sima] 'to prepare leaves . . .' ([ʃima] 'to shave' remained [ʃima]). However, as a result of the merger of *ɨ* and *i*, the *s* and *ʃ* split into separate phonemes, since the different conditioning sounds in their environment (*i* and *ɨ*) which had originally made them predictable variants (allophones) of the single original phoneme /s/, were no longer distinguished (both now *i*), and hence they could no longer serve as the basis for determining when the phoneme /s/ would be pronounced [ʃ] (formerly before *i*) and where it would be [s] (before former *ɨ*). This left these consonants in contrast, thus changing their status from that of variants (allophones) of one distinctive sound (one phoneme, /s/) to being distinctive, contrastive sounds (separate phonemes, /s/ and /ʃ/):

/ʃima/ 'to shave'	/sima/ 'to prepare plant leaves for extracting fibres'

In the case of the split, the two sounds, *ʃ* and *s*, did not themselves change at all (phonetically); they were both present before the change and are still present in the same phonetic form after the change; however, they now contrast with one another and can serve to distinguish words of different meaning, and so their phonemic status has changed; they have, as a result of the merger, now split into separate phonemes.

Actually historical linguists often distinguish two kinds of splits. The examples discussed so far illustrate what is know as *secondary split* (sometimes also called *phonologization*). In secondary splits, the total number of phonemes in the language increases – new phonological contrasts in the language are produced. As seen in the examples above, in this kind of split the environment for understanding the formerly non-contrastive distribution of the sounds (former allophones) changes in such a way that the complementary distribution of the sounds is no longer visible after the mergers which cause the secondary splits, but was visible in an earlier stage of the language, before the merger took place.

The other kind of split is known as *primary split* (also sometimes called *conditioned merger*, which is actually a more representative name, given what happens in this kind of change). Primary splits are often considered more complex and thus more difficult to understand than secondary splits, though the idea is reasonably simple: some variant (allophone) of a sound (a phoneme) abandons that original phoneme and joins some other phoneme instead, leaving a gap in the environments in the language where the phoneme can occur. That is, it could originally occur in certain contexts in which after the change it is no longer found. In this type of split, a variant of a phoneme (an allophone) merges with some other already existing phoneme, but only in certain specific environments. In such changes, the number of phonemes in the language remains unaltered. One of the most cited examples of primary split is rhotacism in Latin (see 2.7.4 below). In rhotacism, intervocalic *s* changes to *r* (*s > r* /V_V), illustrated in such English loans from Latin as *rural* (< *rūs-al*, having undergone rhotacism) but *rustic* (Latin *rūs-ticus*, with no rhotacism, since the *s* of *rūs-* is not intervocalic here), based on the Latin root *rūs* 'country, countryside'. Some other instances of English loans from Latin which illustrate the *r/s* alternation of Latin resulting from rhotacism between vowels are: *opus/opera* (Latin *opus* 'work'), *onus/onerous* (Latin *onus* 'burden'), *corpus/corpora/corporal/corporeal* (Latin *corpus* 'body'), and the less obvious *pus/purulent* (Latin *pūs* 'pus'). Since Latin already had *r* as a distinct phoneme, and since only some instances of *s* (just those intervocalic ones) shifted to *r* and thus join the already existing *r* phoneme of Latin, this is an instance of primary split. Primary splits can be illustrated as in the following diagram:

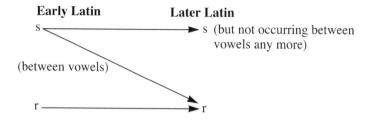

Early Latin   **Later Latin**

s ——————————————→ s (but not occurring between
                                           vowels any more)

(between vowels)

r ——————————————→ r

Another example illustrating primary split is seen in the change of Latin *k* to French *s*, *ʃ* and *k* in different contexts: *k > s* before *i, e* (*centum* [kentum] > *cent* [sã] 'hundred'); *k > ʃ* before *a* (*cantāre* [kanta:re] > *chanter* [ʃãte] 'to sing'); and *k* remaining *k* in other contexts (*clārus* [kla:rus] > *claire* [klɛ:ʀ] 'clear', *cor*

[kor] > *coeur* [kœ:ʀ] 'heart'). For example, since *s* already existed as a distinct phoneme, the transfer of some instances of original *k* to *s* (but not others) represents a primary split (conditioned merger).

2.4.3 Unconditioned phonemic changes

We have already seen several examples which fit this category; for example the merger of Spanish palatalized *l* (/lʸ/) and *y* to *y* (IPA /lʲ/, /j/ > /j/) in most of Latin America was unconditioned – it happened in every environment in the language – and it resulted in fewer contrasting phonemes in the language. In South Island Māori, *ŋ* > *k* (that is, *ŋ*, *k* > *k*); that is, *ŋ* became *k* everywhere, with no limits on where, and the merger of *ŋ* with former *k* resulted in fewer contrastive sounds. Examples of this sort are quite common in languages of the world.

2.4.4 Conditioned phonemic changes

Examples are also abundant of changes in which a sound's phonemic status changes but only in certain circumstances. For example, the well-known 'ruki' rule of Sanskrit is a conditioned change in which original *s* becomes retroflex *ṣ* after the sounds *r*, *u*, *k*, and *i* or *y* (IPA *j*) (s > ṣ / i, y, u, k, r__), for example *agni-* 'fire' + *-su* 'locative plural' > *agniṣu* 'among the fires'; *vāk* 'word' + *-su* > *vākṣu* 'among the words'. There is a version of this rule also in Avestan and Lithuanian in which *s* > *ʃ* and in Old Church Slavonic in which *s* > *x* in contexts similar to that of the Sanskrit rule.

2.5 Sporadic Changes

Sound changes are also sometimes classified according to whether they are *regular* or *sporadic*. *Sporadic* changes affect only one or a few words, and do not apply generally throughout the language; that is, a change is considered sporadic if we cannot predict which words in a language it will affect. A couple of examples of sporadic changes were seen in Chapter 1: Modern English *speech* has lost the *r* of Old English *spræc* 'language, speech', but *r* is not generally lost in this context, as shown by the fact that *spring*, *sprig*, *spree* and so on retain the *r*. *Glamour* comes from *grammar* through the sporadic change of *r* to *l*, but this change is not found regularly in other words; *graft*, *grain*, *grasp* and so forth did not change their *r* to *l*. Sporadic changes are rare and usually not considered very significant.

2.6 General Kinds of Sound Changes

Ultimately, the two distinctions, conditioned/unconditioned and phonemic/non-phonemic, while generally present in the treatments of sound change, are often ignored in discussions of specific sound changes. If a change takes place in all environments, then it is clearly unconditioned whether this is pointed out directly or not; similarly, changes which are limited to particular phonetic contexts are obviously conditioned changes. As for phonemic versus non-phonemic changes, in a great many actual sound changes, it is possible to talk about how one sound changes into another without concern for the phonemic status of the sounds in question, or better said, the resulting phonemic status is often clear even if not pointed out specifically. On the other hand, virtually all treatments present a classification (often just a list) of the kinds of sound changes most often encountered in the languages of the world. These are defined and exemplified in what follows, with some indication of which ones are more important and which terms are used less commonly. Historical linguists often do not bother with the more recondite of these.

2.6.1 Assimilation

Assimilation means that one sound becomes more similar to another, a change in a sound brought about by the influence of a neighbouring, usually adjacent, sound. Assimilatory changes are very common, the most frequent and most important category of sound changes. Assimilatory changes are classified in terms of the three intersecting dichotomies *total–partial*, *contact–distant* and *regressive–progressive*. A change is *total* assimilation if a sound becomes identical to another by taking on all of its phonetic features. The change is *partial* if the assimilating sound acquires some traits of another, but does not become fully identical to it. A *regressive* (*anticipatory*) change is one in which the sound that undergoes the change comes earlier in the word (nearer the beginning, more to the left) than the sound which causes or conditions the assimilation. *Progressive* changes affect sounds which come later in the word than (closer to the end, more to the right of) the conditioning environment. These three parameters of classification interact with one another to give the following combinations of named changes.

2.6.1.1 *Total contact regressive assimilation*

(1) Latin *octo* > Italian *otto* 'eight', *noctem* > *notte* 'night', *factum* > *fatto* 'done'. The *k* (spelled *c*) is before/to the left of the *t* which conditions it to change; thus the change is *regressive*. The *k* is immediately adjacent to the *t*, meaning that this is a *contact* change. And, the *k* assumes all the features of the conditioning *t*, becoming itself a *t*, meaning that the assimilation is *total*. In *septem* > *sette* 'seven', *aptum* > *atto* 'apt, fit for', we see the same sort of assimilation but with *p*.

(2) Latin *somnus* > Italian *sonno* 'sleep, dream'.

(3) In Caribbean dialects of Spanish, preconsonantal *s* typically becomes *h*, which frequently assimilates totally to the following consonant (in casual speech): *hasta* /asta/ > [ahta] > [atta] 'until'; *mismo* > [mihmo] > [mimmo] 'same'.

(4) Swedish *ŋk* > *kk*: **drinka* > *drikka* 'to drink' (compare English *drink*), **tanka* > *takka* 'to thank' (compare English *thank*) (where the spelling *nk* represents [ŋk]) (Wessén 1969:39).

2.6.1.2 *Total contact progressive assimilation*

(1) Proto-Indo-European **kolnis* > Latin *collis* 'hill'. The *n* is after/to the right of the *l* which conditions the change; thus the change is *progressive*. The

n is immediately adjacent to the *l*, thus a *contact* change. The *n* takes on all the features of *l* which conditions the change, a *total* assimilation. The same change is seen in Proto-Germanic **hulnis* (from Proto-Indo-European **kolnis*) > Old English *hyll* > Modern English *hill* 'hill', Old English *myln* > Modern English *mill* 'mill' (ultimately a loan in English from Vulgar Latin *mulina* 'mill'; compare French *moulin* and Spanish *molina* 'mill').

(2) In Finnish, earlier *ln* assimilated to *ll*, as in **falna* > *halla* 'frost'.

2.6.1.3 *Partial contact regressive assimilation*

(1) Proto-Indo-European **swep-no-* > Latin *somnus* 'sleep'. This change is *partial* because *p* only takes on some of the features of the conditioning *n*, namely, it becomes more like the *n* by taking on its feature of nasality, becoming *m*. Because the *p* is next to the *n*, this is a *contact* change; it is regressive because the *p* is before the *n* which conditions the change.

(2) In Spanish (in the non-careful pronunciations of most dialects), *s* > *z* / __voiced C, as in: *mismo* > [mizmo] 'same', *desde* > [dezde] 'since'.

(3) The assimilation of nasals in point of articulation to that of following stops, extremely frequent in the world's languages, is illustrated in English by the changes in the morpheme /in-/ 'not', as in *in-possible* > *im*possible; *in-tolerant* > *in*tolerant; *in-compatible* > *iŋ*compatible (in the last case, the change of *n* to *ŋ* is optional for many speakers).

2.6.1.4 *Partial contact progressive assimilation*

(1) The English suffixes spelled -*ed* formerly had a vowel, but after the change which eliminated the vowel, the *d* very often came to be adjacent to a preceding consonant, and it became voiceless if that preceding consonant was voiceless (and a non-alveolar stop), as in /wɔkt/ 'walked', /træpt/ 'trapped' (d > t / voiceless C__).

(2) English suffixes spelled with -*s* also assimilated, becoming voiced after a preceding voiced (non-sibilant) consonant, as in /dɔgz/ 'dogs', /rɪbz/ 'ribs'.

2.6.1.5 *Distant (non-adjacent) assimilation*

Assimilation at a distance (non-adjacent or non-contact) is not nearly as common as contact assimilation, though some changes having to do with vowels or consonants in the next syllable are quite common. Distant assimilations can be partial or total, and regressive or progressive. These are illustrated in the following examples.

(1) Proto-Indo-European **penkʷe* >Latin *kʷinkʷe* (spelled *quinque*) 'five' (*total distant regressive assimilation*); Proto-Indo-European **pekʷ-* > Italic **kʷekʷ-* 'to cook, ripen' (compare Latin /kokʷ-/ in *coquere* 'to cook').

(2) Proto-Indo-European **penkʷe* >pre-Germanic **penpe* 'five' (compare German *fünf*) (*total distant progressive assimilation*)

(3) Umlaut (see the example above illustrating phonemic split in English) is a well-known kind of change which involves distant assimilation in which a vowel is fronted under the influence of a following front vowel (or a *j*), usually in the

next syllable. Umlaut has been particularly important in the history of Germanic languages.

2.6.2 Dissimilation

Dissimilation, the opposite of assimilation, is change in which sounds become less similar to one another. Assimilation is far more common than dissimilation; assimilation is usually regular, general throughout the language, though sometimes it can be sporadic. Dissimilation is much rarer and is usually not regular (is sporadic), though dissimilation can be regular. Dissimilation often happens at a distance (is non-adjacent), though contact dissimilations are not uncommon. The following examples illustrate these various sorts of dissimilatory changes.

(1) English dialects dissimilate the sequence of two nasals in the word *chimney > chim(b)ley*.

(2) Instances of multiple occurrences of *r* within a word are often sporadically dissimilated in Romance languages; for example, sequences of /r...r/ often become /l...r/, sometimes /r...l/: Latin *peregrīnus* 'foreigner, alien' > Italian *pellegrino* 'foreigner, pilgrim, traveller'; French *pèlerin* (compare Spanish *peregrino* which retained the two *r*'s; English *pilgrim* is a loanword from Old French *pelegrin*); Latin *arbor* > Spanish *árbol* 'tree'. This is distant progressive dissimilation. In a more regular dissimilation involving these sounds, the Latin ending *-al* dissimilated to *-ar* when attached to a root ending in *l*; this is illustrated in the following Latin loans in English, *alveolar, velar, uvular*, which have dissimilated due to the preceding *l*; these can be contrasted with forms in which *-al* remains unchanged because there is no preceding *l*, for example, *labial, dental, palatal*. Some examples from Spanish which illustrate this suffix (though with a different meaning) in both its original and dissimilated form are: *pinal* 'pine grove' (based on *pino* 'pine'), *encinal* 'oak grove' (compare *encino* 'oak'), but *frijolar* 'bean patch' (compare *frijol* 'bean'), *tular* 'stand of reeds' (see *tule* 'reed, cattail'), *chilar* 'chile patch' (based on *chile* 'chili pepper').

(3) *Grassmann's Law*, a famous sound change in Indo-European linguistics, is a case of regular dissimilation in Greek and Sanskrit where in roots with two aspirated stops the first dissimilates to an unaspirated stop. These are voiced aspirated stops in Sanskrit and voiceless aspirated stops in Greek:

Sanskrit *bhabhūva > babhūva* 'became' (reduplication of root *bhū-*)
Greek *phéphūka > péphūka* 'converted' (reduplication of *phŭ-* 'to engender').

Frequently cited Greek examples which show Grassmann's Law in action are:

trikh-ós 'hair'(genitive singular) / *thrík-s* (nominative singular)
tréph-ō 'I rear (nourish, cause to grow)' / *thrép-s-ō* 'I will rear'
trekh-ō 'I walk'/ *threk-s-ō* 'I will walk'

Greek *trikhós* 'hair' (genitive singular) comes from earlier **thrikh-ós*, to which Grassmann's Law has applied to dissimilate the *th* because of the following aspirated *kh* (**th...kh > t...kh*); similarly, *tréphō* 'I rear' is from **thréph-ō*, where *th . . . ph > t . . . ph*. In *thríks* 'hair (nominative singular)', from **thrikh-s*, the *kh* lost its aspiration before the immediately following *s* (the nominative singular ending) (**khs > ks*), and thus Grassmann's Law did not apply in this form. This left initial *th* still aspirated, since there was no longer a sequence of two aspirates in the same root which would cause the first to dissimilate and lose its aspiration. Similarly, in *thrépsō* 'I will rear' (from **thréph-s-ō*) **phs > ps*, and with no second aspirated consonant (no longer a *ph* but now only *p*), the *th* remained aspirated in this word. These changes are seen more clearly in Table 2.3 (nom = nominative, gen = genitive, sg = singular).

TABLE 2.3: Grassmann's Law and its interaction with other Greek changes

	'hair' nom sg	'hair' gen sg	'I will rear'	'I rear'
Pre-Greek	*thrikh-s	*thrikh-os	*threph-s-ō	*threph-ō
deaspiration before *s*	thriks	—	threpsō	—
Grassmann's Law	—	trikhos	—	trephō
Greek forms	thriks	trikhos	threpsō	trephō

Most of the examples presented so far have been cases of distant dissimilations; some additional examples of contact and distant dissimilation are as follows.

(4) Finnish k > h/__ t, d, as in, for example, /tek-dæ/ > *tehdæ* 'to do' (spelled *tehdä*) (compare *teke-e* 'he/she does'); /kakte-na/ > *kahtena* 'as two' (compare *kaksi* 'two') from /kakte-/ to which other changes applied, e > i/__# (*kakte* > *kakti*) and t > s/__i (*kakti* > *kaksi*); since as a result of these changes the *k* no longer appeared before a *t* or *d* in *kaksi*, it remained *k* and so it did not change to *h* (as it did, for example, in *kahtena* 'as two', where it did change to *h*). This is a regular change; all *kt* and *kd* clusters in native words changed to *ht* and *hd* respectively.

(5) In K'iche' (Mayan), the velar stops (*k*, *k'*) were palatalized when the next consonant after an intervening non-round vowel was a uvular (*q*, *q'*, *χ*): *kaq* > *kʲaq* 'red'; *iʃk'aq* > *iʃkʲ'aq* 'fingernail, claw'; *k'aq* > *kʲ'aq* 'flea'; *ke:χ* > *kʲe:χ* 'horse'. The difference between a velar and a uvular stop in the same word is difficult both to produce and to perceive, and for this reason words with *k(')Vq(')* have palatalized the velar (*k*, *k'*) in order to make them more distinguishable from the uvular (*q*, *q'*) in these words. This is a regular change (Campbell 1977).

(6) In the history of Finnish, an /a/ before an /i/ of a following morpheme in non-initial syllables regularly changed to /o/ or /e/, depending on the nature of the vowel in the preceding syllable. If the preceding vowel was non-round, /a + i/ became /oi/, and if it was round, /a + i/ became /ei/, thus dissimilating by taking the opposite value of rounding from that of the vowel of the preceding syllable, as in:

sadoilla 'by hundreds' (< *sata* 'hundred' +*i* 'plural' +*lla* 'by')
sodeissa 'in the wars' (< *sota* 'war' +*i* 'plural' +*ssa* 'in') (later, in
    a further change, the *ei*, as in *sodeissa*, monophthongized to give
    modern Finnish *sodissa*).

(7) Dahl's Law is a sound change which took place in a number of East African Bantu languages in which two voiceless consonants in a word dissimilate so that the first becomes voiced. For example, in Kikuyu the change affects only /k/, as in: *gikuyu* 'Kikuyu' < *kikuyu*; *githaka* 'bush' < **kithaka*; *gukua* 'die' < **kukua* (Newman 2000: 268). The change is commonly stated as involving the dissimilation of aspiration, where the first aspirated stop in adjacent syllables loses its aspiration and becomes voiced, as in Nyamwezi: *-kʰatʰi* 'in the middle' > *gatʰi*, *-pʰitʰ-* 'to pass' > *-bitʰa*, etc. (Mutaka 2000: 253; see also Collinge 1985: 280).

While several of the examples just presented involve dissimilation in regular sound changes, sporadic dissimilations are more frequent on the whole. Another example of sporadic dissimilation is:

(8) In Old French *livel* (from which English borrowed *level*), the sequence of two *l*'s dissimilated, giving *nivel*, which became Modern French *niveau* 'level' through subsequent sound changes which affected the final *l*.

2.7   Kinds of Common Sound Changes

The following is a list of the names for various kinds of sound changes that are used in the literature on language change. In parentheses after each name is a visual representation based on nonsense forms which shows what happens in the change. A number of real examples of each kind of change is presented.

2.7.1   Deletions

2.7.1.1   Syncope (atata > atta)

The loss (deletion) of a vowel from the interior of a word (not initially or finally) is called *syncope* (from Greek *sunkopé* 'a cutting away', *sun-* 'with' + *kopé* 'cut, beat'); such deleted vowels are said to be 'syncopated'. Syncope is a frequently used term.

(1) The change in many varieties of English which omits the medial vowel of words such as *fam(i)ly* and *mem(o)ry* illustrates syncope.

(2) Starting in Vulgar Latin and continuing in the Western Romance languages, the unstressed vowels other than *a* were lost in the interior of words three syllables long or longer, as in *pópulu-* 'people' (*pópulu-* > *poplV-*), reflected by French *peuple* 'people' and Spanish *pueblo* 'people, town' (English *people* is borrowed from French); *fābulare* 'to talk' became *hablar* 'to speak' in Spanish (*fābulare* > *fablar(e)* > *hablar* /ablar/).

While syncope is normally reserved for loss of vowels, some people sometimes speak of 'syncopated' consonants. It is more common in the case of consonants just to speak of *loss* or *deletion*.

(3) For an example of 'syncopation' of consonants, in Swedish (and Scandinavian languages generally), in consonant clusters with three consonants, the middle consonant was lost, as in *norðman* > *norman* (seen, for example, in *Normandy*, and *Norman French*, for the area of northern France where Vikings settled); **norðr-vegi* > **norwegi* (which gives English *Norway*, German *Norwegen*), which went on in Swedish to *Noregi* > *Norge* [norjɛ] 'Norway, Norwegian'; *Västby* 'a town name' [*Väst* 'west' +*by* 'town'] > *Väsby* (Wessén 1969: 68).

2.7.1.2 Apocope *(tata > tat)*

Apocope (from Greek *apokopé* 'a cutting off', *apo-* 'away' + *kopé* 'cut, beat') refers to the loss (apocopation, deletion) of a sound, usually a vowel, at the end of a word, said to be 'apocopated'. Apocope is a frequently used term.

(1) In words which had final *e* in Latin, this *e* was regularly deleted in Spanish in the environment VC__# if the consonant was a dental (*l, r, n, s, θ*) or *y* [j], as in *pane > pan* 'bread', *sōle > sol* 'sun', *sūdāre > sudar* 'to sweat'.

(2) A comparison of the following Old English nouns with their modern counterparts shows the apocope of the final vowels in these words:

Old English	Modern English
sticca	stick
sunu	son
mōna	moon

(3) Estonian (a Finno-Ugric language) lost final vowels in words where this vowel was preceded either by a long vowel and a single consonant or by two consonants:

*jalka > jalg [jalk] 'foot, leg'
*härkä [hærkæ] > härg [hærk] 'bull'
*hooli > hool 'care, worry'
*leemi > leem 'broth'

However, the vowel was not lost when preceded by a short vowel and a single consonant, as in *kala > kala* 'fish', *lumi > lumi* 'snow'.

2.7.1.3 Aphaeresis (or apheresis) *(atata > tata)*

Aphaeresis (from Greek *aphairesis* 'a taking away') refers to changes which delete the initial sound (usually a vowel) of a word. Aphaeresis can be regular or sporadic. The sporadic change where the initial vowel which was present in Latin *apotēca* 'storehouse, wine-store' is lost in Spanish *bodega* 'wine cellar, storeroom, warehouse' illustrates aphaeresis. (In this instance, intervocalic -*p*- > -*b*- in Spanish, but initial *p*- remains *p*-; the *b* of *bodega* shows that the initial *a*- was still present when *p* > *b* and was deleted after this change, *apotēka > abodega > bodega*.) Spanish dialects show many cases of sporadic aphaeresis: *caso < acaso* 'perhaps, by chance'; *piscopal < episcopal* 'episcopal', 'of the bishop'; *ahora > hora* 'now' (especially frequent in *horita < ahorita* 'right now'). The Sapaliga dialect of Tulu (Dravidian) provides an example of regular aphaeresis, where the loss can be seen in comparison with the Shivalli dialect, which has not lost the original vowel. (Here, <c> = [č], IPA [tʃ]; the consonants with dots under them are retroflexed, according to the convention in the Indian linguistic tradition: <ḍ> = IPA [ɖ], <ḷ> = IPA [ɭ]):

Sapaliga Tulu	Shivalli Tulu	
ḍakki	aḍakki	'throw'
lappu	aḷappu	'plough'

Sapaliga Tulu	*Shivalli Tulu*	
laṭṭi	eḷaṭṭi	'tender'
laccilɨ	oḷaccilɨ	'stumble'
daṭṭɨ	eḍaṭṭɨ	'left'

(Bhat 2001: 66)

Aphaeresis is a rarely used term; many prefer just to speak of initial vowel loss.

2.7.2 Epentheses or insertions (asta > asata)

Epenthesis inserts a sound into a word. (*Epenthesis* is from Greek *epi-*'in addition' + *en* 'in' + *thesis* 'placing'.) In sound change, sounds can be inserted in several different ways; several of these have their own names and are considered in the sections that follow, though it is common to refer to them all simply as kinds of epenthesis or insertions.

2.7.2.1 Prothesis (tata > atata)

Prothesis (from Greek *pro-* 'before' + *thesis* 'placing') is a kind of epenthesis in which a sound is inserted at the beginning of a word. This is not a particularly frequent term, and such changes are also referred to as word-initial epentheses.

(1) Starting in the second century, Latin words beginning with *s* + Stop (*sp, st, sk*) took on a prothetic short *i*. The following examples trace the development to modern French and Spanish. The prothetic *i* became *e*, and later in French the *s* was lost when it occurred before other consonants. (a) Latin *scola* [skóla] 'school' > *iskola* > *eskola* > Old French *escole* [eskole] > Modern French *école* [ekol]; for Spanish: *scola* [skóla] > *iskola* > *escuela* [eskuéla]. (b) Latin *scūtum* [skū́tum] 'shield' > *iskutu* > *eskutu* > Old French *escu* > Modern French *écu* [eky] 'shield, money'; the sequence in Spanish was from Latin *scūtum* [skū́tum] > *iskutu* > *eskutu* > *escudo* 'shield'. (c) Latin *stabula* [stábula] 'stable' > *istabula* > *estabula* > Old French *estable* > Modern French *étable* [etábl]; for Spanish: *stabula* [stábula] > *istabula* > *estabula* > Spanish *estable* 'stable'.

(2) In Nahuatl, forms which came to have initial consonant clusters, due to the loss of a vowel in the first syllable, later changed to take on an epenthetic (prothetic) *i*: **kasi* > *kʃi* > *ikʃi* 'foot' (compare *no-kʃi* 'my foot', where no epenthetic *i* occurs because there is no word-initial consonant cluster).

2.7.2.2 Anaptyxis (anaptyctic) (VCCV > VCV̆CV)

Anaptyxis (from Greek *ana-ptussō* 'unfold, open up, expand') is a kind of epenthesis in which an extra vowel is inserted between two consonants (also called a *'parasitic'* vowel or *'svarabhakti'* vowel). This term is used very infrequently, since epenthesis covers this sort of change.

(1) Examples of sporadic anaptyxis are the pronunciation in some dialects of English of *athlete* as ['æθəlit] with the extra vowel and of *film* as ['fɪləm]; in varieties of Spanish, Standard Spanish *Inglaterra* 'England' > *Ingalaterra*, *crónica* 'chronicle' > *corónica*. In the process of borrowing German *Landsknecht* 'mercenary', French inserted an anaptyctic vowel, *lan-*

squenet (from which English borrowed its less well-known *lansquenet* 'mercenary soldier', 'a card game').

(2) In Finnish dialects of eastern Finland, after the first syllable (which bears the stress), a short copy of the preceding vowel is added regularly between consonants of a consonant cluster which begins with *l* or *r*. (The *ä* of Finnish spelling represents [æ].) For example:

Eastern dialects	Standard	Finnish
nelejä	neljä	'four'
kolome	kolme	'three'
pilikku	pilkku	'comma, dot'
jalaka	jalka	'foot, leg'
kylymä	kylmä	'cold'
silimä	silmä	'eye'

(Kettunen 1930: 120; Kettunen 1969: map 199)

2.7.2.3 *Excrescence (amra > ambra; anra > andra; ansa > antsa)*

Excrescence (from Latin *ex* 'out' + *crēscentia* 'growth') is a type of epenthesis which refers to a consonant being inserted between other consonants; usually the change results in phonetic sequences which are somewhat easier to pronounce than the original clusters would be without the excrescent consonant.

(1) Old English *θy:mel* > Modern English *thimble* (compare *humble/ humility*); Old English *θunrian* > Modern English *thunder* (compare the German cognate *Donner* 'thunder'). The example of *chimney* > *chimbley* in English dialects was already mentioned above.

(2) Proto-Indo-European **n̥-m̥r̥t-os* > Greek *ambrotos* 'immortal' (seen in English in *ambrosia* 'food of the gods' (what makes you immortal), a loan with its origin ultimately in Greek).

(3) Spanish *hombre* [ombre] 'man' is from Latin *hominem*, which became *homne* through regular sound changes (syncope, *hominem* > *homne(m)*), then *homre* through dissimilation of the adjacent nasals (*mn* > *mr*), and then *b* was inserted – an example of excrescence – to make the transition from *m* to *r* easier to pronounce ([omre] > [ombre]). Contrast French *homme* 'man', which shows a different history, where at the *homne* stage, the *n* assimilated to the preceding *m* (*homne* > *homme*). Latin *fēmina* 'woman' became *femna* through syncope of the middle vowel; Old French assimilated the *n* to the adjacent *m*, ultimately giving *femme* 'woman'; Spanish, however, dissimilated the two nasals (*femna* > *femra*), and this then underwent excrescence, inserting a *b* between the *m* and *r*, giving modern Spanish *hembra* /embra/ 'female' (in Spanish, *f-* > *h-* > *Ø*, though *h* remains in the orthography). Another example is Latin *nomina⁻re* 'to name' > *nomnar* > *nomrar* > *nombrar* in Spanish; French assimilated *mn* to *mm* in this word, giving *nommer* 'to name'. In a similar example: Latin *numerus* 'number' > Old French *numere* > *numbre*, borrowed into English as *number*.

(4) French *chambre* 'room' comes from Latin *camera* 'arched roof'; when the *mr* cluster was created because of the regular syncope of the medial *e* (*camera*

> *camra*) the *b* was added between the two (this is the source of the loanword *chamber* in English, from French *chambre* 'room').

(5) Greek *andros* 'man (genitive singular)' comes from earlier *anr-os* (compare Greek *anēr* 'man (nominative singular)').

2.7.2.4 Paragoge (tat > tata)

Paragoge (from Greek *paragōgé* 'a leading past') adds a sound (usually a vowel) to the end of a word.

(1) Dialects of Spanish sometimes add a final *-e* (sporadically) to some words that end in *-d*: *huéspede* < *huésped* 'guest'; *rede* < *red* 'net'.

(2) Arandic languages (a branch of Pama-Nyungan, in Australia) regularly added a final *ə* at the end of words that end in a consonant (Ø > ə / C __#), as in **nuŋkarn* > *ŋkwərnə* 'bone' (Koch 1997: 281–2). This is a rarely used term; examples of this kind of change are rare, and many linguists are quite hostile to the use of this term. It is probably best not to have to be bothered with it, since mention of the insertion of a final vowel covers the examples.

2.7.3 Compensatory lengthening (tast > taːt)

In changes of compensatory lengthening, something is lost and another segment, usually a vowel, is lengthened, as the name implies, to compensate for the loss.

(1) In the history of English, a nasal was lost before a fricative with the simultaneous compensatory lengthening of the preceding vowel, as in the following from Proto-Germanic to English: **tonθ* > *tōθ* (> Modern English /tuθ/) 'tooth'; **fimf* > *fīf* (> Modern English /faiv/) 'five'; **gans* > *gōs* (> Modern English /gus/) 'goose' (compare the German cognates, which retain the *n*: *Zahn* [tsaːn] 'tooth', *fünf* 'five' and *Gans* 'goose').

(2) An often-cited example is that of the compensatory lengthening which took place in the transition from Proto-Celtic to Old Irish, as in:

Proto-Celtic	Old Irish	
*magl	maːl	'prince'
*kenetl	ceneːl	'kindred', 'gender'
*etn	eːn	'bird'
*datl	daːl	'assembly'
(Arlotto 1972: 89)		

(3) Old Norse compensatorily lengthened vowels together with the loss of *n* before *s* or *r* (n > Ø / __s, r), as in Proto-Scandinavian **gans* > *gōs* 'goose', **ons* > *ōs* 'us', **þunra-* 'thunder' > *þōr* 'thunder, Thor' (the latter is the name of the Scandinavian god *Thor* and the source of *Thursday*, literally 'Thor's day'; compare English *thunder* and German *Donner* 'thunder', cognates of these Scandinavian forms). (Compare Wessén 1969: 48.)

(4) Middle Indo-Aryan sequences of vowel-nasal-consonant changed to a long nasalized vowel-consonant (VNC > Ṽ:C) in modern Indo-Aryan language, as seen in the following examples:

Middle-Indo-Aryan	Hindi	Bengali	Gujarati	
kampa-	kã:p-	kã:p-	kã:p-	'tongue'
gaṇṭhi	gã:ṭh	gã:ṭh	gã:ṭh	'knot'
bandha	bã:dh	bã:dh	bã:dh	'bond, dam'
sañjha	sã:jh	sã:jh	sã:jh	'twilight'

(Masica 1991: 188)

2.7.4 Rhotacism (VsV > VrV)

Rhotacism (from Greek *rhotakismos* 'use of *r*') refers to a change in which *s* (or *z*) becomes *r*; usually this takes place between vowels or glides; some assume that often cases of rhotacism go through an intermediate stage of -s- > -z- > -r-, where *s* is first voiced and then turned into *r*. The best-known examples of rhotacism come from Latin and Germanic languages.

(1) In the oldest Latin, *s* > *r* / V__V, as seen in *honōr-is* 'honour (genitive singular)' and *honōr-i* 'honour (dative singular)'; *honōs* 'honour (nominative singular)' retains *s*, since it is not between vowels in this form. (In later Latin, *honōs* 'nominative singular' became *honor*, due to analogy with the other forms which contain the intervocalic *r* due to rhotacism; see Chapter 4.)

(2) In West Germanic and North Germanic, *z* > *r*: Proto-Germanic *hauzjan* 'hear' > Old High German *hôren* (Modern German *hören*), Old English *hieran* (Modern English *hear*); contrast the Gothic cognate *hausjan* 'hear' which did not undergo the change (Gothic is East Ger-manic). Proto-Germanic *maizōn* 'greater' (from Proto-Indo-European *mē-is*, comparative of *mē-* 'big') underwent rhotacism to become Old English *māra* 'greater', modern English *more*. (*Most* is from Old English *mæst*, Germanic *maista-* 'most', from Proto-Indo-European *mē-isto-*, the superlative of 'big'.)

While changes involving rhotacism are rare, the term is a frequent one in linguistic textbooks, due no doubt to the examples of rhotacism known from Latin and Germanic.

2.7.5 Metathesis (asta > atsa; asata > atasa)

Metathesis (from Greek *metathesis* 'transposition, change of sides') is the transposition of sounds; it is a change in which sounds exchange positions with one another within a word. Most instances of metathesis are sporadic changes, but metathesis can also be a regular change.

(1) Sporadic examples of metathesis occur in the history of English: Old English *brid* > Modern English *bird*; Old English *hros* > *horse* (rV > Vr).

(2) Spanish has sporadic cases of *l/r* metathesis, as in *palabra* 'word' < Latin *parabola* 'explanatory illustration, comparison' (r . . . l > l . . . r).

(3) Spanish has undergone a reasonably regular change of metathesis in which sequences of *dl*, which were created by vowel loss, shifted to *ld*, as in *tilde* 'tilde, tittle' (the 'swung dash' on *ñ*) < Latin *titulus* 'label, title' (through a series of regular changes: *titulus* > *tidulo* > *tidlo* > *tildo* [metathesis *dl* > *ld*] > *tilde*); *molde* 'mould, pattern' < Latin *modulus* 'small measure' (*modulus* >

modlo > moldo > molde) (Cf. English 'module', borrowing from the same Latin source.)

(4) Some examples of sporadic metatheses in various Spanish dialects are: *probe < pobre* 'poor'; *sequina < esquina* 'corner'; *naide < nadie* 'nobody'; *Grabiel < Gabriel* 'Gabriel'.

2.7.6 Haplology (tatasa >tasa)

Haplology (from Greek *haplo-* 'simple, single') is the name given to the change in which a repeated sequence of sounds is simplified to a single occurrence. For example, if the word *haplology* were to undergo haplology (were to be haplologized), it would reduce the sequence *lolo* to *lo*, *haplology > haplogy*. Some real examples are:

(1) Some varieties of English reduce *library* to 'libry' [laibri] and *probably* to 'probly' [prɔbli].

(2) *pacifism < pacificism* (contrast this with *mysticism < mysticism*, where the repeated sequence is not reduced and does not end up as *mystism*).

(3) English *humbly* was *humblely* in Chaucer's time, pronounced with three syllables, but has been reduced to two syllables (only one *l*) in modern standard English.

(4) Modern German *Zauberin* 'sorceress, female magician' *< Zaubererin* (*Zauber* 'magic, enchantment, charm' + *-er* 'one who does' (like *-er* in English) + *-in* 'female agent' (like *-ess* in English).

2.7.7 Breaking

Breaking refers to the diphthongization of a short vowel in particular contexts. While changes which diphthongize vowels are common (see below), the term 'breaking' is most commonly encountered in Germanic linguistics, used for example in discussions of the history of Afrikaans, English, Frisian and Scandinavian.

(1) For example, Old English underwent the breaking of **i > io*, **e > eo*, **a > ea* before *l* or *r* followed by a consonant, or before *h*, as in **kald- > ceald* 'cold', **erθe > eorþe* 'earth', **næh > nēah* 'near', **sæh > seah* 'saw' (compare Beekes 1995: 275; Hogg 1992: 102–3). (The history of breaking in English is very complex and the phonetic interpretation is disputed; the spelling <ea> probably represented [æa].)

(2) Old Norse *e > ea* (then later *> ia*) before *a* of the next syllable, which is then syncopated, as in **heldaz > hialdr* 'battle', and *e > eo > io > iɔ* before *u* of the next syllable (which also later underwent syncope), as in **erþu > iɔrþ* 'earth' (Beekes 1995: 67).

2.7.8 Other frequent sound changes

There are several other kinds of sound change which are frequently found in discussions of the history of various languages, even though they are usually not included in typical lists of kinds of sound changes. Some of the most common of these follow, described in less detail and with fewer examples. This is by no means an exhaustive listing.

2.7.8.1 Final-devoicing

A very common change is the devoicing of stops or obstruents word-finally; some languages devoice sonorants (*l*, *r*, *w*, *j*, nasals) and some devoice final vowels. In some languages, the devoicing takes place both word-finally and syllable-finally (as in German). In Kaqchikel (Mayan), l, r, w, y > voiceless / __ #. The sonorants *l*, *r*, *w*, *y* (*y* = IPA [j]) underwent the sound change in which they became voiceless at the end of words, for example, *a:l* 'child' [a:l] > [a:l̥], *kar* 'fish' [kar] > [kar̥], *kow* 'hard' [kow] > [kow̥], *xa:y* 'house' [xa:j] > [xa:j̥].

2.7.8.2 Intervocalic voicing (and voicing generally)

It is also very common for various sounds to become voiced between vowels. This affects just stops in some languages, fricatives in others, all obstruents in others. Often the voicing is not just between vowels, but also occurs with the glides *w* and *j*. Many languages also voice stops (some also voice other consonants) after nasals or after any voiced sound; some also voice other sounds when they come before voiced sounds. For example, in the transition from Latin to Spanish (and this includes other Western Romance languages as well), the voiceless stops become voiced between vowels, as illustrated in *lupu* > *lobo* 'wolf' (*p* > *b*), *vīta* > *vida* 'life' (*t* > *d*) and *fīcu* > *higo* 'fig' (*k* > *g*).

2.7.8.3 Nasal assimilation

It is extremely common for nasals to change to agree with the point of articulation of following stops (in some languages with any following consonant): *np* > *mp*, *mt* > *nt*, *nk* > *ŋk*, and so on.

2.7.8.4 Palatalization

Palatalization often takes place before or after *i* and *j* or before other front vowels, depending on the language, although unconditioned palatalization can also take place. Two common kinds of changes are called 'palatalization'. One is the typical change of a velar or alveolar sound to a palato-alveolar sound, as in *k* > *č*, *t* > *č*, *s* > *ʃ* and so on. For example, in colloquial English, sequences of *t* + *y* [j] > *č* [tʃ] and *d* + *y* [j] > *ǰ* [dʒ], as in examples such as *"whatcha doin'"* ['what are you doing?'], *"I betcha"* ['I bet you'], *"didja go"* ['did you go?'], seen also in English varieties where *ty* [tj] word-internal sequences have changed to *č* [tʃ], as in *nature, picture, literature, lecture, fortune*, and *dy* [dj] sequences changed to *ǰ* [dʒ], in *module, grandeur*. English has undergone many changes involving palatalizations throughout its history. For example, Old English *cinn* [kɪn:] > *"chin"* [čɪn] ([tʃɪn]) illustrates the palatalization of *k* before front unrounded vowels (compare the German cognate *Kinn* 'chin, jaw'). In another example, in the history of Spanish the sequence *kt* became *it* (where *i* was the second element of a diphthong), and then the *t* further became palatalized because of the *i*, producing *č*, as in *lakte* > *laite* > *leite* > *leiče* > *leče* 'milk' (spelled *leche*) and *okto* > *oito* > *oičo* > *očo* 'eight' (spelled *ocho*). In a second kind of change called palatalization, a consonant becomes palatalized by taking palatalization as a secondary manner of articulation, as in eastern dialects of Finnish, where consonants are palatalized before *i, susi > sus^j i (sus^j)* 'wolf', *tuli > tul^j i (tul^j)* 'fire'. Slavic languages are well known for a number of palatalization changes. Changes of the first sort of palatalization not conditioned by front vowels are not uncommon. For example, the change of *k > č* spread among several languages of the Northwest Coast linguistic area (see Chapter 12); in Cholan as well as in a few other Mayan languages, **k > č* in general.

2.7.8.5 Diphthongization

Diphthongization refers to any change in which an original single vowel changes into a sequence of two vowel segments which together occupy the nucleus of a single syllable. For example, earlier (in the discussion of splits) we saw the change in English in which original long high vowels /ī/ and /ū/ became /ai/ and /au/ respectively, in /mīs/ > /mais/ 'mice' and /mūs/ > /maus/ 'mouse' (a part of the Great Vowel Shift; see section 2.9, below). In Spanish, the Proto-Romance vowels **ɛ* and **ɔ* diphthongized to *ie* and *ue* respectively when in stressed position, as in **pɛtra > piedra* 'stone', **bɔno > bueno* 'good'. In French, by the ninth century, e > ei, and o > ou. These later changed further; ou > eu > ø (dolor > dolour > doleur > dolør <doleur> 'pain'); ei > oi > oe > we > wa (me > mei > moi > moe > mwe > mwa <moi> 'me', lei > [lwa] <loi> 'law', rei > [rwa] <roi> 'king') (Darmsteter 1922: 96–7, 142–3). The *ī* and *ū* of Middle High German became *ai* and *au* respectively in Modern German, as in *īs > Eis* /ais/ 'ice' and *hūs > Haus* /haus/ 'house'. In Finnish, original long mid vowels diphthongized by raising the first portion of the vowel: *e: > ie* (long vowels in Finnish are spelled orthographically with a double vowel, *tee > tie* 'road'); *o: > uo* (*too > tuo* 'bring'); *ø: > yø* (*tøø > tyø* [spelled *työ*] 'work'). *Breaking* (above) is a kind of diphthongization.

2.7.8.6 Monophthongization

In monophthongization, a former diphthong changes into a single vowel, as in the change from Classical Latin to Vulgar Latin of *au* to *o* which shows up as *o* in the modern Romance languages, as in *auru- >* Spanish *oro*, French *or* 'gold'; *tauru- >* Spanish *toro* 'bull'; *causa- >* 'cause, case, thing' > Italian *cosa*, Spanish *cosa* 'thing', French *chose* [ʃoz] 'thing'. An example from English is the monophthongization of /ai/ to /a:/ before *r* in some dialects, as in [fa:(r)] 'fire', [ta:(r)] 'tire' (cf. Wells 1982: 239). Another case is the Sanskrit change of **ai > e* and **au > o*, as in the first syllable of *kekara* 'squinting' < Proto-Indo-European **kaiko-* 'one-eyed, squinting' (compare Latin *caecus* 'blind'). An instance of monophthongization found in the history of French is somewhat complicated by the other changes and orthographic conventions with which it is represented. At the end of the twelfth century, French changed *al > au* before consonants, as in *altre > autre* 'other'; then later *au* monophthongized to *o*, [otR] (still spelled *autre*) 'other'. Thus, *cheval* [ʃəvál] 'horse' retained *al*, since no consonant follows it, but *chevals > chevaux* [ʃəvó] 'horses' (*als > aus > os > o* in this case) because a consonant (*s*) did follow. Such forms are spelled in Modern French with *x*, which stems from the practice in the Middle Ages of using *x* to abbreviate *-us* (for example, <nox> for *nous* 'we, us'); this gave the spelling <chevax> for 'horses,' which ended in [aus], and when the use of the abbreviation ceased, <x>

came to be understood as a substitute for <s>, and so the *u* heard at that time in the *au* diphthong was reinstated in the writing of such words, hence the modern spelling *chevaux* (Darmesteter 1922: 151–2).

2.7.8.7 Vowel raising

Changes in which low vowels change to mid (or high) vowels, or mid vowels move up to high vowels, are quite common. In particular, long or tense vowels frequently rise. Sometimes these changes can involve rather wholesale changes in much of the vowel system, known as vowel shifts, as in the Great Vowel Shift in English (see Section 2.9 below). One environment in which raising is not uncommon is at the ends of words, such as the Finnish change of *e* to *i* word-finally (for example, *vere-* > *veri* 'blood'). William Labov (1994, 2001) argues that in vowel shifts, long (or tense, or peripheral) vowels tend to rise, as in the Great Vowel Shift in English (considered in section 2.9 below).

2.7.8.8 Vowel lowering

Vowel lowering, the opposite of raising, results in high vowels becoming mid or low vowels, or mid vowels becoming low. For example, vowels are often lowered before uvular and pharyngeal consonants, and when a lower vowel occurs in the next syllable, to mention a few common environments. Also, nasalized vowels are lowered very frequently. For example, Proto-Dravidian *i and *u were lowered before *a in the next syllable in South Dravidian languages, as in *$ilay$ > *elay* 'leaf', *$pukay$ > *pokay* 'smoke' (y = [j]) (Zvelebil 1990: 5–6). However, vowel lowering does not necessarily need to be conditioned.

2.7.8.9 Nasalization

In nasalization, vowels often become nasalized in the environment of nasal consonants. The typical scenario is for the nasalized vowels to become phonemic (contrastive) when later in time the nasal consonant is lost, as in French *bon* > [bõn] > [bõ] 'good' (spelled *bon*).

2.7.8.10 Lenition (weakening)

Lenition is a reasonably loose notion applied to a variety of kinds of changes in which the resulting sound after the change is conceived of as somehow weaker in articulation than the original sound. Lenitions thus typically include changes of stops or affricates to fricatives, of two consonants to one, of full consonants to glides (*j* or *w*), sometimes of voiceless consonants to voiced in various environments, and so on. Lenition can also include the complete loss of sounds. An example of lenition is the change of the intervocalic stops which were voiceless in Latin (*p*, *t*, *k*) to voiced stops (*b*, *d*, *g*) in Spanish, as in *skōpa* > *eskoba* (spelled *escoba*) 'broom', *natāre* > *nadar* 'to swim', *amīka* > *amiga* 'female friend'.

2.7.8.11 Strengthening

The variety of changes which are sometimes referred to as 'strengthening' share a loosely defined notion that, after the change, the resulting sound is somehow 'stronger' in articulation than the original sound was. For example, in the change in Q'eqchi' (Mayan) of *w* > *kw* (*winq* > *kwi:nq* 'person') and *y* > *ty* (IPA [j] > [tj]) (*iyax* > *ityax* 'seed'), the *kw* and *tj* are perceived as being stronger than the original *w* and *j*.

2.7.8.12 Gemination

Gemination (from Latin *geminātiōn-em* 'doubling', related to *geminus* 'twin', seen in the astrological sign *Gemini*) means, as the name suggests, the doubling of consonants, that is, the change which produces a sequence of two identical consonants from a single starting consonant, as in *t* > *tt*. For example, in certain Finnish dialects in a sequence of short vowel–short consonant–long vowel (VCV:) the consonant is regularly geminated (long vowels and long or geminate consonants are written double: /aa/ = [a:], /ss/ = [s:]), as in *osaa* > *ossaa* 'he/she knows', *pakoon* > *pakkoon* 'into flight (fleeing)'.

2.7.8.13 Degemination

When a sequence of two identical consonants is reduced to a single occurrence, the change is often called *degemination*. An example is the change from Latin *pp*, *tt*, *kk* to Spanish *p*, *t*, *k* respectively, as in: *mittere* > *meter* 'to put', *pekkātu-* > *pekado* (spelled *pecado*) 'sin, misfortune'.

2.7.8.14 Affrication

Affrication refers to changes in which a sound, usually a stop, sometimes a fricative, becomes an affricate; for example, *t* > *ts* /__*i*, and *k* > *č* /__*i*, *e* (*č* = IPA [tʃ]) are quite common.

2.7.8.15 Spirantization (fricativization)

Not uncommonly, an affricate will be weakened (lenited) to a fricative, or a stop will become a fricative. In Cuzco Quechua, syllable-final stops become fricatives, as for example in *rapra* > *raɸra* 'leaf, wing'; **suqta* > *soχta* 'six'. A common change is the spirantization of stops between vowels, well known in Dravidian languages (for example, Proto-Dravidian **tapu* 'to perish' > Kannada *tavu* 'to decrease') (Zvelebil 1990:8). Balto-Finnic languages underwent a similar change in closed syllables (that is, in /__CC or /__C#, as in Finnish *tava-n* 'custom-Accusative Singular' < **tapa-n*).

2.7.8.16 Deaffrication

When an affricate becomes a fricative (not an uncommon change), it is sometimes called deaffrication. For example, *č* > *ʃ* in the Spanish of areas of Chile and Panama (in the speech of younger people, varying according to sociolinguistic conditions) (Canfield 1982: 33, 69). In another example, in Chiltiupán Pipil (a Uto-Aztecan language of El Salvador), *ts* > *s*, as in *tsutsukul* > *susukul* 'water jug'.

2.7.8.17 Lengthening

Lengthening refers to the change in which some sound, usually a vowel, is lengthened in some context. For example, in Q'eqchi' (Mayan), vowels are lengthened before a consonant cluster which begins with a sonorant (*l*, *r*, *m* or *n*): *kenq'* > *ke:nq'* 'bean', *ɓalk* > *ɓa:lk* 'brother-in-law'.

2.7.8.18 *Shortening*

Sounds, particularly vowels, often undergo changes which shorten them in a variety of contexts, such as word-finally, before consonant clusters, when unstressed, and so on. Long vowels also often merge with short vowels generally in a language. For example, in Middle English, long vowels were shortened before a consonant cluster, as in Old English *cēpte* > Middle English *kepte* 'kept' (compare modern *keep/kept*), and in trisyllabic forms when followed by two or more syllables, as in *hōliday* > *holiday* 'holiday' (contrast modern *holy* with *holiday*).

2.8 Relative Chronology

A sound change pertains to a particular period of time in the history of the language in which it takes place. This means that some sound changes may take place in the language at some earlier stage and then cease to be active, whereas others may take place at some later stage in the language's history. Often in the case of different changes from different times, evidence is left behind which provides us with the clues with which to determine their relative chronology, that is, the temporal order in which they took place. (For those who are familiar with rule ordering in synchronic phonology, it may be helpful to point out that relative chronology is very similar, but in historical linguistics it refers to the historical sequence in which different changes took place.) Part of working out the phonological history of a language is determining the relative chronology of the changes which have affected the language. A couple of straightforward examples show what is involved.

(1) In the history of Swedish, the change of umlaut took place before syncope, in the sequence:

Umlaut: a > e /__(C)Ci
Syncope: i > Ø/V(C)C__r after a root syllable (approximate form of the changes; they are more general, but only the portions affecting this example are presented here).

From Proto-Germanic to Modern Swedish: **gasti-z* > Proto-Scandinavian **gastiz* > *gestir* > Old Norse *gestr* > Modern Swedish *gäst* 'guest' (*gastiz* > *gestir* > *gestr* > *gest* (spelled *gäst*)) (Wessén 1969: 10–11). We can be reasonably certain that these changes took place in this chronological order, since if syncope had taken place first (*gastir* > *gastr*), then there would have been no remaining *i* to condition the umlaut and the form would have come out as the non-existent ✗*gast*. (Note that ✗ is the symbol used in this book to signal ungrammatical and incorrect forms, distinguished from * which signals reconstructed forms.)

(2) Finnish underwent the two changes:

(1)   e > i /__#
(2)   t > s /__i

In words such as Proto-Finno-Ugric **wete* 'water' which became *vesi* in Finnish, clearly (1) (*e > i /__#*) had to change final *e* into *i* before (2) (*t > s /__i*) could take place, since (2) only applied with *i*, and the *i* of *vesi* would not have been present in this word unless (1) had applied. In *vete-nä* (ä = [æ]) 'water (essive singular case)', the root *vete-* retained its *e* because it is not in word-final position, but rather is followed by the case ending -*nä*; since there is no final *i* in *vete-nä*, the *t* did not become *s* by sound change (2). (Examples involving relative chronology come up again in several places in this text, especially in Chapters 3, 5 and 8.)

2.9   Chain Shifts

Sometimes several sound changes seem to be interrelated, with more far-reaching impact on the overall phonological system of the language. These changes do not happen in isolation from one another, but appear to be connected, dependent upon one another in some way. Such interconnected changes are called *chain shifts*. Several reasons have been put forward for why chain shifts should occur, and the final word about this is surely yet to come, though the connectedness of the changes involved has often been attributed to notions such as 'symmetry in phonemic inventories', 'naturalness' or 'markedness', 'maximum differentiation' and 'a tendency for holes in phonological patterns to be filled'. (See Chapter 13.)

Let's begin to clarify what this means with a brief characterization of what is involved. It is believed that the sounds of a sound system are integrated into a whole whose parts are so interconnected that a change in any one part of the system can have implications for other parts of the system. The general idea behind the chain shifts is that sound systems tend to be symmetrical or natural, and those that are not, that is, those which have a 'gap' in the inventory, tend to change to make them symmetrical or natural (to fill in the gap). However, a change which fills one gap may create other gaps elsewhere in the system which then precipitate other changes towards symmetry/naturalness to rectify its effects, thus setting off a chain reaction.

Chain shifts are classified into two types, *pull chains* (often called *drag chains*) and push chains. In a *pull chain*, one change may create a hole in the phonemic pattern (an asymmetry, a gap) which is followed by another change which fills the hole (gap) by 'pulling' some sound from somewhere else in the system and changing that sound to fit the needs of symmetry/naturalness so that it fills the gap, and, if the sound which shifted to fill the original hole in the pattern leaves a new hole elsewhere in the pattern, then some other change may 'pull' some other sound in to fill that gap.

Behind a *push chain* is the notion that languages (or their speakers) want to maintain differences between sounds in the system in order to facilitate understanding, the processing of what is heard. If a sound starts changing by moving into the articulatory space of another sound, in the push-chain view, this can precipitate a change where the sound moves away from the encroaching one in order to maintain distinctions important to meaning. If the fleeing sound is pushed towards the articulatory space of some other sound, then it too may shift to avoid the encroachment, thus setting off a chain reaction called a push chain. Sometimes the notion of 'maximum differentiation' is called upon in these instances. The idea behind maximum differentiation is that the sounds in a sound system tend to be distributed so as to allow as much perception difference between them as the articulatory space can provide. Thus, if a language has only three vowels, we expect them to be spread out, with *i* (high front unrounded), *u* (high back rounded) and *a* (low central or back unrounded); we do not expect them to be bunched up, for example, all in the high front area (say, *i*, *ɪ* and *y*), and these intuitions are confirmed by the languages of the world, where most of the three-vowel systems have /i, u, a/ or /i, o, a/. If a language has four stops, we do not expect them to be bunched at one point of articulation, say all labials (*p*, *b*, *p'*, *pʰ*) with none at other points of articulation; rather, we expect them to be spread across alveolar, velar and perhaps other points of articulation (see Martinet 1970).

Let's now look at some specific examples to give these abstract notions some substance.

(1) Attic Greek (the Classical Greek dialect of ancient Athens) underwent two changes: *u: > y:* and *o: > u:*. This series of events would be seen as a pull change if the fronting of *u:* to *y:* took place first, 'pulling' ('dragging') original *o:* after it into the phonetic space vacated by original *u:* in the change *o:* to *u:*. Alternatively, if the raising of *o:* to *u:* began first, followed, by *u:* to *y:*, the series of changes could be seen as a push chain, where the move of *o:* towards *u:* 'pushed' former *u:* out of its slot and sent it towards *y:* to avoid merger with the *o:* which was encroaching on the space of *u:*.

(2) Classical Latin had three series of stops intervocalically, the geminates (*pp*, *tt*, *kk*), the single voiceless (*p*, *t*, *k*), and the voiced (*b*, *d*, *g*). These three original series of stops changed from Latin to Spanish in an interrelated fashion:

1. Geminate (double) stops became single voiceless stops: *pp > p*, *tt > t*, *kk > k*, as in Latin *cuppa* [kuppa] > Spanish *copa* [kopa] 'cup'; *gutta > gota* 'drop'; *bucca* [bukka] 'puffed-out cheek' > *boca* [boka] 'mouth'.
2. Plain voiceless stops became voiced stops: *p > b*, *t > d*, *k > g*, as in Latin *sapere* > Spanish *saber* 'to know'; *wīta > vida* 'life'; *amīka > amiga* 'female friend'.
3. Voiced stops (except *b*, which remained) were lost: *d > Ø*, *g > Ø*, (*b > b*), as in Latin *cadere > caer* 'to fall', *crēdere > creer* 'to believe'; *rēgīna > reina* 'queen'.

The series of changes in the stops in the development from Latin to Spanish has been interpreted as a push chain (let *tt*, *t* and *d* represent all the stops in the three respective series), having taken place in the order:

(1) tt > t, (2) t > d, (3) d > Ø.

In this view, as the geminates began to simplify, (1) *tt > t*, this put pressure on the plain voiceless series to get out of the way, (2) *t > d*, which in turn put pressure on the voiced series, causing it to be lost (except for *b*), (3) *d > Ø*. It would also be possible to interpret this series of changes as a pull chain, applying in the temporal sequence:

(3) d > Ø, (2) t > d, (1) tt > t.

In this possible scenario, the loss of the voiced stops, (3) *d > Ø*, left a gap in the inventory, which was filled by the shift of the plain voiceless stops to voiced,

(2) *t > d*; but this then left a gap for the voiceless stops, and a language with voiceless geminates but no plain voiceless stops would be unexpected, so (1) *tt > t* took place.

(3) Grimm's Law is an extremely important set of sound changes in historical linguistics; it is intimately involved in the history of the comparative method and the regularity hypothesis (and so we come back to it in more detail again in Chapter 5). Grimm's Law covers three interrelated changes in the series of stops from Proto-Indo-European to Proto-Germanic:

voiceless stops > voiceless fricatives:

*p	>	f
*t	>	θ
*k, *k̂	>	h (x)
*kʷ	>	hw

voiced stops > voiceless stops

*b	>	p
*d	>	t
*g, *ĝ	>	k
*gʷ	>	kw

voiced aspirated (murmured) stops > plain voiced stops

*bh	>	b
*dh	>	d
*gh, *ĝh	>	g
*gʷh	>	gw, w

(The sounds *k̂ *ĝ and *ĝh represent the "palatal" series in Indo-European. See also section 5.4.1 in Chapter 5.)

This means that words in modern Germanic languages, because they inherit the results of these changes from Proto-Germanic, show the effects of the changes, but when cognate words from other Indo-European languages (not from the Germanic branch) are compared with those from Germanic languages, they do not show the results of these changes. Some examples which illustrate the effects of Grimm's Law are given in Table 2.4, which compares words from English (Germanic) with cognates from Spanish and French (Romance languages, not Germanic). In some cases, Spanish and French have undergone other changes of their own, making the correspondences expected from Grimm's Law not so obvious today, though the connections are clear when we take the full history of these languages into account – this is particularly true of the voiced aspirated sounds, for which examples from Sanskrit and Latin are substituted instead.

Grimm's Law can be interpreted as either a pull chain or a push chain (where *t, d* and *dh* represent all the stops of these series). If the temporal sequence were

(1) t > θ, (2) d > t, (3) dh > d,

then it would be assumed that (1) *t > θ* took place first, leaving the language with the three series, voiceless fricatives (*f, θ, h*), voiced stops (*b, d, g*) and voiced aspirates (*bh, dh, gh*), but no plain voiceless stops (no *p, t, k*). This would be an unnatural situation which would pull in the voiced stops to fill the gap ((2) *d > t*); however, this would leave the language with voiced aspirates but no plain voiced

TABLE 2.4: Grimm's Law in English, Spanish and French comparisons

	Spanish	*French*	*English*
*p > f	pie	pied (Old French pié)	foot
	padre	père	father
	por	per	for
*t > θ	tres	trois	three
	tu	tu	thou
*k > h	(can)	chien (< kani-)	hound (< hūnd)
	ciento	cien (< kent-)	hundred
	corazón	cœur	heart
*b > p	[NOTE: *b was rare in Proto-Indo-European; some say it was		
	missing]		
*d > t	diente	dent	tooth (< tanθ)
	dos	deux	two
*g > k	—	genou	knee
	grano	grain	corn
	Sanskrit	*Latin*	*English*
*bh > b	bhrā́tar	frāter	brother
	bhára-	fer-	bear
		(f < *bh)	
*dh > d	dhā-	facere	do, did, deed
		(f < dh)	
*gh > g	haṃsá (<*gh)	(h)anser	goose
	[hə̃sə]		

stops, also an unnatural arrangement, and so the voiced aspirates would be pulled in to fill the slot of the plain voiced stops ((3) *dh > d*), making a more symmetrical system.

In the push-chain scenario, the voiced aspirates first started to move towards the plain voiced stops, a natural change towards easier articulation ((3) *dh > d*), but the approach of *dh* into the space of *d* forced original **d* to move towards *t* ((2) *d > t*), which in turn pushed original **t* out in order to maintain a distinction between these series of sounds ((1) *t > θ*).

(3) *Mamean shift.* Chain shifts of various sorts, some more complex, some involving only a couple of changes, are known from many languages, not just from Indo-European. One example is the chain shift in Mamean languages (a branch of the Mayan family) in which:

*r > t (for example, Mam *ti:x* < **ri:x* 'old man', the prefix *t-* < **r-* 'his, hers, its')
*t > č (*čap* < **tap* 'crab', *čeʔw* < **teʔw* 'cold')
**č > ç [a laminal retroflex grooved affricate] (*ç'o:ç'* < **č'ohč'* 'earth', *ç'am* < **č'am* 'sour').

(4) The English Great Vowel Shift, mentioned in examples above, is one of the best-known of all chain shifts. Between Chaucer (c. 1400) and Shakespeare (born 1564), English underwent a series of interrelated vowel changes known as the Great Vowel Shift, in which long vowels systematically raised, and the highest long vowels diphthongized, as seen in Figure 2.1.

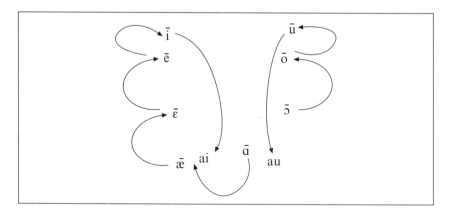

FIGURE 2.1: The Great Vowel Shift in English

These changes are seen in the following words:

Middle English	Chaucer	Shakespeare	Modern English	
bite(n)	/bītə/	/bəit/	/bait/	'bite' (ī > ai)
tide	/tīd/	/təid/	/taid/	'tide'
bete	/bētə/	/bīt/	/bi(:)t/	'beet' (ē > i)
mete	/mɛ̄t/	/mēt/	/mi(:)t/	'meat'(ɛ̄ > ē > i)
bete 'strike'	/bǣt/	/bēt/	/bit/	'beat' (ǣ > i)
name	/nāmə/	/næm/	/neim/	'name'
hous	/hūs/	/həus/	/haus/	'house' (ū > au)
boote	/bōt/	/būt/	/bu(:)t/	'boot' (ō > u)
boat	/bɔ̄t/	/bōt/	/bout/	'boat' (ɔ̄ > ou)

Vowel shifts are found also in a good number of other languages, and have continued in various dialects of English. William Labov has proposed general principles of chain shifting for vowels. Earlier, he argued that (1) long vowels rise, (2) short vowels fall, and (3) back vowels move to the front. This would fit the changes seen in the Great Vowel Shift in English. Later he revised this to (1) tense vowel nuclei rise, (2) lax nuclei fall, and (3) back nuclei move to the front, again illustrated by the English Great Vowel Shift. However, there are exceptions. For example, the short, lax front vowels /æ/ (as in *trap*) and /ɛ/ (as in *dress*) were raised in New Zealand English (æ towards ɛ, and ɛ towards *i*), not lowered (see Gordon et al. 2004).

Later, Labov revised the principles further, referring to the peripherality or non-peripherality of vowels. Labov (1994: 172) explains:

> the term *peripherality* was introduced to describe the path of the high vowels in the Great Vowel Shift ... I will use the term *nonperipheral* and the feature [–peripheral] to describe any type of vowel nucleus that is plainly more distant from the periphery in its mean and distribution than another vowel of the same height.

Labov sees as a central principle that 'in chain shifts, peripheral vowels become more open [lower] and nonperipheral vowels become less open [higher]' (Labov 1994: 601). This is stated later as the principles (1) tense nuclei rise along a peripheral track, and (2) lax nuclei fall long a non-peripheral track (see Labov 2010: 145–50 for details). The definition of peripherality was somewhat imprecise (Labov 1994: 173, 212, 285, 2010: 145–9; cf. Gordon et al. 2004: 271). Peripheral in Labov (2010) is defined in acoustic phonetic terms, in reference to extreme values of F2, extended to include extreme values of F1 as well. In each of these formulations of the principles, it is sometimes difficult to determine whether particular vowels are long or short, tense or lax, or peripheral or non-peripheral. Nevertheless, even if exceptions may exist, Labov's chain shift principles do reflect the fact that very often in vowel shifts, long or tense or peripheral vowels rise and short or lax or non-peripheral vowels fall.

(5) *Northern Cities Vowel Shift*. In the *Northern Cities Vowel Shift* six vowels rotate, as in Figure 2.2: (1) the tensing, raising, and fronting of /æ/ (as in *bat*); (2) the fronting of /ɑ/ (as in *got* or *father*); (3) the lowering and fronting of /ɔ/ (as in *bought*); (4) the lowering and backing of /ɛ/ (as in *bet*); (5) the backing of /ʌ/ (as in *cut* or *but*); and (6) the lowering and backing of /ɪ/ (as in *bit*). This chain shift involves a broad area of the US called the Inland north, around the Great Lakes. William Labov hypothesizes that the shift started in the early nineteenth century during the construction of the Erie Canal, with the migration to the Great Lakes

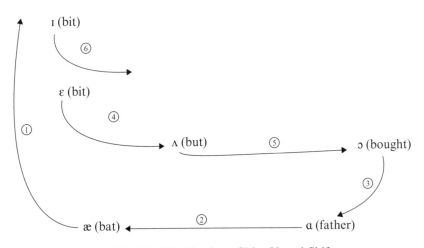

FIGURE 2.2: The Northern Cities Vowel Shift

area of workers from the East Coast representing different varieties of American English. (See Labov 2010, Labov et al. 2006.)

2.10   Exercises

Exercise 2.1   Sound change – Proto-Germanic to Old English

Compare the Proto-Germanic forms with their descendants in Old English and determine what sound changes involving vowels have taken place. Write out the sound change involved, and identify (by name) the kind of change found. Ignore changes involving second syllables. (Note that *ī, ō,* and *ū* are long vowels.)

	Proto-Germanic	*Old English*	
1.	*fimf	fīf	'five'
2.	*gans-	gōs	'goose'
3.	*grinst	grīst 'a grinding'	'grist'
4.	*hanh-	hōh	'heel, hock'
5.	*linθj(az)-	līθe	'mild, lithe'
6.	*munθ-	mūθ	'mouth'
7.	*tanθ-	tōθ	'tooth'
8.	*gang-	gang	'a going'
9.	*grind-	grind	'grind'
10.	*hlink-	hlink	'ridge, links'
11.	*hund-	hund	'dog, hound'
12.	*land-	land	'land'
13.	*sing-	sing-	'sing'
14.	*slink-	slink-	'slink'
15.	*sundan	sund-	'swimming, sea, sound'
16.	*swing-	swing-	'swing'
17.	*θingam	θing-	'assembly, (legal) case, thing'
18.	*wund-	wund	'a wound'

Exercise 2.2   Sound change – Sanskrit to Pali

Compare the Sanskrit forms with their descendants in later Pali; determine what sound changes have taken place. Write out the changes, and identify (by name) the kind of changes where possible.

NOTE: Sanskrit *s* = [s], *ś* = [ʃ], *ṣ* = [ṣ]. Each set is in effect a separate sound change exercise, though some changes may be illustrated in the examples of more than one set.

Set I

	Sanskrit	*Pali*	
1.	śaśa	sasa	'hare'
2.	kēśa	kesa	'hair'
3.	dēśa	desa	'country'

Set I

	Sanskrit	Pali	
4.	dōṣa	dosa	'fault'
5.	dāṣa	dasa	'slave'
6.	śiṣya	sissa	'pupil'
7.	sasya	sassa	'grain'

Set II

	Sanskrit	Pali	
8.	snāna	sināna	'bathing'
9.	sneha	sineha	'friendship'
10.	snihyati	sinihyati	is fond of'
11.	snigdha	siniddha	'oily'

Set III

	Sanskrit	Pali	
12.	āuṣadha	ōsadha	'herbs, medicine'
13.	kāuśika	kōsika	'owl'
14.	gaura	gōra	'pale'
15.	mauna	mōna	'silence'
16.	augha	ōgha	'flood'
17.	tāila	tēla	'oil'
18.	vāira	vēra	'enmity'
19.	śāila	sēla	'rocky'
20.	aikya	ekka	'oneness'

Set IV

	Sanskrit	Pali	
21.	pariṣat	parisā	'assembly'
22.	matimant	matimā	'wise'
23.	ārakāt	ārakā	'from afar'
24.	dharmāt	dhammā	'merit (ablative)'
25.	arthāt	atthā	'that is'
26.	bhagavant	bhagavā	'venerable'
27.	mitravant	mittavā	'having friends'

(Bhat 2001: 67, 68, 70, Masica 1991: 168)

Exercise 2.3   Sound change – Sanskrit to Prakrit

Compare the Sanskrit forms with their descendants in later Prakrit; determine what sound changes have taken place. Write out the changes, and identify (by name) the kind of changes where possible.

NOTE: consonants with subscript dots are retroflex; Sanskrit *s* = [s], *ś* = [ʃ], *ṣ* = [ʂ]. The *dh* in 3. and 6. is a single segment (not a consonant cluster), a breathy voiced stop, traditionally called a voiced aspirate. Each set is in effect a separate

sound change exercise, though some changes may be illustrated in the examples
of more than one set.

Set I

	Sanskrit	Prakrit	
1.	sapta	satta	'seven'
2.	dugdha	duddha	'milk'
3.	udgāra	uggāla	'spit out'
4.	tikta	titta	'pungent'
5.	mudga	mugga	'mung bean'
6.	ardha	addha	'half'
7.	karpaṭa	kappaḍa	'rag, cloth'
8.	kurkura	kukkura	'dog'
9.	darpa	dappa	'arrogance'
10.	parṇa	paṇṇa	'leaf'
11.	karma	kamma	'work'

Set II

	Sanskrit	Prakrit	
12.	saras	sara	'lake'
13.	śara	sara	'arrow'
14.	sapta	satta	'seven'
			(repeated from 1)
15.	śakta	satta	'able'
16.	sarva	savva	'all'
17.	śava	savva	'corpse'
18.	sīsa	sīsa	'lead'
19.	šīla	sīla	'conduct'

Set III

	Sanskrit	Prakrit	
20.	kāśmīra	kamhīra	'Kashmir'
21.	grīṣma	grimha	'summer'
22.	vismaya	vimhaya	'surprise
23.	ūṣman	umhā	'heat'
24.	viṣṇu	viṇhu	'Visnu'
25.	praśna	paṇha	'question'
26.	snāna	ṇhāna	'bath'

(Bhat 2001: 6–7, 32, 83)

Exercise 2.4   *Sound change – Proto-Slavic to Russian*

What sound changes that have taken place in Russian since Proto-Slavic times
are illustrated in the following data? Write rules to account for the palatalization of consonants, the change in the stem vowels, loss of vowels, and change
in voicing of consonants. Do not attempt to write sound change rules for the

changes in the consonant clusters (*bl*, *tl*, *dl*) in examples 1, 2, and 3. More than one change has applied to some forms; for these, state the relative chronology of these changes (the order, temporal sequence) in which the different changes took place. (The breve /˘/ over vowels means 'short'.)

	Proto-Slavic	Russian	
1.	*greblŭ	grʲop	'rowed'
2.	*metlŭ	mʲol	'swept'
3.	*vedlŭ	vʲol	'led'
4.	*nesŭ	nʲos	'carried
5.	*pĭsŭ	pʲos	'dog'
6.	*domŭ	dom	'house'
7.	*grobŭ	grop	'grave'
8.	*nosŭ	nos	'nose'
9.	*rodŭ	rot	'gender'
10.	*volŭ	vol	'bull'
11.	*dĭnĭ	dʲenʲ	'day'
12.	*konĭ	konʲ	'horse'
13.	*vĭsĭ	vʲesʲ	'all'

(Verb forms in these data = 'third person masculine past tense')

Exercise 2.5   Sound change in dialects of Tulu (Dravidian)

The forms in the Sapaliga dialect correspond to those of the oldest stage of the language; therefore, compare the forms in the other dialects to those of Sapaliga and determine what sound changes have taken place in each of the other dialects of Tulu. Write out and list the sound changes for each dialect, and identify (name) the kind of change involved in each instance, wherever this is possible. Do you imagine that some of the dialects went through more than one change in intermediate stages to arrive at some of the individual sounds they now have? If so, what might the intermediate stages have been?

NOTE: <c> = [č] (IPA [tʃ]); consonants with dots beneath = retroflex.

	Sapaliga	Holeya	Setti	Jain 1	Jain 2	
1.	tare	care	sare	hare	are	'wear off'
2.	taḷi	caḷi	saḷi	haḷi	aḷi	'sprinkle'
3	tavḍu	cavḍu	savḍu	havḍu	avḍu	'bran'
4.	tōjɨ	cōjɨ	sōjɨ	hōjɨ	ōjɨ	'appear'
5.	tinɨ	cinɨ	sinɨ	hinɨ	inɨ	'eat'
6.	tudɛ	cudɛ	sudɛ	hudɛ	–	'river'
7.	tōḍu	cōḍu	sōḍu	hōḍu	ōḍu	'stream'
8.	tanɛ	canɛ	sanɛ	hanɛ	anɛ	'conceiving' (of cattle)

	Sapaliga	Holeya	Setti	Jain 1	Jain 2	
9.	tappu	cappu	sappu	happu	appu	'leaf'
10.	tay	cay	say	hay	ay	'die'
11.	tavtɛ	cavtɛ	savtɛ	havtɛ	avtɛ	'cucumber'
12.	tuttu	cuttu	suttu	huttu	uttu	'wear'
13.	tumbu	cimbu	sumbu	humbu	umbu	'carry on head'
14.	tū	cū	sū	hū	ū	'see'

(Bhat 2001: 51)

Exercise 2.6   Sound change – Proto-Indo-European (PIE) to Latin

What sound changes have taken place in the transition from Proto-Indo-European to Latin? Try to formulate the most general, most inclusive statements possible to describe these changes. Concentrate on the sounds at the beginning of roots. (The sounds h_1, h_2, and h_3 refer to the laryngeals reconstructed for Proto-Indo-European; do not be concerned with their phonetic value but just treat them as consonants of a general sort. The laryngeals h_2 and h_3 are thought to represent some sort of fricatives produced in the back of the mouth, with h_1 frequently equated with glottal stop.)

	Proto-Indo-European		*Latin*	
1.	*pórk̂os	'piglet'	porcus /porkus/	'young pig'
2.	*pótis	'capable'	potis	'capable'
3.	*bʰébʰrus	'beaver'	fiber	'beaver'
4.	*bʰréh₂tēr	'brother'	frāter	'brother'
5.	*bʰér-o	'carry'	ferō	'I carry'
6.	*tauros	'bull'	taurus	'bull'
7.	*tréyes	'three'	trēs	'three'
8.	*dl̥kus	'sweet'	dulcis /dulkis/	'sweet'
9.	*dóh₃nom	'gift'	dōnum	'gift'
10.	*dʰeh₁lus	'nourishing'	fēlīx /fe:li:ks/	'fruitful'
11.	*dʰúh₂mos	'smoke;	fūmus	'smoke'
12.	*dʰeh₁-	'to place, set'	faciō /fakio:/	'I do, make'
13.	*k̂m̥tóm	'hundred'	centum /kentum/	'hundred'
14.	*k̂(u)wōn	'dog'	canis /kanis/	'dog'
15.	*ĝénu	'jaw'	gena	'cheek'
16.	*ĝus-tu-	'taste'	gustus	'taste'
17.	*ĝʰans-	'goose'	hanser	'goose'
			(later ānser)	
18.	*ĝʰais-e-	'to adhere'	haerē-	'to stick, cling'

	Proto-Indo-European		Latin	
19.	*kápr̥	'penis'	caper /kaper/	'goat'
20.	*kom	'near, by, with'	cum /kum/	'with'
21.	*genh₁os	'race, kind'	genus	'race, kind'
22.	*gl̥h₁is	'mouse'	glīs	'dormouse'
23.	*gʰaidos	'goat'	haedus	'young goat'
24.	*gʰóstis	'stranger, guest'	hostis	'host'
25.	*kʷis	'who'	quis/kwis/	'who'
26.	*kʷétwor-	'four'	quattuor/ kwattuor/	'four'
27.	*gʷemyo	'come'	veniō/wenio:/	'I come'
28.	*gʷih₃wos	'living'	vīvus/wiwus/	'alive'
29.	*gʷʰermós	'warm'	formus	'warm'
30.	*gʷʰén-	'repel'	(dē-)fen(-dō)	'I repel'
31.	*gʷʰér-	'wild beast'	ferus	'wild'

Exercise 2.7 Sound change – Portuguese

Make the most general statements you can to account for the sound changes which took place intervocalically in the transition from late Latin to modern Portuguese, based on the following examples. (Do not attempt to explain changes in vowels that you see.)

	Late Latin	Modern Portuguese	
1.	lupu	lobo	'wolf'
2.	sapore	sabor	'flavour'
3.	mutu	mudo /mudu/	'dumb, silent'
4.	latu	lado /ladu/	'side'
5.	caritate	caridade	'charity'
6.	pacare /pakare/	pagar	'to pay'
7.	focu /foku/	fogo /fogu/	'fire'
8.	nebula	névoa	'mist'
9.	debere	dever	'to owe'
10.	caballu	cavalo /kavalu/	'horse'
11.	gradu	grau	'degree'
12.	nuda	nua	'nude' (feminine)

	Late Latin	Modern Portuguese	
13.	regale	real	'royal'
14.	cogitare 'to think'	cuidar	'to take care'
15.	palu	pau	'stick'
16.	filu	fio /fiu/	'thread'
17.	salute	saúde	'health'
18.	luna	lua	'moon'
19.	corona	coroa	'crown'
20.	moneta	moeda	'coin'

Exercise 2.8   Sound change – Greek

What happened to the former labiovelar sounds and *w* in Attic Greek? Formulate the most precise, most inclusive statement of the sound change(s) from Proto-Indo-European (PIE) to Attic Greek that you can based on the following data.

	PIE	*Attic Greek*	
1.	*$k^w$is	tis	'who'
2.	*k^we	te	'and'
3.	*k^wetwóres	tettares	'four'
4.	*pénk^{w}e	pente	'five'
5.	*k^wóti- 'how much' 'how many'	pósis	'how much, how many'
6.	*k^wóteros 'which of two'	póteros	'which'
7.	*leik^{w}o-	leipō	'I leave'
8.	*yēk^{w}r̥	hēpar	'liver'
9.	*g^welb^{h}us	delp^{h}ús	'womb'
10.	*g^wous	bous	'cow'
11.	*g^wm̥ti-	basis	'going'
12.	*g^wmye- 'come'	bainō	'I walk, come'
13.	*g^wab^h-	bap-tō [p < p^h]	'I dip in'
14.	*g^{wh}aidrós 'bright, shining'	p^{h}aidrós	'beaming, cheerful'
15.	*g^{wh}ren- 'think'	p^{h}renéō	'I think'
16.	*snig^{wh}-s	nip^{h}a	'snow'
17.	*g^{wh}ermós	t^{h}ermós	'warm'
18.	*g^{wh}el- 'wish, want'	t^{h}élō	'I want, wish'
19.	*g^{wh}en- 'strike'	t^{h}eínō	'I strike'
20.	*g^{wh}ónos 'stiking down'	p^{h}ónos	'murder'

	PIE	Attic Greek	
21.	*woiк̂- 'clan'	oikía	'household'
22.	*wógʰos 'carrier'	okʰos	'wagon'
23.	*h₂ówis	ois	'sheep'
24.	*dʰewo- 'run'	tʰeō	'I run'

Exercise 2.9 Sound change – Balto-Finnic

Determine what sound changes affecting the vowels have taken place in Finnish and Estonian. Write the rules which specify these changes and under what conditions they took place. Identify (name) the changes, where possible.

NOTE: ä = [æ], ö = [ø], ü = [y], õ = [ɨ]. Double vowels (for example *aa*, *oo*, and so on) are long vowels. Orthographic <b, d, g> in Estonian are represented here phonetically as [p, t, k] respectively, although these sounds are between voiced and voiceless, described sometimes as 'semi-voiceless' or 'half-voiced'.

	Proto-Balto-Finnic	Finnish	Estonian	gloss
1.	*maa	maa	maa	'land'
2.	*noori	nuori	noor	'young'
3.	*koori	kuori	koor	'bark, peel'
4.	*hooli	huoli	hool	'care, worry'
5.	*jooni	juoni	joon	'line, direction'
6.	*leemi	liemi	leem	'broth'
7.	*mees	mies	mees	'man'
8.	*meeli	mieli	meel	'mind'
9.	*keeli	kieli	keel	'tongue, language'
10.	*reemu	riemu	rõõm [rɨ:m]	'joy'
11.	*meekka	miekka	mõõk [mɨ:k:]	'sword'
12.	*peena	piena	põõn [pɨ:n]	'slat, rail, cross-piece'
13.	*veeras	vieras	võõras [vɨ:ras]	'foreign'
14.	*luu	luu	luu	'bone'
15.	*hiiri	hiiri	hiir	'mouse'
16.	*kyynärä	kyynärä	küünar	'ell (measure)'
17.	*töö	työ	töö	'work'
18.	*möö-	myö-	möö-	'along, by'
19.	*kala	kala	kala	'fish'
20.	*lapa	lapa	laba [lapa]	'blade'
21.	*kylä	kylä	küla	'village'
22.	*ikä	ikä	iga [ika]	'age'
23.	*isä	isä	isa	'father'
24.	*joki	joki	jõgi [jɨki]	'river'
25.	*kivi	kivi	kivi	'stone'

Proto-Balto-Finnic	Finnish	Estonian	gloss
26. *lumi	lumi	lumi	'snow'
27. *läpi	läpi	läbi [læpi]	'through, hole'
28. *suku	suku	sugu [suku]	'family'
29. *ilma	ilma	ilm 'world'	'weather, world'
30. *jalka	jalka	jalg [jalk]	'foot, leg'
31. *kalma	kalma	kalm	'grave (mound)'
32. *nälkä	nälkä	nälg [nælk]	'hunger'
33. *härkä	härkä	härg [hærk]	'ox, bull'
34. *silmä	silmä	silm	'eye'
35. *marja	marja	mari	'berry'
36. *karja	karja	kari	'cattle'
37. *orja	orja	ori	'slave'
38. *lintu	lintu	lind [lint]	'bird'
39. *hullu	hullu	hull	'crazy'
40. *mänty	mänty	män [mænʲtʲ]	'pine'
41. *synty	synty	sünd [synʲtʲ]	'birth'
42. *hanki	hanki	hang [haŋk]	'crust of snow'
43. *kurki	kurki	kurg [kurk]	'crane'
44. *nahka	nahka	nahk	'leather'
45. *lehmä	lehmä	lehm	'cow'
46. *lehti	lehti	leht	'leaf, sheet'
47. *hauta	hauta	haud [haut]	'grave'
48. *lauta	lauta	laud [laut]	'board'
49. *lava	lava	lava	'platform, frame'
50. *haava	haava	haav	'wound'
51. *hinta	hinta	hind [hint]	'price'
52. *into	into	ind [int]	'passion'
53. *halko	halko	halg [halk]	'piece/block of wood'
54. *kylmä	kylmä	külm	'cold'
55. *hiki	hiki	higi [hiki]	'sweat'
56. *kylki	kylki	külg [kylk]	'side'
57. *kirppu	kirppu	kirp [kirp:]	'flea'
58. *verkko	verkko	võrk [vɨrk:]	'net'

Proto-Balto-Finnic	Finnish	Estonian	gloss
59. *onsi	onsi	õõs [ɨːs]	'a hollow place'
60. *kansi	kansi	kaas	'cover'
61. *kynsi	kynsi	küüs	'fingernail, claw'
62. *mesi	mesi	mesi	'honey'
63. *kuusi	kuusi	kuus	'six'
64. *kusi	kusi	kusi	'urine'
65. *mato	mato 'worm'	madu [matu]	'snake'
66. *elo	elo	elu	'life/building'
67. *hako	hako	hagu [haku]	'evergreen sprig, brushwood'
68. *ilo	ilo 'joy'	ilu	'beauty'
69. *himo	himo	himu	'lust, desire'
70. *iho	iho	ihu	'skin, hide'
71. *vesa	vesa	võsa [vɨsa]	'sprout, brush, weed'
72. *helma	helma	hõlm	'skirt, frock'
73. *terva	terva	tõrv [tɨrv]	'tar'
74. *velka	velka	võlg [vɨlk]	'debt'
75. *perna	perna	põrn [pɨrn]	'spleen'
76. *leuka	leuka	lõug [lɨuk]	'jaw, chin'
77. *tosi	tosi	tõsi [tɨsi]	'true'
78. *solki	solki	sõlg [sɨlk]	'buckle, brooch'
79. *sormi	sormi	sõrm [sɨrm]	'finger'
80. *pohja	pohja	põhi [pɨhi]	'bottom, base'
81. *poski	poski	põsk [pɨsk]	'cheek'
82. *korpi	korpi	kõrb [kɨrp]	'dark woods, wilderness'
83. *metsä	metsä	mets	'woods'
84. *leppä	leppä	lepp [lepː]	'alder'

3

⊯—⊣

Borrowing

⊯—⊣

When a foreign word falls by accident into the fountain of a language, it will get driven around in there until it takes on that language's colour.

(Jakob Grimm)

3.1 Introduction

It is common for one language (actually speakers of the language) to take words from another language and make them part of its own vocabulary: these are called *loanwords* and the process is called linguistic *borrowing*. Borrowing, however, is not restricted to just lexical items taken from one language into another; any linguistic material – sounds, phonological rules, grammatical morphemes, syntactic patterns, semantic associations, discourse strategies or whatever – can be borrowed, that is, can be taken over from a foreign language so that it becomes part of the borrowing language. Borrowing normally implies a certain degree of bilingualism for at least some people in both the language which borrows (sometimes called the *recipient* language) and the language which is borrowed from (often called the *donor* language). In this chapter, we are concerned with answering the questions: (1) what are loanwords?; (2) why are words borrowed?; (3) what aspects of language can be borrowed and how are they borrowed?; (4) what are the methods for determining that something is a loanword and for identifying the source languages from which words are borrowed?; and (5) what happens to borrowed forms when they are taken into another language? (Other aspects of linguistic borrowing are treated in Chapter 10 on syntactic change and in Chapter 12 on areal linguistics.)

3.2 What is a Loanword?

A loanword is a lexical item (a word) which has been 'borrowed' from another language, a word which originally was not part of the vocabulary of the recipient language but was adopted from some other language and made part of the borrowing language's vocabulary. For example, Old English did not have the word *pork*; this became an English word only after it was adopted from French *porc* 'pig, pork', borrowed in the late Middle English period – so we say, as a consequence, that *pork* is a French loanword in English. French has also borrowed words from English, for example *bifteck* 'beefsteak', among many others. Loanwords are extremely common; some languages have many. There are extensive studies of the many Scandinavian and French loans in English; Germanic and Baltic loans in Finnish; Basque, German and Arabic loans in Spanish; Native American loanwords in Spanish and Spanish loans in various Native American languages (called *hispanisms*); Turkic in Hungarian; English in Japanese; Sanskrit in Malay and other languages of Indonesia; Arabic in various languages of Africa and Asia; and so on, to mention just a few cases which have been studied intensively.

A quick glance at the contents of our kitchen pantry will begin to give us an appreciation for the impact of loanwords on English vocabulary:

catsup, ketchup < apparently originally from the Amoy dialect of Chinese *kôe-chiap*, *kè-tsiap* 'brine of pickled fish or shellfish', borrowed into Malay as *kēchap*, taken by Dutch as *ketjap*, the probable source from which English acquired the term.

chocolate < Nahuatl (Mexico, the language of the Aztecs) *čokolātl* 'a drink made from the seeds of the cacao tree', borrowed as Spanish *chocolate* from which other languages of the world obtained the term.

coffee < Arabic *qahwa* 'coffee, wine', from an earlier meaning connected with 'dark'.

Coca-Cola < *coca* < Quechua *kuka* 'coca leaves, coca bush', borrowedvia Spanish *coca*, and *cola* < languages of west Africa *kola* 'cola nut' (for example Temne *kola,* Mandingo *kolo* 'cola (tree species)').

flour < Old French *flour* 'flower' (compare French *fleur de farine* 'flower of meal/flour', that is, the 'best or finest of the ground meal').

juice < French *jus* 'broth, sauce, juice of plant or animal'.

pantry < Old French *paneterie* 'bread-room, bread-closet', based on Latin *pānis* 'bread'.

pepper < ultimately of ancient oriental origin (compare Sanskrit *pippalī* long pepper'); it came early to Germanic peoples via Latin *piper.*

potato < Taino (Cariban language of Haiti) *patata*, borrowed throughSpanish *batata*, *patata* to many other languages.

rice < ultimately from Dravidian **ari/*ariki* 'rice, paddy' (compare Tamil *ari/ari-ci*), via Latin *oriza* and Greek *orúza*.

spaghetti < Italian *spaghetti*, plural of *spaghetto* 'small thread', the diminutive of *spago* 'string, twine'.

sugar < ultimately from Arabic *sukkar*, through Old French *çucre*. Arabic *sukkar* itself is a borrowing from Persian *shakar*, apparently originally from Sanskrit *śarkarā*.

tea < ultimately from Chinese (compare Amoy dialect *te*), probably borrowed through Malay *te/teh* into Dutch and from Dutch to English.

tomato < Nahuatl *tomatl*, through Spanish *tomate*.

These are but a few of the borrowed forms among English foodstuffs.

3.3   *Why do Languages Borrow from One Another?*

Languages borrow words from other languages primarily because of *need* and *prestige*. When speakers of a language acquire some new item or concept from abroad, they *need* a new term to go along with the new acquisition; often a foreign name is borrowed along with the new concept. This explains, for example, why so many languages have similar words for 'automobile' (as in Russian *avtomobilʲ*, Finnish *auto*, Swedish *bil* – from the last syllable of *automobil*); 'coffee' (Russian *kofe*, Finnish *kahvi*, Japanese *kōhii*); 'tobacco' (Finnish *tupakka*, Indonesian *tembakau* [təmbakau], Japanese *tabako* 'cigarette, tobacco', said ultimately to be from Arabic *ṭabāq*, *ṭubāq* 'a herb which produced euphoria' via Spanish *tabaco*); and *Coca-Cola*, for example, since languages presumably needed new names for these new concepts when they were acquired. Of course, most examples of loanwords are not so widespread as these.

The other main reason why words are taken over from another language is for *prestige*, because the foreign term for some reason is highly esteemed. Borrowings for prestige are sometimes called 'luxury' loans. For example, English could have done perfectly well with only native terms for 'pig flesh/ pig meat' and 'cow flesh/cow meat', but for reasons of prestige, *pork* (from French *porc*) and *beef* (from French *bœuf*) were borrowed, as well as many other terms of 'cuisine' from French – *cuisine* itself is from French *cuisine* 'kitchen' – because French had more social status and was considered more prestigious than English during the period of Norman French dominance in England (1066–1300). For example, Udmurt (Votyak, a Finno-Ugric language) borrowed from Tatar (a Turkic language) words for such things as 'mother', 'father', 'grandmother', 'grandfather', 'husband', 'older brother', 'older sister', 'uncle', 'human', among other things. Since Udmurt had native terms for 'father' and 'mother' and these other kin before contact with Tatar, need was not the motivation for these borrowings, rather prestige. Similarly, Finnish borrowed words for 'mother' (*äiti*, from Germanic; compare Gothic *aiþei* [ɛθī], Old High German *eidī*, Proto-Germanic **aiθī*); 'daughter' (*tytär*, from Baltic; compare Lithuanian *dukteř̃s* (genitive form)); 'sister' (*sisar*, from Baltic; compare Lithuanian *seser̃s* (genitive form)); and 'bride', 'navel', 'neck', 'thigh' and 'tooth', among many others from Baltic and Germanic (compare Anttila 1989: 155). Clearly, Finnish had previously had terms for close female kin and for these body parts before borrowing these terms from neighbouring Indo-European languages, and thus it is prestige which accounts for these borrowings and not need.

Some loans involve a third, much rarer (and much less important) reason for borrowing, the opposite of prestige: borrowing due to negative evaluation, the adoption of the foreign word to be *derogatory*. Here are a few examples, all borrowed presumably for derogatory reasons. French *hâbler* 'to brag, to boast' is borrowed from Spanish *hablar* 'to speak'. Finnish *koni* 'nag' [old horse], with negative connotations, is borrowed from Russian *konʲ*, a neutral term for 'horse', with no negative connotations in the donor language. English *assassin* and the similar words with the same meaning in a number of other European languages (see French *assassin*, Italian *assassino*, Spanish *asesino* 'assassin') may be another example; *assassin* is ultimately from Arabic *ḥaʃʃāʃīn* 'hashisheaters' (for the name of an eleventh-century Muslim sect who would intoxicate themselves with hashish or cannabis when preparing to kill someone of public standing; they had a reputation for butchering opponents, hence the later sense of 'murderer for hire or for fanatical reasons'). Korean *hɔstis*, borrowed from English *hostess*, has a negative connotation, meaning the women who work at nightclubs and bars which serve mainly male customers. It is possible, of course, that some examples of this sort were not borrowed with derogatory purposes in mind at all, but rather merely involve things which have low status.

3.4   How do Words get Borrowed?

Borrowed words are usually remodelled to fit the phonological and morphological structure of the borrowing language, at least in early stages of language contact. The traditional view of how words get borrowed and what happens to them as they are assimilated into the borrowing language holds that loanwords which are introduced to the borrowing language by bilinguals may contain sounds which are foreign to the receiving language, but due to *phonetic interference* the foreign sounds are changed to conform to native sounds and phonetic constraints. This is frequently called *adaptation* (or *phoneme substitution*). In adaptation, a foreign sound in borrowed words which does not exist in the receiving language will be replaced by the nearest phonetic equivalent to it in the borrowing language. For example, formerly Finnish had no voiced stops *b*, *d*, *g*; in loans borrowed into Finnish from Germanic languages which contained *b*, *d*, *g*, voiceless stops (*p*, *t*, *k*), the closest phonetic counterparts in Finnish, replaced these sounds, as seen in, for example, *parta* 'beard' (from Germanic **bardaz*) and *humpuuki* 'humbug' (from English *humbug*). Similarly, in Sayula Popoluca (a Mixe-Zoquean language of southern Mexico), which had no native *l* or *r*, the foreign *l* and *r* of borrowed words were replaced by native *n*, as in Sayula Popoluca *kúnu:ʃ* 'cross', borrowed from Spanish *cruz* [krus], *mu:na* 'mule' from Spanish *mula*, and *puná:tu* 'plate, dish' from Spanish *plato*. Occasionally in borrowings, substitutions may spread the phonetic features of a single sound of the donor language across two segments in the borrowing language; for example, Finnish had no *f*, so intervocalic *f* in loanwords was replaced by the sequence *hv*, as in *kahvi* 'coffee' (from Swedish *kaffe*), and *pihvi* 'beef' (from English *beef*). In this instance, some of the features of foreign *f* are represented on the first segment – *h* conveys 'voiceless' – and other features on the second segment – *v* conveys 'labiodental' – and both *h* and *v* signal 'fricative'.

Non-native phonological patterns are also subject to *accommodation*, where loanwords which do not conform to native phonological patterns are modified to fit the phonological combinations which are permitted in the borrowing language. This is usually accomplished by deletion, addition or recombination of certain sounds to fit the structure of the borrowing language. For example, Mayan languages do not permit initial consonant clusters, and consequently Spanish *cruz* / krus/ 'cross' was borrowed as *rus* in Chol (Mayan), where the initial consonant of the donor form was simply left out, and as *kurus* in Tzotzil (another Mayan language), where the consonant cluster has been broken up by the insertion of a vowel between *k* and *r*. Similarly, in the Sayula Popoluca example above, since the language did not have initial consonant clusters, the *kr* and *pl* of Spanish were broken up by the insertion of *u* in, for example, *kunu:ʃ* 'cross' (< Spanish *cruz*, just mentioned) and *puná:tu* 'plate' (< Spanish *plato*). Similarly, Finnish, with no initial consonant clusters in native words, eliminated all but the last consonant of initial consonant clusters in loanwords, for example *Ranska* 'French' (< Swedish *Franska* 'French'), *risti* 'cross' (< Old Russian *kristĭ*), *ruuvi* 'screw' (< Swedish *skruv* 'screw').

However, there are many different kinds of language-contact situations, and the outcome of borrowing can vary according to the length and intensity of the contact, the kind of interaction, and the degree of bilingualism in the populations. In situations of more extensive, long-term or intimate contact, new phonemes can be introduced into the borrowing language together with borrowed words which contain these new sounds, resulting in changes in the phonemic inventory of the borrowing language; this is sometimes called *direct phonological diffusion*. For example, before intensive contact with French, English had no phonemic /ʒ/. This sound became an English phoneme through the many French loans that contained it which came into English, such as *rouge* /ruʒ/ (< French *rouge* 'red') (and added to by the palatalization in the eighteenth century of /zj/ > /ʒ/, as in *vision, Asia* and so on). In the case of *v*, formerly English had an allophonic [v] but no phonemic /v/. It became phonemic due in part to French loans containing *v* in environments not formerly permitted by English. The sound [v] occurred in native English words only as the intervocalic variant (allophone) of /f/; a remnant of this situation is still seen in alternations such as *leaf–leaves, wife–wives* and so on, where the suffix *-es* used to have a vowel in the spoken language. Words with initial *v* of French origin – such as *very* from French *vrai* 'true' and *valley* < Old French *valée* – caused /v/ to become a separate phoneme in its own right, no longer just the allophonic variant of /f/ that occurred between vowels. The phonological patterns (phonotactics, syllable or morpheme structure) of a language can also be altered by the acceptance in more intimate language contact of loans which do not conform to native patterns. For example, while native Finnish words permit no initial consonant clusters, now through intimate contact and the introduction of many borrowings from other languages, especially from Swedish and later from English, Finnish phonology permits loans with initial clusters, as seen in, for example, *krokotiili* 'crocodile', *kruunu* 'crown' (compare Swedish *krona*), *presidentti* 'president' and *smaragdi* 'emerald' (from Swedish *smaragd*), and so on.

While there may be typical patterns of substitution for foreign sounds and phonological patterns, substitutions in borrowed words in a language are not always uniform. The same foreign sound or pattern can be borrowed in one loanword in one way and in another loanword in a different way. This happens for the following reasons. (1) Sometimes different words are borrowed at different times, so that older loans reflect sound substitutions before intimate contact brought new sounds and patterns into the borrowing language, while more recent borrowings may exhibit the newer segments or patterns acquired after more intensive contact. (The extent to which the source language is known by speakers of the borrowing language is relevant here.) An example is Sayula Popoluca *turu* 'bull' (recently from Spanish *toro*), with *r*, where earlier loans would have substituted *n* for this foreign sound (mentioned above). Another example is seen in the comparison of Tzotzil (Mayan) *pulatu* 'dishes' (from Spanish *plato* 'plate, dish'), borrowed earlier when Tzotzil permitted no initial consonant clusters, and Tzotzil *platu* 'plate', borrowed later from the same Spanish source, now containing the initial consonant cluster which was formerly prohibited. (2) In most cases, borrowings are based on pronunciation, as illustrated in the case of Finnish *meikkaa-* 'to make up (apply cosmetics)', based on English pronunciation of *make* /meik/. However, in some cases, loans can be based on orthography ('spelling pronunciations'), as seen in the case of Finnish *jeeppi* [jɛːpːi] 'jeep', which can only be based on a spelling pronunciation of English 'jeep', not on the English pronunciation (/ʤip/) – borrowed nouns that end in a consonant add *i* in Finnish.

Loan words are not only remodelled to accommodate aspects of the phonology of the borrowing language, they are also usually adapted to fit the morphological patterns of the borrowing language. For example, Spanish and French borrowings into some varieties of Arabic have been made to fit Arabic morphological paradigms, which involve alternations in the vowels of the root to signal different morphemes, such as 'singular' and 'plural' difference, as in:

> *resibo* 'receipt' (singular), but *ruāseb* (plural) < Spanish *recibo*
> *bābor* 'a steamship, steamer', but plural *buāber* < Spanish *vapor* /
>   bapor/ 'steam, steamship' (see Vendryes 1968: 95). (Compare Modern
>   Arabic *bābūr* 'steamship, locomotive' (singular), *bwābīr* (plural).)

Chiricahua Apache often has verbs where European languages have adjectives, and as a consequence the Spanish adjectives *loco* 'crazy' and *rico* 'rich' were borrowed but adapted to the verb paradigm, as in:

lô:gò	'he/she is crazy'	*ʒî:gò*	'he/she is rich'
lô:ʃgò	'I am crazy'	*ʒî:ʃgò*	'I am rich'
lóngò	'you are crazy'	*ʒíngò*	'you are rich'

Here, as might be expected, it is the third person verb form ('he is crazy/rich') which phonetically matches the form of the original Spanish adjectives most closely (where *ʒ* is the closest substitution for Spanish *r*, which Apache lacked; the diacritics on the vowels indicate tones and are required by Chiricahua Apache for verbs such as these (see Anttila 1989: 158).

3.5   How do we Identify Loanwords and Determine the Direction of Borrowing?

An important question is: how can we tell (beyond the truly obvious cases) if something is a loanword or not? In dealing with borrowings, we want to ascertain which language is the source (donor) and which the recipient (borrower). The following criteria (perhaps better called rough rules of thumb) address these questions (compare Haas 1969a: 79; Sapir 1949 [1916]).

3.5.1 Phonological clues

The strongest evidence for loanword identification and the direction of borrowing comes from phonological criteria.

(1) Phonological patterns of the language. Words containing sounds which are not normally expected in native words are candidates for loans. For example, in the Chiricahua Apache example just mentioned, the fact that ʒî:gò 'he is rich' has an initial ʒ and that lô:gò 'he is crazy' has an initial l makes these strong candidates for loans, since neither ʒ nor l occurs word-initially in native words. In another example, native Nahuatl words are not expected to begin with p, since Proto-Uto-Aztecan initial *p- was lost through regular sound change in Nahuatl (*p > h > Ø, for example Proto-Uto-Aztecan *pa: > Nahuatl a:- 'water'). For this reason, Nahuatl roots such as petla- 'woven mat', po:čo:- 'silk-cotton tree (ceiba)' and pak- 'to cure' / paʔ- 'medicine' violate expectations for sounds in native forms, making them candidates for possible loans. On further investigation, the sources of these borrowings are found in neighbouring languages: petla- comes from Mixe-Zoquean *pata 'woven mat' (in other words of Nahuatl, a > e in this environment, and t > tl before a); po:čo:- is from Totonac pu:ču:t 'silk-cotton tree (ceiba)'; pak-/paʔ- is from Totonac paʔk 'to cure, get well'. It is the aberrant initial p- of these forms which suggests that they may be loans and which prods us to look for their sources in neighbouring languages.

Words which violate the typical phonological patterns (canonical forms, morpheme structure, syllable structure, phonotactics) of a language are likely to be loans. For example, Mayan languages typically have monosyllabic roots (of the form CVC); the polysyllabic morphemes found in Mayan languages, which violate the typical monosyllabic pattern, turn out mostly to be loanwords or compounds. For example, the polysyllabic monomorphemic tinamit 'town' of Kaqchikel (Mayan) is a loanword from Nahuatl (Uto-Aztecan). Since this polysyllabic form violates the typical monosyllabic structure of Mayan roots, the inference is that it is probably a loan, and indeed its source is found in Nahuatl tena:mi-tl 'fence or wall of a town/city', 'fortified town'.

(2) Phonological history. In some cases where the phonological history of the languages of a family is known, information concerning the sound changes that they have undergone can be helpful for determining loans, the direction of borrowing, and what the donor language was. For example, in the Mayan family, a number of languages have borrowed from Cholan (Mayan), since Cholan speakers were the principal bearers of Classical Maya civilization. Cholan, however, has undergone a number of sound changes which languages of the other branches of the family did not, and this makes it fairly easy to identify many of these Cholan loans. For example, Cholan underwent the sound change *o: > u. Yucatec did not undergo this sound change, although some borrowings from Cholan into Yucatec show the results of this Cholan change; for example, Yucatec kùts 'turkey' < Cholan kuts (from *ko:ts); Yucatec tù:n 'stone, year, stela (monument)' < Cholan tun 'stone' (compare Proto-Mayan *to:ŋ 'stone'). Since these words in Yucatec show the results of a sound change that took place in Cholan but which native Yucatec words did not undergo (compare Cholan suts',

Yucatec *sò:ts'* < Proto-Mayan **so:ts'* 'bat'), it is clear in these cases that Yucatec borrowed the words and Cholan is the donor language (Justeson et al. 1985: 14).

3.5.2 Morphological complexity

The morphological make-up of words can help determine the direction of borrowing. In cases of borrowing, when the form in question in one language is morphologically complex (composed of two or more morphemes) or has an etymology which is morphologically complex, but the form in the other languages has no morphological analysis, then usually the donor language is the one with the morphologically complex form and the borrower is the one with the monomorphemic form. For example, English *alligator* is borrowed from Spanish *el lagarto* 'the alligator'; since it is monomorphemic in English, but based on two morphemes in Spanish, *el* 'the' + *lagarto* 'alligator', the direction of borrowing must be from Spanish to English. *Crocodile* is similar, ultimately from Greek *krókē* 'pebbles' + *drilos* 'worm' (borrowed through Latin, Old French and into English). *Vinegar* in English is a loan from French *vinaigre*, which is from *vin* 'wine' + *aigre* 'sour'; since its etymology is polymorphemic in French but monomorphemic in English, the direction of borrowing is clearly from French to English. English *aardvark* turns out to be borrowed from Afrikaans *aardvark* (composed of *aard* 'earth + *vark* 'pig'), since the Afrikaans form has a morphologically complex etymology while the English form is monomorphemic. *Slogan* is revealed as a loan from Scottish Gaelic *sluaghghairm* 'war-cry'; it is morphologically complex in Gaelic but not in English, from the compound *sluagh* 'army' + *ghairm* 'shout'. Another case is *whisky*, earlier *whiskybae*, from Scottish Gaelic *uisge beatha* 'water of life' (*uisge* 'water' + *bethu* 'life'). French *vasistas* [vazistas] 'fanlight, transom, high window that opens from the top inward' is a loan based on German *was ist das* 'what is that?'; given that the German source has three morphemes (words) but the French word only one, German is the donor.

Spanish borrowed many words from Arabic during the period that the Moors dominated Spain (901–1492). Many Arabic loans in Spanish include what was originally the Arabic definite article *al-* but are monomorphemic in Spanish. A few examples of this are: *albañil* 'mason' (Arabic *bannā́* 'builder, mason'), *albaricoque* 'apricot' (Arabic *barqūq* 'plum'), *albóndiga* 'meat ball' (Arabic *bunduq* 'bullet, hazelnut'), *alcalde* 'mayor' (compare Arabic *qāḍī* 'judge'), *alcoba* 'bedroom, alcove' (Arabic *qubba* 'dome, cupola'), *alcohol* 'alcohol' (Arabic *al-kuḥl* 'collyrium, fine powder used to stain the eyelids'), *alfalfa* 'alfalfa' (from Hispano-Arabic *faṣfaṣa* 'the best sort of fodder', Arabic *fiṣfiṣa* itself a loan from Persian *aspest*), *algodón* 'cotton' (Arabic *quṭn, quṭun* 'cotton'; English *cotton* is also ultimately from Arabic), *alguacil* 'constable, bailiff, peace officer' (Arabic *wazīr* 'minister, vizier', also the source of English *vizier*), *almacén* 'storehouse' (Arabic *maxzan* singular [plural' *maxazīn*] 'storeroom, depository, magazine', itself ultimately from Aramaic *xassen* 'to possess, hoard'; English *magazine* is ultimately from the same source), *almohada* 'pillow' (Arabic *mixadda* 'pillow, cushion', derived from *xadda* 'cheek, side'). Since these are polymorphemic in Arabic, composed of the article *al-* + root, but each is monomorphemic in Spanish, the direction of borrowing is seen to be from Arabic to Spanish.

Frequently, the early loans from Spanish into Native American languages (called *hispanisms*) were based on the Spanish plural forms. A few examples from Mayan languages are: Jakalteko *kaplaʃ* 'goat' (< Spanish *cabras* 'goats'); Huastec *pa:tuʃ*, Tzotzil *patoʃ* (< *patos* 'ducks'), K'iche' *pataʃ* (< Spanish *patas* 'female ducks') 'duck'; Motocintlec *ko:liʃ* 'cabbage' (< *coles* 'cabbages', compare *col* 'cabbage'); Chol *wakaʃ* 'bull, cow', Tojolabal *wakaʃ* 'cattle, beef' (< *vacas* 'cows'). In sixteenth-century Spanish, the sound represented orthographically as *s* was phonetically [ş], an apico-alveolar fricative; it was taken by speakers of these languages as being phonetically closer to their /ʃ/ than to their /s/, which accounts for the /ʃ/ seen in these (monomorphemic) borrowings which corresponds to the (polymorphemic) Spanish plural, *-(e)s*.

The Sanskrit word **kaṇa* 'one-eyed' appears to be borrowed from Proto-Dravidian **kaṇ* 'eye' + **-a* 'negative suffix' (Zvelebil 1990: 79), and it is the morphological complexity of the Dravidian form which shows the direction of the borrowing.

This is a very strong criterion, but not foolproof. It can be complicated by cases of folk etymology (see Chapter 4), where a monomorphemic loanword comes to be interpreted as containing more than one morpheme, though originally this was not the case. For example, Old French monomorphemic *crevice* 'crayfish' was borrowed into English and then later this was replaced by folk etymology with *crayfish*, on analogy with *fish*. Now it appears to have a complex morphological analysis, but this is not original.

3.5.3   Clues from cognates

When a word in two (or more) languages is suspected of being borrowed, if it has legitimate cognates (with regular sound correspondences, see Chapter 5) across sister languages of one family, but is found in only one language (or a few languages) of another family, then the donor language is usually one of the languages for which the form in question has cognates in the related languages. For example, Finnish *tytär* 'daughter' has no cognates in the other branches of the Finno-Ugric family, while cognates of Proto-Indo-European **dhugəter* (**dhughₜer*) 'daughter' are known from most Indo-European languages, including ones as geographically far apart as Sanskrit and English. Therefore, the direction of borrowing is from one of these Indo-European languages (actually from Baltic) to Finnish. Spanish *ganso* 'goose' is borrowed from Germanic **gans*; Germanic has cognates, for example German *Gans*, English *goose*, and so on, but this Spanish word has no true cognate in other Romance languages. Rather, they have such things as French *oie*, Italian *oca*, and others reflecting Latin *ānser* 'goose' (which is cognate with Germanic **gans* 'goose', but not the source of borrowed Spanish *ganso*). Thus, the direction of borrowing is from Germanic to Spanish. (Ultimately, Germanic **gans* and Latin *ānser* are cognates (from Proto-Indo-European **ghans-*), but that does not affect the example of Spanish *ganso* as a loan from German.) In another example, the Proto-Mixe-Zoquean word **tsiku* 'coati-mundi' has cognates throughout the languages of the family; in the Mixe branch of the family, due to sound changes, the cognates reflect **čik*. On the other hand, in the Mayan family (of thirty-one languages in Mexico and

Guatemala), essentially only Yucatecan has the form *či?k* for 'coati-mundi'; the other Mayan languages have native words **ts'uts'*, **si:s* or **kohtom* for 'coati-mundi'. From the general distribution of cognate forms in Mixe-Zoquean, it is concluded that Yucatecan borrowed the word from Mixe-Zoquean, and from its phonological shape, it appears that Yucatecan took the word more directly from the Mixean branch of that family (Justeson et al. 1985: 24).

3.5.4 Geographical and ecological clues

The geographical and ecological associations of words suspected of being loans can often provide clues helpful to determining whether they are borrowed and what the identity of the donor language is. For example, the geographical and ecological remoteness from earlier English-speaking territory of *zebra*, *gnu*, *impala* and *aardvark* – animals originally found only in Africa – makes these words likely candidates for loanwords in English. Indeed, they were borrowed from local languages in Africa with which speakers of European languages came into contact when they entered the habitats where these animals are found – *zebra* is from a Congo language (borrowed through French), *gnu* from a Khoe language, *impala* from Zulu, and *aardvark* from Afrikaans.

It is known that Nahuatl (the language of the Aztecs and Toltecs) started out in the region of northwestern Mexico and the southwestern USA and migrated from there into central Mexico and on to Central America. Since cacao (the source of chocolate, cocoa) did not grow in the original Nahuatl desert homeland, the Nahuatl word *kakawa-* 'cacao' is likely to be a loan. Indeed, it was borrowed from Mixe-Zoquean (Proto-Mixe-Zoquean **kakawa* 'cacao'). Several other loans in Nahuatl reflect the adoption of names for plants and animals not encountered before the migration into lower Mexico, where heretofore unknown items indigenous to the more tropical climate were encountered. In Nez Perce (a Sahaptian language of the north-western USA), *lapatá:t* 'potato' is borrowed from Canadian French *la patate*; it is clearly a loan and clearly from French, not only because it is morphologically analyzable in French but not in Nez Perce, but also because we know that potatoes were introduced to this area after European contact (Callaghan and Gamble 1997: 111). Knowledge of this history suggests that the term for them could be a borrowing. Further investigation shows this to be the case, a borrowing from French into Nez Perce in this case.

Inferences from geography and ecology are not as strong as those from the phonological and morphological criteria mentioned above; however, when coupled with other information, the inferences which they provide can be useful.

3.5.5 Other semantic clues

A still weaker kind of inference, related to the last criterion, can sometimes be obtained from the semantic domain of a suspected loan. For example, English words such as *squaw*, *papoose*, *powwow*, *tomahawk*, *wickiup* and so on have paraphrases involving 'Indian'/'Native American', that is, 'Indian woman', 'Indian baby', 'Indian house' and so on; this suggests possible borrowing from American Indian languages. Upon further investigation, this supposition proves true; these are borrowed from Algonquian languages into English. In another example, in Xinkan (a small family of four languages in Guatemala) most terms for cultivated plants are known to be borrowed from Mayan; this being the case, any additional terms in this semantic domain that we encounter may be suspected of being possible borrowings. This criterion is only a rough indication of possibilities. Sources for the borrowing must still be sought, and it is necessary to try to determine the exact nature of the loans, if indeed borrowings are involved.

3.6   Loans as Clues to Linguistic Changes in the Past

Evidence preserved in loanwords may help to document older stages of a language before later changes took place. An often-cited example is that of early Germanic loans in Finnish which document older stages in the development of Germanic. These loans bear evidence of things in Germanic which can be reconstructed only with difficulty from the evidence retained in the Germanic languages themselves – some of these reconstructed things are confirmed only through comparisons of Germanic with other branches of Indo-European. For example, Finnish *rengas* 'ring' (borrowed; see Proto-Germanic **hreng-az*) reveals two things about Germanic. First, it documents Germanic at the stage before the sound change of *e* to *i* before *n* (*e > i / __n*) – all attested Germanic languages show only the forms with *i*, the result after the change, as in English *ring*. A comparison of Finnish *rengas* and *kuningas* 'king' (also borrowed from Germanic, Proto-Germanic **kuning-az*) shows that Germanic originally contrasted *i* and *e* in the position before *n*, which is not seen in Germanic after the two sounds merged before *n*. Second, both these loans document the Proto-Germanic ending **-az*, suggested by comparative Germanic evidence (but lost in most Germanic languages, seen as *-s* in Gothic). It is only by confirming **-az* through comparisons from other branches of Indo-European (compare the cognates, Latin *-us* and Greek *-os* 'nominative singular') and from borrowings such as these from earlier Germanic into Finnish that we can be certain of the reconstruction. In another case, some loans in Finnish document Germanic before the umlaut change took place. For example, Finnish *patja* 'mattress' (borrowed from Germanic; see Proto-Germanic **badja* 'bed') documents Germanic before umlaut in which *a > e* when followed in the next syllable by *j* or *i* (as seen in English *bed*, German *Bett* – later the **-ja* was lost through a series of changes, **badja > bedja > bed*). The pre-umlaut stage can be reconstructed from other considerations, in particular in comparisons with cognate words from related languages outside of the Germanic branch of Indo-European. In the umlaut context, modern Germanic languages preserve only words which have undergone the change; Gothic is the only Germanic language which did not undergo umlaut. Another loanword in Finnish, *airo* 'oar', preserves evidence of another suffix which is difficult to reconstruct, the Proto-Germanic feminine ending **-ō* (compare Gothic *-a*, Proto-Scandinavian **-u*) (Krause 1968: 53). The loans which bear evidence of the earlier forms before the changes took place, such as these examples from Finnish, help to confirm the accuracy of the reconstructions.

In another example, Spanish used to contrast bilabial stop *b* and fricative *v*, although these are fully merged in modern Spanish (though still spelled differently, <b> and <v>, which are no longer distinct phonemes). The stop *b* came from Latin initial *b* and intervocalic *p*, whereas fricative *v* came from late Latin initial *v* and from intervocalic *v* and *b*; these two phonemes, /b/ and /v/, merged in Spanish to the single /b/ of modern Spanish. However, early loan-words from Spanish into American Indian languages (hispanisms) show clearly that the contrast persisted at least long enough to arrive in America, although soon afterwards the merger took place and later hispanisms reflect only the merged sound. In the early hispanisms, /v/ was borrowed typically as *w*, since most Native American languages lacked *v* (*w* being their sound which is nearest phonetically to *v*), whereas the /b/ of earlier Spanish was borrowed as /b/, /ɓ/ or /p/, depending on the sounds available in the particular borrowing language which could be considered the closest phonetic equivalent to Spanish *b* in each recipient language. The following are a few early hispanisms in Mayan languages which show the earlier contrast in Spanish before these sounds later merged. Forms 1–3 show original intervocalic /b/ (borrowed as *p, b* or *ɓ*):

1. Spanish *jabón* 'soap' (phonetically [ʃabón] in the sixteenth cen-tury), borrowed as: Chol *ʃapum*, Huastec *ʃabu:n*, Q'anjobal *šapon*, Motocintlec *ʃa:puh*, K'iche' *ʃɓon*, Tzeltal *ʃapon*.
2. Spanish *nabo* 'turnip': K'iche' *napuʃ*, Tzotzil *napuʃ* (< *nabos* 'turnips', borrowed from the Spanish plural form).
3. Spanish *sebo* 'tallow, grease': Q'anjobal *ʃepuʔ*, K'iche' *ʃepu*, Tzotzil *ʃepu*.

Forms 4–6 show original intervocalic /v/ (borrowed as *w* or *v*):

4. *navaja* 'knife, razor': Akateko *nawaš*, Chol *ñawaʃaʃ*, Q'anjobal *nawuš*, Tzotzil *navaʃaʃ* (< *navajas*, 'plural' form).
5. *clavo* 'nail': Akateko *lawuʃ*, Chol *lawuʃ*, K'iche' *klawuʃ*, Tzeltal *lawuʃ*, Tojolabal *lawuʃ* ('nail', 'spur'), Tzotzil *lavuʃ* (< *clavos*, borrowed from the plural form).
6. Old Spanish *cavallo* < Latin *cavallus* 'work horse'): Akateko *kawayú* 'horse, beast of burden', Chol *kawayu*, Q'anjobal *kawayo*, Q'eqchi' *kawa:y*, Motocintlec *kwa:yuh* 'horse, mule', Tzeltal *kawu*, Tzotzil *kawayú* 'beast of burden'. (Cf. Modern Spanish *caballo* 'horse'.)

These loans demonstrate (1) the phonetic nature of original sounds, (2) the time when the sounds merged, and (3) the fact that this merger of /b/ and /v/ had not yet taken place in the mid-sixteenth century when these languages began to borrow from Spanish.

Evidence from loanwords can also sometimes contribute to understanding the *relative chronology* of changes in a language (introduced in Chapter 2, and discussed again in Chapters 5 and 8). For example, Motocintlec (Mayan, of the Q'anjobalan branch) *čo:ŋ* 'to sell' is borrowed from Cholan (a different branch of Mayan) *čon* (compare Proto-Mayan **ko:ŋ*). (Recall that Cholan was the principal language of Classical Maya civilization, and as such contributed numerous loans to languages of the region.) We know that Cholan underwent two changes: **k* > *č* and **ŋ* > *n*, though both **k* and **ŋ* remain unchanged in Motocintlec (as seen, for example, in *koŋoɓ* 'market', which retains the native form, from **ko:ŋ* 'to sell' + *-oɓ* 'place of, instrumental suffix'). Therefore, loanwords of Cholan origin such as Motocintlec *čo:ŋ* reveal that in Cholan the change of **k > č* took place earlier than the change of **ŋ > n*, since from the form of the loan in Motocintlec we conclude that Motocintlec borrowed *čo:ŋ* at the stage when **k > č* had already taken place in Cholan, but before Cholan had undergone the change of **ŋ > n*. Thus loans such as this one reveal the relative chronology of Cholan changes, first **k > č*, followed later by **ŋ > n*.

3.7   What Can Be Borrowed?

Not only can words be borrowed, but sounds, phonological features, morphology, syntactic constructions and in fact virtually any aspect of language can be borrowed, given enough time and the appropriate sorts of contact situations. Let's look at a few examples of non-lexical borrowings. (See also Chapter 12.)

3.7.1   Borrowed sounds or features used in native lexical items

Foreign sounds can be borrowed – that is, speakers of one language can borrow sounds from another language with which they are familiar. There are two main ways in which non-native sounds can end up in native words: through areal diffusion (see Chapter 12) and through onomatopoeia and expressive symbolism.

Through intense long-term contact, foreign sounds can be borrowed and come to occur in native words. A few examples are: the clicks borrowed from so-called Khoisan languages (Khoe and San languages) of southern Africa into some neighbouring Bantu languages (for example, Xhosa, Zulu, Sotho; Proto-Bantu had no clicks); glottalized consonants borrowed into Ossetic and Eastern Armenian from neighbouring languages of the Caucasus linguistic area; and the retroflex consonants of Indo-Aryan languages, which owe their origin, at least in part, to contact with Dravidian languages in the South Asian (Indian) linguistic area (see Chapter 12; Campbell 1976).

Expressive symbolism is the use of certain phonetic traits to symbolize affectations, heightened expressive value, or the speaker's attitude. An example of a foreign sound which has been extended into native words through onomatopoeia and affective symbolism is the *r* of Chol and Tzotzil (two Mayan languages). Before contact with Spanish, these languages had no *r*; this sound was introduced through Spanish loanwords which contained it, for example Chol *arus* 'rice' < Spanish *arroz* /aros/, and Tzotzil *martoma* 'custodian' < Spanish *mayordomo*. After *r* was introduced in loanwords, this new sound – which apparently seemed exotic to the speakers of these Mayan languages – came to be employed in certain native words for onomatopoeic or expressive purposes, for example, Chol *buruk-ña* 'buzzing, humming', *burbur-ña* 'noisily', *porok-ña* 'breathing when there is an obstruction', *sorok-ña* 'bubbling'. Some of the expressive Tzotzil words which now have the *r*, which was first introduced through loanwords from Spanish, are native words which formerly had only *l*, for example, *ner-iʃ* 'cross-eyed', where Colonial Tzotzil had only *nel-iʃ* (compare *nel-* 'crooked, twisted, slanted'). The word **kelem* 'strong young man, male' has split into two in modern Tzotzil: *kerem* 'boy (affective)' and *kelem* 'rooster' – Colonial Tzotzil had only *kelem* 'boy, bachelor, servant' (Campbell 1996).

3.7.2 Elimination of sounds through language contact

Not only can foreign sounds be acquired through diffusion, but language contact can also lead to the elimination of sounds (or features of sounds). For example, Proto-Nootkan had nasals, as Nootka still does, but closely related Nitinat and Makah lost nasality – former nasals became corresponding voiced oral stops (*m > b, *n > d, *$\acute{m}$ > b', *$\acute{n}$ > d') – due to diffusion within the linguistic area. Nitinat and Makah are found in a region of the Northwest Coast of North America, where languages of several different families lack nasal consonants. The lack of nasals in Nitinat and Makah is due to the influence of other nasalless languages in the linguistic area (see Chapter 12). Some other examples of loss of this sort due to language contact are the merger of /l/ and /lʲ/ in Czech to /l/, attributed to German influence in the fashionable speech of the cities (Weinreich 1953: 25); and loss of the emphatic (pharyngealized) consonants and of vowel length in Cypriotic Arabic under the influence of Cypriotic Greek (Campbell 1976).

3.7.3 Retention of native sounds due to language contact

In addition to the loss of sounds, language contact can also contribute to the retention of sounds, even if that sound is lost in other areas where the language is spoken which are not in contact with languages which influence the retention. For example, /lʲ/ [spelled <ll>] persists in the Spanish of the Andes region, even though in nearly all other areas of Latin America l^j has merged with j [spelled <y>] (mentioned above). The area where Spanish has maintained this contrast coincides closely with the region where Quechua and Aymara, languages which have /lʲ/, are also widely spoken. Thus, it is due to contact with languages which have the l^j that the Spanish of this region preserves /lʲ/ in contrast with /j/, a contrast lost in most other varieties of Latin American Spanish.

3.7.4 Shifts in native sounds

Another kind of change that can take place in language contact situations is the shift in native sounds to approximate more closely to phonetic traits of sounds in the neighbouring languages. For example, Finnish $ð$ shifted to d under influence from Swedish, due in part to the Swedish reading model with d which was imposed in the Finnish schools. The Nattavaara Finnish dialect shifted native jj to d^jd^j, medial h to $ʔ$, and the geminate (long) stops pp, tt, kk to hp, ht, hk respectively, under influence from Saami. Creek (a Muskogean language of the southern USA) shifted its ϕ (bilabial fricative) to f (labiodental) under English influence (Campbell 1976).

3.7.5 Borrowed rules

Not only can foreign sounds be borrowed, but foreign phonological rules may also be borrowed. For example, borrowed stress rules are not uncommon, such as first syllable stress of many of the languages in the Baltic linguistic area (see Chapter 12), or the rule which places stress on the vowel before the last consonant (V →V́/__C(V)#), shared by several unrelated American Indian languages of southern Mexico and Guatemala. The rule which palatalizes velar stops when followed by a uvular consonant in the same root (for example, *k'aq* → *kʲ'aq* 'flea'; *ke:χ* → *kʲe:χ* 'deer') was borrowed from Mamean languages into the adjacent dialects of several K'ichean languages (two distinct sub-branches of the Mayan family), as shown in Map 3.1. Several Greek dialects of Asia Minor have incorporated a vowel-harmony rule under influence from Turkish. The French spoken in Quimper borrowed a rule of final consonant devoicing from Breton, spoken in that region (see Campbell 1976, 1977). Borrowed phonological rules are not uncommon.

MAP 3.1: Diffusion of Velar palatalization rule in K'ichean languages
(redrawn after Campbell 1977: Map 1)

3.7.6 Diffused sound changes

Related to borrowed phonological rules is the borrowing of sound changes from one language to another. For example, the change of *k* to *č* has diffused throughout the languages of a continuous area of the Northwest Coast of North America from Vancouver Island to the Columbia River, affecting languages of different families. A similar change of *k* to *č* (a laminal palato-alveolar affricate) before front vowels diffused through Telugu, Tamil, Malayalam and some dialects of Tulu

(Dravidian languages), and Marathi (Indo-Aryan) (in several of these languages, *č* before front vowels is in complementary distribution with *ts* before back vowels). The sound change of *ts* to *s* diffused after European contact among neighbouring Q'eqchi', Poqomchi' and Poqomam (Mayan languages) (Campbell 1977).

3.7.7 Calques (loan translations, semantic loans)

In loanwords, something of both the phonetic form and meaning of the word in the donor language is transferred to the borrowing language, but it is also possible to borrow, in effect, just the meaning, and instances of this are called *calques* or *loan translations*, as illustrated by the often-repeated example of *black market*, which owes its origin in English to a loan translation of German *Schwarzmarkt*, composed of *schwarz* 'black' and *Markt* 'market'. Other examples follow.

(1) The word for 'railway' ('railroad') is a calque based on a translation of 'iron' + 'road/way' in a number of languages: Finnish *rautatie* (*rauta* 'iron' + *tie* 'road'); French *chemin de fer* (literally 'road of iron'); German *Eisenbahn* (*Eisen* 'iron' + *Bahn* 'path, road'); Spanish *ferrocarril* (*ferro-* 'iron' in compound words + *carril* 'lane, way'); and Swedish *järnväg* (*järn* 'iron' + *väg* 'road').

(2) English has a number of early calques based on loan translations from Latin, for example: *almighty* < Old English *ælmihtig*, based on Latin *omnipotens* (*omni-* 'all' + *potēns* 'powerful, strong'), and *gospel* < *gōdspell* (*gōd* 'good' + *spel* 'news, tidings'), based on Latin *evangelium* which is from Greek *eu-aggelion* 'good-news/message' (<gg> is the normal transliteration of Greek [ŋg]).

(3) A number of languages have calques based on English *skyscraper*, as for example: German *Wolkenkratzer* (*Wolken* 'clouds' + *kratzer* 'scratcher, scraper'); French *gratte-ciel* (*gratte* 'grate, scrape' + *ciel* 'sky'); and Spanish *rascacielos* (*rasca* 'scratch, scrape' + *cielos* 'skies, heavens').

(4) Some Spanish examples include: (1) varieties of American Spanish have *manzana de Adán* 'Adam's apple', a loan translation from the English name (compare Peninsular Spanish *nuez (de la garganta)*, literally 'nut (of the throat)'). (2) Spanish *plata* 'silver' comes from Latin *platta* 'flat' and is thought to have acquired its sense of 'silver' through loan translation from Arabic where the same term meant both 'thin plate' and 'silver'. (3) More modern loan translations in Spanish from English include *cadena* 'chain' and now also 'chain of stores', *estrella* 'star' and now also 'movie star', *canal* 'canal' and now also 'channel (for television)', *guerra fría* 'cold war', *tercer mundo* 'Third World', *aire acondicionado* 'air conditioning', *desempleo* 'unemployment', *supermercado* 'supermarket'.

(5) A number of calques are shared widely among the languages of the Mesoamerican linguistic area (see Chapter 12); these translate the semantic equations illustrated in the following: 'boa' = 'deer-snake', 'door' = 'mouth of house', 'egg' = 'bird-stone', 'knee' = 'leg-head', 'lime' = 'stone(-ash)', 'wrist' = 'hand-neck' (Campbell, Kaufman and Smith-Stark 1986).

3.7.8 Emphatic foreignization

Sometimes, speakers go out of their way to make borrowed forms sound even more foreign by substituting sounds which seem to them more foreign than the sounds which the word in the donor language actually has. These examples of further 'foreignization' are usually found in loans involving slang or high registers; it is somewhat akin to hypercorrection (see Chapter 4). The phenomenon is illustrated in examples such as the frequent news media pronunciations of *Azerbaijan* and *Beijing* with the somewhat more foreign-sounding ʒ, [azerbaiˈʒan] and [beiˈʒɪŋ], rather than the less exotic but more traditional pronunciation with ǰ (IPA [dʒ]), [beiˈǰɪŋ] and [azerˈbaiǰan] (with penultimate stress in the latter). The English borrowing from French *coup de grace* (literally, 'blow/hit of grace') is more often rendered without the final *s*, as /ku de gra/, than as /ku de gras/, where many English speakers expect French words spelled with *s* to lack *s* in the pronunciation and have extended this to eliminate also the /s/ of *grace*, though in French the *s* of *grace* is pronounced, [gRas]. In borrowings in Finnish slang, sounds which match native Finnish sounds are often replaced with less native-sounding segments; for example, in *bonja-ta* 'to understand', from Russian *ponjatʲ*, and in *bunga-ta* 'to pay for, to come up with the money for', from Swedish *punga*, the *p* – a sound which native Finnish has – was further 'foreignized' by the substitution of more foreign-sounding *b*, a sound not found in native Finnish words. (Compare Hock and Joseph 1996: 261, 271.)

3.8   Cultural Inferences

It is not difficult to see how loanwords can have an important historical impact on a culture – just consider what the evening news in English might be like without *money* and *dollars*, or *sex*, or *religion*, *politicians* and *crime*. These words are all loans:

(1) *money*: borrowed in Middle English times from French (see Old French *moneie*; compare Modern French *monnaie* 'money, coin'), ultimately from Latin *monēta*, from the name of *Juno monēta* 'Juno the admonisher' in whose temple in Rome money was coined (ultimately *admonish* and *money* are related, both involving borrowed forms which hark back to Latin *monēre* 'to admonish') (Anttila 1989: 137).

(2) *dollar*: borrowed into English in the sixteenth century from Low German and Dutch *daler*, ultimately from High German *thaler*, in its full form *Joachimsthaler*, a place in Bohemia, literally 'of Joachim's valley', from where the German *thaler*, a large silver coin of the 1600s, came, from a silver mine opened there in 1516. (Cf. German *Tal* 'valley', English *dale*.)

(3) *sex*: first attested in English in 1382, ultimately from Latin *sexus* 'either of the two divisions of organic beings distinguished as male and female respectively', derived from the verb *secāre* 'to cut, divide'. (English *sect*, *section*, *dissect* and *insect* are borrowings based on the same Latin root.)

(4) *religion*: borrowed from French *religion*, first attested in English in 1200 (ultimately from Latin *religiōn-em*, of contested etymology, said to be from either *relegere* 'to read over again' or *religāre* 'to bind, religate', reflecting the state of life bound by monastic vows).

(5) *politician*: borrowed from French *politicien*, first attested in English in 1588, 'a political person, chiefly in the sinister sense, a shrewd schemer, a crafty plotter or intriguer'.

(6) *crime*: borrowed from French *crime*, first attested in English in 1382; ultimately from Latin *crīmen* 'judgement, accusation, offence'.

A simple example which illustrates the sort of cultural information that can be derived from loanwords comes from the 'Western American' or 'cowboy' vocabulary in English, a large portion of which is borrowed from Spanish: *adobe* 'sun-dried bricks, a structure made of adobe bricks' < *adobe*; *arroyo* 'a water-carved gully in a dry region' < *arroyo* 'brook, small stream'; *bronco* < *bronco* 'rough, rude'; *buckaroo* < *vaquero* 'cowhand'; *burro* < *burro* 'burro', 'donkey'; *calaboose* 'jail, prison' < *calabozo* 'prison cell, dungeon'; *canyon* < *cañón* 'ravine, gorge, canyon'; *cayuse* 'an Indian pony' < *caballo(s)* 'horse(s)' (perhaps first borrowed from Spanish into Chinook Jargon and from there into English); *chaps* [ʃæps] < *chaparreras* 'open leather garment worn by riders over their trousers to protect them'; *cinch* 'saddle-girth' < *cincha* 'belt, sash, cinch'; *corral* < *corral*; *coyote* < Spanish *coyote* (ultimately from Nahuatl *koyōtl* 'coyote'); *desperado* 'a man ready for deeds of lawlessness or violence' < Older Spanish *desperado* 'without hope, desperate' (compare Modern Spanish *desesperado* 'without hope'); *lariat* < Spanish *la reata* 'the rope, lasso'; *lasso* < *lazo* 'knot, bow, lasso'; *mesa* 'flat-topped hill with steep sides' < *mesa* 'table', 'plateau'; *mustang* < *mestenco* 'lacking an owner'; *palomino* 'horse with pale cream-coloured or golden coat and cream-coloured to white mane and tail' < *palomino* 'dove-like', see Mexican Spanish *palomo* 'pale cream-coloured horse'; *pinto* 'a paint (horse), a mottled horse' < *pinto* 'painted, mottled'; *ranch* < *rancho* 'hut or house in the country', *rancher* < *ranchero* 'farmer, rancher'; *rodeo* < *rodeo* 'a round-up' (from *rodear* 'to go round'); *stampede* < Mexican Spanish *estampida* 'crash, uproar'; *vigilante* < *vigilante* '(one who is) vigilant' (from *vigilar* 'to watch, keep an eye on'). Given the large number of loanwords in this semantic domain, we infer that culture and economy of the Old American West were highly influenced by contact with Spanish speakers there.

More extensive examples of this sort are found in Chapter 15, which deals with the information that loanwords can provide for the interpretation of prehistory.

A very revealing case is that of the Romani ('Gypsy') migrations. A good deal is known about the identity, origins, migrations, and history of Romani speakers (the Rom). Historical linguistics is the main source of the information, and much of it comes from loanwords. The comparative method demonstrates that Romani belongs to the Indo-Aryan languages (also called 'Indic', a branch of Indo-European) of northern and central India.

Romani started in north Central India. While there, the language borrowed some Sanskrit words (words meaning 'believe', 'thirst', etc.). The *first move* was to northwest India (before the second century BC), where words from Dardic languages (another branch of Indo-Aryan) were borrowed, for example words for 'man-male', 'whip', 'to arise', 'six', etc. Because of the known history of sound changes and of the break-up of Indic languages, we know that Romani could not have left India later than c. AD 1000.

The *second* move was to Iran (Persia) before AD 650, where Romani borrowed many words from Persian, 'bag', 'blind', 'breath', 'bridge', 'chicken', 'church', 'donkey', 'fortress, town', 'friend', 'goat', 'handful', 'handle', 'honey', 'linen', 'mule', 'pear', 'saddle', 'silk', 'sin', 'sock', 'spur', 'star', 'wax', 'wool', 'worm', and from Kurdish, 'axe', 'forest', 'garlic', 'honey', 'landlord-host', 'nut', 'steel', 'raise', etc. From here the Rom split, with one branch going southwest into the eastern Mediterranean region. Since there are no Arabic loans in European Romani, we infer that they left Iran before the Muslim conquest of AD 650. There are Arabic loans in all the languages in regions where Islam arrived, so the Romani speakers must have migrated from Iran before the arrival of Islam.

The *third* move, if indeed there was one, is less clear. Some scholars hypothesize that Romani moved to the Caucasus region during the Armenian Trebizond Empire, on the Black Sea, before c. AD 1040, where Romani borrowed from languages of the region, Armenian ('bewitch', 'button', 'co-parent-in-law', 'deep', 'dough', 'flax', 'forehead', 'hair', 'heart', 'honour', 'horse', 'leather', 'melon', 'oven', 'tin', 'piece'); Georgian ('plum', 'eyelash', 'tallow', etc.); and Ossetic ('boot', 'sock', 'wagon'). One branch of Romani remained in Armenia. However, other scholars point out that contact with these languages may have been possible in eastern and central Anatolia, eliminating the need to postulate a separate movement into the Caucasus region (Matras 2002: 25).

The invasion of the Seljuk Turks in c. 1040 is thought to have brought about the *fourth* move, to the Byzantine Empire in Anatolia (Turkey), during which time Romani came under Greek influence, taking on some grammatical patterns and borrowing many Greek words, 'anvil', 'bell', 'bone', 'buckle', 'cherry', 'crow', 'dew', 'embrace', 'flower', 'grandmother', 'hour', 'kettle', 'key', 'lead', 'market', 'nail', 'nine', 'road', 'seven', 'Sunday', 'tent', 'town', 'tablecloth', etc. Since Romani shows no Turkish loans (though Seljuks may have used Persian as their lingua franca), it appears that the European Romani speakers left before the Turkish invasions of Anatolia, pushed perhaps by both the Black Death (which reached western Anatolia in 1347) and the invasion of the Ottoman Turks (Ottomans arrived 1265–1328, Byzantium was sacked, and Constantinople fell in 1453).

In their *fifth* move, actually a series of waves, Romani speakers arrived in southeastern Europe, in the Balkans, by c. AD 1350, where they came under the influence of Serbo-Croatian and other South Slavic languages, borrowing many words, for example Serbo-Croatian (perhaps also Bulgarian and Macedonian) 'bean', 'bed', 'body', 'boot', 'cloak', 'dear', 'green', 'gun', 'hut', 'ice', 'inn', 'king', 'mountain', 'old woman', 'onion', 'paper', 'rat', 'room', 'sand-dust', 'sin', 'sheet', 'stable', 'street', 'thick', 'world', 'time', 'vein', 'wild', etc. After this, the European Gypsies do not share a common history.

In the *sixth* move, or wave, documented in historical sources, Romani spread throughout Europe during the fourteenth century. Documentary history establishes Romani as present in Ragusa (Dubrovnik) in 1362, in Hildesheim (Germany) in 1407, in Brussels in 1420, and in Bologna in 1422. (See Hancock 2006, Igla 1997, Kaufman 1973, Matras 2002.)

This remarkable case shows how on the basis of historical linguistic information, and primarily on the evidence of loanwords, we are able to recover a remarkable amount of the history of the identity and migrations of the Romani, ironically the truest 'Aryans' in Europe (despite Nazi views to the contrary).

(See Chapter 16 for other examples of how borrowing can contribute to an understanding of the prehistory of peoples.)

3.9 Exercises

Exercise 3.1

Find ten examples of loanwords (not already mentioned in this chapter) into any language you like, including English. You can consult dictionaries which give historical sources of lexical items or books on the history of particular languages, if you wish. Try to identify the form and meaning of the word in the donor language.

Exercise 3.2 Twentieth-century loans into English

In the history of English, relatively few words were borrowed during the twentieth century when seen in comparison with the large number of loans from earlier times. Still, many did come into the language; here are a few of them. Look up twenty of these (or more if you like) either in a good dictionary of English which indicates the sources from which words come or in a dictionary of the language from which they were borrowed. Try to determine the original meaning and form in the donor language and note any changes (in meaning or form) that the word has undergone as it was adopted into English. The original meanings of many of these may surprise you.

Afrikaans:	apartheid
Chinese:	chow mein, kung fu
Czech:	robot
French:	avant-garde, boutique, camouflage, chassis, cinema, discotheque, fuselage, garage, limousine, sabotage
German:	angst, blitz, ersatz, flak, Nazi, snorkel, strafe, wienerschnitzel
Hawai'ian:	aloha, lei, ukulele
Hebrew:	kibbutz
Italian:	fascism, pasta, pizza
Japanese:	bonsai, kamikaze, karaoke, karate, origami
Russian:	bolshevik, cosmonaut, gulag, intelligentsia, soviet, sputnik
Spanish:	aficionado, burrito, cilantro, macho, nacho
Swedish	(or Scandinavian generally): moped, ombudsman, slalom, smorgasbord
Yiddish:	klutz, maven, putz, schmaltz, tush

Exercise 3.3 Māori and English loanwords

(1) Based on the criteria for establishing loanwords and the direction of borrowing, determine from the following lists of words which are borrowed into

Māori from English and which are borrowed into English from Māori. Note that Māori has the following inventory of sounds: /p, t, k, ɸ, h, r, m, n, ŋ, r, i, e, a, o, u/. In the traditional orthography, /ɸ/ (voiceless bilabial fricative) is spelled *wh*; /ŋ/ is spelled *ng*. Also, native Māori words permit no consonant clusters, rather only syllables of the shape CV (a single consonant followed by a single vowel). (2) Can you say anything about the pronunciation of the variety of English from which Māori took its English loans? (3) What can you say about the social or cultural nature of the contact between speakers of Māori and English? Can you identify semantic domains (areas of meaning) most susceptible to borrowing in either of the languages? (4) How were words from one language modified to fit the structure of the other?

1.	hāhi	'church'
2.	haina	'China; sign'
3.	haka	'haka, Māori dance'
4	haki	'flag' (< Union *Jack*)
5.	hāma	'hammer'
6.	hānara	'sandal'
7.	hāngi	'hangi, oven' (hole in the ground with wrapped food placed on heated stones in the pit with fire)
8.	hānihi	'harness'
9.	hāpa	'harp'
10.	hāte	'shirt'
11.	hēmana	'chairman'
12.	hereni	'shilling'
13.	heti	'shed'
14.	hipi	'sheep'
15.	hiraka	'silk'
16.	hiriwa	'silver'
17.	hoeha	'saucer'
18.	hohipere	'hospital'
19.	hopa	'job'
20.	hōro	'hall'
21.	hū	'shoe'
22.	hui	'meeting for discussion'
23.	huka	'sugar'
24.	hūka	'hook'
25.	hupa	'soup'
26.	hūri	'jury'
27.	iāri	'yard'
28.	ihipa	'Egypt'
29.	ingarangi	'England'
30.	ingarihi	'English'
31.	inihi	'inch'
32.	iota	'yacht'
33.	iwi	'iwi, Māori tribe'
34.	kāka	'cork'

35.	kānara	'colonel'
36.	kapa	'copper, penny'
37.	kāpara	'corporal'
38.	kāpata	'cupboard'
39.	kara	'collar'
40.	karaehe	'grass; glassware, tumbler; class'
41.	karāhi	'glass'
42.	karahipi	'scholarship'
43.	karaka	'clock; clerk'
44.	karauna	'crown'
45.	kāreti	'college; carrot; carriage'
46.	kāta	'cart'
47.	kātaroera	'castor oil'
48.	kātipa	'constable'
49.	kaumātua	'kaumatua, Māori elder'
50.	kauri	'kauri tree'
51.	kāwana	'governor'
52.	kea	'kea' (mountain parrot)
53.	kihi	'kiss'
54.	kirihimete	'Christmas'
55.	kiwi	'kiwi bird'
56.	kōmihana	'commission'
57.	kōti	'court (of law); goat'
58.	kuihipere	'gooseberry'
59.	kūmara	'kumara, sweet potato'
60.	kura	'school'
61.	māhi	'mast'
62.	mana	'mana, influence, prestige'
63.	māori	'Māori, native people' (in Māori *māori* means 'clear, ordinary, native New Zealander')
64.	marae	'marae, enclosed meeting area'
65.	marahihi	'molasses'
66.	moa	'moa' (very large extinct flightless bird)
67.	mokopuna	'mokopuna, grandchild'
68.	motokā	'car, automobile' (< motor car)
69.	nēhi	'nurse'
70.	ngaio	'ngaio, coastal shrub'
71.	ōkiha	'ox'
72.	ōriwa	'olive'
73.	otimira	'oatmeal'
74.	pā	'pa, stockaded village'
75.	pahi	'bus'
76.	paihikara	'bicycle'
77.	paitini	'poison'
78.	pāka	'box'
79.	pākehā	'pakeha, European, non-Māori'

80.	pāmu	'farm'
81.	pāoka	'fork'
82.	parakuihi	'breakfast'
83.	parama	'plumber'
84.	pāua	'paua, abalone shell'
85.	pāuna	'pound'
86.	perakēhi	'pillowcase'
87.	pereti	'plate'
88.	pī	'bee'
89.	pirihi	'priest'
90.	pirihimana	'police(man)'
91.	piriniha	'prince'
92.	piriti	'bridge'
93.	pōkiha	'fox'
94.	pōro	'ball'
95.	pukapuka	'book'
96.	pūkeko	'pukeko, swamp hen'
97.	pune	'spoon'
98.	purū	'blue'
99.	pūru	'bull'
100.	rare	'lolly, sweets'
101.	rata	'doctor'
102.	reme	'lamb'
103.	rērewē	'railroad, railway'
104.	rēwera	'devil'
105.	rīhi	'dish; lease'
106.	rimu	'rimu, red pine'
107.	rōre	'lord' (title)
108.	rori	'road'
109.	takahē	'takahe, bird species' (*Notoris mantelli*)
110.	tana	'ton'
111.	tangi	'tangi, Māori mourning or lamentation' (associated with funerals)
112.	tāone	'town'
113.	taonga	'taonga, heritage, Māori treasure, possessions'
114.	tāra	'dollar'
115.	taraiki	'strike'
116.	tauiwi	'tauiwi, non-Māori'
117.	tēpu	'table'
118.	tiā	'jar'
119.	tiaka	'jug'
110.	tiamana	'chairman; German' (cf. hēmana)
121.	tiāti	'judge'
122.	tīhi	'cheese'
123.	tōtara	'totara' (tree species, *Podocarpus totara*)
124.	tui	'tui, parson bird'

125.	waka	'waka, canoe'
126.	wātene	'warden'
127.	weka	'weka, woodhen'
128.	wētā	'weta, large insect species' (*Hemideina megacephala*)
129.	whakapapa	'whakapapa, genealogy'
130.	whānau	'whanau, extended family' (community of close fellows)
131.	whatura	'vulture'
132.	whira	'violin, fiddle'
133.	whīra	'field'
134.	whurū	'flu'
135.	whurutu	'fruit'
136.	whutupaoro	'football' (rugby)
137.	wihara	'whistle'
138.	wīra	'wheel'
139.	wōro	'wall'
140.	wuruhi	'wolf'

Exercise 3.4 Spanish loanwords

The following is a list of borrowings in Spanish from different languages. What historical and cultural inferences might you suggest about the nature of the contact between speakers of Spanish and each of these other languages based on these? Concentrate on the Germanic and Arabic contacts. Which of the non-Germanic words do you think were further borrowed later from Spanish to English (or from Spanish to French and then on to English)?

From Basque: *boina* 'beret (cap)', *cachorro* 'cub, pup', *chaparro* 'short, chubby, squatty, a scrub', *izquierdo* 'left', *pizarra* 'slate, blackboard', *urraca* 'magpie', *zurdo* 'left-handed'.

Celtic loans, already in Latin (from Gaul), inherited in Spanish: *abedul* 'birch tree', *bragas* 'breeches, trousers', *camisa* 'shirt', *carro* 'cart', *cerveza* 'beer'.

From Germanic (Swabians in Galicia; Vandals, Alans; Franks – Visigoths entered Spain in AD 412). Loans: *eslabón* 'link', *ganar* 'to gain, win, earn', *ganso* 'goose'; *bandera* 'flag', *botín* 'booty', *dardo* 'dart', *espiar* 'to spy', *espuela* 'spur', *guardar* 'guard', *guerra* 'war', *guía* 'guide', *hacha* 'axe', *robar* 'to rob', *yelmo* 'helmet'; *arpa* 'harp', *banco* 'bench', *barón* 'baron', *blanco* 'white', *brasa* 'live coal', *estaca* 'stake', *falda* 'skirt', *gris* 'grey', *guante* 'glove', *rico* 'rich', *ropa* 'clothing', *sopa* 'soup', *tacaño* 'stingy', *toalla* 'towel'; *norte* 'north', *sur* 'south', *este* 'east', *oeste* 'west'; personal names: *Anfonso, Elvira, Federico, Fernando, Francisco, Gonzalo, Matilde, Ricardo, Rodrigo*; and so on.

From Arabic (Moors landed in Spain in AD 711; by 718 they had spread over most of the Peninsula, where they remained until the recapture of Granada in 1492). Loans: *Guad-* 'river' (in place names, for example, *Guadalajara* 'river of stones', *Guadarrama* 'river of sand'); *alcázar* 'castle' (from Latin *castrum* with Arabic article *al-*), *alférez* 'ensign', *alcalde* 'mayor', *atalaya* 'watchtower', *aldea* 'village', *almacén* 'storehouse', *barrio* 'district of city', *adobe* (sun-dried brick), *albañil* 'mason', *alcoba* 'bedroom' (alcove), *alfarero* 'potter', *bazar* 'bazaar', *alfiler* 'pin', *alfombra* 'rug', *almohada* 'pillow', *ataúd* 'coffin', *aceite* 'oil', *aceituna* 'olive', *albaricoque* 'apricot', *alcachofa* 'artichoke', *alfalfa* 'alfalfa', *algodón* 'cotton', *arroz* 'rice', *azúcar* 'sugar', *limón* 'lemon', *naranja* 'orange', *jazmín* 'jasmine', *alcohol* 'alcohol', *cero* 'zero', *cifra* 'cipher', *cenit* 'zenith', *albóndiga* 'meat ball', *azul* 'blue', *matar* 'to kill' (Arabic *mat* 'dead, checkmate'), *mono* 'monkey', *ojalá* 'if Allah will (oh I wish)', *res* 'cattle'.

From Taino (Arawakan): *canoa* 'canoe', *iguana* 'iguana', *nigua* 'nit', *maíz* 'maize, corn', *ají* 'chili pepper', *yuca* 'sweet manioc', *tuna* 'fruit of prickly pear cactus', *barbacoa* 'barbecue', *batata* 'sweet potato', *enagua* 'petticoat, skirt, native skirt', *huracán* 'hurricane', *sabana* 'savanna', *macana* 'club', *cacique* 'chief'; *bejuco* 'vine', *maní* 'peanut'.

From Carib: *caníbal* 'cannibal', *manatí* 'manatee (sea cow)', *loro* 'parrot', *colibrí* 'hummingbird', *caimán* 'cayman, alligator species', *caribe* 'Carib', 'Caribbean'.

From Nahuatl: *hule* 'rubber', *tiza* 'chalk', *petaca* 'covered hamper, trunk, suitcase', *coyote* 'coyote', *ocelote* 'ocelot', *sinsonte* 'mocking bird', *guajolote* 'turkey', *chocolate* 'chocolate', *cacao* 'cacao, cocoa', *chicle* 'gum, chicle', *tomate* 'tomato', *aguacate* 'avocado', *cacahuete* 'peanut', *tamal* 'tamale', *jícara* 'gourd cup, small gourd bowl', *metate* 'quern, grinding-stone', *mecate* 'string, twine', *pulque* 'pulque (drink from century plant juice)', *achiote* 'bixa (food dye)', *camote* 'sweet potato', *ayote* 'pumpkin', *chayote* 'chayote (a vegetable)', *elote* 'ear of corn', *nopal* 'prickly pear cactus', *guacamole* 'guacamole', *cuate* 'buddy, twin', *caite* 'sandal'.

From Quechua: *pampa* 'pampa', *papa* 'potato', *coca* 'coca', *quino* 'quinine', *mate* 'mate (a strong tea)', *guano* 'guano (bird fertilizer)', *llama* 'llama', *vicuña* 'vicuña' (llama species), *alpaca* 'alpaca' (llama species), *cóndor* 'condor', *inca* 'Inca', *gaucho* 'gaucho' (cowboy/ horseman).

From Tupí-Guaraní: *jaguar* 'jaguar', *piraña* 'piranha' (violent fish), *tapioca* 'tapioca', *ananás* 'pineapple'.

From English: *bistec* 'beefsteak', *ron* 'rum', *huisqui/whisky* 'whisky', *orange crush* 'Orange Crush (a soft drink)', *sandwich/sanduche/sanguich* 'sandwich', *panqueque* 'pancake', *lonche* 'lunch', *boicot/boicotear* 'boycott', *clip* 'paper-clip', *piqueteo* 'picketing'/*piquetear* 'to picket', *yate* 'yacht', *parquear* 'to park', *parqueo* 'parking place', *bumper/bómper* 'car bumper', *jet* 'jet', *stop* 'stop', *jeep* 'jeep'; *clóset* 'water closet, toilet', *plywood/plaiwud* 'plywood', *álbum* 'album', *bar* 'bar', *film(e)/filmar* 'film'/'to film', *show* 'show', *ticket/tiquete* 'ticket', *sex appeal/sexapil* 'sex appeal', *stress/estrés* 'stress', *spray/espréi* 'spray', *chequear/checar* 'to check'.

(For some of these and for further examples, see Campbell 1997a; Corominas and Pascual 1980; Lapesa 1981; Resnik 1981; Spaulding 1965.)

Exercise 3.5 *Loanwords in Japanese*

The following is a list of some of the loanwords into Japanese, primarily from English (though some other European languages may be involved in a few of these). How has Japanese modified the foreign sounds to fit its phonology? What arguments can you make to show that the direction of borrowing is indeed from English into Japanese? State your evidence.

NOTE: Japanese permits no syllable-final consonants other than -*n*; it does not tolerate consonant clusters other than -*nC*, though geminates [double consonants] are allowed, and the only word-final consonant is -*n*. In Japanese, /t/ is [ts] before *u*, [č] ([tʃ])before *i*, and [t] elsewhere; similarly, /s/ is [š] ([ʃ])before *i*. Japanese has no *l* or *v*, and no *h* before *u* (only *f*), and no *ə*.

1.	aidea	'idea'
2.	aidoru	'idol' (celebrity)
3.	airon	'iron' (appliance)
4	aisukurīmu	'ice cream'
5.	amachua	'amateur'
6.	ampaia	'umpire'
7.	asuterisuku	'asterisk'
8.	bā	'bar'
9.	baffarō	'buffalo'
10.	bāgen	'bargain, sale'
11.	baiburu	'Bible'
12.	baiorin	'violin'
13.	baitaritī	'vitality'
14.	bajji	'badge'
15.	baketsu	'bucket'
16.	ban	'van'
17.	bando	'band, belt'
18.	baraddo	'balad'
19.	barē-bōru	'volleyball'
20.	basuketto	'basket'
21.	basu-tāminaru	'bus terminal'
22.	batā	'butter'
23.	batterī	'battery'
24.	batto	'(baseball) bat'
25.	bēju	'beige'
26.	bēkon	'bacon'
27.	benchi	'bench'
28.	beruto	'belt'
29.	bifuteki	'beefsteak'
30.	bīru	'beer'
31.	bīrusu	'virus' (cf. uirusu)
32.	bitamin	'vitamin'
33.	bōi sukauto	'Boy Scout'
34.	borantia	'volunteer'
35.	bōru	'ball'
36.	boru	'bowl' (stadium)
37.	borutto	'bolt' (headed metal pin)
38.	bosu	'boss'
39.	botan	'button'

40.	būmu	'boom' (in prosperity)
41.	burajā	'bra' (< brassiere)
42.	burausu	'blouse'
43.	buresuretto	'bracelet'
44.	burijji	'bridge' (card game)
45.	burondo	'blond'
46.	buronzu	'bronze'
47.	chātā	'charter'
48.	chāto	'chart'
49.	channeru	'channel'
50.	chansu	'chance'
51.	chīfu	'chief'
52.	chīmuwāku	'teamwork'
53.	chīzu	'cheese'
54.	chokorēto	'chocolate'
55.	chūbu	'tube'
56.	daietto	'diet'
57.	daiyamondo	'diamond'
58.	dansu	'dance'
59.	depāto	'department store'
60.	dezāto	'dessert'
61.	doa	'door'
62.	doraggu sutoa	'drugstore'
63.	doresu	'dress'
64.	doru	'dollar'
65.	epuron	'apron'
66.	erebētā	'elevator, lift'
67.	fan	'fan' (admirer)
68.	firumu	'film'
69.	fōku	'fork'
70.	fūdo	'hood'
71.	furaipan	'frying pan'
72.	furokku-kōto	'frock-coat'
73.	furūtsu jūsu	'fruit juice'
74.	gādoru	'girdle'
75.	garasu	'glass, pane'
76.	garēji	'garage'
77.	garon	'gallon'
78.	gāru sukauto	'Girl Scout'
79.	gasorin	'gasoline'
80.	gātā	'garter'
81.	gēmu	'game'
82.	gōru	'goal'
83.	gorufu	'golf'
84.	goshippu	'gossip'
85.	gureibī	'gravy'
86.	gurōbu	'glove'

87.	gyamburu	'gamble'
88.	gyaroppu	'gallop'
89.	hābu	'herb'
90.	hādo-weā	'hardware' (computer)
91.	hambāgā	'hamburger'
92.	hammā	'hammer'
93.	hamu	'ham'
94.	hamueggu	'ham and eggs'
95.	handoru	'handle, steering wheel'
96.	hankachi	'handkerchief'
97.	herumetto	'helmet'
98.	hinto	'hint'
99.	hitto	'hit'
100.	hotto doggu	'hotdog'
101.	hyūzu	'fuse'
102.	inchi	'inch'
103.	indekkusu	'index'
104.	infuruenza	'flu'
105.	īsuto	'yeast'
106.	jāji	'jersey'
107.	jakketto	'jacket'
108.	jamu	'jam'
109.	jampā	'jumper'
110.	jazu	'jazz'
111.	jigu-zagu	'zigzag'
112.	jīnzu	'jeans'
113	jippā	'zipper'
114.	kādo	'card'
115.	kāru	'curl'
116.	kāten	'curtain'
117.	kāton	'carton'
118.	kan	'can, tin'
119.	kareji	'college'
110.	katarogu	'catalogue'
121.	kauntā	'counter'
122.	kēki	'cake'
123.	kisu	'caress, kiss'
124.	kōchi	'coach' (trainer)
125.	kōhī	'café, coffee'
126.	kokku	'cook'
127.	komāsharu	'commercial'
128.	komedī	'comedy'
129.	kompakuto disuku	'compact disk'
130.	kompyūta	'computer'
131.	komyunikēshon	'communication'
132.	konkurīto	'concrete' (building material)
133.	kopī	'copy'

134.	koppu	'cup'
135.	kurabu	'club'
136.	kuraimakkusu	'climax'
137.	kuriketto	'cricket' (game)
138.	kyabetsu	'cabbage'
139.	kyabia	'caviar'
140.	kyampasu	'campus'
141.	kyampēn	'campaign'
142.	kyampu	'camp'
143.	kyandī	'candy'
144.	kyaputen	'captain' (chief, leader)
145.	māchi	'march'
146.	māketto	'market'
147.	māmarēdo	'marmalade'
148.	manējā	'manager'
149.	maton	'mutton'
150.	membā	'member'
151.	merodī	'melody'
152.	meron	'melon'
153.	mineraru uōtā	'mineral water'
154.	miruku	'milk'
155.	mishin	'sewing machine'
156.	morutaru	'mortar'
157.	myūjikaru	'musical' (play)
158.	naifu	'knife'
159.	nambā	'number'
160.	napukin	'napkin'
161.	nattsu	'nut'
162.	nekutai	'necktie'
163.	nettowāku	'network'
164.	nikkeru	'nickel'
165.	nūdoru	'noodle'
166.	nyūsu	'news'
167.	ōba	'overcoat'
168.	ōbun	'oven'
169.	ōkē	'O.K.'
170.	ōkesutora	'orchestra'
171.	ofisu	'office'
172.	omuretsu	'omelette'
173.	orenji	'orange'
174.	oribu	'olive(s)'
175.	pai	'pie'
176.	painappuru	'pineapple'
177.	painto	'pint'
178.	paionia	'pioneer'
179.	paipu	'pipe'
180.	paipu-orugan	'organ' (musical instrument)

181.	panchi	'punch' (fruit punch) (cf. also ponchi, ponsu)
182.	paneru	'panel'
183.	panfuretto	'pamphlet'
184.	panikku	'panic'
185.	pantī	'panties'
186.	pantsu	'underpants, shorts, drawers'
187.	parēdo	'parade'
188.	parupu	'pulp (wood-pulp)'
189.	pāsento	'percent'
190.	pasupōto	'passport'
191.	pātī	'party'
192.	patoron	'patron'
193.	paturōru	'patrol'
194.	pējento	'pageant'
195.	pedaru	'pedal'
196.	pen	'pen'
197.	pēsuto	'paste'
198.	perikan	'pelican'
199.	pikunikku	'picnic'
200.	pin	'pin'
201.	pīnatsu	'peanut'
202.	pinku	'pink'
203.	piru	'pill'
204.	pisutoru	'pistol'
205.	poketto	'pocket'
206.	pondo	'pound'
207.	ponsu	'punch' (fruit punch) (cf. also panchi, ponchi)
208.	posutā	'poster'
209.	posuto	'mailbox, postbox'
210.	puragu	'plug' (electric)
211.	puramu	'plum'
212.	purasuchikku	'plastic'
213.	purin	'pudding' (cf. also pudingu)
214.	pūru	'pool'
215.	rādo	'lard'
216.	raberu	'label'
217.	raifuru-	'rifle'
218.	raimu	'lime'
219.	rain	'line'
220.	rajiētā	'radiator'
221.	rajio	'radio'
222.	ramu	'rum'
223.	rampu	'lamp'
224.	rantan	'lantern'
225.	raunji	'lounge'

226.	rejisutā	'register'
227.	rekōdo	'record'
228.	repōto	'report'
229.	renji	'stove' (cooking stove, < range)
230.	rēsu	'lace'
231.	renzu	'lens'
232.	resuringu	'wrestling'
233.	retasu	'lettuce'
234.	ribon	'ribbon'
235.	rinen	'linen'
236.	risuto	'list'
237.	rizōto	'resort'
238.	rizumu	'rhythm'
239.	romansu	'romance'
240.	rosuto chikin	'roast chicken'
241.	sākasu	'circus'
242.	sain	'sign, signal, signature'
243.	sararī	'salary'
244.	sāroin	'sirloin'
245.	sekkusu	'sex'
246.	serori	'celery'
247.	sētā	'sweater'
248.	shaberu	'shovel'
249.	shatsu	'shirt' (cf. waishatsu 'dress shirt' < white shirt)
250.	sherutā	'shelter'
251.	shiringu	'shilling'
252.	shiroppu	'syrup'
253.	shisutā	'sister'
254.	shīzun	'season'
255.	shō	'show' (entertainment)
256.	shokku	'shock'
257.	shōru	'shawl'
258.	sokkusu	'socks'
259.	sōda	'soda'
260.	sōsēji	'sausage'
261.	suchimu	'steam'
262.	suchuwādo	'steward' (airplane)
263.	suchuwādesu	'stewardess'
264.	sukejūru	'schedule'
265.	sukurīn	'screen' (movie screen)
266.	sukuryū	'screw'
267.	sukyandaru	'scandal'
268.	sukāto	'skirt'
269.	sumāto	'smart' (fashionable)
270.	supaisu	'spice'
271.	superu	'spelling'

272.	supīkā	'speaker' (loud speaker)
273.	suponji	'sponge'
274.	supōtsu	'sport'
275.	sūpu	'soup'
276.	supūn	'spoon'
277.	supurē	'spray'
278.	supurinkurā	'sprinkler'
279.	surakkusu	'slacks'
280.	surangu	'slang'
281.	surippā	'slipper(s)'
282.	surōgan	'slogan'
283.	sutā	'star' (film star)
284.	sutairu	'style'
285.	sutajio	'studio'
286.	sutēki	'steak'
287.	sutenresu	'stainless steel'
288.	sutōbu	'stove' (heating stove)
289.	sutoraiki	'strike' (by employees)
290.	sutoraiku	'strike' (in baseball)
291.	sūtsukēsu	'suitcase'
292.	sutsūru	'stool'
293.	taipuraitā	'typewriter'
294.	tairu	'tile'
295.	taiya	'tire'
296.	takkuru	'tackle' (in football)
297.	takushi	'cab, taxi'
298.	tamburā	'tumbler' (drinking glass)
299.	tātorunekku	'turtleneck'
300.	tēburu	'table'
301.	tenisu	'tennis'
302.	terebi(jon)	'television'
303.	tīn-eijā	'teenager'
304.	toire	'toilet' (lavatory)
305.	ton	'ton'
306.	torakku	'truck'
307.	torikku	'trick'
308.	tōsuto	'toast'
309.	tsuīdo	'tweed'
310.	ueitā	'waiter'
311.	ueitoresu	'waitress'
312.	uesuto	'waiste'
313.	uīkuendo	'weekend'
314.	uinku	'wink'
315.	uirusu	'virus' (cf. bīrusu)
316.	wain	'wine'
317.	wakuchin	'vaccine'
318.	wanisu	'varnish'

319.	yādo	'yard (measure)'
320.	yotto	'yacht'
321.	yunifōmu	'uniform'

Exercise 3.6   Hispanisms in Mayan languages

The following is a list of some of the 'hispanisms' (loanwords from Spanish) found in some of the Mayan languages (of Mexico and Guate-mala). The Spanish forms are presented both in current pronunciation and as pronounced in the six-teenth century. Based on these, what evidence can you derive from these loans in the Mayan languages relevant to changes which have taken place in Spanish since these forms were borrowed? By way of illustration, consider the following example involving Sayula Popoluca (a Mixe-Zoquean language):

Spanish *caja* 'box' (modern [kaxa], colonial [kaʃa]): Sayula Popoluca *kaʃa* 'coffin' ('box for the dead').

From this, you would tentatively conclude that Spanish has undergone the change of ʃ > x after this word was borrowed. Of course, it is necessary to keep in mind that the borrowing language will make substitutions, replacing the Spanish sounds with the closest phonetic counterpart available in the recipient language, so that not all differences in the borrowing language will be due to changes which Spanish has subsequently undergone; to determine this, it will be necessary to compare the sixteenth-century and the modern Spanish forms. In regard to this particular example, it is interesting that Sayula Popoluca later borrowed the Spanish word for 'box' again, after the change, as *kaha* 'cardboard box' (note that Sayula Popoluca has no [x], so that [h] is the language's closest approximation to Modern Spanish [x]).

Note the following phonetic symbols found in these examples:
[s̪]dental (fronted) *s*
[s̺]apical alveolar *s*
[š]laminal retroflex *ʃ*

Focus on /lʲ/ and /j/:

1. *llave* 'key' (modern [jaβe], colonial [lʲaβe, lʲave]): Akateko *laweh*, Q'anjobal *lawe*, K'iche' *lawe*.
2. *cebolla* 'onion' (modern [seβoja], colonial [s̺ebolʲa]): Akateko *sewolya*, Q'anjobal *sewolia*, Tzeltal *sebolia* (none of the Mayan languages has /lʲ/, but they do have /l/ and /j/).
3. *cuchillo* 'knife' (modern [kučijo], colonial [kučilʲo]): Chol *kučilu*, Huastec *kuči:l*, Q'anjobal *kučiilu* 'knife, razor', K'iche' *kučiʔl*.
4. *silla* 'chair' (modern [sija], colonial s̺ilʲa]): Akateko *ʃilah*, Huastec *ʃi:laʔ* 'saddle, chair', Q'anjobal *ʃila*, K'iche' *ʃila*, Tzotzil *ʃila*.
5. *castellano* 'Castilian, Spanish' (modern [kastejano], colonial [kastel-ʲano]): Choltí *kaʃtilan čaβ* 'sugar' (literally 'Castilian honey'), *kaʃti-lan wa* 'bread' (literally 'Castilian tortilla'); K'iche' *kaʃtilan, kaʃlan* 'Castilian, Spanish, pure, correct'.

Focus on /ş/, /ş/, and /ʃ/:

6. *sartén* 'frying pan' (modern [saɾtén], colonial [şartén]): Q'anjobal *ʃalten*, *ʃaltin*, Motocintlec *ʃalten*, Tzotzil *ʃalten*.

7. *sebo* 'tallow, fat' (modern [seβo], colonial [şebo]): Q'anjobal *ʃepuʔ*, K'iche' *ʃepu*, *ʃepo*, Tzotzil *ʃepu*.

8. *seda* 'silk' (modern [seða], colonial [şeða]): Chol *ʃelah-* 'ribbon', Tzotzil *ʃela* 'silk, ribbon'. (Mayan languages have no [ð].)

9. *semana* 'week' (modern [semana], colonial [şemana]): Q'eqchi' *ʃama:n*, *ʃema:n*, K'iche' *ʃemano*, Tzotzil *ʃemana*.

10. *señora* 'lady, madam, Mrs' (modern [senʲora], colonial [şenʲora]): Chol *ʃinolah* 'non-Indian woman', Mam *ʃnu:l* 'non-Indian woman', Motocintlec *ʃnu:la:n* 'non-Indian woman', Tzeltal *ʃinola* 'non-Indian woman'.

11. *mesa* 'table' (modern [mesa], colonial [meşa]): Akateko *meʃah*, Huastec *me:ʃa*, Q'eqchi' *me:ʃa*, Motocintlec *me:ʃah*, K'iche' *meʃa*.

12. *patos* 'ducks' (modern [patos], colonial [patoş]): Huastec *pa:tuʃ*, Q'eqchi' *patuʃ*, K'iche' *pataʃ*, Tzotzil *patoʃ*, all 'duck'. (Note that several plant and animal terms, though singular, were borrowed from the Spanish plural form, as in this example and the next.)

13. *vacas* 'cows' (modern [bakas], colonial [βakaş, vakaş]): Akateko *wakaş* 'cattle', Chol *wakaʃ* 'bull, cow', Itzá *wakaʃ* 'cattle', Q'anjobal *wakaş* 'cow, cattle', Q'eqchi' *kwakaʃ* 'cow, cattle', Mopan *wakaʃ* 'cow, bull, cattle', Tzeltal *wakaʃ* 'beef'. (See also 4 and 5 above.)

14. *cidra* 'a grapefruit-like fruit' (modern [siðra], colonial [şiðra]): Chol *silah*, Tzotzil *sila*. (Note that these languages have no *d*, *ð* or *r*).

15. *cocina* 'kitchen' (modern [kosina], colonial [koşina]): Motocintlec *kusi:nah*, Tzotzil *kusina*.

16. *cruz* 'cross' (modern [krus], colonial [kruş]): Chol *rus*, Q'anjobal *kurus*, Q'eqchi' *kurus*, Mam *lu:s*, Motocintlec *kuru:s*, Tzotzil *kurus*.

17. *lazo* 'lasso, rope' (modern [laso], colonial [laşo]): Akateko *lasuh*, Chol *lasoh*, Tzeltal *laso*, Tzotzil *lasu*.

18. *taza* 'cup' (modern [tasa], colonial [taşa]): Chol *tasa* 'piece of glass', Huastec *ta:sa*, Q'eqchi' *ta:s*.

19. *jabón* 'soap' (modern [xaβón], colonial [ʃabón]): Chol *ʃapum*, *ʃapom*, Huastec *ʃabu:n*, Jakalteko *šapun*, Q'anjobal *šapun*, Motocintlec *ʃa:puh*, K'iche' *ʃɓon*, Tzeltal *ʃapon*.

20. *jarro* 'jug, jar' (modern [xaro], colonial [ʃaro]): Jakalteko *ʃalu*, Q'anjobal *ʃalu*, Mam *šar*, Motocintlec *ʃa:ruh*, K'iche' *ʃaruʔ*, Tzeltal *ʃalu*, Tzotzil *ʃalu*.

21. *aguja* 'needle' (modern [aguxa], colonial [aguʃa]): Akateko *akuʃah*, Chol *akuʃan*, Q'anjobal *akuʃa*, Q'eqchi' *aku:ʃ*, *ku:ʃ*, Motocintlec *aku:ʃah*, Tzeltal *akuʃa*, Tzotzil *akuʃa*.

22. *caja* 'box' (modern [kaxa], colonial [kaʃa]): Chol *kaʃa-teʔ* 'chest' (*teʔ* = 'wood'), Q'anjobal *kaʃa* 'box, chest', Q'eqchi' *ka:ʃ* 'chest', Mam *ka:ş* 'box', Motocintlec *ka:ʃah* 'box, chest', K'iche' *kaʃa* 'box, chest, trunk', Tzeltal *kaʃa*.

Focus on /v/ and /b/:

23. *ventana* 'window' (modern [bentana], colonial [βentana, ventana]): Chol
     wentana, Q'anjobal *wentena*, Motocintlec *wanta:nah*.
24. (= 13 above) *vacas* 'cows' (modern [bakas], colonial [βakaṣ, vakaṣ]):
     Akateko *wakaš* 'cattle', Chol *wakaʃ* 'bull, cow', Itzá *wakaʃ* 'cattle',
     Q'anjobal *wakaš* 'cow, cattle', Q'eqchi' *kwakaʃ* 'cow, cattle', Mopan
     wakaʃ 'cow, bull, cattle', Tzeltal *wakaʃ* 'beef'.
25. *calvario* 'Calvary' (modern [kalβario], colonial [kalβario, kal-vario]):
     Q'anjobal *karwal* 'cemetery, graveyard', K'iche' *kalwar*.
26. *clavos* 'nails' (modern [klaβos], colonial [klaβoṣ, klavoṣ]): Akateko
     lawuʃ, Chol *lawuʃ*, Tzeltal *lawuʃ*, Tojolabal *lawuʃ*. (Note that these
     forms mean 'nail', but are borrowed from the Spanish plural form.)
27. *rábanos* 'radishes' (modern [ráβanos], colonial [ráβanoṣ, rávanoṣ]):
     Tojolabal *lawuniʃ*, Motocintlec *luwaʔnʃa* 'rábano', Tzotzil *alavanuʃ*.
     (Note that these all mean 'radish', though borrowed from the Spanish
     plural form. Tzotzil has a phonemic contrast between /v/ and /b/, but has
     no /w/; the other languages have no /v/, but do have /w/.) (See also 1
     above.)
28. *botón(es)* 'button(s)' (modern [botón], colonial [botón]): Q'eqchi'
     ɓoto:nʃ, K'iche' *ɓotona, ɓotoniʃ*, Tojolabal *ɓoton* 'button, knot in
     wood', Tzotzil *ɓoton*.
29. *bolsa* 'bag, pocket' (modern [bolsa], colonial [bolṣa, borṣa]): Chol *borʃa*,
     Q'eqchi' *ɓo:ʃ* 'pocket', K'iche' *ɓorʃa*, Tzeltal *ɓolsa*.
30. *nabos* 'turnips' (modern [naβos], colonial [naboṣ]): K'iche' *napuʃ*,
     Tzotzil *napuʃ*, Motocintlec *kolinaʔwa*. (See also 2 and 7 above.)

4

Analogical Change

They have been at a great feast of languages, and stolen the scraps.
(Shakespeare [1564–1616],
Love's Labour's Lost, V, 1, 39)

4.1 Introduction

Sound change, borrowing and analogy have traditionally been considered the three most important (most basic) types of linguistic change. In spite of the importance of analogy, linguistics textbooks seem to struggle when it comes to offering a definition. Some do not even bother, but just begin straight away by presenting examples of analogical change. Some of the definitions of analogy that have been offered run along the following lines: analogy is a linguistic process involving generalization of a relationship from one set of conditions to another set of conditions; analogy is change modelled on the example of other words or forms; and analogy is a historical process which projects a generalization from one set of expressions to another. Arlotto (1972: 130), recognizing the problem of offering an adequate definition, gives what he calls 'a purposely vague and general definition': '[analogy] is a process whereby one form of a language becomes more like another with which it is somehow associated'. The essential element in all these definitions, vague and inadequate though this may sound, is that *analogical change involves a relation of similarity* (compare Anttila 1989: 88).

For the Neogrammarians, sound change was considered regular, borrowings needed to be identified, and analogy was, in effect, everything else that was left over. That is, almost everything that was not sound change or borrowing was analogy. Analogy became the default (or wastebasket) category of changes. In analogical change, one piece of the language changes to become more like another pattern in the language where speakers perceive the changing part as similar to the pattern that it changes to be more like. Analogy is sometimes described as 'internal borrowing', the idea being that in analogical change a language may 'borrow' from some of its own patterns to change other patterns.

By way of getting started, let us consider some examples of analogy. Originally, *sorry* and *sorrow* were quite distinct, but in its history *sorry* has changed under influence from *sorrow* to become more similar to *sorrow*. *Sorry* is from the adjective form of 'sore', Old English *sārig* 'sore, pained, sensitive' (derived from the Old English noun *sār* 'sore'), which has cognates in other Germanic languages. The original *ā* of *sārig* changed to *ō* and then was shortened to *o* under influence from *sorrow* (Old English *sorh* 'grief, deep sadness or regret'), which had no historical connection to *sorry*. This is an analogical change, where the form of *sorry* changed on analogy with that of *sorrow*.

There are many kinds of analogical change. In this chapter, we explore the different types of analogy and the role of analogy in traditional treatments of linguistic change, and we see how it interacts with sound change (and to a more limited extent with grammatical change, looking forward to Chapter 10 on syntactic change).

Some equate analogical change with morphological change, though this can be misleading. While it is true that many analogical changes involve changes in morphology, not all do, and many changes in morphology are not analogical. In this book, aspects of morphological change are treated not only in this chapter, but also in Chapters 2, 3, 10 and 11.

4.2 Proportional Analogy

Traditionally, two major kinds of analogical changes have been distinguished, *proportional* and *non-proportional*, although the distinction is not always clear or relevant. Proportional analogical changes are those which can be represented in an equation of the form, a : b = c : x, where one solves for 'x' – *a* is to *b* as *c* is to what? (*x* = 'what?'). For example: *ride : rode = dive : x*, where in this instance *x* is solved with *dove*. In this analogical change, the original past tense of *dive* was *dived*, but it changed to *dove* under analogy with the class of verbs which behave like *drive : drove, ride : rode, write : wrote, strive : strove*, and so on. (Today, both *dived* and *dove* are considered acceptable in Standard English, though the use of these forms does vary regionally.) The four-term analogy of the form a : b = c : x is also sometimes presented in other forms, for example as: *a : b :: c : x*; or as:

$$\frac{a}{c} = \frac{b}{x}$$

Not all cases considered proportional analogy can be represented easily in this proportional formula, and some cases not normally thought to be proportional analogical changes can be fitted into such a formula. In the end, the distinction may not be especially important, so long as you understand the general notion of analogy. Let us turn to examples of four-part proportional analogy, which will make the concept clearer.

(1) A famous example comes from Otto Jespersen's observation of a Danish child 'who was corrected for saying *nak* instead of *nikkede* ('nodded'), [and] immediately retorted "stikker, stak, nikker, nak," thus showing on what analogy he had formed the new preterit' (Jesperson 1964: 131). That is, the child produced the proportional formula: *stikker* 'sticks' : *stak* 'stuck' = *nikker* 'nods' : *nak* 'nodded'.

(2) In English, the pattern of the verb *speak/spoke/spoken* ('present tense'/'past tense'/'past participle') developed through remodelling on analogy with verbs of the pattern *break/broke/broken*. In Old English, it was *sprec/spræc/gesprecen* (compare the *spake* 'past tense' of Early Modern English with present-day *spoke*).

(3) Finnish formerly had *laksi* 'bay (nominative singular)'; its possessive form ('genitive singular') was *lahde-n*, just as words such as *kaksi* (nominative singular) : *kahde-n* (genitive singular) 'two'. However, under the weight of Finnish words with the different nominative–genitive pattern as in *lehti* : *lehde-n* 'leaf', *tähti* : *tähde-n* 'star', the *laksi* nominative singular of 'bay' changed to *lahti*, as in the proportional fomula: *lehden : lehti :: lahden : lahti* (< *laksi*). The past tense form of the verb 'to leave' had the same fate: originally the pattern was *lähte-* 'leave' : *läksi* 'left', but this alternation was shifted by the same analogical pattern to give *lähti* 'left' (past tense) in Standard Finnish.

(4) A more grammatical example of proportional analogical change is found in some Spanish dialects in the non-standard pronoun pattern called *laísmo*. Standard Spanish has distinct masculine and feminine third person pronominal direct object forms, but the indirect object pronominal forms do not distinguish gender, as in:

lo vi 'I saw him' [him I.saw], *la vi* 'I saw her' [her I.saw]
le di 'I gave him/her (something)' [him/her I.gave].

In the dialects with *laísmo*, the change created a gender distinction also in the indirect object pronoun forms:

le di 'I gave him (something)', *la di* 'I gave her (something)'.

The proportional analogy in the formula would be:

lo vi 'I saw him' : *la vi* 'I saw her' :: *le di* 'I gave him (something) : *x* where *x* is solved for *la di* 'I gave her (something)'.

(5) Proto-Nahua had a single verbal prefix to signal reflexives, **mo-*, still the basic pattern in a majority of the modern varieties of Nahua, as in Pipil *ni-**mu**-miktia* 'I kill myself', *ti-**mu**-miktiat* 'we kill ourselves', and ***mu**-miktia* 'he/she kills himself/herself'. However, on analogy with the subject pronominal verbal prefixes (*ni-* 'I', *ti-* 'we'), Classical Nahuatl has created distinct reflexive pronouns, *-no-* 'myself', *-to-* 'ourselves' and *(-)mo-* 'himself/herself', as in: *ni-**no**-miktia* 'I kill myself', *ti-**to**-miktia?* 'we kill ourselves' and ***mo**-miktia* 'he/she kills himself/herself'.

4.3 Analogical Levelling

Many of the proportional analogical changes are instances of analogical levelling. (Others are extensions; see below.) Analogical levelling reduces the number of allomorphs a form has; it makes paradigms more uniform. In analogical levelling, forms which formerly underwent alternations no longer do so after the change.

(1) For example, some English 'strong' verbs have been levelled to the 'weak' verb pattern, as for instance in dialects where *throw/threw/ thrown* has

become *throw/throwed/throwed*. There are numerous cases throughout the history of English in which strong verbs (with stem alternations, as in *sing/ sang/sung* or *write/wrote/written*) have been levelled to weak verbs (with a single stem form and *-ed* or its equivalent for 'past' and 'past participle', as in *bake/baked/baked* or *live/lived/lived*). Thus *cleave/clove/cloven* (or *cleft*) 'to part, divide, split' has become *cleave/cleaved/cleaved* for most, while *strive/ strove/striven* for many speakers has changed to *strive/strived/strived*. (*Strive* is a borrowing from Old French *estriver* 'to quarrel, contend', but came to be a strong verb very early in English, now widely levelled to a weak verb pattern.)

(2) Some English strong verbs have shifted from one strong verb pattern to another, with the result of a partial levelling. For example, in earlier English the 'present'/'past'/'past participle' of the verb *to bear* was equivalent to *bear/bare/ born(e)*, and *break* was *break/brake/broke(n)*. They have shifted to the *fight/ fought/fought*, *spin/spun/spun* pattern, where the root of the 'past' and 'past participle' forms is now the same (*bear/bore/born(e)*, *break/broke/broken*).

(3) In a rather large class of verbs in Standard Spanish, *o* (unstressed) alternates with *ue* (when stressed), as in *volár* 'to fly', *vuéla* 'it flies'. Some speakers of Chicano Spanish have levelled the alternation in favour of *ue* alone in these verbs: *vuelár* 'to fly', *vuéla* 'it flies'.

(4) In English, the former 'comparative' and 'superlative' forms of *old* have been levelled from the pattern *old/elder/eldest* to the non-alternating pattern *old/ older/oldest*. Here, *o* had been fronted by umlaut due to the former presence of front vowels in the second syllable of *elder* and *eldest*, but the effects of umlaut were levelled out, and now the words *elder* and *eldest* remain only in restricted contexts, not as the regular 'comparative' and 'superlative' of *old*.

(5a) *Near* was originally a 'comparative' form, meaning 'nearer', but it became the basic form meaning 'near'. If the original state of affairs had persisted for the pattern 'near'/'nearer'/'nearest', we should have had *nigh/near/next*, from Old English *nēah* 'near'/*nēarra* 'nearer'/*nēahsta* 'nearest'. However, this pattern was levelled out; *nearer* was created in the sixteenth century, then *nearest* substituted for *next*. Both *nigh* and *next* remained in the language, but with more limited, shifted meanings. (5b) Similarly, *far* was also comparative in origin (originally meaning 'farther'), but this became the basic form meaning 'far', which then gave rise to the new comparative *farrer*, which was replaced by *farther* under the influence of *further* 'more forward, more onward, before in position'. (5c) The pattern *late/later/latest* is also the result of an analogical levelling without which we would have had instead the equivalent of *late/latter/last*, with the 'comparative' from Old English *lætra* and the 'superlative' from Old English *latost*. (In this case, *later* replaced *latter*, which now remains only in restricted meaning; and *last*, though still in the language, is no longer the 'superlative' of *late*.)

(6) In Greek, $*k^w$ became *t* before *i* and *e*, but became *p* in most other environments. By regular sound change, then, the verb 'to follow' in Greek should have resulted in forms such as: *hépomai* 'I follow', *hétēi* 'you follow', *hétetai* 'he/she/ it follows'. However, by analogy, the *p* (from original $*k^w$ before *o* in this case) spread throughout the paradigm, levelling all the forms of 'to follow': *hépomai* 'I follow', *hépēi* 'you follow', *hépetai* 'he/she/it follows' (Beekes 1995: 73).

(7) Many verbs which have the same form in the singular and plural in Modern German once had different vowels, which were levelled by analogy. Thus, for example, Martin Luther (1483–1546) still wrote *er bleyb* 'he stayed'/*sie blieben* 'they stayed' and *er fand* 'he found'/*sie funden* 'they found', where Modern German has *er blieb/sie blieben* and *er fand/sie fanden* (Polenz 1977: 84).

4.4 Analogical Extension

Analogical extension (rarer than analogical levelling) extends the already existing alternation of some pattern to new forms which did not formerly undergo the alternation. An example of analogical extension is seen in the case mentioned above of *dived* being replaced by *dove* on analogy with the 'strong' verb pattern as in *drive/drove*, *ride/rode* and so on, an extension of the alternating pattern of the strong verbs. Other examples follow.

(1) Modern English *wear/wore*, which is now in the strong verb pattern, was historically a weak verb which changed by extension of the strong verb pattern, as seen in earlier English *werede* 'wore', which would have become modern *weared* if it had survived.

(2) Other examples in English include the development of the non-standard past tense forms which show extension to the strong verb pattern which creates alternations that formerly were not there, as in: *arrive/arrove* (Standard English *arrive/arrived*), and *squeeze/squoze* (Standard *squeeze/squeezed*).

(3) In some Spanish verbs, *e* (unstressed) alternates with *ie* (when in stressed positions), as in *pensár* 'to think', *piénso* 'I think'. In some rural dialects, this pattern of alternation is sometimes extended to verbs which formerly had no such alternating pairs, for example: *aprendér* 'to learn'/*apriéndo* 'I learn', where Standard Spanish has *aprendér* 'to learn'/*apréndo* 'I learn'. Others include *compriendo* 'I understand' for *comprendo*, *aprieto* 'I tighten' for *apreto*; this also extends to such forms as *diferiencia* for *diferencia* 'difference'.

(4) Where Standard Spanish has no alternation in the vowels in forms such as *créa* 'he/she creates'/*creár* 'to create', many Spanish dialects undergo a change which neutralizes the distinctions between *e* and *i* in unstressed syllables, resulting in alternating forms as seen in *créa* 'he/she creates'/*criár* 'to create'. This alternation has been extended in some dialects to forms which would not originally have been subject to the neutralization. Thus, for example, on analogy with forms of the *créa/criár* type, illustrated again in *menéa* 'he/she stirs'/*meniár* 'to stir', some verbs which originally did not have the stress pattern have shifted to this pattern, as seen in dialect *cambéa* 'he/she changes'/ *cambiár* 'to change', replacing Standard Spanish *cámbia* 'he/she changes'/*cambiár* 'to change'; *vacéo* 'I empty'/*vaciár* 'to empty', re-placing Standard Spanish *vácio* 'I empty'/*vaciár* 'to empty'.

From the point of view of the speaker, analogical levelling and extension may not be different, since in both the speaker is making different patterns in the language more like other patterns that exist in the language.

4.5   The Relationship between Analogy and Sound Change

The relationship between sound change and analogy is captured reasonably well by the slogan (sometimes called 'Sturtevant's paradox'): *sound change is regular and causes irregularity; analogy is irregular and causes regularity* (Anttila 1989: 94). That is, a regular sound change can create alternations, or variant allomorphs. For example, umlaut was a regular sound change in which back vowels were fronted due to the presence of a front vowel in a later syllable, as in *brother* + *-en* > *brethren*; as a result of this regular sound change, the root for 'brother' came to have two variants, *brother* and *brethr-*. Earlier English had many alternations of this sort. However, an irregular analogical change later created *brothers* as the plural form, on analogy with the non-alternating singular/plural pattern in such nouns as *sister/sisters*. This analogical change is irregular in that it applied only now and then, here and there, to individual alternating forms, not across the board to all such alternations at the same time. This analogical change in the case of *brethren* in effect resulted in undoing the irregularity created by the sound change, leaving only a single form, *brother*, as the root in both the singular and plural forms; that is, analogy levelled out the alternation left behind by the sound change (*brethren* survives only in a restricted context with specialized meaning). In this context, we should be careful to note that although analogical changes are usually not regular processes (which would occur whenever their conditions are found), they can sometimes be regular.

The history of the verb *to choose* in English shows the interaction of analogy and sound change well. Old English had the forms *cēosan* [čēozan] 'infinitive', *cēas* [čǣas] 'past singular', *curon* [kuron] 'past plural' and *coren* [koren] 'past participle'. These come from the Proto-Indo-European root **geus-* 'to choose, to taste' (which had vowel alternations in different grammatical contexts which gave also **gous-* and **gus-* – the latter is the root behind Latin *gustus* 'taste' and the loanword *gusto* in English). From this Indo-European root came Proto-Germanic **keus-an* (and its alternates in different grammatical contexts, **kaus-* and **kuz-*). The differences in the consonants among the Old English forms of 'to choose' come from two sound changes. The past plural and past participle forms had undergone Verner's law (see Chapter 5), which changed the **s* to **z* when the stress followed (as it did in the 'past plural' and 'past participle' in Pre-Germanic times), and then intervocalic *z* changed to *r* by rhotacism. The other change was the palatalization in English of *k* to *č* before the front vowels. Together, these changes resulted in different allomorphs with different consonants in the paradigm, *čVs-* and *kVr-*. Analogical levelling later eliminated these consonant differences, leaving Modern English *choose/chose/chosen* uniformly with the same consonants. (In dialects, even the difference in vowels of the strong verb pattern was sometimes levelled, to *choose/choosed/choosed* or similar forms, though these have not survived well in the face of competition from Standard English.) In this example, clearly the regular sound changes, rhotacism (after Verner's law) and palatalization, created different allomorphs (irregularity in the paradigm for 'choose' in Old English), and subsequent analogical changes restored uniformity to the consonants of this paradigm.

A somewhat more complicated but more informative example is seen in Table 4.1. (See also section 2.7.4 in Chapter 2.)

In this example, the regular sound change in Stage 2, rhotacism (s > r / V__V), created allomorphy (*honōs/honōr-*), that is, irregularity in the paradigm. Later, irregular analogy changed *honōs* and *labōs* (nominative singular forms) to *honor* and *labor*, both now ending in *r*, matching the *r* of the rest of the forms in the paradigm. Thus irregular analogy has regularized the form of the root, eliminating the allomorphic alternations involving the final consonant of the root.

TABLE 4.1: Latin rhotacism and the interaction of analogy with sound change

Stage 1: Latin before 400BC		
honōs 'honour'	labōs 'labour'	nominative singular
honōsem	labōsem	accusative singular
honōsis	labōsis	genitive singular
Stage 2: rhotacism: s > r /V__V		
honōs	labōs	nominative singular
honōrem	labōrem	accusative singular
honōris	labōris	genitive singular
Stage 3: after 200BC, analogical reformation of nominative singular		
honor	labor	nominative singular
honōrem	labōrem	accusative singular
honōris	labōris	genitive singular

4.6   Analogical Models

In discussions of different sorts of analogical change, it is common to distinguish between *immediate models* and *non-immediate models*. These have to do with the place in the language where we find the 'relation of similarity' which is behind the analogical change. Cases involving *non-immediate models* are, like those of the Latin *labōs > labor* of Table 4.1, due to the influence of whole classes of words or paradigms which do not normally occur in discourse in the near vicinity of the form that changes. In a case such as *honōs > honor* under analogy from other forms in the paradigm, such as *honōrem, honōris* and so on, in normal discourse these forms would not occur adjacent to (or nearby) one another. For the majority of analogical changes no immediate model exists, but rather the model is a class of related forms.

An *immediate model* refers to a situation in which the 'relation of similarity' upon which the analogical change is based is found in the same speech context as the thing that changes. This refers to instances where the thing that changes and the thing that influences it to change are immediately juxtaposed to one another or are located very near each other in frequently repeated pieces of speech. Thus, analogical changes based on an immediate model are typically found in frequently recited routines, such as sequences of basic numbers, days of the week, months of the year, or in phrases used so frequently they can almost be taken as a unit. For example, month names are frequently said together in sequence; as a result, for many English speakers, because of the immediate model of *January*, *February* has changed to *Febuary* [fɛbjuwɛɹi], becoming more like *January* [jænjuwɛɹi].

(1) In English, *female* ['fimeil] was earlier *femelle* [fɛ'mɛl]; however, in the immediate model of *male and female*, frequently uttered together, the earlier *femelle* (the Middle English form) changed to be more similar to *male*.

(2) Modern Spanish has the following days of the week which end in *s*: *lunes* 'Monday', *martes* 'Tuesday', *miércoles* 'Wednesday', *jueves* 'Thursday', *viernes* 'Friday'; however, *lunes* and *miércoles* come from forms which originally lacked this final *s*, but took it by analogy to other day names which ended in *s* in this immediate context, where the days of the week are commonly recited as a list. The day names are derived from shortened versions of the Latin names which originally contained *dies* 'day', as in the following, where the last sound in these compounds reveals which forms contained the original final *s* and which lacked it: Spanish *lunes* < Latin *dies lunae* 'moon's day' [no final -*s*], *martes* < *dies martis* 'Mars' day', *miercoles* < *dies mercurī* 'Mercury's day' [no final-*s*], *jueves* < *dies jovis* 'Jupiter's day', *viernes* < *dies veneris* 'Venus' day'.

(3) Many examples of analogical changes based on an immediate model are found in numbers. For example, (1) Proto-Indo-European had *$*k^w etwor-$* 'four', *$*penk^w e-$* 'five'; *$*p$* became Germanic *$*f$* by Grimm's law, and *$*k^w$* should have become *$*h^w$*, but we get *four* (with *f*, not expected *whour*) by influence from the *f* of following *five*. (2) Latin *quinque* /$k^w ink^w e$/ 'five' (from *$*penk^w e-$*) may be due in part to influence from preceding *quattuor* 'four' (from *$*k^w etwor-$*). (3) In some Greek dialects, the sequence *hepta* 'seven', *oktō* 'eight' has become *hepta*, *hoktō*; in others, *oktō* has become *optō* 'eight', becoming more like the preceding *hepta* 'seven'. (4) In Slavic, originally 'nine' began with *n-* and 'ten' with *d-*, but they shifted so that 'nine' now begins with *d-*, making it more similar to following 'ten', as in Russian *$d^j ev^j at^j$* 'nine' (< Proto-Indo-European *$*new\underset{\circ}{n}$*) *$d^j es^j at^j$* 'ten' (< Proto-Indo-European *$*dek\underset{\circ}{m}$*).

The numbers in several Mayan languages illustrate this tendency for numbers counted in sequence to influence each other, as immediate models for analogical change. For example, Poqomchi' numbers have come to have the same vowel in *kiʔi:ɓ* 'two', *iʃi:ɓ* 'three', *kixi:ɓ* 'four', from earlier forms with distinct vowels: Proto-K'ichean *$*kaʔi:ɓ$* 'two', *$*oʃi:ɓ$* 'three', *$*ka\underset{.}{x}i:ɓ$* 'four'. In Q'eqchi', 'ten' has been influenced by 'nine': *ɓeleheɓ* 'nine', *laxe:ɓ* 'ten', from Proto-K'ichean *$*ɓe:le\underset{.}{x}eɓ$* 'nine', *$*laxu\underset{.}{x}$* 'ten'. The Proto-Mayan forms *$*waq-$* 'six' and *$*huq-$* 'seven' have influenced each other in several Mayan languages: for example, the *w* of 'six' has influenced 'seven' to take *w* instead of its original *$*h$*, as seen in Teco *wu:q* 'seven' and Tzotzil *wuk* 'seven'.

(4) An often-repeated example is Cicero's *senātī populīque Romanī* 'of the Roman senate and people', where *senātūs* 'senate (genitive singular)' is expected. In this case, different noun classes are involved, which had different 'genitive singular' forms:

'nominative singular':	animus 'soul, heart'	senātus 'senate'
'genitive singular':	animī	senātūs

The *senātus* class was small, and only a few nouns belonged to it. The class to which *animus* belonged was much larger. A frequent phrase, in the nominative case, was *senātus populusque romanus* 'the Roman senate and people' (the clitic *-que* means 'and'). Cicero gave it in the genitive case, not with expected *senātūs* 'senate (genitive singular)', but *senatī* based on the immediate model of *populī* 'people (genitive singular)' in this phrase (compare Paul 1920: 106).

4.7   Other Kinds of Analogy

Many different kinds of change are typically called analogy; some of these have little in common with one other. It is important to have a general grasp of these various kinds of changes which are all lumped together under the general heading of analogy, for these terms are used very frequently in historical linguistic works. As pointed out above, the proportional analogical changes which involve levelling and extension, though often irregular, can in some instances be quite regular and systematic. Most of the other kinds of analogy, normally considered non-proportional, are mostly irregular and sporadic (and many of these can be interpreted as proportional, too). There is nothing particularly compelling about this classification of kinds of analogical changes. The names are standard, but one type is not necessarily fully distinct from another, so that some examples of analogical changes may fit more than one of these kinds of change.

4.7.1   Hypercorrection

Hypercorrection involves awareness of different varieties of speech which are attributed different social status. An attempt to change a form in a less prestigious variety to make it conform with how it would be pronounced in a more prestigious variety sometimes results in overshooting the target and coming up with what is an erroneous outcome from the point of view of the prestige variety being mimicked. That is, hypercorrection is the attempt to correct things which are in fact already correct and which already match the form in the variety being copied, resulting in overcorrection and getting the form wrong.

(1) Some dialects in the western United States have: *lawnd* < *lawn*; *pawnd (shop)* < *pawn*; *drownd* (present tense)/*drownded* (past tense) < *drown*/*drowned*; and *acrost* (or *acrossed*) < *across*. These changes came about by hypercorrection in an overzealous attempt to undo the effects of final consonant cluster simplification found to one extent or another in most varieties of English, for example the loss of final *d* after *n*, *han'* for *hand* (common, for example, in *han(d)made*), *fin'* for *find*, *roun'* for *round*, and of *t* after *s*, *firs'* for *first* (for example, in *firs(t) thing*), and so on.

(2) The frequently heard instances in English of things like *for you and I* for what in Standard English is *for you and me* involve hypercorrection; schoolteachers have waged war on the non-standard use of *me* in subject positions, in instances such as *me and Jimmy watched 'Star Trek'* and *me and him ate popcorn* and so on. Speakers, in attempting to correct these to *I* when it is part of the subject of the clause, sometimes go too far and hypercorrect instances of *me* in direct or indirect objects to *I*, as in *Maggie gave it to Kerry and I*.

(3) Some English dialects in the southern United States have *umbrellow* for 'umbrella' and *pillow* for 'pillar', a hypercorrection based on the less prestigious pronunciations of words such as *fella* and *yella*, changing to match to more formal (more prestigious) *fellow* and *yellow*.

(4) In many rural Spanish dialects, *d* before *r* has changed to *g* (d > g /__ r), as in: *magre* 'mother' (< *madre*), *pagre* 'father' (< *padre*), *piegra* 'stone' (< *piedra*), *Pegro* 'Pedro'. Sometimes speakers of these dialects attempt to change these *gr* pronunciations to match the standard and prestigious *dr* counterpart; however, in doing this, they sometimes hypercorrect by changing instances of *gr* to *dr* where the standard language in fact does have *gr*, as for example *suedros* 'parents-in-law', where Standard Spanish has *suegros*, and *sadrado* 'sacred' instead of Standard *sagrado*.

(5) Standard Finnish has /d/, but many regional dialects do not; several have /r/ instead. An attempt to correct dialectal *suren* 'wolf (accusative singular)' to Standard Finnish *suden* would work out well through the replacement of dialect *r* by *d*. However, this sort of substitution leads to hypercorrections such as *suuden* 'big' (accusative singular) where Standard Finnish actually does have /r/, *suuren* (Ravila 1966: 57).

(6) In regional dialects of Spanish, *f* has become *x* before *u*, and this leads to the following sorts of hypercorrections, since the standard language preserves *f* in these cases, but also has other legitimate instances of *xu* as well (where [x] is spelled in Spanish with *j*): *fugo* < *jugo* 'juice', *fueves* < *jueves* 'Thursday', *fuicioso* < *juicioso* 'judicious'.

4.7.2 Folk etymology (popular etymology)

We might think of folk etymologies as cases where linguistic imagination finds meaningful associations in the linguistic forms which were not originally there and, on the basis of these new associations, either the original form ends up being changed somewhat or new forms based on it are created.

(1) An often-cited example is that of English *hamburger*, whose true etymology is from German *Hamburg* + *-er*, 'someone or something from the city of Hamburg'; while hamburgers are not made of 'ham', speakers have folk-etymologized *hamburger* as having something to do with *ham* and on this basis have created such new forms as *cheeseburger*, *chilliburger*, *fishburger*, *vegiburger* or *vegie burger*, *Gainsburgers* (a brand of dog food in North America), just *burger*, and so on.

(2) In Spanish, *vagabundo* 'vagabond, tramp' has given rise also to *vagamundo* (same meaning), associated by speakers in some way with *mundo* 'world' and *vagar* 'to wander, roam, loaf', since a tramp wanders about in the world, or so it may seem.

(3) Jocular Spanish has created *indiosingracia* 'idiosyncrasy' (for *idiosincrasia*), based on *indio* 'Indian' + *sin* 'without' + *gracia* 'grace'.

(4) The original name of the city of *Cuernavaca* in Mexico was *kwāwnawak* in Nahuatl, but it was folk-etymologized by the Spanish as *cuernavaca*, based on *cuerno* 'horn' + *vaca* 'cow', though the place had no connection with either 'horns' or 'cows'. Its true etymology is Nahuatl *kwaw-* 'trees' + *nāwak* 'near, adjacent to', that is, 'near the trees'.

(5) *(Beef) jerky, jerked beef* in English comes from Spanish *charqui*, which Spanish borrowed from Quechua *č'arqi* – nothing is 'jerked' in the preparation of this dried meat, as the folk etymology seems to assume.

(6) *Handiwork* comes from Old English *handġeweorc*, composed of *hand* 'hand' + *ġeweorc* 'work (collective formation)', where *ġe* > *y* [j] or *i* in Middle English, and then was lost elsewhere. The word was reformulated by folk etymology in the sixteenth century on the basis of *handy* + *work* (compare Palmer 1972: 240).

(7) Many today (mis)spell *harebrained* as *hairbrained*, apparently having shifted the original etymology from 'one having a brain like a hare (rabbit)' to a new folk etymology based on *hair*, 'one having a brain associated in some in way with hair'.

(8) Some dialects of English have *wheelbarrel* for *wheelbarrow*, folk-etymologizing it as having some association with *barrel*. A similar example is the saying applied to things requiring two parties, *it takes two to tangle*, folk-etymologized from *it takes two to tango*, made popular from the 1952 song 'Takes Two to Tango', recorded independently by Pearl Bailey and Louis Armstrong.

(9) Some speakers have changed *cappuccino* to *cuppacino*, influenced analogically by the word *cuppa* 'cup of tea', unknown in American English but widely used elsewhere, from *cup of* (*tea* or *coffee*); a seven-year-old boy called it *caffeccino* (based on *coffee*).

(10) Old Spanish *tiniebras* 'darkness' changed to Modern Spanish *tinieblas* through the folk-etymological assumption that it had something to do with *niebla* 'fog' (cf. Spanish *tenebroso* 'dark, gloomy' < Latin *tenebrōsus*).

(11) The true etymology of English *outrage* has nothing to do with *out* or *rage*, which are due to folk etymology. Rather, *outrage* is in origin a borrowing from French *outrage* 'outrage, insult', which is based on Latin *ultrā* 'beyond' + the nominalizing suffix *-agium* (cf. *-age*).

(12) The English *country-dance* was borrowed in France between 1715 and 1723, and in the process was folk-etymologized as *contre danse* (*contre* 'counter, against' + *danse* 'dance'). From France it passed to Italian, Spanish and Portuguese (cf. Spanish *contradanza*, Portuguese *contradança*). Later it was borrowed back into English from French as *contre-dance, contra-dance*.

(13) One of the glosses of the *Appendix Probi*, which warns against what the author considered improper pronunciations in Latin (see Exercise 14.1 in Chapter 14), says it should be *effeminatus* 'effeminate' (derived form *femina* 'woman') rather than the folk-etymologized version *infiminatus* (derived from *infimus* 'low, below').

4.7.3 Back formation

In back formation (*retrograde* formation), a type of *folk etymology*, a word is assumed to have a morphological composition which it did not originally have, usually a root plus affixes, so that when the affixes are removed, a new modified root is created, as when children, confronted with a plate of pieces of cheese, often say 'can I have a chee?', assuming that *cheese* is the plural form, and therefore creating the logical singular root, *chee*, by removing the final *s*, which they associate with the *s* of plural. Examples which result in permanent changes in languages are quite common.

(1) *Cherry* entered English as a loan from Old French *cherise* (Modern French *cerise*) where the *s* was part of the original root, but was interpreted as representing the English 'plural', and so in back formation this *s* was removed, giving *cherry*.

(2) English *pea* is from Old English *pise* 'singular'/*pisan* 'plural'; later the final *s* of the singular was reinterpreted as 'plural' and the form was backformed to *pea*. Compare *pease-pudding* and *pease porridge* (preserved in the nursery rhyme, 'Pease porridge hot, pease porridge cold, . . .'), which retain the *s* of the earlier singular form.

(3) A number of new English verb roots have been created by back formations based on associations of some sounds in the original word with a variant of *-er* 'someone who does the action expressed in the verb': *to burgle* based on *burglar*; *to chauf* 'to drive someone around, to chauffeur', based on *chauffeur* (*-eur* reinterpreted as English *-er* 'agent'), *to edit* from *editor*; *to escalate* based on *escalator*; *to letch* from *lecher*; *to orate* backformed from *orator*; *to peddle* based on *pedlar*; *to sculpt* from *sculptor*.

(4) Some varieties of English have a verb *to orientate*, backformed from *orientation* (competing with or replacing Standard English *to orient*). *Disorientated* is less established, but is sometimes said, derived analogically from *orientated*.

(5) Swahili *kitabu* 'book' is originally a loanword from Arabic *kitāb* 'book'. However, on analogy with native nouns such as *ki-su* 'knife'/*vi-su* 'knives' (where *ki-* and *vi-* represent the noun-class prefixes for which Bantu languages are well known), Swahili has backformed *kitabu* by assuming that its first syllable represents the *ki-* singular noun-class prefix and thus creating a new plural in *vitabu* 'books'. Setswana, another Bantu language (in Botswana and northern South Africa), has *sekole* 'school', borrowed from English (Setswana does not permit initial *sk-* consonant clusters); however, since *se-* is also a noun-class prefix for 'singular', this word has undergone back formation, as seen in *dikole* 'schools', where *di-* is the 'plural' prefix for this class of nouns (cf. Janson 2002: 48).

4.7.4 Metanalysis (reanalysis)

Traditionally two things are treated under the title of metanalysis, *amalgamation* and *metanalysis proper* (today more often called *reanalysis*). Since amalgamation is also a kind of lexical change, it is not treated here, but rather in Chapter 9. *Metanalysis* is from Greek *meta* 'change' + *analysis* 'analysis', and as the name suggests, metanalysis involves a change in the structural analysis, in the interpretation of which phonological material goes with which morpheme in a word or construction.

(1) English provides several examples: *adder* is from Old English *nǣddre*; the change came about through a reinterpretation (reanalysis) of the article–noun sequence *a + nǣddre* as *an + adder* (compare the German cognate *Natter* 'adder,

viper'). English has several examples of this sort. *Auger* is from Middle English *nauger*, *naugur*, Old English *nafo-gār* (*nafo-* 'nave [of a wheel]' + *gār* 'piercer, borer, spear', literally 'nave-borer'). *Apron* is from Middle English *napron*, originally a loan from Old French *naperon*, a diminutive form of *nape*, *nappe* 'tablecloth'. The related form *napkin* (from the French *nape* 'tablecloth' + *-kin* 'a diminutive suffix', apparently ultimately from Dutch) still preserves the original initial *n-*. *Umpire* < *noumpere* (originally a loanword from Old French *nonper* 'umpire, arbiter', *non* 'not' + *per* 'peer'). Finally, *newt* is from Middle English *ewt* (*an* + *ewt* > *a* + *newt*).

(2) Shakespeare (in *King Lear* I, iv, 170) had *nuncle* 'uncle', a form which survives in dialects today. It is derived from a metanalysis based on the final *-n* of the possessive pronouns *mine* and *thine*. In earlier English the form with the final nasal was required when the following word began in a vowel (*mine eyes*) but the nasalless form was employed before words beginning in a consonant (*my lips*). In *nuncle* the original *mine uncle* was reanalyzed so that the *-n* was no longer seen as the end of the possessive pronoun *mine* but as the beginning of the following word, hence *mine + uncle > my nuncle*.

(3) Latin *argent-um* 'silver' and *argent-arius* 'silversmith' became in French *argent* [aʁʒã] 'silver, money' and *argentier* [aʁʒãtje] (with the analysis *argent + ier*); however, a reanalysis of this form as *argen+tier* is the basis of the *-tier* of newer forms such as *bijoutier* 'jeweller', based on *bijou* 'jewel'; another example is the addition of *-tier* to *café* to create *cafetier* 'coffee house keeper', based on *cabaretier* 'cabaret owner, publican, innkeeper', which bears what was originally the *-ier* suffix, construed as *-tier* from comparison with *cabaret* [kabaʁe] 'cabaret, tavern, restaurant'.

(4) Swedish *ni* 'you' (plural, formal) comes from Old Swedish *I* 'you', where it often came after verbs which ended in *-n* 'plural agreement' and the *-n + I* combination was reinterpreted as together being the pronoun *ni*, as in *veten I > veten ni > vet ni* 'you know', *vissten I > visten ni > visste ni* 'you knew' (Wessén 1969: 219).

Reanalysis is one of the most important mechanisms of syntactic change, and is treated in more detail in Chapter 11.

4.7.5 Blending (or contamination)

In *blends*, pieces of two (or more) different words are combined to create new words. Usually the words which contribute the pieces that go into the make-up of the new word are semantically related in some way, sometimes as synonyms for things which have the same or a very similar meaning. Some blends are purposefully humorous or sarcastic in their origin; others are more accidental, sometimes thought to originate as something like slips of the tongue which combine aspects of two related forms which then catch on. Examples of blending and contamination are sometimes treated as lexical change (see Chapter 9). The following English examples illustrate these various origins and outcomes.

(1) Often-cited examples include: *smog* < *smoke* + *fog*; *brunch* < *breakfast* + *lunch*; *motel* < *motor* + *hotel*, *splatter* < *splash* + *spatter*; *flush* < *flash* + *blush*.

(2) *(computer) bit* < *binary digit*.

(3) It is popular to create blends based on *cappuccino*, for example *mochaccino/mocaccino*, *muggaccino*, *frappaccino*, *cyberccino* (involving an internet coffeeshop), *skinniccino/skinnyccino* (small black coffee), *skimmuccino* (cappuccino made with skim milk), *decaphaccino* (cappuccino made of decaffeinated coffee), *soyaccino*, *kiddiccino*, and others.

(4) Based on a portion of *magazine*: *fanzine* (fan group newsletter-magazine), *videozine* (videotape featuring items comparable to print magazines), *webzine* (Internet sites in magazine format), *e-zine/ezine*.

(5) A suffix-like element was created on the basis of a portion of *marathon*: *telethon*, *walkathon*, *bik(e)athon*, *danceathon*, and so on.

(6) *newscast < news + broadcast*; also *sportscast*, *sportscaster*.

(7) Based on part of *alcoholic*: *workaholic*, *chocaholic*, *foodaholic*, *gumaholic*, *shoppaholic*, and so on.

(8) *sexting < sex + texting*.

(9) From combinations based on *hijack*: *skyjack(ing)* and *car-jack(ing)*.

(10) *not* < an Old English compound composed of *ne* 'Negative' + *ōwiht* 'anything'; *neither* < Old English *nāhwæther*, composed of *nā* 'not' + *hwæther* 'whether', through influence from *either*.

(11) *-gate* (a new suffix-like element created on the basis of *Watergate* of the Richard Nixon Watergate scandal): *Contragate*, *Koreagate*, *Irangate*, *Camillagate* (involving a telephone call between Prince Charles and his then close friend and now spouse, Camilla Parker Bowles, Duchess of Cornwall), *nipplegate* (also called *boobgate*, involving the revealing of Janet Jackson's breast in a wardrobe malfunction during the Super Bowl XXXVIII halftime show), *Monicagate* (for Monica Lewinsky, made famous by US President William J. Clinton's indiscretions with her), etc.

(12) *refudiate*, a blend of *refute* and *repudiate*, from a famous 2010 tweet from Sarah Palin.

(13) *gaydar*, the assumed ability to determine by intuition whether someone is homosexual, a blend of *gay* and *radar*.

(14) *webinar*, for web-based seminar, a seminar, workshop, lecture, or presentation that is transmitted over the web, a blend of *web* and *seminar*.

Some non-English examples are:

(15) An often-cited case: Latin *reddere* 'to give back' and *pre(he)ndere* 'to take hold of, seize' influenced one another and resulted in the blend in Romance languages illustrated by Spanish *rendir* 'to yield, produce, render', Italian *rendere* 'to render, yield', French *rendre* 'to render' (English *render* is a borrowing from French).

(16) Spanish jocular *indioma* 'language' (from Cantinflas' films) is a blend of *indio* 'Indian' and *idioma* 'language'.

(17) Names of languages which borrow extensively from others or are highly influenced by others are the sources of such blends as *Spanglish < Spanish + English*, *Finnglish < Finnish + English*; *manglish* was created in feminist discourse to reflect male biases in English, *< man + English*; *Franglais < français* 'French' + *anglais* 'English'.

There are also syntactic blends. Neogrammarians presented many examples (for example, Paul 1920: 165). Some are:

(1) *I'm friends with him*, from a contamination based on *I'm a friend with him* and *we are friends* (Paul 1920: 150).

(2) Non-standard German *mich freut deines Mutes*, from a contamination of the two perfectly normal constructions *ich freu-e mich dein-es Mut-es* [I please-first.person me.Reflexive your-Genitive courage-Genitive], roughly 'I'm pleased over your courage', and *mich freu-t dein Mut* [me.Accusative please-third.person your courage], roughly 'your courage pleases me' (Paul 1920: 149).

(3) Finnish has two alternative constructions for verbs meaning 'to command, order', as in 'she told/commanded the boy to come':

> *hän käski poikaa tulemaan* (*poika-a* 'boy-Partitive.Singular' *tule-ma-an* 'come-third.Infinitive-Illative.case')
> *hän käski pojan tulla* (*poja-n* 'boy-Genitive.Singular' *tul-la* 'come-first. Infinitive').

These two have blended for some dialects to give a third construction:

> *hän käski pojan tulemaan* (*poja-n* 'boy-Genitive.Singular' *tule-ma-an*'come-third.Infinitive-Illative') – not accepted in Standard Finnish.

4.8 Exercises

Exercise 4.1
Observe the language of your friends and of newspapers, television and so on, and attempt to find examples of your own of the various sorts of analogy.

Exercise 4.2 Identifying analogical changes
Determine what kind of analogical change is involved in the following examples. Name the kind of change, and attempt to explain how it came about, if you can.

(1) In some dialects of English, the pattern *bring/brought/brought* has become *bring/brang/brung*.

(2) Where Standard English has *drag/dragged*, some varieties of English have *drag/drug*. It appears in this case that the Standard English pattern is older.

(3) Old Spanish *siniestro* 'left' changed from Latin *sinister* 'on the left' to take on *ie* under the influence of the antonym *diestro* 'right', since *diestro* and *siniestro* frequently occurred together.

(4) In many Spanish dialects, an intervocalic *d* is regularly lost, as in *mercado* > *mercao* 'market'; in some instances, however, there are changes of the following sort: dialect *bacalado* < Standard *bacalao* 'codfish'; dialect *Bilbado* < Standard *Bilbao* (a place name).

(5) In the Dominican Republic, forms such as Standard Spanish *atras* 'behind' become *astras*; in this variety of Spanish, preconsonantal *s* is often lost, as in *ata* < *asta* (spelled *hasta*) 'until'.

(6) English *Jerusalem artichoke* (a kind of sunflower, with some similarities to an artichoke) is in origin from Italian *girasóle articiocco*, where Italian *girasóle* /jirasóle/ contains *gira-* 'turn around, revolve, rotate' + *sole* 'sun', and *articiocco* 'artichoke', with nothing associated with *Jerusalem*; originally.

(7) In English, *Key West* (in Florida) comes from the Spanish name *cayo hueso*, where *cayo* is 'key, small island' and *hueso* is 'bone'.

(8) English *heliport* < *helicopter* + *airport*; *snazzy* < *snappy* + *jazzy*; *jumble* < *jump* + *tumble*.

(9) Colloquial and regional varieties of Spanish have *haiga* where Standard Spanish has *haya* (subjunctive, 'there may be') and *vaiga* where Standard Spanish has *vaya* (subjunctive, 'may go'). These have been influenced by Standard Spanish verb forms such as *traiga* (subjunctive of *traer* 'to bring', 'may bring') and *caiga* (subjunctive of *caer* 'to fall', 'may fall').

(10) Middle English had *help-* 'present tense', *holp* 'past tense'; Modern English has *help*, *helped* for these.

(11) English to *emote* is derived from *emotion*; to *enthuse* is derived from *enthusiastic*.

(12) Many varieties of English have a new verb *to liaise* based on *liaison*.

(13) English *to diagnose* is derived from *diagnosis*.

(14) Finnish *rohtia* 'to dare' resulted from both *rohjeta* 'to be bold enough, to dare' and *tohtia* 'to dare'.

(15) English *hangnail* is derived from Old English *angnægl* 'painful corn (on foot)'. When *ang* 'pain' as an independent word was lost (though later reborrowed in *anguish*), the *angnægl* form was reinterpreted as having something to do with 'hanging', with painful detached skin of toes and then also hands.

5

The Comparative Method and Linguistic Reconstruction

Linguistic history is basically the darkest of the dark arts, the only means to conjure up the ghosts of vanished centuries. With linguistic history we reach furthest back into the mystery: humankind.

(Cola Minis 1952: 107 [Euphorion 46])

5.1 Introduction

The comparative method is central to historical linguistics, the most important of the various methods and techniques we use to recover linguistic history. In this chapter the comparative method is explained, its basic assumptions and its limitations are considered, and its various uses are demonstrated. The primary emphasis is on learning how to apply the method, that is, on how to reconstruct. The comparative method is also important in language classification, in linguistic prehistory, in research on distant genetic relationships, and in other areas; these topics are treated in later chapters.

We say that languages which belong to the same language family are *genetically related* to one another: this means that these related languages derive from (that is, 'descend' from) a single original language, called a *proto-language*. In time, dialects of the proto-language develop through linguistic changes in different regions where the language was spoken – all languages (and varieties of language) are constantly changing – and then later through further changes the dialects become distinct languages.

The aim of reconstruction by the comparative method is to recover as much as possible of the ancestor language (the proto-language) from a comparison of the related languages, the descendants of the original language, and to determine what changes have taken place in the various languages that developed from the proto-language. The work of reconstruction usually begins with phonology, with an attempt to reconstruct the sound system; this leads in turn to reconstruction of the vocabulary and grammar of the proto-language. As can be seen from the way languages are classified, we speak of linguistic relationships in terms of kinship; we talk about 'sister languages', 'daughter languages', 'parent language' and 'language families'. If reconstruction is successful, it shows that the assumption

that the languages are related is warranted. (See Chapter 6 for family-tree classification and Chapter 13 for methods of determining whether languages are
related.)

With the genealogical analogy of your family tree in mind, we can
see how modern Romance languages have descended from spoken Latin
(better said, from Proto-Romance, which is reconstructed via the comparative
method), illustrated in the family tree for the Romance languages in Figure
5.1. (The biological kinship terms added here under the language names in
Figure 5.1 are just a trick to reveal the pedigree of the languages; in this case
the focus is on Spanish. This is certainly not conventionally done in linguistic
family trees.)

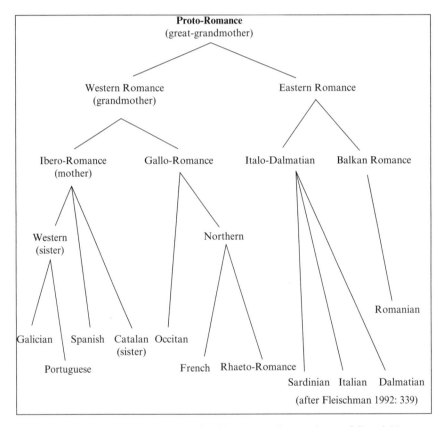

FIGURE 5.1: Proto-Romance family tree (and genealogy of Spanish)

By comparing what these sister languages inherited from their ancestor, we
attempt to reconstruct the linguistic traits which Proto-Romance possessed.
(Proto-Romance is equivalent to the spoken language at the time when Latin
began to diversify and split up into its descendant branches, essentially the same
as Vulgar Latin at the time. The 'Vulgar' of Vulgar Latin means 'of the people'.)
If we are successful, what we reconstruct for Proto-Romance by the comparative

method should be similar to the Proto-Romance which was actually spoken at the time before it split up into its daughter languages. Of course, our success is dependent upon the extent to which evidence of the original traits is preserved in the descendant languages (daughter languages) which we compare and upon how astute we are at applying the techniques of the comparative method, among other things. In this case, since Latin is abundantly documented, we can check to see whether what we reconstruct by the comparative method accurately approximates the spoken Latin we know about from written sources. However, the possibility of checking our reconstructions in this way is not available for most language families, for whose proto-languages we have no written records. For example, for Proto-Germanic (from which English descends), there are no written attestations at all, and the language is known only from comparative reconstruction.

Currently existing languages which have relatives all have a history which classifies them into language families. By applying the comparative method to related languages, we can postulate what that common earlier ancestor was like – we can reconstruct that language. Thus, comparing English with its relatives, Dutch, Frisian, German, Danish, Swedish, Icelandic and so on, we attempt to understand what the proto-language, in this case called 'Proto-Germanic', was like. Thus, English is, in effect, a much-changed 'dialect' of Proto-Germanic, having undergone successive linguistic changes to make it what it is today, a different language from Swedish and German and its other sisters, which underwent different changes of their own. Therefore, every proto-language was once a real language, regardless of whether we are successful at reconstructing it or not.

5.2   The Comparative Method Up Close and Personal

To illustrate the application of the comparative method, let's begin by applying it briefly in a simplified fashion to some Romance languages. (There are many more Romance languages, but for illustration's sake, this miniature introduction is limited to just a few of the better-known of these.) First, consider some data, the words compared among Romance languages given in Table 5.1. (The first line represents conventional spelling; the second is phonemic.)

Latin is *not* a Romance language; the Latin forms in Table 5.1 are presented only so that ultimately we can check the reconstructions which we postulate for Proto-Romance to see how close they come to the forms in the actual spoken proto-language, which was essentially the same as Latin in this case.

To understand the comparative method and to be able to apply it, we need to control some concepts and technical terms:

Proto-language: (1) the once spoken ancestral language from which aughter languages descend; (2) the language reconstructed by the comparative method which represents the ancestral language from which the compared languages descend. (To the extent that the reconstruction by the comparative method is accurate and complete, (1) and (2) should coincide.)

TABLE 5.1: Some Romance cognate sets

	Italian	Spanish	Portuguese	French	(Latin)	English gloss
1.	capra	cabra	cabra	chèvre	capra	'goat'
	/kapra/	/kabra/	/kabra/	/ʃɛvr(ə)/		
2.	caro	caro	caro	cher	caru	'dear'
	/karo/	/karo/	/karu/	/ʃɛr/		
3.	capo	cabo	cabo	chef	caput	'head, top'
	/kapo/	/kabo/	/kabu/	/ʃɛf/		
	'main, chief'	'extremity'	'extremity'	'main, chief'		
4.	carne	carne	carne	chair	carō/carn-	'meat, flesh'
	/karne/	/karne/	/karne/	/ʃɛr/		
				(cf. Old French charn /čarn/)		
5.	cane	can (archaic)	cão	chien	canis	'dog'
	/kane/	/kan/	/kãw̃/	/ʃjɛ̃/		

Sister language: languages which are related to one another by virtue of having descended from the same common ancestor (proto-language) are sisters; that is, languages which belong to the same family are sisters to one another.

Cognate: a word (or morpheme) which is related to a word (morpheme) in sister languages by reason of these forms having been inherited by these sister languages from a common word (morpheme) of the proto-language from which the sister languages descend.

Cognate set: the set of words (morphemes) which are related to one another across the sister languages because they are inherited and descend from a single word (morpheme) of the proto-language.

Comparative method: a method (or set of procedures) which compares forms from related languages, *cognates*, which have descended from a common ancestral language (the *proto-language*), in order to postulate, that is *to reconstruct*, the form in the ancestral language.

Sound correspondence (also called *correspondence set*): in effect, a set of 'cognate' sounds; the sounds found in the related words of cognate sets which correspond from one related language to the next because they descend from a common ancestral sound. (A sound correspondence is assumed to recur in various cognate sets.)

Reflex: the descendant in a daughter language of a sound of the proto-language is said to be a *reflex* of that original sound; the original sound of the proto-language is said to be reflected by the sound which descends from it in a daughter language.

For ease of description, we will talk about 'steps' in the application of the comparative method. Strictly speaking though, it is not always necessary to follow all these steps in precisely the sequence described here. In practice, the comparative linguist typically jumps back and forth among these steps.

Step 1:   Assemble cognates

To begin to apply the comparative method, we look for potential cognates among related languages (or among languages for which there is reason to suspect relatedness) and list them in some orderly arrangement (in rows or columns). In Table 5.1, this step has already been done for you for the few Romance cognates considered in this exercise. In general, it is convenient to begin with cognates from 'basic vocabulary' (body parts, close kinship terms, low numbers, common geographical terms), since these resist borrowing more than other sorts of vocabulary, and for the comparative method we want to compare only true cognates, words which are related in the daughter languages by virtue of being inherited from the proto-language. For successful reconstruction, we must eliminate all other sets of similar words which are not due to inheritance from a common ancestor, such as those which exhibit similarities among the languages because of borrowing, chance (coincidence) and so on (for details, see Chapter 13). Ultimately, it is the systematic correspondences which we discover in the comparative method (in the following steps) which demonstrate true cognates.

Step 2:   Establish sound correspondences

Next, we attempt to determine the sound correspondences. For example, in the words for 'goat' in cognate set 1 in Table 5.1, the first sound in each language corresponds in the way as indicated in SOUND CORRESPONDENCE 1 (here now we concentrate on the phonemic representation of the sound and not on the conventional spelling):

> *Sound correspondence* 1:
> Italian *k-* : Spanish *k-* : Portuguese *k-* : French *ʃ-*

Note that historical linguists often use the convention of a hyphen after a sound to indicate initial position, as *k-* here signals initial *k*; a preceding hyphen indicates that the sound is word-final (for example, *-k*); and a hyphen both before and after refers to a medial sound, one found somewhere in the middle of a word but neither initially nor finally (for example, *-k-*).

It is important to attempt to avoid potential sound correspondences which are due merely to chance. For example, languages may have words which are similar only by accident, by sheer coincidence, as the case of Kaqchikel (Mayan) *mes* 'mess, disorder, garbage' : English *mess* ('disorder, untidiness'). To determine whether a sound correspondence such as that of SOUND CORRESPONDENCE 1 is real (reflecting sounds inherited in words from the proto-language) rather than perhaps just an accidental similarity, we need to determine whether the correspondence recurs in other cognate sets. In looking for further examples of this particular Romance sound correspondence, we find that it recurs in the other cognate sets (2–5) of Table 5.1, all of which illustrate SOUND CORRESPONDENCE 1 for their first sound. If we were to attempt to find recurrences of the seeming *m-* : *m-* correspondence between Kaqchikel and English (seen in the comparison of their words meaning 'mess'), we would soon discover that there are no other instances of it, that it does not recur, as illustrated by the compared words of

TABLE 5.2: Kaqchikel–English comparisons

English	Kaqchikel
man	ači
mouse	č'oy
moon	qati?t
mother	nan

Table 5.2, where the English forms begin with *m*, but the Kaqchikel forms begin with various sounds.

Of course, in principle in a situation such as this, it is possible that the compared languages could be related but that we accidentally chose the few words to compare in Table 5.2 where one or the other of the related languages has not retained the cognate due to borrowing or lexical replacement. To be certain that this is not the case, we would need to look at many comparisons (not just the handful presented in Table 5.2 for illustration's sake). However, in the case of English and Kaqchikel lexical comparisons, we will never find more than one or two which exhibit what initially might have been suspected of being an *m-* : *m-* correspondence based on the words meaning 'mess' in the two languages, and this is precisely because these two languages are not genetically related and therefore the *m* : *m* matching does not recur and is not a true correspondence. Similarly, we need to attempt to eliminate similarities found in borrowings which can seem to suggest sound correspondences. Usually (though not always), loanwords do not exhibit the sort of systematic sound correspondences found in the comparison of native words among related languages, and loans involving basic vocabulary are much rarer than borrowings in other kinds of vocabulary (see Chapter 13 for details).

Given that SOUND CORRESPONDENCE 1 recurs frequently among the Romance languages, as seen in the forms compared in Table 5.1, we assume that this sound correspondence is genuine. It is highly unlikely that a set of systematically corresponding sounds such as this one could come about by sheer accident in a large number of words so similar in sound and meaning across these languages.

Step 3: Reconstruct the proto-sound

There is no fixed rule about what should be done next. We could go on and set up other sound correspondence sets and check to see that they recur; that is, we could repeat step 2 over and over until we have found all the sound correspondences in the languages being compared. Or, we could go on to step 3 and attempt to reconstruct the proto-sound from which the sound in each of the daughter languages (represented in SOUND CORRESPONDENCE 1) descended. In the end, to complete the task, we must establish all the correspondences and reconstruct the proto-sound from which each descends, regardless of whether we do all of step 2 for each set first and then step 3 for all the sets, or whether we do step 2 followed by step 3 for each set and then move on to the next set, repeating step 2, then step 3.

In either case, as we shall soon see, the initial reconstructions which we postulate based on these sound correspondences must be assessed in steps 5 and 6, when we check the fit of the individual reconstructed sounds which we initially postulate in step 3 against the overall phonological inventory of the proto-language and its general typological fit; it is often the case that some of the reconstructions for sounds postulated in step 3 need to be modified in steps 5 and 6.

The different sounds (one for each language compared) in the sound correspondence set reflect a single sound of the proto-language which is inherited in the different daughter languages; sometimes the sound is reflected unchanged in some daughters, though often it will have undergone sound changes in some (or even all) of the daughter languages which make it different from the original proto-sound. We reconstruct the proto-sound by postulating what the sound in the proto-language most likely was on the basis of the phonetic properties of the descendant sounds in the various languages in the correspondence set. The following are the general guidelines that linguists rely on to help them in the task of devising the best, most realistic reconstruction.

Directionality

The known directionality of certain sound changes is a valuable clue to reconstruction (see Chapter 2). By 'directionality' we mean that some sound changes which recur in independent languages typically go in one direction ($A > B$) but usually are not (sometimes are never) found in the other direction ($B > A$). Some speak of this as 'naturalness', some changes 'naturally' taking place with greater ease and frequency cross-linguistically than others. For example, many languages have changed $s > h$, but change in the other direction, $h > s$, is almost unknown. In cases such as this, we speak of 'directionality'. If we find in two sister languages the sound correspondence s in Language$_1$: h in Language$_2$, we reconstruct *s and postulate that in Language$_2$ *$s > h$. The alternative with *h and the change *$h > s$ in Language$_1$ is highly unlikely, since it goes against the known direction of change. Usually, the directionality has some phonetic motivation. Some idea of the typical direction of many of the more commonly recurring sound changes can be gathered from a look at the examples considered in Chapter 2.

In the case of SOUND CORRESPONDENCE 1, we know that the direction of change from k to $ʃ$ is quite plausible and has been observed to occur in other languages, but that $ʃ$ essentially never changes to k. Actually, even more typical would be for k to change to $ʃ$ by first going through the intermediate stage of $č$, that is, $k > č > ʃ$; documentary evidence shows that the sound change in French did go through this intermediate $č$ stage. Old French documents had for the words in Table 5.1: *čjɛvr(ə)* 'goat', *čjɛr* 'dear', *čjɛf* 'head', *čarn* 'meat' and *čjɛŋ* 'dog'. This intermediate stage is preserved in many English loans from French from that time, for example, *chief* and *Charles* with [č], where more recent loans from the same French sources have [ʃ], the result of the later French change of $č > ʃ$, as in *chef* and *Charlene*, with [ʃ].

In another example of the way in which directionality aids in reconstruction, we know that very often voiceless stops (p, t, k) are voiced (b, d, g) between vowels. If we compare two related languages, Language$_1$ and Language$_2$, and we find intervocalic -b- in Language$_1$ corresponding to intervocalic -p- in Language$_2$, then we reconstruct *-p- and assume that Language₂ underwent the common sound change of intervocalic voicing of stops ($p > b$ /V__V, in this case). If we tried to reconstruct *-b- in this situation, we would have to assume that Language₂ had changed -b- to -p-, but this goes against the direction most commonly taken in changes involving these sounds between vowels. This example comes up in SOUND CORRESPONDENCE 2 (below).

The phonetic motivation for the directionality in this case is clear. It is easy to voice stops between vowels, since vowels are inherently voiced, and therefore the change (1) $p > b$/V__V is very common, while it is not so easy to make stops voiceless between vowels, which makes the change (2) $b > p$ /V__V very rare indeed – for (2) the vocal cords would be vibrating for the first vowel, then we would need to stop them from vibrating in order to produce the voiceless [p], and then start the vocal-cord vibration up again for the second vowel; for (1) we merely leave them vibrating for all three segments, the two vowels and the intervening [b]. The known directionality, then, with (1) encountered frequently across languages and (2) hardly at all, is natural and phonetically motivated. As a beginning linguist's experience with language changes and phonological systems increases, a stronger understanding of the directionality of changes develops.

Majority wins

Another guiding principle is that, all else being equal, we let the majority win – that is, unless there is evidence to the contrary, we tend to pick for our reconstructed proto-sound the particular sound in the correspondence set which shows up in the greatest number of daughter languages. Since in SOUND CORRESPOND-ENCE 1, Italian, Spanish and Portuguese all have *k*, and only French diverges from this, with *ʃ*, we would postulate *k* for the Proto-Romance sound, under the assumption that the majority wins, since the majority of the languages have *k* in this correspondence set. This reconstruction assumes that French underwent the sound change *$k > ʃ$, but that the other languages did not change at all, *k* remaining *k*. The underlying rationale for following the majority-wins principle is that it is more likely that one language would have undergone a sound change (in this case, French *$k > ʃ$) than that several languages would independently have undergone the sound change. In this case, if *ʃ were postulated as the proto-sound, it would be necessary to assume that Italian, Spanish and Portuguese had each independently undergone the change of *$ʃ > k$.

Caution is necessary, however, in the use of the majority-wins guideline to reconstruction. Some sound changes are so common (and languages undergo them so easily) that several languages might undergo one of these kind of changes independently of one another (for example, loss of vowel length, nasalization of vowels before nasal consonants, and so on). It is also possible that only one of the daughter languages might have preserved the original sound unchanged while the others all changed it in some way. It is also possible that all the daughter languages may undergo various changes so that none reflects the proto-sound unchanged. Clearly, in these situations there is no majority to do the winning. Moreover, majority rule may not work if some of the languages are more closely related to one another. If some of the languages belong to the same branch (subgroup) of the family (see Chapter 6), then they have a more immediate ancestor which itself is a daughter of the proto-language. This inter-mediate language (a parent of its immediate descendants but itself a daughter of the proto-language) could have undergone a change and then later split up into its daughters, the members of the subgroup, and each of these would then inherit the changed sound that their immediate common ancestor (once a single daughter of the proto-language) had undergone. For example, French, Spanish and Portuguese all share some sounds which are the results of sound changes that took place in Western Romance before it split up further into French, Spanish and Portuguese. Italian does not share these because it comes from a separate branch of Romance. For example, Western Romance changed syllable-final *k* to *i̯*, seen in Spanish, Portuguese and French, which separated from one another only after this Western Romance change had taken place, as in **lakte > lai̯te* 'milk', which gives us French *lait*, Portuguese *leite* and Spanish *leche* (where later changes were *ai > ei > e* in these languages, and *i̯t > č* in Spanish); Italian (not a Western Romance language) underwent a different change, *kt > tt*, giving *latte* 'milk' – we see the results of these changes in choices of kinds of coffee on menus, with *cafe au lait* (French), *cafe latte* (Italian) and *cafe con leche* (Spanish). Now if we compare Italian *tt* with the *i̯t* of Portuguese, French and formerly also of Spanish, 'majority wins' would seem to suggest **i̯t* as the reconstruction with *i̯ > t / __ t* in Italian; but knowing that Portuguese, Spanish and French are closely related, all members of the Western Romance branch, we no longer need to compare three separate instances of *i̯t* to one of *tt*, but only one *i̯t* case (the result of the single change,**kt > i̯t*, in Western Romance) to one *tt* case (in Italian). It is only with the aid of other information that we discover that the best reconstruction is **kt*, from which both the Italian and Western Romance languages departed due to their separate sound changes. As will be seen in Chapter 6, it is the results of the com-parative method which provide the basis for arriving at the classification which tells us which of the related languages belong to the same branches of the family.

So, 'majority wins' is an important principle, but it is easily overridden by other considerations. Still, it would seem to work in the case of SOUND CORRESPOND-ENCE 1 above, suggesting **k* as the best reconstruction, since it is found in a majority of the languages compared.

Factoring in features held in common

We attempt to reconstruct the proto-sound with as much phonetic precision as possible; that is, we want our reconstruction to be as close as possible to the actual phonetic form of the sound as it was pronounced when the proto-language was spoken. We can never know for sure how accurately our reconstructed sound matches the actual sound of the formerly spoken proto-language, but in general, the more information available upon which to base the reconstruction, the more likely it is that we may be able to achieve a reasonably accurate reconstruction. We attempt to achieve as much phonetic realism as possible by observing what phonetic features are shared among the reflexes seen in each of the daughter languages in the sound correspondence. We determine which phonetic features are common to the reflexes in the daughter languages (and features which can be derived from others by the known direction of sound changes, in Step 2), and then we attempt to reconstruct the proto-sound by building into it these shared phonetic features. To illustrate this, let us consider another sound correspondence from Table 5.1, seen to recur here in the words for (1) 'goat' and (2) 'head' (and in many other cognates not given in Table 5.1):

Sound correspondence 2:
Spanish *b* : Portuguese *b* : French *v* : Italian *p*

The reflexes in all four languages share the feature 'labial'; the Spanish, Portuguese and Italian reflexes share the feature 'stop' (phonemically). Factoring the features together, we would expect the proto-sound to have been a 'labial stop' of some sort, a *p* or *b*. Given that the reflex in Spanish, Portuguese and French is 'voiced', under the principle of 'majority wins' we might expect to reconstruct a 'voiced bilabial stop' (*b). In this case, however, other considerations – especially directionality – override the majority-wins principle. The directionality is that it is easy for *p* to become voiced between voiced sounds (between vowels in cognate set 3, and between a vowel and *r* in cognate set 1 in Table 5.1), but the reverse is very rare. Therefore, by directionality, *p is a better choice for the reconstruction, phonetically more plausible; Italian maintained *p* while the others underwent the change to voicing (*p > *b* in Spanish and Portuguese; *p > *v* in French, actually *p > *b* > *v*). From directionality, we also know that stops frequently become fricatives between vowels (or between continuant sounds), but that fricatives rarely ever become stops in this environment. Thus, it is very likely that the French reflex *v* is the result of this sort of change. Taking these considerations into account, for correspondence set 2, we reconstruct *p and postulate that in Spanish and Portuguese *p > *b*, and French *p > *v* (or *p > *b* > *v*). SOUND CORRESPONDENCE 2, then, illustrates how the comparative linguist must balance the various rules of thumb for reconstruction, majority wins, directionality, and factoring in the features shared among the reflexes. (Ultimately, we find out that Western Romance underwent the change of *p > *b* in this position, and then after Western Romance split up, the change of *b* > *v* in French took place. That is, taking the degree of relatedness (the subgrouping; see Chapter 6) into account, there is no longer a majority with the reflex *b*, but rather only Western Romance *b* as opposed to Italian *p*.)

Economy

What is meant by the criterion of economy is that when multiple alternatives are available, the one which requires the fewest independent changes is most likely to be right. For example, if for SOUND CORRESPONDENCE 1 we were to postulate *ʃ, this would necessitate three independent changes from *ʃ > *k*, one each for Italian, Spanish and Portuguese; however, if we postulate *k for the Proto-Romance sound, we need assume only one sound change, *k > ʃ in French. The criterion of economy rests on the assumption that the odds are greater that a single change took place than that three independent changes took place. Of course, sometimes independent changes do take place, so that the criterion does not always guarantee correct results; but all else being equal, the chances of a reconstruction which embodies more economical assumptions being correct are greater than for a reconstruction which assumes less economical developments. (See below for other examples of the use of the economy criterion.)

The other two general considerations (rules of thumb) which linguists use in reconstructing sounds involve checking to see whether the individual sounds postulated to represent the various sound correspondences fit the overall phonological pattern of the proto-language and to see whether this reconstructed pattern is consistent with linguistic universals and typological expectations. These are *phonological fit* and *typological fit* respectively (steps 5 and 6, below). These two considerations come into play mostly after the full set of sound correspondences has been dealt with and the overall inventory of reconstructed sounds that are being postulated can be considered. For this reason, let's deal first with the other correspondences of Table 5.1, and then come back to these two considerations later.

Let us continue steps 2 and 3, then, for the forms in Table 5.1, and establish the remaining sound correspondences illustrated in these forms and set up reconstructions for them. It does not matter in which order we investigate the sound correspondences. We could first look only at initial consonants for all of the cognate sets, then medial consonants, then final consonants, and finally the various vowels; or, we could proceed by investigating the sound correspondence representing the next sound (the second) in the first cognate set, then go on to the third sound in that set, and so on until all the sounds of that cognate set have been addressed, and then proceed to the next cognate set, dealing with each of the sound correspondences for each of the sounds found in that set in sequence (though some of these may recur in other cognate sets and thus may already have been established in the consideration of the previous cognate sets already dealt with). We continue in this way until all the recurring sound correspondences have been examined and proto-sounds to represent them have been postulated. In this way, we will eventually come to reconstruct the full inventory of sounds in the proto-language.

In the example in Table 5.1, let us continue with the corresponding sounds in cognate set 1, for 'goat'. The first vowel in the forms in cognate set 1 shows SOUND CORRESPONDENCE 3:

Sound correspondence 3:
Italian *a* : Spanish *a* : Portuguese *a* : French *ɛ*.

We check this to see if it recurs, and we see that it is also found in the other cognate sets of Table 5.1, for 'dear', 'head' and 'meat'. (It is also found again, in effect, in the last vowel of cognate set 1 for 'goat', though we must deal with the later change in French of final *ɛ* to *ə*/Ø.) Under the majority-wins principle, for this sound correspondence we reconstruct **a* for the Proto-Romance sound, assuming that French has undergone the sound change **a > ɛ*.

The third sound in cognate set 1 'goat' has, in fact, already been dealt with in SOUND CORRESPONDENCE 2 (where we reconstructed **p* for the correspondence set Spanish *b* : Portuguese *b* : French *v* : Italian *p*).

The next sound in the sequence of sounds in the 'goat' cognates gives correspondence set 4:

Sound correspondence 4:
Italian *r* : Spanish *r* : Portuguese *r* : French *r*

SOUND CORRESPONDENCE 4 also recurs, in 'goat', 'dear' and 'meat' (in Table 5.1). For it, we would postulate Proto-Romance **r*, under 'majority wins', since all the languages have this reflex. (To be absolutely accurate, we would have to deal with the fact that in Standard French the *r* became a uvular, but for now we ignore this detail.)

The last sound in 'goat' in effect repeats SOUND CORRESPONDENCE 3, although French later changed final *ɛ* further (to *ə* or *Ø*). Though technically this must be considered a separate sound correspondence, to make it easier we will just assume here that we would easily discover that the two correspondence sets, for the first and last vowel in the 'goat' cognate set, belong together due to a later conditioned change in French.

To complete the task, we would need to establish the sound correspondences for all the cognate sets and reconstruct sounds to represent them. For example, we would find:

Sound correspondence 5:
Italian *o* : Spanish *o* : Portuguese *u* : French *Ø*.

This recurs, as in 'dear', 'head'. For SOUND CORRESPONDENCE 5, we would reconstruct **o* (majority wins), assuming that Portuguese changed final **o* to *u*, and that French lost final **o*.

With more extensive data (many more cognate sets than presented in Table 5.1), we would confirm these reconstructions, with their attendant sound changes and the conditions under which they took place, and we would eventually find all the sound correspondences and postulate reconstructions for all the sounds of the proto-language and work out its phonemic inventory and phonological patterns.

Step 4: Determine the status of similar (partially overlapping) correspondence sets

Some sound changes, particularly conditioned sound changes, can result in a proto-sound being associated with more than one correspondence set. These must be dealt with to achieve an accurate reconstruction. To see how this is done, we will work through an example. For this, let us consider some additional cognate sets in Romance languages, those of Table 5.3 (numbered to follow those of Table 5.1).

Based on the forms of Table 5.3, we set up a sound correspondence for the initial sound in these forms:

Sound correspondence 6:
Italian *k* : Spanish *k* : Portuguese *k* : French *k*

For SOUND CORRESPONDENCE 6, since all the languages have the same sound, *k*, we would naturally reconstruct **k*. However, SOUND CORRESPONDENCE 6 is quite similar to SOUND CORRESPONDENCE 1 (in Table 5.1), for which we also tentatively reconstructed **k*, repeated here for comparison with SOUND CORRE-SPONDENCE 6:

Sound correspondence 1:
Italian *k* : Spanish *k* : Portuguese *k* : French *ʃ*

The two sets overlap partially, since both sets share some of the same sounds. In fact, the only difference between the two is in French, which has *k* in SOUND

CORRESPONDENCE 6 but ʃ in SOUND CORRESPONDENCE 1. In cases such as this of similar (partially overlapping) correspondence sets, we must determine whether they reflect two separate proto-sounds or only one which split into more than one sound in one or more of the languages. In the case of SOUND CORRESPONDENCES 1 and 6, we must determine whether both sets reflect *k, or whether we must reconstruct something distinct for each of the two. Because we assume that sound change is regular, the options for possible solutions here are restricted to essentially only two. One possible solution would be for us to find evidence to show that the two correspondence sets are different today but represent only a single proto-sound. To show this, it would be necessary to explain away the difference between the two sets, that is, to show how a single original sound could change in ways that would result in the two different correspondence sets. For this, we would need to show that a single original sound ended up as ʃ in certain specific environments in French but as k in other circumstances – since the other languages all have only the single reflex, k, the most likely candidate is a *k assumed not to have changed in these languages, but, under this hypothesis, changed to ʃ in French only in specific instances. If we cannot succeed in showing this – in being able to predict where the postulated original *k became ʃ and where it remained k in French – then we cannot reconstruct a single sound for the two sets and we are forced to consider the other possible solution. In this other possible solution, the two correspondence sets represent two distinct sounds in the proto-language which merged to k in all contexts in Italian, Spanish and Portuguese, but remained distinct in French.

In this case, we are able to determine the context in which French sometimes but not always changed *k to ʃ. We notice that in the cognate sets of Table 5.1 which exhibit SOUND CORRESPONDENCE 1, this sound comes before ε in French and a in the other languages (SOUND CORRESPONDENCE 3), while in SOUND CORRESPONDENCE 6, illustrated by the cognate sets in Table 5.3, the initial sound is not before a or ε (as in SOUND CORRESPONDENCE 1), but before o or u (French u or y). There-fore, we determine that French underwent a conditioned sound change, that *k > ʃ before the vowel of correspondence set 3 (*a which became ε in French), but retained *k unchanged before the round vowels seen in the cognates of Table 5.3 (essentially *u and *o, though we need to go through

TABLE 5.3: Some additional Romance cognate sets

	Italian	Spanish	Portuguese	French	(Latin)	English gloss
6.	colore	color	côr	couleur	colōre	'colour'
	/kolore/	/kolor/	/kor/	/kulœr/		
7.	correre	correr	correr	courir	currere	'to run'
	/korere/	/kořer/	/korer/	/kuri(r)/		
8.	costare	costar	costar	coûter	co(n)stāre	'to cost'
	/kostare/	/kostar/	/kostar/	/kuter/	['stand firm']	
9.	cura	cura	cura	cure	cūra	'cure'
	/kura/	/kura/	/kura/	/kyr/	['care']	

the steps to reconstruct these). So, in spite of two distinct sound correspondences (1 and 6), we reconstruct a single proto-sound and show that one of these (SOUND CORRESPONDENCE 1) is the result of a conditioned change which affected only some of the instances of original **k* in French (those before original **a*) but not the other cases of **k* (those before **u* and **o*).

In some cases, however, we are forced to reconstruct separate protosounds in instances of similar, partially overlapping correspondence sets. Consider for example the two sound correspondences illustrated by the initial sounds in additional cognates in Table 5.4.

TABLE 5.4: Further Romance cognate sets

	Italian	Spanish	Portuguese	French	(Latin)	English gloss
10.	battere	batir	bater	battre	battuere	'to beat'
	/battere/	/batir/	/bater/	/batr/		
11.	bolla	bola	bola	boule	bulla	'ball, bubble'
	/bolla/	/bola/	/bola/	/bul/		
12.	bontà	bondad	bondade	bonté	bonitāte	'goodness
	/bonta/	/bondad/	/bõdaǰi/	/bõte/		
13.	bev-	beber	beber	boire	bibere	'to drink'
	/bev-/	/beber/	/beber/	Old French beivre		
14.	venire	venir	vir	venir	venīre	'to come'
	/venire/	/benir/	/vir/	/vənir/		
15.	valle	valle	vale	val	valle	'valley'
	/valle/	/baʎe/	/vale/	/val/		
16.	vestire	vestir	vestir	vêtir	vestīre	'to dress'
	/vestire/	/bestir/	/vestir/	/vetir/		

Cognate sets 10 to 13 show the sound correspondence in (7):

Sound correspondence 7:
Italian *b* : Spanish *b* : Portuguese *b* : French *b*

Cognate sets 14 to 16 show the sound correspondence in (8):

Sound correspondence 8:
Italian *v* : Spanish *b* : Portuguese *v* : French *v*

Clearly the best reconstruction for SOUND CORRESPONDENCE 7 would be **b*, since all the languages have *b* as their reflex. SOUND CORRESPONDENCE 8 partially overlaps with this in that Spanish has *b* for its reflex in this set as well, corresponding to *v* of the other languages. As in the case of Proto-Romance **k* (above), either we must be able to explain the difference in these two sets by showing that those languages with *v* changed an original **b* to *v* under some clearly defined circumstances, or we must reconstruct two separate sounds in the proto-language, presumably **b* and **v*, where Spanish would then be assumed to have merged its original *v* with *b*. In this case, to make a long story short, if we look for factors which could be the basis of a conditioned change in Italian, Portuguese and French, which could explain how a single original **b* could become *v* in certain circumstances but remain *b* in others in these languages, we are unable to find any. We find both *b* and *v* at the beginnings of words before all sorts of vowels, and with more extensive data we would find that both sounds occur quite freely in the same environments in these languages. Since no conditioning factor can be found, we reconstruct **b* for the cognates in correspondence set 7 and **v* for those in correspondence set 8, two distinct proto-sounds. From this, it follows that **v* merged with **b* in Spanish, accounting for why *b* is the Spanish reflex in both cognate sets 14–16 and 10–13 of Table 5.4.

A somewhat more revealing example of the problem of overlapping correspondence sets which prove to contrast and thus require separate sounds to be reconstructed is seen in the example in Table 5.5, from Mayan languages (of which only a few, each representing a major branch of the family, are represented).

TABLE 5.5: Some Mayan cognate sets

	K'iche'	Tzeltal	Yucatec	Huastec	Proto-Mayan	English gloss
1.	ra:h	ya	yah	yah-	*ra:h	'hot, spicy'
2.	ri?x	yix	yi?ih	yeh-	*ri?ix	'old (old man)'
3.	r-	y-	y-	—	*r-	'his/her/its'
4.	raš	yaš	ya?aš	yaš-	*ra?aš	'green'
5.	war	way	way	way	*war	'to sleep'
6.	ya:x	yah	yah	ya?	*ya:h	'sick'
7.	yaš	yaš	—	—	*yaš	'crab, pincers'
8.	k'ay-	k'ay-	k'ay-	č'ay-	*k'ay	'to sell'
		['sing']	['sing, sell']	['buy']		

(NOTE: y = IPA [j], š = [ʃ], č = [tʃ], C' = glottalized (ejective) consonants.)

Note that the 'dash' (–) is the convention used by linguists to mean that either no cognate is known or the data are unavailable. In such instances, we must rely on information from the other cognate sets in order to determine features of those languages where the forms are missing. (In the examples that follow from Mayan, y = IPA [j].)

Cognate sets 1–5 show SOUND CORRESPONDENCE 1:

Sound correspondence 1:
K'iche' *r* : Tzeltal *y* : Yucatec *y* : Huastec *y*

Cognate sets 6–8 show SOUND CORRESPONDENCE 2:

Sound correspondence 2:
K'iche' *y* : Tzeltal *y* : Yucatec *y* : Huastec *y*

Clearly, by our standard criteria, the best Proto-Mayan reconstruction for SOUND CORRESPONDENCE 2 would be *y (preserved unchanged in all the languages). However, all the languages except K'iche' also have y as their reflex in SOUND CORRESPONDENCE 1, whereas K'iche' has r in this case. As in the discussion of the Proto-Romance *k case (above), we must either explain how the difference in these two sets arose by showing that K'iche' had changed original *y to r in some clear set of phonetic circumstances, or we must reconstruct two separate sounds in the proto-language. In this case, to make a long story short, if we look for factors which could be the basis of a conditioned change in K'iche', we are unable to find any. We find both r and y at the beginning and end of words, before all sorts of vowels, and so on, and basically either sound can occur in any context without restrictions. Since no conditioning factor can be found, we reconstruct *r for the SOUND CORRESPONDENCE 1 and *y for SOUND CORRESPONDENCE 2, two distinct proto-sounds. From this, it follows that *r merged with y in Tzeltal, Yucatec and Huastec, accounting for why they have y as the reflex also in cognate sets 6–8 of Table 5.5. When we look at still other Mayan languages, we find this distinction further supported, since, for example, Mam has t and Motocintlec has č where K'iche' has r in the cognates that illustrate SOUND CORRESPONDENCE 1, but they both have y in cognates where K'iche' has y in SOUND CORRESPONDENCE 2. That is, K'iche' turns out not to be the only witness of the distinction between the two sounds of these correspondence sets (Campbell 1977).

TABLE 5.6: Central Algonquian sound correspondences and Bloomfield's reconstruction

	Fox	Ojibwa	Plains Cree	Menomini	PCA
1.	hk	sk	sk	čk	*čk
2.	ʃk	ʃk	sk	sk	*ʃk
3.	hk	hk	sk	hk	*xk
4.	hk	hk	hk	hk	*hk
5.	ʃk	ʃk	hk	hk	*çk

There is a famous case which confirms this way of treating partially overlapping sound correspondence sets. Leonard Bloomfield's (1925, 1928) famous proof of the applicability of the comparative method in unwritten ('exotic') languages was based on the correspondence sets from Central Algonquian languages presented with his reconstructions in Table 5.6 (PCA = Proto-Central Algonquian). Bloomfield (1925) postulated the reconstruction of *çk for set 5 as distinct from the others on the basis of scant evidence, but under the assumption that sound change is regular and the difference in this correspondence set (though exhibiting only sounds that occur in different combinations in the other sets) could not plausibly be explained away. Later, his decision to reconstruct something different for set 5 was confirmed when Swampy Cree was discovered, which contained the correspondence htk in the morpheme upon which set 5 was based, distinct in Swampy Cree from the reflexes of the other four reconstructions. Based on this discovery, Bloomfield (1928: 100) concluded:

> As an assumption, however, the postulate [of sound-change without exception] yields, as a matter of mere routine, predictions which otherwise would be impossible. In other words, the statement that *phonemes change* (sound-changes have no exceptions) is a tested hypothesis: in so far as one may speak of such a thing, it is a proved truth.

Mayan languages provide a somewhat clearer and more compelling case of the need to reconstruct distinct proto-sounds if the difference between two partially overlapping correspondence sets cannot be explained away. Consider the following two K'ichean (a subgroup of Mayan) sound correspondences:

	Tz'utujil	Kaqchikel	K'iche'	Poqomam	Uspanteko	Q'eqchi'
(1)	x	x	x	x	x	x
(2)	x	x	x	x	x-/-(V̀)x	h

For example, the correspondence set in (1) is illustrated by:

Kaqchikel	K'iche'	Poqomam	Uspanteko	Q'eqchi'	gloss
čax	čax	čax	čax	čax	'pine'
k'ax	k'ax	k'ax	k'ax	k'ax	'flour'
k'o:x	k'o:x	k'o:x	k'o:x	k'o:x	'mask'

The correspondence set in (2) is seen in:

Kaqchikel	K'iche'	Poqomam	Uspanteko	Q'eqchi'	gloss
ča:x	ča:x	ča:x	čà:x	čah	'ashes'
ka:x	ka:x	ka:x	kà:x	—	'sky'
o:x	o:x	o:x	ò:x	o:h	'avocado'
q'i:x	q'i:x	q'i:x	q'ì:x	-q'ih	'day, sun'
				(in compounds)	

In (1), all the languages have *x* as the reflex, and we would naturally expect to reconstruct **x* for the Proto-K'ichean sound. However, (2) overlaps considerably with (1), where each language also has *x* except Q'eqchi', which has *h*; Uspanteko has *x* too; however, if there is a vowel preceding this *x*, it has falling tone (V̀), which is not the case for vowels preceding the *x* of correspondence set (1). Since no conditioning factor can be found to explain away the difference between the two sets in Q'eqchi' and Uspanteko, separate proto-sounds must be reconstructed. It has been proposed that correspondence set (2) represents a sound which is further forward than *x*, the sound of correspondence set (1), and thus **x̣* (a somewhat fronted velar fricative) has been proposed to represent correspondence set (2). While the reconstruction with **x* and **x̣* for these two sets is not phonetically ideal, nevertheless the decision to reconstruct something different for the two is confirmed when cognates are compared from other branches of Mayan beyond K'ichean, which exhibit the following corresponding sounds:

	Yucatec	Chol	Chuj	Jakalteko	Mam	K'ichean
(3)	x	h	x	x	x	*x
(4)	n	n	ŋ	ŋ	x	*x̣

The correspondence set in (3) (which matches the K'ichean set in (1)) is exemplified by:

Yucatec	Chol	Chuj	Jakalteko	Mam	K'ichean	gloss
tax	tah	tax	tah	tsax	*čax	'pine'
k'ax	č'ah	k'ax	k'ah	k'ax	*k'ax	'flour, pinole'
k'o:x	k'o:h	k'o:x	k'oh	k'o:x	*k'o:x	'mask'

In Proto-Mayan these have *x; they are, respectively: *ṭax 'pine', *k'ax 'flour, pinole', and *k'o:x 'mask' (where ṭ represents a fronted dental or palatalized 't').

The correspondence set in (4) (which matches K'ichean set (2)) is seen in:

Yucatec	Chol	Chuj	Jakalateko	Mam	K'ichean	gloss
taʔan	tan-	taʔaŋ	taŋ	tsaʔx	*čax̣	'ashes'
kaʔan	čan	čaʔaŋ	kaŋ	kyaʔx	*kax̣	'sky'
ò:n	un	oŋ	oŋ	o:x	*o:x̣	'avocado'
k'ì:n	k'in	q'iŋ-	q'iŋ-	q'i:x	*q'i:x̣	'sun, day'

In Proto-Mayan these all have *ŋ; they are, respectively: *ṭaʔŋ 'ashes', *kaʔŋ 'sky', *o:ŋ 'avocado', and *q'i:ŋ 'sun, day'.

That is, the sounds of correspondence set (3) reflect Proto-Mayan *x, whereas those of set (4) reflect Proto-Mayan *ŋ. Since the two sounds are clearly distinguished in the other branches of the family and descend from distinct sounds in Proto-Mayan, the validity of the decision to reconstruct different sounds for Proto-K'ichean, one branch of Mayan, is confirmed. Perhaps also the phonetics of this reconstruction could be refined. Since the *x* of K'ichean (and several other Mayan) languages is phonetically [χ] (voiceless uvular fricative), it may seem appealing to reconstruct *χ for set (3) in K'ichean and then let *x (velar) represent set (4). Since K'ichean languages contrast uvular and velar stops, a similar contrast in the fricative series may make some sense (see step 5).

Step 5: Check the plausibility of the reconstructed sound from the perspective of the overall phonological inventory of the proto-language

Steps 5 and 6 are related. The rule of thumb in step 5 takes advantage of the fact that languages tend to be well behaved, that is, they tend to have symmetrical sound systems with congruent patterns. For example, in the reconstruction of sounds for the individual sound correspondences in step 3, we can reconstruct each sound of the proto-language with little regard for how these sounds may relate to one another or how they may fit together to form a coherent system. Often in step 5 when we consider the broader view of these sounds in the context of the overall inventory, we refine and correct our earlier proposals. For example, if two related languages have the correspondence set Language$_1$ *d* : Language$_2$ *r*, we might initially reconstruct **r* and assume **r* > *d* in Language$_1$, since *r* > *d* is known to take place in languages, though the alternative of **d* with the assumption that Language$_2$ underwent the change **d* > *r* is just as plausible, since the change *d* > *r* is also found in languages. Suppose, however, that in step 5 we discover that we have reconstructed sounds based on other sound correspondences which would give the following phonological inventory for the proto-language:

**p	**t	**k
**b		**g
	**r	
	**l	

There is a gap in this inventory where **d* would be expected to complete the stop series, where the voiceless stops (**p*, **t*, **k*) would each be matched by a voiced counterpart (**b*, **d*, **g*), if a **d* existed, which would make the stop series symmetrical, the pattern congruent. The proto-language as tentatively reconstructed so far, with both **r* and **l* and **b* and **g*, but no **d*, would be unusual and unexpected. However, by revising our earlier tentative reconstruction of **r* for the *d* : *r* sound correspondence to the equally plausible **d* (assuming **d* > *r* in Language$_2$), we arrive at a much more coherent and likely set of sounds for the proto-inventory, where the two stop series are congruent:

**p	**t	**k
**b	**d	**g
	**l	

While this instance is presented as a hypothetical possibility, it is in fact encountered in a number of real language families, for example in branches of Austronesian. It is important, however, to keep in mind that while languages tend to be symmetrical and have pattern congruity, this is by no means always the case.

Let's consider one other hypothetical instance, also actually found in real language families. If in a family of two languages we encounter the correspondence set Language$_2$ *s* : Language$_2$ *ʃ*, either we could reconstruct **s* (assuming **s* > *ʃ* in Language$_2$) or we could postulate **ʃ* (and assume **ʃ* > *s* in Language$_1$). Both of these changes (**s* > *ʃ* and **ʃ* > *s*) are frequently found in other languages. Suppose, however, that in step 5 we discover that the other sound correspondences justify the reconstruction of several proto-sounds in the alveolar series, including **ts*, but no other palato-alveolar sound. This would give a proto-language with alveolar **ts* but palato-alveolar **ʃ* and no **s*, but this system would be asymmetrical and odd. However, a proto-language with **ts* and **s* but lacking **ʃ* would be normal and not at all unusual. Therefore, in step 5 we would revise the

preliminary reconstruction of Step 3 to make sure that we reconstructed *s for the
s : ʃ correspondence set (assuming *s > ʃ in Language₂) to ensure a more plausible overall phonological inventory for the proto-language which we reconstruct.
A real example which fits precisely this situation comes from Mixe-Zoquean (a
family of languages from southern Mexico), where the languages of the Zoquean
branch have s corresponding to ʃ of the Mixean languages. So, for Proto-Mixe-
Zoquean, *s is a better reconstruction for the s : ʃ correspondence set.

Of course, languages do not have to be symmetrical or fully natural, though
they tend to be. Also, it is conceivable that a proto-language might have gaps
(such as the missing *d in the first example) and asymmetries (*ts and *ʃ rather
than *ts and *s in the second example); however, unless there is strong evidence
to compel us to accept a less expected reconstruction, we are obliged to accept
the ones motivated by pattern congruity, symmetry and naturalness. That is,
languages in general have symmetrical (natural) systems much more often than
not. Therefore, in the case of two possibilities, one with a more expected inventory and the other with a less expected, less normal inventory, the probability
that the reconstruction with the symmetrical, natural system accurately reflects
the structure of the formerly spoken proto-language is much higher than that
the asymmetrical one does. Given the greater odds of the first being right, we
choose it, not the second, which is less likely to have existed.

Step 6: Check the plausibility of the reconstructed sound from the perspective of linguistic universals and typological expectations

Certain inventories of sounds are found with frequency among the world's
languages while some are not found at all and others only very rarely. When
we check our postulated reconstructions for the sounds of a proto-language, we
must make sure that we are not proposing a set of sounds which is never or only
very rarely found in human languages. For example, we do not find any languages which have no vowels whatsoever. Therefore, a proposed reconstructed
language lacking vowels would be ruled out by step 6. There are no languages
with only glottalized consonants and no plain counterparts, and therefore a
reconstruction which claimed that some proto-language had only glottalized
consonants and no non-glottalized counterparts would be false. Languages do
not have only nasalized vowels with no non-nasalized vowels, and so we never
propose a reconstruction which would result in a proto-language in which there
are only nasalized vowels.

Let us look at an actual case. The Nootkan family has the sound correspondences seen in Table 5.7. Since no other guidelines help here, we might
be tempted, based on the majority-wins principle, to reconstruct voiced stops
for Proto-Nootkan for these four correspondence sets and postulate that these
changed to the nasal counterparts in Nootka. However, only a very few languages
of the world lack nasal consonants; therefore, we do not expect a nasalless
proto-language, and any postulated proto-language which lacks nasals altogether
must be supported by very compelling evidence. In this case, Nitinat and Makah
belong to the area of the Northwest Coast of North America where languages
of several different families lack nasal consonants. The lack of nasals in these

languages is due to the influence of other nasalless languages in the linguistic area (see Chapter 12); Proto-Nootkan had nasals, as Nootka still does, but Makah and Nitinat lost nasality – their former nasals became corresponding voiced oral stops (*$m > b$, *$n > d$, *$\dot{m} > b$', *$\acute{n} > d$'). The knowledge of universals and typological expectations in this case would direct us to reconstruct the proto-language with nasals and to assume a subsequent change in Makah and Nitinat.

Of course, in step 5, we also relied on general typological patterns in language and evaluated proposed proto-inventories on this basis; that is, steps 5 and 6 are not really distinct.

TABLE 5.7: Nootkan correspondences involving nasals

	Makah	*Nitinat*	*Nootka*
1.	b	b	m
2.	d	d	n
3.	b'	b'	ṁ
4.	d'	d'	ṅ

Step 7: Reconstruct individual morphemes

When we have reconstructed the proto-sounds from which we assume that the sounds in the sound correspondences descend, it is possible to reconstruct lexical items and grammatical morphemes. For example, from the cognate set for 'goat' in Table 5.1, the first sound (in SOUND CORRESPONDENCE 1) was reconstructed as *k (based on the $k : k : k : \int$ correspondence set); for the second sound in the cognates for 'goat', we reconstructed *a, as in SOUND CORRESPONDENCE 3 (with $a : a : a : \varepsilon$); the third sound is represented by SOUND CORRESPONDENCE 2 ($p : b : b: v$), for which we reconstructed *p; the next sound in cognate set 1, as represented by SOUND CORRESPONDENCE 4, reflects Proto-Romance *r (based on the $r : r : r : r$ correspondence set); and the last sound in the 'goat' cognates reflects SOUND CORRESPONDENCE 2 (or actually a modification of it involving final vowels in French) which was reconstructed as *a. Putting these reconstructed sounds together following the order in which they appear in the cognates for 'goat' in set 1, we arrive at *$kapra$. That is, we have reconstructed a word in Proto-Romance, *$kapra$ 'goat'. For cognate set 2 'dear' in Table 5.1, we would put together *k (SOUND CORRESPONDENCE 1), *a (SOUND CORRESPONDENCE 3), *r (SOUND CORRESPONDENCE 4) – all seen already in the reconstruction of 'goat' – and *o (SOUND CORRESPONDENCE 5, with $o : o : u : \emptyset$), giving us the Proto-Romance word *$karo$ 'dear'. For cognate set 3 'head', we have combinations of the same correspondence sets already seen in the reconstructions for 'goat' and 'dear', SOUND CORRESPONDENCES 1, 3, 2 and 5, giving the Proto-Romance reconstructed word *$kapo$ 'head'. In this way, we can continue reconstructing Proto-Romance words for all the cognate sets based on the sequence of sound correspondences that they reflect, building a Proto-Romance lexicon.

The reconstruction of a sound, a word or large portions of a proto-language is, in effect, a hypothesis (or better said, a set of interconnected hypotheses) concerning what those aspects of the proto-language must have been like. Aspects of the hypothesized reconstruction can be tested and proven wrong, or can be modified, based on new insights. These insights may involve new interpretations of the data already on hand, or new information that may come to light. The discovery of a heretofore unknown member of the family may provide new evidence, a different testimony of the historical events which transpired between the proto-language and its descendants, which could change how we view the structure and content of the proto-language. There are a number of well-known cases where this has happened which illustrate this point. Bloomfield's Swampy Cree case has already been mentioned. With the discovery and decipherment of Hittite (or better said, the languages of the Anatolian branch of Indo-European), the whole picture of Proto-Indo-European phonology changed; this included clearer evidence of several new proto-sounds (the laryngeals).

5.3   A Case Study

Let us apply the comparative method in a somewhat more complex example (though still simplified) which illustrates what we have until now been considering mainly through a simplified comparison of Romance languages. The forms in Table 5.8 are cognates found in Finnish, Hungarian and Udmurt (Votyak). These languages belong to the Finno-Ugric family, but since there are many other languages also in this family (see Figure 6.2 in Chapter 6), the data in this example are far from complete enough to offer a full perspective on the proto language – these three are compared here only for illustration's sake. These languages separated from one another a very long time ago, which explains why some of these cognates are not as immediately apparent based on mere superficial similarity. The languages have undergone many changes and are now quite different, and we would need much more information than presented here to reconstruct all the sounds of Proto-Finno-Ugric. Therefore, here we will be concerned only with the initial sounds in these data.

Step 1 is already done; the cognates have been assembled in Table 5.8. In step 2, we compare these cognates and set up sound correspondences. It is helpful to keep a good record of what we have looked at, either by noting with each sound correspondence the numbers which identify the cognate sets in which it is found, or if we do not use numbers, then the glosses. This is just a matter of bookkeeping – a means of being able to go back and check things without having to search back through all the data to find the cognates which exhibit the correspondence in question, particularly useful, for example, in steps 5 and 6.

Sound correspondences found in the cognates of Table 5.8 are:

(1)   Finnish *p-* : Hungarian *f-* : Udmurt *p-* (in Set I, nos 1–11)
(2)   Finnish *t-* : Hungarian *t-* : Udmurt *t-* (in Set II, nos 12–17)
(3)   Finnish *k-* : Hungarian *h-* : Udmurt *k-* (in Set III, nos 18–26)
(4)   Finnish *k-* : Hungarian *k-* : Udmurt *k-* (in Set IV, nos 27–35)
(5)   Finnish *s-* : Hungarian *s-* : Udmurt *ç-* (in Set V, nos 36–41)
(6)   Finnish *s-* : Hungarian Ø- : Udmurt *s-* (in Set VI, nos 42–48)

TABLE 5.8: Some Finno-Ugric cognate sets

Finnish	Hungarian	Udmurt (Votyak)	gloss
Set I			
1. pää [pæ:]	fej [fej]	pum, puŋ	'head, end'
2. pata [pata]	fazék [fɔze:k]	—-	'pot'
3. pato 'dam, wall'	fal [fɔl] 'wall'	—	
4. pääsky- [pæ:sky]	fecske [fečke]	poçkɨ-	'swallow' (bird)
5. pelkää- [pelkæ:-]	fél [fe:l]	pulɨ-	'to fear'
6. pesä [pesæ]	fészek [fe:sek]	puz-	'nest'
7. pii [pi:] 'tooth of rake'	fog [fog]	pinʲ	'tooth'
8. pilvi [pilvi]	felhő [felhø:]	pilʲem	'cloud'
9. poika [poika]	fiú [fiu:]	pi	'boy'
10. puno- [puno-]	fon [fon]	pun-	'spin, braid'
11. puu [pu:]	fa [fɔ]	pu	'tree'
Set II			
12. tä- [tæ-]	té- [te:-] (cf. tétova 'here and there')	ta	'this'
13. täi [tæi]	tetű [tety:]	tei	'louse'
14. talvi [talvi]	tél [te:l]	tol	'winter'
15. täyte- [tæyte-]	tel- [tel-] (in derived forms)	—	'full'
16. tunte- [tunte-]	tud [tud]	tod	'to know, sense'
17. tyvi [tyvi]	tő [tø:]	[dinʲ]	'base'
Set III			
18. kala [kala]	hal [hɔl]	—	'fish'
19. kalime- [kalime-]	háló [ha:lo:]	[Komi kulem]	'fishnet'
20. kamara [kamara]	hám- [ha:m-]	kəm	'peel'
21. koi [koi]	haj- [hɔj-]	[Komi kɨa]	'dawn'
22. kolme [kolme]	három [ha:rom]	kuinʲm-	'three'
23. kota [kota]	ház [ha:z]	kwa-/-ko/-ka 'summer hut'/ 'house'	'hut'
24. kunta [kunta] 'community, group, society'	had [hɔd] 'army'	—	

TABLE 5.8: continued

Finnish	Hungarian	Udmurt (Votyak)	gloss
Set III			
25. kuole- [kuole-]	hal [hɔl]	kul-	'to die'
26. kusi [kusi]	húgy [hu:dʲ]	kiż	'urine'
Set IV			
27. käte- [kæte-]	kéz [ke:z]	ki	'hand'
28. keri [keri]	kér [ke:r]	kur	'(tree-) bark'
29. kerjää- [kerjæ:]	kér [ke:r]	kur-	'to beg'
30. kii- [ki:-] 'rut, mating'	kéj [ke:j] '(carnal) pleasure'	[*Komi* koj-] 'to make mating call'	
31. kivi [kivi]	kő [kø:]	kə 'mill stone'	'stone'
32. kyynel [ky:nel]	könny [kønnj]	-kiłʲi- (in çin-kiłʲi; çin(m)- 'eye')	'tear' (noun)
33. kytke- [kytke-]	köt [køt]	kitk-i 'to harness'	'to tie'
34. kyy [ky:] 'adder'	kígyó [ki:dʲo:]	kij	'snake'
35. kyynär [ky:nær]	könyök [kønʲøk]	[gir-]	'elbow'
Set V			
36. salava [salava] 'willow'	szil [sil] 'elm'	—	
37. sarvi [sarvi]	szarv [sɔrv]	çur, çir	'horn'
38. sata [sata]	száz [sa:z]	çu	'hundred'
39. silmä [silmæ]	szem [sem]	çinm-	'eye'
40. suu [su:]	szá(j) [sa:j]	çu- (?) (in compounds)	'mouth'
41. sydäme- [sydæme-]	szív [si:v]	çulem	'heart'
Set VI			
42. sappi [sappi]	epe [epe]	sep	'gall'
43. sää [sæ:] 'weather'	ég [e:g] 'sky' <'weather'	[*Komi* sinəd] 'sunshine haze, mist'	
44. säynä- [sæynæ-]	őn [ø:n]	son- (son-tçorig, tçorig 'fish')	'fish (*Leuciscus idus*)'

TABLE 5.8: continued

Finnish	Hungarian	Udmurt (Votyak)	gloss
Set III			
45. sula-[sula]	olva- [olvɔ-]	silm-	'to melt'
46. suoni [suoni]	ín [i:n]	sin	'sinew'
47. syksy [syksy]	ősz [ø:s]	sizʲil	'autumn'
48. syli [syli]	öl [øl]	sul, sil	'lap, bosom'

Note that in a few cases where Udmurt has no cognate or the cognate is unknown, cognate forms from closely related Komi have been included for comparison.)

In Step 3 we attempt to reconstruct the proto-sound which we believe is reflected in each of these correspondence sets. For SOUND CORRESPONDENCE (1) ($p : f : p$) our choices are: [1] reconstruct $*p$ and assume Hungarian changed to f; [2] reconstruct $*f$ and assume Finnish and Udmurt changed this to p; or [3] reconstruct some third thing (say $*p^h$) and assume that it changed in all three languages, that Hungarian changed in one way to give f while Finnish and Udmurt changed in another to give p. From directionality of change as a guideline, we conclude that possibilities [1] ($*p$) and [3] (some third thing, like $*p^h$) are plausible, but not [2] ($*f$), since in sound changes familiar from languages around the world we see that voiceless bilabial stops (p, p^h) frequently become f, but extremely rarely do we find instances of f changing to p or p^h. In the majority-wins guideline, since Finnish and Udmurt both have p, against Hungarian alone with f, majority wins suggests $*p$ as a more likely reconstruction than $*f$. In the guideline of factoring in features held in common, we may conclude from the sounds p and f in the sound correspondence that the proto-sound was voiceless and a labial of some kind, but this is consistent with all three of the possibilities [1]–[3]. In this case, then, factoring in the common features provides no basis for choosing among the alternatives. The guideline of economy also urges us towards [1] ($*p$). With $*p$ (as in [1]), we would need to postulate only a single change, $*p > f$ in Hungarian; in choice [2] ($*f$) we would have to assume the change of $*f > p$ twice, in Finnish and again in Udmurt. Choice [3] ($*p^h$) would require us to postulate the change $*p^h > p$ twice, in Finnish and Udmurt, and another change, $*p^h > f$, in Hungarian. Steps 4 and 5 can help us resolve which of these possibilities is the best reconstruction; however, we have sufficient reason now for selecting [1], with $*p$, based on these considerations from directionality of change, majority wins, and economy.

SOUND CORRESPONDENCE (2) (t- : t- : t-) appears to reflect $*t$- (where none of the language has changed).

SOUND CORRESPONDENCES (3) (k- : h- : k-) and (4) (k- : k- : k-) could present more of a challenge. In (4) we reconstruct $*k$-, since all three languages have k- and thus none of them appears to have changed. However, if (4) were not present to complicate the picture, then (3) would also seem to be best reconstructed as *k-. Directionality of change would support this possibility, since the change *k* > *h* (as would be required for Hungarian in this hypothesis) is very common and not unexpected, whereas a change *h-* > *k-* is all but unknown. Also the majority-wins criterion supports *k-, with *k-* in two languages but *h-* in only one. We move to Step 4 to attempt to resolve the difficulty of the partially overlapping sound correspondences (3) and (4). If we can show that both sound correspondence sets reflect the same original sound because one of the languages has undergone a conditioned change where that sound changed in some environments but not in others, then we can reconstruct just a single sound, the same one for both correspondence sets. We would explain the difference between the two correspondences by pointing out the conditions under which one of the languages changed and thus resulted in two different outcomes from the single original sound. If we cannot explain the difference in this way, then we are obligated to reconstruct two distinct proto-sounds, one to represent each of the two sound correspondences, with the assumption that these two originally distinct sounds merged to *k-* in Finnish and Udmurt. This, then, requires us to take a closer look at the cognates in question (those of Sets III and IV). We notice that in the cognates of Set III the *h* of Hungarian appears only before back vowels (*u, o, a*), whereas in the cognates of Set IV Hungarian's *k* occurs only before front vowels. We conclude that Hungarian had a single original sound which changed to *h* before back vowels (as in Set III) but remained *k* before front vowels (as in Set IV). We reconstruct *k. Someone might wonder whether the proto-language could not have had an *h which then changed to *k* before front vowels in Hungarian and to *k* in all environments in Finnish and Udmurt. First, directionality argues against this possibility (since the change *h* > *k* is essentially unknown anywhere). Second, the criterion of economy also go against this alternative; it is more likely that only one change took place, *k > h before back vowels in Hungarian, than that several independent changes occurred, one of *h > k before front vowels in Hungarian and independently of the Hungarian development the changes of *h > k in all contexts in Finnish and in Udmurt.

The SOUND CORRESPONDENCES (5) (*s-* : *s-* : *ç-*) and (6) (*s-* : *Ø-* : *s-*) present a similar problem of partially overlapping correspondence sets. However, the partial overlap in this instance is not like that seen in the sound correspondences (3) and (4), both of which come from a single original sound in different positions due to conditioned sound change. Both sound correspondences (5) and (6) in the cognates of Sets V and VI occur essentially in the same environments: both before the various vowels, front and back, and both before the same sorts of consonants in the following syllable (for example, *l*, of 36, 45, and 48), which would be clearer if we had more cognates in the data presented here. Careful scrutiny in this case eventually shows that it is not possible to explain the difference between the two sound correspondence sets as conditioned phonetic change in some environment, given that both occur in essentially the same environments. This being the case, we have no choice but to reconstruct a different proto-sound to represent each of these two sound correspondences. Let us see how the general guidelines for reconstruction fare in these partially overlapping but ultimately contrastive cases, first applied to (5), then to (6), with the results then compared.

By *directionality*, for (5) (*s*- : *s*- : ç-) we might assume either **s* which became ç in Udmurt, or **ç* which became *s* in Finnish and Hungarian. Both are known changes, though *s* > ç is not common without some conditioning environment, say before front vowels. Thus, while not compellingly strong, the directionality in this instance gives a slightly stronger vote for **ç* than for **s*, that is, for the change **ç* > *s* being the most likely. On the other hand, *majority wins* clearly votes for **s*, since two languages have *s* (Finnish and Hungarian) and only one has ç (Udmurt). The criterion of examining the *features held in common* avails little in this instance, since *s*- and ç- share all their features except palatalization, meaning the proto-sound presumably had all these same shared features – some kind of *s*-like sound. *Economy* would clearly favor **s*, since this would require only one change, **s* > ç in Udmurt; the postulation of **ç* would require the change of **ç* > *s* in Finnish and again in Hungarian. In sum, the guidelines do not all unanimously point in one direction, but appear to favor **s* for (5), which presumes the change **s* > ç in Udmurt.

However, the existence of sound correspondence (6) (*s*- : Ø- : *s*-) complicates this picture, since it, too, appears to point to **s* as the best probable reconstruction, and yet we were unable to combine the two as possibly coming from the same original sound with some conditioned changes in particular contexts. *Directionality* clearly favors **s* for (6), since *s* > Ø is a relatively frequent change (often through the intermediate stage of *s* > *h* > Ø), but Ø > *s* is unknown and there is no phonetic motivation for why such a change should take place. *Majority wins* also clearly favors **s*, given the two cases with *s* (Finnish and Udmurt) but only one with Ø (Hungarian). Similarly, the *features held in common* suggest **s*, since *s* is the sound in two of the languages, and the features of Ø do not contribute insight here. Finally, *economy* also supports **s* for (6), since this would require only the single change of **s* > Ø in Hungarian. Postulation of **Ø* , for example, because that is the reflex in Hungarian, would require the change of Ø to *s* in Finnish and again in Udmurt. Postulation of some third alternative, say **ʃ*, would require even more changes, **ʃ* > s in Finnish and in Udmurt, and , **ʃ* > Ø in Hungarian. In sum, then, the guidelines support **s* for (6), with the presumed change **s* > Ø in Hungarian.

However, this cannot be right. As already indicated, the two correspondences (5) and (6) occur in contrastive environments and apparently cannot be combined as separate outcomes from the same original sound due to conditioned change. This means that we cannot, then, reconstruct **s* both for (5) and for (6), since sound change is regular and such a reconstruction would afford no means of explaining why the proposed single original **s* behaves differently in the two different correspondence sets, why in Hungarian it is sometimes *s* (in Set V cognates) and sometimes Ø (in Set VI cognates), why in Udmurt sometimes ç, sometimes *s*, and so on. We must reconstruct a separate sound for each of these distinct correspondence sets. While the decision about what to reconstruct for each is not as straightforward as we might like, all the guidelines clearly suggest **s* for (6) (*s*- : Ø : *s*), where for (5) (*s*- : *s*- : ç-) there was not such agreement – directionality appeared to favour **ç*. Let us then propose these reconstructions: **ç* for (5) (postulating the sound changes **ç* > *s* in Finnish and in Hungarian), and **s* for (6) (with the changes **s* > Ø in Hungarian). In fact, with the aid of much additional evidence from other Finno-Ugric languages, specialists reconstruct *ś (IPA [sʲ] or aveolo-palatal [ç]) for the sound correspondence of (5) and *s for that of (6) (Sammallahti 1988).

Let us return to SOUND CORRESPONDENCES (1), (2), (3) and (4) and apply Steps 5 and 6. Not enough cognate sets are given in the data here to reconstruct the full phonological inventory of Proto-Finno-Ugric, so that we are unable to apply Steps 5 and 6 fully. However, for now let us assume that we at least have available in the cognates of Table 5.8 the evidence for the voiceless stops and apply these steps to these to illustrate the procedures. Our tentative reconstructions to this point based on the sound correspondences were:

*p (1) Finnish p- : Hungarian f- : Udmurt p- (in Set I, nos 1–11)

*t (2) Finnish t- : Hungarian t- : Udmurt t- (in Set II, nos 12–17)

*k (before back vowels) (3) Finnish k- : Hungarian h- : Udmurt k- (in Set III, nos 18–26)

*k (before front vowels) (4) Finnish k- : Hungarian k- : Udmurt k- (in Set IV, nos 27–35).

We check these in Step 5 to see how plausible the resulting inventory of voiceless stops would be with these sounds in the proto-language. A language with the stops p, t, k would be quite normal, with an internally consistent pattern of voiceless stops. If we did attempt to reconstruct possibility [3] (some third thing from which to derive p and f plausibly, say *pʰ) for sound correspondence (1), we would no longer have a natural, symmetrical phonemic inventory of voiceless stops (*p, *t, *k), but rather the unlikely *pʰ, *t, *k. In Step 5, we would see that this would result in a series of stops which is not internally consistent, where the presence of aspirated pʰ (with no plain p) is incongruent with t and k (with no tʰ and kʰ). In Step 6, we would check this pattern to see how well it fits typologically with what we know of the sound systems of the world's languages. Here we would find that languages with only the stops pʰ, t, k (but no p and no other aspirated stops) are very rare, while a large majority of languages have a stop series with p, t, k. For possibility [2] (which would reconstruct *f), Step 5 tells us a language with f, t, k (but no p) is also internally not as consistent as one with p, t, k, and therefore not as good a reconstruction. Step 6 tells us the same thing; in looking at the sound systems of the world's languages, we find few with f, t, k (and no p), but hundreds with p, t, k. Putting these considerations of directionality, economy, internal consistency and typological realism together, we conclude that the reconstruction of *p is the best of the alternatives for SOUND CORRESPONDENCE (1). In turn, we apply steps 5 and 6 to the reconstructions with *t and *k and we find these to be supported in similar fashion in these steps. We find that the possible alternative with *h for SOUND CORRESPONDENCES (3) and (4) which might have been considered, would be inconsistent internally and typologically (leaving a system with p, t, h, but no k) not to mention being against economy, the known directionality of change, and the majority-wins guidelines.

5.4   Indo-European and the Regularity of Sound Change

The development of historical linguistics is closely associated with the study of Indo-European. *Grimm's Law, Grassmann's Law* and *Verner's Law* are major milestones in the history of Indo-European and thus also in historical linguistics, and traditionally all linguists have had to learn these laws – indeed, knowledge of them is helpful (some might say essential) for understanding the comparative method and the regularity hypothesis. (These laws have been considered in preliminary form in Chapter 2.) In this section, each is taken up individually and the development of the claim that sound change is regular based on these laws is considered.

5.4.1   Grimm's Law

The forms of Table 5.9 illustrate Grimm's Law, a series of changes in the stops from Proto-Indo-European to Proto-Germanic:

voiceless stops > voiceless fricatives:

*p	>	f
*t	>	θ
*k, *k̂	>	h (x)
*kʷ	>	hw

voiced stops > voiceless stops

*b	>	p
*d	>	t
*g, *ĝ	>	k
*gʷ	>	kw

voiced aspirated (murmured) stops > plain voiced stops

*bh	>	b
*dh	>	d
*gh, *ĝh	>	g
*gʷh	>	gw, w

Note here that many scholars believe that the voiced aspirates did not become plain voiced stops directly, but rather went through an intermediate stage of becoming voiced fricatives, which then later hardened to voiced stops (or became *w* in the case of *gʷh*): *bh > β > b, *dh > ð > d, *gh > γ > g, *ĝh > γʲ > ĝ, *gʷh > γʷ > w. (The sounds *k̂, *ĝ and *ĝh represent the 'palatal' series in Indo-European.)

(Not all the stops are included in Table 5.9.) In Table 5.9, the Gothic and English forms show the results of these changes in Germanic, while the Sanskrit, Greek and Latin forms for the most part reflect the Indo-European stops unchanged; that is, they did not undergo Grimm's Law as the Germanic forms did.

Grimm's Law embodies systematic correspondences between Germanic and non-Germanic languages, the results of regular sound changes in Germanic. So, for example, as a result of the change *p > f* in the examples in Set Ia of Table 5.9, Gothic and English (the Germanic languages) have the reflex *f* corresponding to

TABLE 5.9: Indo-European cognates reflecting Grimm's Law

Sanskrit	Greek	Latin	Gothic	English
Set Ia: *p > f				
pad-	pod-	ped-	fōtus	foot
páñča	pénte	[quinque]	fimf	five
[pán̐ča]		[kʷinkʷe]		
pra-	pro-	pro-	fra-	fro
pū-'make clear, bright'	pur	pūrus 'pure'	[OE fȳr]	fire
pitár-	patḗr	pater	fadar [faðar]	father [OE fæder]
nápāt-'descendant'		nepōs 'nephew, grandson'	[OHG nefo]	nephew [OE nefa]
Set Ib: *t > θ				
trī-/tráyas	treīs/tría	trēs	þrija	three
tv-am	tū (Doric)	tu	þu	thou
-ti-	-ti-	-tis/-sis		-th 'nominalizer'
gátis	básis	mor-tis		[health, birth, death]
'gait'	'going'	'death'		
Set Ic: *k, *k̂ > h (or [x])				
śván- [ʃvən-]	kúōn	canis [kanis]	hunds	hound 'dog'
śatám [ʃətə́m]	(he-)katón	centum [kentum]	hunda (pl.)	hundred
kravís	kré(w)as	cruor		raw [OE hrāw]
'raw flesh'	'flesh, meat'	'raw, blood, thick'		'corpse'
dáśa	déka	decem	taíhun	ten
[dɔ́ʃə]		[dekem]	[tɛxun]	

Set IIa: *b > p (*b* was very rare in Proto-Indo-European, and many doubt that it was part of the sound system; some Lithuanian forms are given in the absence of cognates in the other languages)

		(Lithuanian)		
		dubùs	diups	deep [OE dēop]
		(*Lithuanian*)		
	kánnabis	kanapḗs]		hemp (borrowing?)
		Latin		
		lūbricus	sliupan	slip

TABLE 5.9: continued

Sanskrit	Greek	Latin	Gothic	English
Set IIb: *d > t				
d(u)vá-	dúo/dúō	duo	twái [twai]	two
dánt-	odónt-	dent-	tunþus	tooth
dáśa [dɔ́ʃə]	déka	decem [dekem]	taíhun [tɛxun]	ten
pad-	pod-	ped-	fōtus	foot
ad- 'eat'	édō 'I eat'	edō 'I eat'		eat [OE etan]
véda 'I know'	woĩda 'I know'	videō 'I know'	wáit [wait] 'I know'	wit 'to know'
Set IIc: *g, *ĝ > k				
janás	génos	genus	kun-i 'race, tribe'	kin
jánu-	gónu	genū	kniu	knee
jnātá	gnōtós	(g)nōtus	kunnan 'to know'	known
ájra- 'country'	agrós	ager	akrs	acre 'field'
mr̥j- 'to milk'	(a-)mélgō 'to squeeze out'	mulgeō 'I milk'	miluk-s 'milk'	milk
Set IIIa: *bh > b				
bhar-	phér-	fer-	baír-an [bɛran] 'to bear'	bear
bhrátar	phrátēr	fráter	brōþar	brother
a-bhū-t 'he was'	é-phū 'he grew, sprang up'	fu-it 'he was'	bau-an [bɔ́-an] to dwell'	be
Set IIIb: *dh > d				
dhā- 'put'	ti-thē-mi 'I put'	fē-cī 'I made'		do [OE dō-n]
dhr̥ṣnóti 'he dares'	thrasús 'bold'	(fest-)	(ga-)dars 'he dares'	dare
dvār-	thúr-a	for-ēs	daúr- [dor-]	door

TABLE 5.9: continued

Sanskrit	Greek	Latin	Gothic	English
vidhávā	ē-wíthewos 'unmarried youth'	vidua	widuwo	widow
mádhu	méthu			mead
madhya-	mésos	medius	midjis	mid
Set IIIc: *gh, *ĝh > g				
haṁs-á- [hə̃sə́] 'swan, goose'	khēn	āns-er	Gans [*German*]	goose
stigh- 'stride'	steíkhō 'I pace'		steigan [stīgan] 'to climb'	
vah- 'carry'	wókh-os 'chariot'	veh-ō 'I carry'	ga-wig-an 'to move, shake'	weigh/wain

p in Sanskrit, Greek and Latin (the non-Germanic languages), all from Proto-Indo-European *p*. While Grimm's Law accounts for the systematic correspondences seen in Table 5.9, nevertheless these are not entirely without exceptions. However, as we will see, these exceptions all have satisfactory explanations. One set of forms which seem to be exceptions to Grimm's Law involves stops in consonant clusters, and examples of these are given in Table 5.10. (An Old

TABLE 5.10: Exceptions to Grimm's Law in consonant clusters

	Sanskrit	Greek	Latin	Gothic	English
1.	páś-	[skep-]	spec-	[OHG speh-]	spy (?) 'to see'
2.	(ṣṭhiv-)	pū	spu-	speiw-an [spīw-an]	spew 'to spit'
3.	aṣṭāu [əṣṭáu]	oktō	octō [oktō]	ahtau [axtau]	eight
4.	nákt-	nukt-	noct- [nokt-]	nahts [naxts]	night
5.			capt(īvus)	(haft)	[OE hæft] 'prisoner'
6.	-ti- gátis 'gait'	-ti- básis 'going'	-tis/-sis mor-tis 'death'		-t 'nominalizer' thrift, draught, thirst, flight, drift
7.			piscis [piskis]	fisks	[OE fisc] 'fish'

High German (OHG) form is sometimes substituted when no Gothic cognate is available; OE = Old English.)

In these forms, by Grimm's Law, corresponding to the *p* in (1) and (2) of Sanskrit, Greek and Latin we should expect to find *f* in Gothic and English, not the *p* seen in these forms. (And given the *p* of Gothic and English, the Germanic languages, we expect the correspondence in Sanskrit, Greek and Latin to be *b*, not the *p* that actually occurs.) In (3–6) we expect Gothic and English to have /θ/ (not the actually occurring *t*) corresponding to the *t* of Sanskrit, Greek and Latin. And in (7), we would expect Latin *k* to correspond to Germanic *x*, not to the *k* of the Gothic and English words in this cognate set. These exceptions are explained by the fact that Grimm's Law was actually a conditioned change; it did not take place after fricatives (**sp* > *sp*, not ✗*sf*) or after stops (**kt* > *xt*, not ✗*xθ*; the **k*, the first member of the cluster, does change to *x* as expected by Grimm's Law, but the **t*, the second member, does not change). In the case of (6), the difference between *thrift, draught, thirst, flight, drift* of Table 5.10 and the *health, birth, death* of Table 5.9 is explained in the same way. The /θ/ forms (as in Table 5.9) underwent Grimm's Law (**t* > *θ*); the forms with *-t* (in Table 5.10) are exempt from Grimm's Law because this **t* comes after a fricative in English (the <gh> of *draught* and *fight* was formerly [x], which was later lost; see Chapter 15). Thus, when Grimm's Law is correctly formulated – written to exclude stops after fricatives and other stops in consonant clusters, since that environment did not enter the change – the stops in clusters are not, in fact, exceptions to the sound change.

5.4.2 Grassmann's Law

Another set of forms which earlier had seemed to be exceptions to Grimm's Law is explained by Grassmann's Law (seen already in Chapter 2). In Greek and Sanskrit, Grassmann's Law regularly dissimilated the first of two aspirated stops within a word so that the first lost its aspiration, as in the change from Proto-Indo-European **dhi-dhē-mi* (**dhi-dheh$_i$-mi*) 'I put, place' (with reduplication of root *dhē-* (**dheh$_i$-*)) to Sanskrit *da-dhā-mi* and Greek *ti-thē-mi*. As a result of Grassmann's Law, some sound correspondences between Sanskrit, Greek and Germanic languages do not match the expectations from Grimm's Law, as, for example, in the following cognates:

Sanskrit	Greek	Gothic	English
bōdha	peutha	biudan	bid 'to wake, become aware'
bandha		bindan	bind 'to bind'.

The first is from Proto-Indo-European **bheudha-*, the second from **bhendh-*; both have undergone dissimilation of the first **bh* due to the presence of a second aspirated stop in the word (**dh* in this case). This gives the SOUND COR-RESPONDENCE in (1):

(1) Sanskrit *b* : Greek *p* : Gothic *b* : English *b*.

By Grimm's Law, we expect the *b* of Sanskrit to correspond to *p* in Germanic (Gothic and English in this case), and we expect Germanic *b* to correspond to

Sanskrit *bh* and Greek *ph*. So SOUND CORRESPONDENCE (1) in these cognate sets appears to be an exception to Grimm's Law. The cognate sets with correspondence (1) (and others for the originally aspirated stops at other points of articulation), then, are not real exceptions to Grimm's Law; rather, their reflexes in Germanic are correct for Grimm's Law, and the Sanskrit and Greek reflexes are not those expected by Grimm's Law only because Grassmann's Law regularly deaspirated the first aspirated stop when it occurred before another aspirated stop in the word in these languages. That is, SOUND CORRESPONDENCE (1) (and the others like it at other points of articulation) is the result of regular changes, Grimm's Law in Germanic, and Grassmann's Law in Sanskrit and Greek.

5.4.3 Verner's Law

A final set of what earlier had seemed to be exceptions to Grimm's Law is explained by Verner's Law (called *grammatical alternation* in older sources; see Chapter 2). Some forms which illustrate Verner's Law are seen in the cognate sets of Table 5.11 (OE = Old English; OHG = Old High German).

TABLE 5.11: Examples illustrating Verner's Law

	Sanskrit	*Greek*	*Latin*	*Gothic*	*English*
(1)	saptá	heptá	septem	sibun [siβun]	seven
(2)	pitár-	patár	pater	fadar [faðar]	OE fæder 'father'
(3)	śatám [ʃatəm]	(he-)katón	centum [kentum]	hunda (pl.)	hundred
(4)	śrutás 'heard'	klutós 'heard'			OE hlud 'loud'
(5)		makrós 'long, slender'	macer [maker]	[OHG magar]	meagre

In cognate set (1), by Grimm's Law we expect the *p* of Sanskrit, Greek and Latin to correspond to *f* in Germanic (Gothic and English), but instead we have Gothic *b* ([β]) and English *v*; given Gothic *b*, we expect the correspondence in Sanskrit to be *bh* and in Greek to be *ph*. Similarly, in cognate sets (2–4) we have the correspondence of Sanskrit, Greek and Latin *t* to Germanic *d*, not the θ expected by Grimm's Law in Germanic (and not the Sanskrit *dh* and Greek *th* we would expect, given Germanic *d*). These apparent exceptions to Grimm's Law are explained by Verner's Law. Verner's Law affects medial consonants; when the Proto-Indo-European accent followed, medial fricatives in a root – both original ones and those resulting from Grimm's Law – became voiced in Germanic, (*)f > β, (*)θ > ð, (*)x > γ, and *s > z. Since later in Proto-Germanic the accent shifted to the root-initial syllable, the earlier placement of the accent can only be seen when the cognates from the non-Germanic languages are compared. Thus, in the cognate sets of Table 5.11, we see in the Sanskrit and Greek cognates that the accent is not on the initial syllable but is on a later syllable, after the sound that changed, and that the Germanic forms do not match expectations from Grimm's Law in these instances. In (1), we would not expect Gothic *sibun*, but rather something like *sifun*, given the *p* of Sanskrit *saptá* and Greek *heptá*; however, since the accent is on the last syllable in the Sanskrit and Greek forms, Verner's Law gives Gothic *β* (spelled *b*) in this case. The forms of Table 5.12 show how the forms with the accent later in the word (which undergo Verner's Law, symbolized as ...C... ′) contrast with forms with the accent before the sound in question (indicated as ′...C...), cases which have undergone Grimm's Law), but where Verner's Law does not apply because they do not fit the environment for it.

TABLE 5.12: Examples showing the effects of Grimm's Law and further effects of Verner's Law on medial consonants in different contexts

Grimm's Law	*Verner's Law*
′...C...	...C...′
*p > f	*p > f > β
(1a) OE hēafod 'head'	(1b) Gothic sibun [siβun] 'seven'
Latin cáput [káput]	Sanskrit saptá-
*t > θ	*t > θ > ð
(2a) Gothic brōþar [brōθar] 'brother'	(2b) OE fæder 'father'
Sanskrit bhrátar-	Sanskrit pitár-
*k > x	*k > x > ɣ
(3a) Gothic taíhun 'ten'	(3b) Gothic tigus 'decade'
Greek déka	Greek dekás

It is easy to see why Verner's Law was also often called 'grammatical alternation' (*grammatischer Wechsel* in German). The accent in Proto-Indo-European fell on different syllables in certain grammatically related forms, as seen in the forms compared in Table 5.13 (PIE = Proto-Indo-European; P-Germ = Proto-Germanic). As a result, Germanic languages have different allomorphs in grammatical paradigms which depend upon whether or not Verner's Law applied, and these grammatical alternations further support Verner's Law and its correlation with the place of the accent in the proto-language.

Just as expected by Grimm's Law, the Old English forms in the first two columns have /θ/ (spelled <þ>), where the accent in Proto-Indo-European preceded the original *t* (as illustrated by the Sanskrit forms). However, in the last two columns, Old English does not have the /θ/ expected by Grimm's Law, but the /d/ of Verner's law because the accent came after this medial *t* in Proto-Indo-European, again as shown by the Sanskrit forms. The Old High German forms subsequently underwent other sound changes of their own, but the difference between those with /d/ and those with /t/ has its origin in Verner's Law just as the alternations seen in the Old English cognates. The allomorphic variation which resulted, as for example that seen in the verb paradigm in Table 5.13, illustrates the 'grammatical alternation' that comes from Verner's Law.

TABLE 5.13: Verner's Law in grammatical alternations

	'I become'	*'I became'*	*'we became'*	*'became [participle]'*
PIE	*wértō	*(we)wórta	*(we)wr̥təmé	*wr̥tonós
Sanskrit	vártāmi	va-várta	vavr̥timá	vr̥tānáh
	'I turn'	'I have turned'	'we have turned'	'turned'
P-Germ	*werθō	*warθa	*wurðum(i)	*wurðan(a)z
OE	weorþe	warþ	wurdon	worden
OHG	wirdu	ward	wurtum	wortan

So, the Verner's Law cases (as in Tables 5.11, 5.12 and 5.13), which originally appeared to be exceptions to Grimm's Law, turn out also to be explained by regular sound change – by Verner's Law, a conditioned change having to do with the earlier location of the accent.

5.4.4   Indo-European sound laws and regularity of sound change

The laws just considered played an important role in the history of Indo-European studies and as a consequence in the overall history of historical linguistics. Grimm's Law, which was published first (in 1822), was quite general and accounted for the majority of sound correspondences involving the stop series between Germanic and non-Germanic languages. However, as initially formulated, it did appear to have exceptions. When Hermann Grassmann discovered his law (in 1862), a large block of these 'exceptions' was explained, and then Karl Verner through Verner's Law (in 1877) explained most of the remaining exceptions. This success in accounting for what had originally appeared to be exceptions led the Neogrammarians to the confidence that sound change was regular and exceptionless (see Chapter 2). This is one of the most significant conclusions in the history of linguistics.

5.5   Basic Assumptions of the Comparative Method

What textbooks call the 'basic assumptions' of the comparative method might better be viewed as the consequences of how we reconstruct and of our views of sound change. The following four basic assumptions are usually listed.

(1) The proto-language was uniform, with no dialect (or social) variation. Clearly this 'assumption' is counterfactual, since all known languages have regional or social variation, different styles, and so on. It is not so much that the comparative method 'assumes' no variation; rather, it is just that there is nothing built into the comparative method which would allow it to address variation directly. This means that what is reconstructed will not recover the once-spoken proto-language in its entirety. Still, rather than stressing what is missing, we can be happy that the method provides the means for recovering so much of the original language. This assumption of uniformity is a reason-

able idealization; it does no more damage to the understanding of the language than, say, modern reference grammars do which concentrate on a language's general structure, typically leaving out consideration of regional, social and stylistic variation. Moreover, dialect differences are not always left out of comparative considerations and reconstructions, since in some cases scholars do reconstruct dialect differences to the proto-language based on differences in daughter languages which are not easily reconciled with a single uniform starting point. This, however, has not been common practice outside of Indo-European studies.

Assumptions (2) and (3) are interrelated, so that it is best to discuss them together.

(2) Language splits are sudden.

(3) After the split-up of the proto-language, there is no subsequent contact among the related languages.

These 'assumptions' are a consequence of the fact that the comparative method addresses directly only material in the related languages which is inherited from the proto-language and has no means of its own for dealing with borrowings, the results of subsequent contact after diversification into related languages. Borrowing and the effects of subsequent language contact are, however, by no means neglected in reconstruction. Rather, we must resort to other techniques which are not formally part of the comparative method for dealing with borrowing and the results of language contact (see Chapters 3, 7 and 12). It is true that the comparative method contains no means for addressing whether the language of some speech community gradually diverged over a long period of time before ultimately distinct but related languages emerged, or whether a sudden division took place with a migration of a part of the community so far away that there was no subsequent contact between the two parts of the original community, resulting in a sharp split and no subsequent contacts between the groups. (Assumptions (2) and (3) are better seen as the consequence of the family-tree model for classifying related languages, dealt with in Chapters 6 and 7, since the tree diagram depicts a parent language splitting up sharply into its daughters.)

(4) Sound change is regular. The assumption of regularity is extremely valuable to the application of the comparative method. Knowing that a sound changes in a regular fashion gives us the confidence to reconstruct what the sound was like in the parent language from which it comes. If a sound could change in unconstrained, unpredictable ways, we would not be able to determine from a given sound in a daughter language what sound or sounds it may have come from in the parent language, or, looking at a particular sound in the parent language, we could not determine what its reflexes in its daughter languages would be. That is, if, for example, an original *p of the proto-language could arbitrarily for no particular reason become f in some words, y in others, q' in others, and so on, in exactly the same phonetic and other linguistic circumstances, then it would not be possible to reconstruct. In such a situation, comparing, say a p of one language with a p of another related language would be of no avail, if the p in each could have come in an unpredictable manner from a number of different sounds.

5.6   How Realistic are Reconstructed Proto-languages?

The success of any given reconstruction depends on the material at hand to work with and the ability of the comparative linguist to figure out what happened in the history of the languages being compared. In cases where the daughter languages preserve clear evidence of what the parent language had, a reconstruction can be very successful, matching closely the actual spoken ancestral language from which the compared daughters descend. However, there are many cases in which all the daughter languages lose or merge formerly contrasting sounds or eliminate earlier alternations through analogy, or lose morphological categories due to changes of various sorts. We cannot recover things about the proto-language via the comparative method if the daughters simply do not preserve evidence of them. In cases where the evidence is severely limited or unclear, we often make mistakes. We make the best inferences we can based on the evidence available and on everything we know about the nature of human languages and linguistic change. We do the best we can with what we have to work with. Often the results are very good; sometimes they are less complete. In general, the longer in the past the proto-language split up, the more linguistic changes will have accumulated and the more difficult it becomes to reconstruct with full success.

A comparison of reconstructed Proto-Romance with attested Latin provides a telling example in this case. We do successfully recover a great deal of the formerly spoken language via the comparative method. However, the modern Romance languages for the most part preserve little of the former noun cases and complex tense–aspect verbal morphology which Latin had. Subsequent changes have obscured this inflectional morphology so much that much of it is not reconstructible by the comparative method.

5.7   Exercises

Exercise 5.1   Aimaran

Consider the following data from the two major branches of the Aimaran language family (Peru and Bolivia). Focus your attention on the sibilant fricatives (*s* and *š*) only (ignore *x* and *χ* for this exercise). What will you reconstruct? How many sibilant fricatives do you postulate for Proto-Aimaran? State your evidence.
NOTE: *š* = IPA [ʃ], *č* = IPA [tʃ]; *χ* = voiceless uvular fricative; *C'* = glottalized [ejective] consonants.

	Central Aimara	Southern Aimara	gloss
1.	saxu	sawu-	'to weave'
2.	sa(wi)	sa(ta)	'to plant'
3.	asa	asa-	'to carry flat things'
4.	usu	usu-	'to become sick'
5.	nasa	nasa	'nose'
6.	aski	hiskʰi	'to ask'
7.	muxsa	muχsa	'sweet'

	Central Aimara	Southern Aimara	gloss
8.	suniqi	sunaqi	'small spring'
9.	šanq'a	sanqa	'to snuffle'
10.	waša	wasa	'silent place'
11.	iši	isi	'dress'
12.	muši	musi	'to take care (of)'
13.	puši	pusi	'four'
14.	išt'a	hist'a-	'to close'
15.	išapa	isapa-	'to hear, listen'

(Cerrón-Palomino 2000: 145–6)

Exercise 5.2   Tulu

Tulu is a Dravidian language (of India) which has several varieties. Consider the following data from two principal varieties. Focus your attention only on the nasals. What will you reconstruct for these? How many nasals do you postulate for Proto-Tulu? State your evidence.

NOTE: *j* = [j], IPA [dʒ]; *ṇ* = IPA [ɳ].

	Shivalli	Sapaliga	gloss
1.	aːṇɨ	aːnɨ	'male'
2.	uṇɨ	uːnɨ	'dine'
3.	maṇṇɨ	mannɨ	'soil'
4.	koːṇɛ	koːnɛ	'room'
5.	eːnɨ	yaːnɨ	'I'
6.	ninɛ	ninɛ	'wick'
7.	jaːnɛ	daːnɛ	'what'
8.	sanɛ	tanɛ	'conceiving'

(Bhat 2001: 11)

Exercise 5.3   Polynesian

The Polynesian languages of the Pacific form a subgroup of the Oceanic branch of the Austronesian family of languages. (1) What are the sound correspondences found in these data? What sound do you reconstruct for the proto-language to represent each sound correspondence set? (2) What sound change or changes have taken place in each of these languages? (3) What is the best reconstruction (proto-form) for 6, 16, 20 and 32? Show how your postulated sound changes apply to each of these to produce the modern forms. Note that not all sounds of the proto language are represented in these cognate sets with their sound correspondences. For example, in one not represented clearly here, Tongan has Ø corresponding to *l* or *r* of the other languages (reflecting what is usually reconstructed as **r* of Proto-Polynesian), distinct from the set in which Tongan has *l* corresponding to *l* or *r* in these sister languages (reflecting Proto-Polynesian **l*). This distinction may not be clearly visible in the data presented in this exercise.

NOTE: <'> = [ʔ].

Māori	Tongan	Samoan	Rarotongan	Hawai'ian	gloss
1. tapu	tapu	tapu	tapu	kapu	'forbidden', 'taboo'
2. pito	pito	—	pito	piko	'navel'
3. puhi	puhi	—	pu'i	puhi	'blow'
4. taha	tafa 'edge'	tafa	ta'a	kaha	'side'
5. tae 'trash'	ta'e	tae	tae	kae	'excrement'
6. taŋata	taŋata	taŋata	taŋata	kanaka	'man, person'
7. tai	tahi	tai	tai	kai	'sea'
8a. kaha	kafa	'afa	ka'a	'aha	'strong'
8b. ma:rohi-	ma:lohi	ma:losi	ma:ro'i	—	'strong'
9. karo	kalo	'alo	karo	'alo	'dodge'
10. aka	aka	a'a	aka	a'a	'root'
11. au	'ahu	au	au	au	'gall'
12. uru 'tip of weapon'	'ulu	ulu	uru	ulu 'centre'	'head'
13. uhi	ufi	ufi	u'i	uhi	'yam'
14. ahi	afi	afi	a'i	ahi	'fire'
15. ɸa:	fa:	fa:	'a:	ha:	'four'
16. ɸeke	feke	fe'e	'eke	he'e	'octopus'
17. ika	ika	i'a	ika	i'a	'fish'
18. ihu	ihu	isu	puta-i'u 'nostril' (puta 'hole')	ihu	'nose'
19. hau 'wind' (hauku: 'dew' [-ku: 'showery weather'])	hau	sau	'au	hau	'dew'
20. hika	—	si'a	'ika	hi'a	'firemaking'
21. hiku 'fishtale'	hiku	si'u	'iku	hi'u	'tail'
22. ake	hake	a'e	ake	a'e	'up'
23. uru	—	ulu	uru	ulu	'enter'
24. maŋa	maŋa	maŋa	maŋa	mana	'branch'
25. mau 'fixed'	ma'u	mau	mau	mau	'constant'
26. mara 'marinated'	—	mala	mara	mala	'fermented food'
27. noho	nofo	nofo	no'o	noho	'sit'
28. ŋaru	ŋalu	ŋalu	ŋaru	nalu	'wave'
29. ŋutu	ŋutu	ŋutu	ŋutu	nuku	'mouth'
30. waka	vaka	va'a	vaka	wa'a	'canoe'
31. wae	va'e	vae	vae	wae	'leg'
32. raho 'testicle'	laho	laso	ra'o	laho	'scrotum'
33. rou 'long forked stick'	lohu	lou	rou	lou	'fruit-picking pale'

	Māori	*Tongan*	*Samoan*	*Rarotongan*	*Hawai'ian*	*gloss*
34.	rua	ua	lua	rua	lua	'two'

Exercise 5.4   Orokolo-Toaripi

Orokolo and Toaripi are two closely related Eleman languages (usually assigned to the Trans-New Guinea grouping, though this is as yet uncertain). Compare the data presented here and reconstruct Proto-Orokolo-Toaripi. (1) List the sound correspondences you find. (2) Give the proto-sounds you reconstruct to represent these. (3) Present the sound changes which you postulate that each language has undergone. (4) If there is any relative chronology involved among these changes, state what it is and the evidence for it. (5) Give your reconstruction of 12, 25 and 35 together with how the individual sound changes apply to these to produce the modern forms.

Many find this problem very difficult. When looking for conditioning factors that may distinguish overlapping correspondence sets, consider TOGETHER AT THE SAME TIME the environments BOTH before and after the sounds in question.

NOTE: for this problem, consider Orokolo *r* and *l* the same sound. Do not struggle over the difference between *ae* and *ai* in no. 38.

	Toaripi	*Orokolo*	*gloss*
1.	uti	uki	'bone'
2.	ete	eke	'vagina'
3.	tete	keke	'fish scales'
4.	tao	kao	'tooth'
5.	toare	koare	'senior'
6.	tola	kora	'tree'
7.	tolotolo	korokoro	'leaves'
8.	tapare	kapare	'grease'
9.	torea	korea	'theft'
10.	turuturu	kurukuru	'thundering'
11.	aite	aire	'after'
12.	kite	kile	'mat'
13.	lauta	laura	'flame tree'
14.	ita	ila	'pig'
15.	puta	pura	'cloth'
16.	uta	ura	'hole'
17.	fi	hi	'cry'
18.	firu	hiru	'portion'
19.	fe	he	'penis'

	Toaripi	Orokolo	gloss
20.	fere	here	'betel nut'
21.	fapai	hapa	'open'
22.	fave	have	'stone'
23.	forerai	horera	'appear'
24.	furi	huri	'pus'
25.	afutae	ahurae	'ashes'
26.	sisia	hihia	'sour'
27.	siri	hiri	'mildew'
28.	ase	ahe	'sugarcane'
29.	seseroro	heheroro	'thin'
30.	sare	hare	'sun, day'
31.	sarea	harea	'sorcery'
32.	soa	hoa	'time'
33.	sua	hua	'pigeon'
34.	susu	huhu	'plank'
35.	farisa	harita	'arrow'
36.	marisa	marita	'girl'
37.	taisa	kaita	'paddle'
38.	saesa	haita	'dish'
39.[=12]	kite	kile	'mat'
40.	kiva	kiva	'care'
41.	koko	koko	'narrow'
42.	ekaka	ekaka	'fish'

Exercise 5.5 Lencan

Compare the cognates from the two Lencan languages (both of which have recently become extinct: Chilanga was spoken in El Salvador; Honduran Lenca was spoken in Honduras). Work only with the consonants in this problem (the changes involving the vowels are too complex to solve with these data alone). (1) Set up the correspondence sets; (2) reconstruct the sounds of Proto-Lencan; (3) find and list the sound changes which took place in each language; and (4) determine what the relative chronology may have been in any cases where more than one change took place in either individual language, if there is evidence which shows this.

NOTE: *t'*, *k'* and *ts'* are glottalized consonants. Also, these data do not provide enough information for you to recover all the consonants of the proto-language, so that it will be difficult to apply steps 5 and 6 here.

	Honduran Lenca	Chilanga	gloss
1.	pe	pe	'two'
2.	lepa	lepa	'jaguar'
3.	puki	puka	'big'
4.	ta	ta	'cornfield'
5.	tem	tem	'louse'
6.	ke	ke	'stone'
7.	kuma	kumam	'fingernail, claw'
8.	katu	katu	'spider'
9.	waktik	watih	'sandals'
10.	kakma	k'ama	'gourd'
11.	siksik	sisih	'shrimp'
12.	nek	neh	'tooth'
13.	insek	ints'eh	'beak'
14.	taw	t'aw	'house'
15.	tutu	t'ut'u	'flea'
16.	kin	k'in	'road'
17.	kunan	k'ula	'who'
18.	kelkin	k'elkin	'tortilla griddle'
19.	sewe	ts'ewe	'monkey'
20.	saj	ts'aj	'five'
21.	musu	muts'u	'liver'
22.	sak-	ts'ih-	'to wash'
23.	lawa	lawa	'three'
24.	liwa-	liwa-	'to buy'
25.	tal-	tal-	'to drink'
26.	wala	wala	'raccoon'
27.	was	wal	'water'
28.	asa	alah	'head'
29.	wasan	wila	'urine'
30.	wara	wara	'river'
31.	siri	sirih	'star'
32.	sili	sili	'iron tree' (tree species)
33.	suri-sur	ʃurih	'squirrel'

[NOTE: *suri-sur* involves reduplications; just compare the *suri-* segment of it]

	Honduran Lenca	Chilanga	gloss
34.	saj-	ʃej-	'to want'
35.	so	ʃo	'rain'
36.	suna	ʃila	'flower'
37.	soko	ʃoko	'white'
38.	sak	ʃah	'firewood'
39.	wewe	wewe	'baby'
40.	jet-	jete-	'to laugh'
41.	juku	juku	'coyol palm' (palm tree species)
42.	sa	ʃam	'good'

Exercise 5.6 Uto-Aztecan

1. State the sound correspondences.
2. Present the sound that you reconstruct for Proto-Uto-Aztecan for each sound correspondence.
3. List the sound changes that you observe in the various languages.

Ignore vowel length and do not attempt to reconstruct the vowels for this exercise. There are not sufficient examples in the data given here to be able to reconstruct the full set of Proto-Uto-Aztecan sounds. Assume that correspondences found in only a single cognate set would recur if more data were present. Attempt to reconstruct the consonants in initial and medial position and state the sound changes you postulate to get from your reconstructed consonants to the actual forms in the various daughter languages. Given the paucity of forms cited here, you may have to postulate some sound changes on the basis of poor evidence, in hopes of confirming (or disconfirming) them when more data are brought into the picture. It is often the case that the historical linguist must work with incomplete or imperfect data, so the challenge here of attempting to reconstruct with less than complete information is a realistic experience.

NOTE: a few examples have been regularized, slightly modified, in order to avoid complications for the reconstruction.

	Cupeño	Hopi	Comache	Tohono O'odham	Huichol	Nahuatl	
1.	paqa	pa:qa-	paka 'arrow'	wa:-pka	haka	a:ka	'reed'
2.	pa-	pa:hɨ	pa:	wa-	ha:	a:	'water'
3.	pah	pa:y-	pahi-	—	hai-	e:y	'three'
4.	puš	po:si	pui	wuhi	hiši	i:š	'eye'
5.	pi-	pöhɨ	puʔe	wo:g	hu:ye:	oʔ	'road'
6.	—	pɨtɨ	pɨhtɨ	we:č	he:te	ete-	'heavy'
7.	tama	tama	ta:ma	ta:-tami	tame	tla:n	'tooth'
8.	—	teni	—	čini	teni	te:n	'mouth'
9.	tuu-, tula	tö:vɨ	(kuh-)tu:bi	ču:d	tɨ:	ti:l	'charcoal'

	Cupeño	Hopi	Comache	Tohono O'odham	Huichol	Nahuatl	
10.	—	tös-	tus(oyuni) 'grindstone'	čuhi	tɨsi	tiš	'grind, flour'
11.	—	qa:si	—	kahio	—	ikši	'leg, thigh'
12.	qʷaše	kʷasi	kʷasɨ-pɨ	bahi	kʷaši	ikʷši	'cooked, ripe'
13.	qʷaš	—	kʷasi	bahi	kʷaši	—	'tail'
14.	qʷeʔ-	kʷɨʔɨ	—	baʔa	-kʷaʔa	kʷa	'eat'
15.	—	kʷita	kʷita-	bi:t	kʷita	kʷitla	'excre- ment'
16.	maqa	maqa	maka	ma:k	—	maka	'give'
17.	—	mo:ki	—	mu:ki	mɨki	miki	'kill, die'
18.	mala	mata	—	mač ˇud	ma:ta:	matla	'grind- stone'
19.	naqa	na:qa	na:ki	na:k	naka	nakas	'ear'
20.	nema	nɨ:ma	nɨ:ma	nem	nema	—	'liver'
21.	waxe	la:ki	—	gaki	-waki	wa:ki	'dry'
22.	wexi-	lökö	woko	—	huku	oko	'pine'

(Based on Stubbs 2011)

Exercise 5.7   *Jicaquean*

Jicaquean is a family of two languages in Honduras. Jicaque (Jicaque of El Palmar) is extinct; Tol (Jicaque of La Montaña de la Flor) is still spoken by a few hundred people, but has become extinct or nearly so everywhere except in the village of La Montaña de la Flor. Reconstruct Proto-Jicaquean; state the sound correspondences which you encounter in the following cognate sets, and reconstruct a proto-sound for each. State the sound changes that have taken place in each language.

HINT: your reconstruction should include the following sounds:

p	t	ts	k	ʔ		i	ɨ	u
pʰ	tʰ	tsʰ	kʰ			e		o
p'	t'	ts'	k'				a	
		s						
		l						
m	n							
w		j		h				

What happens to each of the proto-sounds which you reconstruct in initial and in final position in these two languages? Can you make guesses about an appropriate reconstruction and sound changes to account for sounds in medial positions? NOTE: the correspondences involving affricates and sibilants are quite complex, and you will need to pay special attention to the possibilities for combining some of the initial correspondence sets with some of the medial ones as reflecting the same proto-sound. The consonants *p'*, *t'*, *ts'*, *k'* are glottalized. The accent mark on a vowel (for example *á*) means that it is stressed; this is not relevant to the sound changes. In a few cases, a non-initial *h* does not match well in the two languages; ignore this, since it is due to changes for which you do not have enough evidence in these data. The hyphen (-) before some words, as in 9 (-*rɨk*), means that these occur with some other morpheme before them which is not relevant and so is not presented here.

	Jicaque	*Tol*	*gloss*
1.	pe	pe	'stone'
2.	pit	pis	'meat'
3.	pɨné	pɨné	'big'
4.	pɨga-	pɨʔa-	'jaguar'
5.	pen	pel	'flea'
6.	kamba	kampa	'far, long'
7.	arba-	alpa	'above'
8.	to-bwe	to-pwe	'to burn'
9.	-rɨk	-lɨp	'lip'
10.	kek	kep	'woman'
11.	ik	hip	'you'
12.	huruk	hulup	'grain' (of corn)
13.	huk	hup	'he, that'
14.	nak	nap	'I'
15.	-kuk	-kup	'we'
16.	te	te	'black'
17.	tek	tek	'leg'
18.	tebé	tepé	'he died'
19.	tɨt	tɨt'	'louse'
20.	mandɨ	mantɨ	'vulture'
21.	n-gon	n-kol	'my belly'
22.	harek	halek	'arrow'
23.	mak	mak	'foreigner'
24.	n-abuk	n-ajpʰuk	'my head'
25.	kon	kom	'liver'
26.[=6]	kamba	kampa	'far, long'
27.	pɨrɨk	pɨlɨk	'much'
28.	keré	kelé	'nephew'
29.	mik	mik	'nose'
30.	korok	kolok	'spider'
31.	pʰe	pʰe	'white'

	Jicaque	Tol	gloss
32.	pʰen	pʰel	'arm, shoulder'
33.	-pʰa	-pʰa	'dry'
34.	pʰɨja	pʰɨja	'tobacco'
35.	m-bat	m-pʰats'	'my ear'
36.	lɨbɨ-	lɨpʰɨ	'wind'
37.	pʰɨbɨh	pʰɨpʰɨh	'ashes'
38.	urubana	(j)ulupʰana	'four'
39.	ten	tʰem	'boa constrictor'
40.	tut	tʰutʰ	'spit'
41.	peten	petʰel	'wasp'
42.	kun	kʰul	'fish'
43.	ke-ke	(kʰ)ekʰe	'agouti'

[NOTE: *keke* is a reduplicated form and should be treated as the root *ke-* repeated, rather than as having an intervocalic -*k*-]

	Jicaque	Tol	gloss
44.	kan	kʰan	'bed'
45.	kere	kʰele	'bone'
46.	to-gon-	to-kʰol	'to grind'
47.	kujuh	kʰujuh	'parrot'
48.	pɨt	p'ɨs	'deer'
49.	m-bɨj	m-p'ɨj	'my body'
50.	pɨčá	p'ɨsá	'macaw'
51.	-te	-t'e	'to cut'
52.[=19]	tɨt	tɨt'	'louse'
53.	-tja	-t'ja	'to be late'
54.	mata	mat'a	'two'
55.	kat	ʔas	'blood'
56.	kot	ʔos	'I sit, am'
57.	kaw-	ʔaw-a	'fire'
58.	kona	ʔona	'sour'
59.	kan	ʔan	'zapote' (fruit)
60.[=4]	pɨga-	piʔa-	'jaguar'
61.	te-ga	te-ʔa	'to give'
62.	čok	sok'	'tail'
63.	čorin	tsolin	'salt'
64.	ču(h)	tsu	'blue'
65.	čiwiri	-tsiwil-	'to lie'
66.	čigin-	tsikin	'summer'
67.	čoʔ-	tsoʔ-	'to nurse'

	Jicaque	*Tol*	*gloss*
68.	čuba	tsupa	'to tie'
69.	nočot	notsots	'fly'
70.	ʃeme	tsʰeme	'horn'
71.	ʃijó	tsʰijó	'dog'
72.	ʃe(w)	tsʰew	'scorpion'
73.	čin	ts'il	'hair, root'
74.	-čun	ts'ul	'intestines'
75.	čoron	ts'olol	'oak'
76.	čih	ts'ih-	'caterpillar'
77.	te-neče	te-nets'e	'to sing'
78.	ločak	lots'ak	'sun'
79. [=35]	m-bat	m-pʰats'	'my ear'
80.	čot	sots'	'owl'
81.	-čɨ	-sɨ	'water'
82. [=62]	čok	sok'	'tail'
83.[=2]	pit	pis	'meat'
84.	-mut	mus	'smoke'
85.	hoč(uruk)	hos-	'his heart'
86.[=50]	pɨčá	p'ɨsá	'macaw'
87.	mon	mol	'cloud'
88.[=25]	kon	kom	'liver'
89.	ma	ma	'land'
90.	wa	wa	'house'
91.	wara	wala	'forehead'
92.	jo	jo	'tree'
93.	he	he	'red'
94.[=22]	harek	halek	'arrow'

(Data from Campbell and Oltrogge 1980)

Exercise 5.8 *K'ichean languages*

K'ichean is a subgroup of the Mayan family. Compare these cognate forms and set up the sound correspondences; propose the most appropriate reconstruction for the sound in the proto-language for each, and write the sound changes which account for the developments in the daughter languages. Are any instances found in any of the individual languages in which it is necessary to state what the relative chronology of changes was?

NOTE: ɓ = voiced imploded bilabial stop; t', ts', č', k', q', m', w' = glottalized consonants. In Uspanteko, the accent mark over the vowel, as in ò:x 'avocado', indicates falling tone. Although the correspondence set in which Q'eqchi' *h* corresponds to *x* of the other languages is not found in these data before *u*, ignore this – this correspondence occurs in general with no restrictions that have anything to do with *u*.

NOTE: *y* = [j], *š* = IPA [ʃ], *č* = IPA [tʃ] *C'* = glottalized [ejective] consonants.

	Kaqchikel	Tz'utujil	K'iche'	Poqomam	Uspanteko	Q'eqchi'	gloss
1.	pak	pak	pak	pak	pak	pak	'custard apple'
2.	pur	pur	pur	pur	pur	pur	'snail'
3.	pim	pim	pim	pim	pim	pim	'thick'
4.	toʔ	toʔ	toʔ	toʔ	toʔ	toʔ	'to help'
5.	tox	tox	tox	tox	tox	tox	'to pay'
6.	kiʔ	kiʔ	kiʔ	kiʔ	kiʔ	kiʔ	'sweet'
7.	ka:ʔ	ka:ʔ	ka:ʔ	ka:ʔ	ka:ʔ	ka:ʔ	'quern'(metate)
8.	k'el	k'el	k'el	k'el	k'el	(k'el)	'parrot'
9.	qa-	qa-	qa-	qa-	qa-	qa-	'our'
10.	qul	qul	qul	—	qul	—	'neck'
11.	q'o:l	q'ol	q'o:l	q'o:l	q'o:l	q'o:l	'resin, pitch'
12.	q'an	q'an	q'an	q'an	q'an	q'an	'yellow'
13.	si:p	si:p	si:p	si:p	si:p	si:p	'tick'
14.	saq	saq	saq	saq	saq	saq	'white'
15.	tsuy	tsuy	tsuh	suh	tsuh	suh	'water gourd'
16.	uts	uts	uts	us	uts	us	'good'
17.	tsats	tsats	tsats	sas	tsats	sas	'thick'
18.	ts'iʔ	ts'iʔ	ts'iʔ	ts'iʔ	ts'iʔ	'ts'iʔ'	'dog'
19.	če:ʔ	če:ʔ	če:ʔ	če:ʔ	če:ʔ	če:ʔ	'tree, wood'
20.	ču:n	ču:n	ču:n	ču:n	ču:n	ču:n	'lime'
21.	č'o:p	č'o:p	č'o:p	č'o:p	č'o:p	č'o:p	'pineapple'
22.	xul	xul	xul	xul	xul	xul	'hole, cave'
23.	winaq	winaq	winaq	winaq	winaq	kwinq	'person'
24.	we:š	we:š	we:š	we:š	—	kwe:š	'trousers'
25.	ya:x	ya:x	ya:x	ya:x	ya:x	ya:x	'genitals, shame'
26.	mu:x	mu:x	mu:x	mu:x	mù:x	mu:h	'shade'
27.	o:x	o:x	o:x	o:x	ò:x	o:h	'avocado'
28.	ča:x	ča:x	ča:x	ča:x	čà:x	ča:h	'ashes'
29.	tu:x	tu:x	tu:x	tu:x	tù:x	tu:h	'steambath'
30.	q'i:x	q'i:x	q'i:x	q'i:x	q'ì:x	(-q'ih)	'day, sun'
31.	ka:x	ka:x	ka:x	ka:x	kà:x	—	'sky'
32.	čax	čax	čax	čax	čax	čax	'pine'
33.	k'ax	k'ax	k'ax	k'ax	k'ax	k'ax	'flour'
34.	k'o:x	k'o:x	k'o:x	k'o:x	k'o:x	k'o:x	'mask'
35.	ɓa:y	ɓa:y	ɓa:h	w'a:y	ɓa:h	ɓa:h	'gopher'

	Kaqchikel	Tz'utujil	K'iche'	Poqomam	Uspanteko	Q'eqchi'	gloss
36.	6a:q	6a:q	6a:q	w'a:q	6aq	6aq	'bone'
37.	6e:y	6e:y	6e:h	w'e:h	6e:h	6e:h	'road'
38.	si6	si6	si6	sim'	si6	si6	'smoke'
39.	xa6	xa6	xa6	xam'	xaŋ	haŋ	'rain'
40.	xuku:ʔ	xuku:ʔ	xuku:6	xuku:m'	xuku:6	xuku6	'canoe, trough'
41.	a:q'aʔ	a:q'aʔ	a:q'a6	a:q'am'	a:q'a6	(a:q'6)	'night'
42.	xal	xal	xal	xal	xal	hal	'ear of corn'
43.	xe:y	xe:y	xe:h	xe:h	xe:h	he:h	'tail'
44.	č'o:y	č'o:y	č'o:h	č'o:h	č'o:h	č'o:h	'mouse, rat'
45.	k'yaq	k'yaq	k'yaq	k'aq	k'aq	k'aq	'flea'
46.	kyaq	kyaq	kyaq	kaq	kaq	kaq	'red'
47.	(i)kyaq'	(i)kyaq'	kyaq'	kaq'	—	—	'guava'
48.	išk'yaq	šk'yaq	išk'yaq	išk'aq	išk'aq	—	'fingernail'
49.	winaq	winaq	winaq	winaq	winaq	kwinq	'person'
50.	šikin	šikin	šikin	šikin	šikin	(šikn)	'ear'
51.	išoq	išoq	išoq	išoq	—	išq	'woman'
52.	nimaq	nimaq	nimaq	nimaq	nimaq	ninq	'big' (plural)
53.	sanik	sanik	sanik	(sanik)	sanik	sank	'ant'
54.	suʔt	suʔt	suʔt	suʔt	sù:t'	(suʔut)	'cloth, kerchief'
55.	poʔt	poʔt	poʔt	poʔt	pò:t'	poʔot	'blouse'
56.	piʔq	piʔq	piʔq	piʔq	pì:q'	—	'corncob'
57.	atiʔt	atiʔt	atiʔt	atiʔt	atì:t'	atiʔt	'grandmother'
58.	k'ax	k'ax	k'ax	k'ax	k'ax	k'ax	'flour'
59.	k'ay	k'ay	k'ah	k'ah	k'ah	k'ah	'bitter'
60.	k'ay	k'ay	k'ay	k'ay	k'ay	k'ay	'to sell'
61.	mo:y	mo:y	mo:y	mo:y	mo:y	mo:y	'blind' (dark)
62.	ča:x	ča:x	ča:x	ča:x	čà:x	ča:h	'ashes'
63.	čax	čax	čax	čax	čax	čax	'pine'
64.	č'ax	č'ax	č'ax	—	č'ax	č'ax	'to wash'
65.	č'ay	č'ay	č'ay	č'ay	—	—	'to hit'

Exercise 5.9   Quechuan

Quechuan is a family of several languages spoken in the Andes region of South America, with varieties found in Columbia, Ecuador, Peru, Bolivia and Argentina.

Compare the cognates from the languages listed here. Set up the correspondence sets; reconstruct the sounds of Proto-Quechuan; find and list the sound changes which took place in each language (variety); determine what the relative chronology may have been in any cases where more than one change took place in an individual language (variety), if there is evidence which shows this. What do you think the inventory of Proto-Quechuan sounds was? (Note that there is some controversy about the historical status of glottalized consonants (p', t', č', k', q') and aspirated consonants (pʰ, tʰ, čʰ, kʰ, qʰ) in Quechuan. For the purposes of this exercise do not try to reconstruct them, but rather treat those few which occur (in the Cuzco variety) as though they were equal to the plain counterparts.) (NOTE: [ɴ]= uvular nasal; y = IPA [j]; lʸ = IPA [lʲ]; nʸ = IPA [nʲ].)

	Ancash	Junín	Cajamarca	Amazonas	Ecuador	Ayacucho	Cuzco	gloss
1.	paka-	paka-	paka-	paka-	paka-	paka-	paka-	'begin'
2.	apa-	apa-	apa-	apa-	apa-	apa-	apa-	'wash'
3.	rapra	lapla	rapra	rapra	—	rapra	raɸra	'leaf, wing'
4.	pampa	pampa	pamba	pamba	pamba	pampa	pampa	'plains'
5.	tapu-	tapu-	tapu-	tapu-	tapu-	tapu-	tapu-	'ask'
6.	wata-	wata-	wata-	wata-	wata-	wata-	wata-	'tie'
7.	utka	utka	utka	utka	—	utka	uskʰa	'cotton'
8.	inti	inti	indi	indi	indi	inti	inti	'sun'
9.	kimsa	kimsa	kimsa	kimsa	kimsa	kimsa	kimsa	'three'
10.	puka	puka	—	puka	puka	puka	puka	'red'
11.	haksa-	saksa-	saksa-	saxsa-	saxsa-	saksa-	saxsa-	'be full, fed up'
12.	kuŋka	kuŋka	kuŋga	kuŋga	kuŋga	kuŋka	kuŋka	'neck'
13.	qam	am	qam	kam	kaŋ	χam	qaŋ	'you' (sg.)
14.	qoha	usa	qosa	kusa	kusa	χosa	qosa	'husband'
15.	waɢa-	waʔa-	waɢa-	waka-	waka-	waχa-	waqa-	'cry'
16.	hoχta	suʔta	soχta	sukta	suxta	soχta	soχta	'six'
17.	heŋɢa	siŋʔa	seŋɢa	siŋga	siŋga	seŋχa	seŋqa	'nose'
18.	tsaki	čaki	čaki	čaki	čaki	čaki	č'aki	'dry'
19.	mutsa-	muča-	muča-	muča-	muča-	muča-	muč'a-	'kiss'
20.	mantsa-	manča-	manča-	manča-	manča-	manča-	manča-	'fear, be afraid'
21.	putska-	pučka-	pučka-	pučka-	puʃka-	pučka-	puska-	'to thread'
22.	e:tsa	ayča	ayča	e:ča	ayča	ayča	ayča	'meat'
23.	čaki	çaki	çaki	çaki	çaki	čaki	čaki	'foot'
24.	kača-	kača-	kača-	kača-	kača-	kača-	kača-	'send'
25.	učpa	učpa	učpa	učpa	uʃpa	učpa	uspʰa	'ashes'
26.	kički	kiçki	kiçki	kiçki	kiʃki	kički	k'iski	'narrow'
27.	haru-	salu-	saru-	saru-	saru-	saru-	saru-	'to step on'
28.	hara	sala	sara	sara	sara	sara	sara	'maize, corn'
29.	qaha	asa	qasa	kasa	kasa	χasa	qasa	'ice'

	Ancash	Junín	Cajamarca	Amazonas	Ecuador	Ayacucho	Cuzco	gloss
30.	isqoŋ	isʔuŋ	esqoŋ	iʃkuŋ	iʃkuŋ	isχoŋ	esqoŋ	'nine'
31.	—	aysa-	aysa-	e:sa-	aysa-	aysa-	aysa-	'pull'
32.	waʃa	waʃa	waʃa	waʃa	waʃa	wasa	wasa	'behind'
33.	iʃke:	iʃkay	iʃkay	iʃke:	iʃkay	iskay	iskay	'two'
34.	hatuŋ	hatuŋ	atuŋ	atuŋ	hatuŋ	hatuŋ	hatuŋ	'big'
55.	hutsa	huča	uča	uča	huča	huča	huča	'fault'
36.	humpi	humpi	—	umbi	humbi	humpi	hump'i	'sweat'
37.	laki	lʸaki	ʒaki	ǰaki	ʒaki	lʸaki	lʸaki	'pain, trouble'
38.	kila	kilʸa	kiʒa	kija	kiʒa	kilʸa	kilʸa	'moon'
39.	alba	alʸpa	aʃpa	aǰpa	aʒpa	alʸpa	halʸp'a	'land'
40.	aylu	aylʸu	ayʒu	e:ǰu	ayʒu	aylʸju	aylʸu	'family'
41	rima-	lima-	rima-	rima-	rima-	rima-	rima-	'to speak'
42.	karu	kalu	karu	karu	karu	karu	karu	'far'
43.	warmi	walmi	warmi	warmi	warmi	warmi	warmi	'woman'
44.	waχra	waʔla	waχra	wakra	—	waχra	waχra	'horn'
45.	nina	nina	nina	nina	nina	nina	nina	'fire'
46.	yana	yana	yana	yana	yana	yana	yana	'black'
47.	wayna	wayna	wayna	wayna	wayna	wayna	wayna	'young man'
48.	aŋya-	aŋya-	aŋya-	aŋya-	aŋya-	aŋya	aŋya-	'to reprove'
49.	nawi	nʸawi	nʸawi	nʸawi	nʸawi	nʸawi	nʸawi	'eye'
50.	wanu-	wanʸu-	wanʸu-	wanʸu-	wanʸu-	wanʸu-	wanʸu-	'to die'
51.	qepa	ipa	qepa	kipa	kipa	χepa	qʰepa	'behind'
52.	weɢe	wiʔi	—	wiki	wiki	weχe	weqe	'tear (drop) (noun)'
53.	qeʃpi-	iʃpi-	—	kiʃpi-	kiʃpi-	χespi-	qespi-	'to escape'
54.	qo-	u-	qo-	—	ku-	χo-	qo-	'to give'
55.	qoŋɢa-	uŋʔa-	qoŋɢa-	kuŋga-	kuŋga-	χoŋχa-	qoŋqa-	'to forget'

6

Linguistic Classification

Stability in language is synonymous with rigor mortis.

(Ernest Weekley)

6.1 Introduction

How are languages classified and how are family trees established? *Subgrouping*, as the classification of which languages are more closely related to one another in a language family is called, is an important part of historical linguistics, and methods and criteria for subgrouping are the focus of this chapter. Before turning to these methods, however, let us first look briefly at some of the *language families* around the world.

6.2 The World's Language Families

There are around 420 distinct language families (including language isolates) in the world, listed in Table 6.1. The count is by no means absolute, since there are languages about which we do not yet know enough to be able to classify them, and others where reasonable opinions about classification differ, and there are abundant hypotheses about potential but unconfirmed more inclusive groupings which attempt to combine some of these into higher-order, more inclusive families. Some of the proposals of distant affiliation are more plausible than others; some are controversial (see Chapter 14). It is possible that as research progresses, some of these families and isolates may be shown to be related to others, reducing the total number. This is quite possible for some language groups in New Guinea, and also for some in Australia and South America. It is unlikely that the total number of independent language families (including isolates) will change much for Europe, most of Asia, or North and Central America. The classification of languages in Africa will probably change, though the number of families there is unlikely to be reduced. Also, there are many extinct languages with so little attestation that we will probably never be able to classify them successfully, and, as mentioned, there are also living languages for which so little information is known that they remain unclassified, at least until better descriptive material for

TABLE 6.1: Language families of the world (including isolates)

Africa

1.	Afroasiatic	28.	Laal
2.	Aroid (South Omotic)	29.	Maban
3.	Bangi Me (Bangime) (isolate)	30.	Mande
4.	Berta	31.	Mao
5.	Birri†?	32.	Mpra (Mpre)
6.	Central Khoisan (Khoe)	33.	Meroitic† (isolate)
7.	Central Sudanic	34.	Meyobe (Miyobe)
8.	Daju	35.	Nara
9.	Dizoid	36.	Narrow Talodi?
10.	Dogon	37.	Niger-Congo
11.	Dompo	38.	Nilotic
12.	Furan	39.	Nubian
13.	Gimojan	40.	Nyimang
14.	Gongan	41.	Ongota (isolate)
15.	Gumuz	42.	Rashad?
16.	Hadza (isolate)	43.	Saharan
17.	Heiban	44.	Sandawe
18.	Ijoid	45.	Shabo
19.	Jalaa (isolate)	46.	Songhay
20.	Kadu (Kadugli-Krongo)	47.	Southern Khoisan†?
21.	Koman	48.	Surmic
22.	Kresh-Aja (?)	49.	Taa (!Xoon cluster)
23.	Kujargé	50.	Tama (Taman)
24.	Kuliak	51.	Tegem?
25.	Kunama	52.	Temein
26.	Kwadi (isolate)	53.	!Ui (!Kwi)
27.	Kx'a (Ju [!Xun] + ‡Huan)	54.	‖Xegwi†

Asia

55.	Ainu (isolate)	70.	Miao-Yao (Hmong-Mien)
56.	Burushaski (isolate)	71.	Mongolian
57.	Chukotko-Kamchatkan	72.	Nakh-Daghestanian
58.	Dravidian	73.	Nihali (isolate)
59.	Elamite† (isolate)	74.	Nivkh (Gilyak) (isolate)
60.	Etruscan† (Tyrsenian)	75.	Northwest Caucasian
61.	Hattic† (isolate)	76.	Sino-Tibetan
62.	Hurro-Urartian†	77.	Sulung (Tibeto-Burman?)
63.	Iberian†	78.	Sumerian† (isolate)
64.	Indo-European	79.	Tai-Kadai
65.	Japanese (Japonic)	80.	Tungusic
66.	Jamao?	81.	Turkic
67.	Kartvelian	82.	Uralic
68.	Korean (isolate)	83.	Yeniseian
69.	Kusunda (isolate)	84.	Yukaghir

TABLE 6.1: continued

Australia

85.	Anindilyakwa (Enindhilyagwa) (isolate)	101.	Marrku-Wurrugu
86.	Anson Bay†?	102.	Mirndi (Mindi)
87.	Bunaban	103.	Northern Daly (Daly)
88.	Eastern Daly†	104.	Nyulnyulan
89.	Gaagudju† (isolate)	105.	Pama-Nyungan
90.	Garrwan	106.	Southern Daly
91.	Giimbiyu†	107.	Tangkic
92.	Gunwinyguan	108.	Tiwi (isolate)
93.	Iwaidjan	109.	Umbugarla† Umbugarla/ Ngurmbur† (isolate)
94.	Jarrakan	110.	Wagiman
95.	Kungarakany† (isolate)	111.	Wardaman
96.	Larrakiyan†	112.	Western Daly
97.	Limilngan†	113.	Worrorran
98.	Mangarrayi† (isolate)	114.	Tasmanian 1†
99.	Maningrida	115.	Tasmanian 2†
100.	Maran		

Europe

116. Basque (isolate)

Pacific

117.	Austroasiatic	132.	Bosavi (Trans-New Guinea Phylum?)
118.	Abinomn (isolate)		
119.	Abun (isolate) (maybe West Papuan?)	133.	Bulaka River
		134.	Burmeso (isolate)
120.	Amto-Musan	135.	Busa (Odiai) (isolate)
121.	Anêm (isolate)	136.	Dagan (Trans-New Guinea Phylum?)
122.	Angan (Trans-New Guinea Phylum?)	137.	Dem (isolate)
123.	Ata (isolate)	138.	Dibiyaso-Doso-Turumsa (maybe Trans-New Guinea Phylum?)
124.	Austronesian		
125.	Awin-Pa (Awin-Pare?) (Trans-New Guinea Phylum?)	139.	Duna-Bogaya (Trans-New Guinea Phylum?)
126.	Baibai		
127.	Baining (?)	140.	Duranmin (Trans-New Guinea Phylum?)
128.	Bayono-Awbono (Trans-New Guinea Phylum?)	141.	East Bird's Head
		142.	East Bougainville
129.	Bilua	143.	East Kutubu (Trans-New Guinea Phylum?)
130.	Binanderean (Trans-New Guinea Phylum?)	144.	East New Britain
131.	Border (Trans-New Guinea Phylum?)	145.	East Strickland (Trans-New Guinea Phyum?)

TABLE 6.1: continued

Pacific

146. East Timor
147. Eastern Trans-Fly
148. Eleman (Trans-New Guinea Phylum?)
149. Fasu (Trans-New Guinea Phylum?)
150. Geelvik Bay (Cenderawasih Bay)
151. Goilalan (Trans-New Guinea Phylum?)
152. Guriaso (isolate)
153. Hatam (isolate)
154. Inland Gulf (maybe Trans-New Guinea Phylum?)
155. Kaki Ae (Trans-New Guinea Phylum?)
156. Kapauri (isolate)
157. Kaure (Kaure-Narau-Kosare)
158. Kayagar (Trans-New Guinea Phylum?)
159. Kazukuru† (Austronesian?)
160. Kembra† (isolate)
161. Kimki (isolate)
162. Kiwai
163. Koiarian (Trans-New Guinea Phylum?)
164. Kol (isolate)
165. Kolana (isolate) (possibly Timor-Alor-Pantar)
166. Kolopom
167. Kuot (isolate)
168. Kwalean (Trans-New Guinea Phylum?)
169. Kwerba (maybe Trans-New Guinea Phylum?)
170. Kwomtari
171. Lakes Plain
172. Lavukaleve
173. Left May (Arai)
174. Lepki (isolate)
175. Lower Mamberamo (maybe Austronesian?)
176. Lower Sepik-Ramu

177. Mailuan (Trans-New Guinea Phylum?)
178. Mairasi (Trans-New Guinea Phylum?)
179. Manubaran (Trans-New Guinea Phylum?)
180. Marind
181. Masep (isolate)
182. Mawes (isolate)
183. Molof (isolate)
184. Mombum (maybe Trans-New Guinea Phylum?)
185. Monumbo (Torricelli?)
186. Mor (of Bomberai) (isolate)
187. Moraori (isolate)
188. Morehead and Upper Maro Rivers
189. Morwap (Elseng) (isolate)
190. Mpur (isolate)
191. Murkim (isolate)
192. Namla (isolate)
193. Nimboran
194. North Bougainville
195. Oksapmin (Trans-New Guinea Phylum?)
196. Pahoturi
197. Pawaia (Trans-New Guinea Phylum?)
198. Pauwasi (includes Karkar(-Yuri))
199. Porome (Kibiri) (Trans-New Guinea Phylum?)
200. Sause (isolate)
201. Savosavo
202. Senagi (Trans-New Guinea Phylum?)
203. Sentani (maybe Trans-New Guinea Phylum?)
204. Sepik
205. Shom Pen (Austro-Asiatic?)
206. Skou
207. South Bougainville

TABLE 6.1: continued

Pacific	223. Turama-Kikori (Trans-New Guinea Phylum?)
208. South Bird's Head (maybe Trans-New Guinea Phylum?)	224. Uhunduni (isolate)
209. Suki-Gogodala (Trans-New Guinea Phylum?)	225. Upper Sepik (Biksi or Yefta/ Biksi, Pyu related to Biksi??)
210. Sulka	226. Urim (Torricelli?)
211. Taiap (isolate)	227. Usku
212. Tambora† (isolate)	228. West Bomberai (maybe Trans-New Guinea Phylum?)
213. Tanglapui (isolate)	
214. Tanahmerah (of Bomberai)	229. West Papuan
215. Taulil-Butam (Baining-Taulil?)	230. Yalë (Nagatman) (isolate)
216. Teberan (Trans-New Guinea Phylum?)	231. Yareban (Trans-New Guinea Phylum?)
217. Timor-Alor-Pantar	232. Yélî Dnye (Yele) (isolate)
218. Tofanma (isolate)	233. Yuat River
219. Touo	234. Onge-Jarawa (Jarawa-Onge) (of Andaman Islands)
220. Tor (Tor-Orya) (Trans-New Guinea Phylum?)	
221. Torricelli	235. Great Andamanese (of Andaman Islands)
222. Trans New Guinea	

North America	
237. Alsean†	261. Kalapuyan†
238. Atakapan†	262. Karankawa† (isolate)
239. Beothuk† (isolate)	263. Karuk (isolate)
240. Caddoan	264. Keresan
241. Calusa† (isolate)	265. Kiowa-Tanoan
242. Cayuse† (isolate)	266. Kootenai (isolate)
243. Chimakuan	267. Maiduan
250. Chimariko† (isolate)	268. Muskogean
251. Chinookan	269. Na-dene (Tlingit + Eyak-Athabaskan)
252. Chitimacha† (isolate)	270. Natchez† (isolate)
253. Chumashan†	271. Palaihnihan†
254. Cochimí-Yuman	272. Plateau
255. Comecrudan†	273. Pomoan
256. Coosan†	274. Salinan† (isolate)
257. Eskimo-aleut	275. Salishan
258. Esselen† (isolate)	276. Shastan†
259. Haida (isolate)	277. Siouan-Catawba
260. Iroquoian	

TABLE 6.1: continued

North America

278.	Siuslaw† (isolate)	286.	Wakashan
279.	Takelman†	287.	Washo (isolate)
280.	Timucuan†	288.	Wintuan
281.	Tonkawa† (isolate)	289.	Yana† (isolate)
282.	Tsimshianic	290.	Yokutsan
283.	Tunica† (isolate)	291.	Yuchi (isolate)
284.	Utian (Miwok-Costanoan)	292.	Yukian†
285.	Uto-Aztecan	293.	Zuni (isolate)

Central America and Mexico

294.	Coahuilteco† (isolate)	303.	Misumalpan
295.	Cotoname† (isolate)	304.	Mixe-Zoquean
296.	Cuitlatec† (isolate)	305.	Otomanguean
297.	Guaicurian†	306.	Seri (isolate)
298.	Huave (isolate)	307.	Tarascan (Purépecha) (isolate)
299.	Jicaquean (Tol)		
300.	Lencan†	308.	Tequistlatecan
301.	Maratino† (unclassified)	309.	Totonacan
302.	Mayan	310.	Xinkan (Xincan) †

South America

311.	Aikaná (isolate)	334.	Chipaya-Uru
312.	Andaquí† (isolate)	335.	Chiquitano (isolate)
313.	Andoque (isolate)	336.	Chocoan
314.	Arawakan	337.	Cholonan†
315.	Arawan	338.	Chonan
316.	Atacameño† (isolate)	339.	Chono† (isolate)
317.	Awaké† (isolate)	340.	Cofán (A'ingaé) (isolate)
318.	Aymaran	341.	Culle† (isolate)
319.	Baenan† (isolate)	342.	Esmeralda† (isolate)
320.	Barbacoan	343.	Gamela† (isolate)
321.	Betoi† (isolate)	344.	Guaicuruan
322.	Boran	345.	Guajiboan
323.	Bororoan	346.	Guamo† (isolate)
324.	Cahuapanan	347.	Guató (isolate)
325.	Camsá (isolate)	348.	Harákmbut-Katukinan
326.	Candoshi (isolate)	349.	Huamoé† (Wamoé) (isolate)
327.	Canichana† (isolate)		
328.	Cañar-Puruhá†	350.	Huarpean†
329.	Cariban	351.	Irantxe†?? (Münkü) (isolate)
330.	Cayuvava† (isolate)		
331.	Chapacuran	352.	Itonama (isolate)
332.	Charruan†	353.	Jabutían
333.	Chibchan	354.	Jêan (Jê family)

TABLE 6.1: continued

South America

355.	Jeikó (isolate)	388.	Pankararú† (isolate)
356.	Jirajaran†	389.	Pano-Tacanan
357.	Jivaroan	390.	Puquina† (isolate)
358.	Jotí (isolate)	391.	Purían†
359.	Kaliana† (Sapé) (isolate)	392.	Quechuan
360.	Kamakanan†	393.	Rikbaktsá (Canoeiro)
361.	Kapixaná (Kanoé) (isolate)		(isolate)
362.	Karajá (isolate)	394.	Sabela (Auishiri) (isolate)
363.	Karirian†	395.	Sáliban
364.	Katembrí	396.	Sechura-Catacaoan†
365.	Kawesqaran	397.	Tarairiú† (isolate)
366.	Koayá (Kwaza) (isolate)	398.	Taruma† (Taruamá)
367.	Krenákan		(isolate)
368.	Leco (isolate)	399.	Taushiro (Pinchi) (isolate)
369.	Lule-Vilelan†	400.	Tequiraca† (isolate)
370.	Máko† (isolate)	401.	Ticuna-Yuri
371.	Makúan (Puinavean)	402.	Timotean†
372.	Mapudungu (isolate)	403.	Tiniguan†
373.	Mascoyan	404.	Trumai (isolate)
374.	Matacoan	405.	Tucanoan (Tukanoan)
375.	Matanawí† (isolate)	406.	Tupían
376.	Maxakalían	407.	Tuxá† (isolate)
377.	Mochica (Yunga)† (isolate)	408.	Urarina (isolate)
378.	Mosetenan	409.	Warao (isolate)
379.	Movima (isolate)	410.	Witotoan
380.	Munichi† (isolate)	411.	Xukurú† (isolate)
381.	Muran	412.	Yagan† (isolate)
382.	Nambiquaran	413.	Yaguan
383.	Natú† (Peagaxinan)	414.	Yanomaman
	(isolate)	415.	Yaruro (isolate)
384.	Ofayé† (Opayé)	416.	Yaté (Furniô) (isolate)
	(isolate)	417.	Yuracaré (isolate)
385.	Omurano† (isolate)	418.	Yurumangui† (isolate)
386.	Otomacoan†	419.	Zamucoan
387.	Paezan	420.	Zaparoan

them is obtained and compared with other languages to determine whether they may belong to larger families.

In Table 6.1, the cross (†) after a language family indicates that all the languages of that family are now extinct.

It will be noticed that all the languages of an even 100 of these families are extinct (marked with † after the name). This means that essentially a quarter (24 per cent) of the linguistic diversity of the world is gone. In the following section the relationship of language isolates to language families is clarified.

Historical linguistic research has reached an advanced state for only a few of these language families. For example, Sino-Tibetan (c. 300 languages) is an extremely important family, since its languages are spoken by more people than those of any other language family in the world except Indo-European. Nevertheless, comparative linguistic research in this family is actually quite recent, flourishing only since the early 1980s or so. Its classification has been and continues to be controversial, with many Chinese scholars placing languages of the Hmong-Mien (Miao-Yao) and Tai-Kadai families also in Sino-Tibetan, where most other scholars limit the family to the Sinitic (Chinese) and Tibeto-Burman languages, and a few even feel that it has not yet been adequately demonstrated that the Chinese and Tibeto-Burman branches belong to a single language family. Table 6.1 presents a consensus view of language families, as accepted by most specialists in each region, but by no means by all.

6.2.1 Language isolates and their history

A language isolate is a language which has no known relatives, that is, that has no demonstrable genetic relationship with any other language. Consequently, language isolates are in effect language families with only a single member. The best-known and most cited are Basque, Burushaski, and Ainu, though there are many others, as just seen – 136, one third of all language families when isolates are included in the number of language families. Language isolates have often been misunderstood and so it is important to clarify them and their status in language classification schemes.

Language isolates are not very different from language families which have multiple members. Some language isolates may have had relatives in the past which have disappeared without coming to be known, leaving these languages isolated, though if we had information about their lost relatives, they would not be isolates but rather members of families of more than one member. For example, Ket in Siberia is the only surviving language of the Yeniseian family. Nevertheless, there were other Yeneseian languages, now extinct: Arin, Asan, Kott, Pumpokol, and Yugh. If these languages had disappeared without a trace, today Ket would be considered an isolate. However, since data from these other now extinct Yeniseian languages were registered before the languages disappeared, Ket was not left an isolate, rather it is a member of a family of languages, albeit the only surviving member of that family.

Language isolates and language families are not so different from one another in another sense, too. Some languages which were thought to be isolates have turned out not to be; rather, they have proven to be members of small families of related languages as previously unknown relatives became known. For example, Japanese would be a language isolate if not for the fact that Ryukyuan languages (of Okinawa and the other Ryukyu islands) proved to be separate languages, sisters of Japanese. Thus Japanese belongs to a family of related languages, often called Japonic, and is thus no longer a language isolate. A second example is Etruscan, long thought to be an isolate; however, Lemnian has been shown to be related to Etruscan. Lemnian is known from a stella and ceramic fragments from the Greek island of Lemnos, dating from c.400 BC.

Some other cases of small families no longer considered language isolates because related languages have come to be known are:

Atakapan Texas and Louisiana (two languages: Atakapa, Akokisa)
Jicaquean (Tol) Honduras (two languages: Eastern Jicaque, Jicaque of El Palmar [Western Jicaque])
Lencan El Salvador, Honduras (two languages: Chilanga, Honduran Lenca)
Xinkan Guatemala (four languages: Chiquimulilla, Guazacapán, Jumaytepeque, and Yupiltepeque)
Hurrian (Hurro-Urartian) Northeast Anatolia, from the state of Mitanni, known from the second and first millennium BC.
(There are numerous others.)

As mentioned, it is necessary to distinguish language isolates from *unclassified* languages, languages so poorly known that they cannot be classified, though they are sometimes also called language isolates. An unclassified language is one for which there are not enough data (attestation) available to know whether it has relatives or not – these languages lack enough data for them to be compared meaningfully with other languages and therefore their possible kinship remains unknown. For isolated languages, sufficient data do exist; these languages are not grouped in larger genetic classifications with any other language because comparisons of these languages, from known data, with other languages do not reveal any confirmable linguistic kinship.

There are two sorts of unclassified languages. To the first belong those extinct languages which are too poorly attested to group with any other language or language group. Some examples include:

Adai, Louisiana
Aranama-Tamique, Texas
Camunico, Northeast Italy (survived to the second half of the first millennium BC)
Eteocretan, Crete, fourth to third centuries BC
Ibrerian, Iberian Penninsula (second half of first millennium BC to first half of first millennium AD)
Kaskean, Northeast Anatolia, second millennium BC
Ligurian, Northeast Italy, few words, 300 BC–AD 100
Maratino, Northeast Mexico
Minoan Linear A, undeciphered, 1800–1450 BC
Mysian, Western Anatolia, before first century BC
Naolan, Tamaulipas, Mexico
Northern Picene, Adriatic coast of Italy, first millennium BC
Pictish, Scotland, seventh to tenth centuries AD, few inscriptions
Quinigua, Northeast Mexico

Raetic, Northern Italy, Switzerland, Austria, first millennium BC
Sicanian, Central Sicily, pre-Roman epoch
Solano, Texas, Northeast Mexico
Sorothaptic, Iberian Peninsula, pre-Celtic, Bronze Age
Tartessian, Spain, first millennium BC

The second kind of unclassified language includes still extant languages not classified for lack of data, living languages that are so unknown that the data available do not permit them to be compared with other languages in order to determine whether they may be related or not. Examples of this sort of unclassified language include:

In Africa: Bung, Lufu, Kujargé, perhaps Mpre, Oropom, Rer Bare, Weyto
In Asia and the Pacific: Sentinelese (Andaman Islands), Bhatola (India), Waxianghua (China), Doso (Papua New Guinea), Kehu (Indonesia Papua), Tirio (Papua New Guinea)
In South America: Amikoana, Ewarhuyana, Himarimã, Iapama, Korubo, Miarrã, Papavô, Potiguara, Tremembé, Wakoná, Wasu, Yarí, and several others.

It should be noted that some of these unclassified languages could also be language isolates, but without data on them we cannot know. Table 6.2 provides a list of the language isolates of the world. The total number of language isolates is 136. Language isolates thus make up 32 per cent of all the c. 420 'language families'. Seen from this perspective, isolates are not at all weird; rather they have as their 'cohorts' one third of the world's 'language families'.

TABLE 6.2: The language isolates of the world

Africa (6)		
1. Bangi Me (Bangime)	4. Kwadi	
2. Hadza	5. Meroitic†	
3. Jalaa	6. Ongota	
Asia (9)		
7. Ainu	12. Kusunda	
8. Burushaski	13. Nihali	
9. Elamite†	14. Nivkh (Gilyak)	
10. Hattic†	15. Sumerian†	
11. Korean		
Australia (6)		
16. Anindilyakwa (Enindhilyagwa)	19. Mangarrayi†	
17. Gaagudju†	20. Tiwi	
18. Kungarakany†	21. Umbugarla† Umbugarla/Ngurmbur†	
Europe (1)		
22. Basque		

TABLE 6.2: continued

Pacific (33)

23.	Abinomn	40.	Mawes
24.	Abun	41.	Molof
25.	Anêm	42.	Mor (of Bomberai)
26.	Ata	43.	Moraori
27.	Burmeso	44.	Morwap (Elseng)
28.	Busa	45.	Mpur
29.	Dem	46.	Murkim
30.	Guriaso	47.	Namla
31.	Hatam	48.	Sause
32.	Kapauri	49.	Taiap
33.	Kembra†	50.	Tambora†
34.	Kimki	51.	Tanglapui
35.	Kol	52.	Tofanma
36.	Kolana	53.	Uhunduni
37.	Kuot	54.	Yalë (Nagatman)
38.	Lepki	55.	Yélî Dnye (Yele)
39.	Masep		

North America (19)

56.	Beothuk†	66.	Natchez†
57.	Calusa†	67.	Salinan†
58.	Cayuse†	68.	Siuslaw†
59.	Chimariko†	69.	Tonkawa†
60.	Chitimacha†	70.	Tunica†
61.	Esselen†	71.	Washo
62.	Haida	72.	Yana†
63.	Karankawa†	73.	Yuchi
64.	Karuk	74.	Zuni
65.	Kootenai		

Central America and Mexico (6)

75.	Coahuilteco	78.	Huave
76.	Cotoname†	79.	Tarascan (Purépecha)
77.	Cuitlatec†	80.	Seri

South America (56)

81.	Aikaná	90.	Canichana†
82.	Andaquí†	91.	Cayuvava†
83.	Andoque	92.	Chiquitano
84.	Atacameño†	93.	Chono†
85.	Awaké†	94.	Cofán (A'ingaé)
86.	Baenan†	95.	Culle†
87.	Betoi†	96.	Esmeralda†
88.	Camsá	97.	Gamela†
89.	Candoshi	98.	Guamo†

TABLE 6.2: continued

South America (56)

99. Guató	118. Omurano†
100. Huamoé† (Wamoé)	119. Pankararú†
101. Irantxe† (Münkü)	120. Puquina†
102. Itonama	121. Rikbaktsá (Canoeiro)
103. Jeikó	122. Sabela (Auishiri)
104. Jotí	123. Tarairiú†
105. Kaliana† (Sapé)	124. Taruma† (Taruamá)
106. Kapixaná (Kanoé)	125. Taushiro (Pinchi)
107. Karajá	126. Tequiraca†
108. Koayá (Kwaza)	127. Trumai
109. Leco	128. Tuxá†
110. Máko†	129. Urarina
111. Mapudungu	130. Warao
112. Matanawí†	131. Xukurú†
113. Mochica (Yunga) †	132. Yagan†
114. Movima	133. Yaruro
115. Munichi†	134. Yaté (Furniô)
116. Natú† (Peagaxinan)	135. Yuracaré
117. Ofayé† (Opayé)	136. Yurumangui†

How do we explain the general attitude that language isolates are commonly considered highly unusual, so weird that they should be treated with suspicion? How do we account for the frequent sentiment that it is not to be tolerated that there should be languages with no relatives? It may be suspected that these feelings stem from lack of knowledge about how many isolates there are and lack of understanding about how little isolates differ from other language families in their basic character, as seen above.

6.2.2 How can we advance knowledge of the history of language isolates?

How can we learn about the history of a language without relatives? The means that can be employed to learn about the history of language isolates include:

Internal reconstruction (see Chapter 8)
The philological study of the attestations (see Chapter 15)
Evidence from toponyms (see Chapter 16)
Names (personal names, names of rivers, deities, etc.) (see Chapter 16)
Early historical reports about the language (see Chapter 15)
Comparative reconstruction based on dialects (see Chapter 5)
Evidence from loanwords (see Chapter 3)

Language contact and areal linguistics (see Chapter 12)
Wörter und Sachen techniques (see Chapter 16).

It will be instructive to look at a few of these in a bit more detail.

(1) *Internal reconstruction.* Internal reconstruction is the best-known and most used tool for investigating the history of language isolates. Here is a simple example of a single word offered for illustration's sake. In standard Basque (the most famous isolated language) 'wine' has two variant forms, *ardo* in isolation and *ardan-* in compounds. Internal reconstruction (Chapter 8) based on these would suggest something like **ardano* (or at least something in which the *n* is present), and indeed this is confirmed in the reconstruction by the comparative method of **ardano* based on comparison of the variants in Basque dialect of *ardo, ardao, arno,* and *ardu* (cf. Lakarra 1995: 195). Internal reconstruction postulates a change of *-n-* > Ø (loss of intervocalic *n*), which is confirmed by comparative evidence in the dialects and other historical evidence.

(2) *Comparative reconstruction.* A less well-known but extremely valuable tool for investigating the history of language isolates is the comparative method applied in the case of language isolates, not to separate related languages, but to forms from regional dialects, as seen in the case of 'wine' in Basque just mentioned. Successful and instructive examples this kind of reconstruction for isolates include:

Ainu (Vovin 1993)
Basque (Gorrochategui and Lakarra 1996, 2001, Michelena 1988, 1995, Trask 1997)
Huave (Suárez 1975)
Tarascan (Friedrich 1971).

(3) *Loanwords.* Loanwords can provide excellent evidence of the history of isolates. For example, from the semantic content of the more than 300 ancient loanwords from Latin into Basque it is clear that the Romans had much influence in the domains of laws, administration, technology, religion, and refined culture. Moreover, the relative age of many of these loanwords in Basque is known from phonological traits they exhibit.

(4) *Wörter und Sachen.* *Wörter und Sachen* strategies can also provide information on the history of language isolates. (For details, see Chapter 16.) It is believed that words which can be analyzed into multiple morphemes were created more recently in the history of the language than words which have no such internal composition. For example, Basque *garagardo* 'beer' is analyzable morphologically, from *garagar* 'barley' + *ardo* 'wine'; however, *ardo* 'wine' has no evident morphological analysis; therefore, it is inferred that the word for 'wine' is probably older in Basque than the word for 'beer'. Similarly, Basque *gari* 'wheat' is inferred to be probably older in the language than *garagar* 'barley', since *garagar* is a reduplicated form of the word for 'wheat' and thus morphologically analyzable. And the word for 'wheat' too must be older than the one for 'beer', since the 'barley' component of 'beer' is morphologically

complex, with the morpheme for 'wheat' in it. In another example, Basque *janarbi* 'radish' is analyzable as *jan* 'to eat + *arbi* 'turnip'; however, *arbi* 'turnip' has no such internal structure; it is inferred that probably the word for 'turnip' is older than the word for 'radish'.

It is also inferred that place names that can be analyzed into component parts probably came to be known more recently than those which have no such internal analysis. In Basque, since the names of several rivers in the French Basque area have no clear etymology (cannot easily be analyzed into parts), it is inferred that they are old names in the language, for example *Atturri (Adour), Bidasoa, Biduze, Errobi*. The names of several rivers of the Biscaya region, on the other hand, are analyzable, for example *Ibaizabal* from *ibai* 'river' + *zabal* 'wide', and *Artibai* from *arte* 'between + *ibai* 'river'. It is inferred that these latter names are not as old as the former.

Words which bear non-productive (irregular) morphemes are assumed to be possibly older than words composed only of productive morphemes. In Basque, for example, the morph -*di* is frozen, no longer productive, and its presence in the names of the animals *ardi* 'sheep', *zaldi* 'horse', *idi* 'ox', and *ahardi* 'sow' suggests that these animals have been known to Basque speakers for a long time. Thus, for example *zaldi* 'horse', with the non-productive -*di*, appears potentially older than *zamari* 'horse', which on further investigation is confirmed as a loanword (from Latin *sagmariu* 'pack-horse'). Nothing can be inferred about the age of words lacking such forms, so for *otso* 'wolf' and *ahuntz* 'goat', lacking the non-productive morpheme, it is not possible to say anything of their relative age in the language.

It is important to be aware of these ways of obtaining information about the history of language isolates, since it is often asserted that since they have no known relatives, nothing can be known of their history.

6.3 *Terminology*

Linguistic classification is about the relationships among languages (and language varieties); to see how it works, it is important to understand the terminology used.

Subgrouping is about the internal classification of the languages within language families; it is about the branches of a family tree and about which sister languages are most closely related to one another. The terminology employed in linguistic classifications can be confusing, since the terms are not always used consistently and there is controversy concerning the validity of some of the kinds of entities which some labels are intended to identify. Therefore, it is important to begin by clarifying this terminology. In linguistic classification, we need names for a range of entities which distinguish language groups of greater and lesser relatedness, that is, entities with different degrees of internal diversity (time depth), each more inclusive than the level below it.

Dialect means only a variety (regional or social) of a language, which is mutually intelligible with other dialects of the same language. 'Dialect' is not used in historical linguistics to mean a little-known ('exotic') or minority language, and it is no longer used to refer to a daughter language of a language family, though the word has sometimes been used in these senses. (See Section 7.4, Chapter 7.)

Language means any distinct linguistic entity (variety) which is mutually unintelligible with other such entities.

A language *family* is a group of genetically related languages, that is, languages which share a linguistic kinship by virtue of having developed from a common ancestor. Many linguistic families are designated with the suffix *-an*, as in, for example, *Algonquian, Austronesian, Indo-European, Sino-Tibetan* and so on. In recent times, many scholars have begun to use the term *genetic unit* to refer to any language family or isolate. An *isolate* is a language which has no known relatives, that is, a family with but a single member. (See Section 6.2.1, above.)

Language families can be of different magnitudes; that is, they can involve different time depths, so that some larger-scale families may include smaller-scale families among their members or branches. Unfortunately, however, a number of confusing terms have been utilized in attempts to distinguish more inclusive from less inclusive family groupings.

The term *subgroup* (also called *subfamily, branch*) is relatively straightforward; it is used to refer to a group of languages within a language family which are more closely related to each other than to other languages of that family–that is, a subgroup is a branch of a family. As a proto-language (for example, Proto-Indo-European) diversifies, it develops daughter languages (such as Proto-Germanic, Proto-Celtic and so on, in the case of Indo-European); if a daughter (for instance Proto-Germanic) then subsequently splits up and develops daughter languages of its own (such as English, German and so on), then the descendants (English, German and others, in the case of Germanic) of that daughter language (Proto-Germanic) constitute members of a subgroup (the Germanic languages), and the original daughter language (Proto-Germanic) becomes in effect an intermediate proto-language, a parent of its own immediate descendants (its daughters, English, German and so on), but still at the same time a descendant (daughter) itself of the original proto-language (Proto-Indo-European).

A number of terms have also been used for postulated but undemonstrated higher-order, more inclusive families (proposed but as yet unproven distant genetic relationships); these include *stock, phylum, macrofamily,* and the compounding element '*macro-*' (as in *Macro-Mayan, Macro-Penutian, Macro-Siouan* and the like). These terms have proven confusing and controversial, as might be expected when names are at stake for entities that have been postulated but where agreement is lacking. In order to avoid confusion and controversy, none of these terms should be used. That is, the term *family* is sufficient and clear. Since the entities called 'stock', 'phylum' and 'macro-' would be bona fide language families if they could be established (demonstrated) on the basis of the linguistic evidence available, and they will not be families if the proposals which they embody fail to hold up, it is much clearer to refer to these proposed but as yet unsubstantiated proposed relationships as 'proposed distant genetic relationships' or 'postulated families'. The question of distant genetic relationships – how to determine whether languages not yet known to be related to one another may be distantly related – is much debated (see Chapter 14). (See Chapter 17 for other terminology, used in quantitative approaches.)

6.4   How to Draw Family Trees: Subgrouping

Subgrouping is the internal classification of language families to determine which sister languages are most closely related to one another. It is common for a language over time to diversify, that is, to split up into two or more daughter languages (with the consequence that the earlier language ceases to be spoken except as reflected in its descendants) – this means that the original language comes to constitute a proto-language. After the break-up of the original proto-language, a daughter language (for example, Western Romance, which split off from Proto-Romance) may itself subsequently diversify into daughters of its own (Western Romance split up into Spanish, Portuguese, French and others). This gives the first daughter language to branch off (Western Romance in our example) an intermediate position in the family tree – it is a daughter of the original proto-language (Proto-Romance) and it is an ancestor to its own daughters (Western Romance is the parent of Spanish, Portuguese and French). So, the languages which branch off from the intermediate language (Western Romance) belong to the same subgroup (Spanish, Portuguese and French are more immediate daughters of Western Romance, thus belonging to the Western Romance subgroup, which itself belongs to the Romance family). A subgroup, then, is all the daughters which descend from an ancestor (intermediate proto-language) which itself has at least one sister. To say that certain languages belong to the same subgroup means that they share a common parent language which is itself a daughter of a higher-order proto-language, just as English is a descendant of Proto-Germanic (together with its other Germanic sister languages, such as German, Swedish, Icelandic and others) and so is a member of the Germanic subgroup, which in turn is a daughter of (branch of) Proto-Indo-European, together with other subgroups (such as Slavic, Italic, Celtic, Indo-Iranian and so on, which have their own later daughter languages). Also, after the break-up of the original proto-language, a daughter language may remain unified; such a language which branches off directly from the proto-language and does not later split up into other languages constitutes a subgroup (branch) of the family all by itself, a subgroup with only a single member. The goal of subgrouping is to determine which languages belong to intermediate parents. The purpose of subgrouping is to determine the family tree for genetically related languages. An example of a family tree has already been seen in Chapter 5 in Figure 5.1 for the Proto-Romance family tree. Since examples from the Indo-European and Uralic families are cited frequently in this book, and because so much historical linguistic work has been done on these, their family trees are presented in Figures 6.1 and 6.2. The Austronesian family tree is also presented, in Figure 6.3. Frequent examples from Mayan languages are also cited here; the Mayan family tree is given in Figure 6.4.

The particular family trees presented here for Indo-European (Figure 6.1) and Uralic (Figure 6.2) are representative, but far from universally agreed upon. In both families, there is general agreement about the major lower-level subgroups (subfamilies), where the evidence is fairly clear. However, there is disagreement about the higher-order branches. In both families, the evidence for the higher branches, those closer to the proto-language, is limited and often unclear. The most common tree given traditionally for Indo-European usually presents some ten separate subgroups branching directly from Proto-Indo-European with little intermediate branching for higher-order subgroups. The Indo-European family tree presented in Figure 6.1 incorporates some recent hypotheses about higher-order branching, but this is still inconclusive. The position of Albanian, in particular, is unclear. Other ancient Indo-European languages should also be represented, for example, Phrygian, Thracian, Illyrian, Messapic and Venetic, though where they should appear in the tree is less clear. For more details about the internal branchings in the Romance subgroup, see Figure 5.1 in Chapter 5. (For discussion of the classification of Indo-European, see Clackson 2007: 5–15, Garrett 1999, Jasanoff 2003, Mallory and Adams 1997: 550–6, and Ringe, Warnow and Taylor 2002.)

The Uralic tree given in Figure 6.2 represents a more traditional classification of the family, though recent opinion is divided. Some find little support for the branching classification with its higher-order intermediate subgroups (see Häkkinen 1984, 2001: 169–71, Salminen 2001). Others are sympathetic to the problems pointed out due to the limited evidence for higher-order internal branches, but nevertheless see sufficient evidence to support much of the branching classification (see Sammallahti 1988, 1998: 119–22). There is fairly general agreement that the former Volgaic branch (not given here), which would group Mari and Mordvin more closely together, should be abandoned. Salminen (2001) would prefer to drop not just this branch, but most of the others, leaving several groups diverging directly from the proto-language with very little intermediate branching in any of these. (For discussion, see Abondolo 1998, Häkkinen 1984, 2001, Janhunen 2001, Salminen 2001, Sammallahti 1988, 1998: 119–22.)

The Austronesian family tree is given in Figure 6.3. It provides another example of a family tree and the subgrouping which it represents (after Ross, Pawley and Osmond 1998: 6). In this figure, note that the names in italics indicate groups of languages which have no exclusively shared common ancestor. Thus, for example, *Formosan languages* refers to a collections of languages all descended from Proto-Austronesian (along with Proto-Malayo-Polynesian), but there is not assumed to be any 'Proto-Formosan'.

The only generally accepted criterion for subgrouping is *shared innovation*. A shared innovation is a linguistic change which shows a departure (innovation) from some trait of the proto-language and is shared by a subset of the daughter languages. It is assumed that a shared innovation is the result of a change which took place in a single daughter language which then subsequently diversified into daughters of its own, each of which inherits the results of the change. Thus the innovation is shared by the descendants of this intermediate parent but is not shared by languages in other subgroups of the family. This is because the languages of other subgroups do not descend from the intermediate parent that underwent the change which is inherited from this more immediate parent by its daughter languages. The fact that they share the innovation means that they

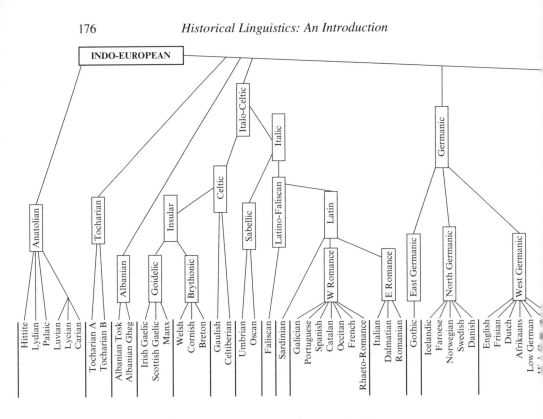

FIGURE 6.1: The Indo-European family tree

contain evidence which suggests that they were formerly a unified language which underwent the change and then subsequently split up, leaving evidence of this change in its daughters.

The classification of the Mayan languages will serve as a guided exercise to illustrate how subgrouping is done, and we will examine how shared innovations among these languages determine their subgrouping. Let us look first at the classification which has been established, given in the family tree in Figure 6.4, and then we will consider some of the shared innovations upon which the subgrouping is based.

Given that there are thirty-one Mayan languages and each has undergone several sound changes, we consider only a subset of the many shared innovations to give an idea of how subgroups are established. The following is a list of the major sound changes which are innovations shared among some but not others of the languages of the family. These form the basis for subgrouping the Mayan languages.

(1) *w > Ø / #__ (before *u, o, i, a*) (for example, *winaq* > Huastec *inik* 'person')

(2) *ŋ > w / #__, h /__# (*ŋe:h* > Huastec *we:w* 'tail', *o:ŋ* > Huastec *uh* 'avocado')

(3) *ts, *t̯ > t; *ts', *t̯' > t' (The *t̯* represents a fronted "*t*", perhaps palatal-

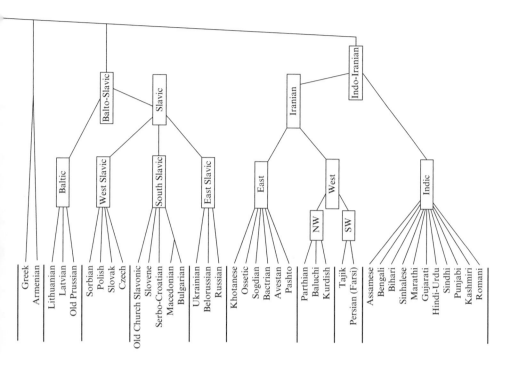

ized, in traditional Mayan reconstructions.) (*tseʔ- > Huastec teʔ- 'laugh')

(4)   *-h > -y (final *h* became *y*) (*ɓa:h > Kaqchikel ɓa:y 'gopher')

(5)   *-ɓ > -ʔ / VCV__# (in polysyllabic forms final imploded *b* became a glottal stop) (Kaqchikel xuna:ʔ 'year' <*xun + ha:ɓ 'one year')

(6)   *h > ʔ (*haʔ > Mam ʔaʔ 'water',

(7)   *r > t (*ri:x > Mam ti:x 'old man')

(8)   *t > č (*tap > Mam čap 'crab')

(9)   *č' > ҫ̌ (alveopalatal affricate > laminal retroflex affricate) (*č'am > Mam ҫ̌'am 'sour')

(10) *-t > -č (word-final *t* changed to *č*) (*naxt > Yucatec ná:č 'far')

(11) *e: > i, *o: > u (long mid vowels raised to high vowels) (*so:ts' > Chol suts' 'bat')

(12) *ŋ > x̱ (velar nasal > a kind of velar fricative) (*ŋa:h > K'iche' xa:h 'house')

(13) *ṭ > ć (a fronted *t* [dental or palatalized] changed to *ć* [a prepalatal affricate]) (*ṭe:ʔ > Mam tse:ʔ, K'iche' *če:ʔ 'tree')

(14) *CVʔVC > CVʔC (*xoʔoq > K'iche' xoʔq 'corn husk, maize leaf')

(15) ć > č (the prepalatal affricates became palato-alveolar) (*ṭe:ʔ > *će:ʔ > K'iche' *če:ʔ 'tree')

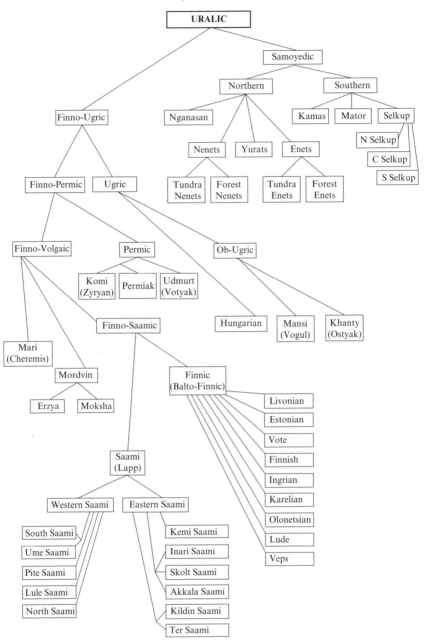

FIGURE 6.2: The Uralic family tree

(16) *q > k, *q' > k' (the uvular stops became velars) (*saq > Huastec θak,
      Yucatec sak, Chol sak 'white')

(17) *ŋ > n (*ŋe:h > Chol neh 'tail')

(18) *ts > s (*tsuh > Q'eqchi' suh 'bottlegourd')

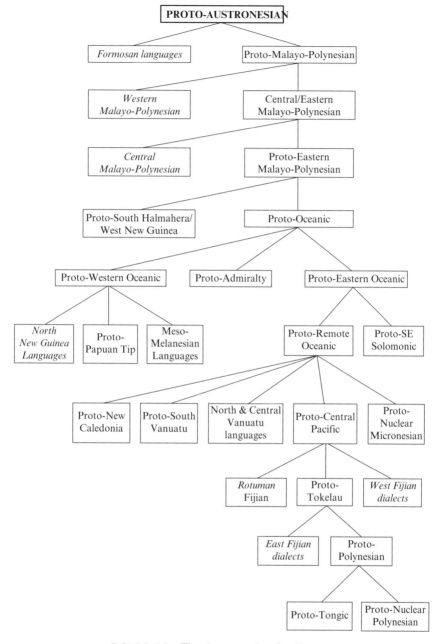

FIGURE 6.3: The Austronesian family tree

(Note that innovations in morphology and syntax are just as important as phonological innovations. Examples involving sound change are utilized here only because it takes less space to describe them than changes in other areas of the grammar usually do.)

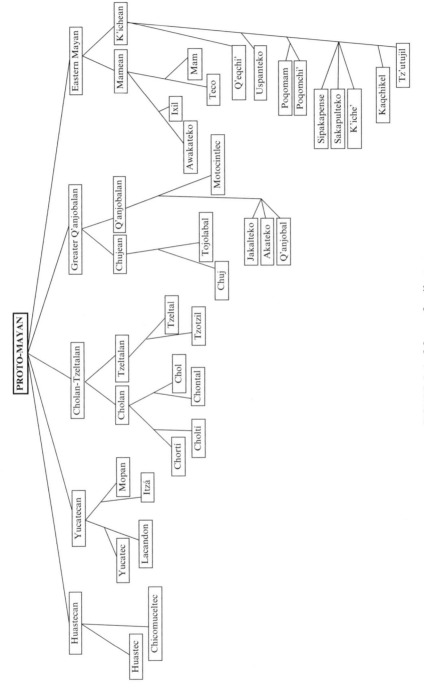

FIGURE 6.4: Mayan family tree

Let us begin by looking at the lower-level groupings (the languages most closely related) for ease of illustration. In the Huastecan subgroup, Huastec and Chicomuceltec share the changes (1), (2) and (3). Other Mayan languages did not undergo these changes. We interpret this to mean that Huastec and Chicomuceltec belong together as members of a single subgroup: while Proto-Huastecan was still a unified language, it underwent these sound changes (and others not presented here). After having undergone these changes, Proto-Huastecan split up into its two daughter languages, Huastec and Chicomuceltec. As a consequence of this shared history, when we examine cognates, we see in both Huastec and Chicomuceltec that the cognates show the results of these sound changes, shared innovations, not shared by the cognates in the other Mayan languages. Looking backwards, it is because they share these innovations that we postulate that there was an earlier unified Proto-Huastecan language which underwent these changes before it diversified into the two daughter languages of this branch of the family.

Kaqchikel and Tz'utujil share the two innovations (4) and (5), which show that these two languages are more closely related to one another than to the others, since none of the others has evidence of these changes. Here we assume that there was a unified language which underwent the two changes and then later split up into Kaqchikel and Tz'utujil, accounting for why these two languages share the results of these changes. The alternative would require us to assume that these two languages are not closely related but just happened independently to undergo changes (4) and (5). Such a coincidence is not likely.

The four Mamean languages, Ixil, Awakateko, Mam and Teco, share a series of innovations, (6) through (9) (and others not mentioned here); these include a chain shift in which Proto-Mayan (PM) *r became t (7), while *t in turn became $č$ (8), and *$č$ in turn changed to Mamean $\check{s}$ (9) (a chain shift mentioned in Chapter 2).

The four Yucatecan languages (Yucatec, Lacandon, Mopan and Itzá) share innovation (10) (final -t > -$č$), among others.

The Cholan languages, but no others, share change (11) (raising of long mid vowels, *e: > i, *o: > u).

At higher, more inclusive levels of the classification, all the languages of the K'ichean and Mamean groups share the innovations (12) through (14), showing that they all descend from a common parent language, Proto-Eastern Mayan, which had itself branched off from Proto-Mayan.

We proceed in this fashion (not all the evidence is presented here) until we have worked out the classification of all the Mayan languages and subgroups, both lower-level and higher-order ones, and it is on this basis that we draw the family tree presented in Figure 6.4.

It might be asked, why would just a list of shared similarities not be enough to distinguish more closely related languages from more distantly related ones within a language family? Because not just any similarity provides reliable evidence of closer affinity. For example, it is important to keep in mind that *shared retentions* are of practically no value for subgrouping. A shared retention is merely something that different daughter languages inherit unchanged from the proto-language regardless of whether the daughters belong to the same subgroup or not. For example, Huastec, Mam and Motocintlec (which, as seen in Figure 6.4, belong to separate branches of the family) retain the vowel-length contrast, but this is not evidence that these three necessarily belong to a single subgroup of Mayan, sharing a period of common history not shared by the other languages of the family. Rather, since Proto-Mayan had contrastive vowel length, the fact that Huastec, Mam and Motocintlec share this trait means only that these three still retain unchanged something that Proto-Mayan had, and they could retain this inherited trait regardless of whether they belonged together to a single subgroup or to separate subgroups each of which independently retained this feature of the proto-language. Shared retentions just do not reveal which languages share a period of common history *after* the break-up of the proto-language.

Although shared innovation is the only generally accepted criterion for sub-grouping, not all shared innovations are of equal value for showing closer kinship. Some shared innovations represent sound changes that are so natural and happen so frequently cross-linguistically that they may easily take place independently in different branches of a language family and thus have nothing to do with a more recent common history. For example, in Mayan, change (16) (*$*q > k$, *$*q' > k'$) took place in all the languages of the Huastecan, Yucatecan and Cholan-Tzeltalan branches, as well as in some of the Greater Q'anjobalan languages. However, since uvular stops (q and q') are rarer in languages in general than velars and are more difficult to produce than velars (k and k'), and since they easily and frequently change to velars, the fact that change (16) is shared by languages of these branches does not necessarily mean that a single change took place in some more immediate ancestor of these languages before they split up; it is just as likely that the uvulars changed to velars independently in different languages within the family. Change (17) (*$*\eta > n$) took place in the Yucatecan, Cholan-Tzeltalan and some of the Greater Q'anjobalan languages, but velar nasals (η) can easily become alveolar nasals (n), a change frequently found in the world's languages. In these two cases (changes (16) and (17)), it is assumed that these branches of Mayan independently underwent these very common sound changes, and that they therefore provide no strong evidence for subgrouping. They merely represent independent, convergent innovations. Obviously, such changes are not of as much value for subgrouping as other less expected changes are.

A very telling example of this sort is the loss of the vowel-length contrast through the merger of long vowels with their short counterparts in Cholan and in some dialects of Kaqchikel. This is perfectly understandable, since the loss of vowel length is a very common change which languages seem easily to undergo. In this case, it would be ludicrous to imagine that Chol and the Kaqchikel dialects without the length contrast formed one branch of the family while the other Kaqchikel dialects which maintain the contrast belong to a totally distinct branch. Clearly, the seemingly shared innovation of loss of vowel length came about independently in the two instances. The very natural, very frequent changes are candidates for convergent development (innovations shared due to independent change rather than to inherited results from a single change in the immediate parent), changes such as nasalization of vowels before nasal consonants, intervocalic voicing, final devoicing, palatalization before *i* or *j* and so on.

Finally, some sound changes can be borrowed among related languages, and this can complicate the subgrouping picture. For example, Q'eqchi', Poqomam and Poqomchi' share change (18) (*$ts > s$); however, documents from the sixteenth and seventeenth centuries reveal that this change took place long after these three were independent languages and that the change is borrowed, diffused across language boundaries (see Chapters 3 and 12). Naturally, if the change is borrowed from one language to another after they had become separate languages, this does not reflect a time of common history when a single language underwent a change and then subsequently split up, leaving evidence of the change in its daughter languages. Therefore, borrowed changes, which may appear to be shared innovations, are also not evidence of subgrouping.

While shared innovation as the only reliable criterion for subgrouping is clear, it must be kept in mind that the subgrouping can be only as successful as the reconstruction upon which it is based. That is, what constitutes an innovation depends crucially on what is reconstructed, and if the reconstruction is wrong, there is a strong possibility that the subgrouping which depends on it will be wrong as well. Let's consider an example illustrated by Nootkan (a family of three languages, Makah, Nitinat and Nootka, spoken in the Northwest Coast area of North America). Consider the sound correspondences presented in Table 6.3. (See Haas 1969b; some of the Nootkan correspondences and changes were seen in Chapter 5.)

TABLE 6.3: Some Nootkan sound correspondences

	Makah	Nitinat	Nootka	Proto-Nootkan
(1)	q'	ʕ	ʕ	*q'
(2)	χ	χ	ħ	*χ
(3)	b	b	m	*m
(4)	d	d	n	*n

Let us begin with what is considered the correct reconstruction and subgrouping before considering the consequences of erroneous alternatives. Proto-Nootkan is reconstructed with *q' for (1), *$χ$ (voiceless uvular fricative) for (2), *m for (3) and *n for (4); Nitinat and Nootka are subgrouped together, with Makah as a separate branch of the family first. This interpretation is based on the fact that Nitinat and Nootka share, for example, the innovation in (1) in which glottalized uvular stops (q') changed to pharyngeal ʕ. While Makah and Nitinat seem to share the innovation (in (3) and (4)) that the Proto-Nootkan nasals (represented by *m and *n here) became corresponding voiced oral stops (b and d, respectively), this change came about through diffusion in the linguistic area after Makah and Nitinat had separated. Nitinat and Makah belong to the area of the Northwest Coast of North America where several languages lack nasal consonants (see Chapters 2 and 12). In (2), since only Nootka changed (*$χ > ħ$), Makah and Nitinat share only the retention of $χ$, not evidence for subgrouping. However, suppose now that for (2) we were to reconstruct (erroneously) *$ħ$ (pharyngeal fricative) for Proto-Nootkan; this would presuppose the change of *$ħ$ to $χ$ in Makah and Nitinat, and this would be a shared innovation, evidence to support subgrouping them together and Nootka apart. As this shows, subgrouping is very much at the mercy of how accurate the reconstruction upon which it is based is. In this case, if we did not recognize that the change from nasals to corresponding voiced stops in (3) and (4), *m > b and *n > d, was due to borrowing and we reconstructed erroneously *b and *d instead, with the assumption that Nootka changed these to nasals, nothing would follow for subgrouping, since Nootka alone would change and Makah and Nitinat would only share a retention.

The Mayan subgrouping, considered above, provides a final example, though it is simplified here in that we will consider only one of many sound correspondences together with the changes and the reconstruction based on it. In the Mayan family, the lower-level subgroups are well established; these include Huastecan, Yucatecan, Cholan-Tzeltalan, Greater Q'anjobalan, K'ichean and Mamean. Some of these are grouped together in higher-order, more inclusive branches of the family; we must ask what the evidence for these larger subgroupings is and whether it is accurate. Consider the following sound correspondence (encountered earlier, in Chapter 5):

Huastecan *h* : Yucatecan *n* : Cholan-Tzeltalan *n* : Q'anjobalan *ŋ* : K'ichean *x̱* : Mamean *x*

The generally accepted reconstruction in this case is Proto-Mayan *ŋ (where it is assumed that Huastecan independently changed *ŋ > h (change (2) in the list above), and so we will leave it out of the rest of the discussion). K'ichean and Mamean share the change of *ŋ > x̱ (change (12) above; x̱ then later changed to x in Mamean and in most of the K'ichean languages), and this shared innovation (together with others mentioned above) supports subgrouping K'ichean and Mamean together; the group is usually called Eastern Mayan. In this reconstruction for the correspondence set that Proto-Mayan *ŋ is based on, Yucatecan, Cholan-Tzeltalan and Q'anjobalan each retain the nasal (where it is assumed that the change of ŋ > n is so natural and easy that Yucatecan and Cholan-Tzeltalan probably underwent it independently), and since this is a shared retention (if viewed this way), nothing follows for whether or not these three groups may have a closer kinship or not. However, K'ichean and Mamean share the innovation *ŋ > x̱, which is grounds for subgrouping them together. Suppose hypothetically now that this reconstruction were wrong and that Proto-Mayan actually had *x̱ (although this is highly unlikely). In this case, K'ichean and Mamean would share not an innovation but merely a retention, and nothing would follow from this for their position within the family. However, Yucatecan, Cholan-Tzeltalan and Greater Q'anjobalan would all share an innovation to a nasal (*x̱ > ŋ, then later ŋ > n in Yucatecan and Cholan-Tzeltalan), and this would be evidence for classifying Yucatecan, Cholan-Tzeltalan and Greater Q'anjobalan as members of the same subgroup. That is, if the reconstruction of *ŋ is wrong, then the subgrouping based on the shared innovations which depart from this reconstruction is also not founded; if the alternative reconstruction with *x̱ is wrong (which is almost certainly the case), then any subgrouping which presupposes it must also be wrong (unless other shared innovations can be found which do support it).

See Chapter 17 for discussion of subgrouping and classification involving glottochronology and its problems and of more recent quantitative approaches to the topic.

6.5 Exercises

Exercise 6.1 Polynesian subgrouping

There are numerous Polynesian languages, of which the ones in this exercise are only a sample. Polynesian is a branch (subgroup) of the Austronesian family. Consider the two cognate sets from these five Polynesian languages. What sound change has taken place? Observe which languages underwent the change and which ones did not, and on this basis draw all the alternative possible family trees that could account for the subgrouping of these languages. (Clue: which languages share an innovation? Which languages share a retention?) Note that the medial consonant, spelled <ng> or <g>, is /ŋ/ in all the languages.

Proto-Polynesian	*songi 'smell'	*sae 'to tear'
Tongan	hongi	hae
Niuean	hongi	hee
Samoan	sogi	sae
East Futuna	sogi	sae
Luangiua	songi	sae

(Data from Otsuka 2005)

Exercise 6.2 Barbacoan subgrouping

Barbacoan is a small family of languages spoken in Colombia and Ecuador; its members include Awa Pit, Cha'palaachi, Guambiano, Totoró, and Tsafiqui. Consider the following sound changes in the various Barbacoan languages. On the basis of these, draw the most likely family tree which represents the subgrouping of the Barbacoan family.

NOTE: č = IPA tʃ, š = IPA ʃ.

1. Proto-Barbacoan *t > č / __ i (when before *i*) in Guambiano
2. Proto-Barbacoan *t > č / __ i (when before *i*) in Totoró
3. Proto-Barbacoan *t > š / __ i (when before *i*) in Awa Pit
4. Proto-Barbacoan *t > tʂ elsewhere (when not before *i*) in Guambiano
5. Proto-Barbacoan *t > tʂ elsewhere (when not before *i*) in Totoró
6. Proto-Barbacoan *t > s elsewhere (when not before *i*) in Awa Pit
7. Proto-Barbacoan *š > Ø /__ # (lost word-finally) in Guambiano
8. Proto-Barbacoan *š > Ø /__ # (lost word-finally) in Totoró
9. Proto-Barbacoan *l > n / #__ i (before *i*) in Guambiano
10. Proto-Barbacoan *l > n / #__ i (before *i*) in Totoró
11. Proto-Barbacoan *l > n / #__ i (before *i*) in Awa Pit
12. Proto-Barbacoan *p, *t, *k > Ø/__ # (stops lost word-finally) in Cha'palaachi
13. Proto-Barbacoan *p, *t, *k > Ø/__ # (stops lost word-finally) in Tsafiqui
14. Proto-Barbacoan *s > h in Cha'palaachi
15. Proto-Barbacoan *s > h in Tsafiqui

(From Curnow and Liddicoat 1998)

Exercise 6.3　Other subgrouping exercises

Return to your reconstructions of Proto-Polynesian (Exercise 5.3), Proto-Uto-Aztecan (Exercise 5.6), Proto-K'ichean (Exercise 5.8), and Proto-Quechuan (Exercise 5.9), and based on your reconstruction and the sound changes that you postulated for each language, attempt to establish the subgrouping in these language families. These subgrouping exercises may prove difficult, depending on what you reconstructed and on the number and kind of sound changes which you postulated in each of these reconstruction exercises.

7

Models of Linguistic Change

It is now an axiom of scientific philology that the real life of language is in many respects more clearly seen and better studied in dialects and colloquial forms of speech than in highly developed literary languages.

(Henry Sweet 1900: 79)

7.1 Introduction

When textbooks on historical linguistics talk about 'models of change', they invariably mean the traditional 'family-tree' model and the 'wave theory', and the conflict that is assumed to exist between them. These are described in this chapter and the conflict between them is reconciled. In particular, the contrasting (but actually complementary) approaches taken by dialectologists and traditional Neogrammarians are examined and clarified, sociolinguistic approaches to language change are brought into the picture, and the related notion of 'lexical diffusion' is put in perspective.

7.2 The Family-tree Model

The family tree (sometimes called *Stammbaum*, its German name) is the traditional model of language diversification. The family-tree model attempts to show how languages diversify and how language families are classified (as described in Chapter 6). A family-tree diagram's purpose is to show how languages which belong to the same language family are related to one another. *Linguistic diversification* refers to how a single ancestor language (a proto-language) develops dialects which in time through the accumulation of changes become distinct languages (sister languages to one another, daughter languages of the proto-language), and how through continued linguistic change these daughter languages can diversify and split up into daughters of their own (members of a subgroup of the family). The family-tree diagram represents this diversification, being a classification of the languages of a family and the degree of relatedness among the various languages.

The family-tree model is often associated with August Schleicher, prominent in the history of Indo-European linguistics and teacher of several founders of Neogrammarianism, as well as of well-known opponents to Neogrammarian thinking (see Schleicher 1861–2). This model is typically linked in the litera-ture with the development of the comparative method and eventually with the Neogrammarian notion of regularity of sound change. At the heart of the conflict over models are two of the basic assumptions of the comparative method (dis-cussed in Chapter 5), that sound change is regular (the Neogrammarian hypoth-esis) and that there is no subsequent contact among the sister languages after the break-up of the proto-language.

The Neogrammarian slogan, *sound laws suffer no exceptions* (declared virtu-ally as doctrine in the so-called 'Neogrammarian manifesto', in the foreword to Hermann Osthoff and Karl Brugmann (1878), written mostly by Brugmann), became an important cornerstone of reconstruction by the comparative method (as explained in Chapter 5). There is nothing inherently hostile to language contact and borrowing in the comparative method or the regularity of sound change; it is just that there is no provision in the comparative method for dealing directly with borrowings. For this, it is necessary to resort to considerations that are not properly part of the comparative method itself (see Chapters 3 and 12). Nevertheless, this neglect of language contact in the comparative method is the source of dispute about which models are assumed most appropriate for dealing with kinds of changes and kinds of relationships among languages. Clearly, genetic relationship, the only thing represented in family-tree diagrams, is not the only sort of relationship that exists among languages – for example, languages do also borrow from one another.

7.3   The Challenge from Dialectology and the 'Wave Theory'

Some scholars, many of them dialectologists, did not accept the Neo-grammarian position that sound change is regular and exceptionless, but rather opposed this and the family-tree model. The slogan associated with opponents of the Neogrammarian position is *each word has its own history* ('*chaque mot a son histoire*'). (This slogan is often attributed to Jules Gilliéron, author of the *Atlas linguistique de la France* (1902–10), the dialect atlas of France (see Gilliéron 1921; Gilliéron and Roques 1912), although it should be credited to Hugo Schuchardt, a contemporary of the Neogrammarian founders, of whose claims he was critical.) The alternative to the family-tree model which was put forward was the 'wave theory'. The wave theory is usually attributed to Johannes Schmidt (1872), though it, too, was actually developed slightly earlier by Hugo Schuchardt (in 1868 and 1870; this history is documented in Alvar 1967: 82–5) – Schuchardt and Schmidt were both students of Schleicher. The 'wave theory' was intended to deal with changes due to contact among languages and dialects. According to Schmidt's wave model, linguistic changes spread outward concentrically like waves, which become progressively weaker with the distance from their central point. Since later changes may not cover the same area, there may be no sharp boundaries between neighbouring dialects or languages; rather, the greater the distance between them, the fewer linguistic traits dialects or languages may share. The dialectologists' slogan, that every word has its own history, reflects this thinking – a word's history might be the result of various influences from various directions, and these might be quite different from those involved in another word's history, hence each word has its own (potentially quite different) history. It is easy to see that this model would reduce historical linguistics to etymology, since etymology is the study of the idiosyncratic particular properties in the history of individual words.

The dialectologists believed that their findings contradicted the regularity hypothesis of the Neogrammarians. However, this was not really the case. What is at stake here is, in the traditional view, the difference between regular sound change internal to a particular language or dialect and dialect borrowing, change that can be irregular and comes from outside the particular language or dialect. Labov (2010: 305) describes it well, speaking of the distinction 'between transmission within the speech community and diffusion across communities'. Both types of change are important. The first is subject to 'the normal type of [regular] internal language change; it is termed "change from below" or change from within the system, as opposed to "change from above" or the importation of elements from other systems' (Labov 2010: 307) – or for short, the distinction between transmission and diffusion.

To see what is meant, let us consider an instructive example from English dialects. The velar fricative /x/ of earlier English is gone from Standard English, either lost (for example, by the rule that deleted the velar fricative before following consonants, $x > \emptyset /\_\_ C$, as in 'light': /lixt/ > /liːt/ > lait [by the Great Vowel Shift]) or in some cases changed to /f/ (as in /trox/ > /trɒf/ 'trough'). However, in southern West Yorkshire, the *Survey of English Dialects* (Orton et al. 1962–71) recorded 'occasional relic forms such as [trɒx] for *trough* (RP [British Received Pronunciation] /trɒf/) and [lɪçt] for *light*' (Wells 1982: 190) ([ç] is the allophone of /x/ which appeared after a front vowel such as the /ɪ/ in *light*). That is, a handful of words, which maintain /x/, appear to be exceptions to this change, though the overwhelming majority of words with original /x/ in this geographical region did undergo the changes, deleting /x/ or turning it into /f/. Some dialectologists took cases such as this one as evidence that the Neogrammarian idea of exceptionless sound change must be wrong. A dialectologist might say that each of these words has its own history. For example, a 'homey' word such as *trough*, characteristic of rural life, might more successfully resist the wave of change affecting /x/ which had spread from other, more prestigious dialects. However, there are two important things to notice about this case. First, we can identify these words as exceptions only if we recognize the sound changes which affected /x/ – without acknowledging the sound change, it would be impossible to recognize these few words in southern West Yorkshire, found at the time of the *Survey of English Dialects*, as exceptions. While these words are exceptions to strict exceptionlessness of sound change, we cannot explain their individual histories, that they are exceptions, without reference to the sound changes themselves. Second, it is possible that a situation like this one can tell us something more about how some sound changes take place – in this case apparently through the spread of the prestige norm (without /x/) to more remote locations.

This sort of change is traditionally called *dialect borrowing*. Most importantly, this example shows that neither model – neither the family tree nor the wave theory – is sufficient to explain all linguistic change and all the sorts of relationships that can exist between dialects or related languages. Without recognizing the sound change, we would not be able to identify these dialect forms as exceptional, and without the information from dialectology, our knowledge of how some changes are transmitted or diffuse would be incomplete. Clearly, both are needed. This being the case, it will pay us to look more closely at some basic aspects of dialectology. (Other aspects of the explanation of change are deferred until Chapter 13.)

7.4 Dialectology (Linguistic Geography, Dialect Geography)

Dialectology deals with regional variation in a language. Some concepts of dialectology that need to be understood are the following.

Isogloss: a line on a map which represents the geographical boundary (limit) of regional linguistic variants. By extension, the term 'isogloss' also refers to the dialect features themselves, an extension of the original sense of the word from dealing with a line on a map to reference to the actual linguistic phenomena themselves. For example, in the USA the *greasy/greazy* isogloss is a line roughly corresponding to the Mason–Dixon line which separates the North Midlands from the South Midlands; it runs across the middle of the country until it dives down across south-eastern Kansas, western Oklahoma and Texas (see Map 7.1). North of the line, *greasy* is pronounced with *s*; south of the line it is pronounced with *z*. Another isogloss has to do with a contrast versus lack of

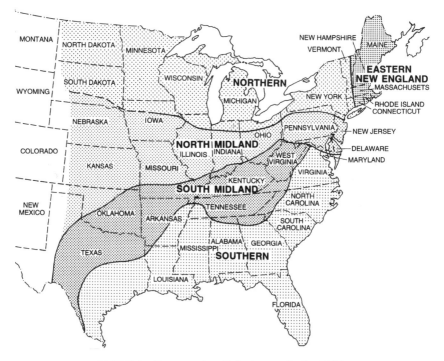

MAP 7.1: Some major dialect areas in the USA

contrast in the vowels in such word pairs as *pin/pen* and *tin/ten*. In these words, [ɪ] and [ɛ] before nasals contrast in other dialects, but in the South Midlands and Southern dialect areas there is no contrast – these vowels have merged before nasals in these dialects. This explains how country-music songs, many of whose writers and singers are from the dialect areas which lack the contrast, can rhyme words such as *win* and *end*, both phonetically [ĭn] (*end* also loses the final consonant [nd > n]), as in the well-known song, 'Heartaches by the Number', where the last line of the refrain goes: 'I've got heartaches by the number for a love that I can't *win*, but the day that I stop countin' is the day my world will *end*.'

Bundle of isoglosses: several isoglosses whose extent coincides at the same geographical boundary; such bundling of isoglosses is taken to constitute the boundary of a dialect (or dialect area). The two examples of isoglosses just mentioned happen to bundle, both along the Mason–Dixon line, with *greasy* and the *pin/pen* contrast north of the line (for example, in the North Midlands dialect area), and with *greazy* and lack of the vowel contrast south of the line (for example, in the South Midlands dialect area) (see Map 7.1).

Focal area: zone of prestige from which innovations spread outwards.

Relic area (*residual area*): an area (usually small) which preserves older forms that have not undergone the innovations that the surrounding areas have; relic areas are often regions of difficult access for cultural, political or geographical reasons, and thus resistant to the spread of prestige variants from elsewhere. The southern West Yorkshire area which retained *x* in certain words is a relic area.

Lect: some scholars feel the need for a more open-ended term which signifies any linguistic variety, whether defined by its geographical distribution or by its use by people from different social classes, castes, ages, genders and so on. *Lect* is intended to cover all such varieties (geographical dialect, sociolect, idiolect – the language characteristic of a single individual – and so on).

Mutual intelligibility: when speakers of different linguistic entities can understand one another. This is the principal criterion for distinguishing dialects of a single language from distinct languages (which may or may not be closely related). Entities which are totally incomprehensible to speakers of other entities clearly are mutually unintelligible, and for linguists they therefore belong to separate languages. However, the criterion of mutual intelligibility is often not so straightforward. For example, there are cases of non-reciprocal intelligibility (for instance, Portuguese speakers understand Spanish reasonably well, while many Spanish speakers do not understand Portuguese well at all) and of non-immediate intelligibility, where upon first exposure understanding is limited, but after a time intelligibility grows. There are many studies in the sociolinguistic and dialectological literature of cases of various sorts having to do with how to determine to which language various dialects belong, often having to do with the relationship of regional varieties to some standard or *superordinate* language or to their position within a dialect chain. We do not have the space to get into the details of this here, though these various relationships among varieties are relevant to linguistic change.

Language: the definition of 'language' is not strictly a linguistic enterprise, but sometimes is determined more by political or social factors. For this reason, Max Weinreich's definition of language is very frequently reported: *a language is a dialect which has an army and a navy.* This emphasizes that the definition of a 'language' is not merely a linguistic matter. For example, while speakers of Norwegian and Swedish have little difficulty understanding one another (the languages are mutually intelligible), these are considered separate languages for political reasons. On the other hand, Chinese has several so-called 'dialects' which are so different one from another that their speakers do not easily understand each other's language. By the criterion of mutual intelligibility, linguists consider these separate languages; however, official policy in China regards these as representing the same language.

Although the literature on the history of linguistics often disposes us to think that dialectology played an important role in the making of the wave theory, giving us the slogan 'every word has its own history', in fact the study of dialects also significantly influenced the Neogrammarians and the origin of their slogan, that 'sound laws suffer no exceptions'. The Neogrammarian founders were impressed by Winteler's (1876) study of the Kerenzen dialect of Swiss German, in which he presented phonological statements as processes (following the ancient rules for Sanskrit of Pāṇini, an important Hindu grammarian from around the fifth century BC, which Winteler studied in his linguistic training). This 'regularity' which Winteler saw in the dialect's (synchronic) rules – for example, in Kerenzen every *n* became *ŋ* before *k* and *g* – inspired the Neogrammarian founders to have confidence in the exceptionlessness of sound changes (Weinreich et al. 1968: 115). Of course, as we saw, Gilliéron (1921), who opposed regularity, also based his objections on the study of dialects, arguing against the Neogrammarians with the other slogan, 'every word has its own history'. Ironically, both these famous orientations to historical linguistics were influenced significantly by dialect studies.

The conflict between the Neogrammarians' 'exceptionless sound change' and the dialectologists' 'every word has its own history' is implicated in more recent controversies over how sound change is transmitted. This controversy will be considered presently, but first it will be helpful to have in mind the general framework which has most influenced thinking in this area, that of Weinreich, Labov and Herzog (1968).

7.5 *A Framework for Investigating the Causes of Linguistic Change*

The framework presented by Weinreich et al. (1968) has been very influential in historical linguistic thought concerning 'why' and 'how' linguistic changes take place. They asked a number of questions, which they also called 'problems', which must be answered (or 'solved') by any theory which hopes to explain language change. These are:

(1) *The constraints problem*: what are the general constraints on change that determine possible and impossible changes and directions of change? For example, among the constraints on change, Weinreich et al. (1968: 100) postulate that 'no language will assume a form in violation of such formal principles as are ... universal in human languages'. The constraints problem is a central issue in linguistic change for many scholars; it takes the form of a search for the

kinds of linguistic change that will *not* take place. The irreversibility of mergers (see Chapter 2) is a good example of such a constraint.

(2) *The transition problem*: how (or by what route or routes) does language change? What intermediate stages or processes does a language go through to get from a state before the change began to the state after the change has taken place? For example, a much-debated question is whether certain kinds of changes must be seen as gradual or abrupt.

(3) *The embedding problem*: how is a given language change embedded in the surrounding system of linguistic and social relations? How does the greater environment in which the change takes place influence the change? That is, the parts of a language are tightly interwoven, often in complex interlocking relationships, so that a change in one part of the grammar may impact on (or be constrained by) other parts of the grammar (see Chapter 13). Also, language change takes place in a social environment, where differences in language may be given positive or negative sociolinguistic status, and this sociolinguistic environment plays a very important role in change.

(4) *The evaluation problem*: how do speakers of the language (members of a speech community) evaluate a given change, and what is the effect of their evaluation on the change? What are the effects of the change on the language's overall structure? (How does the system change without damage to its function of serving communication?)

(5) *The actuation problem*: why does a given linguistic change occur at the particular time and place that it does? How do changes begin and proceed? What starts a change and what carries it along? The actuation question is the most central, since the other questions relate to it; and if we succeed in answering it, we will be able to explain linguistic change (see Chapter 13).

7.6 Sociolinguistics and Language Change

Changes typically begin with variation, with alternative ways of saying the same thing entering the language. Variation is the specific subject matter of sociolinguistics, and while sociolinguists are interested in many other things in addition to linguistic change, sociolinguistics is extremely relevant to understanding how and why languages change. Sociolinguistic concerns underlie several of the questions in Weinreich et al.'s framework (just considered). Sociolinguistics deals with systematic co-variation of linguistic structure with social structure, especially with the variation in language which is conditioned by social differences. The most important dimensions which can condition variation have to do with social attributes of the sender (speaker), the receiver (hearer) and the setting (context). Variation in a language can be conditioned by such social characteristics of the speaker as age, gender, social status, ethnic identity, religion, occupation, self-identification with a location, and in fact almost any important social trait.

Let's consider just a couple of examples of some of these to get a flavour of what is involved. Grammars of Classical Nahuatl report that where Aztec men pronounced *w*, women spoke the same words with *v*. This is linguistic variation conditioned by the gender of the speaker. Since Proto-Uto-Aztecan had **w* in these words, it is necessary to conclude that the *w/v* variation in Classical

Nahuatl is due to a linguistic change which women adopted, *w > v, but men did not. An example reflecting the social status of the speaker is the variation in the Hindi of Khalapur village in India (in Uttar Pradesh) where in words with a stressed vowel in the next syllable, the higher castes contrast /ʊ/ and /ə/, but the lower castes have only /ə/ both in words with /ʊ/ and those with /ə/ in the speech of the higher castes (as seen in, for example, higher caste *dʊtə́i* / low caste *dətə́i* 'blanket'). Here, it appears that there has been a sound change in which ʊ and ə have merged with ə (ʊ, ə > ə) in the language of the low-caste speakers, affecting the language of only a portion of the population, leading to the variation in speech characteristic of the different castes. Similar examples could be presented for the various other social attributes of speakers. Similarly, social attributes of hearers can condition linguistic variation. This sort of variation is often indicative of changes in progress in a speech community, and this makes the study of such variation and its implications for understanding linguistic change in general extremely important.

Sociolinguistic investigations of change have been of two types: *apparent-time* and *real-time* studies. In apparent-time research, by far the more common, a *variable* (a linguistic trait subject to social or stylistic variation) is investigated at one particular point in time. To the extent that the variation correlates with age, it is assumed that a change in progress is under way and that the variant most characteristic of older speakers' speech represents the earlier stage and the variant more typical of younger speakers' speech shows what it is changing to. The age-gradient distribution shows the change in progress. An example of this sort is the ongoing merger of diphthongs /iə/ (as in *ear*, *cheer*) and /ɛə/ (as in *air*, *chair*) in New Zealand English, where in general older speakers maintain the contrast more, most younger speakers merge the two to /iə/, hence jokes based on the homophony of 'beer' and 'bear', for example (see Maclagan and Gordon 1996). Real-time studies compare samples of language from different times; for example, a comparison of recordings from fifty years ago with comparable samples of speech today can reveal changes (see Labov 1994 for discussion of several examples).

Some general claims about linguistic change which have been made based on large-scale sociolinguistic investigations in urban settings are:

1. Linguistic changes originate in the intermediate social classes (the upper working class or lower middle class), not in the highest or the lowest classes.
2. The innovators of change are usually people with the highest local status, who play a central role in the speech community.
3. These innovators have the highest density of social interactions within their communication networks and they have the highest proportions of contacts outside the local neighbourhood, as well.
4. Women lead most linguistic changes (women accept and help to propagate the linguistic changes earlier than men do).
5. Different ethnic groups who newly enter a speech community participate in changes in progress only to the extent that they begin to gain local rights and privileges in jobs and housing, and access to or acceptance in the society. (See Labov 1994, 2001.)

Several of these claims are currently being challenged or refined – for example, there is a range of opinion concerning whether (3) holds up, even in the urban settings for which it is designed. Some of these claims may be appropriate only to modern settings; it is important to determine to what extent these and other claims may be true of changes which take place in languages spoken in societies and social settings with very different social organizations, subsistence patterns and economic practices, less nucleated settlements, and so on.

A number of influential historical linguists (for example, Henning Andersen, Eugenio Coseriu, James Milroy) hold that speakers change, and not languages, making all linguistic change social change, rather than language change per se. Some go so far as to deny any language-internal motivation (arising from the structural aspects of the language itself) for language change, but most historical linguists disagree with this, since there is strong evidence that the explanation of some aspects of linguistic change requires appeal to non-social factors. For example, how could the approach which views linguistic change as merely a kind of social change explain why certain changes (for example, intervocalic voicing of stops) recur in language after language, despite the vastly different social settings in which these different languages are used? The explanation of linguistic change is not found solely in conscious change by speakers for social purposes, rather only rarely so. Both internal and external factors are important (see Chapter 13).

Different conceptions of linguistic change are often closely linked with the stand taken on the *actuation problem* (mentioned above). For example, James Milroy (1992: 10) stresses network theory's emphasis on language *maintenance*: 'In order to account for differential patterns of change at particular times and places [that is, to solve the actuation problem], we need first to take account of those factors that tend to maintain language states and resist change'. Strong network ties are seen as norm-enforcement mechanisms, a model for maintenance of local language norms against encroaching change from outside the network. How can the actuation problem, the question about how changes get started in the first place, be approached with a model based solely on norm maintenance, that is on resistance to change but not on change itself? In Milroy's view, linguistic change takes place in strong-tie networks only to the extent that they fail at their primary mission of maintaining the network norms and resisting change from outside. If the social network can only resist but not initiate change, with all change entering from without, how could network theory contribute to solving the actuation problem? The origins of these changes in the broader community from where they flow into the strong-tie networks appear to be more relevant to the actuation problem and generally to understanding how and why languages change.

7.7 The Issue of Lexical Diffusion

For the Neogrammarians, the three primary mechanisms of change were regular sound change, analogy and borrowing. Regularity for them meant that every instance of a sound changes mechanically, irrespective of particular words in which it is found, that is, that it affects every word in which the sound occurs in the same phonetic environment. Cases where a change does not affect all words in the same way at the same time were not seen to be the result of regular sound change, but as due to analogy or to dialect borrowing, as in the case of the variable result of the *x > Ø change in different words in southern West Yorkshire (see above) due to the differential impact of dialect borrowing from the prestige variety. This, in essence, constitutes an attempt to answer the transition question, of how change is implemented. The concept of *lexical diffusion*, promoted by William Wang and his associates (Wang 1969; see Labov 1994: 421–543 for an extensive survey and evaluation), challenges Neogrammarian regularity. They see sound change as being implemented not by mechanically affecting every instance of a sound regardless of the particular words in which instances of the sound are found (as in the Neogrammarian position), but rather as change affecting the sound in certain words and then diffusing gradually to other words in the lexicon. Fully regular sound changes, in this view, are those in which the change diffuses across the lexicon until it reaches all words. This is like 'dialect borrowing', but with some words borrowing from others in the same dialect. It constitutes a different outlook on the transition problem. It should be kept in mind, however, that in spite of strong claims that lexical diffusion is a more basic mechanism by which change is transmitted than Neogrammarian regularity, very few cases of lexical diffusion have actually been reported, and most of these are doubtful.

While several cases have been analyzed as lexical diffusion, most mainstream historical linguists have not been convinced. They see these cases as being better explained as the results of dialect borrowing, analogy and erroneous analysis. On closer scrutiny, most of these cases prove not to be real instances of lexical diffusion but to be more reliably explained by other means. Often it turns out that the phonetic conditioning environments are quite complex – important phonetic environments were missed in several of the cases for which lexical diffusion was claimed. Detailed studies of the same cases by people aware of the claims for lexical diffusion have found sounds behaving regularly in change in these environments and no evidence of lexical conditioning. When the environments are understood, Neogrammarian regularity is what was behind the changes and not lexical diffusion after all. In the examples from the history of Chinese, which had been influential support for lexical diffusion, it turns out that the extent of borrowing from literary Chinese into the varieties of Chinese studied was vastly more extensive than originally thought. That is, like the southern West Yorkshrine case, they amounted to just dialect borrowing, which proponents of lexical diffusion later called 'intimate borrowing'; these cases were a misreading of the influence of stylistic choices, language contact and sociolinguistic conditions in general. (See Labov 1994: 444–71.)

With this background, consider again the irregularities so commonly pointed out in the dialect atlases of various languages and the assumed hostility of dialect atlas data to the Neogrammarian regularity hypothesis. The collectors of the data did not take into account the fact that commonly the data collected from local dialects was the result of long interaction between local dialect forms and the dominant prestige or standard language, as in the case of the English forms recorded in southern West Yorkshire. These atlas forms did not come to us recorded with tags identifying which words represent an uninterrupted inheritance from an original form versus which were replaced due to influence from an external source. Also, the methods involved in collecting the data for the atlases were not sufficiently sensitive to different styles and socially conditioned variation and were not geared to looking for complex phonetic conditioning environments. It is little wonder, then, that with dialect atlas evidence alone we seem to see support for the slogan 'each word has its own history'; but with more detailed information on social interaction of different varieties/dialects and on phonetic conditioning factors, we find the Neogrammarian regularity more firmly supported. The irregularities seem to develop not internally to a system, but through interaction or interference among systems (Labov 1994: 474). The Neogrammarians with their 'dialect borrowing' account were right all along! In fact, evidence of regular, phonetically conditioned sound change (and not lexical diffusion) in dialect geography turns out to be strong in the cases which have been investigated in detail (Labov 1994: 501).

Labov has attempted to reconcile the mostly regular changes with the few which seem to involve sound changes which affect some lexical items but not others. He notes that 'earlier stages of change are quite immune to such irregular lexical reactions [as implied in lexical diffusion]; and even in a late stage, the unreflecting use of the vernacular preserves that regularity' (Labov 1994: 453). This he calls 'change from below', below the level of awareness. Only in later stages of a change do speakers become aware of the change and give it sociolinguistic value (positive or negative), and this often involves the social importance of words. Change of this sort is what Labov calls 'change from above'. For him, lexical diffusion can involve only the later stages and change from above, the same changes which are often characterized by dialect mixture and analogical change, by a higher degree of social awareness or of borrowing from another system (Labov 1994: 542–3).

In summary, sound change is regular within its own system, though dialect borrowing and various influences from outside the system can result in changes which are less like regular exceptionless sound change. Consequently, to explain change we need both 'sound laws suffer no exceptions' and 'every word has its own history' – they address different things, both of which are important for the full picture of linguistic change.

Some of the topics of this chapter are considered further in relation to the explanation of linguistic change, treated in Chapter 13.

8

Internal Reconstruction

Language is the armoury of the human mind, and at once contains the trophies
of its past and the weapons of its future conquests.

(Samuel Taylor Coleridge)

8.1 Introduction

Internal reconstruction is like the comparative method but applied to a single
language. It is a technique for inferring aspects of the history of a language from
what we see in that language alone. Lying behind internal reconstruction is the
fact that when a language undergoes changes, traces of the changes are often left
behind in the language's structure, as allomorphic variants or irregularities of
some sort. The things that are compared in internal reconstruction, which correspond to the cognates of the comparative method, are the forms in the language
which have more than one phonological shape in different circumstances, that is,
the different allomorphs of a given morpheme, such as those found in alternations
in paradigms, derivations, stylistic variants and the like. Internal reconstruction is
frequently applied in the following situations where it can recover valuable information: (1) to isolates (languages without known relatives); (2) to reconstructed
proto-languages; and (3) to individual languages to arrive at an earlier stage to
which the comparative method can then be applied to compare this with related
languages in the family. In this chapter, we will learn how to apply internal
reconstruction, and we will take its uses and limitations into account.

8. 2 Internal Reconstruction Illustrated

Lying behind internal reconstruction is the assumption that the variants (allomorphs) of a morpheme are not all original, but that at some time in the past
each morpheme had but one form (shape) and that the variants known today have
come about as the result of changes that the language has undergone in its past.
We internally reconstruct by postulating an earlier single form together with
the changes – usually conditioned sound changes – which we believe to have
produced the various shapes of the morpheme that we recognize in its alternants.

The language reconstructed by internal reconstruction bears the prefix *pre-* (as opposed to the *proto-* of comparative-method reconstructions). For example, we would call the results of an internal reconstruction of English *Pre-English*. (Note, though, that *pre-* is sometimes used in historical linguistics where it has nothing to do with internal reconstruction; for example, it is possible to read about the 'Pre-Greeks' where what is intended is the Greeks before they appear in recorded history, or about 'Pre-English' which is not reconstructed but refers to a stage of English assumed to have existed before the earliest Old English texts but after the break-up of West Germanic.)

The steps followed in internal reconstruction, broadly speaking, consist of the following:

Step 1: Identify alternations, that is, forms which have more than one phonological shape (different allomorphs) in paradigms, derivations, different styles and so on.

Step 2: Postulate a single, non-alternating original form.

Step 3: Postulate the changes (usually conditioned sound changes) which must have taken place to produce the alternating forms. (Where relevant, determine the relative chronology – the sequence in which these changes took place.) As in the comparative method, we use all the information at our disposal concerning directionality of change and how natural or likely (or unexpected and unlikely) the changes we postulate are in order to evaluate the reconstruction and the changes we propose.

Step 4: Check the results to make certain that the changes we posulated do not imply changes for other forms that they do not in fact undergo; that is, we must guard against proposing changes which might seem to work for certain morphemes but which, if allowed to take place, would produce non-existent forms of other morphemes. We must also check to make certain that the postulated reconstructions are typologically plausible and do not imply things that are impossible or highly unlikely in human languages.

In actual practice, these steps are typically applied almost simultaneously and with little attempt to distinguish one step from the other. The best way to gain an understanding of internal reconstruction is through examples of its application, and several follow.

8.2.1 First example

Let us begin with a rather easy example from Tojolabal (Mayan). Compare the following words and notice the variants for the morpheme that means 'I':

(1)	h-man	I buy	man	to buy
(2)	h-lap	I dress	lap	to dress
(3)	h-k'an	I want	k'an	to want
(4)	k-il	I see	il	to see
(5)	k-uʔ	I drink	uʔ	to drink
(6)	k-al	I say	al	to say

In step 1, we identify *h*- and *k*- as alternants of the morpheme meaning 'I'; *h*- is the variant which occurs before consonants, and *k*- is the form which appears before vowels. In step 2, we attempt to postulate the original form of the morpheme for 'I' in Pre-Tojolabal. Three hypotheses suggest themselves: (1) **h*- (which would presuppose a change to *k*- before vowels to derive the other form of the morpheme, the *k* allomorph); (2) **k*- (with a change **k*- > *h*- before consonants to account for the *h*- variant); or (3) possibly some third thing (which would change into *h*- before consonants and into *k*- before vowels). The third alternative would require two independent changes (and thus would go against the criterion of economy, discussed in Chapter 5), whereas hypotheses (1) and (2) would each need only one change; therefore we abandon (3) under the assumption that it is less likely that two independent changes took place than it is that only one did. There is no particular phonetic motivation for *h*- to change into *k*- before vowels, as presupposed by hypothesis (1) (and if we had more data, we would see that there are plenty of words with initial *h*- before a vowel, for example, *haʔ* 'water', *hune* 'one', *hiʔ* 'unripe ear of maize', etc.). However, a change of *k*- to *h*- before consonants is not phonetically unusual, a dissimilation encountered in other languages (and if we had more data, we would see there are no consonant clusters in Tojolabal with initial *k*-; the general directionality of *k* > *h* and not *h* > *k* was seen in Chapter 5). Therefore, we assume that hypothesis (2) with **k*- is more plausible. In step 3, we postulate that the **k*- which we reconstruct for 'I' in Pre-Tojolabal undergoes the change **k*- to *h*- before consonants and that this accounts for the *h*- variant of this morpheme. So, for example, we would reconstruct **k-man* 'I buy', and then the change of **k*- to *h*- before consonants would give modern *h-man*; for 'I see', however, we reconstruct **k-il*, and since this *k*- 'I' is before a vowel, it does not change, leaving modern Tojolabal with *k-il*. This reconstruction and the derivation of the modern forms are seen in Table 8.1.

TABLE 8.1: Internal reconstruction and derivation of Tojolabal *k*-

	'*I buy*'	'*I see*'
Pre-Tojolabal:	*k-man	*k-il
Change k > h /__C:	hman	—
Modern Tojolabal:	hman	kil

8.2.2 Second example

In Nahuatl (Uto-Aztecan), a large number of morphemes have two variant shapes, one with an initial *i* and one without, of the sort illustrated in 'foot', with its two allomorphs, *ikʃi* when without prefixes and *kʃi* when it occurs with prefixes (as in *ikʃi-* foot', but *no-kʃi* 'my foot'). In internal reconstruction, we must reconstruct a single form as original and attempt to account for the variants which occur by postulating changes which will derive them from the single reconstructed form. In this case, the two most likely choices are: (1) to reconstruct **ikʃi* together with some rule to delete the initial *i* in order to provide for the *kʃi* variant, as in *no-kʃi* 'my foot'; (2) to reconstruct **kʃi* and posit some rule to insert the initial *i* in appropriate contexts to give *ikʃi*. Since in Nahuatl there are numerous forms with initial *i* which do not lose this vowel with prefixes (for example, *n-ihti* 'my stomach' – the change of *no-* to *n-* before vowels is a general trait of the language, that is, *o > Ø / n__+V*), it turns out to be impossible to write a rule which assumes the *i* of *ikʃi* was originally present but got lost due to the presence of the prefix (**no-ikʃi > no-kʃi* 'my foot'). This would wrongly predict, in step 4, that the non-alternating forms such as *ihti* should also lose their initial *i* (*no-ihti > no-hti*), but this does not happen (there is no ✗*no-hti* 'my stomach'; rather, the initial *i* is preserved in the form with the possessive prefix, *n-ihti*). (The notation ✗ is used here for 'non-occurring', 'erroneous' or 'ungrammatical' forms). The second hypothesis, however, encounters no such problem. We get the right results if we assume that the initial *i* was not originally present in the morpheme for 'foot' and reconstruct the words **kʃi* 'foot' and **no-kʃi* 'my foot', with *i* added to the first later by a rule of initial epenthesis, **kʃi > ikʃi* 'foot'. In looking at the phonological pattern of the language, we find that there are no initial consonant clusters and we therefore assume that a change added *i* to the beginning of words which formerly began in a consonant cluster:

Epenthesis rule: $Ø > i \; / \; \#\_\_CC$

Thus we reconstruct the forms and apply the epenthesis rule to produce the modern forms as shown in Table 8.2.

TABLE 8.2: Internal reconstruction and derivation of Nahuatl roots with initial *i*

	'foot'	'my foot'	'stomach'	'my stomach'
Pre-Nahuatl:	*kʃi	*no-kʃi	*ihti	*no-ihti
Epenthesis:	ikʃi	—	—	—
Vowel-loss ($o > Ø / n\_\_+V$):	—	—	—	n-ihti
Modern Nahuatl:	ikʃi	no-kʃi	ihti	n-ihti

8.3 Relative Chronology

Sometimes in internal reconstruction when more than one change can apply to a particular form it is necessary to pay attention to the order in which the changes took place in the forms in question. The identification of the sequence (temporal order) of different changes in a language is called *relative chronology* (seen also in Chapters 2, 3 and 5). When more than one change is involved in the reconstruction, sometimes they can each affect a form, and in such situations it may be necessary to figure out which change or changes took place earlier and which later. There is no hard-and-fast procedure for working out the relative chronology of the changes. However, the criterion of *predictability* is the most useful – determining a chronological sequence of changes which, when applied in order to the words of that language, does not produce any non-occurring forms. This is illustrated in the next example.

8.3.1 Third example: Finnish

Consider the forms in Table 8.3. They provide a straightforward illustration of relative chronology (compare the discussion of this example in section 2.8 of Chapter 2).

TABLE 8.3: Finnish internal reconstruction

Essive singular		*Nominative singular*	
1. onne-na	'as happiness'	onni	'happiness'
2. sukse-na	'as (a) ski'	suksi	'ski'
3. vete-nä	'as water'	vesi	'water'
4. käte-nä	'as (a) hand'	käsi	'hand'
5. tuoli-na	'as (a) chair'	tuoli	'chair'

(NOTE: /ä/ = [æ]. The -*na* / -*nä* alternation is the result of vowel harmony in Finnish and is of no relevance to the discussion here.)

In these data, we note the alternants (allomorphs) of each root: *onne-* / *onni*, *sukse-/ suksi*, *vete-/ vesi*, amd *käte-/ käsi*. In internal reconstruction, we must postulate some unique, single form for each root in Pre-Finnish together with the changes we believe took place to produce the modern alternant forms of each root. We postulate that in 1–4 the stem-final vowel *e* must have been original and the forms with final *i* (those in the nominative singular case) are derived by the change of final *e* to *i*:

Rule 1: e > i / __#.

This is clearer in 1 and 2:

Pre-Finnish:	*onne-na	*onne	*sukse-na	*sukse
Rule 1:	—	onni	—	suksi
Modern Finnish:	onnena	onni	suksena	suksi

A conceivable alternative solution in which *i* would become *e* when not final (Rule X: *i* > *e* / __+ C (or something similar)) is impossible, since by Rule X, 5 *tuoli-na* should become **X***tuole-na*, but that does not happen. If we postulate for Pre-Finnish *tuoli-na* and *tuoli*, then Rule 1 simply does not apply to them, since there is no *e* in these forms to which it could apply. (Ultimately, *tuoli* 'chair' is a loanword in Finnish, but this does not change the results as far as this example is concerned.)

Rule 1, then, accounts for the *e* / *i* alternation in the forms in 1 and 2 (and indirectly for the lack of alternation in 5), but for 3 and 4 an additional rule is required:

Rule 2: t > s /__ i.

Both Rule 1 and Rule 2 apply to the forms in 3 and 4. With Rules 1 and 2 in the right sequence – Rule 1 as the first change, followed later in time by the change in Rule 2 – we can account for modern *vesi* and *käsi*, as shown in Table 8.4:

TABLE 8.4: Derivation showing Finnish relative chronology

Pre-Finnish:	*vete-nä	*vete	*käte-nä	*käte
Rule 1:	—	veti	—	käti
Rule 2:	—	vesi	—	käsi
Modern Finnish:	vetenä	vesi	käte-nä	käsi

However, if we were to imagine that perhaps the changes had taken place in the reverse order, Rule 2 earlier and then Rule 1 later, we would get the wrong results, as seen in the hypothetical derivation in Table 8.5.

TABLE 8.5: Hypothetical derivation of Finnish with the wrong relative chronology

Pre-Finnish:	*vete-nä	*vete	*käte-nä	*käte
Rule 2:	—	—	—	—
Rule 1:	—	veti	—	käti
Modern Finnish:	vetenä	✗veti	käte-nä	✗käti

That is, in this hypothetical application of the changes in reverse order (in Step 4), we end up with the erroneous ✗*veti* 'water' and ✗*käti* 'hand'. Rule 2 cannot create the *s* in these words until after Rule 1 creates a final *i*, since Rule 2 requires an *i* after the *t* for it to become *s* (and in these words the *i* comes into existence only with the prior application of Rule 1). In this example, then, we conclude that the relative chronology was that Rule 1 (*e* > *i* /__#) took place first (**vete* > *veti*, **käte* > *käte* > *käti*) and then later in time the change in Rule 2 (*t* > *s* /__*i*) took place (*veti* > *vesi*, *käti* > *käsi*).

8.3.2   Fourth example: Classical Greek

In Classical Greek paradigms, we find alternative forms of morphemes such as:

genes-si 'race, family (dative plural)'
gene-os 'race, family (genitive singular)'

Here we see two variants (allomorphs) of the root: *gene-* when followed by a vowel-initial suffix (as in *gene-os*, with the 'genitive singular' *-os*), and *genes-* when followed by a consonant-initial suffix (as with 'dative plural' *-si* in *genes-si*). (In later developments, *geneos* changed to end up as *genūs* in major dialects, but that does not affect the story here.) Since there is no compelling phonetic motivation for a language to insert precisely an *s* before consonants (not *gene-si*

> *genes-si*), we assume that the original form had the root-final *s* and that this *s* was lost between vowels, represented in Rule 1:

Rule 1 (Deletion of intervocalic *s*): s > Ø / V__V

The reconstruction and the result of this change are seen in the historical derivation presented in Table 8.6.

TABLE 8.6: Derivation showing loss of intervocalic *s* in Classical Greek

	'dative plural'	*'genitive singular'*
Pre-Greek:	*genes-si	*genes-os
Rule (1) (Deletion of intervocalic *s*):	—	geneos
Classical Greek	genessi	geneos

However, in a different set of forms in Classical Greek, we encounter morphemes with different variants (allomorphs) in which *t* and *s* alternate, where *s* is found intervocalically, as in:

ambros-ia 'food of the gods' (that is, 'immortality')/*ambrotos* 'immortal'
pos-is 'drink, beverage/*potēs* 'a drinking, a drink'

In this instance, we might first attempt to reconstruct internally by choosing the variant with *s* as original with a rule to show how it changed to *t* under certain circumstances; or vice versa, we might assume that the original forms are to be reconstructed with *t* with a rule to change this original *t* to *s* in appropriate contexts. The sound change of *s* to *t* before various vowels is extremely rare, and therefore, based on the known directionality of change, the reconstruction which presupposes **s* is unlikely. However, the change of *t* to *s* before *i* is found in many languages around the world, and in these data we see that the alternant with *s* is always before *i*, which leads us to reconstruct **t* as original and to postulate Rule 2:

Rule 2: t > s /__i

The reconstruction of these forms and the application of this change to them are illustrated by the historical derivation shown in Table 8.7.

TABLE 8.7: Derivation showing *t* to *s* before *i* in Classical Greek

	'immortality'	*'immortal'*	*'drink'*	*'drinking'*
Pre-Greek:	ambrot-ia	ambrot-os	pot-is	potēs
Rule 2 (*t* to *s* before *i*):	ambrosia	—	posis	—
Greek:	ambrosia	ambrotos	posis	potēs

Now that we have postulated two changes which affect Pre-Greek, Rules 1 and 2, the question of relative chronology comes up: which change took place earlier, which later? If we assume that the relative chronology was that first the change in Rule 2 took place and then later the change of Rule 1 occurred, we end up with the wrong result for forms such as *ambrosia* and *posis*, as shown in the hypothetical historical derivation of Table 8.8.

TABLE 8.8: Hypothetical derivation showing wrong chronological order in Classical Greek

Pre-Greek:	*ambrot-ia	*pot-is	*genes-os	*genes-si
Rule 2 (*t* to *s* before *i*):	ambrosia	posis	—	—
Rule 1 (Deletion of intervocalic *s*):	ambroia	pois	geneos	—
Erroneous Greek:	✗ambroia	✗pois	geneos	genessi

Since ✗*ambroia* and ✗*pois* are erroneous, the relative chronology must be that first the change of Rule 1 (s > Ø/V__V) took place and then sometime later, after the change in which intervocalic *s* was deleted had run its course, Rule 2 (t > s /__i) created some new forms with intervocalic *s*, the result of the change *t* > *s*/__*i*, as seen in the correct historical derivation in Table 8.9.

TABLE 8.9: Derivation showing the correct chronological order in Classical Greek

Pre-Greek:	*ambrot-ia	*pot-is	*genes-os	*genes-si
Rule 1 (Deletion of intervocalic *s*):	—	—	geneos	—
Rule 2 (*t* to *s* before *i*):	ambrosia	posis	—	—
Greek:	ambrosia	posis	geneos	genessi

Often, if comparative evidence from related languages is available, we can check the accuracy of our internal reconstructions. In the case of Greek *geneos* 'race, family (genitive singular)', which we postulated to be from Pre-Greek *genes-os*, the presence of an original *-s-* which we reconstructed for the Pre-Greek form is confirmed by cognates in some of Greek's sister languages, as in Sanskrit *jánas-as* and Latin *gener-is* (both 'genitive singular'), which show the -s- that we reconstructed in Pre-Greek *genes-* (in Latin the -r- of *gener-is* is due to the rhotacism of an earlier intervocalic -s- – *genesis* > *generis*).

8.3.3 Fifth example

Let us look at one more example, also from Classical Greek. Consider first the following forms:

Nominative singular	*Genitive singular*	
(1) ait^híops	ait^híopos	'Ethiopian'
(2) kló:ps	klo:pós	'thief'
(3) p^hléps	p^hlebós	'vein'

Nominative singular		Genitive singular	
(4)	pʰúlaks	pʰúlakos	'watchman'
(5)	aíks	aigós	'goat'
(6)	sálpiŋks	sálpiŋgos	'trumpet'
(7)	tʰɛ́ːs	tʰɛːtós	'serf'
(8)	elpís	elpídos	'hope'
(9)	órniːs	órniːtʰos	'bird'
(10)	kórus	kórutʰos	'helmet'
(11)	hríːs	hriːnós	'nose'
(12)	delpʰíːs	delpʰíːnos	'dolphin'

Throughout these data, we see the non-alternating suffixes *-s* 'nominative singular' and *-os* 'genitive singular'; since they do not alternate, the best that we can do is tentatively reconstruct these to Pre-Greek as *-s and *-os, respectively. In (1), (2) and (4), we also see no alternations in the roots, only the non-alternating morphemes, *aitʰíop* 'Ethiopian', *kloːp-* 'thief' and *pʰúlak-* 'watchman', presumably from Pre-Greek *aitʰíop, *kloːp and **pʰúlak-*, respectively. However, in the other forms, we see alternations: (3) *pʰlep-/pʰleb-*, (5) *aik-/aig-*, (6) *sálpiŋk-/ sálpiŋg-*, (7) *tʰɛː-/tʰɛːt-*, (8) *elpí-/elpíd-*, (9) *órniː-/órniːtʰ-*, (10) *kóru-/kórutʰ-*, (11) *hriː-/hriːn-* and (12) *delpʰíː-/delpʰíːn-*. These each require us to reconstruct a single original form in internal reconstruction and to postulate changes which derive the variant forms. In the case of (3) *pʰlep-/pʰleb-*, two hypotheses suggest themselves: Hypothesis I: reconstruct for (2) **pʰlep-* and assume the *pʰleb-* allomorph is the result of intervocalic voicing, since it is found with *-os* in *pʰleb-ós*. Let's call this Rule A:

Rule A (intervocalic voicing): p > b / V__V

TABLE 8.10: Derivation for Hypothesis I for Classical Greek 'vein'

	'nominative singular'	*'genitive singular'*
Pre-Greek	*pʰlép-s	*pʰlep-ós
Rule A (p > b/V__V):	—	pʰleb-ós
Classical Greek	pʰléps	pʰlebós

This hypothesis would give us the derivation in Table 8.10. Hypothesis I would be fine if it only had to account for the alternation in *pʰléps/pʰlebós*. The sound change postulated in Rule A would account for the *p/b* alternation in this form, but it makes the further prediction that Pre-Greek *aitʰíop-os 'Ethiopian (genitive singular)' should have become *aitʰíobos* by the intervocalic voicing of Rule A. However, this is wrong; ✗*aitʰíobos* does not occur – the correct form is *aitʰíopos*. This means that we must abandon (or at least seriously modify) Hypothesis I. Let us now look at Hypothesis II.

Hypothesis II: reconstruct **pʰleb-* for (3) and assume that the *pʰlep-* allomorph is the result of devoicing before *s*, since it is found with *-s* in *pʰlep-s* (nominative singular). Let's call this Rule B:

Rule B (devoicing before *s*): b > p/__s (also g > k and d > t, as in examples below)

TABLE 8.11: Derivation for Hypothesis II for Classical Greek 'vein'

	'nominative singular'	*'genitive singular'*
Pre-Greek	*pʰléb-s	*pʰleb-ós
Rule B (b > p /__s):	pʰléps	—
Classical Greek	pʰléps	pʰlebós

This hypothesis would give the derivation in Table 8.11. Hypothesis II accounts for the *p/b* alternation in *pʰléps/pʰlebós*, but does not erroneously predict in (1) that Pre-Greek **aitʰíop-os* 'Ethiopian (genitive singular)' should become ✗*aitʰíobos* (as the intervocalic voicing of Rule A in Hypothesis I does). Rather, in Hypothesis II we postulate Pre-Greek **aitʰíop-s* and **aitʰíop-os*, and since these words have no *b*, nothing will change in Rule (B), which affects only forms with *b* (such as *pʰlebós/pʰléps*), as illustrated in Table 8.12.

TABLE 8.12: Derivation of **aitʰíop-* 'Ethiopian' in Hypothesis II

	'nominative singular'	*'genitive singular'*
Pre-Greek	**aitʰíop-s	**aitʰíop-os
Rule B (b > p /__s):	—	—
Classical Greek	aitʰíops	**aitʰíopos

Thus, Hypothesis II makes correct predictions, while Hypothesis I makes erroneous predictions; therefore Hypothesis II is accepted and Hypothesis I rejected. Since the forms in (2) follow the same pattern, we reconstruct **klo:p-* 'thief' for its root (**klo:p-s* 'nominative singular' and **klo:p-ós* 'genitive singular').

Turning now to the alternants in the forms in (5) for 'goat', *aík-/aig-*, we follow the pattern in Hypothesis II further, reconstructing Pre-Greek **aig-* 'goat' and applying Rule B (devoicing before *s*) to derive the *aík-* variant found in *aík-s* 'nominative singular'. That is, we reconstruct **aig-s* 'goat (nominative singular)' which becomes *aiks* by Rule B, and **aig-ós* 'goat (genitive singular)' which remains *aigós*, since no changes apply to it. The two variants of the root in (6), *sálpiŋk-/sálpiŋg-* 'trumpet', follow the same pattern, and we therefore reconstruct **sálpiŋg-s* 'nominative singular' and **sálpiŋg-os* 'genitive singular' in this case.

If we continue to follow the pattern in Hypothesis II, given *tʰɛ:t-ós* 'serf (genitive singular)' in (7), we would reconstruct Pre-Greek **tʰɛ:t-ós* and we would expect the nominative singular to be ✗*tʰɛ:t-s*; however, the actually occurring nominative singular form is *tʰɛ:s*. Similarly in (8), from *elpíd-os* '(genitive singular)' we would expect the nominative singular to be the non-occurring ✗*elpits*, that is, a Pre-Greek form **elpid-s* to which Rule (B) (devoicing before *s*) applied would give ✗*elpits*. However, we do not get *elpits*, but rather *elpís*. Similarly, from *órni:tʰ-os* in (9), *kórutʰ-os* in (10), *hri:n-ós* in (11) and *delpʰí:n-os* in (12) we would expect the corresponding nominative singular forms to be ✗*órni:tʰ-s*, ✗*kóruthʰ-s*, ✗*hri:n-s* and ✗*delpʰí:n-s*, respectively, not the actually occurring *órni:s*, *kórus*, *hrí:s* and *delpʰí:s*. Unlike the forms in (1–6) whose roots end in labials (*p* or *b*) or velars (*k* or *g*), what the forms in (7–12) have in common is that their root-final consonant is an alveolar (*t, d, tʰ, n*) in the genitive singular forms, which is missing from the nominative singulars. It would not be possible, starting with the nominative singular forms which lack these root-final consonants, to write a plausible account to predict just which consonant would be added in each instance to derive the genitive singular forms. Therefore, we reconstruct for Pre-Greek roots the forms reflected in the genitive singulars (as we did for the forms in (1–6) in Hypothesis II), and then derive the nominative singular variants by postulating Rule (C), deletion of alveolars before *s*:

Rule C (alveolar deletion before *s*): t, d, tʰ, n > Ø /__s

Note that in this case we cannot tell whether Rule B took place before Rule C or whether the historical events happened in the reverse order, since in either sequence we obtain correct results. In the order Rule B followed by Rule C, reconstructed **elpid-s* would first be devoiced by Rule B, giving *elpits*, and then the *t* would be lost by Rule C (alveolar loss before *s*), giving the correct form *elpís* (that is, **elpid-s* > by Rule B *elpits* > by Rule C *elpís*). In the order Rule C followed by Rule B, reconstructed **elpid-s* would become *elpís* by Rule C, in which the final alveolar (*d* in this case) is lost before the *-s* of the nominative singular; Rule B would then not apply to this form, since there would no longer be a *d* which could be made voiceless (*t*) by this rule (that is, **elpid-s* > by Rule C *elpís*; Rule B not applicable; result: Classical Greek *elpís*).

The derivation of the nominative singular forms from the postulated Pre-Greek internal reconstruction to Classical Greek is illustrated in Table 8.13.

TABLE 8.13: Internal reconstruction of Classical Greek 'nominative singular' forms

	Pre-Greek	Rule B (devoicing)	Rule C (alveolar loss before *s*)	Classical Greek form
(1)	*aitʰíop-s	—	—	aitʰíops
(2)	*klóp-s	—	—	klóps
(3)	*pʰléb-s	pʰlép-s	—	pʰléps
(4)	*pʰúlak-s	—	—	pʰúlaks
(5)	*aíg-s	aík-s	—	aík-s
(6)	*sálpiŋg-s	sálpiŋk-s	—	sálpiŋks
(7)	*tʰét-s	—	tʰés	tʰés
(8)	*elpíd-s	elpíts	elpís	elpís
(9)	*órnītʰ-s	—	órnīs	órnīs
(10)	*kórutʰ-s	—	kórus	kórus
(11)	*hrín-s	—	hrís	hrís
(12)	*delpʰín-s	—	delpʰís	delpʰís

8.4 The Limitations of Internal Reconstruction

In attempting to apply the method of internal reconstruction, we need to keep in mind the circumstances in which we can expect more reliable results and those where it is of limited or no value for recovering a language's history. Let us examine some of these limitations.

(1) The strongest limitation is that, while internal reconstruction is often able to recover conditioned changes, *internal reconstruction cannot recover unconditioned changes*. For example, in the unconditioned merger of **e*, **o*, **a* to *a* in Sanskrit (seen in Chapter 2), these original vowels ended up as *a*. If we attempt to reconstruct internally the Pre-Sanskrit forms of *dánta* 'tooth' or *dva* 'two', we find no alternations in these vowels which would provide clues to the fact that *danta* originally had **e* (Proto-Indo-European **dent*, compare Latin *dent-*) but that *dva-* had **o* (Proto-Indo-European **dwo*, compare Latin *duo-*). It is simply impossible to recover via internal reconstruction the unconditioned change which these Sanskrit vowels underwent: if *a* is all we ever see, there is no basis in Sanskrit itself for seeing anything else in the past of the *a* which occurs in these words.

(2) The method may be reliable if later changes have not eliminated (or rendered unrecognizable) the context or contexts which condition the change that we would like to recover as reflected in alternations in the language. We have seen several examples of this in the cases discussed in this chapter. However, internal reconstruction can be difficult or impossible if later changes have severely altered the contexts which conditioned the variants that we attempt to reconstruct. For example, some splits are impossible to recover due to subsequent changes, as illustrated by the case of voiced fricatives in English. We observe in English such forms as *breath/breathe* ([brɛθ]/[brið]), *bath/bathe* ([bæθ]/[beið]), *wreath/wreathe* ([[riθ]/[rið]) which suggest an alternation between θ and ð (voiceless and voiced dental fricative). Because we can identify alternations, we would like to be able to reconstruct a single original form, but since in these forms both alternants can occur in exactly the same phonetic environment, we have no basis for reconstruction. From other sources of information, however, we know that the voiced fricatives in Old English were allophones of the voiceless fricatives in intervocalic position. Remnants of this rule are seen in such forms as *mouths* (with [ð], compare *mouth* with [θ]) and *paths* (with [ð], compare *path* with [θ]), and so on. The problem is that, due to later sound changes which eliminated certain vowels, these voiced fricatives are no longer intervocalic: these later changes have so altered the context which conditioned the change to voicing of fricatives between vowels that, in spite of the alternations we find which propel us to attempt to reconstruct, we are unable to do so with any reliability in this case. Moreover, later loanwords have also made the original context which conditioned the alternation no longer clearly visible. For example, in looking at *mother*, *rather* and *either* (each with intervocalic [ð]), we might be tempted to see evidence of the former intervocalic voicing (θ > ð/ V__V); however, later loanwords such as *lethal*, *ether*, *method*, *mathematics* and so on, with intervocalic [θ], obscure the former intervocalic voicing beyond recognition, since, after the borrowings entered the language, [θ] and [ð] are

both found between vowels, and the former complementary distribution with only [ð] intervocalically and [θ] elsewhere no longer holds. In short, subsequent sound changes and borrowings have rendered the conditioning of the former intervocalic voicing of fricatives in English unrecognizable, making internal reconstruction in this case unsuccessful.

Another example (already considered in a different context in Chapter 2) which illustrates this point is that of such singular–plural alternations as seen in *mouse/mice* and *goose/geese*. Given the alternations, we would like to be able to apply internal reconstruction, but the context which originally produced these variant forms is now totally gone, due to subsequent changes. Though today such plurals are irregular, they came about in a relatively straightforward way. In most Germanic languages (except Gothic), back vowels were fronted (underwent 'umlaut') when followed by a front vowel or glide (semivowel) in the next syllable, and the plural suffix originally contained a front vowel, as in Proto-Germanic **mu:s* 'mouse'/**mu:s-iz* 'mice' and **go:s* 'goose'/**go:s-iz* 'geese'. In the plural, the root vowels were fronted in Pre-English times: *mu:s-i > my:s-i* and *go:s-i > gø:s-i*. Two later changes took place: this final vowel was lost, and the front rounded vowels *y* and *ø* became unrounded to *i* and *e* respectively, merging with *i* and *e* from other sources. These changes produced the alternations, *mi:s* and *ge:s* as the plurals, but *mu:s* and *go:s* as the singulars. Finally, all these forms underwent the Great Vowel Shift, giving Modern English /maus/ 'mouse', /mais/ 'mice', /gus/ 'goose' and /gis/ 'geese' (see Chapter 2). This sequence of changes is represented in Table 8.14.

TABLE 8.14: Historical derivation of 'mouse', 'mice', 'goose', 'geese'

	'mouse'	*'mice'*	*'goose'*	*'geese'*
Proto-Germanic:	*mu:s	*mu:s-iz	*go:s	*go:s-iz
Early Pre-English:	mu:s	mu:s-i	go:s	go:s-i
Umlaut:	—	my:s-i	—	gø:s-i
Loss of -*i*:	—	my:s	—	gø:s
Unrounding:	—	mi:s	—	ge:s
Great Vowel Shift:	maus	mais	gus	gis
Modern English:	/maus/	/mais/	/gus/	/gis/

However, since the environment for umlaut was lost in subsequent changes which deleted the-*i* which had caused the umlauting, we are unable to recover this history through internal reconstruction, even though the alternations seen in these singular–plural pairs provoke us to imagine that some historical explanation which we cannot recover by this method alone lies behind these different forms of the same root.

Finally, while the examples presented in this chapter deal with sound changes, it is important to mention that internal reconstruction of morphology and aspects of syntax is also possible in favourable circumstances.

8.5 *Internal Reconstruction and the Comparative Method*

Sometimes it is suggested that internal reconstruction should be undertaken first and the comparative method applied afterwards. In this view, internal reconstruction would help us to see beyond the effects of many recent changes so that we would have access to an earlier stage of the language for use in the comparative method when sister languages are compared with one another. This is often the case. Usually, both internal reconstruction and the comparative method lead in the same direction. However, in reality there is no rigid principle about which method is to be applied first – they can be applied in either order. Often, reconstruction by the comparative method reveals alternations which the proto-language underwent, and it is perfectly legitimate to apply internal reconstruction to these proto-alternations in order to reach even further back in time, to a pre-proto-language. In this event, the sequence would be the comparative method first, followed by internal reconstruction, or perhaps first internal reconstruction to the individual languages, then the comparative method to related languages, and then internal reconstruction again to the reconstructed proto-language. In any event, it is important to check, when internal reconstruction is applied before the comparative method, that it does not factor out alternations which were present in the proto-language.

A case from Balto-Finnic will illustrate the point. Finnish had alternations such as *jalka* 'leg (nominative singular)' / *jalan* 'leg (genitive singular)'. This has been internally reconstructed as **jalka* / **jalka-n*, under the assumption that **k* was lost in non-initial closed syllables (in this case in the genitive form, the syllable is closed by *n*, causing the change). (Some postulate that **k* in closed syllables first changed to ɣ and then later was lost (**k > ɣ > Ø*), and this view is no doubt aided by the fact that there are older written materials which document that this is precisely what happened in the history of these words.) If the comparative method is applied after internal reconstruction, then the forms utilized by the comparative method will be Pre-Finnish **jalka* and **jalka-n*, and evidence of the alternation will have been factored out. However, if we turn to sister languages of Finnish in the Balto-Finnic subgroup, we find the following forms: Estonian *jalg* [*jalk*] 'leg (nominative singular)' and *jala* 'leg (genitive singular)'. Estonian underwent two additional changes which Finnish did not, loss of final vowels in certain contexts (*jalka* > [*jalk*] 'nominative singular') and loss of final -*n* (*jalan* > *jala* 'genitive singular'). An internal reconstruction of Estonian results in **jalka* 'leg (nominative singular)' and **jalka(X)* 'leg (genitive singular)', where from other forms it is known that the alternation normally takes place in closed syllables and therefore something now missing, signalled here by *X*, is posited as formerly having closed the syllable and causing the alternation. Finally, Northern Saami, a related language, has the forms *juolʲke* 'leg (nominative singular)' / *juolʲge* 'leg (genitive singular)', where Saami, too, has lost final *n* in an independent change, and internal reconstruction gives **juolʲke* 'leg (nominative singular)' / **juolʲke(X)* 'leg (genitive singular)'. Notice now that if we compare only the results of internal reconstruction in these three sister languages, we have no access to the alternation, as seen in Table 8.15.

TABLE 8.15: Comparison of Balto-Finnic 'leg' forms after internal
　　　　　　　　reconstruction

	nominative singular	*genitive singular*
Pre-Finnish	*jalka	*jalka-n
Pre-Estonian	*jalka	*jalka(X)
Pre-Lapp	*juolke	*juolke(X)
Proto-Balto-Finnic	**jalka	**jalka-n

However, if the comparative method is applied before internal reconstruction, the alternation is revealed to have been part of the proto-language, as seen in Table 8.16. The moral is clear: internal reconstruction can help by offering forms to be compared in the comparative method which see past the disruptions of many recent changes; nevertheless, caution should be exercised so that alternations which should legitimately be reconstructed to the proto-language by the comparative method are not factored out by previous internal reconstruction and then lost sight of. (See Anttila 1989: 274.)

TABLE 8.16: Comparison of Balto-Finnic 'leg' forms before internal
　　　　　　　　reconstruction

	nominative singular	*genitive singular*
Finnish	jalka	jala-n
Estonian	jalg [jalk]	jala
Lapp	juolke	juolge
Proto-Balto-Finnic	*jalka	*jalɣa-n

8.6   Exercises

Exercise 8.1   German internal reconstruction

Compare the following German words; find the variants of forms of the roots (do not be concerned with the forms of the suffixes), and apply internal reconstruction to these. Reconstruct a single original form for the morphemes which have alternate forms, and postulate the changes which you think took place to produce the modern variants. Present your reasoning; why did you choose this solution? (Hint: the criterion of predictability is important in this case.) (German traditional orthography is given in parentheses after the forms, which are presented in phonemic transcription. The 'e' of the final syllable in these forms is phonetically closer to [ə] in most dialects, though this is not a relevant fact for solving this problem.)

　　1. tyːp (Typ)　　　'type'　　　tyːpen (Typen)　　　'types'
　　2. toːt (tot)　　　'dead'　　　toːte (Tote)　　　'dead people'

3. lak (Lack)	'varnish'	lake (Lacke)	'kinds of varnish'
4. tawp (taub)	'deaf'	tawbe (Taube)	'deaf people'
5. to:t (Tod)	'death'	to:de (Tode)	'deaths'
6. ta:k (Tag)	'day'	ta:ge (Tage)	'days'

Exercise 8.2　*Kaqchikel internal reconstruction*

Kaqchikel is a Mayan language of Guatemala. Compare the following words;
find the forms which have variants; apply internal reconstruction to these forms.
Reconstruct a single original form for the morphemes which have alternate
forms, and postulate the changes that you think must have taken place to produce
these variants. Present your reasoning; why did you choose this solution and
reject other possible hypotheses? (Note that -*ir* is the inchoative suffix, meaning
'to become/turn into', and-*isax* is the causative suffix.)

1.	nax	'far'	naxt-ir-isax	'to distance (to make it become far)'
2.	čox	'straight'	čoxm-ir	'to become straight'
			čoxm-il	'straightness'
3.	war	'sleep'	wart-isax	'to put to sleep (to cause to sleep)'
4.	ax	'ear of corn'	axn-i	'of corn (-*i* 'adjective suffix')'

Exercise 8.3　*Sanskrit internal reconstruction*

Compare the following forms from Sanskrit. Identify the variants of the various
roots and attempt to reconstruct a Pre-Sanskrit form for each root. Note that the
reconstructions for the forms in 10–16 are not straightforward and may require
some creative thinking on your part. What change do you think took place to
produce these forms? Why did you choose this particular analysis and not some
other?

NOTE: *j* = [j], IPA [dʒ]; consonants with dots underneath are retroflex.)

		Nominative		*Instrumental*	
1.		šarat	'autumn'	šarad-ā	'by autumn'
2.		sampat	'wealth'	sampad-ā	'by wealth'
3.		vipat	'calamity'	vipad-ā	'by calamity'
4.		marut	'wind'	marut-ā	'by wind'
5.		sarit	'river'	sarit-ā	'by river'
6.		jagat	'world'	jagat-ā	'by world'
		Nominative		*Ablative*	
7.		suhṛt	'friend'	suhṛd-ā	'from friend'
8.		sukṛt	'good deed'	sukṛt- ā	'from good deed'
9.		sat	'being'	sat- ā	'from being'
10.		bhiṣak	'physician'	bhiṣaj- ā	'from physician'
11.		ṛtvik	'priest'	ṛtvij- ā	'from priest'
12.		yuk	'yoke'	yuj- ā	'from yoke'
13.		srak	'garland'	sraj- ā	'from garland'
14.		rāṭ	'king'	rāj- ā	'from king'

	Nominative		Ablative	
15.	iṭ	'worship'	ij- ā	'from worship'
16.	sṛṭ	'creation'	sṛj- ā	'from creation'

(Bhat 2001: 33, 91, 94)

Exercise 8.4 *Internal reconstruction of Finnish vowels*

Compare the following words; what happens when the *i* 'plural' or *i* 'past tense' morphemes are added to these roots? State what the variants (allomorphs) of the roots are; apply internal reconstruction to these forms. Reconstruct a single original form for each root morpheme and postulate the changes which you think must have taken place to produce these variants. Present your reasoning; why did you choose this solution and reject other possible hypotheses?

NOTE: double vowels, such as *aa*, *yy*, and so on, are phonetically long vowels ([a:], [y:], etc.). Finnish *ä* = IPA [æ], *ö* = [ø].

HINT: Native Finnish words do not have (surface) *oo*, *ee*, or *öö* [øø]; rather, Finnish has *uo*, *ie*, and *yö* [yø] where long mid vowels would be expected. The correct answer for words containing these diphthongs does NOT involve the first vowel being lost when *i* is added (that is, NOT *suo* + *i* > *soi* by loss of *u*).

1.	saa	'gets'	sai	'got'
2.	maa	'land'	mai-	'lands'
3.	puu	'tree'	pui-	'trees'
4.	luu	'bone'	lui-	'bones'
5.	pii	'tooth (of rake)'	pii-	'teeth'
6.	pää	'head'	päi-	'heads'
7.	pyy	'wood grouse'	pyi-	'wood grouses'
8.	täi	'louse'	täi-	'lice'
9.	suo	'grants'	soi	'granted'
10.	suo	'swamp'	soi-	'swamps'
11.	luo	'creates'	loi-	'created'
12.	syö	'eats'	söi	'ate'
13.	lyö	'hits'	löi	'hit'
14.	tie	'road'	tei-	'roads'
15.	vie	'takes'	vei	'took'
16.	talo	'house'	taloi-	'houses'
17.	hillo	'jam'	hilloi-	'jams'
18.	halu	'desire'	halui-	'desires'
19.	hylly	'shelf'	hyllyi-	'shelves'
20.	nukke	'doll'	nukkei-	'dolls'
21.	hölmö	'fool'	hölmöi-	'fools'

22.	sata	'hundred'	satoi-	'hundreds'	
23.	pala	'piece'	paloi-	'pieces'	
24.	hella	'stove' ('cooker')	helloi-	'stoves' ('cookers')	
25.	hilkka	'hood'	hilkkoi-	'hoods'	
26.	hiha	'sleeve'	hihoi-	'sleeves'	
27.	sota	'war'	sotei-	'wars' (soti- in Modern Finnish)	
28.	pora	'drill'	porei-	'drills' (pori- in Modern Finnish)	
29.	muna	'egg'	munei-	'eggs' (muni- in Modern Finnish)	
30.	rulla	'roll'	rullei-	'rolls' (rulli- in Modern Finnish)	
31.	tupa	'cabin'	tupei-	'cabins' (tupi- in Modern Finnish)	
32.	jyvä	'grain'	jyvei-	'grains' (jyvi- in Modern Finnish)	
33.	hätä	'distress'	hätei-	'distresses' (häti- in Modern Finnish)	
34.	mökä	'hullabaloo'	mökei-	'hullabaloos' (möki- in Modern Finnish)	

Exercise 8.5   Nahuatl internal reconstruction

Nahuatl is a Uto-Aztecan language, spoken by over 1,000,000 people in Mexico; it was the language of the Aztecs and the Toltecs. Compare the following words. Find the forms which have variants; apply internal reconstruction to these forms. Reconstruct a single original form for the morphemes which have alternate shapes, and postulate the changes which you think must have taken place to produce these variants. Can you establish a relative chronology for any of these changes? Present your reasoning; why did you choose this solution and reject other possible hypotheses? (NOTE: *tl* is a single consonant, a voiceless lateral affricate; *kʷ* is a labialized velar stop and is a single segment; *č* = IPA *tʃ*; *š* = IPA *ʃ*.) Note that the morpheme which has the allomorphs *-tl, -tli, -li* is traditionally called the 'absolutive'; it has no other function than to indicate a noun root which has no other prefixes or suffixes.

1a	tepos-tli	'axe'	4a	mis-tli	'cougar'
1b	no-tepos	'my axe'	4b	mis-tlān	'place of cougars'
1c	tepos-tlān	'place of axes'	5a	kal-li	'house'
2a	kak-tli	'shoe, sandal'	5b	no-kal	'my house'
2b	no-kak	'my shoe, sandal'	6a	tlāl-li	'land'
3a	teʃ-tli	'flour'	6b	no-tlāl	'my land'
3b	no-teʃ	'my flour'	7a	čīmal-li	'tortilla griddle'

7b	no-čīmal	'my tortilla griddle'		16a	ihti-tl	'stomach'
7c	čīmal-lān	'place of tortilla griddles'		16b	n-ihti	'my stomach'
				17a	īʃte-tl	'eye'
8a	mīl-li	'cornfield'		17b	n-īʃte	'my eye'
8b	no-mīl	'my cornfield'		18a	ihwi-tl	'feather'
8c	mīl-lan	'place of cornfields'		18b	n-ihwi	'my feather'
9a	āma-tl	'paper, fig tree'		19a	itskʷin-tli	'little dog'
9b	n-āma	'my paper, fig tree'		19b	n-itskʷin	'my little dog'
9c	āma-tlān	'place of paper, fig trees'		20a	ička-tl	'cotton'
				20b	no-čka	'my cotton'
10a	e-tl	'bean'		21a	okič-tli	'male, man'
10b	n-e	'my bean'		21b	n-okič	'my husband'
10c	e-tlān	'place of beans'		22a	kaʃi-tl	'bowl'
11a	siwā-tl	'woman'		22b	no-kaʃ	'my bowl'
11b	no-siwā	'my wife'		23a	kʷawi-tl	'tree, wood'
11c	siwā-tlan	'place of women'		23b	no-kʷaw	'my tree, wood'
12a	ol-li	'rubber'		24a	māyi-tl	'hand'
12b	n-ol	'my rubber'		24b	no-māy	'my hand'
12c	ol-lān	'place of rubber'		25a	ʃāmi-tl	'brick'
13a	ikʃi-tl	'foot'		25b	no-ʃān	'my brick'
13b	no-kʃi	'my foot'		26a	pāmi-tl	'flag'
14a	ikni-tl	'fellow'		26b	no-pān	'my flag'
14b	no-kni	'my fellow'		27a	kōmi-tl	'jug'
15a	isti-tl	'fingernail'		27b	no-kōn	'my jug'
15b	no-sti	'my fingernail'				

Exercise 8.6   *Indonesian internal reconstruction*

Identify the morphemes which have more than one variant in the following data from Indonesian (an Austronesian language). Apply internal reconstruction to these forms; reconstruct a single original form for each of the roots and for the prefix, and postulate the changes you think must have taken place to produce these variants. Can you establish a relative chronology for any of these changes? Provide sample derivations which show your reconstruction and how the changes apply to it for both the simple and the prefixed forms in 2, 12, 13, 15 and 19. (The prefix in the second column has a range of functions, among them, it places focus on the agent ('doer') of a verb, derives transitive or causative verbs, and derives verbs from nouns.)

HINT: relative chronology is important to the solution of this problem. (/ɲ/ = palatal nasal.)

	simple form	*prefixed form*	*gloss*
1.	lempar	məlempar	'throw'
2.	rasa	mərasa	'feel'
3.	wakil	məwakil-	'represent'
4.	yakin	məyakin-	'convince'

	simple form	prefixed form	gloss
5.	masak	məmasak	'cook'
6.	nikah	mənikah	'marry'
7.	ŋačo	məŋačo	'chat'
8.	ɲaɲi	məɲaɲi	'sing'
9.	hituŋ	məŋhituŋ	'count'
10.	gambar	məŋgambar	'draw a picture'
11.	kirim	məŋirim	'send'
12.	dəŋar	məndəŋar	'hear'
13.	tulis	mənulis	'write'
14.	bantu	məmbantu	'help'
15.	pukul	məmukul	'hit'
16.	ǰahit	məɲǰahit	'sew'
17.	čatat	məɲčatat	'note down'
18.	ambil	məŋambil	'take'
19.	isi	məŋisi	'fill up'
20.	undaŋ	məŋundaŋ	'invite'

Exercise 8.7   Tol (Jicaque) internal reconstruction

Jicaque (called Tol by its speakers) is spoken in Honduras. State the variants (allomorphs) of the roots and of the possessive pronominal prefixes; apply internal reconstruction to these forms. Reconstruct a single original form for each root morpheme and write the changes which you think must have taken place to produce these variants. Present your reasoning; why did you choose this solution and reject other possible hypotheses? (HINT: the original form of the possessive pronouns was: *n- 'my', *hi- 'your', *hu- 'his'; original *n+h > n.) Note that what is structurally a labialized w is realized phonetically as [wⁱ], but is written as wʷ in this problem. This phonetic fact should not affect your analysis. Note that y = IPA j, including superscript ʸ which is equivalent to IPA ʲ, the diacritic for palatalization.

	my	your	his	Meaning of the noun root
1.	mbata	peta	pota	'duck'
2.	mbapay	pepay	popay	'father'
3.	ndaʔ	teʔ	toʔ	'man's brother'
4.	ndarap	terap	torap	'woman's younger sister'
5.	ŋkʰan	kʰen	kʰon	'bed'
6.	nlara	lera	lora	'mouth'
7.	ntsʰam	tsʰem	tsʰom	'foot'
8.	mbe	hepe	pʷe	'rock, stone'
9.	mbep	hepep	pʷep	'fingernail'
10.	mberam	heperam	pʷeram	'tongue'
11.	mpʰel	hepʰel	pʰʷel	'arm'

	my	*your*	*his*	*Meaning of the noun root*
12.	ŋgerew	hekerew	kʷerew	'cousin'
13.	ŋkʰere	hekʰere	kʰʷere	'bone'
14.	ŋgiway	hikiway	kʷiway	'woman's brother'
15.	njič	hičič	čʷič	'tendon'
16.	njipe	hičipe	čʷipe	'paired sibling'
17.	mbomam	pʸomam	hopomam	'chokecherry'
18.	mpʰok	pʰʸok	hopʰok	'cheek'
19.	ŋgol	kʸol	hokol	'belly'
20.	nts'ul	ts'ʸul	huts'ul	'intestines'
21.	mpʰɨya	pʰʸeya	hipʰɨya	'tobacco'
22.	mp'ɨs	p'ʸes	hip'ɨs	'deer'
23.	ndɨm	tʸem	hɨtɨm	'heel'
24.	mbasas	wesas	wosas	'woman's sister-in-law'
25.	mbis	hiwis	wʷis [wⁱis]	'tooth'
26.	mbin	hiwin	wʷin [wⁱin]	'toad'
27.	mboyum	wʸoyum	howoyum	'husband'
28.	namas	mes	mos	'hand'
29.	nemen	hemen	mʷen	'neck'
30.	nimik	himik	mʷik	'nose'
31.	nɨmɨnɨ	mʸenɨ	himɨnɨ	'yam'
32.	namap	hemap	homap	'aunt'
33.	nasunu	hesunu	hosunu	'chest'

Exercise 8.8   *Samoan internal reconstruction*

Compare words in the two columns. Identify the morphemes which have more than one variant. Reconstruct a single original form for all the morphemes here, and postulate the changes you think must have taken place to produce these forms. Can you establish a relative chronology for any of these changes? Why did you choose this solution and reject other possible hypotheses?

NOTE: many roots will have two allomorphs; the suffix also has more than one variant in several of the cases.

HINT: think 'predictability' and exploit gaps in the inventory of the consonants that can occur as the last consonant in these words.

1.	alofa	'love'	alofaŋia	'loved'
2.	taŋo	'grasp'	taŋofia	'grasped'
3.	fua	'measure'	fuatia	'measure'
4.	au	'reach'	aulia	'reached'
5.	faitau	'read'	faitaulia	'read'
6.	u	'to bite'	utia	'bitten
7.	ula	'smoke'	ulafia	'smoked'
8.	na	'hide'	natia	'hidden'
9.	fau	'bind'	fausia	'bound'
10.	ʔata	'laugh'	ʔataŋia	'laughed'

11.	inu	'drink'	inumia	'drunk'
12.	taofi	'hold'	taofia	'held'
13.	mu	'burn'	muina	'burned'
14.	tuʔu	'put'	tuʔuina	'put'
15.	faŋa	'feed'	faŋaina	'fed'
16.	sauni	'prepare'	saunia	'prepared'
17.	siʔi	'raise'	siʔitia	'raised'
18.	pisi	'splash'	pisia	'splashed'
19.	ao	'gather'	aofia	'gathered'
20.	ilo	'perceive'	iloa	'perceived'
21.	ʔave	'take'	ʔavea	'taken'
22.	oso	'jump'	osofia	'jumped'
23.	ʔino	'hate'	ʔinosia	'hated'
24.	filo	'mix'	filoŋia	'mixed'
25.	fasioti	'kill'	fasiotia	'killed'
26.	utu	'fill'	utufia	'filled'
27.	ufi	'cover'	ufitia	'covered'
28.	ʔai	'eat'	ʔaiina	'eaten'
29.	afio	'come in'	afioina	'(has) come in'
30.	laʔa	'step over'	laʔasia	'stepped over'
31.	manaʔo	'want'	manaʔomia	'wanted'
32.	mataʔu	'destroy	mataʔutia	'destroyed'
33.	milo	'twist	milosia	'twisted'
34.	taŋi	'cry'	taŋisia	'cried'
35.	vavae	'divide'	vavaeina	'divided'

Exercise 8.9 *Nivaclé internal reconstruction*

Nivaclé (also called Chulupí) is a Matacoan language of northern Argentina and Paraguay. Compare the forms in the two columns; identify the morphemes which have more than one phonological shape (variant). Attempt to reconstruct a unique form for each of these words in Pre-Nivaclé, and state the changes which have taken place, according to your analysis, in the transition from Pre-Nivaclé to modern Nivaclé. Is there any relative chronology involved in the changes you postulate? If so, state what it is and show sample derivations of at least four word pairs (for example both words of 12, 14, 18, and 20). Do not bother with trying to reconstruct the exact nature of the vowel of the plural suffixes; also do not try to reconstruct a single original form for 'plural', as the different forms seen here depend in part on gender classification and in part on noun classes in the language.

NOTE: /kl/ is a single segment, both phonemically and phonetically – the velar closure and the lateral articulation are released simultaneously as a single sound; /ts/ is also a single segment, an alveolar affricate. /ɑ/ is a back low vowel, and contrasts with /a/, a cental low vowel; ɬ = voiceless *l*; *C'* = glottalized [ejective] consonants. The š is IPA ʃ, the č IPA tʃ. The plural suffixes, in the second column, have several different forms, but do not attempt to reconstruct them.

Set I

1.	xutsax	'vulture'	xutsx-as	'vultures'
2.	ɸatsux	'centipede'	ɸatsx-us	'centipedes'
3.	snomax	'ash'	snomx-as	'ashes'
4.	ɬtɑsex	'seed'	ɬtɑsx-ey	'seeds'
5.	kutsxanax	'thief'	kutsxanx-as	'thieves'
6.	ipɑset	'my lip'	ipɑst-es	'my lips'
7.	nasuk	'guayacán (tree)'	nask-uy	'guayacans'
8.	ɸaʔayuk	'algarrobo (acacia tree)'	ɸaʔayk-uy	'algarrobos'
9.	axɑyuk	'mistol (tree)'	axɑyk-uy	'mistols '

Set II

10.	inkɑʔp	'year'	inkɑp-es	'years'
11.	ɬuʔp	'nest'	ɬup-is	'nests'
12.	k'utxaʔn	'thorn'	k'utxan-is	'thorns'
13.	ɬsɑʔt	'vein'	ɬsɑt-ay	'veins'
14.	tisuʔx	'quebracho (tree)'	tisx-uy	'quebrachos'
15.	k'utsaʔx	'old man'	k'utsx-as	'old men'

Set III

16.	towɑk	'river'	towx-ɑy	'rivers'
17.	ɸinɑk	'cigarrette'	ɸinx-ɑy	'cigarrettes'
18.	ituʔk	'my arm'	itx-uy	'my arms'
19.	tsanuʔk	'duraznillo (tree)'	tsanx-uy	'duraznillos'
20.	namač	'axe'	namx-ay	'axes'
21.	šateč	'head'	šatx-es	'heads'

Set IV

22.	titeč	'plate'	titx-ey	'plates'
23.	k'atseč	'wood chip'	k'atsx-es	'wood chips'
24.	axpɑyič	'your house'	axpɑyx-ey	'your houses'

9

Semantic Change and Lexical Change

They that dally [= converse idly] nicely [= foolishly] with words may quickly make them wanton [= unmanageable].

(Shakespeare, *Twelfth Night* III, 1)

9.1 Introduction

Changes in meaning and vocabulary excite people. Non-linguists are fascinated by why *bloody* and *bugger* are obscene in Britain and not in America – the words don't even mean the same thing in the two places – and why *pissed* means 'angry' in the USA but 'drunk' in the UK, and why *pissed* is so much less obscene and more tolerated than it was a generation ago in both countries. People want to know how words such as *ditz, dork, dweeb, geek, nerd, twit, wimp, wuss* and *yutz* get added to the language so fast and why their meanings seem to change so rapidly, and whatever happened to the *groovy* of late 1960s love songs, anyway? Some find a certain delight (some would say a twisted satisfaction) in the seeming irony in the semantic history of *to bless*, from Old English *blēdsian* (earlier *blǭdsian*), which originally meant 'to mark with blood' in an act of consecration in pagan sacrifice. With umlaut in mind, it is easy to see the connection between *blood* and the *blēd-* part of *blēdsian* (just think *to bleed* to see the connection more clearly). Some are charmed (perhaps perversely so) by a favourite example of handbooks, the story behind *cretin*. English *cretin* is borrowed from French *crétin* 'stupid', which comes, to the surprise and delight of etymology-lovers, ultimately from Latin *christiānum* 'Christian'. In Romance languages, the term for 'Christian' was used also for 'human being' to distinguish people from beasts; the semantic shift which gives the modern sense of *cretin* 'a stupid person' apparently came about in Swiss French dialects especially in reference to a class of dwarves and physically deformed idiots in certain valleys of the Alps, used euphemistically to mean that even these beings were human, and from this came the semantic shift from 'Christian' to 'idiot'. Those who learn other languages often ask how true cognates can come to have such different meanings in related languages, as in the English–German cognates *town/Zaun* 'fence', *timber/Zimmer* 'room', *bone/Bein* 'leg', *write/reissen* 'to tear, rip'. They ask why a seemingly innocent French word such as *baiser*, which the dictionary says means 'to kiss', has changed its meaning to 'to copulate' with no warning to save the unsuspecting language learner from embarrassment. Vocabulary change can be a matter of alarm and deep emotional concern. This is evidenced by the creation of language academies and the appointment of language commissions to protect the purity of languages such as French and Spanish, and as seen, for example, in letters to the press in Canada, Britain, New Zealand and South Africa which denounce on the one hand the invidious creeping encroachment of Americanisms in vocabulary and on the other hand decry the degeneration of young people's all-too-limited vocabulary into nothing but slang (so they claim), holding up writers of famous literature as models of how we all should talk in order to be considered proper human beings who uphold our moral and linguistic obligations to the language. This chapter is about what linguists think about changes in meaning and in vocabulary, the topic which non-linguists find both exciting and alarming.

In linguistics (also in anthropology, philosophy and psychology), there are many approaches to semantics, the study of meaning. Unfortunately, these various theoretical approaches to semantics and the traditional historical linguistic treatments of change in meaning have typically had little in common, though clearly we would be in a better position to explain semantic change if we could base our understanding of change in meaning on a solid theory of semantics. Some recent approaches do attempt, with limited success, to reconcile the differences. Given the importance of semantic change, this chapter presents both a traditional classification of kinds of semantic changes and some more recent thinking concerning regularities and general tendencies in meaning change. Semantic change deals with change in meaning, understood to be a change in the concepts associated with a word, and has nothing to do with change in the phonetic form of the word. However, there are also aspects of lexical change which do not fall under this definition of semantic change, and we will look into them as well. Note that some aspects of semantic change and vocabulary change have already come up in previous chapters, under analogy in Chapter 4 and calques (semantic borrowing) in Chapter 3; we will consider grammaticalization in Chapter 10.

9.2   Traditional Considerations

Work in semantic change has been almost exclusively concerned with lexical semantics (change in the meaning of individual words), and that is the focus in this chapter. Semantic change is mostly concerned with the meaning of individual lexical items, whereas much of semantic theory involves logical relations among items in longer strings. There are various classifications of types of semantic change, and there is nothing special about the classification presented here. Some of the categories overlap with others, and some are defined only vaguely, meaning that some instances of semantic change will fit more than one type while others may fit none comfortably. It is probably best to consider this classification as offering a sort of broad scheme for organizing kinds of semantic change, but with no pretensions of being particularly complete or adequate, only (it is hoped) useful.

9.2.1 Widening (generalization, extension, broadening)

In semantic changes involving widening, the range of meanings of a word increases so that the word can be used in more contexts than were appropriate for it before the change. Changes from more concrete to more abstract meanings fit here.

(1) *Dog.* English *dog* first appeared with the more specific meaning of 'a (specific) powerful breed of dog', which generalized to include all breeds or races of dogs.

(2) *Salary.* Latin *salārium* was a soldier's allotment of salt (based on Latin *sal* 'salt'), which then came to mean a soldier's wages in general, and then finally, as in English, wages in general, not just a soldier's pay.

(3) *Cupboard.* In Middle English times, *cupboard* meant 'a table ("board") upon which cups and other vessels were placed, a piece of furniture to display plates, a sideboard', whose meaning then became 'a closet or cabinet with shelves for keeping cups and dishes', and finally in America it changed to mean any 'small storage cabinet'. In parts of Canada, *cupboard* has been extended to mean also what others call a 'wardrobe' or 'clothes closet'. Spanish *armario* 'cupboard' was borrowed from Latin in the Middle Ages where it had to do with 'arms', 'weapons', and meant 'armoury'; later its meaning widened to include present-day 'clothes closet, cupboard'. French *armoire* 'wardrobe, locker, cabinet' (also borrowed into English form French) has the same history.

(4) Spanish *caballero*, originally 'rider, horseman', expanded to include also 'gentleman, man of upper society' (since only men of means could afford to be riders of horses).

(5) Spanish *estar* 'to be' (especially 'to be in a location') < Latin *stāre* 'to stand'.

(6) Spanish *pájaro* 'bird' < Latin *passer* 'sparrow'.

(7) Finnish *raha* 'money' originally meant 'a fur-bearing animal' and its 'pelt'. The skins were an important means of exchange in the past, and *raha* came to mean 'skin used as medium of exchange'; when new means of exchange took the place of the old ones, *raha* shifted its meaning to 'money', its only meaning today (Ravila 1966: 105).

9.2.2 Narrowing (specialization, restriction)

In semantic narrowing, the range of meanings is decreased so that a word can be used appropriately only in fewer contexts than it could before the change. Changes of more abstract meanings to more concrete ones fit this category.

(1) *Meat* originally meant 'food' in general (as in the King James translation of the Bible) and later narrowed its meaning to 'meat' ('food of flesh'); this original meaning is behind compounds such as *sweetmeat* 'candy'. (Compare the Swedish cognate *mat* 'food'.)

(2) *Hound* 'a species of dog (long-eared hunting dog which follows its prey by scent)' comes from Old English *hund* 'dog' in general.

(3) *Wife* meant 'woman' in Old English times (as in the original sense of *midwife*, literally a 'with-woman'). It narrowed to mean 'woman of humble rank

or of low employment, especially one selling commodities of various sorts'. The former meaning is preserved in *old wives' tales* and the second in *fishwife*. Finally it shifted to 'married woman, spouse'.

(4) *Deer* narrowed its sense from Old English *dēor* 'animal' (compare the German cognate *Tier* 'animal').

(5) *Fowl* 'bird (especially edible or domestic)' has narrowed its sense from Old English *fugol* which meant 'bird' in general (compare the German cognate *Vogel* 'bird').

(6) *Girl*, which meant 'child or young person of either sex' in Middle English times, narrowed its referent in Modern English to 'a female child, young woman'.

(7) *Starve* 'to suffer or perish from hunger' is from Old English *steorfan* 'to die'. (Compare the German cognate *sterben* 'to die').

(8) French *soldat* 'soldier' comes from *solder* 'to pay' and thus meant 'a paid person', a narrowing from 'any paid person' to 'someone in the military'.

(9) French *drapeau* 'flag' meant first 'the piece of cloth fastened to a staff' (derived from *drap* 'cloth, sheet'; compare English *drape*, borrowed from French).

(10) Spanish *rezar* 'to pray' < Old Spanish *rezar* 'to recite, say aloud' (from Latin *recitāre* 'to recite, say aloud', the source from which *recite* in English is borrowed).

As will be seen in Chapter 10, many examples of grammaticalization involve semantic narrowing, from a broader lexical meaning to a narrower grammatical function.

9.2.3 Metaphor

Definitions of 'metaphor' (from Greek *metaphorā* 'transference') vary and are often vague; that is, it is often difficult to determine whether a given instance fits the definition or not. Metaphor involves understanding or experiencing one kind of thing in terms of another kind of thing thought somehow to be similar in some way: that is, A is like B. Metaphor in semantic change involves extensions in the meaning of a word that suggest a semantic similarity or connection between the new sense and the original one. Metaphor is considered a major factor in semantic change. It has been likened to analogy where one thing is conceptualized in terms of another, with a leap across semantic domains. The semantic change of *grasp* 'seize' to 'understand', thus can be seen as such a leap across semantic domains, from the physical domain ('seizing') to the mental domain ('comprehension') (see Traugott and Dasher 2002: 28). A much-repeated example is English *bead*, now meaning 'small piece of (decorative) material pierced for threading on a line', which comes from Middle English *bede* 'prayer, prayer bead', which in Old English was *beode*, *gebed* 'prayer' (compare the German equivalent *Gebet* 'prayer'). The semantic shift from 'prayer' to 'bead' came about through the metaphoric extension from the 'prayer', which was kept track of by the rosary bead, to the rosary bead itself, and then eventually to any 'bead', even including 'beads' of water. Frequently mentioned examples of metaphoric extensions involve expressions for 'to kill': *dispose of, do someone in, liquidate, terminate, take care of, eliminate* and others. In slang, there are many metaphoric changes for 'drunk' based on forms whose original meaning is associated with being 'damaged' in some way: *blasted, blitzed, bombed, hammered, obliterated, ripped, shredded, smashed, tattered, wasted* and many more. Another area of metaphor for 'drunk' involves being saturated with liquid: *pissed, sauced, sloshed, soaked*.

Other examples are:

(1) French *feuille* 'leaf, sheet of paper' < 'leaf (of plant)'; Spanish *hoja* 'leaf, sheet of paper' < 'leaf' (both from Latin *folia* 'leaves, plural of *folium* 'leaf').

(2) French *entendre* 'to hear' comes by metaphor from original 'to understand' (compare the Spanish cognate *entender* 'to understand').

(3) Spanish *sierra* 'saw' was applied by metaphor to 'mountain range'; now there is *sierra* 'saw' and *sierra* 'mountain range'.

(4) Spanish *pierna* 'leg' < Latin *perna* 'ham'.

(5) *root* (of plant) > 'root of plant, root of word, root in algebra, source'.

(6) French *fermer* 'to close' originally meant 'to fix, make firm or fast'. Spanish *firmar* 'to sign (with one's signature)' has the same source.

(7) Latin *captāre* 'to catch, to try to seize, to trap' became in French *chasser* 'to hunt, to chase, to drive away, to cause a hurried departure' (the source from which English *chase* is borrowed, which means both 'to go after, try to catch' and 'to drive (away)').

(8) French *chapeau* 'hat, bonnet' originally meant 'garland'.

(9) English *stud* 'good-looking, sexy man' of slang origin, derived by metaphor from *stud* 'a male animal (especially a horse) used for breeding'.

(10) English *chill* 'to relax, calm down' of slang origin came about by metaphoric extension of the original meaning of *chill* 'to cool'.

(11) English *thrill*, whose original meaning was 'to make a hole in, to pierce', shifted metaphorically to 'to pierce with emotion', later 'to fill with pleasure'.

9.2.4 Metonymy

Metonymy (from Greek *metōnomia* 'transformation of the name') is a change in the meaning of a word so that it comes to include additional senses which were not originally present but which are closely associated with the word's original meaning, although the conceptual association between the old and new meanings may lack precision: that is, A is associated with B, but need not be like B. Metonymy traditionally was held to be an important factor in semantic change, though less important than metaphor. Metonymy might be thought to be conceptual shifts within the same semantic domain (Traugott and Dasher 2002: 28–9). That is, metonymic changes typically involve some contiguity in the real (non-linguistic) world. They involve shift in meaning from one thing to another that is present in the context (though being present may be a conceptual judgement call not necessarily immediately apparent to us before the change takes place). For example, English *tea* means, in addition to the drink, 'the evening meal' in many English-speaking locations. A much-repeated example is English *cheek* 'fleshy side of the face below the eye'; Old English *cēace* meant 'jaw, jawbone', which over time shifted to the sense of Modern English *cheek*.

Traugott and Dasher (2002) give metonymy a more important role in

semantic change than is traditionally the case. They do not believe that metaphor and metonymy in principle exclude each other, since easily understood
metaphors can also be seen as typical associations – in some instances the
notion of a leap across semantic domains (metaphor) and change within the
same domain (metonymy) may not be clear or even relevant. Traugott and
Dasher believe that it must be possible for the target (the semantic concept
after the change) and/or the source (before the change) of a potential metaphor
to be understood or conceptualized metonymically for metaphor to be possible
(p. 29).

Some examples of metonymy are:

(1) French *jument* 'mare' < 'pack horse'.

(2) Spanish *cadera* 'hip' < 'buttocks' < ultimately Latin *cathedra* 'armchair'.
(Compare the French cognate *chaise* 'chair', from earlier *chaire*, from the same
Latin source.)

(3) Spanish *mejilla* 'cheek' < Latin *maxilla* 'jaw'.

(4) Spanish *plata* 'silver' has been extended to mean also 'money'.

(5) Spanish *acera* 'sidewalk' < Old Spanish *façera* 'façade, front of buildings
on a street or square'.

(6) Spanish *timbre* 'bell (as a telephone bell or doorbell), postage stamp' originally meant 'drum'; by metonymy this extended to include a 'clapperless bell'
(struck on the outside with a hammer), then 'the sound made by this sort of bell',
and then 'the sonorous quality of any instrument or of the voice', then 'tone' (of a
sound); from the round shape of a bell, it also extended to mean 'helmet-shaped',
then 'the crest of a helmet', 'the crest in heraldry' (the ornament placed above the
shield), and from this the meaning was extended to include 'the official mark
stamped on papers', to 'the mark stamped by the post office upon letters', and
finally to 'postage stamp'. (French *timbre* 'tone, postage stamp' has the same
history of semantic changes; English *timbre* 'the distinctive quality of a sound' is
borrowed from French.)

(7) English *flake* 'irresponsible person' of slang origin is by metonymy from the
original meaning of *flake* 'a small, loose, flat bit' – 'flaking' is usually considered an unfortunate thing to happen to most things.

(8) English *elope* originally applied to a married woman running off with
a lover, and later shifted to apply to a couple running away from home to get
married without a parent's permission (related etymologically to *leap*).

A common sort of metonymy, sometimes thought to be connected with *clipping* or *ellipsis* (see Section 9.4.9), is the use of the name of the place for a product
characteristic of it, as in French *champagne* 'champagne', from the name of the
region, *Champagne*. (For other examples, see sections 9.2.6 and 9.4.9.)

9.2.5 Synecdoche

Synecdoche (from Greek *sunekdokhé* 'inclusion'), often considered a kind of
metonymy, involves a part-to-whole relationship, where a term with more comprehensive meaning is used to refer to a less comprehensive meaning or vice
versa; that is, a part (or quality) is used to refer to the whole, or the whole is used
to refer to part, for example *hand*, which was extended to include also 'hired

hand, employed worker'. Some common examples found in various languages are 'tongue' > 'language', 'sun' > 'day', 'moon' > 'month'.

(1) Spanish *boda* 'wedding' comes from Latin *vōta* 'marriage vows', where the term for part of the whole, namely the 'vows', came to signal the whole, in this case the 'wedding'.

(2) German *Bein* 'leg' originally meant 'bone' (cognate with English *bone*).

(3) French *tableau* 'picture, panel, board' < Latin *tabula* 'board' (compare English *table*, a loanword ultimately from this same source).

(4) English *mail*, originally 'bag, pouch', underwent a series of shifts; borrowed from Old French with the meaning 'bag, pouch' (see modern French *malle* 'bag'), it shifted to 'bag for carrying letters', then to 'letters carried in that way' and to 'mail' generally; *email* is a step further removed from the original 'bag' meaning.

9.2.6 Displacement (ellipsis)

Displacement (also called *ellipsis*) involves changes where one word absorbs part or all of the meaning of another word with which it is linked in a phrasal constituent (usually Adjective–Noun), for example, *contact(s)* from *contact lens(es)* and *a capital* from *a capital city*, where the notion of 'city' has been absorbed into the word *capital* (English *capital* is a loan from French). Displacement is sometimes considered a special kind of synecdoche. (Some see this also as a kind of syntactic change.)

(1) French *succès* 'success' comes from *succès favorable* 'favourable issue, event' (derived from *succéder* 'to follow, transpire'; compare Latin *successus* 'advance, result', derived from *succēdere* 'to follow, undergo, replace'). (French is the source of borrowed *success* in English.)

(2) French *journal* 'newspaper' is a displacement from *papier journal* 'daily paper' (*papier* 'paper' + *journal* 'daily'). In English, *a daily* (from *daily paper*) has the same meaning and has developed in the same way.

(3) Spanish *hermano* 'brother' < Latin *frāter germānus* 'brother of the same parent', where *germānus* 'of the same parent' was used in the sense of 'true, authentic' and eventually displaced the expected form from Latin *frāter* 'brother'.

(4) *sexual intercourse* > *intercourse*.

(5) French *foie* 'liver' and Spanish *higado* 'liver' < Latin *iecur ficatum* 'fig-stuffed liver' by ellipsis so that only the reflex of *ficatum* 'fig-stuffed' remains in the meaning 'liver'.

(6) Finnish *yskä* 'cough' comes from original *yskä tauti*, literally 'chest sickness', *yskä* 'breast, lap' + *tauti* 'sickness', where *yskä* now no longer has the connotation of 'breast, chest' (Ravila 1966: 106).

(7) An often-cited example is *private soldier* > *private*, where *private* after the change came to mean 'ordinary/regular soldier' (contrasted with 'officer'), taking on the meaning of the whole phrase.

9.2.7 Degeneration (pejoration)

In degeneration (often called *pejoration*), the sense of a word takes on a less positive, more negative evaluation in the minds of the users of the language – an increasingly negative value judgement. A famous, oft-cited example is English *knave* 'a rogue', from Old English *cnafa* 'a youth, child', which was extended to mean 'servant' and then ultimately to the modern sense of *knave* 'rogue, disreputable fellow' (compare the German cognate *Knabe* 'boy, lad'). Examples of the degeneration of terms for women are well known and are often cited as examples in works dealing with social issues. For example, in colloquial German, *Weib* means 'ill-tempered woman' though in Standard German it just means 'woman' (the English cognate *wife* also formerly meant 'woman'). A great many of the terms for women which initially were neutral (or at least not so negative) degenerated so that today they are quite negative in connotation:

spinster 'unmarried older woman' < 'one who spins'.

mistress < originally from a borrowing from Old French *maistresse* 'a woman who rules or has control'; earlier in English it meant 'a woman who employs others in her service, a woman who has the care of or authority over servants or attendants'.

madam 'the female head of a house of prostitution' < 'a title of courtesy used as a polite form of address to a woman' (from *Madame*, originally borrowed from Old French *ma dame* 'my lady').

harlot was originally 'tramp, beggar' (borrowed from Old French *harlot, herlot* 'vagabond').

Italian *putta* and Spanish *puta* 'whore' earlier meant just 'girl' (compare Old Italian *putta* 'girl', *putto* 'boy'; Latin *putus* 'boy', *puta* 'girl').

Spanish *ramera* 'prostitute' earlier meant 'innkeeper's wife, female innkeeper'.

Some other examples of degeneration are:

(1) English *silly* 'foolish, stupid' comes from Middle English *sely* 'happy, innocent, pitiable', from Old English *sǣlig* 'blessed, blissful' (compare the German cognate *selig* 'blissful, happy').

(2) English *churl* 'a rude, ill-bred person' is from Old English *ceorl* 'man, man without rank, lowest rank of freemen', which became 'serf, tenant farmer' in Middle English, later 'countryman, peasant, rustic', then debased to 'base fellow, villain', and finally it came to have the modern sense of 'rude, ill-bred fellow' (compare the German cognate *Kerl* 'guy, chap, fellow').

(3) English *villain* 'criminal, scoundrel' was borrowed from French *villein* 'person of the villa/farm/homestead, serf, farm worker', and in Middle English meant 'low-born, base-minded rustic, a man of ignoble ideas or instincts', but later came to mean 'unprincipled or depraved scoundrel' and 'a man naturally disposed to criminal activities'.

(4) Spanish *siniestro* 'sinister' < Old Spanish *siniestro* 'left' (from Latin *sinister* 'left', the source of the loanword *sinister* in English).

(5) English *dilettante* did not originally have a negative connotation, but meant 'devoted amateur, one with love of a subject'; it shifted its meaning to 'a dabbler, amateur who lacks the understanding of professionals', and then to 'one with superficial interest in an area of knowledge'. *Amateur* is similar, originally a lover of the topic (a French loan into English, from Latin *amator* 'lover, one who loves'), then it acquired the meaning of 'a non-professional who engages in an

activity for pleasure', and eventually was extended also so that now it includes the meaning of 'an incompetent person'.

(6) English *disease* 'illness' formerly meant 'discomfort' (*dis-* + *ease*, like *un-easy* today).

(7) English *evil* had the original sense of 'uppity, exceeding due limits', related etymologically to *up* and *over*.

9.2.8 Elevation (amelioration)

Semantic changes of elevation involve shifts in the sense of a word in the direction towards a more positive value in the minds of the users of the language – an increasingly positive value judgement.

(1) *pretty* < Old English *prættig* 'crafty, sly'.

(2) *fond* < past participle of Middle English *fonnen* 'to be foolish, silly'.

(3) English *knight* 'mounted warrior serving a king', 'lesser nobility (below baronet)' comes from Old English *cniht* 'boy, servant', which shifted to 'servant', then 'military servant', and finally to the modern senses of 'warrior in service of the king' and 'lesser nobility'. (Compare the German cognate *Knecht* 'servant, farm hand'.)

(4) Spanish *caballo* 'horse' < Latin *caballus* 'nag, workhorse'.

(5) Spanish *calle* 'street' < Latin *calle* '(cattle-)path'.

(6) Spanish *casa* 'house' < Latin *casa* 'hut, cottage'.

(7) Spanish *corte* 'court' < Latin *cohortem, cortem* 'farmyard, enclosure', which came to mean 'division of a Roman military camp', which was extended to include 'body of troops (belonging to that division)' to 'imperial guard' and then further to 'palace' (see English *court*, a loan from Old French *court*, Modern French *cour* 'court (legal, royal), courtship' with the same Latin origin as the Spanish forms).

(8) The *villa* of the Middle Ages meant 'farm, homestead', but was elevated in French *ville* to 'city, town', Spanish *villa* 'village, town, country house' (compare Italian *villa* 'country house').

(9) English *dude* 'guy, person' (slang in origin) was in 1883 a word of ridicule for 'a man who affects an exaggerated fastidiousness in dress, speech and deportment, concerned with what is aesthetically considered "good form", a dandy'.

(10) English *nice* originally meant 'foolish, stupid, senseless', borrowed from Old French *ni(s)ce* 'foolish, stupid' (from Latin *nescius* 'ignorant, unaware'; compare Spanish *necio* 'foolish, imprudent', from the same Latin source).

9.2.9 Taboo replacement and avoidance of obscenity

Much is written about semantic changes and changes in vocabulary which involve responses to taboo and obscenity, and euphemism in general, though many of these changes might better be treated merely as examples of degeneration and metaphor and so on. In the sorts of semantic changes considered so far, focus is on changes in the meaning of words whose phonetic form mostly remains unaltered. There are cases of lexical replacement where a meaning remains but the phonetic realization of it is changed in some way, usually by substituting some other lexical item which had other denotations of its own before the change. Thus, lexical replacements involve more than meaning shifts, although change in the meaning may also be involved. Changes involving taboo and obscenity are prime examples of this sort. For instance, in English, *ass* 'long-eared animal related to a horse' has essentially been replaced in America by *donkey* (or *burro*) because it is considered too close for comfort to obscene *ass* 'derriere, arse'; *cock* 'adult male chicken' is replaced by *rooster* due to discomfort from the obscene associations of *cock* with 'penis'. In dialects of English where *bloody* is obscene, what is generally called a *bloody nose* in North America becomes *blood nose* or *bleeding nose* in order to avoid the taboo word. The following two examples were mentioned in Chapter 6.

(1) Spanish *huevo* 'egg' came to mean both 'egg' and 'testicle', but because of the obscene associations of 'testicle', in colloquial Mexican Spanish *huevo* as 'egg' was avoided and replaced by *blanquillo* 'egg', originally 'small white thing' (*blanco* 'white' + *-illo* 'diminutive').

(2) Latin American Spanish *pájaro* 'bird' came to be associated obscenely also with 'penis', and for this reason *pajarito* is usually substituted for 'bird', from *pájaro* 'bird' + *-ito* 'diminutive'. This taboo avoidance is carried even further in Kaqchikel and K'iche' (Mayan languages of Guatemala), where in many dialects the native term *ts'ikin* 'bird' has become taboo due to influence from Spanish *pájaro* 'penis, bird' (Spanish is the politically dominant language of the region), and therefore has been replaced by *čikop* '(small) animal'. Thus the meaning of *čikop* has been extended to include both '(small) animal' and 'bird', while that of *ts'ikin* has been restricted now to only or predominantly 'penis', with the meaning 'bird' either eliminated or now very recessive.

Changes involving *euphemism*, the replacement of words regarded as unpleasant, are part of this discussion. Favoured examples involve the many euphemistic replacements of words meaning 'toilet'. Terms for 'toilet' frequently come to be considered indelicate, and substitutions lacking the distressing sentiments are made. The room where indoor toilets were installed was called *water closet* (abbreviated *WC*) in Britain; this was soon replaced by *toilet*, originally a loan from French *toilette* 'small cloth' (diminutive of *toile* 'cloth, towel') which in English originally meant 'a wrapper for clothes, a night-dress bag', then 'a cloth or towel thrown over the shoulders during hairdressing', then 'a cloth cover for a dressing table', then 'articles used in dressing', 'furniture of the toilet' 'toilet-table', 'toilet service', and then 'the table upon which these articles are placed', 'the action or process of dressing', 'a dressing room with bathing facilities', and finally 'toilet/WC/bathroom'. Other euphemistic replacements include *lavatory*, *bathroom, restroom, washroom, commode, loo, john* and many others.

Spanish *embarazada* 'pregnant' (originally meaning 'encumbered') has essentially replaced earlier *preñada* 'pregnant'. (English *embarrass* also earlier meant 'to encumber, impede, hamper [movements, actions]', a borrowing from French *embarrasser* 'to block, to obstruct'.)

Not only can words be replaced or lost due to avoidance of obscenities and taboo, but also they are often changed phonetically to give more euphemistic outcomes, one source of new vocabulary. English has many such 'deflected' forms, for example: *blasted, darn, dang, dadnabbit, fudge, gadzooks, gosh, jeez, shucks, zounds* and many others. Varieties of Spanish have *pucha, puchis, púchica, futa* and the like as euphemistic replacements for *puta* 'whore' (very obscene); *chin* in Mexican Spanish replaces the very obscene *chingar* 'to have sexual intercourse (crudely)'. Examples of this sort are found in many languages. (Other cases of avoidance of taboo and obscenity are also seen in the discussion of *avoidance of homophony*, Chapter 13.)

9.2.10 Hyperbole

Hyperbole (*exaggeration*, from Greek *hyperbolē* 'excess') involves shifts in meaning due to exaggeration by overstatement.

(1) English *terribly, horribly, awfully* and other similar words today mean little more than 'very' (a generic intensifier of the adjective which they modify); by overstatement they have come to have no real connection with their origins, *terror, horror, awe* and so on.

(2) German *sehr* 'very' < 'sorely'.

(3) German *quälen* 'to torment, torture' < Proto-Germanic **kʷaljan* 'to kill' (compare the English cognate *quell*, from Old English *cwellan* 'to kill, slay').

(4) English slang *lame* 'stupid, awkward, socially inept', from the original meaning 'crippled, having an impaired limb'.

9.2.11 Litotes

Litotes (*understatement*, from Greek *litótēs* 'smoothness, plainness') is exaggeration by understatement (such as 'of no small importance' when 'very important' is meant). In many languages, examples of litotes are found involving verbs meaning 'to kill'. For example, English *kill* originally meant 'to strike, beat, hit, knock'. If you were to say *hit* but intend it to mean 'kill', this would be an understatement.

(1) French *meurtre* 'murder, homicide' comes via litotes from 'bruise', still seen in the etymologically related verb *meurtrir* 'to bruise' (compare the Spanish cognate *moretón* 'bruise, black-and-blue spot').

(2) French *poison* 'poison' originally meant 'potion, draught' (English *poison* was borrowed from French after this semantic shift).

(3) English *bereaved, bereft* 'deprived by death' < 'robbed' (Old English *be-* + *rēafian* 'to rob, plunder, spoil').

(4) English slang *inhale* 'to eat something fast' < 'to breathe in, draw in by breathing'.

9.2.12 Semantic shift due to contact

Though it is not generally found in traditional classifications of semantic change, examples of semantic shift due to language contact are occasionally pointed out in work on the history of specific languages. The following are a few examples.

(1) Spanish *pavo* originally meant 'peacock'; however, when the Spanish came to the New World, the newly discovered turkey was also called *pavo*,

and eventually to distinguish the two birds, *pavo* remained for 'turkey', while 'peacock' became *pavo real*, literally 'real turkey' (also 'royal turkey').

(2) In K'iche' (Mayan), *kye:x* originally meant 'deer'; however, with the introduction of horses with European contact, *kye:x* came to mean 'horse'. Eventually, to distinguish 'deer' from 'horse', the term for 'deer' became *k'iče' kye:x*, literally 'forest horse'. (NOTE: *y* = IPA [j], [kje:x].)

(3) In Lake Miwok (in California, of the Miwok-Costanoan family), with the introduction of European guns, the word *kó:no*, which originally meant 'bow', shifted to include 'gun'; the 'gun' meaning then extended so fully that 'bow' is now *hintí:l kó:no*, literally 'old-time gun' (*hintí:l* is a borrowing from Spanish *gentil* 'pagan', originally used to refer to unchristianized Indians) (Callaghan and Gamble 1997: 112). See also calques, in Chapter 3 (3.7.7).)

9.2.13   Summary of traditional classification

As is easy to see, the categories of semantic change in this classification are not necessarily distinct from one another; rather, some of them overlap and intersect. For this reason, some scholars consider 'narrowing' and 'widening' to be the principal kinds of semantic change, with others as mere subtypes of these two. Some emphasize the tendency for change to be in the direction from *concrete* to *abstract* (see below). Instances of overlapping and intersection are easily found in the examples listed here. For example, a semantic change could involve widening, degeneration and metonymy all at once, as in instances where terms for male and female genitals have taken on negative meanings for a man or woman of negative character, though often obscene (as in the meanings of English *prick* as 'penis' and 'miscreant male'). Another case is Yiddish *schmuck* 'penis, fool, stupid person', which originally meant 'jewel' (compare German *Schmuck* 'jewel, ornament'), but shifted to mean 'penis' (roughly analogous to the English jocular expression *the family jewels* to refer to the same general thing), then, as in the previous example, was extended further to 'fool, stupid person' (and along the way lost the original meaning of 'jewel'). *Schmuck* has been borrowed into English, primarily with the meaning of 'miscreant male'.

9.3   Attempts to Explain Semantic Change

Such general classifications of semantic change seem to offer little in the way of explaining how and why these changes take place in the ways they do. Nevertheless, many scholars have called for a search for regularities and explanations in semantic change, and some general tendencies have been discussed and some generalizations proposed. It is important to see what general understanding they may offer. The more traditional classifications of kinds of semantic change are generally thought to be useful for showing what sorts of changes might occur, but some of the generalizations that have been based on them amount to little more than a repetition in different form of the classification on which they are based. Others point out that semantic change and lexical change will not be explained in a vacuum, but will require appeal to and coordination with analogy, syntax (especially in the form of grammaticalization; see Chapter

11), discourse analysis, pragmatics and social history. Because sociocultural historical facts are often relevant, some insist that it is useless to seek generalizations to explain semantic change, although most would admit that some general statements about how and why meanings change may be possible even if not all semantic changes are regular or predictable.

Earlier work on semantic change was not totally without attempts at generalization. A general mechanism of semantic change was believed to be the associative patterns of human thought, and thus traditional approaches to meaning change typically had a psychological-cognitive orientation, though social context and pragmatic factors were emphasized by others. All of these factors play a role in more recent work on semantic change.

In the past, it was rarely asked how semantic change might come about, what pathways it might follow, and how it was to be explained, but many now recognize that semantic change must go through a stage of *polysemy*, where a word has more than one meaning. Thus in a historical shift a word might expand its sphere of reference to take on additional readings, becoming polysemous. Alternatively in a semantic change, a polysemous form may lose one (or more) of its meanings. A view which some have of semantic change combines both these situations: the word starts out with an original meaning, then acquires additional, multiple meanings, and then the original sense is lost, leaving only the newer meaning. Schematically this can be represented in three stages, beginning with form *a* which has meaning 'A':

Stage 1:	a	'A'	
Stage 2:	a	'A', 'B'	('A' > 'A', 'B')
Stage 3:	a	'B'	('A', 'B' > 'B')

Some examples will be helpful.

(1) English *timber*, German *Zimmer* 'room'. In Stage 1, form *a* = Germanic **tem-ram*, meaning *A* = 'building' (originally from Proto-Indo-European **dem-rom*; compare Latin *dom-us* 'house' and Old English *timrian* 'to build'). In Stage 2, English *a* = *timber*, *A* = 'building', *B* = 'material for building', 'wood which supplies building material'. Similarly in Stage 2, German *a* = *Zimmer*, *A* = 'building', *B* = 'room'. In Stage 3, English *a* = *timber*, *B* = 'material for building', 'wood which supplies building material' (meaning *A* 'building' was lost). In Stage 3, German *a* = *Zimmer*, *B* = 'room' (meaning *A* 'building' was lost).

(2) English *write*. In Stage 1, *write* meant 'to cut, score' (compare the German cognate *reissen* 'to tear, split'). In Stage 2, the meaning was extended to include both 'to cut, scratch' and 'to write'; the connection is through runic writing, which was carved or scratched on wood and stone (compare Old Icelandic *ríta* 'to scratch, to write'). This stage is attested in Old English *wrītan* 'to write', 'to cut'. Stage 3 is illustrated by modern English *write* meaning 'to write' only, where the sense of 'to cut' or 'to scratch' has been lost.

(3) Spanish *alcalde* 'mayor', when first borrowed from Arabic *qāḍī* meant 'judge (in Islamic law)' ('A'), but was later broadened to mean 'an official who is magistrate and mayor' ('B', added with 'A'), and then eventually the term was restricted in meaning to only 'mayor' (only 'B', since 'A' was lost).

This view recognizes (at least implicitly, and often explicitly) an intervening stage of polysemy as necessary in semantic changes. Others do not emphasize this view so much; rather, they recognize that lexical items typically have a core meaning (or group of related core concepts) but also various less central, more peripheral senses when used in a variety of discourse contexts, and they see semantic change as a less central sense becoming more central and the original core concept receding to be more peripheral, often being lost altogether. Still others see meaning as a network or semantic map where items within a semantic domain and from other domains are related by various overlappings in the polysemous choice which each lexical item has. Semantic change in this view follows paths of connections in the network, selecting and emphasizing different senses which the items have in different contexts. These are not really different approaches, but rather just more realistic versions of the view that holds that polysemy is a necessary intermediate step in semantic change.

Most linguists, past and present, have looked to structural (linguistic) and psychological factors as a primary cause of semantic change; however, historical factors outside of language have also been considered important causes of semantic change. Changes in technology, society, politics, religion and in fact all spheres of human life can lead to semantic shifts. Thus, for example, *pen* originally meant 'feather, quill' (a loan from Old French *penne* 'feather, writing quill'; compare Latin *penna* 'feather'), but as times changed and other instruments for writing came into use, the thing referred to by the word *pen* today is not remotely connected with 'feathers'. As guns replaced older hunting implements and weapons, terms meaning 'bow' (or 'arrow') shifted to mean 'gun' in many languages. Thus in the Lake Miwok (a Miwok-Costanoan language of California) example mentioned above, *kó:no* 'gun' originally meant 'bow'. The word for 'blowgun' in K'iche' (Mayan), *uɓ*, shifted its meaning to include 'shotgun'. In the wake of automobiles and aeroplanes, *fly* and *drive* have taken on new meanings.

There are countless such examples, of words whose meanings have changed due to sociocultural and technological change in the world around us, and several of the examples presented here in the classification of kinds of semantic changes are of this sort. For example, changes in religion and society are behind the shift from *blēdsian* 'to mark with blood in an act of consecration in pagan sacrifice' to modern *to bless*; and, as 'pelts' were replaced as a medium of exchange, Finnish *raha* shifted its meaning from 'pelt' to 'money'. In the historical events that brought English-speaking settlers to America, Australia, New Zealand, South Africa and so on, new plants and animals were encountered and sometimes native English words which originally referred to very different species were utilized for these new species, leading to semantic shifts in the meaning of these words. Thus, for example, *magpie* and *robin* refer to totally different species of birds in North America, in the UK and in Australia and New Zealand. *Magpie* in Europe is *Pica caudata* (of the family of *Corvidae*); the American magpie is *Pica pica hudsonia*; and the New Zealand and Australian magpie is *Gymnorhina tibicen* (of the *Cracticidae* family). *Robin* in England is of the genus *Erithacus*; in North America *robin* refers to *Turdus migratorius*; the New Zealand robin is *Petroica australis* (of the family *Muscicapidae*). The American *possum* (or *opossum*) (*Didelphis virginiana*) and Australian *possum* (*Trichosurus vulpecula*, and other species) are very different animals. Many Spanish words have undergone semantic changes as the result of similar historical events; for example, *gorrión* means a 'sparrow' in Spain, but shifted its meaning to 'hummingbird' in Central America; *tejón* means 'badger' in Spain, but 'coati-mundi' in Mexico; *león* refers to 'lion' in Spain, but has shifted to 'cougar, mountain lion' in many areas of Latin America; similarly, *tigre*, originally 'tiger', means 'jaguar' in much of Latin America. It is this sort of shift in meaning which makes it so difficult to generalize about semantic change. Since changes in society and technology are for the most part unpredictable, their affects on semantic change are also not predictable.

More recent work concentrates on the general directionality observed for some kinds of semantic changes, and attempts based on these are being made to elaborate a more explanatory approach, one which might predict possible and impossible changes or directions of change. Eve Sweetser's and Elizabeth Closs Traugott's work in this area has been the most influential (see Sweetser 1990, Traugott 1989, Traugott and Dasher 2002, Traugott and Heine 1991, and Traugott and König 1991; see also Hopper and Traugott 2003). Some general claims about semantic change which have been formulated are the following.

1. Semantically related words often undergo parallel semantic shifts. For example, various words which meant 'rapidly' in Old English and Middle English shifted their meaning to 'immediately', as with Old English *swifte* 'rapidly' and *georne* 'rapidly, eagerly', both of which changed the meaning to 'immediately' in about 1300 (Traugott and Dasher 2002: 67).
2. Phonetic similarity (especially cases of phonetic identity, homophony) can lead to shifts which leave the phonetically similar forms semantically more similar (sometimes identical). Note the confusion and lack of contrast in many English dialects for such sets of related words as *lie/lay* and *sit/set*.
3. Spatial/locative words may develop temporal senses: *before, after, behind*. Also, spatial terms often develop from body-part terms, as in *ahead of, in the back of, at the foot of*.
4. Some common semantic shifts typically (though not absolutely always) go in one direction and not the other; cases which recur and are found in numerous languages include the following.

(1) Words having to do with the sense of touch may typically develop meanings involving the sense of taste: *sharp, crisp, hot* ('spicy').

(2) Words involving the sense of taste may develop extended senses involving emotions in general: *bitter, sour, sweet*.

(3) Obligation > possibility/probability – more precisely, *root* senses of modals, also called *deontic* senses, by which is meant real-world forces, such as obligation, permission and ability, typically develop *epistemic* meanings (where epistemic means 'speaker's assessment' and denotes necessity, probability and possibility involving reasoning). For example, in the history of *may*, the meaning was first physical ability (*Jane may come* = 'Jane is able to come'); then the sense of social permission developed ('Jane is allowed to come'); finally the epistemic, logical possibility sense came about ('it is perhaps the case that Jane will come'). The history of *must* is similar: first, *Bess must sing* had the root

meaning 'it is a requirement that Bess sing'); second, an epistemic sense was added, 'that Bess must sing is a reasoned conclusion based on the evidence that her father and mother and brothers and sisters all sing, so it is likely that she, too, sings'. In these examples, the root senses are original and the epistemic senses developed later.

(4) Propositional > textual – things with propositional meanings tend to develop textual and later expressive meanings. For example, *while* in modern English means (1) 'a period of time' (propositional, a specific temporal situation), (2) 'during the time that' and (3) 'although' (textual, connecting clauses); however, *while* comes from Old English *þa hwīle þe* [that.Accusative while/time.Accusative Subordinate.particle] 'at the time that', which had only the propositional sense, not the later textual one. This phrase was reduced by late Old English times to *wile*, a simple conjunction (Traugott and König 1991: 85).

(5) 'see' > 'know, understand'.

(6) 'hear' > 'understand', 'obey'.

(7) Physical-action verbs (especially with hands) > mental-state verbs, speech-act verbs. For example, verbs such as 'grasp', 'capture', 'get a hold on', 'get', 'catch on to' very commonly come to mean 'understand'; thus, *feel* goes from 'touch, feel with hands' to 'feel, think, have sympathy or pity for'; Spanish *captar*, originally 'capture, seize', added the sense 'to understand'; Finnish *käsittää* 'to comprehend' is derived from *käsi* 'hand'; Spanish *pensar* 'to think' comes from Latin *pēnsāre* 'to weigh'. English *fret* 'worry, be distressed' formerly meant 'to eat, gnaw' (compare the German cognate *fressen* 'to eat, devour, consume (of animals, or rudely of people)').

(8) Mental-state verbs > speech-act verbs (*observe* 'to perceive, witness' > 'to state, remark').

(9) 'man' > 'husband' (German *Mann* 'man, husband' < 'man').

(10) 'woman' > 'wife'.

(11) 'body' > 'person' (compare *somebody*).

(12) 'finger' > 'hand'.

(13) 'left(-handed, left side)' > 'devious, evil, foreboding' (English *sinister*, ultimately from Latin *sinister* 'left').

(14) 'know' > 'find out', 'taste' (compare Spanish *saber* 'to know, to taste, to find out' < Latin *sapere* 'to know').

(15) animal names > inanimate objects. For example, Spanish *gato* 'jack (for raising cars)' < *gato* 'cat'; in Central American Spanish *mico* 'jack'< *mico* 'monkey'; Spanish *grúa* '(construction) crane' < Old Spanish *grúa* 'crane' (bird) (compare Modern Spanish *grulla*, *grúa* 'crane (bird)' (compare English *crane* '(bird) crane', 'building crane').

Traugott speaks of broad explanatory tendencies:

1. Meanings based on the external situation > meanings based on the internal situation (evaluative/perceptual/cognitive). This would cover, for example, the cases called degeneration and elevation, which involve value judgements on the part of the users of the language. It would also include many of the examples from (5–7) above.
2. Meanings based on external or internal situations > meanings based on

textual or (meta)linguistic situations. This would include many instances from (4), (7) and (8) above.

3. Meanings tend to become increasingly based on speakers' subjective beliefs/states/attitudes towards the proposition. Instances of (1), (2) and especially (3) above illustrate the change of meaning involving increase in subjective reaction. Many metonymic semantic changes fall under this. (See Traugott 1989.)

It is frequently claimed that semantic shifts typically go from more *concrete* to more *abstract*. For example, there are many semantic changes which extend body-part notions to more abstract meanings, but not the other way around, as with German *Haupt* originally meaning only 'head' (body part, concrete), which was later extended to mean 'main' or 'principal', as in *Hauptstadt* 'capital' (*Haupt* 'head' + *Stadt* 'town, city'), *Hauptbahnhof* 'central station' ((*Haupt* 'head' + *Bahnhof* 'railway station'), and then later *Haupt* lost its primary original meaning of 'head' in most contexts. While this is an interesting and important claim, a number of the traditional classes of semantic change, for example narrowing in particular, often involve change towards more concreteness, and therefore the claim needs to be understood as only a broad general tendency which can easily have exceptions.

In their explanatory treatment of semantic change, Traugott and Dasher (2002) emphasize the typical direction of certain kinds of semantic change. They identify 'regular' tendencies in semantic change, that is changes that are encountered frequently across languages and also repeatedly within single languages. They propose an 'Invited Inferencing Theory of Semantic Change'. Polysemy is central in this theory, and it typically arises out of the pragmatic forces of *invited inferences* and *subjectification*. *Invited inferences* arise in the pragmatic use of language in given contexts. For example, *as long as* and *so long as* formerly had only spatial and temporal meanings, as in *King Alfred's long ships were almost twice **as long as** the other ships* (spatial) and *Squeeze the medication through a linen cloth onto the eye **as long as** he needs* (temporal). But such temporal sentences could invite the inference that *as/so long as* might also mean conditional ('provided that'), 'squeeze the medication on the eye for the length of time that he needs it' or 'if/on the condition that he still needs it'. Later, in some contexts the conditional sense became the only one possible, as in *He told the jury that it is proper for police to question a juvenile without a parent present **so long as** they made a reasonable effort to notify the parent*. In *subjectification*, speakers come to develop meanings for words 'that encode or externalize their perspectives and attitudes as constrained by the communicative world of the speech event, rather than by the so-called "real-world" characteristics of the event or situation referred to' (Traugott and Dasher 2002: 30). For example, an increase in subjectivity is seen in semantic changes involving *indeed*: first as in *dede* 'in action', then 'certainly, in actuality'; second, *indeed* changed to include 'in truth' (subjective, reflecting speaker's attitude) in its meaning; third, *indeed* changed to add 'what's more', 'adding to that' (a discourse marker). Another example is the verb *promise*. Its original sense was as 'a directive imposing obligation on oneself as speaker', as in *I promise to do my* *best*. Semantic change added later the sense 'speaker's high degree of certainty' (more subjective, internalizing the speaker's perspective/attitude), as in *She promises to be an outstanding student*.

9.4   Other Kinds of Lexical Change – New Words

There are many kinds of lexical change that are not limited to semantic change. Several sources of new vocabulary have already come up in the treatment of various kinds of analogy, borrowing and the semantic changes. We will not bring these up again here, but will concentrate on other sources of *neologisms* (new words in a language), presenting a more or less traditional classification of kinds of lexical change together with examples. Abundant examples involving the more productive sources of neologisms are found especially in slang, advertising and political discourse.

9.4.1   Creations from nothing (root creations)

Creations of new words from nothing, out of thin air, are rare, but putative examples exist. Examples that are often cited of this include:

1. *blurb* coined by Gelett Burgess (American humorist) in 1907.
2. *gas* coined by Dutch chemist J. B. van Helmont in 1632, inspired by Greek *khāos* 'chaos', where the letter *g* of Dutch is pronounced [x], corresponding to the pronunciation of the Greek letter χ, the first of the word for 'chaos'.
3. *paraffin* invented by Karl Reichenbach in 1830, based on Latin *parum* 'too little, barely' + *affīnis* 'having affinity'.

It might be objected that in most cases of this sort, the creation isn't really fully out of 'nothing'; for example, *gas* has Greek 'chaos' lying in some way behind it; the creation of *paraffin* utilized pieces from Latin. Probably better examples of creations from nothing could be found in certain slang terms (*zilch*, *pizazz*) and product names (see below).

A related source of new words is *literary coinage*, new words created by (or at least attributed to) authors and famous people.

1. *blatant* < Edmund Spenser (between 1590 and 1596).
2. *boojum* < Lewis Carroll.
3. *chortle* < Lewis Carroll (a blend of *chuckle* + *snort*).
4. *pandemonium* 'the abode of all the demons, the capital of Hell', from John Milton's *Paradise Lost*, 1667 (the pieces from which this was created are Greek).
5. *yahoo* < Jonathan Swift's *Gulliver's Travels*, the name created for an imaginary race of brutes with human form.

9.4.2   From personal names and names of peoples

From names of individuals we have examples such as:

1. *guillotine* borrowed from French *guillotin*, named after the French physician Joseph-Ignace Guillotin, who suggested that the instrument be used in executions in 1789.
2. *macadam (road)* named after John Loudon McAdam (1756–1836) for the kind of road he invented and the kind of material used in it.
3. *sandwich* said to be named after John Montagu, the 4th Earl of Sandwich (1718–92), who spent twenty-four hours gambling with no other food than slices of cold meat between slices of toast.
4. *volt* named after Alessandro Volta, Italian scientist and physician (1745–1827).

There are also words which originate from names of groups of people:

gothic from the Goths (Germanic tribes);
cannibal, first recorded by Christopher Columbus, as *caniba*, a name of the feared Carib Indians, who, Columbus reports, were called *Carib* on Hispaniola. English borrowed the word from Spanish *canibal* 'cannibal'.
to gyp 'to cheat, swindle' from 'Gypsy' (today considered improper, racist);
to jew (a price down) from 'Jew' (now avoided because of its negative stereotype of an ethnic group);
vandal, vandalize from the Vandals (another Germanic tribe);
welch, welsh 'to cheat by avoiding payment of bets', said to be from 'Welsh'.

5. Other examples derived from names of persons or peoples – some mythical or fictional – include:

cereal from Latin *cereālis* 'of grain', derived from *Ceres*, the Roman goddess of agriculture;
chauvinism from Nicholas Chauvin of Rochefort, French soldier (possibly legendary) known for excessive patriotic zeal;
lynch from William Lynch of Virginia, who set up unofficial tribunals to try suspects;
mesmerize from Austrian physician Franz Anton Mesmer (1734–1815), whose experiments induced trance-like states in his subjects;
nicotene from Jean Nicot, French ambassador in Lisbon, who sent samples of a new 'tobacco' to the French queen Catherine de Medici in 1560 (in his honour, plants of the genus are all called *nicotiana*); nicotene, the addictive alkaloid, comes from *nicotiana* plants;
panic from the Greek god *Pan*;
quixotic from Cervantes' *Don Quixote*.

9.4.3 From place names

1. *canary* < Canary Islands.
2. *currant* ultimately from *Corinth*, a loan from Old French *raisins de Corauntz* (Modern French *raisins de Corinthe*) 'raisins of Corinth'.
3. *denim* ultimately from French *serge de Nîmes* 'serge (a woollen fabric) of Nîmes' (a manufacturing town in southern France).
4. *jeans* < Genoa (for a twilled cotton cloth associated with Genoa).

5. *peach* < Persia. English *peach* is a loan from French *pêche* which derives from Latin *malum persicum* 'Persian apple'; 'Persia' as the source of words for 'peach' is more visible in German *Pfirsich* and Finnish *persikka*.
6. *sherry* < Jerez (a place in Spain associated with this fortified Spanish wine).
7. *spa* < Spa (place in Belgium celebrated for the curative properties of its mineral water).
8. *tangerine* < Tangier, Morocco.
9. *turkey* < Turkey (shortened from *turkeycock, turkeyhen,* originally a guinea-fowl imported through Turkey, later applied erroneously to the bird of American origin).
10. Other examples derived from place names include:

champagne from *Champagne,* the name of a province in northern France for which the wine produced there is named;
frank from the Franks, Germanic conquerors of Gaul, whose name is seen in the name *France*;
meander from the river Maeander, Turkey (through Greek *maíandros,* which came to mean 'winding course');
muslin from Mosul, Iraq, where fine cotton fabric was made (< Arabic *mūslin*);
pheasant named for the river Phasis in the Caucusus, where in legend pheasants come from.

9.4.4 From brand (trade) names

1. *coke, cola* (drink), *coca-cola* < Coca-Cola.
2. *frig, frigidaire* < Frigidaire (in the USA).
3. *jello* (jelly crystals, a gelatin dessert in North America) < Jell-O.
4. *kleenex* (tissue) < Kleenex.
5. *levis, levi jeans* < Levi Strauss.
6. *xerox* < Xerox.
7. *hoover* (vacuum cleaner) < Hoover.
8. *to google* < Google.

9.4.5 Acronyms

Acronyms are words derived from the initial letters or syllables of each of the successive parts of a compound term or word: *ASAP* < 'as soon as possible'; *beemer* < 'BMW automobile'; *Benelux* < Belgium–Netherlands–Luxembourg; *BS* < 'bullshit'; *CD* < 'compact disc'; *CIA* < 'Central Intelligence Agency'; *DJ* < 'disc jockey'; *emcee* < 'master of ceremonies'; *FYI* < 'for your information'; *Gestapo* < from German *Geheime Staatspolizei* 'secret state's police', borrowed into English; *Hummer* < HMMWV 'High Mobility Multipurpose Wheeled Vehicle', an abbreviation of which was pronounced *Humvee,* which General Motors changed to *hummer* when it bought the rights to make the vehicle, in order to market it better; *lol* (*LOL*) < 'laughing out loud'; *MD* < 'medical doctor'; *MP* < 'military police', *MP* < 'member of parliament'; *OJ* < slang for 'orange juice'; *OMG* < 'oh my God' (or 'oh my goodness' for some); *PDQ* 'fast'

< 'pretty damned quick'; *radar* 'radio direction and ranging'; *RAM* < 'random access memory'; *ROM* < 'read-only memory'; *scuba* (diving) < 'self-contained underwater breathing apparatus'; *TMJ* 'temporomandibular-joint disorder'; *UK*; *USA*; *yuppie* < 'young urban professional'; and many more.

Some forms are turned into acronym-like words even though they do not originate as such; these usually involve sequences of letters from principal syllables in the word, for example: *TV* < television; *PJs* < pyjamas.

9.4.6 Compounding

Compounds are words (or better said, lexical items) formed from pieces or units that are (or were) themselves distinct words. Compounding is a productive process in English and many other languages. A number of examples of compounds that are relatively new in English include the following: *all-nighter* (*to pull an all-nighter* 'to stay up all night long, usually to study for exams'); *bad(-)ass*; *bag lady*; *boombox*; *brain-dead* 'stupid, unable to think'; *buttload*; *cashflow*; *couch potato* 'lazy person, someone who just lies around'; *cyberbullying*; *downmarket* 'less expensive, less sophisticated'; *downside*; *glass ceiling* 'hypothetical barrier which allows a goal to be viewed but denies access to it'; *-head* (as in *airhead, butthead, deadhead, dickhead, doughhead*); *knee-jerk* (adjective); *mad cow disease*; *meltdown*; *motormouth*; *-person* (as in *busperson, chairperson, clergyperson, minutepersons*); *red-eye* 'cheap whisky', *red-eye* 'early-morning or late-night flight'; *scumbucket* 'despicable person'; *shareware*; *slamdunk*; *stargaze*; *studmuffin* 'a muscular or attractive male'; *tummytuck*; *waterboarding*; and so on.

In the case of older compounds, later changes often make the original components of the compound no longer recognizable, for example:

1. *elbow* < Proto-Germanic **alinō* 'forearm' + **bugōn* 'bend, bow' (compare Old English *eln* 'forearm, cubit').
2. *gamut* < *gamma*, the name of the Greek letter *G*, introduced in the Middle Ages to represent a note on the musical scale one note lower than *A*, which began the scale, + *ut*, the first of a series of six syllables used to name the six notes of a hexachord.
3. *gossip* < Old English *godsībb* (*God* + *sib* 'related') 'one who has contracted spiritual affinity with another by agreeing to act as sponsor at a baptism', which came to mean 'family acquaintance, friend' and 'a woman's female friends invited to be present at a birth', and to 'someone, usually a woman, of light and trifling character' to 'the conversation of such a person', 'idle talk'.
4. German *Elend* 'misery, miserable' < Old High German *elilenti* 'sojourn in a foreign land, exile' (compare Gothic *alja-* 'other' + *land* 'land').

In others, the source of the compounding is only partially perceived today: *cobweb* < Middle English *coppe* 'spider' + *web*; *nickname* < *an* + *eke* 'additional' + *name*; *werewolf* < Old English *wer* 'man' (cognate with Latin *vir* 'man') + *wolf*.

9.4.7 Other productive word-formation and derivational devices

In addition to compounding, new words are derived more or less productively through the employment of various derivational affixes in word-formation processes. Others involve what have been called 'neo-classical' compounds (involving elements from Greek or Latin (such as *auto-*, *trans-*, *bio-* and so on). A few examples illustrating these processes are: *-able* (*bankable*, *billable*, *bloggable*, *doable*, *getatable* (*get-at-able*), *microwav(e)able*); *auto-* (*autopilot*, *auto-suggestion*); *-belt* (*banana belt*, *bible belt*, *cow belt*); *mega-* (*mega-sound*, *mega-show*, *mega-event*); *micro-* (*microenvironment*, *microbiotic*, *microcapsule*, *microprocessor*, *microsurgery*); *mini-* (*minibike*, *minicomputer*, *minimart*, *miniskirt*, *mini-series*); *pan-* (*pandemic*, *pan-galactic*, *pan-national*); *pre-* and *post-* (*pre-packaged*, *pre-washed*, *post-colonialist*, *post-structuralism*); *pseudo-* (*pseudo-friend*, *pseudo-psychological*, *pseudo-scholar*, *pseudo-Western*); *trans-* (*transmigration*, *transnationals*, *transpacific*); *ultra-* (*ultraliberal*, *ultramodern*, *ultraradical*, *ultrashort*); *-ism/-ist* (*racist*, *sexism*, *fattist*, *neologism*); among many others. Some of these overlap with blends, such as *bio-*: *biodegradable*, *biodiversity*, *biosphere*; and *eco-* (< *ecology*, *ecological*): *ecotourism*, *eco-friendly*, *ecofreak*.

9.4.8 Amalgamation

Amalgamations are forms which formerly were composed of more than one free-standing word (which occurred together in some phrase), which as a result of the change get bound together in a single word. For example, English *nevertheless* and *already* are now single words, but come from the amalgamation of separate words, of *never + the + less* and *all + ready*. English has many words of this sort in whose background lies the amalgamation of earlier separate words into a single lexical item. Amalgamation is often considered a kind of analogy. (Similarly, cases of blending and contamination are sometimes treated as kinds of lexical change, as discussed in Chapter 4 on analogy.) We can see amalgamation under way in the frequent (mis)spellings of *alright* for *all right* (probably influenced by analogy with *already*), *alot* for *a lot* meaning 'many, much', and *no-one* for *no one*.

(1) Some examples of amalgamations in English are: *almost* < *all most*, *alone* < *all one*, *altogether* < *all together*, *always* < *all ways*, *however* < *how ever*, *without* < *with out*.

(2) English *don* < *do on*; *doff* < *do off*.

(3) Spanish *usted* 'you (formal, polite)' < *vuestra merced* 'your grace'.

(4) Spanish *también* 'also' < *tan bene* 'as well', *todavía* 'still, yet' < *tota via* 'all way(s)'.

(5) Latin *dē mānē* (*dē* 'of' + *manus* 'good (ablative)'), meaning 'in good time', is behind amalgamated forms meaning 'morning, tomorrow' in some of the Romance languages, for example French *demain* 'tomorrow' and Italian *domani* 'morning, tomorrow'. Later, French underwent further amalgamations: *en demain* ('in' + 'tomorrow') > *l'endemain* (*l(e)* 'the' + *endemain*) > *le lendemain* 'tomorrow, the next day'.

(6) Latin *hodie* 'today' should have ended up in French as *hui*, but this was

further amalgamated, first to *jour d'hui* (from *jour* 'day' + *d(e)* 'of' + *hui* 'today') and then on to *aujourd'hui* 'today, nowadays' (from *au* 'to the' + *jour d'hui* – even *au* is an amalgam of *a* 'to' + *le* 'the').

(7) Spanish *hidalgo* 'noble', Old Spanish *fijodalgo*, come from *fijo* 'son' (Latin *filiu-*, compare Modern Spanish *hijo* 'son') + *d(e)* 'of' + *algo* 'something/ wealth'.

(8) French *avec* 'with' comes from Latin *apud* 'with, by, beside' + *hoc* 'this, it', literally 'with/by this'.

(9) Spanish *nosotros* 'we' comes from *nos otros* 'we others', *vosotros* 'you (familiar plural)' from *vos otros* 'you others'.

(10) English *wannabe(e)* of slang origin ('someone who tries to be accepted by a group, adopting its appearance and manners') < *want to be.*

Note that many of the cases today called *grammaticalization* (see Chapter 11) are instances of amalgamation, where formerly independent words are amalgamated with the result that one becomes a grammatical affix.

(11) For example, in Spanish and other Romance languages, forms of the verb *haber* 'have' (from Latin *habēre*) were amalgamated with infinitives to give the 'future' and 'conditional' morphological constructions of today, for example *cantar he* > *cantar-hé* > *cantaré* 'I will sing' (*he* 'first person singular' of *haber*), *cantar has* > *cantar-has* > *cantarás* 'you will sing' (*has* 'second person singular' of *haber*); *cantar habías* > *cantarías* 'you would sing' (*habías* 'you had').

(12) In another example, *mente* 'in mind' (from the ablative of Latin *mens* 'mind') was grammaticalized in Romance languages as an adverbial clitic (in Spanish) or suffix (in French). From *absoluta mente* 'in absolute mind' we get Spanish *absolutamente* and French *absolument* 'absolutely'. (For discussion and other examples, see Chapter 11.)

Blending (contamination), included with analogy (see Chapter 4), is sometimes also considered a kind of lexical change, sometimes linked loosely with amalgamation.

9.4.9 Clipping (compression, shortening)

Often, new words or new forms of old words come from 'clipping', that is, from shortening longer words. The several examples from English which follow show this process: *ad* < advertisement, *app* < application, *bike* < bicycle, *bus* < Latin *omnibus* 'for everyone' (*-bus* dative plural case ending – this is a much-cited example), *condo* < condominium, *decaf* < decaffeinated coffee, *dis(s)* (*dissing*) < 'to be disrespectful towards someone', *fan* < fanatic, *fridge* < refrigerator, *gas* < gasoline, *gym* < gymnasium, *jock* ('athlete') < jockstrap, *limo* < limousine, *math/ maths* < mathematics, *mod* < modern, *nuke* (*nukes, to nuke*) < nuclear weapons, *a perm, to perm* < permanent wave, *perp* < perpetrator, *phone* < telephone, *prep* < prepare, preparation, *pro* < professional, *psycho* < psychotic, *pub* < public house, *rad* < radical, *schizo* [skɪtso] < schizophrenic, *stats* < statistics, *sub* < substitute ('a substitute, to substitute'), *telly* < television, *veg, to veg out* < vegetate. Popular on restaurant menus (in North America) is *shrooms*, a clipped form of *mushrooms*; it remains to be seen whether it will survive.

9.4.10 Expressive creations

Onomatopoeia is another source of new words, creations with only sounds in nature as a model, thought to be the source of words such as *buzz*, *gag* and so on. Interjections (ejaculations) are another source, exemplified by *ah*, *oh*, *wow*, *pow*, *whew*, *shush* and many others. Some expressive words seem to develop out of nothing, as for example *bodacious* 'remarkable, fabulous' and *humongous* (also spelled *humungous*) 'very large'. In most cases such as these, blending is involved, and while the origin of these two words is uncertain, it is possible that *bodacious* is connected in some way to *bold* and *audacious*, and that *humongous* perhaps involves *huge* in some way.

9.4.11 Obsolescence and loss of vocabulary

Those who work on lexical change are interested not only in the adoption of new vocabulary, but also in the question of why vocabulary items become archaic and sometimes disappear altogether from a language. While the use of particular words can fade for a number of social and stylistic reasons, the primary cause is the disappearance in society of the thing they refer to – that is, historical changes in society can lead to vocabulary loss as well as to semantic shifts (mentioned above). For example, there was a large range of vocabulary involving falconry, armour, feudal society and other institutions and technologies of the Middle Ages which in effect has become totally forgotten, as these things faded from modern life. Replacement of one word by another for the same meaning is another frequent means by which vocabulary is lost. A few examples of older words now essentially lost to modern English vocabulary are the following (though some are occasionally resurrected for special purposes in fantasy literature and games reflecting medieval themes):

> *dorbel*: a dull-witted pedant, a foolish pretender to learning; from Nicholas Dorbellus, a fifteenth-century professor of scholastic philosophy at Poitiers and follower of Duns Scotus, whose name gave us *dunce*.
> *dousabell*: a common name in sixteenth-century poetry for a sweetheart, especially an unsophisticated country girl < French *douce et belle* 'sweet and beautiful'.
> *fribbler*: a trifler; one who professes rapture for a woman yet dreads her consent.
> *jarkman*: he that can write and read, and sometimes speak, Latin and uses these skills to make counterfeit licences, which they call *gybes*, and sets to seals, in their language falsified documents called *jarks*; sixteenth-century slang for an educated beggar able to forge passes, licences, etc. *Jark* was rogues' cant for a seal, whence also a licence of the Bethlehem Hospital ('Bedlam') to beg.
> *kelchyn*: a fine paid by one guilty of manslaughter, generally to the kindred of the person killed.
> *kexy*: dry, brittle, withered.
> *mulligrubs*: a twisting of the guts, so called from the symptomatic fever attending it.

palliard: a vagabond who slept on the straw in barns, hence a dissolute rascal, a lecher, a debauchee < French *paille* 'straw'.

parnel: a punk, a slut; the diminutive of Italian *petronalla*; a priest's mistress.

rogitate: to ask frequently.

thural: of or pertaining to incense.

towrus: among hunters a roebuck eager for copulation is said to 'go to his towrus'.

tyromancy: divining by the coagulation of cheese.

wittol: a husband who knows of and endures his wife's unfaithfulness; a contented cuckold; from *woodwale*, a bird whose nest is invaded by the cuckoo, and so has the offspring of another palmed off on it for its own.

yelve: dung-fork; garden-fork; to use a garden fork.

9.5 Exercises

Exercise 9.1

Attempt to find examples of your own of new vocabulary items which represent some of the categories of lexical and semantic change discussed in this chapter. Try to name or identify the categories involved. You can do this by listening for words that you think are new in the speech of your friends and family or by asking others if they can think of any examples. Slang is a fertile area for new vocabulary and semantic shifts.

Exercise 9.2 Lexical change

The following are a few of the many new words (neologisms) that have been added to English recently. Can you determine where these come from, that is, how they came about? What processes of vocabulary creation, semantic change or other kinds of linguistic changes do you think lie behind the creation of these new words? (You may need to look some of these up to find their meanings, or ask your friends who might know what they mean.)

blogosphere, bridezilla, buzzword, de-friend/unfriend, emoticon, guesstimate, mouse, peops, tweet, wiki, WMD.

Exercise 9.3 Semantic change

Look up the following words in a dictionary which provides basic etymologies for words. (*The Oxford English Dictionary* is generally recognized as the primary authority in this area and is recommended here, although a number of other dictionaries also provide useful etymological information.) Determine what change in meaning has taken place in each word. State which type of semantic change is involved (from among the types defined in this chapter).

For example, if you were to see *villain* in the list, you would look it up and find out that it originally meant 'person of the villa/farm' but has changed its meaning to 'criminal, scoundrel', and you would state that this is an example of *degeneration* (or *pejoration*).

corpse; crafty; disease; fame; journey; officious; science; starve; thing; vulgar.

Exercise 9.4

In the following examples of semantic change, identify the kind of semantic change involved (widening, narrowing, metonymy and so on).

1. Spanish *cosa* 'thing' < Latin *causa* 'matter, cause, question'.
2. Spanish *dinero* 'money' < Latin *dēnāriu* 'coin (of a particular denomination)'.
3. Spanish *pariente* 'relative' < Old Spanish *pariente* 'parent'.
4. Spanish *segar* 'to reap (to cut grain, grass with a scythe)' < Latin *secāre* 'to cut'.
5. Old Spanish *cuñado* 'relation by marriage' shifted to 'brother-in-law' in Modern Spanish. (This Spanish word comes ultimately from Latin *cognātus* 'blood-relation'.)
6. Mexican Spanish *muchacha*, formerly only 'girl', now has a primary meaning 'maid, servant woman' in some contexts.
7. Modern Spanish *siesta* 'afternoon nap (rest period during the heat of the day)' < Old Spanish *siesta* 'midday heat' (ultimately from Latin *sexta (hōra)* 'sixth (hour)').
8. English *gay* 'homosexual' is the result of a recent semantic shift, where the original sense, 'cheerful, lively', has become secondary; the shift to the 'homosexual' sense perhaps came through other senses, 'given to social pleasures, licentious', which the word had.
9. English *to spill* formerly meant (from c. 1300 to 1600) 'to destroy by depriving of life, to put to death, to slay, to kill'.
10. French *cuisse* 'thigh' < Latin *coxa* 'hip' (Spanish *cojo* 'lame, crippled' is thought also to be from Latin *coxa* 'hip').
11. Spanish *cadera* 'hip' < Latin *cathedra* (from Greek) 'seat'.
12. Spanish *ciruela* 'plum' < Latin *prūna cēreola* 'waxy plum' (*prūna* 'plum' + *cēreola* 'of wax').
13. French *viande* 'meat' formerly meant 'food' in general. (This change parallels English *meat* which originally meant 'food'.)
14. Spanish *depender* 'to depend' < Latin *dēpendere* 'to hang'.
15. English *lousy* 'worthless, bad' < 'infested with lice'.

10

Morphological Change

10.1 Introduction

How and why do morphemes change? How do new morphemes emerge and old ones get lost? This chapter is about answering those questions, about morphological change. There is no generally accepted view of how morphological change should be talked about. Many textbooks do not have chapters dedicated directly to the topic at all, and in a good number of others what is labelled morphological change is in fact mostly limited to just analogy (see Chapter 4). It is easy to understand, however, why this might be the case, since changes that affect morphology also can involve sound change, analogy, grammaticalization, syntactic change, and lexical change – indeed, many aspects of morphological change have already been seen in previous chapters. For that reason, some of what is presented here will cover familiar ground, but will also review the kinds of changes that affect morphology in a different light, which may help to clarify some already familiar concepts and reinforce others. Some of the other topics involving morphological change treated in this chapter are not discussed in other chapters of this book.

To state the obvious, morphological change involves change in morphemes. 'Morpheme', from Greek *morphe* 'form, shape', has to do with the shape of words, or more precisely, with the form of words and their meaningful elements. A morpheme, as students of linguistics know, is the smallest unit of meaning, and can involve roots or stems and affixes, the meaningful pieces of words. So for example, English *hunters* is composed of three morphemes, *hunt*, the root, + *-er* 'agent' (who does the action), a derivational suffix, + *-s* 'plural', an 'inflectional' suffix. Roots, derivation, and inflection have different properties of their own and some scholars believe that each of them may be subject to different kinds of change.

In this chapter, some of the topics often judged to be involved in morphological change are examined. (See also Chapter 4.)

10.2   Change in Allomorphs

An *allomorph* is one of the forms (phonological shapes) that a morpheme can have. Differences among allomorphs of a single morpheme are typically conditioned by phonological or grammatical context, though, also, morphemes may have just a single allomorph, one invariant form. Change in an allomorph of a morpheme typically involves change in the contexts (environments) in which the allomorph occurs, but can also affect the form of the allomorph itself.

A common kind of change involving allomorphy is the creation of *new allomorphs* of a morpheme when a conditioned sound change takes place. For example, Nahuatl (a Uto-Aztecan language of Mexico) has three phonologically conditioned allomorphs of the 'absolutive' morpheme, a suffix attached to noun roots when they bear no other bound morphology (their 'absolute' state): *-li* following *l*, *-tli* following other consonants (not *l*), and *-tl* following vowels. Historically, these three come from a single invariant form, *-tli*, which underwent sound changes which produced the later allomorphs: *tl* became *l* before another *l* (*tl > l / __ l*), giving the allomorph *-li* as in *či:l-li < či:l-tli* 'chilli pepper'. The final vowel of the suffix was lost when the suffix was attached to a root ending in a vowel (V > Ø /V+C__#; note that *tl* is a single consonant), resulting in *-tl*, as in *toma-tl < toma-tli* 'tomato'). The *-tli* occurred after other consonants, where there was no change in its original form, as in *sen-tli* 'maize'. These sound changes produced three allomorphs where formerly there was only one.

A commonly cited example from English is the allomorphs of the 'past tense' morpheme (also the 'past participle', phonologically identical for many verbs, not all), where earlier unstressed vowels were lost in a context which resulted in *-ed* ending up as a single consonant next to the final consonant of the root to which it was attached (except roots ending in *t* and *d*, where the vowel was not lost), and then this *d* changed to agree in voicing with the preceding consonant, resulting in phonologically conditioned allomorphs, /-d/ after voiced consonants, as in /bɛg-d/ *begged*, but /-t/ after voiceless consonants, as in /beik-t/ *baked*. The sound change that assimilated these sounds to the voicing of the preceding consonant resulted in multiple allomorphs of the 'past tense' morpheme (also of the 'past participle'), *-d* and *-t* (and *-ed,* with a vowel, after *t* and *d*, as in /nid-əd/ *needed*).

As is readily apparent, it is possible to talk about allomorphic change in examples such as these, but in fact the morphology itself did nothing on its own. Rather, morphemes simply ended up with new variant forms (additional allomorphs) as an automatic consequence of the sound changes which changed the shapes of these morphemes because they happened to be found in contexts to which the sound changes applied.

Another kind of change in allomorphy is the *loss of allomorphs*, which can result both from sound change and from analogical change. Analogical levelling (Chapter 4) very often has as its result the loss of allomorphs, as, for example, when the different allomorphs of the strong verb *strive : strove : striven* /straiv/ : /strouv/ : /strɪv-/ are levelled in the speech of many speakers to one allomorph, / straiv/, to the *strive : strived : strived* pattern of weak verbs, like *arrive : arrived : arrived*.

Also, a sound change can sometimes modify the phonological shape of an allomorph so that it ceases to be distinct from other allomorphs, causing that allomorph to be lost. For example, standard Estonian underwent a sound change in which the front vowels *ü* [y], *ö* [ø], and *ä* ([æ]) in non-initial syllables shifted to the corresponding back vowels *u, o,* and *a,* respectively. This resulted in the loss of the earlier vowel harmony rule that vowels in words must all be combinations of only front vowels or combinations of only back vowels, but not a mixture of some front and some back vowels in the same word (though /i/ and /e/ were neutral and could appear in words with either front or back vowels). Before this change, many bound morphemes had two allomorphs, one with front vowels when attached to forms containing non-neutral front vowels, and another with back vowels when attached to forms which had back vowels in the preceding syllable. After the sound change (which resulted in loss of the vowel harmony rule), the allomorphs of these morphemes with front vowels were simply lost, as seen in the following examples:

-*ja* < -*ja* / -*jä* 'agent, one who performs the action' (like -*er* in English): *tuli-ja* 'one who comes', but *pesi-ja* < *pesi-jä* 'washer', *tegi-ja* < *tegi-jä* 'maker, doer'

-*kas* < -*kas* / -*käs* 'having in abundance' (somewhat like -*ful* of English *cheerful, colourful*): *edu-kas* 'successful' (*edu* 'success, advantage'), but *tüli-kas* 'bothersome, inconvenient' < *tüli-käs* (compare *tüli* 'bother')

-*nud* < -*nud* / -*nüd* 'past active participle': *luge-nud* 'read [have read]', but *vii-nud* 'taken' < *vii-nüd.*

-*ta* < -*ta* / -*tä* 'infinitive' (one of several infinitive forms): *vasta-ta* 'to answer', but *hüpa-ta* 'to jump'< *hüpä-tä*

-*ta* < -*ta* / -*tä* 'causative': *kooli-ta-* 'to school, educate' (*kooli-* 'school' + -*ta* 'causative'), but *käi-ta-* 'to use, keep in use' < *käi-tä-* (*käi-* 'go, run, work, function' + -*tä-* 'causative)

-*tar* < -*tar* / -*tär* 'female' (like English -*ess* of *countess, lioness*): *tantsi-ja-tar* 'woman dancer' (*tantsi-* 'dance'+ -*ja* 'agent' + *tar* 'female'), but *näitle-ja-tar* 'female actor, actress' < *näitle-jä-tär* (*näitle-* 'perform, show' + -*ja* 'agent' + *tar* 'female').

In these cases of loss of allomorphs, again, the morphology does nothing in and of itself, but rather is the victim (or beneficiary, depending on one's point of view) of analogy in the former case and of sound change in the latter.

Sometimes allomorphs are 'lost' when former allomorphs are no longer recognized as allomorphs of a particular morpheme but instead become identified with separate independent morphemes, as in cases where a paradigm splits into separate words. For example, originally *mead* and *meadow* were not separate words, but rather involved different allomorphs of a single morpheme. *Mead* (in the sense of 'meadow', now archaic) is from Old English *mǣd* 'meadow' (Middle English *mede*); *meadow* is from Old English *mǣdwe,* a member of the paradigm of *mǣd* 'meadow', the allomorph that occurred when the root was inflected for non-nominative case forms; this became Middle English *medwe,* the oblique (that is, non-nominative) case of *mede.* The vowel of the first syllable of *mede* was long. However, that vowel was shortened in *medwe* because of the Middle English sound change which shortened vowels before two consonants, /dw/ here. Later *medwe* became *medowe*. Subsequently, the two forms split into separate words, giving the *mead* and *meadow* of Modern English. The case of *shade* and *shadow* is the same, perhaps even clearer. *Shade* is from Old English *sceadu* 'shade, shadow, darkness, shady place, protection from glare or heat', which became Middle English *schade*, with a long first vowel in the open syllable. *Shadow* is from Old English *sceadwe*, Middle English *schadwe*, with the vowel shortened before the two consonants, /dw/, then later it became *schadewe*, and then *shadowe*, the oblique case of *schade*. In both *mead* and *shade*, the vowels were raised in the Great Vowel Shift, which affected long vowels, but not the short vowels of *meadow* and *shadow*. The phonological distance between *mead* and *meadow*, and between *shade* and *shadow*, facilitated their split from a single paradigm into separate words, with different meanings of their own, resulting in loss of allomorphy. This sort of splitting of allomorphs in paradigms into distinct lexical roots is not common, however.

10.3   Boundary Changes

Morphological change can involve morpheme boundaries, and the boundaries between morphemes can change in several ways.

(1) *Boundary loss.* A morpheme boundary can simply be lost. Sometimes forms that were formerly composed of multiple morphemes change so that the boundary separating morphemes disappears. For example, in Pipil (a Uto-Aztecan language of El Salvador) the boundary separating the former *ta-* 'indefinite object' prefix from the verb root has been lost in some words, leaving *ta* a frozen part of the root. An example is *ni-k-takwi:ka* [I-it-sing] 'I sing it', originally *ni-ta-kwi:ka* [I-Indefinite.Object-Sing.] 'I sing something', contrasted with *ni-k-kwi:ka* '[I-3rd.Pers.Definite.Object-Sing.] 'I sing it' (compare *ni-ta-čiwa* 'I make something' with *ni-k-čiwa* 'I make it'). Now *ta* of *takwi:ka* 'sing' is just part of the root, frozen, though formerly a separate morpheme. A case in English is that of the loss of the former morpheme boundary for the morpheme *a-* 'on', as in *acknowledge*, historically connected with Old English *oncnawan* 'to understand', composed of *on-* 'on' + *cnawan* 'to recognize', where the former morpheme boundary with *a-* is simply lost in Modern English and the *a* is now just a frozen part of the root. A few other examples with the former morpheme *a-* 'on' include *abroad, alive, aloud, around, athwart, aware,* and *away*.

(2) *Morpheme boundary shift.* Sometimes the position of a morpheme boundary can shift within forms. The most commonly cited examples of this involve metanalysis (seen in Chapter 4), as for example when forms which earlier were equivalent to *a nadder, a napron, a nuncle* became *an adder, an apron, an uncle*, respectively, and *an ewte, an ekename* became *a newt* and *a nickname*, respectively. These examples involve reanalysis of the morpheme boundary, in the first set of examples reassigning the *-n* of the article *an* as the initial consonant of the root which formerly began in a vowel, and in the second set of examples reassigning the initial *n-* of these noun roots to the article *a*, leaving these noun

roots as vowel-initial after the change. *Back formation*, another kind of analogy (again, seen in Chapter 4), also results in shifts in morpheme boundaries, as in the well-known examples of *pea* and *cherry*, formerly *pise* and *cerise*, singular forms, which were reanalyzed under the assumption that they contained a plural 's', creating a different boundary, the equivalent of *peas* > *pea-s* and *cherris* > *cherri-es*, leaving *pea* and *cherry* as the singular forms of these morphemes.

Changes by *folk etymology*, another kind of analogy (Chapter 4), can also result in morpheme boundary shifts, as for example in the change from Old English *handġeweorc* to modern *handywork*, shifting the original morpheme boundary of *hand* 'hand'+ *ġe-weorc* 'work' to *hand-y* + *work*, after *ġe* > *y* (IPA *j*) or *i* in Middle English.

(3) *New boundary creation*. New morpheme boundary creation is not especially common, but in cases of folk etymology, sometimes morpheme boundaries are inserted that formerly were not there. In fact the examples of back formation that created singular *pea* and *cherry* (above) could be seen as inserting a new morpheme boundary in the former singular *peas* (or actually *pise*) and *cherris*, that is, for example, *peas* > *pea-s*. An example of new morpheme boundary insertion in folk etymology is *hamburger*, from original *Hamburg-er* 'someone or something from Hamburg', where the folk etymological association with 'ham' resulted in a new morpheme boundary, *ham-burger*, and then with various replacements for the newly segmented *ham-* morpheme, as in *cheeseburger*, *fishburger*, and just plain *burger*.

(4) *Change in kind of boundary*. An element that was formerly a fully independent word can become a clitic or an affix. Clitics can also become fully bound affixes, and can sometimes go on to end up as an unanalyzable part of a word. Among various sorts of examples, it is not uncommon for a postposition to become a case suffix. For example, the Estonian comitative case was in its earlier history a postposition, **kansak* 'with', as in **poja-n kansak* [boy-Genitive.Sg. with] 'with the boy', originally as in closely related Finnish *poja-n kanssa* [boy-Genitive.Sg. with] 'with the boy'. This changed to the modern Estonian comitative case suffix, *poja-ga* [boy-Comitative] 'with the boy' (orthographic *g* is [k]). The postposition **kansak* lost its status as an independent word and became a case suffix (also in some Finnish dialects). (See Oinas 1961: 12–23; see Chapter 11.)

The cases generally involve change from a stronger boundary towards a weaker kind of boundary (as expected in grammaticalization changes, for example; see Chapter 11). Change in the opposite direction, from a weaker to a stronger boundary, is less common, though examples exist. English *teen* 'teenager' resulted in the bound *-teen* in numbers between 'thirteen' and 'nineteen' being segmented and becoming an independent word. *Ex*, as in *ex-husband* or *ex-girlfriend*, originally had no independent status and was a bound morpheme, part of a larger word. In Northern Saami, a former case suffix became an independent word: *-taga* 'abessive case', meaning 'without', still a suffix in related languages, has become a clitic, and in Enontekiö Saami it has become both a postposition and an independent adverb, for example *mun báhcen taga* [I go without] 'I remain without', that is, it underwent the changes *case affix* > *clitic* > *postposition* > *independent adverb* (Nevis 1985). In Estonian, a former bound clitic *-pa* / *-pä* 'emphatic' changed to independent free-standing *ep* 'indeed, just so' (Campbell 1991).

Examples such as these go against the assumption of unidirectionality of grammaticalization (see Chapter 11), and so are matters of much discussion in the grammaticalization literature. They are not frequent, but their existence is undeniable.

10.4   Change in Morpheme Order

Another kind of morphological change affects the order of bound morphemes. Morphemes can shift from one position to another within words under certain conditions. An example involves what was originally the verb *nemi* 'to live, to walk (around)' in varieties of Nahuatl (Uto-Aztecan). In Tetelcingo, Michoacán, and North Puebla varieties, *nemi* became attached to the verb stem, becoming the 'ambulative' morpheme, meaning 'to go around doing, to go about doing, to be currently or habitually engaged in doing', as illustrated by North Puebla Nahuatl in (1):

(1)   čoka-ti-*nemi*
      cry-Connective-*Ambulative*
      'he/she goes about crying'

Huasteca Nahuatl developed further, reanalysing *-nemi* as a 'habitual' morpheme and shifting it to the position before the verb root, a morphological slot occupied by directionals which include morphemes meaning 'towards', 'away from', etc., as in (2):

(2)   ki-*nen*-palewiya
      3rd.Pers.Object-*Habitual*-help
      'he/she helps him/her continually'

(Note that *-nen-* is a regular allomorph of *nemi* in environments when followed by morphemes beginning in a single consonant, as in, for example, *nen-ki* 'he/she lived/walked' (*nemi-ki* > *nem-ki* by vowel loss, *nen-ki* by *m* > *n* when syllable-final.)

Such a change in the order of morphemes does not happen without reason. In this case it appears that *nen-* 'habitual' (originally 'ambulative') was attracted by analogy to the slot in the verb morphology where other verbal directional morphemes occurred, as in (3):

(3)   ni-k-*on*-ita-s
      1st.Pers.Subject-3rd.Pers.Object-*Directional.away*-see-Future
      'I will see him there' ('I'll go see him')

With respect to change in morpheme order, it is good to keep in mind, also, that related languages can come to have morphological categories whose positions do not match in the different languages. For example, in some Uralic languages the order among suffixes on nouns does not correspond directly to their order in other languages of the family. Some have *case* + *possessive* order where others have *possessive* + *case*, as seen in the comparison of Finnish *kodi-ssa-ni* [home-in-my] with Hungarian *ház-am-ban* [house-my-in], both meaning 'in my house'. The reason for this difference is that these languages underwent different changes in their independent histories. In Hungarian, some former postpositions changed into case suffixes later on (as did *-ban* 'in' in this example), and came to be attached at the end of nouns which could bear possessive suffixes that were already there, whereas in Finnish, possessive markers (such as *-ni* 'my' in this example) came to be attached to nouns later in the history of the language, so that if a noun already bore a case suffix, the possessive marker was attached after the case morpheme. The different order of suffixes in these two related languages corresponds to the different temporal order in which the languages underwent grammaticalizations (see Chapter 11) that created new suffixes that came to be attached to the end of nouns, with their earlier suffixes already attached closer to the noun stem. This is important, since the order of bound morphemes in different languages has sometimes been misunderstood and claimed to be evidence of distant genetic connections (see Chapter 14) when in fact the orders can have different explanations.

10.5 Morphological Levelling

Morphological change often involves the attraction or influence of one form or group of forms over another, that is, analogy (see Chapter 4). Morphological levelling, a very common sort of morphological change, is just analogical levelling that affects morphologically related forms. For example, in inflectional paradigms, many examples of strong verbs have been levelled by analogy, attracted to the pattern of the weak verbs, as in the change of *help* : *holp* : *holpen* to *help* : *helped* : *helped*. How analogical levelling can result in the loss of allomorphs has already been seen above. Analogical levelling can also result in loss of entire morphological categories (see below).

10.6 Morphological Loss

We have seen how analogical levelling can result in the loss of allomorphs and in the loss of whole morphemes. There are also other ways in which morphological categories can be lost. Whole morphemes, morphological categories in a language, can be lost as a result of regular sound change. For example, Old High German and Middle High German marked partially affected objects with the genitive case, as in (4):

(4) ich   will   im   mîn-es   brôt-es   geben
     I   want   to.him   my-Genitive   bread- Genitive   to.give
     'I want to give him some of my bread'
     (From Hartmann von Aue, cited by Ebert 1978: 52)

In Middle High German, this partitive construction began to fade and was lost due to a phonological merger which had the effect of eliminating the contrast between former *-es* 'genitive singular' and *-ez* 'nominative/accusative' of neuter adjectives, and as a result the old *-es* 'genitive' was reanalyzed as 'accusative' in this construction, with the result that the partitive construction was lost from the language (Ebert 1978: 51–2).

In another example, English used to have a contrast between present participles (as in *writing*) and gerunds (verbal nouns, for example *the writing*), seen in Old English *wrīt-ende* 'writing' (present participle) and *wrīt-ing* 'writing' (gerund). Earlier, the gerund ending was *-ung*, seen in Old English *leorn-ung* 'learning', equivalent to the *-ung* of modern German, as in *Lernung* 'learning' (*Lern* 'learn, study' + *-ung* 'Gerund'). There was a period of much variation in the history of English, with *-ende* in the Midlands, *-inde* in the south, and *-and* in the north. In Middle English, the present participle *-ende/-inde* came to vary with *-ing(e)*, presumably under analogical influence from the gerund *-ing*, and by 1450 had changed to *-ing*, eliminating the formal difference between present participle and gerund, resulting in the loss of the formal (phonological) distinction between the two categories (Lass 1992: 144–6).

10.7   Suppletion

Suppletion is the convergence of what were in origin two or more different lexical items so that the two or more originally unconnected roots (or stems) come to be used in the inflectional paradigm of a single lexical item. An example is *go/went*. Originally *went* had nothing to do with the past tense of *go*, but rather was the past tense of the verb *wend*, which was taken over as the past of 'to go' and incorporated into its inflectional paradigm. This is the most common inter-pretation of suppletion, though irregular forms that have other sorts of origins are also sometimes talked about as suppletion. For example, sometimes forms which originally come from a single source are left seeming to be irregular or unrecognizable due to phonological or analogical change. An example is English *was/were*, forms which today are irregular but come from a single Old English lexical item, *wæs/wæron*, where the *r* of the plural came about through rhotacism (*s* to *r* between vowels), and is not due to the convergence of separate lexical roots. Analogical extension can make new irregularities of the *dive/dove* sort, on analogy with the pattern in strong verbs such as *drive/drove*, from the former single verb root *dive/dived*, still the standard form for many speakers. Another popular example is *snuck* (replacing former regular *sneaked*), which appears to have become the past tense of *sneak* for a good number of English speakers, apparently extending the past tense form by analogy based on similarities with verbs such as *strike/struck* and *stick/stuck*. Though these examples do not involve suppletion in the sense of formerly independent lexical items coming to be used in the inflectional paradigm of a single lexical item, sometimes, nevertheless, they are also called suppletive.

Here, the focus is on suppletion of the first, more standard sort. The other kinds of cases sometimes called suppletion, such as *was/were* or *dive/dove*, have their explanations in sound change (Chapter 2) and analogy (Chapter 4). Suppletion can be characterized as involving complete replacement of one lexical form by another in a set of paradigmatically related forms, an extreme form of stem modification. Suppletion involves the lexicon, semantics, and grammar. Suppletive forms are not frequent in most languages, but when they do occur they often involve quite frequent words in the language, as in the case of *go/went* and *be/am/is/are/was* in English. The suppletive nature of these verbs is highlighted when compared to the paradigmatically related forms of regular verbs, as *bake* in (5):

(5) *bake*   *go*   *be*

    I bake   I go   I am

    we bake   we go   we are

    she bakes   she goes   she is

    he baked   he went   he was

    they baked   they went   they were

    have baked   have gone   have been

Some examples of suppletion in some other languages are:

Finnish: *hyvä* 'good' / *parempi* 'better' / *paras* 'best'

French: *avoir* 'to have' / *eu* 'had' (past participle)

German: *gut* 'good' / *besser* 'better' / *best* 'best'

Spanish: *ir* 'to go' / *va* '(he/she/it) goes' / *fue* '(he/she/it) went'

Nivaclé: (Matacoan language, Argentina and Paraguay) verb root /-ɑk/ 'to go' (as in *x-ak* 'I go') / *y-ič* [he/she/it-go] 'he goes' / *ma* 'you don't go' / *meʔ-* 'go!'; verb root /-ʔaw/ 'be, live' (as in *xa-ʔaw* [I-am] 'I am, I live (here)' / *y-iʔeʔ* [he/she is] 'she is, she lives (here)'.

Not just any two lexical items can converge to create a single one involving suppletion. To explain suppletive changes, it would be necessary to be able to answer the question: what might cause two (or more) lexical items to converge? Answers that have been offered include frequency, semantic factors, and phonological factors, where the relationship of the two (or more) lexical elements before the change is crucial. In some cases, sheer *phonetic similarity* may be enough to bring about changes that result in suppletion, as for example in the ongoing change in Australian and New Zealand English in which *brought* is being replaced by phonetically similar *bought*, resulting in an even stranger strong-verb pattern with suppletion: *bring/bought/bought*.

It is sometimes said that when forms become too small phonetically to be perceived easily, a suppletion helps remedy the picture. For example, several of the forms of the Latin verb *ire* 'to go' that regular sound changes reduced to monosyllables in Romance languages were replaced through suppletion by polysyllabic forms derived from the Latin verb *vadere* 'to walk, rush', so for example Classical Latin forms from *ire* remained in Spanish when polysyllables were still in play:

Classical Latin	*Old Spanish*	
imus	imos	'we go'
itis	ides	'you (Pl.) go'

However, forms of *ire* were replaced with forms from *vadere* when monosyllabic forms of *ire* were involved:

Classical Latin	*Old Spanish*	
eo (became jo)	vo (modern Spanish voy) < vado	'I go'
is	vas < vadis	'you (Pl.) go'
it	va < vadit	'he/she goes'
eunt (became junt)	van < vadunt	'they go'

This is an interesting hypothesis, though it would be difficult to demonstrate conclusively that this assumed motivation for the change comes from the perceptual difficulty because of the small phonological size of the words, compensated for by the recruitment of polysyllabic forms from a semantically similar verb. (See Börjars and Vincent 2011.)

As for other suggested explanations, it has been thought that *frequency* might be a factor determining which forms are recruited to replace others in a paradigm, presumably with forms from less frequent lexical items being imported to the paradigms of more frequent ones that are semantically similar, as in *went* from less frequent *wend* being taken over as the past tense of *go*. This does not, however, offer much to help to explain why a form of *go* would be replaced at all. *Semantic scope* has also been mentioned as a possible factor, involving the difference in generality between the meanings of the forms involved, where, for example, *ire* 'to go' has a broader, more general meaning than narrower *vadere* 'to walk, rush', allowing the *ire* paradigm with its broader sense to import forms from *vadere*, more narrow in its meaning, but not permitting the paradigm of *vadere* to take over forms from semantically broader *ire*.

Finally, suppletion of this sort involves *semantic loss*, where forms of one lexical item lose their original meaning as they are substituted into the paradigm of another lexical item, whose broader meaning wins out in the change, where now *went* no longer has anything to do with *wend* and is just the past tense form of 'to go'.

10.8   Morphological Change and Grammaticalization

Many cases of grammaticalization involve morphological change, where a former lexical item becomes a bound grammatical morpheme (see Chapter 11 for examples and discussion). Examples of this have been seen already in the change in Estonian of the postposition **kansak* 'with' to the bound comitative case suffix /-ka/ (orthographic *-ga*), and in varieties of Nahuatl where the independent verb *nemi* 'to live, to walk (around)' became attached to other verbs as the 'ambulative' morpheme, meaning 'to go around doing, to go about doing, to be currently or habitually engaged in doing'; the process is seen in the change in Romance languages where the independent auxiliary 'to have' became bound to infinitive forms to become the new 'future', as in Spanish *cantaré* 'I will sing' < *cantar +* *hé* [to.sing + I.have].

Grammaticalizations also often involve cases of the change in boundary status, from a former word boundary to a clitic boundary or to a bound morpheme boundary. Indeed, some enthusiasts for grammaticalization believe that essentially all bound morphemes formerly derive from independent lexical sources. Of course some bound morphemes have other origins, as seen in the development of the new *-s(i)* 'past tense' morpheme in Estonian, Votic, Livonian, and some Finnish dialects. This new morpheme came from *-t*, a part of root of many verbs, + *-i* the former 'past tense' morpheme, where a sound change in these languages turned *t* into *s* before *i* ($t > s$ /__i), resulting in allomorphic variation when the root appeared before the old *-i* 'past tense', as in Finnish *palas-i* 'returned' (< *palat-i*; compare *palata* 'to return') and *kielsi* 'forbad' (< *kielt-i*; compare the root *kieltä-* 'forbid'). By analogy with those verbs with *t* in the root which legitimately became *s* before the past tense marker *i*, the past tense in general was reanalyzed as *-si*, and this was extended to verbs which originally had no *t* in the root, as in examples from Finnish dialects: *astu-s(i)* 'stepped', *istu-s(i)* 'sat'; compare Standard Finnish *astu-i, istu-i* (Ravila 1975: 86, Laalo 1988: 5, 47–9). In some of these languages, final *i* of polysyllabic forms was lost, motivating the reanalysis. For example, when *palas-i* 'returned' became *palas*, losing the final *i* that originally signalled the 'past tense', it was easy for speakers to assume that the *s* of *palas* must mark 'past tense', as it contrasted with the root with *t* as in *palata* 'to return', and this reanalyzed *s* 'past tense' was extended to other verbs which formerly had no *t* or *s* at all in the root, compensating for the lost past tense (*-i*) which was deleted by the sound change that eliminated final vowels from these forms. However, the new *-s(i)* 'past tense' has no prior history as a lexical item that became grammaticalized, as expected by those who believe that the origin of all bound morphemes is due to the grammaticalization of former lexical items.

Examples of grammatical affixes (and bound clitics) that come from former independent lexical items by grammaticalization abound, as in the cases mentioned above of the development of the comitative case in Estonian from an independent postposition, the future tense marker in Romance language from a former auxiliary verb, and the 'ambulative' and 'habitual' grammatical morphemes in varieties of Nahuatl from a former verb meaning 'to live, walk around'. Some additional examples which illustrate this are:

(6) French *-ment* 'adverb' (like English *-ly*), as in *absolument* 'absolutely' < Latin *absoluta mente* 'in absolute mind', from the ablative of *mens* 'mind'

(7) Swedish *-s* 'passive, impersonal' < *sig* '3rd person accusative reflexive pronoun' (see Old Norse *sik*), originally like English *self*, as in *hoppa-s* 'it is hoped, one hopes', and *dörren öppna-s* 'the door opens'.

10.9 Change from One Kind of Morpheme to Another

Now that we have seen examples of various kinds of changes that can affect morphemes, we can turn to the question of whether morphemes of one kind can change into morphemes of another kind. The simple answer is 'yes'; in practice any kind of morpheme can change into any other kind of morpheme, though some of these kinds of changes are commonplace while others are rare. We take up each of the possibilities in turn.

10.9.1 Free and Bound Morphemes

(1) *Free > bound*. Free (independent) morphemes often lose their independence and become bound. Many examples of grammaticalization are of this sort (see Chapter 11). Several examples seen earlier in this chapter or elsewhere in this book illustrate this.

1. The change of the free-standing word *nemi* 'to live, to walk (around)' in varieties of Nahuatl (Uto-Aztecan) to a bound suffix meaning 'ambulative' or 'habitual' in varieties of Nahuatl (illustrated above in (1) and (2)).

2. (repeated from (6) above) French *-ment* 'adverb', as in *absolument* 'absolutely' and Spanish *abolutamente* < Latin *absoluta mente* 'in absolute mind', from the ablative of *mens* 'mind'.

3. (mentioned above) Estonian comitative case *-ga* (/-ka/) < **kansak* 'with', formerly a postposition, as in *poja-ga* [boy-Comitative] 'with the boy' < **pojan kansak*.

Changes of this sort are sometimes called *univerbation*, the change in which a single word is produced from a construction or expression that originally contained multiple words.

(2) *Bound > free*. Cases of a bound morpheme becoming a free-standing independent word are rare and go against the expected direction of grammaticalization from lexical > grammatical and not grammatical > lexical. Nevertheless, a number of cases are known.

1. In Irish, the first person plural suffix *-mid/-muid* was freed from being restricted as a bound suffix and became an independent pronoun, replacing the original independent first person plural pronoun *sinn* (Bybee et al. 1994: 19–20).

2. (mentioned above) In Enontekiö Saami, the inherited *-taga* 'abessive case suffix' ('without') (still a suffix in sister languages) become a completely unbound postposition and an independent adverb, for example *mun báhcen taga* [I go without] 'I remain without', that is, it underwent the changes *case affix > clitic > postposition > independent adverb* (Nevis 1985).

3. (mentioned above) In Estonian, former *-pa/-pä* 'emphatic' (bound) > *ep* 'emphatic' (free). Estonian now has an independent adverb *ep* 'yes, indeed, just so, then', from the bound form *-p, -pa, -pä*, as in *seep* 'that is it indeed' > *see ep*, *pealle-p* 'on top of indeed' > *peall ep*; later this word *ep* could change its position in the sentence to precede, *ep see, ep peall* (Campbell 1991).

(See Chapter 11.)

10.9.2 Roots, Affixes, and Clitics

(1) *Root > affix*. Several examples of this sort of change have already been seen in the changes of free > bound, above. Such changes are very common in grammaticalization (see Chapter 11).

(2) *Affix > root*. Some well-known examples (mentioned above) are *ex* (from *ex-*, as in *ex-wife, ex-boyfriend*); *ism(s)* (from *-ism*, as in *racism, sexism*); and *teen* (from the numbers *thirteen* to *nineteen*). Examples illustrating this kind of change were also seen in the changes above of bound > free.

(3) *Affix > clitic*. Clitics are essentially halfway between bound affixes and free words. A clitic is a morpheme that functions at the phrase level with syntactic characteristics like a word, but is pronounced like an affix, depending phonologically on another word or phrase. Affixes are usually limited in their distribution, attached to specific word classes (parts of speech), whereas clitics are often able to attach phonologically to words of several different classes (parts

of speech). For example, the *-s* 'plural' affix in English attaches essentially only to nouns (*dragons, ogres, trolls, unicorns*); however, the possessive *-'s* is a clitic which attaches to whole phrases and can have different parts of speech as its phonological host (for example, *the king's, the king of Middle-earth's fortress, the king of Middle-earth who lost his fortress's knights*). This morpheme was originally a more tightly bound genitive case suffix which became a clitic. As Otto Jespersen (1894: 317–18) explained long ago:

> In modern English . . . (compared to Old English) the *-s* is much more independent: it can be separated from its main word by an adverb such as *else* (as in *somebody else's hat*), by a prepositional clause such as *of England* (as in *the queen of England's power*), or even by a relative clause such as *I saw yesterday* (as in *the man I saw yesterday's car*) . . . the English genitive is in fact no longer a flexional form . . . a development – not, indeed, from an originally self-existent word to a mere flexional ending, but the exactly opposite development of what was *an inseparable part of a complicated flexional system to greater and greater emancipation and independence.* (Jespersen's emphasis.)

Middle Swedish *-s* 'genitive' affix also became a phrasal clitic in Modern Swedish, parallel to the English genitive *-'s*.

Examples such as these also go against the usual directionality of grammaticalization (see Chapter 11).

10.9.3   Derivational and Inflectional Morphemes

(1) *Derivational > derivational.* English *-ly* of adverbs (as in *underhandedly*) started life as an independent noun, Old English *lic* 'body, form', which entered into compounds from which an adjectival function developed – Old English *cildlic* corresponding structurally to Modern English *childlike*. With the addition of *-e*, these adjectives functioned as adverbs, *cildlice*, though later the *-e* was lost, and the remaining *-ly* (as in adjectives *manly, kingly, slovenly*) also assumed an adverbial function, as for example in *bravely, royally, cleanly, rapidly*, giving the change of derivational *-ly* 'adjective' to *derivational -ly* 'adverb'. This kind of change is reasonably common.

(2) *Inflectional > inflectional.* Examples of this kind of change are not uncommon.

The partitive case in Finnish, which signals objects only partially affected, developed from an earlier ablative case, meaning 'from'. Since both cases are inflectional, this is an instance of change of inflectional > inflectional. This change is clear from the comparative evidence in Finnish's sister languages, though the change is also seen in Finnish in relics of the partitive case in its former 'ablative' function. The 'separation' cases *-sta/-stä* 'from within' (elative) and *-lta / -ltä* 'from without' (ablative) come from locatives **-s* and **-l* + the old ablative **-ta / *-tä*. Relics of the partitive in its old ablative function are seen in some combinations of adjectives or demonstratives which in general must agree in case and number with the nouns they modify, exemplified here by nouns that bear the newer separation cases (note that **t* was lost invervocalically after a short unstressed vowel, giving allomorphs *-ta, -a, -tä, -ä* of the 'partitive'), as in the examples in (8):

(8a)   sii-*tä* talo-*sta* [it-From (= Partitive)] house-From (= Elative)] 'from that house'

(8b)   talo-n taka-*a* [house-Genitive back-From (= Partitive)] 'from behind the house'

(8c)   isä-n luo-*ta* [father-Genitive presence-From (= Partitive)] 'from father's presence, away from father'

Relics of the partitive in its old ablative function are also seen in some frozen sayings, and in (9) and (10):

(9)   mies   on   suur-*ta*   suku-*a*
        man   is   big-Partitive   family-Partitive
        'the man is from an important family'

(10)   kärsiä   nälkä-*ä*
        to.suffer   hunger-Partitive
        'to suffer from hunger'

(Hakulinen 1968: 437, Laanest 1982: 299)

Another example is the development of the essive case in Finnish from an earlier locative. The locative was **-na/*-nä*, seen in such frozen forms as *koto-na* 'at home', *sii-nä* 'in it', *taka-na* 'behind it', *ulko-na* 'outside'. It took on the 'essive' function, giving, for example, *lapse-na* [child-Essive] 'as a child', *miehe-nä* [man-Essive] 'as a man'.

(3) *Derivational > inflectional*. Examples of morphemes changing from being derivational to being inflectional are not unusual, though also not frequent. To mention one example, in Proto-Yuman, verbal plurality was a derivational category; its use was optional, and it was limited to certain lexical items. In most of the Pai languages (a subgroup of Yuman), use of plural verbs became more regular, becoming an inflectional category where plurality is obligatorily marked on verbs when semantically appropriate. Langdon (1992) presents evidence that the Proto-Yuman category of verb plurality was derivational and not obligatory. There were a large number of different ways to modify verb stems to show plurality, and it was impossible to predict which verbs require which plural marking, so that plural stems had to be listed in the dictionary. In the Pai languages, verb plurality became grammatically required, that is, inflectional, also relying mostly on the suffixation of *-č*, rather than the former seven unpredictable derivational plural forms.

(4) *Inflectional > derivational*. The inflectional category of 'present active participle' in Classical Latin was based on the verb present tense stem + *-ns* 'nominative' (from *-nt-s*), *-nte-m* 'accusative'), as in *cane-m curre-nte-m* [dog-Accusative run-Present.Active.Participle-Accusative] 'the running dog, the dog that is running'. In Spanish, the reflexes of this morpheme are no longer inflectional but have shifted to being a derivational suffix which derives adjectives or nouns, as in *corriente* 'current, ordinary, running' (< Classical Latin *currens/currentem* 'running'); *amante* 'lover' (cf. *amar* 'to love', from Latin *amans/amantem* 'loving'); *chocante* 'shocking' (cf. *chocar* 'to collide, to shock'); *hablante* 'speaker' (cf. *hablar*

'to speak'). As a derivational suffix today, it is much less productive in modern Spanish than it was in Classical Latin as an inflexional suffix.

Changes of this sort go against the grammaticalization expectation that changes should go from less grammatical (more lexical) to more grammatical, and not the other direction. Derivational morphology is usually considered less tightly integrated into the fabric of a grammar than inflectional morphology, so a change from inflectional to derivational morphology is from more grammar-like to less grammar-like.

10.10 Exaptation

Exaptation in linguistics refers to cases where phonological material takes on a new function, unrelated to its original or obsolete function in the language. Gould and Vrba (1982) coined the term 'exaptation' in biological evolution to refer to the co-opting for new functions of structures originally developed for other purposes, for example the co-opting in the evolution of vertebrates of respiratory and digestive structures for sound production. Roger Lass, who adopted the term for linguistics, characterizes it as the opportunistic renovation of material that was already there but served some other purpose or served no purpose at all, so that both structures in use and 'junk of various kinds' can be exapted for other purposes (Lass 1997: 316–24). For example, Lass presents as a case in point the changes in *you* versus *thou*. When the number opposition was marginalized (originally *thou* 'singular' versus *you* 'plural'), the then mostly useless opposition was exapted so that *thou* found new uses when it took on senses of affectation and contempt, more common in earlier times; for example, when in 1603 at the trial of Sir Walter Raleigh, Sir Edward Coke, prosecuting for the crown, insulted Raleigh, saying, 'thou viper, for I thou thee, thou traitor'. (See also section 10.14 below.)

An often-repeated example illustrating exaptation of morphological material involves an Indo-European suffix for forming present tense, sometimes with iterative value (but no inchoative meaning), *-sk̑-, which was exapted as an inchoative in Latin. It acquired the inchoative function in Latin, on the model of *crescō* 'grow', also in *senescō* 'I get old, I grow old'. This became the Latin derivational morpheme -*ēsc-/-īsc-* and later in Italian became part of the inflectional system 'to mark the singular persons and the third person plural in the present tense conjugation, in subjunctive and imperative' (Giacalone Ramat 1998: 110) – another example of derivational > inflectional. This chain of events illustrates two exaptations, one from present tense stem formation to marking inchoative from Proto-Indo-European to Latin, and the other from inchoative marking to person marking in Italian.

10.11 Morphological Conditioning

Non-phonetic properties affecting sound change are typically called *morphological conditioning* (or grammatical conditioning) of sound change. Such changes involve sounds in their morphological or grammatical contexts, but are not really about morphological change per se. (For discussion and examples, see Chapter 13.)

A sound change is said to be morphologically or grammatically conditioned when it takes place regularly except in a certain morphological context, or, in another sense, when it takes place in a particular morphological environment rather than in strictly phonologically determined contexts. A well-known example illustrating morphological conditioning in the former, more general sense is the loss of intervocalic *s* in Classical Greek except in certain 'future' and 'aorist' verb forms, where the *s* was not lost (for details, see Chapter 13). Loss of *s* by regular sound change here would have obliterated the phonological form of the 'future' morpheme, *-s-*. In the interpretation which calls on morphological conditioning, this sound change was prevented from obliterating intervocalic *s* in just those cases where the meaning distinction between 'future' and 'present' would have been lost, intervocalic *s* being morphologically conditioned, that is, not lost when the *s* in question represented the 'future' in these verbs. However, the *s* of the 'future' was freely lost with verb stems ending in a nasal or a liquid, where the future/present distinction could be signalled formally by the *e* which these future stems bear. Thus in *poié-ō* 'I do' / *poié-s-ō* 'I will do', the *s* of the 'future' was maintained, since otherwise the two would be identical and it would not be possible to distinguish the 'present' from the 'future'; however, in *mén-ō* 'I remain' / *mené-ō* [< *mene-s-ō] 'I will remain', the *s* was lost, since the 'future' could be distinguished from the 'present' based on the difference in the stems, *mén-* in 'present' / *mené-* in 'future'.

Not all scholars agree that morphologically conditioned sound changes are possible; some believe instead that such changes reflect analogy. In Greek verb roots which end in consonants (other than liquids and nasals) the *s* of the 'future' was not threatened, since it was not between vowels, for example *trép-s-ō* 'I will turn' (contrast *trép-ō* 'I turn'). In this view, forms such as *poié-s-ō* are seen as actually at one time having lost the intervocalic *s* which marked 'future' by the regular sound change, but later in time, the *s* 'future' was restored by analogy based on the *s* 'future' of consonant-final verb stems such as *trép-s-ō*, thus for 'I will do': *poié-s-ō* > *poiéō* by regular sound change, then *poiéō* > *poié-s-ō* by analogy, restoring the *s* 'future'.

In Q'eqchi' (Mayan) a sound change deleted short vowels of the final syllable of words of more than one syllable (V > Ø /VC__C#), as in:

išq	<	išoq	'woman'
winq	<	winaq	'person, man'
wark	<	warik	'sleep'
šulɓ	<	šuluɓ	'flute, whistle'

([š] = IPA [ʃ])

In certain final consonant clusters produced by this change the final consonant was lost (C > Ø /C__#), as for example in *ts'ikin* 'bird' > *ts'ikn* (by vowel loss) > *ts'ik* (by final-consonant cluster reduction), where a final nasal was lost. The vowel-loss change applied to all words except verb roots, where the vowel was retained, as in (11) to (13):

(11)   t-at-in-k'am
       Aspect-2nd.Absolutive-1st.Ergative-carry
       'I will carry you'

(12) t-at-in-muq
Aspect-2nd.Absolutive-1st.Ergative-bury
'I will bury you'

(13) t-at-w-il
Aspect-2nd.Absolutive-1st.Ergative-see
'I will take care of you'

Thus, *t-at-in-k'am* 'I will carry you' did not become ✗*t-at-in-k'm*, nor did it go on to become ✗*t-at-in-k'* by loss of the final nasal in a final consonant cluster. It is assumed that the loss of the vowel in the verb root was blocked – morphologically conditioned – because if it had been lost, it would be difficult to recognize the verb root, especially difficult if the loss of the final consonant in clusters had also taken place. (See Campbell 1996: 79–80.)

In this example, it is difficult to imagine that the language went by regular sound change to a stage where it had *t-at-in-k'* but then later by analogy restored the missing sounds of the root to bring it back to *t-at-in-k'am*, though of course it is not possible to declare definitively that this could not have been what happened. Whether sound change can be morphologically conditioned is disputed and remains an empirical question. (See Chapter 13 for more discussion and details.)

10.12 Directionality in Morphological Change

The question of whether there is directionality to morphological change has been of interest to a number of scholars, and it has been addressed in a number of ways and on different levels. While there is no simple wholesale directionality to changes in morphology, there have been claims that particular kinds of morphological change have directional tendencies. These are considered in what follows, beginning with more specific claims and then moving to more general ones.

10.12.1 Specific claims of directional morphological changes

There are some claims of directionality for changes affecting certain specific kinds of constructions; only a few examples of these kinds of changes are considered here.

(1) *Postposition > case suffix*. One example that seems to hold true is that postpositions can become case suffixes, but grammatical case suffixes very rarely become postpositions. An example was seen above in the change in Estonian of a postposition to the comitative case, where **poja-n kansak* [boy-Genitive.Sg. with] 'with the boy' changed to modern *poja-ga* [boy-Comitative] 'with the boy' (orthographic *g* is [k]). The postposition **kansak* was reduced to the comitative suffix /-ka/. Numerous such cases are attested of postpositions evolving into case suffixes in numerous languages.

(2) *Partitive < ablative*. Another example which seems to have support is that partitive morphemes typically develop from ablative or ablative-like forms (mentioned above). Thus, for example, in the history of Finnic and Baltic languages, the partitive case comes from a former ablative case. The partitive case

basically signals only partially affected objects, not fully affected ones, as in the contrast in Finnish of *Leena söi omena-a* [Leena ate apple-Partitive] 'Leena ate (some of the) apple' versus *Leena söi omena-n* [Leena ate apple-Accusative] 'Leena ate the (whole) apple'. Originally, forms meaning, for example, 'eat from the meat' or 'drink from the water' came to mean 'eat some meat' and 'drink some water'. Partitive cases or constructions with ablative-like origins are found in, as mentioned, Baltic, Finnic, older forms of some Germanic languages, and some Romance languages, to mention a few examples. Instances are not known where the direction is reversed, where a former partitive has changed to an ablative in meaning or function. (See Harris and Campbell 1995: 362–3.)

(3) *Watkin's Law*. A directional change of a different sort is Watkin's Law, the principle that 'the third person occupies the pivotal position in the historical development of a verbal paradigm' (Arlotto 1972: 156). What this means is that the form of the third person becomes the basic form of the verb paradigm or that the third person form is incorporated into the verb stem. Examples abound, as in forms in various dialects of English which have, for example, *I says*, *we goes*, *they makes, the farmers makes*, etc. (based on third person singular forms, *he/she/ it says, he/she/it makes*). The historical narrative style in colloquial English also often utilizes third person singular forms of the verbs, as in story-telling about past events when the narrator uses the historical narrative present tense with third person verbs; for example, *and then we sees'em charge the enemy, and they runs away from our boys, but our boys keeps chasing them*. For example, the third person form has taken over the verb root in changes from Avestan to Modern Persian (Farsi) and from Proto-Slavic to Polish, as in (14):

(14)	*Avestan*	*Modern Persian*	*Proto-Slavic*	*Polish*	
	ah-mi	hast-am	*es-mi	jest-em	'I am'
	ah-ti	hast-i	*es-i	jest-eś	'you are'
	as-ti	hast	*es-ti	jest	'he/she is'
(Arlotto 1972: 155)					

Why the third person forms should have this pivotal role in verb paradigms is uncertain. It has been thought that the third person form may tend to be simpler, more frequent, or in some unexplained way psychologically more salient or basic.

(4) *Directional laws of analogy*. Some of Jerzy Kuryłowicz's (1947) and Witold Mańczak's (1958) well-known laws of analogy involve explicit directionality. Several of Kuryłowicz's six laws are unclear and not particularly helpful, where the same law is sometimes interpreted in opposing ways by different scholars – and all of his laws were controversial. Law 4, the most famous, is clearly directional. It states that 'given a morphological derivation resulting in two differentiated forms, the derived form takes over the primary function and the old form is reserved from secondary function' (Collinge 1985: 249; see Winters 1995: 136 for a different translation). This law is intended to explain why, for example in the case of English *brothers/brethern*, the form *brothers*, derived by analogical change based on other forms with regular -*s* plural, takes over primary function, and the former *brethren* is relegated to more marginal,

secondary functions, mainly associated with religious contexts and fraternal orders (see details in Chapter 4).

Mańczak's nine 'tendencies' of analogy were clearer, several with very definite directionality (repeated here from Trask 1996: 114–15; see Collinge 1985: 250 and Winters 1995: 117–18 for different treatments and versions).

The *first* is: 'longer words are more often reshaped on the model of shorter words, rather than vice versa, except in inflectional paradigms'. The idea here is that a longer word such as *housewife* is based on the model of shorter words, *house* + *wife*. Thus the process which first created *hussy* from two parts of a compound has been replicated in the creation of Modern English *housewife*, conjoining *house* and *wife*, where *hussy* originally had the same origin, coming from Old English *hūswīf* 'housewife' (composed of *hūs* 'house' + *wīf* 'woman, wife'), which underwent sound changes to end up as *hussy*, now reserved for a secondary, more restrictive function/meaning, as expected from Kuryłowicz's fourth law (see Trask 1996: 114). Put more briefly, longer words tend to be made up of originally shorter words.

The *second* tendency is that 'root alternation is more often abolished than introduced'. This in effect states that analogical levelling is more likely than analogical extension, an idea held by many scholars.

Tendency *four* holds that 'zero-endings are more frequently replaced by overt ones than vice versa'. This would hold true for English, where the class of nouns with zero for plural has reduced over time, and even now there is a tendency among some to replace plural *deer, sheep, fish* with *deers, sheeps, fishes*, respectively.

Tendency *six* states that 'the forms of the indicative more often bring about the reshaping of other moods than vice versa'. It is relatively easy to find examples that illustrate this. Even in English, the traditional subjunctive verb forms are no longer very productive for many people, so that for many speakers subjunctive forms such as in *If I were a rich man, I wouldn't have to work hard* have been replaced by the indicative *If I was a rich man, I wouldn't have to work hard*.

The *seventh* tendency is: 'the forms of the present more often bring about the reshaping of other tenses than vice versa'. For example, in analogical levelling of strong verbs in English, it is the form of the present tense stem that wins out, not that of the past or past participle; so, for example, in the levelling of *strive/ strove/striven* or *cleave/clove/cloven* (or *cleft*), it is the present tense stem that wins out in *strive/strived/strived* and *cleave/cleaved/cleaved*, not the past stem ✗*strove*/✗*stroved*/✗*stroved* or the past participle stem ✗*striv*/✗*strivved*/✗*strivved*, for example.

(6) *Grammaticalization and directionality.* Numerous pathways of grammaticalization are inherently directional, involving particular lexical items as the source from which grammatical morphemes evolve (see, for example, Heine and Kuteva 2002; see also Chapter 11). For example, in a number of languages, grammatical markers of 'future' developed from independent verbs meaning 'come', 'go', or 'have', but future markers in languages do not normally change into verbs with the meaning of 'come' or 'go' or 'have'.

Grammaticalization, of course, involves directionality on a higher, more abstract level, too, where the very definition of grammaticalization implies the direction from independent lexical source to grammatical item. The claim of 'unidirectionality' in grammaticalization – *lexical > grammatical*, but not *grammatical > lexical* – is much discussed and disputed. Most changes are in this direction, lexical to grammatical, though there are some well-known exceptions (see Chapter 11 for more detail).

Givón's (1971: 413) slogan, 'today's morphology is yesterday's syntax', involves broad directionality, and grammaticalization is typically invoked when it is discussed. It means that bound grammatical morphemes tend to come from former independent words that took on grammatical functions, and many of the properties of the morphemes actually reflect the syntax of the independent words lying behind them, their order and meaning or function, for example.

10.13   Typological Cycles and Directionality

In the traditional morphological classification of languages, following the nineteenth-century scholars Friedrich von Schlegel, August Schleicher, and Wilhelm von Humboldt, languages were classified according to their predominating morphological tendencies into:

Isolating, where each morpheme is a separate word, where there is no bound morphology, and grammatical markers are independent words.

Agglutinative, characterized by *agglutination*, the addition of affixes to roots, with no significant phonological changes in the root and where the different affixes are readily identifiable and easily segmented from the root and from each another.

Inflectional, where the language undergoes inflection, which is the modification or marking of a word so that it reflects grammatical information, such as grammatical gender, tense, person, number, etc.

Related to these types are two processes which further characterize languages by morphological types. One is *analysis* (*analytic languages*), for constructions which employ independent words rather than bound morphemes to express grammatical relationships. An *analytic language* is one characterized by a predominance of analytic constructions and relative lack of bound morphology. This contrasts with *synthesis* (*synthetic languages*), where *portmanteau* inflectional morphemes are prevalent, that is, single morphemes with multiple components of meaning. For example, in Spanish *voy a comer* 'I am going to eat' is the analytic future, expressed by independent words (*voy* 'I go', *a* 'to', *comer* 'eat'), while *comeré* 'I will eat' is the synthetic future, where the suffix *-ré* 'first person agreement, singular, indicative mood, future tense' combines subject agreement, tense, mood, and aspect.

Throughout the nineteenth and early twentieth centuries it was often assumed that there was a unidirectional evolution of language type from isolating to agglutanitive to inflectional, though Franz Boas, Edward Sapir, and others showed that this was not valid. Nevertheless, a notion of an evolutionary cycle involving movement from one type to another persists and many believe there is a general tendency of this sort at play in language change. A change from analytic to synthetic structure is illustrated in the Romance languages, where, for example,

Latin *cantare* 'to sing' + *habeō* 'I have' became the new analytic future; the new analytic constructions in turn become synthetic, as in the change in Romance languages reflected in Spanish *cantaré* < *cantar* + *hé* and French *chanterai* < *chanter* + *ai* (Spanish *hé* and French *ai* from Latin *habeō* 'I have'). New synthetic forms can undergo phonological erosion, thus starting the directional typological cycle again – at least according to this view.

A problem with this directional cycle view of morphological change is that languages can change in both directions at once, where some new synthetic constructions are created while at the same time other new analytic constructions are created, as in the case of Spanish *comeré* and *voy a comer*, both future constructions meaning 'I will eat', where both are relatively new in the language and both coexist, but the synthetic one (*comeré*) seems not to be experiencing any erosion that might justify moving to the next stage of importing a new analytic construction.

Those who support the idea of a directional cycle in the evolution of morphological type see a cyclic sequence of changes, where, for example, a language with inflections experiences erosion of these markers through sound change and other sorts of linguistic change, as in the case of Latin *am-abo* [love-1st.Pers. Sg.Future] 'I will love', where the intervocalic *b* of the future suffix was lost; if eroded too much, the eroded inflectional forms come to be replaced by new analytic constructions, in this view.

10.14   One Form, One Meaning

The principle of 'one form, one meaning' has also been called Humboldt's Universal and the Principle of Isomorphism. It is thought by many scholars to guide morphological and perhaps several other kinds of linguistic change broadly. It claims that there is a tendency for languages to change in ways that maximize the one-to-one relationship between form and meaning, where each form (the phonological shape of a morpheme) has only one meaning and each meaning has only one phonological shape, that is, a single form. This assumes that a single form should not have multiple meanings or functions, so, for example, -*s* should not function to signal both noun plurals (as in the *s* of *rats*) and possession (as in the *s* of *rat's*, or *Gandalf's*, and *Gollum's*). Similarly, it assumes that a single meaning (or function) should not be signalled by more than one form, so that the past participle of English should not be marked by both -*ed* (as in *waited*) and -*en* (as in *eaten*). These cases illustrate violations of the principle.

Conforming examples are very easy to find, however, along with linguistic changes which bring former violations in line with the principle. For example, all the cases discussed above in which allomorphs are lost or reduced in number conform – there should not be, according to the principle, multiple forms (allomorphs) to signal a single meaning (that of the morpheme). Similarly, the cases of analogical levelling conform, reducing multiple forms of a morpheme (or morphemes in paradigms) to one-to-one matches of form and meaning. The idea can be illustrated with straightforward examples from English. Originally, English *will* meant 'want', just as it still does in German; however, *will* was grammaticalized (see Chapter 11) to 'future'; at one stage, *will* meant both 'want' and 'future', *I will eat* for 'I want to eat' and 'I will eat', but the 'want' meaning was eliminated, leaving *will* 'future' in conformity with the one-form-one-meaning principle – the multiple meanings for the form *will* were reduced to a single meaning. Changes in form to conform to the principle are also easy to find. Formerly there were multiple forms for the possessive pronouns, *my* and *thy*, with *mine* and *thine* before nouns beginning in a vowel (as in *mine eyes*) but with *my* and *thy* when before nouns beginning in a consonant (as in *my teeth*); with the loss of the final *n* of these forms, they were brought into conformity, only one form to match a single meaning, no longer two forms, *my* and *mine*, for a single meaning of 'my' before nouns.

While there are far too many conforming examples in languages everywhere to doubt the principle, nevertheless, the tendency to conform is not overpowering. It is also easy to find examples of changes where new instances of multiple forms for one meaning or multiple meanings for one form are created – for example, analogical extensions, to mention one kind of changes which result in new instances not conforming to the principle of 'one form, one meaning'.

10.15   Morphological Reconstruction

Basically, the reconstruction of morphology follows directly from normal lexical reconstruction by the comparative method (as in Chapter 5), with morphological analysis applied to reconstructed lexical items that happen to be morphologically complex. Lexical reconstruction based on the sequence of sound correspondences in cognate words frequently results in the reconstruction of polymorphemic words. Morphological analysis of these reconstructed proto-words provides the reconstructed morphology free, so to speak. (See Chapter 11 for other examples and more detail.) This can be illustrated in a comparison of some cognate verb forms which contain more than one morpheme in Romance languages, in Table 10.1, where a paradigm with the infinitive and forms from the present indicative conjugation are given.

TABLE 10.1: Comparison of some verb morphology in some Romance languages

	Spanish	Portuguese	French	Italian	
Infinitive	amar	amar	aimer	amare	'to love'
Present	amo	amo	aime	amo	'I love'
indicative	amas	amas	aimes	ami	'you love'
	ama	ama	aime	ama	'(he/she/it) loves'
	amamos	amamos	aimons	amiamo	'we love'
	aman	amam	aiment	amano	'(they) love'

For the 'infinitive' form, we would presumably reconstruct **amare*, based on sound correspondences. The vowels of French *aimer* [ɛmɛR] reflects the sound change of **a* > ɛ (as seen in Chapter 5). The *m* and *r* correspond across all these languages, reconstructed as **m* and **r*. As for the final *e* of Italian, it is more likely that Western Romance (Spanish, Portuguese, and French) lost the final *e* than that Italian added it. External comparison with Classical Latin *amāre* 'to love' confirms this (though perhaps without the Latin form, some might imagine that **amar* rather than **amare* would be the best reconstruction and that the final *e* of Italian had been added later).

The reconstruction of **ama* for third person singular 'he/she/it loves' is also straightforward, where the reflexes of the sound correspondences in each of the languages, *a* of the others to *French* /ɛ/ (*aime* [ɛm(ɛ)]), and *m* in all the languages, allow for the reconstruction of **ama*. The other forms in Table 10.1 allow reasonably clear reconstruction, but are not quite as straightforward.

The *amo* of Spanish, Portuguese, and Italian would seem to suggest **amo* based on the straightforward sound correspondences with Spanish *a* : Portuguese *a* : Italian *a*, and again with *o* in all three languages, and with *m* corresponding to *m* in all four. The correspondences with the /ɛ/ of the first syllable of French *aime* of the 'first person singular' form to *a* in the other languages also supports the **a* reconstruction for the first syllable, as already seen. However, the final <e> of *aime* in contrast to the *o* of the other forms suggests something has changed in the individual history of French, since the ending of French *aime* does not fit the expected correspondences with *o* (see Chapter 5). On the basis of majority wins, we can still reconstruct **amo* 'I love', and seek an explanation for the difference in the separate history of French. We might hypothesize, for example, that the unexpected form has to do with Watkins' Law, that third person forms tend to take over other parts of verbal paradigms, in this case making the first person singular and third person singular forms essentially the same in shape (both *aime*).

We would be tempted to reconstruct **amas* 'you love' for 'second person singular', based on the regular sound correspondences, if we left Italian out of the picture. However, the *ami* 'you love' of Italian does not fit the expected reflexes, where *amas* might otherwise be expected. Again, we might seek an explanation in the separate history of Italian. It is not as straightforward this time, though, since Spanish, Portuguese, and French are all members of a single branch, Western Romance, while Italian is a member of Eastern Romance. It could be the case that Italian innovated in some special way and the other three reflect the original form of the 'second person singular' verb form, or it could be that Western Romance changed and Italian reflects a truer picture of the original Proto-Romance suffix for this form. This may be a case where the data we have to compare do not easily allow us to come to a definitive conclusion. Nevertheless, when we compare these with Classical Latin *amās* 'you love', the reconstruction with **amas* seems vindicated by the external evidence. An explanation for the change to *-i* in Italian needs to be sought.

The original 'first person plural' form of this verb is a bit less straightforward. The endings are *-mos*, *-mo*, and *-ons*, which, once we look into the sound changes in the individual histories of the separate languages in these contexts, reflect **-mos*, and we would reconstruct **amamos* based on the rest of the correspondences. However, we need to look further afield for an explanation of why Italian *amiamo* has the *i*. Though opinion differs, it is agreed that it started with Latin subjunctives *-iamus* and *-eamus* (each in a different conjugation class), as for example in Latin *sapiamus* 'let us taste' > Italian *sappiamo* 'let us know', and the *i* of *-iamo* eventually extended from there to indicatives of all conjugation classes by analogy (cf. Maiden 1995: 128). The reconstruction *amamos* receives support again from the external comparison with Classical Latin *amāmus* 'we love'. We miss the vowel length and the *u* rather than *o*, but in fact by later Common Romance (or Vulgar Latin) times, the reconstruction with *amamos* is actually accurate.

Finally, for 'third person plural', the reconstruction is also not completely straightforward, but it is not difficult to propose a reasonable hypothesis. The forms we compare are Spanish *aman*, Portuguese *amam* [amã], French *aiment* [ɛmã / ɛmãt-], and Italian *amano*. The Portuguese final nasalized vowel comes from /an/, taking us to earlier *aman*, just as in Spanish. French third person plural verb endings are complex; in the colloquial language the pronominal suffix is present in the spelling but is not pronounced, but it is present in formal French and historically was pronounced. As seen in Chapter 5 and again here, the French /ɛ/ corresponds to /a/ in the other languages and comes from *a. The nasalized vowel [ã] is from /ɛn/, again with /ɛ/ from *a. This would take us to earlier *aman*; however, what of the final <t> in the spelling of *aiment*, which can be pronounced [ɛmãt] if followed by a word or clitic beginning in a vowel, as in the question, *aiment-ils* 'do they love?', for example *Les Français aiment-ils le futur?* 'Do the French like the future?' This final *t* presents a problem, since the forms in the other languages do not have anything corresponding to it. We could imagine it was somehow added in the separate history of French, reconstructing *aman*, or we could imagine it was originally present, from *amant*, and the other languages lost it. Since there is no easy phonetic explanation for why French might have added a *t* here, perhaps the best hypothesis is to reconstruct the form with *t* and propose that final *t* after *n* was lost in the other languages. While this is not entirely satisfying, the external comparison with Classical Latin *amant* reveals that the reconstruction with *t* was in fact the correct conclusion. Italian *amano* requires explanation. Italian lost final *-t*, so *amant > aman*. As a result of this change and of a change in which final *m > n*, Latin *sunt* 'they are' and *sum* 'I am' became homophonous in Italian, both *son*. By analogy, the first person singular ending *-o* (as in *amo* 'I love') was added to *son* 'I am', to give *sono*. However, because *son* 'they are' was identified with *son* 'I am', when *son* 'I am' became *sono* by analogy with other first person singular verb forms, *son* 'they are' also became *sono* based on analogy with *sono* 'I am'. Then by analogy with *sono* 'they are', the *o* was added to other third person plural verb forms, resulting in *amano* (see Maiden 1995: 130–1). After sorting through the various sound changes and changes by analogy, we reconstruct *amant* '(they) love', which matches Classical Latin *amant*.

These verb form were reconstructed just as we reconstruct ordinary lexical items based on the sound correspondences they exhibit and the phonemes postulated to reconstruct each of the sounds, as in Chapter 5. If, however, we compare the reconstructed verb forms with one another, we can do a standard morphological analysis just as we would for any other language. Thus, comparing the reconstructed words, contrasting the parts that recur which have different meanings, we come up with a morphological analysis where what is after the hyphen (-) reflects the reconstructed bound morphemes:

ama-re 'to love' (*-re* 'infinitive')
am-o 'I love' (*-o* 'first person singular indicative')
ama-s 'you love' (*-s* 'second person singular indicative')
ama 'he/she/it loves' (*-Ø* 'third person singular indicative')
ama-mos 'we love' (*-mos* 'first person plural indicative')
ama-nt '(they) love' (*-nt* 'third person plural indicative').

That is, a standard morphological analysis of the reconstructed words based on the cognate forms in the related languages gives this proto-morphology free, so to speak.

This look at this portion of the verb paradigm compared in some Romance languages gives a good sense of what can be reconstructed and of some of the kinds of problems such morphological reconstruction can encounter. Morphological reconstruction faces difficulties that mean that it is not always as straightforward or as easy as lexical reconstruction. If some of the bound morphemes have been lost or have changed their function in all or most of the compared sister languages, it may be impossible to recover those earlier affixes. For example, Latin had a 'future' verbal affix as seen in *amābō* 'I will love', *amābis* 'you will love', *amābit* 'he/she/it loves', *amābimus* 'we love', etc. This morpheme, however, did not survive in the modern Romance languages and thus simply cannot be reconstructed from a comparison of the languages we have looked at. Also, if languages add new grammatical affixes through grammaticalization, that can complicate reconstruction, particularly if related languages undergo parallel grammaticalization after they have split up into separate languages. If the related languages have clear phonological reflexes of particular bound morphemes but their function changes dramatically across the languages, it may be impossible to reconstruct what the original function (meaning) of the affix was. Again, if different languages in the family have a grammatical morpheme with the same function across the related languages, but the phonological shapes of the morphemes are different in the different languages, it can be impossible to reconstruct the morpheme. Still, enough of the original phonetic form and comparable function is often preserved across related languages so that it is possible to reconstruct some aspects of the morphology with confidence. In general, the further back in time we go, the more opportunity related languages have had to undergo changes which can make it harder to recover past morphology by comparative reconstruction.

Some of these difficulties are evident in the examples presented here in Table 10.2, a comparison of some forms from the conjugation of the verb 'to bear, carry' in several branches of Indo-European.

Without going into details, it is clear that there are similarities among the related forms in Table 10.2, but that there are also considerably greater differences than seen the comparison of Romance verb forms in Table 10.1, which makes reconstruction of the affixes here more difficult. Nevertheless, the forms have been reconstructed: *bhér-o-h₂* '1st person singular', *bhér-e-si* '2nd person singular', *bhér-eti* '3rd person singular', *bhér-o-me* '1st person plural', *bhér-e-te(-)* '2nd person plural', *bhér-o-nti* '3rd person plural', with sound changes

TABLE 10.2: Comparison of some verb forms in some Indo-European languages

Sanskrit	Greek	Latin	Gothic	Old Church Slavonic	
bhárāmi	phérō	ferō	baíra	berǫ	1st person singular
bhárasi	phéreis	fers	baíris	bereši	2nd person singular
bhárati	phérei	fert	baíriþ	beret	3rd person singular
bhárāmas	phéromen	ferimus	baíram	beremŭ	1st person plural
bháratha	phérete	fertis	baíriþ	berete	2nd person plural
bháranti	phérousi	ferunt	baírand	bertŭ	3rd person plural

(Based on Fortson 2011: 89)

and analogical reformations to explain the forms in the individual languages (Fortson 2011: 89). (See also Chapter 11, section 11.5.3.)

10.16　Exercises

No explicit exercises for morphological change are given here. Several of the exercises in other chapters involve aspects of morphological change, in particular in those in Chapters 4, 8, and 11.

11

Syntactic Change

Our speech hath its infirmities and defects, as all things else have. Most of the
occasions of the world's troubles are grammatical.

(Montaigne, *Essays* II, xii)

11.1 Introduction

The study of syntactic change is currently an extremely active area of historical
linguistics. Nevertheless, there has been no generally recognized approach to the
treatment of syntactic change, such as there is for sound change. While there
were some excellent studies in historical syntax in the nineteenth century and
many in the last twenty years or so, syntactic change was very often not represented (or present only superficially) in the textbooks on historical linguistics.
The approach followed in this book is that of Harris and Campbell (1995) (on
which this chapter relies heavily). In this chapter, we learn about the mechanisms
of syntactic change – reanalysis, extension and borrowing – and the common
pathways that grammatical changes take; that is, we are interested in the more
commonly occurring kinds of syntactic changes found in the world's languages.
Grammaticalization, an approach currently of much interest, is also considered
together with its limitations. Finally, the possibilities for syntactic reconstruction
are described and defended.

11.2 Mechanisms of Syntactic Change

There are only three *mechanisms* of syntactic change: *reanalysis, extension* and
borrowing. Let us consider these mechanisms in turn, first with a brief characterization of each, followed by additional examples.

11.2.1 Reanalysis

Reanalysis changes the underlying structure of a syntactic construction, but does
not modify surface manifestation. The *underlying structure* includes (1) con-
stituency, (2) hierarchical structure, (3) grammatical categories, (4) grammatical

relations and (5) cohesion. We will come to examples illustrating changes in each of these shortly. *Surface manifestation* includes (1) morphological marking (for example, morphological case, agreement, gender) and (2) word order.

An important axiom of reanalysis is: *reanalysis depends on the possibility of more than one analysis of a given construction*. The following example from English exemplifies both reanalysis and this axiom. A new construction with a 'future' auxiliary (seen here in (2)) was derived through reanalysis from the construction in (1) which has a main verb (a verb of motion with a purposive sense):

(1) *Hermione is going to marry Ron.*
     Structure: Hermione is going$_{\text{VERB OF MOTION}}$ to marry Ron

The purposive *be going (to)* was reanalyzed as a 'future auxiliary':

(2) *Hermione is going to marry Ron.*
     Structure: Hermione is going$_{\text{FUTURE AUXILIARY}}$ to marry Ron

In the reanalysis which produced (2), the surface manifestation remained unchanged – (1) and (2) are identical in form, but are not the same in internal structure or meaning, which changed in the reanalysis. In this case, (1) came to be interpreted as having more than one possible structural analysis – it underwent reanalysis, yielding (2) with its different structural analysis.

For another example, in Finnish, a new postposition (seen here in (2)) was derived through reanalysis from what was formerly an ordinary noun root with a locative case (as in (1)):

(1) *miehe-n rinna-lla*
     man-Genitive chest-Adessive ('Adessive' is a locative case)
     'on the man's chest'   (Original)

(2) *miehe-n rinna-lla*
     man-Genitive Postposition-Adessive
     'beside the man'   (Reanalyzed)

In this case there is nothing ambiguous or opaque at all about (1), and in fact it is still fully grammatical in the language. However, it came to be interpreted as having more than one possible analysis, as a regular noun in locative case (as in (1)), but also as a postposition (as in (2)). This new postposition in Finnish is quite parallel to the development of the preposition *abreast of* in English, which comes historically from *a-* 'on' + *breast*. Such developments are common in English and other languages, as seen in English *beside* < *by + side*, *behind* < *by + hind*, and so on. In this instance, an original construction with an ordinary lexical noun in a locative case, as in (1), was the basis of the reanalysis which produced the new construction with the postposition, as in (2). Notice, however, that (1) and (2) are the same except for their internal analysis; that is, though a reanalysis took place to produce (2), the surface manifestation remained unchanged – (1) and (2) are identical in form, but not in their internal structure.

11.2.2 Extension

Extension results in changes in surface manifestation, but does not involve immediate modification of underlying structure. This can be seen in the reanalysis mentioned above in which a new future auxiliary came from 'be going to'. After this reanalysis took place, there was a subsequent extension so that *be going to* as a future auxiliary could appear with new verbs that were not possible earlier. Before it could occur only with verbs which could be the complements in the purposive and motion verb constructions, for example, *I am going to eat* (as in, *going there to eat* or *going in order to eat*). However, the new construction was extended so that it could occur with complement verbs which were not possible in the former sense of a verb of motion, for example, *It is going to rain on the muggles, Ron is going to like Hermione, Hermione is going to go to Hogwarts.*

11.2.2.1 First example: change in some Finnish subordinate clauses

Finnish subordinate clauses provide an example which underwent first reanalysis and then extension. Old Finnish had sentences of the form illustrated in (3) (NOTE: orthographic ä is phonetically [æ]):

(3) näen   miehe-m   tule-va-m
    I.see   man-Accusative.Singular   come-Participle-Accusative.Singular
    'I see the man who is coming'

Here, the noun *miehe-m* 'man' is the direct object of the verb *näen* 'I see', and the participle *tule-va-m* 'coming/who comes' modifies this noun ('man') and agrees with it in case and number (both take the 'accusative singular' suffix *-m*). Later, Finnish underwent a sound change in which final *-m* > *-n*, and as a result the accusative singular *-n* (formerly *-m*) and genitive singular *-n* became homophonous, both *-n*. After this sound change, the resulting form, shown in (4), was seen as having two possible interpretations, in (4a) and (4b) (Acc = Accusative, Part = Participle, Pl = Plural, Sg = Singular):

(4)   näen miehe-n   tule-van
(4a) I.see man-Acc.Sg   come-Part
(4b) I.see man-Gen.Sg   come-Part
      'I see the man who is coming'

This led to a change in which the older interpretation in (4a) was eventually eliminated and this subordinate clause construction was reanalyzed as (4b). That is, *miehe-n* was reinterpreted not as the direct object (in accusative case) of the verb *näen* 'I see' as it had originally been in Old Finnish (as in the example in (3)), but as the subject (in genitive case) of the participle *tulevan* (as in (4b)). (The change is somewhat like starting with the equivalent of *I saw the man coming* and changing it to *I saw the man's coming*.) At this stage there is still no visible difference in the surface manifestation ((4a) of older Finnish and (4b) of modern Finnish are in form the same, though different in analysis).

The next phase was the *extension* of the reanalyzed structure to other instances where the surface manifestation was visibly changed, as seen in the comparison of Old Finnish (5) with modern Finnish (6):

(5) näin venee-t   purjehti-va-t
     I.saw boat-Acc.Pl   sail-Part.Acc.Pl
     'I saw the boats that sail'
(6) näin vene-i-den   purjehti-van
     I.saw boat-Pl-Gen   sail-Part
     'I saw the boats that sail'

In Old Finnish, sentence (5), with *venee-t* in the 'accusative plural', did not permit a second interpretation, as (4) did, where the 'accusative singular' had the same form as the 'genitive singular'; however, the reanalysis (from accusative to genitive) that began with the homophonous singular form was extended to include the plurals, so that in modern Finnish *venee-t* 'accusative plural' is no longer possible in this construction (as it was in (5) in Old Finnish), but was replaced through extension by *vene-i-den* 'genitive plural', as in (6). Where formerly the singular had two possible interpretations, accusative singular direct object of the main verb or genitive singular subject of the participle, after the change had been extended to the plural making it also genitive, the original (accusative) interpretation was no longer available. The shift from *veneet* 'accusative plural' to *veneiden* 'genitive plural' made the change very evident, now visible in the surface manifestation.

11.2.2.2 Second example: Spanish reflexive to passive

A second example which shows both reanalysis and extension involves changes in the reflexive in Old Spanish. Old Spanish had only the reflexive as in (7), with none of the other functions that the Spanish reflexive later came to have:

(7) Yo no vestí   a   Juanito; Juanito se   vistió
     I   no dressed   OBJECT   Johnny;   Johnny   REFLEXIVE   dressed
     'I didn't dress Johnny; Johnny dressed himself '

A reanalysis of the reflexive took place in which *se* could also be interpreted as a passive. In the first stage of this change, certain transitive verbs with *se* and a human subject came to have multiple interpretations as either a reflexive of volitional/consentive action, or as a passive, as illustrated in (8) and (9) (REFL = reflexive):

(8) El   rico se   entierra   en   la   iglesia
     the   rich REFL   bury   in   the   church
     (8a) 'The rich person has himself interred/buried in the church'
          (volitional reflexive; literally: 'the rich person inters himself in
          the church')
     (8b) 'The rich person gets buried/is buried in the church' (*passive*)
(9) Cum esto se   vençen   moros del   campo
     with this REFL   they.conquer Moors of.the countryside
     (9a) 'Therefore Moors of the countryside give themselves up for
          conquered' (*consentive*; literally: 'with this Moors of the
          countryside conquer themselves')

(9b) 'Therefore Moors of the countryside get conquered/are conquered' (*passive*)

In (8) and (9), different interpretations are possible, either reflexive or passive; the surface manifestation is unaltered in the new, reanalyzed passive interpretation of these sentences. Also, the original reflexive construction (as in (7)) remains grammatical in Spanish. In the next step, the passive interpretation of the former reflexive *se* was extended to include not just human subjects, but also non-animate subjects, where no reflexive interpretation was possible, as in (10) and (11):

(10) Los vino-s   que en esta ciudad se   vende-n . . .
     the wine-PL that in this city   REFL sell-3rd.PERS.PL
     'The wines that are sold in this city . . .'

(11) Cautiváron-se   quasi dos mil   persona-s
     they.captured-REFL almost two thousand person-Plural
     'Almost two thousand persons were captured'

These sentences are now clearly passive and not reflexive; in (10) the 'wines' cannot 'sell themselves', and in (11) the 'two thousand persons' are not 'capturing themselves'.

11.2.3 Syntactic borrowing

Syntactic borrowing is much more frequent and important than some scholars have thought in the past, though others have gone to the other extreme of assuming that everything not otherwise readily explained in a language's grammar is due to borrowing. It is important to avoid such excesses but also to recognize the proper role of syntactic borrowing in syntactic change. The following is a straightforward example of syntactic borrowing. Pipil (a Uto-Aztecan language of El Salvador) borrowed the comparative construction, *mas . . . ke*, from Spanish, as in (12):

(12) ne siwa:t *mas* galá:na *ke*   taha
     the woman more pretty   than you
     'That woman is prettier than you are'

Compare the Spanish equivalent in (12'):

(12') esa mujer es *más* linda *que* tú (/mas . . . ke/)
      that woman is more pretty than you

Pipil had several different comparative expressions before its contact with Spanish, but these have been eliminated, replaced by this borrowed comparative construction.

Another case involves the extensive borrowing of grammatical elements and constructions among the Australian aboriginal languages of Arnhem

Land, in particular among Ritharngu, Ngandi, Nunggubuyu and Warndarang. This includes the direct borrowing of case affixes (for example, for ergative markers, instrumental, ablative, genitive-dative- purposive, comitative), number affix, noun-class affixes (with discourse functions of reference and anaphora), diminutive affix, derivational verbal affixes, negative affix, postpositions and the inchoative verbalizer, among others (Heath 1978). (For several more examples of syntactic borrowing and discussion, see Harris and Campbell 1995:120–50.)

11.3   Generative Approaches

Most work on historical syntax since 1960 has taken the perspective of Generative Grammar (or its descendants). Generative linguists generally associate syntactic change with child language acquisition, seeing syntactic change as part of what happens in the transition of grammars from one generation to the next. In this view, child language learners hear the output of adults around them and on the basis of these data they must construct their own grammar. The grammar which the children acquire reproduces the output which they hear from the adults' grammar more or less accurately, but it does not necessarily coincide with the internal structure of adults' grammar. After learning an optimal grammar as children, adults may later add rules to their grammars which make them no longer optimal. Children of the next generation, hearing the output of this non-optimal adult grammar, restructure it as they construct their own internal grammars, making it more optimal.

We can illustrate this approach with a somewhat hypothetical example, but one that figured in early generative work on syntactic change (cf. Klima 1964). Suppose that an earlier generation of English speakers had learned a grammar with the rule that pronouns, including *who*, require an object case marking (*me, him, whom*) when they occur as the object of a verb (*Harry saw him/me, Whom did Harry see?*) or a preposition (*to him, to me, to whom*). Let us call this Grammar$_1$, informally characterized as in Table 11.1 (Pro = Pronoun, Prep = Preposition).

TABLE 11.1: Derivation of whom in Grammar$_1$

Underlying:	*saw who*	*to who*
	[Verb + Pro]$_{\text{VERB PHRASE}}$	[Prep +Pro]$_{\text{PREPOSITIONAL PHRASE}}$
Rule 1:	*saw whom*	*to whom*
(Case-marking)	[Verb + Pro-Case]$_{\text{VERB PHRASE}}$	Prep + Pro-Case]$_{\text{PREPOSITIONAL PHRASE}}$
Result:	*saw whom*	*to whom*

(A later rule which fronts question words such as *who(m)* gives, for example, *Whom did Harry see?*)

Now suppose that later in life, as adults, speakers of Grammar$_1$ changed their grammar by adding a rule which deletes the case marking with *whom*; let's call this Grammar$_{1a}$, characterized informally as in Table 11.2.

The next generation of children learning the language would hear only *who*

TABLE 11.2: Derivation of *who(m)* in Grammar$_{1a}$

Underlying:	*saw who*	*to who*
	[Verb + Pro]$_{\text{VERB PHRASE}}$	[Prep + Pro]$_{\text{PREPOSITIONAL PHRASE}}$
Rule 1:	*saw whom*	*to whom*
(Case-marking)	[Verb + Pro-Case]$_{\text{VERB PHRASE}}$	[Prep + Pro-Case]$_{\text{PREPOSITIONAL PHRASE}}$
Rule 2:	*saw who*	*to who*
(Delete Case from *whom*)		
Result:	*saw who*	*to who*

as the output of the adult grammar, Grammar$_{1a}$, and therefore for their own grammar would simply learn *who* in all contexts, having no need for Rule 2 of adult Grammar$_{1a}$. That is, the adults' non-optimal Grammar$_{1a}$, would have two rules, Rule 1 to add object case marking (*whom*) to pronoun objects of verbs and prepositions, and Rule 2 to convert *whom* into *who* (deletion of the object case marking for *who*). The children learning the language, hearing only the output *who*, would not learn Rule 2, but would simply learn to use *who* in all contexts. They thus construct their grammar with simpler internal structure. They have no Rule 2 to eliminate case marking from *who*, and their Rule 1 is modified to apply only to personal pronouns (*me, him, us*, etc.) but to leave *who* out. Let us call these children's grammar Grammar$_2$, which can be characterized informally as in Table 11.3.

TABLE 11.3: Derivation of *who* in Grammar$_2$

Under-lying:	*saw who*	*to who*
	[Verb + Pro]$_{\text{VERB PHRASE}}$	[Prep + Pron]$_{\text{PREPOSITIONAL PHRASE}}$
Rule 1:	[Verb + PersPro-Case]$_{\text{VERB PHRASE}}$	[Prep + PersPro-Case]$_{\text{PREPOSITIONAL PHRASE}}$

(Case-marking): (Not applicable with *who*: *saw who, to who*; but *saw him, to him*)

Result:	*saw who*	*to who*

(A later rule which fronts question words gives, for example, *Who did Harry see?*)

The children's grammar (Grammar$_2$) achieves the same output as the adult grammar (Grammar$_{1a}$) but is now more optimal again.

David Lightfoot's (1979, 1991) work has been very influential and is considered a major representative of generative views. His scenario for the explanation of syntactic change is that grammatical complexity builds up gradually in a language (through minor changes of little importance) until eventually a sudden catastrophic and far-reaching restructuring of the grammar takes place which eliminates this complexity that made the language's grammar difficult for children to learn. One criticism of this view is that there is no reliable means of distinguishing the catastrophic changes (which overhaul grammars that become too complex, Lightfoot's major interest) from the gradually accumulating less significant changes. Another criticism is that catastrophic changes of this sort are extremely rare in the attested history of most languages. A central feature of Lightfoot's (1979) treatment is the claim that syntactic change (and syntax in general) is autonomous, meaning that syntactic change takes place independently of semantic relations, pragmatic considerations, discourse functions or sociolinguistic considerations. For Lightfoot, syntactic changes operate independently of considerations of meaning and use. This claim has been much criticized because syntactic rules and changes do not operate independently of meaning, use, pragmatics, sociolinguistic value judgements, foreign-language influences and so on.

Central to the generative view of language change is the notion that linguistic change in general, and therefore also syntactic change, takes place in the language acquisition process and in the transition of grammars from one generation to the next. Many cases of syntactic changes would seem to conform to this view, though others seem at odds with it. This approach assumes that many of the kinds of changes are the results of the child language learners just getting it wrong, making mistakes. For example, this view claims for the change in the Finnish participle construction (sentences (3–6) above) that in language acquisition children incorrectly assumed that sentence (4) was to be analyzed as containing the genitive singular because they incorrectly perceived what was (formerly) the accusative singular (in (4)) and then they carried through with this assumption (by extension) by imposing their new and erroneous genitive interpretation on sentences with the plurals (as in (6)) as well, which were not ambiguous at all, as the singulars had been (where the suffix -*n* might be seen as either 'accusative singular' or 'genitive singular'), resulting in a restructuring of the grammar. However, this view is simply not available for many kinds of syntactic change where after the change the original construction still remains grammatical and unchanged alongside the innovative construction that the change is based on; the development of the new Finnish postposition (above) is such a case. In such changes, the original construction remains but in effect gains additional interpretations, that is, multiple analyses. In the development of the new Finnish postposition ((1) and (2) above), the source construction (in (1)) and the new postpositional construction based on it (in (2)) both survive; the same is true of the changes involving the Spanish reflexive (in (7) above) and the new passive construction derived from it (in (10–11)). In these changes, there is nothing which requires the assumption that the child language learner got it wrong which resulted in the grammar with a different construction (a new and different analysis of the old construction) which eliminates the original interpretation of the construction from the grammar. In these examples, there is nothing that requires child language acquisition to be the driving force behind the changes. Adult speakers could just as easily initiate the new analyses alongside the pre-existing ones. If these changes did begin with adults, their results would be part of the language which the next generation would hear around them, and consequently the children would simply learn these new, additional constructions together with any others that happen to be around as part of the grammar which they acquire. The argument that the language acquisition process need not be seen as the crucial locus of syntactic change challenges assumptions of the generative approach to syntactic change.

11.4 Grammaticalization

Grammaticalization is a topic of extensive current interest. The famous French Indo-Europeanist Antoine Meillet (1912:132) introduced the term 'grammaticalization' with the sense of 'the attribution of a grammatical character to a formerly independent word', where an independent word with independent meaning may develop into an auxiliary word and, if the process continues, it ends up as a grammatical marker or bound grammatical morpheme. Jerzy Kuryłowicz's (1965:52) much-cited definition is: 'Grammaticalization consists in the increase of the range of a morpheme advancing from a lexical to a grammatical or from a less grammatical to a more grammatical status'. This process is often characterized by a concurrent 'weakening' of both the meaning and the phonetic form of the word involved. In grammaticalization, two related processes are the typical objects of investigations: (1) changes of the lexical-item-to-grammatical-morpheme sort, which can involve phonological reduction and exhibit change from independent word to clitic or affix; and less commonly (2) the discourse-structure-to-morpho-syntactic-marking sort, the fixing of discourse strategies in syntactic and morphological structure (Traugott and Heine 1991:2). In both kinds, grammaticalization is typically associated with *semantic bleaching* and *phonological reduction* (to which we return below). Thus, Heine and Reh (1984:15) define grammaticalization as 'an evolution whereby linguistic units lose in semantic complexity, pragmatic significance, syntactic freedom, and phonetic substance'.

A frequently cited example is English *will*, which originally meant 'want', as its German cognate, *will* '(he/she) wants', still does. We can see remnants of the former 'want' meaning in such things as *have the will* [= desire], *if you will* [= if you want to] and *good will* [= wishes, desires]. English *will* became semantically bleached (lost its sense of 'want') and was grammaticalized as a 'future' marker. Grammaticalized forms are also often associated with 'phonetic erosion' (reduction of fuller forms to phonologically shorter ones). In this example, grammaticalized *will* 'future' can also be reduced in form, as in contractions such as *I'll*, *she'll*, *my dog'll do it*, and so on. Meillet presented a parallel example in Greek of the grammaticalization of a verb 'to want' as a future marker, though its history is more complex than the change in English and is coupled with the loss of infinitives in Greek. Modern Greek *θa* 'future marker' began life as the Classical Greek main verb *thélei* 'want'. Greek lost its original infinitive construction and replaced it with a subordinate clause construction: *thélō hina gráphō* 'I want to write' [literally 'I want that I write'], *thélei hina gráphei* 'he/she wants to write' ['he/she wants that he/she writes']. Though *thélei* continued as a main verb meaning 'want', it also came to mean 'will' (future), so that *thélō hina gráphō*, for example, could mean either 'I want to write' or 'I will write'. Later, the 'future' became restricted to the 'third person' form only, /θeli/ (from *thélei*), and eventually the combination of /θeli hina/ changed to /θa/, going through the steps: /θeli hina/ > /θeli na/ > /θe na/ > /θa na/ > /θa/, giving Modern Greek /θa ɣráfo/ 'I will write' (Joseph 1990). Another example is the frequent grammaticalization of lexical 'go' to 'future', as with English *(be) going to* which originally referred only to the verb of motion, but then acquired a sense of 'future'/'future intention', which can be reduced phonologically to *gonna* in spoken language.

11.4.1 Examples of typical grammaticalization changes

It may be helpful to mention some of the sorts of grammaticalization changes, and the pathways they typically take, that are seen to recur with some frequency in languages around the world.

(1) Auxiliary < main verb (as in English *will* 'future auxiliary' < 'want').

(2) Case suffixes < postpositions (as in Estonian *–ga* (/-ka/) 'comitative case' suffix < **kansak* 'with' postposition).

(3) Between < 'centre', 'middle'.

(3) Case marking < serial verbs.

(4) Causatives < causal verb ('make, have, get, cause, force') + Clause with another verb.

(5) Classifiers (numeral and noun) < concrete nouns ('man', 'woman', 'child', 'animal', 'tree', etc.)

(6) Complementizer/subordinate conjunction < 'say'; demonstrative, relative clause markers.

(7) Coordinate conjunction ('and') < 'with'.

(8) Copula ('to be') < positional verbs 'stand', 'sit', or 'give', 'exist' (Spanish *estar* 'to be' < Latin *stāre* 'to stand'; varieties of Quechua *tiya-* 'to be' < **tiya-* 'to sit'). Note that Spanish *ser* 'to be' comes from a blending of Latin *sedēre* 'to sit' and *esse* (*essere* in Vulgar Latin) 'to be'.

(9) Dative case marker < 'give'.

(10) Definite article < demonstrative pronoun.

(11) Direct object case markers < locatives, prepositions (for example, a dative marker has become an accusative marker in Spanish, Kwa, Bemba and others; compare Spanish *Harry vio **a** Ron* [Harry saw OBJECT.MARKER Ron] 'Harry saw Ron' with *Harry lo dio **a** Ron* [Harry it gave TO Ron] 'Harry gave it to Ron').

(12) Dual < 'two'.

(13) Durative, habitual, iterative < 'stay'; durative aspect < 'remain, stay, keep, sit'.

(14) Existential/presentational constructions < 'have', 'be' (often with no inflection or only third person present inflection allowed), or < locative pronoun (Spanish *hay* 'there is/are' < *haber* 'to have'; French *il y a* < *y* 'there' + *a* 'has'; English *there is/are*).

(15) Future < 'want', 'have', 'go', 'come' (English *will* 'future auxiliary' < 'want'); adverbs ('quickly', 'tomorrow', 'then', 'after-wards').

(16) Grammatical gender < noun (masculine < 'man, male, boy'; feminine < 'woman, female, girl').

(17) Habitual < 'to live', 'stay', 'go', 'sit', 'use'; continuous.

(18) Hortative < 'come', 'go', 'leave' ('abandon').

(19) Impersonal/agentless verb forms: the following constructions are interrelated in many languages and changes frequently go from one to another among these, though directionality is not strongly determined in most cases: reflexive ~ reciprocal ~ spontaneous/automatically occur-

ring ~ potential ~ honorific ~ plural ~ detransitivizing constructions ~ middle/medio-passive/pseudo-passive ~ passive ~ defocusing ~ non-agent topicalization ~ impersonal verb ~ first person plural imperative/hortatory ~ causative ~ transitive (for example, 'Mr. Weasley had/got his car stolen') ~ stative/resultative ~ perfect ~ ergative. A directionality is frequently attested in which reflexive > reciprocal > passive > impersonal (where reflexive > passive, or reflexive > impersonal are possible and occur with frequency).

(20) Indefinite article < 'one'(English *a(n)* comes from 'one').

(22) Indefinite pronoun < 'person', 'man', 'body', 'thing'; 'one'; 'you'; 'they' (as with English *somebody, anybody* which incorporate 'body').

(23) Infinitive < 'to', 'for' (purpose).

(24) Locative constructions < body-part terms (compare English *at the head of, at the foot of*, etc.).

(25) Negative < negative intensifiers (for example, French *ne pas,* originally 'not a step' where *pas* was a negative intensifier much like English *not a bit* is today; similar changes are attested in many languages).

(26) Negative < 'leave', 'abandon', 'lack'.

(27) Quotative < 'say'.

(28) Obligation < 'need', 'necessity', 'owe' (for example, English *ought (to)* from Old English *āhte,* past tense of *āgan* 'to owe').

(29) Obligation < copula (for example, *you are to go to the doctor tomorrow*).

(30) Passive < 'get', 'obtain', 'receive'; 'they'.

(31) Perfect(ive) < 'finish', 'complete', 'have/possess', 'end'.

(32) Preposition/postpositions < verb (preposition < VO; postposition < OV).

(33) Progressive < locative + non-finite verb (English, for example, *is hunting* < *is a-hunting* < *is on hunting*; Pennsylvania German, Cologne German *ist am Schreiben* [is on.the to.write] 'is writing').

(34) Progressive/habitual < durative verbs ('keep'), 'do', copula, positional verb.

(35) Reflexive pronoun < some body-part noun ('body', 'head', 'belly', 'person') + possessive; 'reciprocal' < 'body'.

(36) Relative pronouns < *wh*-question words/interrogative pronouns (compare English relative pronouns *who, which* with question words *who?, which?*).

(37) Relative clause markers < demonstratives.

(38) Third person pronoun < demonstrative, 'man', 'person'.

(39) *Wh*-questions < cleft or pseudo-cleft (equivalents to 'what did she do?' < 'what is it that she did?'

(40) Yes–no question < 'or'; negation.

These are just a few of the many. Also, these are not the only paths by which many of these elements can develop. (For actual examples of these and others, see especially Heine and Kuteva 2002, also Harris and Campbell 1995, and Hopper and Traugott 2003.)

11.4.2   The status of grammaticalization

Some argue that grammaticalization has no independent status of its own, that there is nothing special or unique about it, that it merely involves other kinds of linguistic changes which are well understood and not inherently connected with grammaticalization: sound change, semantic change and reanalysis. It is important to understand the basis for this challenge to grammaticalization.

Most scholars agree that grammaticalization is not a mechanism of change in its own right, but relies on the other mechanisms, primarily on reanalysis, but also sometimes on extension and borrowing. There are, however, many reanalyses which do not involve grammaticalization, for example those involving word-order changes, affixes becoming independent words (which is rare, but a number of examples are known from various languages), changes from one syntactic structure to another, and so on – that is, any reanalysis which does not involve lexical items shifting towards having a more grammatical status or discourse structure becoming more fixed morphosyntactically.

That grammaticalization is often associated with 'semantic bleaching' (also called *fading, weakening*) should perhaps not be seen so much as a special attribute of grammaticalization as just regular semantic change in action (see Chapter 9). Semantic bleaching in grammaticalization can hardly be seen as very remarkable, since it is essentially part of the definition of grammaticalization, a shift from more lexical meaning to more grammatical content. The types of semantic change involved in grammaticalization are primarily narrowing, sometimes coupled with metaphor, metonymy, and others (see Chapter 9). The emphasis on semantic loss or weakening is perhaps unwarranted, however, since in the process of grammaticalization forms also take on new meanings, such as 'future' in the case of *will* and *gonna*, and it is not necessarily the case that any lexical meaning is lost, since often the source of the grammaticalization remains in the language with its former meaning alongside the new grammaticalized form, as *be going to*, the original directional verb, has in English alongside the new 'future' meaning acquired in the grammaticalization. The semantic bleaching (the semantic change) in grammaticalization can in no way be considered independent of semantic change in general.

The phonological reduction ('erosion' of form) which many associate with grammaticalization is also best not seen as unique to grammaticalization, but as normal phonological change. Phonological reduction processes apply to items of the appropriate phonological character generally in a language, not just to certain items which happen to be involved in processes of grammaticalization. Reduction often follows grammaticalization because it is at that stage that the conditions favourable to changes of phonological reduction first come about, for example where the forms which get reduced no longer have an independent lexical meaning and hence come to be in relatively unstressed positions.

In short, grammaticalizations involve reanalysis, but reanalysis is a much more powerful mechanism of change and is by no means limited to nor coextensive with grammaticalization. Sound change and semantic change apply to all sorts of things in addition to grammaticalizations. For this reason, many find grammaticalization derivative, perhaps an interesting intersection of these various sorts of change, but with no special explanatory status of its own. (For general treatments of grammaticalization, see C. Lehmann 1995, Hopper and Traugott 2003, and Traugott and Heine 1991; for critiques of grammaticalization as an explanatory theory, see the articles in Campbell 2001.)

11.5 Syntactic Reconstruction

Opinions are sharply divided concerning whether syntax is reconstructible by the comparative method. Nevertheless, the evidence available for comparison is often sufficient for successful reconstruction of many aspects of the syntax of a proto-language. To understand why there has been doubt about reconstruction of syntax and to see the real potential which we have for successful reconstruction in this area, we need to look at some of the obstacles to such reconstruction that are sometimes mentioned and at ways of surmounting the difficulties which they raise. Following this, we will consider some beneficial things which can help in syntactic reconstruction.

11.5.1 Reanalysis as an obstacle to reconstruction

Instances of traditional analogy sometimes pose obstacles in phonological and lexical reconstruction. Reanalysis in syntactic change is like analogy, and cases of reanalysis can make syntactic reconstruction difficult. However, in instances where analogy changes the form in one language so that it does not fit those of the related languages with which it is compared, we seek an explanation for the non-fitting form, and often we find the analogical reformation which caused the form to deviate, as in the following cognate set from Germanic:

English	German	Gothic	Old Norse	
adder	*natter*	*nadr-*	*naðra*	'adder'/'snake'

The weight of the evidence in German, Gothic and Old Norse suggests an initial **n-* in the proto-form, and this bids us seek an explanation for why no reflex of this *n-* is seen in the English cognate. In seeking an explanation, we eventually discover that the pattern of the English indefinite article with *a* before words beginning in a consonant (as *a plum*) and *an* before vowel-initial words (*an apple*) suggests analogical reinterpretation, from *a #nadder* to *an #adder* (compare Old English *næddre* 'snake'). In a situation such as this one, the analogical change is not devastating to lexical reconstruction, and it is precisely the comparative method and the evidence from the other languages which helps us to unravel the complication. We reconstruct initial **n-* and posit an analogical change to account for the deviance of the English cognate.

Using the same procedure, in many instances where one of the languages being compared has undergone reanalysis in some particular construction, we can discover the reanalysis and explain it so that it no longer prevents us from reconstructing the syntactic pattern in question. Earlier in this chapter, we saw the example in which a Finnish participle construction was reanalyzed so that the noun that had originally been an accusative direct object of the main verb (as in (3) and (5)) came to be interpreted as the genitive subject of the participle (as in (4b) and (6)). If we compare cognate constructions among the Balto-Finnic languages, which include Finnish and its close relatives, we soon discover that Finnish stands out as not fitting the pattern of the other languages, as seen in the following examples (Acc = accusative, Gen = genitive, Part = participle):

(13a) *Finnish*:   näin häne-n tule-van   [genitive]
                      I.saw he-Gen come-Part
                      'I saw him coming/that he comes'

(13b) *Estonian*:   nägin te-da tule-va-t   [accusative]
                      I.saw he-Acc come-Part-Acc
                      'I saw him coming/that he comes'

(13c) *Vote*:   näin me:s-sä tuɬə-va-a te:tä mö   [accusative]
                      I.saw man.Acc come-Part-Acc street along
                      'I saw a man coming/who comes along the street'

      Compare *Finnish*:   näin miehe-n tule-van tietä pitkin
                            [genitive]
                            I.saw man-Gen come-Part road along
                            (same meaning)

(13d) *North*   son oia'dna boc'cu-i-d vuol'-ga-m   [accusative]
      Saami: he see reindeer-Pl-Acc leave-Past.Part-Acc
                      'he sees that the reindeer have left'

      Compare *Finnish*:   hän näkee poro-j-en lähte-neen   [genitive]
                            he sees reindeer-Pl-Gen leave-Past.Part

The cognate constructions in Balto-Finnic languages, except for Finnish, present the noun phrase which plays the role of the subject of the subordinate clause syntactically as a direct object in accusative case of the main verb, not as a genitive subject of the participle, as in Finnish. The difference in Finnish demands an explanation. In seeking an explanation, we soon discover that the accusative singular and genitive singular cases are both signalled by *-n*, allowing for multiple interpretations. Given this and the difference between Finnish and the other languages with respect to this construction, we encounter little difficulty in determining that Finnish has undergone a reanalysis and does not reflect the original form. We reconstruct the construction as reflected in the other Balto-Finnic languages, with the noun phrase as accusative object of the main verb, and we write out the changes of reanalysis and extension that have caused Finnish to depart from this structure.

11.5.2 Borrowing as an obstacle to syntactic reconstruction

Just as borrowing can complicate lexical reconstruction, it can be a serious obstacle to syntactic reconstruction as well. However, the techniques for identifying borrowing (in Chapter 3) can often help to identify syntactic borrowing and thus get beyond this obstacle. For example, a comparison of the words for 'mother' across Finno-Ugric languages reveals reflexes of **ema* 'mother' in most of them; however, Finnish has *äiti* 'mother' instead, and this difference turns out to be the result of borrowing. Closer investigation reveals that Finnish did indeed borrow this word from Germanic 'mother' (Gothic *aiþei* [ɛθī] Old High German *eidī*,

Proto-Germanic *aiθī). Since it is borrowed, it is not a legitimate witness of what the form in the proto-language may have been; to determine that, we rely rather on the information available from the other languages which did not replace the original cognate word through borrowing. In syntactic reconstruction, we do the same thing. For example, in most varieties of Finnish, verbal constructions involving obligation require the subject to be in the genitive case and the verb to be in a third person singular form (that is, the verb does not agree with this genitive subject), as in the following example from Standard Finnish (Gen = genitive, Sg = Singular, Nom = nominative, Pl = Plural, Part = Participle):

(14a) minu-n täyty-y mennä
       I-Gen must-3rd.Person.Present to.go
       'I must go'

(14b) minu-n pitä-ä mennä
       I-Gen must-3rd.Sg.Present to.go

However, Western Finnish lacks this obligation construction; rather, it has borrowed its construction from neighbouring Swedish, now with a subject in nominative case and with the verb agreeing in person with this subject, as in the following examples:

Western Finnish:

(14c) mä täydy-n mennä
       I.Nom must-I to.go
       'I must go'

(14d) mä pidä-n mennä
       I.Nom must-I to.go
       'I must go'

When we compare the many regional varieties of Finnish (in (15–16)), Western Finnish (illustrated in (14c–d)), with its nominative subjects and verb agreement, stands out as inconsistent with the others, which take genitive subjects and no verb agreement. This is illustrated here with an example from just two of the many dialects, Vermland (in Sweden) and Koprina (Inkeri, former Soviet Union):

Vermland:

(15a) nii-j-en ois pitän-nä lahata oamus´e-lla
       these-Pl-Gen would.have must-Past.Part to.slaughter
           morning-on
       'they should have slaughtered in the morning'
       Compare *Standard Finnish*:

(15b) nii-den olisi pitä-nyt lahdata aamu-lla
       these-Pl.Gen would.have must-Past.Part to.slaughter
           morning-on
       Inkeri (Koprina):

(16a) sulhaśe-n pitʲ antaa kolme ruplaa pojil viinarahaa
       bridegroom-Gen had to.give three roubles boys.to wine.money. of
       'The bridegroom had (was supposed) to give three roubles
           of drinking money to the boys'

Compare *Standard Finnish*:

(16b)   sulhase-n piti antaa pojille kolme ruplaa viinarahaa
        bridegroom-Gen had to.give three roubles boys.to wine.money.of

Given that all other varieties of Finnish have the genitive subject and non-agreeing third person verb form in verbal obligation constructions, we reconstruct this pattern and we explain the Western Finnish one with nominative subjects and verbs that agree in person with their subjects as a later change due to borrowing from the Swedish model. The evidence from other varieties shows that Western Finnish is inconsistent, and further research reveals that it is due to borrowing. Therefore, in spite of the borrowing in this case, we are able successfully to reconstruct the older stage of the language, with genitive subjects and non-agreeing verbs, based on the weight of the comparative evidence from the other varieties compared.

In summary, there are many obstacles to reconstruction of syntax, but they are largely the same sort that we encounter in phonological and lexical reconstruction, and often it is possible to see beyond the obstacles. Let us turn now to some considerations which prove beneficial in efforts to reconstruct syntax.

11.5.3   Morphological reconstruction as clues to syntactic reconstruction

Morphology and syntax are so interrelated that to the extent that morphology can be reconstructed, many aspects of the proto-syntax in many cases will automatically become clear. The techniques used for lexical reconstruction (Chapter 5), based on the sequence of sound correspondences in cognate words, can frequently be used to reconstruct polymorphemic words. Morphological analysis of these reconstructed proto-words provides the proto-morphology free, so to speak. An example of this sort is seen in Table 11.4, where some polymorphemic cognate words for the paradigm for the verb 'to read' in Balto-Finnic are

TABLE 11.4: Balto-Finnic comparative verbal morphology

Finnish	*Vote*	*Estonian*	*Proto-Balto-Finnic*
1. luen lugən		loen	*luɣe-n
'I read (indicative)'			
2. olen lukenut ələn lukənnu		olen lugenud	*ole-n luke-nut
'I have read' (first person perfect indicative)			
3. luettiin lugəti:		loeti [loetti]	*luɣe-ttiin
'(it) was read' (past passive)			
4. lukemaan lukəma:		lugema [lukema]	*luke-ma-han
'third infinitive'			
5. lukeva lukəva		lugev [lukev]	*luke-vaʔ
'reading' (present active participle, basis of relative clauses)			

The 'third infinitive' is an infinitival form (formerly nominal) used especially with verbs of motion.

compared. With just these few compared words, we see indications of such aspects of Proto-Balto-Finnic morphosyntax as tenses and aspects, passive, embedded clauses with the third infinitive, and the participle (which is also used in relative clauses). This is enough to illustrate how the technique of reconstructing the proto-morphology can help us to obtain aspects of the proto-syntax.

While in some situations this technique can recover a considerable amount of the proto-syntax, it works less well where the cognate grammatical morphemes have undergone functional or positional shifts or have been lost due to other changes in the languages. Successful reconstruction here, as with phonological and lexical reconstruction, depends on the nature of the evidence preserved in the languages being compared. For example, when we compare the modern Romance languages, we are able to recover much less of the original morphology because so much has been lost in the various languages. This being the case, the technique of morphological reconstruction which worked well for aspects of Proto-Balto-Finnic syntax provides less for Proto-Romance syntax. (See Section 10.15, Chapter 10.)

11.5.4 Directionality

Just as knowing the characteristic direction of change in various sound changes provides clues to the best reconstruction in phonology, the directionality of a number of grammatical changes is also known, and this provides clues for the best grammatical reconstruction. An example of this is the fact that postpositions frequently become attached to roots and lose their independent status, becoming case suffixes; however, case suffixes hardly ever become independent postpositions. With the directionality Postposition > Case in mind, consider the comparisons of forms meaning 'with' in Table 11.5, where Postp = Postposition; Com = Comitative case ('with'). In this example, given the known directionality of Postposition > Case, it is incumbent upon us to reconstruct the postposition as original and to postulate that the comitative case endings which are the cognates in Veps and Estonian are due to a grammatical change, 'postposition' > 'comitative' case or clitic.

TABLE 11.5: Comparison of Balto-Finnic 'with' forms

Finnish	Karelian	Veps	Estonian	Vote	Livonian	Proto-Balto-Finnic
kanssa	kanssa	-ka	-ga [-ka]	ka:sa	ka:zu	*kans(s)aʔ
(Postp)	(Postp)	(Com)	(Com clitic)	(Postp)	(Postp)	(Postp)

11.5.5 Archaisms

An *archaism* (also often called *relic*) is something characteristic of the language of the past, a vestige, which survives chiefly in specialized uses. Archaisms are in some way exceptional or marginal to the language in which they are found.

They are most commonly preserved in certain kinds of language such as in proverbs, folk poetry, folk ballads, legal documents, prayers and religious texts, very formal genres or stylistic variants, and so on. A straightforward example is English *pease* for 'pea', an archaism preserved in the nursery rhyme 'Pease porridge hot, pease porridge cold, pease porridge in the pot nine days old'; it reflects the older *pease* before it was changed by analogical back formation to *pea* (mentioned in Chapter 4). As examples of archaisms in English more relevant to historical grammar, we might mention the verb forms with the *-eth* third person and *-st* second person agreement markers and the auxiliary forms *hath, hast, art, doth* (*doeth*), and the archaic second singular pronoun forms, *thou, thee, thy, thine*. These are all archaic and no longer productive. Some examples of these are:

> *Hell* **hath** *no fury like a woman scorned.* (Proverb)
>
> *What therefore God* **hath** *joined together, let not man put asunder.* (Marriage ceremony, Biblical, from Matthew 19:6.)
>
> *The lady* **doth** *protest too much, methinks.* (*Hamlet*)
>
> *O Romeo, Romeo!* **wherefore art thou***?* (*Romeo and Juliet*)

Several of these are illustrated in the 23rd Psalm, oft repeated in literature, poetry and song:

> *The Lord is my shepherd . . . He* **maketh** *me to lie down in green pastures; He* **leadeth** *me beside the still waters. He* **restoreth** *my soul; he* **leadeth** *me in the paths of righteousness for . . .* **thou art** *with me;* **thy** *rod and* **thy** *staff they comfort me.* **Thou preparest** *a table . . .* **thou anointest** *my head . . . my cup* **runneth** *over.*

As exceptions, archaisms have somehow been bypassed or exempted from the general changes which the language has undergone. Grammatical archaisms are favoured in syntactic reconstruction – some scholars believe them to be the single most useful source of evidence. Naturally, if we can tell what is archaic – by definition 'old' – it affords us extremely valuable information for historical reconstruction.

A difficulty with using archaisms (relics) for reconstruction is that it can be difficult to tell whether we are dealing with a legitimate archaism or something that is exceptional for other reasons but is not old. Another difficulty comes from the frequent situation in which we easily identify exceptions, but where the archaism provides too little information for reliable reconstruction.

Let us look at a slightly more complicated example. As we saw above, Proto-Balto-Finnic had a participle construction in which the logical subject of the participial verb was originally a direct object (in accusative case, as in (3) and (5)) of the main verb, but this was reanalyzed in Finnish so that the noun phrase came to be interpreted as the subject (in genitive case) of the participle (as in (4b) and (6)). This reanalysis was made possible by the homophony of the accusative and genitive singular case endings, both *-n*. Finnish archaisms preserve evidence of the construction before the change with the accusative. For example, in folk poems there are instances of relics such as (17a) (Acc = 'accusative', Pass = 'passive', Pl = 'plural', Part = 'participle', Gen = 'genitive'):

(17a) kuul-tihin kala-t kute-van, lohenpursto-t loiskutta-van
       hear-Past.Pass fish-Acc.Pl spawn-Part salmon.tail-Acc.Plsplash-Part
       'the fish were heard spawning, salmon-tails splashing'

Instead of the accusative plural of 'fish' (*kala-t*) and 'salmon-tails' (*lohenpursto-t*), modern Standard Finnish has the genitive plural, as in (17b):

(17b) kuul-tiin kalo-j-en kute-van, lohenpursto-j-en loiskutta-van
       hear-Past.Pass fish-Pl.Gen spawn-Part salmon.tail-Pl.Gen splash-Part

The relic contained in this folk poem provides additional support for the reconstruction above with the accusative pattern which was securely established on the basis of comparative evidence from the related languages. However, if other supporting evidence from related languages were not available, this archaism alone would be insufficient for a reliable reconstruction. We would not be certain whether this was in fact an archaism (and thus evidence of a former state of the language) or perhaps just some exception to the normal pattern for expressive or poetic purposes.

11.5.6 What can be successfully reconstructed

Another way of appreciating the possibilities for successful syntactic reconstruction is by evaluating the results of attempts to reconstruct the syntax of language families. The application of the comparative method to languages of the Uralic family reveals a proto-language with the following grammatical features. There were three contrasting grammatical numbers, 'dual' (*-kə(-)*), 'plural' (*-t* and *-j*) and 'singular' (Ø). Direct objects of finite verbs were marked by the 'accusative' case (*-m*), but the objects of an imperative verb bore no accusative marker. Case and definiteness were related; the genitive and accusative cases implied definiteness, while indefinite nouns took no marking (that is, in form they were not distinct from the nominative case). The 'genitive' case marked not only the possessor but also served to signal an adjective attribute before its head noun. Proto-Uralic verb tenses included: *-j* 'past', *-mə* 'past (perfect)', *-pA* 'present' and *-śA* 'past' ('*A*' denotes vowel harmony with the attached root). There was a negative verb, *e-*. Sentences minimally had a nominal subject and a predicate (verbal or nominal); the subject could be signalled by personal pronominal suffixes attached to the predicate. The predicate agreed with its subject (in person and number); there was no other agreement. The predicate of embedded clauses was in form a verbal noun, where personal possessive pronominal suffixes were used to signal its subject. The role of the embedded clause in the overall sentence was shown by case markings on the verbal noun (a nominalization) which was the core of the embedded clause. Proto-Uralic had no overt conjunctions or relative pronouns; embedded verbal nouns, nominalizations, were the only means of showing subordination. In brief, the application of the comparative method to the reconstruction of Proto-Uralic morphosyntax has proven quite successful and this case shows that, at least in some instances, we are capable of syntactic reconstruction (Janhunen 1982; Campbell 1990).

In summary, there are many obstacles to successful syntactic reconstruction, but many of these are like the obstacles encountered in phonological and lexical reconstruction, and in many instances, using normal historical linguistic techniques (recognition of borrowing, analogy and so on), we can get beyond the obstacles through the weight of the comparative evidence from related languages. Reliance on the known directionality of many grammatical changes helps, and reconstructed morphology and syntactic archaisms can provide very valuable information. In short, while syntactic reconstruction can be very difficult, it is clearly possible.

11.6 Exercises

Exercise 11.1 Syntactic change in Panare

Consider the following from Panare (a Cariban language of Venezuela). (NOTE: *y* = IPA [j], *ñ* = IPA [ɲ], *č* = IPA [tʃ].) The basic word order is verb first and subject final.) When the subject is 'I' or 'you', no copula (form of the verb 'to be') is required in the present tense, as in:

(1) maestro   yu   (2) maestro   amǝn
     teacher   I   teacher   you
     'I am a teacher'   'You are a teacher.'

However, with a third-person subject, a copula is obligatory. With an inanimate subject, the copula is *mǝn*, as in (3):

(3) eʔčipen   mǝn   manko
     fruit   mǝn   mango
     'Mango is a fruit'

For this exercise, such examples with inanimate subjects are not so relevant. However, with an animate subject, the copula is either *kǝh* or *nǝh*, with a difference in meaning. Sentences (4) and (5) show that sentences with third-person subjects but with no copula are ungrammatical (here /✗/ means ungrammatical):

(4) ✗maestro   eʔñapa   (5) ✗eʔčipen   manko
      teacher   Panare   fruit   mango

Sentences (6) (7), and (8) illustrate the *kǝh* and *nǝh* copulas and their difference:

(6) maestro   kǝh   eʔñapa   (7) eʔčipen   mǝn   manko
     teacher   kǝh   Panare   fruit   mǝn   mango
     'This Panare here is a teacher'   'Mango is a fruit'

(8) maestro   nǝh   eʔñapa
     teacher   nǝh   Panare
     'That Panare there is a teacher'

Now consider some demonstratives. The demonstratives *mǝh* 'this person whom I can see now' and *kǝn* 'that person whom I can't see now' at first glance appear to behave straightforwardly, as in (9) and (10):

(9) maestro   *kəh*   <u>məh</u>   (10) maestro   *nəh*   <u>kən</u>
     teacher   *kəh*   this.guy   teacher   *nəh*   that.guy
     'This guy is a teacher here'   'That guy is a teacher there'

But consider the additional Panare copular sentences in (11) through (14) (note here that /y/ changes to /č/ after /h/, so that *yu* 'I' in this example is *ču* in this context):

(11) maestro   *nəh*   məh   (12) maestro   *nəh*   ču
      teacher   *nəh*   this.guy   teacher   *nəh*   I
      'This guy was a teacher'   'I was a teacher'

(13) maestro   *nəh*   amən   (14) maestro   *kəh*   kən
      teacher   *nəh*   you   teacher   *kəh*   that.guy
      'You were a teacher'   'That guy is being a teacher right
                                              now'(that is, he is off somewhere
                                              performing his teaching duties at
                                              this very moment)

Though originally not possible, notice also that *kəh* and *nəh* now can also occur with ordinary verbs, as in (15) through (18) (the question mark indicates a sentence which sounds very strange to native speakers):

(15) əʔ púmanəpəh   *kəh*   Toman   (16) ? əʔ púmanəpəh   *nəh*   Toman
      be-falling   *kəh*   Thomas   be-falling   *nəh*   Thomas
      'Tom is falling'   'Tom is falling (but I can't see him)'

(17) yɨupúmən   *kəh*   Toman   (18) yɨupúmən   *nəh*   Toman
      fall   *kəh*   Thomas   fall   *nəh*   Thomas
      'Tom is going to fall!'   'Tom is going to fall one day' or
                                              'Tom fell'

State the syntactic changes which have affected *kəh* and *nəh*. Explain the historical development of these items as best you can using the terms and mechanisms presented in this chapter.

(Based on Gildea 1993.)

Exercise 11.2   *Syntactic change in Estonian*

Compare the sentences in this exercise, which represent different stages of Estonian (a Finno-Ugric language); explain what changed and identify the kinds of changes or the mechanisms involved.

Stage I: Estonian had two alternative constructions for subordinate clauses involving the complements of speech-act and mental-state main verbs, illustrated in (1) and (2) (Gen = 'genitive', Nom = 'nominative', Part = 'participle', Pres = 'present indicative'):

(1)   sai   kuulda,   et   seal   üks   mees   ela-b
      got   to.hear   that   there   one.Nom   man.Nom   live-3rd.Pres
      'he/she came to hear that a man lives there'
(2)   sai   kuulda   seal   ühe   mehe   ela-vat
      got   to.hear   there   one.Gen   man.Gen   live-Part
      (same meaning as (1))

Stage II: (1) and (2) remain possible, but the construction in (3) also became possible (note that 'participle' became 'indirect'):

(3)   sai   kuulda,   (et)   seal   üks   mees   ela-vat
      got   to.hear   (that) there   one.Nom   man.Nom   live-Indirect
      (3a) 'he/she came to hear that they say a man lives there'/
      (3b) 'he/she came to hear that reportedly a man lives there'

Stage III: (1), (2) and (3) are all possible now, but forms formerly found only in subordinate clauses, as in (3), came to be found also in main clauses, as in (4):

(4)   ta   tege-vat   töö-d
      he.Nom   do-Indirect   work-Partitive
      'They say he is working' / 'Reportedly he is working'

Exercise 11.3   The development of perfect auxiliaries in Spanish

In the following, the stages in the development of perfect auxiliaries in Spanish from their Latin origins are described and illustrated. On the basis of this information, compare the stages and attempt to determine the changes which took place and to identify the kinds of changes or the mechanisms involved. (Fem = 'feminine', Masc = 'masculine', Part = 'participle', Pl = 'plural', PPP = 'past passive participle').

Stage I: Latin used expressions with 'past passive participle' (PPP) in combination with the verbs *tenēre* 'hold', *habēre* 'keep, hold' and others meaning 'hold, possess, own', to represent something as ready or kept in a completed condition, as in (1):

(1)   Metuō enim   nē   ibi   vos   habeam   fatigā-tō-s (Late Latin)
      fear.I truly lest there   you   have.   I fatigue-PPP.Masc-Pl
      'I fear that I have you tired'/'that I have tired you'/'that you are tired'

This construction with 'past passive participle' was quite limited in its occurrence in Classical Latin, but became associated with 'perfect' aspect in combination with the development of *habēre* as an auxiliary. Originally this construction had *habēre* 'keep, hold, have' (a main verb) with the 'past passive participle' form as an adjective which modified the direct object (both the logical and surface object) of this main verb (*habēre*), which agreed in number and gender with this object as its head,

(2a) [habe-ō] [litter-ā-s   scrip-t-ā-s]
     have-I   letter-Fem-Pl.Acc   write-PPP-Fem-Pl.Acc
     'I have written letters' = ('I have letters which are written')

(2b) [habe-ō] [scrip-tum   libr-um}
     have-I   write-PPP.Masc.Acc.Sg. book-Masc.Acc.Sg.
     'I have (a) written book'

As seen here, the past passive principles *scriptās* in 2(a) and *scriptum* in 2(b) are declined as adjectives that agree in case, gender, and number with the head nouns, *litterās* in 2(a) and *librum* in 2(b); the past passive principle is not part of the main verb (*habeō* 'I have, hold' here), but functions as an adjective modifying the noun (*litterās* in 2(a) and *librum* in 2(b)).

Stage II: In Old Spanish, *haber* (spelled *aver* in Old Spanish, from Latin *habēre* 'to have, hold') in such constructions began to lose its possessive meaning and to consolidate the auxiliary function, resulting in compound tenses, but still with agreement in gender and number between the participle and the direct object until the mid-sixteenth century, as illustrated in (3) (where the *-o-s* 'masculine plural' of *hechos* 'made' agrees with the *-o-s* 'masculine plural' of *enemigos* 'enemies'):

(3) Los   había . . . he-ch-_o-s_   enemig-_o-s_   de estotros
    Them had   make-Past.Part-Masc-Pl enemy-Masc-Pl of these.others
    'He had made enemies of these others' (from Hernán Cortés)

Stage III: Gradually, the *haber* + PPP construction changed, eliminating the requirement that 'past passive participle' must agree in number and gender with the noun which it modified, losing its passive sense, with the verb *haber* becoming the 'perfect auxiliary', and Modern Spanish no longer permits agreement between the participle and the object, as in (4):

(4) Hemos   escri-to   cart-a-s
    have.we write-Past.Part letter-Fem-Pl
    'We have written letters'

The adjectival participle source with number and gender agreement still survives in other contexts (but not in the perfect construction with forms of the verb *haber*), for example:

(5) Tenemos cart-_a-s_   escri-t-_a-s_   en tint-a   roj-a
    have.we letter-Fem-Pl write-Past.Part-Fem-Pl in ink-Fem.Sg red-Fem.Sg
    'We have letters written in red ink'.

In the series of changes described here, the meaning is no longer 'X possesses that which has been done', but 'X has done', and is accompanied by the structural change of *haber* from main verb to an auxiliary.

Stage IV: Additional changes in connection with the new 'perfect' construction also came about. First, the verb *ser* 'to be' had formerly also been a an auxiliary used with certain intransitive verbs (especially verbs of motion) (as in (6a) and (7a)), but this was replaced by the auxiliary *haber*, as seen in the Modern Spanish equivalents in (6b) and (7b):

(6a) Old Spanish   ella   *es*   naci-d-*a*
                           she   is   born-Past.Part-Fem

(6b) Modern Spanish   ella   ha   naci-do
                           she   has   born-Past.Part
                           'she has been born'

(7a) Old Spanish   ellos   *son*   i-d-*o-s*
                           they   are   go-Past.Part-Masc-Pl

(7b) Modern Spanish   ellos   *han*   i-do
                           they   have   go-Past.Part
                           'they have gone' (Lapesa 1981: 212)

Second, the word order changed, placing the participle closer to the auxiliary, for example from the equivalent of 'I have a letter written' (as in (2)) to 'I have written a letter' (as in (4)).

Exercise 11.4   *Finding examples of grammaticalization*

The following are some of the most common pathways of grammaticalization (that is, lexical sources which often become grammatical morphemes as a result of grammaticalization changes). Attempt to find examples from English (or from other languages you may be familiar with) which might illustrate these processes. (A few which are extremely common around the world are also included even though English alone may not offer examples.) As an example, for 'go to' > Future, you might list English 'going to' > Future as in 'Hermione is going to marry Ron.'

   (1) Allative ('to') > complementizer (for example, marker of infinitives)
   (2) 'come' > future
   (3) Copula ('to be') > obligation (such as 'must', 'should')
   (4) Demonstrative pronoun (such as 'this', 'that') > definite article (such as 'the')
   (5) 'get' > passive
   (6) 'have' (possession) > obligation
   (7) 'have' (possession) > perfect or completive aspect
   (8) 'keep' ('hold', 'grasp') > continuous
   (9) 'keep' > possession ('have')
   (10) 'man' > indefinite pronoun
   (11) 'need' > obligation
   (12) 'one' > indefinite pronoun, indefinite article
   (13) 'owe' > obligation
   (14) 'say' > quotative

(15) 'say' > conditional
(16) 'want' > future
(17) Wh-question word (such as 'what?', 'which?', 'who') > relative pronoun, relative clause marker.

12

Language Contact

Es gibt keine Mischsprache. [There is no mixed language.]

(Max Müller 1871: 86)

Es gibt keine völlig ungemischte Sprache. [There is no totally unmixed language.]

(Hugo Schuchardt 1884: 5)

12.1   Introduction

We speak of *language contact* when two or more languages (or varieties of languages) interact with one another. When historical linguists speak of language contact, they usually mean change in languages caused by this interaction among languages, and some prefer to speak of *contact-induced language change*. Some call the study of language contact 'contact linguistics'. This usually includes borrowing, multilingualism, areal linguistics, pidgin and creole languages, language shift and maintenance, language endangerment, and mixed languages in particular, and sometimes also other topics. In this chapter we look at how historical linguists deal with change due to language contact. In particular, we look at areal linguistics, pidgin and creole languages, mixed languages, and language endangerment here. (For borrowing see Chapter 3; examples of syntactic change due to language contact are presented in Chapter 11.)

12.2   Areal Linguistics

Areal linguistics, related to borrowing (Chapter 3), is concerned with the diffusion of structural features across language boundaries within a geographical area. This section defines areal linguistics, surveys the features of a few of the better-known linguistic areas of the world, and then addresses issues concerning how areally diffused features are identified, how linguistic areas are established, and what impact areal linguistics has on other aspects of historical linguistics – its implications for subgrouping, reconstruction and proposals of distant genetic relationship. Areal linguistics is very important because the goal of historical linguistics is to determine the full history of languages, to find out what really happened. The full history includes understanding both inherited traits (traits shared in genetically related languages because they come from a common parent language) and diffused features (traits shared because of borrowing and convergence among neighbouring languages). This is important in many ways. For example, in order to reconstruct proto-languages accurately or to determine family relationships, it is necessary to distinguish material which is borrowed from that which is inherited from a common ancestor.

12.2.1 Defining the concept

The term *linguistic area* refers to a geographical area in which, due to borrowing and language contact, languages of a region come to share certain structural features–not only borrowed words, but also shared elements of phonological, morphological or syntactic structure. Linguistic areas are also referred to at times by the terms *Sprachbund*, *diffusion area*, *adstratum relationship* and *convergence area*. The central feature of a linguistic area is the existence of structural similarities shared among languages of a geographical area (where usually some of the languages are genetically unrelated or at least are not all close relatives). It is assumed that the reason why the languages of the area share these traits is because at least some of them are borrowed.

The studies of linguistic areas that have been undertaken are of two sorts. The more common approach, called *circumstantialist*, mostly just lists similarities found in the languages of a geographical area, allowing the list of shared traits to suggest diffusion. In this approach, firm evidence that the shared traits actually are due to diffusion is typically not required. Circumstantialist areal linguistics has been criticized, since it does not eliminate chance, universals, and possibly undetected genetic relationships as alternative possible explanations for shared traits. The other approach, called *historicist*, attempts to find concrete evidence showing that the shared traits are diffused (borrowed). The historicist approach is preferred because it is more rigorous and reliable, although the lack of clear historical information in many cases makes it necessary to fall back on the less reliable circumstantialist approach (Campbell 1985).

While some linguistic areas are reasonably well established, more investigation is required for nearly all of them. Some other linguistic areas amount to barely more than preliminary hypotheses. Linguistic areas are often defined, surprisingly, by a rather small number of shared linguistic traits.

12.2.2 Examples of linguistic areas

A good way to get a solid feel for linguistic areas and how they are defined is to look at some of the better-known ones. In what follows, some are presented with the more important of the generally accepted defining traits shared by the languages of each linguistic area.

(1) *The Balkans.* The languages of the Balkans linguistic area are Greek, Albanian, Serbo-Croatian, Bulgarian, Macedonian and Romanian (to which

some scholars also add Romani [the language of the Gypsies] and Turkish). Some salient traits of the Balkans linguistic area are:

1. A central vowel /ɨ/ (or /ə/) (not present in Greek or Macedonian).

2. Syncretism of dative and genitive (dative and genitive cases have merged in form and function); this is illustrated by Romanian *fetei* 'to the girl' or 'girl's' (compare *fată* 'girl'; *ă* represents a short or reduced *a*), as in *am data o carte fetei* 'I gave the letter to the girl' and *frate fetei* 'the girl's brother'.

3. Postposed articles (not in Greek); for example, Bulgarian *mɔʒ-ət* 'the man' / *mɔʒ* 'man'.

4. Periphrastic future (futures signalled by an auxiliary verb corresponding to 'want' or 'have'; not in Bulgarian or Macedonian), as in Romanian *voi fuma* 'I will smoke' (literally 'I want smoke') and *am a cínta* 'I will sing' (literally 'I have sing').

5. Periphrastic perfect (with an auxiliary verb corresponding to 'have').

6. Absence of infinitives (instead, the languages have constructions such as 'I want that I go' for 'I want to go'); for example, 'give me something to drink' has the form corresponding to 'give me that I drink', as in: Romanian *dă-mi să beau*, Bulgarian *daj mi da pija*, Tosk Albanian *a-më të pi*, Greek *dós mu na pjó*.

7. Use of a personal pronoun copy of animate objects so that the object is doubly marked, as illustrated by Romanian *i-am scris lui Ion* 'I wrote to John', literally 'to.him-I wrote him John', and Greek *ton vlépo ton jáni* 'I see John', literally 'him.Acc I see the/him.Acc John' (Joseph 1992; Sandfeld 1930).

(2) *South Asia (Indian subcontinent).* This area is composed of languages belonging to the Indo-Aryan, Dravidian, Munda and Tibeto-Burman families. Some traits shared among different languages of the area are:

1. Retroflex consonants, particularly retroflex stops.

2. Absence of prefixes (accept in Munda).

3. Presence of a 'dative-subject construction' (that is, dative-experiencer, as in Hindi *mujhe maaluum thaa* I knew it' [*mujhe* 'to me' + know + Past], *mujhe pasand hai* 'I like it' [to.me + like + Past]).

4. Subject–Object–Verb (SOV) basic word order, including post-positions.

5. Absence of a verb 'to have'.

6. The 'conjunctive or absolutive participle' (tendency for subordinate clauses to have non-finite verb forms and for them to be preposed; for example, relative clauses precede their heads).

7. Morphological causatives.

8. So-called 'explicator compound verbs' (where a special auxiliary from a limited set is said to complete the sense of the immediately preceding main verb, and the two verbs together refer to a single event, as in, for example Hindi *kho baithnaa* 'to lose' ['lose' + 'sit'], *le jaanaa* 'to take away' ['take' + 'go']).

9. Sound symbolic (phonesthetic) forms based on reduplication, often with *k*

suffixed (for example in Kota, a Dravidian language: *kad-kadk* '[heart or mind] beats fast with guilt or worry'; *a:nk-a:nk* 'to be very strong [of man, bullock], very beautiful [of woman]').

Some of these proposed areal features are not limited to the Indian subcontinent, but can be found in neighbouring languages (for example, SOV basic word order is found throughout much of Eurasia and northern Africa) and in languages in many other parts of the world, while some of the other traits are not necessarily independent of one another (for example, languages with SOV basic word order tend also to have non-finite subordinate clauses (as in (6)), especially relative clauses, and not to have prefixes). (Compare Emeneau 1980.)

(3) *Mesoamerica*. The language families and isolates which make up the Mesoamerican linguistic area are: Nahua (branch of Uto-Aztecan), Mixe-Zoquean, Mayan, Xinkan, Otomanguean, Totonacan, Tarascan, Cuitlatec, Tequistlatecan and Huave. Five areal traits are shared by nearly all Mesoamerican languages, but not by neighbouring languages beyond this area, and these are considered particularly diagnostic of the linguistic area. They are:

1. Nominal possession of the type *his-dog the man* 'the man's dog', as illustrated by Pipil (Uto-Aztecan): *i-pe:lu ne ta:kat*, literally 'his-dog the man'.

2. Relational nouns (locative expressions composed of noun roots and possessive pronominal affixes), of the form, for example, *my-head* for 'on me', as in Tz'utujil (Mayan): *(č)r-i:x* 'behind it, in back of it', composed of *č-* 'at, in', *r-* 'his/her/its' and *i:x* 'back', contrasted with *č-w-i:x* 'behind me', literally 'at-my-back'.

3. Vigesimal numeral systems based on combinations of twenty, such as that of Chol (Mayan): *hun-k'al* '20' (1x20), *čaʔ-k'al* '40' (2x20), *uʃ-k'al* '60' (3x20), *hoʔ-k'al* '100' (5x20), *hun-bahk'* '400' (1x400), *čaʔ-bahk'* '800' (2x400) and so on.

4. Non-verb-final basic word order (no SOV languages) – although Mesoamerica is surrounded by languages both to the north and south which have SOV (Subject–Object–Verb) word order, languages within the linguistic area have VOS, VSO or SVO basic order.

5. A large number of loan translation compounds (calques) are shared by the Mesoamerican languages; these include examples such as 'boa' = 'deer-snake', 'egg' = 'bird-stone/bone', 'lime' = 'stone(-ash)', 'knee' = 'leg-head' and 'wrist' = 'hand-neck' (mentioned also in 3.7.7, Chapter 3). Since these five traits are shared almost unanimously throughout the languages of Mesoamerica but are found almost not at all in neighbouring languages outside of Mesoamerica, they are considered strong evidence in support of the validity of Mesoamerica as a linguistic area.

Additionally, a large number of other features are shared among several Mesoamerican languages but are not found in all the languages of the area, while other traits shared among the Mesoamerican languages are found also in languages beyond the borders of the area. Some widely distributed phonological phenomena of these sorts are:

1. Devoicing of final sonorant consonants (*l, r, w, y*) (K'ichean, Nahuatl, Pipil, Xinkan, Totonac, Tepehua, Tarascan and Sierra Popoluca), as for example in Nahuatl /no-mi:l/ [no-mi:l̥] 'my cornfield'.

2. Voicing of obstruents after nasals (most Otomanguean languages, Tarascan, Mixe-Zoquean, Huave, Xinkan), as in Copainalá Zoque /n-tɨk/ [ndɨk] 'my house'.

3. Predictable stress; most Mesoamerican languages have predictable stress (contrastive stress is rare in the area). Some of the languages share the rule which places the stress on the vowel before the last (rightmost) consonant of the word (V́/__C(V)#) (Oluta Popoluca, Totontepec Mixe, Xinkan and many Mayan languages (by default in these Mayan languages, where stress falls on final syllables, but roots do not end in vowels)).

4. Inalienable possession of body parts and kinship terms (in almost all Mesoamerican languages, but this feature is characteristic of many languages throughout the Americas).

5. Numeral classifiers (many Mayan languages, plus Tarascan, Totonac, Nahuatl and so on), as in Tzeltal (Mayan) *oʃ-tehk teʔ* [three plant-thing wood] 'three trees', *oʃ-k'as teʔ* [three broken-thing wood] 'three chunks of firewood'.

6a. Noun-incorporation, a construction where a general nominal object can become part of the verb, is found in some Mayan languages (Yucatec, Mam), Nahua and Totonac. An example is Nahuatl *ni-tlaʃkal-čiwa* [I-tortilla(s)-make] 'I make tortillas'.

6b. Body-part incorporation (Nahuatl, Totonac, Mixe-Zoquean, Tlapanec, Tarascan), a sort of noun-incorporation where specific forms for body parts can be incorporated in the verb, usually as instrumentals, though sometimes also as direct objects, as for example in Pipil (Uto-Aztecan): *tan-kwa* [tooth-eat] 'bite', *ikʃi-ahsi* [foot-arrive] 'to reach, overtake', *mu-yaka-pitsa* [Reflexive-nose-blow] 'to blow one's nose'. This type of construction is found also in various languages elsewhere in the Americas.

7. Directional morphemes ('away from' or 'towards') incorporated into the verb (Mayan, Nahua, Tequistlatec, Tarascan, some Otomanguean languages, Totonac), as in Kaqchikel (Mayan) *y-e-ɓe-n-kamisax* [Aspect-them-thither-I-kill] 'I'm going there to kill them'.

8. An inclusive–exclusive contrast in the pronoun system (Chol, Mam, Akateko, Jakalteko, Chocho, Popoloca, Ixcatec, Otomí, Mixtec, Trique, Chatino, Yatzachi Zapotec, Tlapanec, Huave, several Mixe-Zoquean languages), as, for example, in Chol (Mayan) *honon la* 'we (inclusive)', *honon lohon* 'we (exclusive)'.

9a. 'Zero' copula (no form of the verb 'to be'). An overt copula is lacking from most Mesoamerican languages in equational constructions, as in K'iche' (Mayan) *saq le xah* [white the house] 'the house is white'. This feature is also found widely elsewhere in the Americas and beyond.

9b. A pronominal copular construction (Mayan, Nahua, Chocho, Chinantec, Mazatec, Otomí, several Mixe-Zoquean languages). Copular sentences with pronominal subjects are formed with pronominal affixes attached directly to the complement, as in Q'eqchi' (Mayan) *iʃq-at* [woman-you]

'you are a woman', *kwinq-in* [man-I] 'I am a man'; Pipil *ti-siwa:t* [you-woman] 'you are a woman' (Campbell, Kaufman and Smith-Stark 1986).

(4) *The Northwest Coast of North America.* As traditionally defined, the Northwest Coast linguistic area includes Tlingit, Eyak, the Athabaskan languages of the region, Haida, Tsimshian, Wakashan, Chimakuan, Salishan, Alsea, Coosan, Kalapuyan, Takelma and Lower Chinook. This is the best-known of North American linguistic areas. The languages of this area are characterized by elaborate systems of consonants, which include series of glottalized stops and affricates, labiovelars, multiple laterals (*l, ł, tl, tl'*) and uvular stops in contrast to velars. The labial consonant series typically contains fewer consonants than those for other points of articulation (labials are completely lacking in Tlingit and Tillamook and are quite limited in Eyak and most Athabaskan languages); in contrast, the uvular series is especially rich in most of these languages. The vowel systems are limited, with only three vowels (*i, a, o,* or *i, a, u*) in several of the languages, and only four vowels in others. Several of the languages have pharyngeals (*ʕ, ħ*), and most have glottalized resonants and continuants.

Shared morphological traits include extensive use of suffixes; nearly complete absence of prefixes; reduplication processes (often of several sorts, signalling various grammatical functions, for example iteration, continuative, progressive, plural, collective and so on); numeral classifiers; alienable/inalienable oppositions in nouns; pronominal plural; nominal plural (distributive plural is optional); verbal reduplication signifying distribution, repetition and so on; suffixation of tense–aspect markers in verbs; evidential markers in the verb; and locative–directional markers in the verb; plus masculine/feminine gender (shown in demonstratives and articles); visibility/invisibility opposition in demonstratives; and nominal and verbal reduplication signalling the diminutive. Aspect is relatively more important than tense (and aspect includes at least a momentaneous/durative dichotomy). All but Tlingit have passive-like constructions. The negative appears as the first element in a clause regardless of the usual word order. Northwest Coast languages also have lexically paired singular and plural verb stems (that is, an entirely different lexical root may be required with a plural subject from the root used with a singular subject).

Some other traits shared by a smaller number of Northwest Coast languages include:

1. A widely diffused sound change of **k > č*, which affected Wakashan, Salishan, Chimakuan and some other Northwest Coast languages.
2. Tones (or pitch-accent contrasts), found in a number of the languages (Tlingit, Haida, Bella Bella, Upriver Halkomelem, Quileute, Kalapuyan and Takelma).
3. Ergative alignment in several of the languages (where the subject of intransitive verbs and the object of transitives have similar morphosyntactic marking, while the subject of transitive verbs is marked differently) (Tlingit, Haida, Tsimshian, some Salishan languages, Sahaptin, Chinookan, Coosan).
4. 'Lexical suffixes', found in a number of the languages (Wakashan and Salishan); lexical suffixes designate such familiar objects (which are

ordinarily signalled with full lexical roots in most other languages) as body parts, geographical features, cultural artifacts and some abstract notions. Wakashan, for example, has some 300 of these.

5. In the grammar of these languages, one finds a severely limited role for a contrast between nouns and verbs as distinct categories (some assert the total lack of a noun–verb distinction for some of the languages).

The sub-area of the Northwest which lacks primary nasals includes the languages Twana and Lushootseed (Salishan languages), Quileute (Chimakuan) and Nitinat and Makah (Nootkan, of the broader Wakashan family). The last two, for example, have changed their original *m > b, *ṁ > b', *n > d and *n' > d' due to areal pressure, but closely related Nootka has retained the original nasals (Haas 1969b; Campbell 1997a: 333–4) (mentioned also in Table 5.7 in Chapter 5.).

(5) *The Baltic.* The Baltic linguistic area is defined somewhat differently by different scholars. It includes at least (Balto-)Finnic languages (especially Estonian and Livonian) and Baltic languages (Indo-European), and usually also Baltic German. Some have included all of the following (and others) in their treatment of the Baltic linguistic area: Old Prussian (now extinct), Lithuanian, Lavian (Baltic, branch of Indo-European); the ten Saami (Lapp) languages, Finnish, Estonian, Livonian, Vote, Veps, Karelian and others (of the Balto-Finnic branch of Finno-Ugric); High German, Low German, Baltic German, Yiddish (West Germanic); Danish, Swedish, Norwegian (North Germanic); Russian, Belorussian, Ukranian, Polish, Kashubian (Slavic); Romani (Indo-Aryan, branch of Indo-European); and Karaim (Turkic).

The Baltic area is defined by several shared features, some of which are:

1. First-syllable stress.
2. Palatalization of consonants.
3. Tonal contrasts.
4. Partitive case/partitive constructions (to signal partially affected objects, equivalent to, for example, 'I ate (some) apple', found in Finnic, Lithuanian, Latvian, Russian, Polish, etc.
5. Nominative objects in a number of constructions which lack overt subjects (Finnic, Baltic, North Russian).
6. Evidential mood ('John works hard [it is said/it is inferred]': Estonian, Livonian, Latvian, Lithuanian).
7. Prepositional verbs (as German *aus-gehen* [out-to.go] 'to go out': German, Livonian, Estonian, Baltic and others.
8. Subject-Verb-Object (SVO) basic word order.
9. Agreement of adjectives in number with the nouns which they modify (all languages of the area except Saami languages and Karaim); adjectives also agree in case in all except the Scandinavian languages (which have lost case distinctions for adjectives); they also agree in gender in Baltic, Slavic, Scandinavian, and German, Yiddish, and some others.

(For a more complete list of traits which have been attributed to this linguistic area, see Zeps 1962, Dahl and Koptjevskaja-Tamm 2001, and especially Koptjevskaja-Tamm and Bernhard Wälchli 2001.)

(6) *Ethiopia*. Languages of the Ethiopian linguistic area include: Cushitic (Beja, Awngi, Afar, Sidamo, Somali, etc.), Ethiopian Semitic (Ge'ez, Tigre, Tigrinya, Amharic, etc.), Omotic (Wellamo [Wolaytta], Kefa, Janjero [Yemsa], etc.), Anyuak, Gumuz and others. Among the traits they share are the following:

1. SOV basic word order, including postpositions.
2. Subordinate clause preceding main clause.
3. Gerund (non-finite verb in subordinate clauses, often inflected for person and gender).
4. A 'quoting' construction (a direct quotation followed by some form of 'to say').
5. Compound verbs (consisting of a noun-like 'preverb' and a semantically empty auxiliary verb).
6. Negative copula.
7. Plurals of nouns are not used after numbers.
8. Gender distinction in second and third person pronouns.
9. Reduplicated intensives.
10. Different present tense marker for main and subordinate clauses.
11. The form equivalent to the feminine singular is used for plural concord (feminine singular adjective, verb or pronoun is used to agree with a plural noun).
12. A singulative construction (the simplest noun may be a collective or plural and it requires an affix to make a singular).
13. Shared phonological traits such as *f* but no *p*, palatalization, glottalized consonants, gemination, presence of pharyngeal fricatives (ħ and ʕ).

(Ferguson 1976; cf. Tosco 2000; see also Thomason 2001: 111–13.)

12.2.3 How to determine linguistic areas

On what basis is it decided that something constitutes a linguistic area? Scholars have at times utilized the following considerations and criteria: the number of traits shared by languages in a geographical area, bundling of the shared traits in some significant way (for example, clustering at roughly the same geographical boundaries), and the weight of different areal traits (some are counted differently from others on the assumption that some provide stronger evidence than others of areal affiliation).

With respect to the number of areal traits necessary to justify a linguistic area, in general the rule is: the more, the merrier – that is, linguistic areas in which many diffused traits are shared among the languages are generally considered more strongly established; however, some argue that even one shared trait is enough to define a weak linguistic area (Campbell 1985). Regardless of debate over some arbitrary minimum number of defining traits, it is clear that some areas are more securely established because they contain many shared traits, whereas other areas may be weaker because their languages share fewer areal traits. In the linguistic areas considered above, we see considerable variation in the number and kind of traits they share which define them.

With respect to the relatively greater weight or importance attributed to some traits than to others for defining linguistic areas, the borrowed word order patterns in the Ethiopian linguistic area provide an instructive example. Ethiopian Semitic languages exhibit a number of areal traits diffused from neighbouring Cushitic languages. Several of these individual traits, however, are interconnected due to the borrowing of the SOV (Subject–Object–Verb) basic word order patterns of Cushitic languages into the formerly VSO Ethiopian Semitic languages. Typologically, the orders Noun–Postposition, Verb–Auxiliary, Relative Clause– Head Noun and Adjective–Noun are all correlated and they tend to co-occur with SOV order cross-linguistically. If the expected correlations among these con- structions are not taken into account, we might be tempted to count each one as a separate shared areal trait. Their presence in Ethiopian Semitic languages might seem to reflect several different diffused traits (SOV counted as one, Noun– Postposition as another, and so on), and they could be taken as several independ- ent pieces of evidence defining a linguistic area. However, from the perspective of expected word order co-occurrences, these word order arrangements may not be independent traits, but may be viewed as the result of the diffusion of a single complex feature, the overall SOV word order type with its various expected coordinated orderings of typologically interrelated constructions. However, even though the borrowing of SOV basic word order type may count only as a single diffused areal trait, many scholars would still rank it as counting for far more than some other individual traits based on the knowledge of how difficult it is for a language to change so much of its basic word order by diffusion.

With respect to the criterion of the bundling of areal traits, some scholars had thought that such clustering at the boundaries of a linguistic area might be necessary for defining linguistic areas correctly. However, this is not correct. Linguistic areas are similar to traditional dialects in this regard (see Chapter 7). Often, one trait may spread out and extend across a greater territory than another trait, whose territory may be more limited, so that their boundaries do not coincide ('bundle'). This is the most typical pattern, where languages within the core of an area may share a number of features, but the geographical extent of the individual traits may vary considerably one from another. However, in a situation where the traits do coincide at a clear boundary, rare though this may be, the definition of a linguistic area which matches their boundary is relatively secure. As seen earlier, several of the traits in the Mesoamerican linguistic area do have the same boundary, but in many other areas, the core areal traits do not have the same boundaries, offering no clearly identifiable outer border of the linguistic area in question.

In the end, what is important is to try to answer the question, 'what happened?' If we succeed in determining what changes have taken place, and how, when and where they took place, we will have provided the information upon which lin- guistic areas depend. If we succeed in finding out what happened, we will know which changes are due to borrowing and which to other factors, and we will know how the changes are distributed in the languages involved. The geographi- cal patterning characteristic of linguistic areas will be a natural consequence of this fuller historical account. In the end, areal linguistics is not distinct from borrowing; rather, it depends on an understanding of the patterns of borrowing. Therefore, a full account of the linguistic changes in the languages involved, including in particular contact-induced changes, is a sufficient goal, even if in the end the definition of a linguistic area based on these traits is not entirely clear. It is the borrowed traits that tell us about linguistic areas; linguistic areas are not necessary to understand these traits themselves and to answer the question of what really happened.

12.2.4 Implications of areal linguistics for linguistic reconstruction and subgrouping

Areal diffusion can have important implications for reconstruction and for subgrouping within known language families (see Chapter 6). Nootkan provides a good example which illustrates this. The sound correspondences upon which Nootkan subgrouping is based are given in Table 12.1 (some of which have been seen in other chapters). Nitinat and Makah appear to share the innovation which changed nasals to corresponding voiced stops (in (1–4)), while Nitinat and Nootka appear to share the change of the glottalized uvulars to pharyngeals (in (5) and (6)). Makah and Nitinat also share the retention of uvular fricatives, which Nootka has changed to a pharyngeal (in (7) and (8)); however, shared retentions are not valid evidence for subgrouping (see Chapter 6). That is, one innovation (denasalization) suggests a subgrouping of Makah–Nitinat, with Nootka as more distantly related, while the other innovation (pharyngealization) suggests Nitinat–Nootka, with Makah less closely related. This seeming impasse is solved when we take into account the fact that the absence of nasals is an areal feature shared by several other languages of the area; it diffused into both Makah and Nitinat under areal pressure and is thus not solid evidence of a shared common development before the languages separated, but rather diffused after these languages split up. The innovation shared by Nitinat and Nootka of glottalized uvulars changing to pharyngeals (in (5) and (6)) is real evidence of subgrouping – a true (non-diffused) shared innovation. So, Nitinat and Nootka together constitute one branch of the family, Makah the other branch. Moreover, with respect to areal implications for reconstruction, if we did not know about the areal diffusion in this case, we might be tempted to reconstruct the voiced stops in Proto-Nootkan and postulate a change of these to nasals in Nootka (for

TABLE 12.1: Nootkan sound correspondences

	Makah	*Nitinat*	*Nootka*	*Proto-Nootkan*
(1)	b	b	m	*m
(2)	b'	b'	ṁ	*ṁ
(3)	d	d	n	*n
(4)	d'	d'	ṅ	*ṅ
(5)	q'	ʕ	ʕ	*q'
(6)	q'ʷ	ʕ	ʕ	*q'ʷ
(7)	χʷ	χʷ	ħ	*χʷ
(8)	χ	χ	ħ	*χ

(Haas 1969b)

(1–4)), getting it wrong in this case. Thus, recognition of areal linguistic traits can be important for how we classify (subgroup) and how we reconstruct. (See also 3.7.2 in Chapter 3, Table 5.7 in Chapter 5, and Table 6.3 in Chapter 6.)

12.2.5 Areal linguistics and proposals of distant genetic relationship

Unfortunately, it is not uncommon to find cases of similarities among languages which are in reality due to areal diffusion but which are mistakenly taken to be evidence of a possible distant family relationship among the languages in question. One example will be sufficient to illustrate this. The Mosan hypothesis proposes a genetic connection between the Salishan, Wakashan and Chimakuan language families of the Northwest Coast of North America. Several scholars had noted structural similarities among these languages and a number accepted Mosan as a genetic grouping, though today this hypothesis has for the most part been abandoned. A big part of why the Mosan hypothesis was not found convincing has to do with the fact that much of the evidence originally presented in its favour turns out to be widely borrowed traits of the Northwest Coast linguistic area. For example, Morris Swadesh (1953) presented sixteen shared structural similarities in support of the proposed Mosan genetic grouping, but most of these features turn out to be traits of the linguistic area (others of Swadesh's traits are typologically expected correlations with other traits and are widely found in languages throughout the world, not just in putative 'Mosan' languages). Typologically commonplace traits are also not good evidence of genetic relationship, since they can easily develop independently in languages.)

For illustration's sake, we look at just a few of the putative 'Mosan' features which Swadesh presented which turn out to be Northwest Coast areal traits (identified above in the discussion of the Northwest Coast linguistic area):

(1) 'Extensive use of suffixes.'
(2) 'Nearly complete absence of functioning prefixes in Chimakuan and Wakashan, minor role in comparison to the suffixes in Salish.' (Notice that typologically it is quite common for suffixing languages to lack prefixes.)
(3) 'Extensive use of stem reduplication, including initial reduplication . . . and . . . full stem reduplication.'
(4) 'Aspect, including at least the dichotomy of momentaneous and durative.'
(5) 'Tense is an optional category.'
(6) 'Distributive plural is an optional category. This is very different from the European kind of plurality.'
(7) 'Dichotomy of non-feminine versus feminine gender shown in demonstratives and articles.'
(8) 'Numeral classifier notions, shown by suffixes.'
(9) 'Two alternate stems for number' (lexically paired distinct singular and plural verb stems).
(10) 'Lexical suffixes (sometimes called field suffixes), referring to body parts and other space references.'

(11) 'Predicative use of nouns.'

(12) 'Demonstrative distinctions such as the present versus absent, or visible versus invisible.'

As is clear, these traits which Swadesh listed as evidence for the Mosan hypothesis of remote linguistic relationship are better explained as the results of borrowing within the Northwest Coast linguistic area (see Campbell 1997a for details).

Much of the evidence upon which the Altaic hypothesis was based when it was originally formed also turns out to be probably due to areal diffusion, one of the reasons why specialists have not found it convincing (see details in Chapter 14). The core Altaic hypothesis holds that Turkic, Mongolian, and Tungusic are genetically related. Problems for the proposal include, among several others, the extensive lexical borrowing among these language groups and extensive areal diffusion. Traits that were cited in support of 'Altaic' include vowel harmony, relatively simple phoneme inventories, agglutination, exclusively suffixing, (S)OV word order, postpositions, no verb 'to have' for possession, no articles, no gender, and the use of non-finite (participial) verb forms for subordinate clauses. All these shared features are considered areal traits, shared by a number of languages in surrounding regions whose structural properties were not well known when the hypothesis was first framed. Clearly, failure to distinguish areal linguistic traits is a considerable obstacle to the Altaic hypothesis. (See Chapter 14 for details.)

From these examples, it is easy to see why the identification of areal traits is so important in historical linguistics. In this case, failure to recognize the areal borrowings led to an erroneous proposals of genetic relationship among neighbouring language families. (The methods for investigating distant genetic relationship are treated in detail in Chapter 14.)

12.3   Pidgins and Creoles

Definitions of *pidgin* and of *creole* differ. It is said to be a law of pidgin and creole studies that almost everyone else's definition of a creole sound absurd and arbitrary (DeCamp 1977: 4). A pidgin language is traditionally seen as a minimal contact language, for example used for trade, though it is not the native language of either trading group; instead, it is often based largely on a simplified version of one of the languages, usually a European one, perhaps mixed with some elements from the other language or languages in the contact situation. Thus, according to one definition, a pidgin 'is a marginal language which arises to fulfill certain restricted communication needs among people who have no common language' (Todd 1974: 1). In contrast, a creole language in the traditional view arises from a pidgin that has become the native language of its community of speakers – it is a pidgin that has acquired native speakers, usually through marriage of individuals who only have the pidgin language in common, and whose children grow up with this pidgin as their primary means of communication. In this situation, it is believed that the former pidgin expands from its simplified origins and becomes a fuller language able to meet all the communicative needs of its speakers. In this view, while a pidgin is not the native language of its speakers, a creole is the native language of many of its speakers. As we will see shortly, however, this traditional view of how pidgins and creoles arise and the relationship between the two is not universally accepted.

The etymology of *pidgin* is uncertain, but there is no shortage of hypotheses about the origin of the word. Among proposals, many assume it is derived from a Chinese corruption of English *business*; some think it is a Chinese corruption of Portuguese *ocupação* 'business'. The etymology of *creole* is clearer, from Portuguese *crioulo* or Spanish *criollo* 'person born in the (American) colonies'.

There are many pidgin and creole languages around the world; a few that are more commonly talked about are:

Bajan Creole (English based, Barbados)
Belizean Creole (English based, Belize)
Bislama (English based, Vanuatu)
Chavacano (Spanish based, Philippines)
Chinese Pidgin English (English based)
Chinook Jargon (Chinuk Wawa) (based on Lower Chinook, Pacific Northwest of North America)
Gullah (English based, sea islands of North Carolina, South Carolina, and Georgia)
Guyanese Creole (English based, Guyana)
Haitian Creole (French based, Haiti)
Hawaiian Pidgin (also called Hawaii Pidgin English, Hawaii Creole English) (English based, Hawai'i)
Hiri Motu (Police Motu) (based on Motu, an Austronesian language of Papua New Guinea)
Jamaican Creole (Jamaican Patois) (English based, Jamaica)
Krio, Sierra Leone Krio (English based, Sierra Leone)
Louisiana Creole (French based, Louisiana)
Mauritian Creole (French based, Mauritius)
Mobilian Jargon (based on Choctaw and Chickasaw, Muskogean languages, used as a lingua franca in the Southeastern USA along the Gulf of Mexico)
Ndyuka (English based, Suriname)
Palenquero (Spanish based, Colombia)
Papiamento (Portuguese or Spanish based, Aruba, Bonaire, Curaçao)
Pitcairnese (English based, Pitcairn Island, Norfolk Island)
Réunion Creole (French based, Réunion)
Russenorsk (Russian based, northern Norway and Russian Kola Peninsula)
Saramacca (English based, Suriname, French Guiana)
Seychellois Creole (French based, Seychelles)
Sranan Tongo (English based, with a later layer of words from Dutch, Suriname)
Tok Pisin (English based, Papua New Guinea; the name is from *talk pidgin*)

Some of these have remarkable stories. For example, Pitcairnese on Pitcairn Island comes straight out of adventure annals. Pitcairn Island was settled by the mutineers from the *Bounty*, led by Fletcher Christian in 1790 – a story so captivating that it became the subject of five different films. The group was made up of eight English sailors, their Tahitian and Tubuaian wives, and nine others who were Tahitian or Tubuaian. Most of the males killed each other within a few years; by 1808 John Adam was the only survivor among the original English sailors. The language developed in isolation; at that time there was no Pidgin English in the Pacific. Pitcairnese differs in some respects from other pidgins and creoles.

Pidgins and creoles are often looked down upon as not being 'real' languages, or as being corrupt. This attitude is changing. There is strong popular and political support for these languages in some areas, and creoles have become official languages in some countries, for example Haitian Creole in Haiti, Papiamento in Aruba and Curaçao, Sranan Tongo in Suriname, Tok Pisin and Hiri Motu in Papua New Guinea, and Bislama in Vanuatu.

12.3.1 Structural characteristics of pidgins and creoles

Scholars of pidgin and creole languages typically believe that the data of other scholars are messy, or just that the data seen in these languages in general are complex and chaotic, and it is often said that pidgin and creole scholars prefer unruly data. Pidgins are often characterized as contrasting with 'full' or 'normal' (non-pidgin) languages by having the following traits, among others: (1) being simpler, more regular; (2) having fewer resources – a small number of lexical items, sounds, and grammatical constructions; (3) relying almost exclusively on 'content' words – on nouns and verbs, not on grammatical morphemes; (4) having little if any morphology; and (5) not differentiating forms of pronouns that are distinguished in their 'lexifier' languages. The *lexifier* language is the one from which they take most of their lexical material. These assumed traits are exemplified and examined in what follows. It should be kept in mind, though, that they are not necessarily true.

The idea of *simple phonology* can be seen in comparisons of some pidgins with their lexifier languages. For example, Tok Pisin of Papua New Guinea lacks phonological contrasts that are present in English, its lexifier language, seen in examples such as: *hat* 'hat', 'hard', 'heart', coming from words in English distinguished by several phonological contrasts: *hat, hot, hard, heart*; and in *wok* 'work', but *wokabaut* 'walk' (from *walk about*). The lack of the /p/-/f/ contrast is seen in *pis* 'fish' versus *pispis* 'urinate'; the lack of contrast between /ʃ/ and /s/ is also seen in this last pair, and in *sua* 'sore' versus *sua* 'shore', *sip* 'ship' versus *sipsip* 'sheep'. Simplified phonological structure is seen in the break-up or elimination of consonant clusters, as in Tok Pisin examples where a vowel is inserted to break up a consonant cluster in the corresponding word in the lexifier language, as in *supia* 'spear' and *bokis* 'box', or a sound is lost to simplify the cluster, as in *pain* 'find' (where final *d* was eliminated).

The trait of *limited vocabulary*, with extensive periphrasing, said to characterize pidgins, can be seen in the following from Tok Pisin:

Based on *gras* from *grass* in English:

gras bilong ai 'eyebrow', 'eyelash' (literally, 'grass belong eye';
structurally 'eye's grass')

gras bilong dok 'fur (dog's fur)'

gras bilong het 'hair' (cf. 'grass belong head'; structurally 'head's
grass')

gras bilong maus 'moustache' (cf. 'grass belong mouth')

gras bilong pisin 'feather' (cf. 'grass belong bird [< *pigeon*]')

gras bilong sipsip 'wool' (cf. 'grass belong sheep')

gras bilong solwara 'seaweed' (cf. 'grass belong sea [< *saltwater*]')

gras nogut 'weeds' (cf. 'grass no good')

Based on *haus* 'house, building, hut' from English *house*:

haus bilong king 'palace'

haus bilong pisin 'nest' (cf. 'house belong bird [< *pigeon*]')

haus bilong wasim klos 'laundry' (cf. 'house belong wash clothes')

haus mani 'bank' (cf. 'house money')

haus marasin 'pharmacy' (cf. 'house medicine')

haus piksa 'cinema, theatre' (cf. 'house picture [pictures, picture
show]')

haus sik 'hospital' (cf. 'house sick')

In support of the notion of *lack of morphology* or very limited morphology, often examples of the lack of inflectional morphology are cited where bound morphemes of the lexifier language are signalled by independent words in the pidgin or creole. For example, Tok Pisin grammar uses *bai* for 'future' (etymologically from *by and by*), *bin* 'past tense' (from *been*), and *stap* 'present progressive' as in *kaikai stop* 'is eating' (etymologically from *stop* as in 'stay, continue'). Nevertheless, Tok Pisin does have some inflectional morphology, not parallel to standard English, for example *-im* 'transitive verb' (etymologically from *him*), as in *mi laik wok-im haus* 'I want to build a house' (etymologically *I like work-him house*).

Pronoun underdifferentiation is also often pointed out as evidence of limited grammar and of the lack of morphology. This can be illustrated by the single form of a pronoun where in the lexifier language there are distinctions, as for example Tok Pisin *em* for 'he', 'she', 'it', 'him', 'her', as in *em i-save* 'he/she/ it knows'; and *mi* for 'I' and 'me', as in *mi lukim yu* 'I see you' versus *yu lukim mi* 'you see me' (*lukim* 'see' etymologically from *look-him*, *-im* 'transitive verb suffix').

Nevertheless, the very common view that pidgins and creoles are maximally simple is inaccurate and so is misleading. For example, we find that Tok Pisin has a complex pronominal system, contrasting singular, dual, trial, and plural pronouns, as seen in those pronouns for which English has only *we*: *mitupela* 'we exclusive dual' (he or she and I), *mitripela* 'we exclusive trial' (both of them and I), *mipela* 'we plural exclusive' (all of them and I), *yumitupela* 'we inclusive dual' (you singular and I), *yumitripela* 'we inclusive trial' (both of you and I), and *yumi* (or *yumipela*) 'we inclusive plural' (all of you and I). Chinook Jargon, for example, has a rather complex phoneme inventory, including glottalized stops and affricates, uvular stops and fricatives, voiceless 'ł', and a glottalized lateral affricate /tl'/ (IPA [t͡ɬʔ]), etc. – it is not simple phonologically.

12.3.2 Pidgin and creole origins

There have been a number of different ideas about the origins of pidgin languages, from which creoles were generally assumed to have developed later. As mentioned above, a very common view has been the general notion of pidgins arising as minimal contact languages among groups with no language in common, usually for trading. Another idea, now generally discarded, was that pidgins derive from foreigner talk, a kind of spontaneous simplified communication that might occur any time people lacking a common language have to communicate. This is the sort of baby-talk-like simplification of one's own language a European might use with a taxi-cab driver in some Asian country where the European traveller does not know the local language, for example.

Ideas of origins have also differed in that some have argued for *monogenesis* while most now insist on *polygenesis*. The theory of monogenesis holds that all pidgins and creoles ultimately have a single origin, coming from a pidgin language based on Portuguese that was used on board ships from the fifteenth to the eighteenth century in the slave trade, and is often called West African Pidgin (or West African Pidgin Portuguese). Supporters of this view believe that this explains why many pidgin and creole languages share a number of grammatical similarities and especially why there are some words of Portuguese origin in many of these languages. A couple of examples from Tok Pisin include *pikinini* 'baby, child' (ultimately from Portuguese *pequenino* 'small, little'), and *save* 'know' (seen in the Tok Pisin example above of *em i-save* 'he/she/it knows', ultimately from Portuguese *sabe* 'knows'). These are even found as loanwords into English from creole languages, English *savvy* 'practical knowledge, intelligence, to know, understand', and *pickaninny* 'black child'. The theory of monogenesis is coupled with *relexification*, the idea that the original Portuguese-based vocabulary came to be replaced by words from another lexifier language without changing the basic grammatical structure. So, for example, the English-based creoles of today, in this view, would mostly be relexified from this assumed original Portuguese pidgin.

Often the theory of monogenesis assumes an even earlier original contact language, called *Sabir* or *Lingua Franca* of the Mediterranean, from which the later Portuguese pidgin and all others are ultimately derived according to this view. Sabir was a pidgin language used in the Crusades (1095 to c. 1450) and in the Mediterranean region from the eleventh to the nineteenth century, with vocabulary mostly from Provençal and Italian in the eastern Mediterranean, and later with more vocabulary from Spanish and Portuguese, especially on the Barbary coast (the Berber lands of north Africa, today's Algeria, Libya, Morocco, and Tunisia), but also with borrowings from Arabic, French, Greek, and Turkish. It was used throughout the Middle East in the Middle Ages (and until the nineteenth century) as a language of commerce and diplomacy, and also by slaves and the famous Barbary pirates of this region. In the monogenesis hypothesis, this Lingua Franca was known by Mediterranean sailors, including the Portuguese, who carried it with them in exploring Africa and beyond, and in settling New World colonies.

From this Lingua Franca comes the modern sense of *lingua franca* as any language used for speakers of different languages to be able to communicate with each other, a bridge language among people of different mother tongues. 'Franca' in Romance languages referred to the Franks, the Germanic rulers for whom modern France is named. 'Lingua Franca' meant language of the Franks, but in Arabic and Greek from quite early on Roman Christians and later all Western Europeans were called 'Franks', the source of the word for 'foreigner' in several languages, *faranji* in Arabic, *farangi*, *firang* in Persian, 'foreigner', presumably also behind the name of the *Ferengi*, a race of extraterrestrials in some of the Star Trek series.

Of course, a serious problem for the monogenesis hypothesis is that there are a number of pidgin or creole languages which are not based on any European language and cannot have come about via relexification of a former Portuguese vocabulary, for example Chinook Jargon, Hiri Motu, and Mobilian Jargon.

A different view about the origins of creoles comes from the *bioprogramme* or *language bioprogramme hypothesis*, proposed by Derek Bickerton. He claimed that the structural similarities among various creole languages are not due just to the languages upon which they are based, but that creolization involves the innate language-learning capacity of children operating on a variable and unstructured pidgin. As a consequence, a pidgin changes – according to this view – into a fully fledged, normal, more elaborated language with a structured grammar that follows the principles of universal grammar built into the children's innate language capacity, assumed to be the explanation for similarities among many creole languages. Many exceptions to this explanation of similarities among creoles have been discussed, and the theory of the bioprogramme for the origin of creoles is now not widely followed.

Under the more traditional view, it was typically held that creole languages have multiple parents, with most of the lexicon from the lexifier language and much of the grammar due to the 'substrate' languages, for example the West African languages of slaves in the case of Caribbean creoles. This would mean that creoles present a problem for classification, since genetic classification assumes one parent per language, a single ancestor, but creoles in this view seemingly have multiple ancestor languages for different parts. Thomason and Kaufman (1988) proposed a solution to the problem. They say that only languages which have a single parent qualify for classification into language families, that is, only languages which have normal transmission. Creoles are, they say, not changed forms of some single parent language; they do not arise in direct transmission from one speaker to another, and because of their imperfect transmission, genetic relationship by definition does not apply to them.

The traditional view of the origin of pidgins and creoles and of their relationship to one another is rejected by a number of scholars today, Salikoko Mufwene in particular. They believe, for example, that pidgins and creoles have different origins from one another and arise under different conditions. They do not believe that a creole must evolve from a prior pidgin. In this view, pidgins come about in trade contact among people who keep their native languages for everyday communication. Many creoles, these scholars believe, developed in a different way, namely in colonies where speakers of some European language – often indentured servants who spoke non-standard versions of the European language involved – and non-European slaves interacted intensely. The language they used took on some traits and words from non-European native languages, but remained essentially a version of the European language underlying it. The creole that started out in this way would then became the daily language of slaves and workers, not just used for contact with speakers of the non-creole version of the European language lying behind the creole in restricted contexts. In this view, each creole has a single ancestor. It is the language of the founder population, speakers of the dominant European language, that predominates in the formation of the creole language and in its content. In this view, creoles present no particular problem for genetic classification; they are classified in the same way as any other language would be. So, for example, Jamaican Creole and Tok Pisin are Germanic languages, closely related to English, and Haitian Creole and Mauritian Creole are Romance languages, closely related to French.

It is perhaps too soon to tell, but it might be suspected that this latter view, in which creoles can be classified as genetically related to the dominant language upon which they are based, may prevail among historical linguists.

12.4 Mixed Languages

In recent years another challenge has arisen to the ability to classify languages according to the families to which they belong, namely *mixed languages*. Until around the early 1980s, most linguists believed that truly mixed languages did not exist. A mixed language is one which has two source languages for different components or parts of its grammar and as a result has no single ancestor; consequently it cannot easily be classified as belonging exclusively to the language family of one or of the other of its source languages. There are very few true mixed languages, which makes linguists believe that probably they can arise only in very limited circumstances. Mixed languages seem often to correlate with how newly developed ethnic groups identify themselves.

Unlike pidgins and creoles, in the case of mixed languages both source languages are well known by members of the community involved. Also, mixed languages are not structurally simplified and can have complex morphology.

The best-known cases of mixed languages are the following.

(1) *Mbugu (Ma'a)*, spoken in Tanzania in two forms; so-called 'normal Mbugu' is fully Bantu, whereas 'inner' Mbugu (Ma'a) has much of its vocabulary from Southern Cushitic, but has Bantu grammar.

(2) *Media Lengua*, spoken in Salcedo, Ecuador (the name is from Spanish meaning 'half language'). It is composed of Spanish lexicon and Quechua morphology and pronunciation. Its speakers give themselves a separate ethnic identity, neither Quechua nor Spanish, but in between.

(3) *Mednyj Aleut* (Copper Island Aleut), originally spoken on Copper Island, from where the population was moved to Bering Island, and now highly endangered. The original population was made up of Russians who settled there for seal hunting and Aleuts brought there from the Aleutian Island chain by a Russian-

American company in 1826, and of children of Russian men and Aleut women. The language has Russian verbal morphology but mostly Aleut vocabulary.

(4) *Michif*, spoken by the Métis in North Dakota, Manitoba, and Saskatchewan, descendants of mostly Cree women and European fur traders. The nouns, adjectives, and noun phrase syntax are taken from French and have French lexical items, pronunciation, and morphology (such as agreement, gender marking); verbs and verb phrase grammar are from Plains Cree, with the complex morphology and pronunciation of Cree.

As yet there is no generally agreed upon solution to the problem of the mixed ancestry of mixed languages, though there are a few proposals. Their existence constitutes a problem for comparative linguistics, where it is assumed that each language indeed has only one parent and therefore can be classified as belonging to that parent's language family. If systematic comparisons with other languages sometimes point to correspondences in the language family to which one parent belongs and sometimes to the family of the other parent, reconstruction by the comparative method is frustrated. The directions to which some have looked to solve this difficulty include the following.

(1) They rely on the vocabulary and classify the mixed language with the parent that provides the bulk of the vocabulary. Some have thought that in mixed languages it is usually the mother's language which provides the grammar while the father's supplies the vocabulary. The thinking behind this is that children usually have more access to their mother's language and learn it better, while men in these situations are often immigrants. There are some difficulties with this line of thought, however. First, the number of confirmed mixed languages is so small that it is questionable to what degree generalizations are possible. Second, even given the small number of mixed languages, some do not fit the scenario envisaged – Michif has its noun vocabulary and associated grammar from one language, French, that of the original fathers, and its verb vocabulary and associated grammar from Plains Cree, the language of the mothers in the early mix. Mbugu (Ma'a) has two sets of vocabulary, one from Bantu and one in the mixed variety of Mbugu from Southern Cushitic. And worse, Mednyj Aleut has the opposite, not the mothers' grammar, but the mothers' Aleut vocabulary and the fathers' Russian verbal morphology.

(2) They consider the grammar, especially the morphology, to be basic and thus classify the mixed language with the parent language which supplies most of the grammar. There is no agreement among linguists that either the vocabulary or the grammar should be considered somehow basic for language classification purposes. In any event, Michif would still raise difficulties, with its nominal grammar (and nominal lexicon) from French but its verbal grammar (and verbal vocabulary) from Plains Cree.

(3) They consider mixed languages as not truly mixed but as basically having only one parent with exceptionally heavy lexical borrowing. This last approach may prove a reliable reflection of how some of these languages were formed, letting the historical linguist off the hook with respect to the assumed indeterminacy of the genetic classification of these languages. It is unclear whether such a solution holds promise for all cases of mixed languages.

12.5   Endangered Languages and Linguistic Change

Language extinction can be seen as the most extreme outcome of language contact, where typically one language replaces another (see below for more details on ways in which this can happen). The highly accelerated rate of language extinction in recent times has made language endangerment the highest concern for many linguists, a crisis of enormous proportions. Of the c. 420 independent language families (including isolates) of the world, at least 100 are already extinct – that means that nearly a quarter (24 per cent) of the linguistic diversity of the world in terms of unique lineages is gone. Worse, predictions are that even in the best-case scenario no less that 50 per cent of the world's languages will be doomed within the next hundred years. It is clear that language extinction will continue, since many languages in various parts of the world are no longer being learned by children. To understand fully what is possible in human languages, we need reliable descriptions of languages representing the full range of independent language families (including language isolates – families with only a single member). The loss without documentation of a language isolate or of the last language of a language family whose other languages are unknown is a substantial blow. The loss of a single language with relatives can be compared to the loss of a single species, say the Bengal tiger or the right whale – it would be a blow to biodiversity. However, the loss of whole language families (including isolates) means the loss of complete lineages, analogous to losing whole branches of the animal kingdom. Trying to work out the full range of structural possibilities in human languages and the ways they reflect the history of humankind when undocumented families and isolates have become extinct is analogous to trying to understand the animal kingdom with major branches missing, for example all the felines or cetaceans. Language endangerment and extinction are important to historical linguistics for this and several other reasons, to which we now turn.

12.5.1   Language change and endangered languages

Though there are various ways in which languages can become extinct, the most typical is when a language gradually over time comes to have fewer and fewer speakers who use the language in ever fewer domains until finally no one is able to speak it in any context. There can be considerable impact on the structure of the endangered language in these situations (see Campbell and Muntzel 1989, Palosaari and Campbell 2011). The kinds of variation and changes found in endangered languages are addressed here. Of particular relevance is the impact that language endangerment can have on the structure of languages and the kinds of changes they can undergo in contrast to the changes that affect fully viable, non-endangered languages. Important to much of this discussion is the concept of *semi-speaker*, a person who has learned to a language incompletely or imperfectly in the context of language endangerment.

(1) *Normal changes.* Some changes which endangered languages can undergo are the 'normal' or natural sorts of changes that also take place in non-endangered languages. For example, highly endangered Mam of Tuxtla Chico (Mayan, southern Mexico) (and also several non-endangered Mayan languages)

merged uvular and velar consonants (*q*, *k* > *k*, and *q'*, *k'* > *k'*). In moribund
Chiltiupan Pipil (Uto-Aztecan, El Salvador), *ts* changed to *s*. The change of an
affricate to a fricative (*ts* > *s*) is not an uncommon sound change, also found in
languages that are not endangered. Similarly, Pipil speakers today, none fully
fluent, have lost the vowel length contrast (V: > V) and most have lost the
rule that devoices final *l* (for example /mi:l/ [mi:l̦] > /mil/ [mil] 'cornfield'),
all structural traits of earlier, fully viable Pipil. The loss of these things from
the phonology of these languages might be motivated by the tendency to avoid
sounds that are hard to produce, hard to learn, and to replace them with sounds
that are easier to produce and to acquire. However, such changes can also be
accelerated in endangered languages by influence from the dominant language,
by the fact that the sounds being lost are absent from the dominant language
replacing the endangered one – Spanish in the case of the endangered languages
in the examples just seen.

While influence from the dominant language (or languages) must always be
taken seriously into consideration as possibly affecting the structure of endangered languages, as we shall see presently, not all changes involving endangered
languages can be attributed to influence from the dominant language.

(2) *Variability*. Variation that was not found before the language became
endangered can develop. Things that are obligatory in the fully viable language can become optional in the language of semi-speakers. For example,
semi-speakers of Tlahuica (also called Ocuilteco, an Otomanguean language of
Mexico) sometimes fail to voice stops after nasals (*nt* → *nd*, which is obligatory in viable Tlahuica), producing free variation of *nd* ~ *nt* which for fully
fluent speakers was not possible, with *nd* as the only option. In Pipil before
endangerment, as mentioned, /l/ was always voiceless in final position. In highly
endangered Cuisnahuat Pipil, however, speakers started not devoicing the *l* word-
finally, resulting in free variation between voiced *l* and voiceless *l* ([l̦]) in this
position. As Swadesh (1934, 1946) observed in Chitimacha (isolate, Louisiana)
in his work with the last two speakers, glottalized consonants could vary freely
with their non-glottalized counterparts, though consonants which were originally
plain did not vary with glottalized equivalents.

(3) *Overgeneralization of unmarked features* (or loss of marked features
through replacement with unmarked counterparts). Marked features are traits
of language which tend to be more unusual cross-linguistically, more difficult
for children to learn, and more easily lost in language change. They tend to be
replaced by less marked ones (more common cross-linguistically, more easily
learned) in language change. That is, difficult contrasts may not be learned, or not
learned well. For example, as mentioned, in endangered Mam of Tuxtla Chico
(Mayan), marked uvular stops were replaced by unmarked velars (*q* > *k*; *q'* >
k'), that is, uvulars merged with velars. Chipewyan (Athabaskan, Canada) semi-
speakers change glottalized consonants to their plain counterparts (C' > C) (Cook
1989). As already seen, many of these sorts of changes are also quite normal and
can be found in languages which are not threatened.

(4) *Overgeneralization of marked features*. In several situations, things that
seem 'exotic' from the point of view of speakers of the dominant language are
used overly much in inappropriate contexts in the endangered languages. For

example, one Jumaytepeque (Xinkan, Guatemala) semi-speaker arbitrarily glottalized nearly every possible consonant (C > C'). This is not a natural change and would definitely not be expected to occur in fully viable languages. In moribund Teotepeque Pipil, some speakers overgeneralized voiceless *l*, employing it everywhere at the expense of voiced *l*, though in fully viable Pipil the voiceless *l* is only an allophone of /l/ in word-final position. In instances such as these, it seems that the semi-speakers are aware of the unusual traits but have not learned precisely where they belong, and so use them excessively in inappropriate contexts from the point of view of the structure of the language as spoken by fully viable speakers, a consequence of the imperfect learning.

(5) *Loss or reduction in phonological contrasts (mergers)*. Some cases of such mergers have already been seen, as for example, Pipil *ts* > *s*, V: > V, (that is, *ts, s* > *s*; V:, V > V), and Mam of Tuxtla Chico (Mayan, Mexico) *q* > *k*; *q'* > *k'* (or, put differently, *q, k* > *k*; *q', k* > *k*). Descriptions of both Chitimacha (isolate, Louisiana) (Swadesh 1934, 1946), mentioned above, and Tonkawa (isolate, Texas) (Hoijer 1933, 1946), endangered at the time they were described, both now extinct, revealed that the last speakers often merged glottalized consonants with the non-glottalized counterparts.

(6) *Both overgeneralization and undergeneralization*. In some instances both overgeneralization and undergeneralization can affect structural properties. For example, viable Pipil devoices non-nasal sonorants (*l, w, y*) word-finally; as mentioned above, moribund Teotepeque Pipil, however, overgeneralized voiceless *l*, devoicing *l*'s in all environments, not just word-final ones, but undergeneralized in the case of *w* and *y* by not devoicing them finally (nor anywhere else). Through overgeneralization (of voiceless *l*) and undergeneralization (of voiceless *w* and *y*), the sonorant final-devoicing process was eliminated from the language of these speakers. In some other Pipil dialects, as mentioned above, the final *l* also ceased to be devoiced, along with *w* and *y*, meaning that the rule of final devoicing of sonorants was also completely lost in these dialects, though through undergeneralization only, failure to learn the rule.

(7) *Acts of reception*. Some structural changes may be due to influence from the dominant language in which the minority language takes on structural traits otherwise quite foreign to it. For example, Teotepeque Pipil underwent the change *š̫* > *r* (where /š̫/ is a retroflex non-apical laminal fricative, equivalent to a [š] (IPA [ʃ]) that is retracted to the hard palate), due to the stigmatized variant [ş] of the trilled *r* phoneme in local Spanish, the dominant language. The negative evaluation of this [ş] variant of Spanish /r/ caused moribund Pipil to shift pronunciation of its native sound to match the Spanish prestige variant [r] (trilled *r*) of its /r/. A change of a sibilant such as *š̫* to a trilled *r* is highly unnatural and unexpected (there are no *r* sounds in native words in viable Pipil). In another example, some semi-speakers and non-native learners of Pipil pronounce Pipil initial /y/ (/j/ in IPA) as [ž] (IPA [ʒ]), as in [žek] for /yek/ [yek] 'good', to make it match the [ž] prestige pronunciation of initial /y/ in Spanish, totally alien to viable Pipil, which has [y] as the only pronunciation of this sound.

Acts of reception can also influence the lexicon, as for example in the case of native words which are neutral in their meaning but, because they sound like words that are obscenities in the dominant language, are avoided or replaced. For example, Nivaclé (Matacoan, Argentina and Paraguay) *puta* 'rabbit' sounds like obscene *puta* 'whore' in dominant Spanish, which has led speakers to replace it by *nanxatetax* (derived from *nanxate* 'hare, jack rabbit' + *-tax* 'similar to'). Examples of lexical avoidance of this sort are not difficult to find.

(8) *Morphological reduction.* Two changes observed with some frequency across endangered languages are the decay of inflectional systems and the tendency to change towards more rigid grammatical word order. For example, semispeakers of American Finnish failed to make adjectives agree with nouns in case and number, producing instances such as *vanha miehe-n* [old man-Genitive.Sg.] 'the old man's' and *vanha miehe-ltä* [old man-from] 'from the old man', where fully competent speakers have *vanha-n miehe-n* [old-Genitive.Sg. man-Genitive. Sg.] and *vanha-lta miehe-ltä* [old-from man-from], respectively, with case agreement also signalled on the adjective. In another example, imperfect speakers of Tlahuica (mentioned above) often eliminate the dual and plural markers which fully fluent speakers do not leave out, as in the following examples where the material missing in the speech of semi-speakers is indicated in parentheses:

(1) kiat-kwe-p-tyɨɨ(-nkwe(-βi))
FUT.-1st.PL.-EXCL.-sing(-DUAL(-EXCL.))
'We (two, but not you) will sing'

(2) kiat-kwe-p-tyɨɨ(-hñə(-βi))
FUT.-1st.PL.-EXCL.-sing(-PL.(-EXCL.))
'We (all, but not you) will sing'
(Campbell and Muntzel 1989: 191–2)

(9) *Preference for analytic constructions over ones with bound morphology.* Sometimes endangered languages develop analytic constructions in preference to ones involving bound morphology (see Campbell and Muntzel 1989: 192–4). For example, Pipil used to have a morphological 'future':

(3a) ni-panu-s [I-pass-Fut.] 'I will pass'
(3b) ti-panu-ske-t [we-pass-Fut.-Pl.] 'we will pass'.

However, later in its more moribund stage, Pipil lost the morphological 'future' and had in its place only the analytic syntactic 'future':

(4a) ni-yu ni-panu [I-go I-pass] 'I will pass' (literally 'I'm going to pass')
(4b) ti-yawi-t ti-panu-t [we-go-Pl. we-pass-Pl.] 'we will pass' ('we're going to pass').

Scottish Gaelic semi-speakers replaced the morphological conjugated prepositions (*riu-m* 'to-me', *bhu-atha* 'from-them') with analytic constructions of freestanding preposition and pronoun (*ri mis* 'to me', *bho aid* 'from them') (Dorian 1981: 15).

(10) *Syntactic reduction.* Loss of certain grammatical categories and syntactic options, particularly complex constructions, is common in endangered language situations. The loss of the morphological 'future' in Pipil, just seen, is also an example of this. It is sometimes thought that complex linguistic structures typically learned later in childhood may be lost from an endangered language because it is at this age that children in many communities often stop using the

endangered language. One example is the reduced use and loss of subordinate clauses in threatened languages. Since speakers of moribund languages produce few complex sentences, a child exposed to their speech may have an inadequate model for acquiring constructions found in this sort of sentence. Certain subordinate clauses tend to be used in higher (more formal) styles, but the endangered language often comes to be used in only less formal contexts, with 'lower' styles. The complex constructions may simply disappear as these more formal styles cease to be used. When there are competing structures with the same function (meaning), they may tend to be reduced to a single structure in endangered language situations.

(11) *Stylistic shrinkage*. Correlated with reduction in grammar is reduction of speech genres and stylistic alternatives (such as verbal art, oral literature, ritual language, formal registers, and figurative language). Stylistic shrinkage often begins at the formal end of the stylistic continuum, 'polystylism' moving to 'mononstylism', where finally only casual speech remains.

In short, language endangerment can have a considerable impact on the structure of the languages involved. An important question is: can endangered languages change in ways that are different from change in non-endangered languages? The answer seems to be 'yes', endangered languages can undergo kinds of changes not usually available to fully viable languages. Under normal circumstances, for example, we would not expect a language to change $š$ to a trilled r, or a replace a plain l with a voiceless one everywhere, or for all plain consonants to become glottalized, as in some of the examples seen here. Thus, it appears that the languages learned by semi-speakers of endangered languages can undergo kinds of changes not typical of fully viable languages. Another important question is: is sound change in endangered languages always regular? The answer to this question would appear to be 'no'. For example, semi-speakers in several of the changes presented here did not change all instances of a particular sound in the same way, but rather introduced considerable variation, and sometimes changed a particular sound in some words and did not change the sound in other words. This would seem to go against the Neogrammarian regularity hypothesis, that sound laws suffer no exceptions (see Chapter 2). However, given that the regularity of sound change holds so well in non-endangered languages, we would not give up such a valuable principle because sometimes the speech of imperfect learners may fail to conform, just as we would not abandon the principle if we found irregularities in the speech of small children still acquiring their first language, of persons with various speech pathologies, of adult second language learners, etc. In general, though, these two questions merit much more investigation.

13

⊨

Explanation

⊨

These phonetic changes [in Grimm's Law] have, it is true, been brought about by the influence of climate, food, laziness or the reverse, analogy, and fashion; but we are still ignorant of the relative power of these causes, and the precise manner in which they affect the phonology of a language.

(Sayce 1874: 16)

13.1 Introduction

This chapter is concerned with the explanation of linguistic change or, perhaps better said, with attempts that linguists have made towards explaining why languages change as they do. The explanation of linguistic change is usually understood as the search for causes; it is central to the study of language change, though it is a topic of much debate and considerable disagreement. In this chapter, we try to cut through the disagreements to see how linguists have attempted to explain linguistic change and to see whether the different kinds of explanations that are proposed provide a foundation for understanding why languages change. Until the early 1970s, it was common to find statements in historical linguistic works to the effect that we should be concerned with 'how' languages change, but that the question of 'why' languages change could not be answered and therefore should be avoided. For example, from Joos (1958: v) we read: 'If the facts have been fully stated, it is perverse or childish to demand an explanation into the bargain' (intended perhaps more of descriptive linguistics); in Lehmann's introduction to historical linguistics, we are told: 'A linguist establishes the facts of change, leaving its explanation to the anthropologist' (1962: 200, in a discussion of semantic change). What is behind the comment about leaving explanation to the anthropologist is the once widely shared notion that the reasons for linguistic change were like those for change in fashion–in one year new cars might have fins and in another not, or the hemlines of women's dresses might be higher one year and lower in another. So, the driving force behind language change was held to be cultural, to do with social choices and thus outside of the structure of language itself and hence not primarily even a linguist's concern. However, not everyone had such a pessimistic view, and many causal factors in linguistic change had been identified and discussed earlier, and in the last few decades much has been done to consolidate what we know about the causes of linguistic change. In this chapter, the term *causal factors* is used to designate both factors which always bring about change and those which create circumstances which are known to facilitate change but the change is not always obligatory when the factors are present. Much current research is directed at revealing the factors which help to explain language change.

In this chapter, we examine some of the better-known efforts in the direction of explaining linguistic change. We begin with a brief look at some of the earlier and less successful claims about why languages change, the ones we can safely eliminate from any theory of linguistic change.

13.2 Early Theories

Almost anything affecting humans and their language has at one time or another been assumed to be behind some change in language. Some of these today seem hilarious–for example, nearly all the 'causes' given by Sayce in the quote at the head of this chapter–some socially or morally disturbing, but fortunately some seem pointed, if only vaguely, in the right direction.

Climatic or *geographical determinism* was thought by some to lie behind some linguistic changes. A revealing example is the claim that the consonantal changes of Grimm's Law were due to life in the Alps, where all that running up and down mountains caused huffing and puffing which led to the voiceless stops becoming fricatives (the changes $*p > f$, $*t > \theta$, $*k > h$). Since examples of the same change are known in languages not found in mountainous regions and many other languages found in mountains are known where changes of this sort have not taken place, the suggested cause is neither necessary (given the existence of such changes in non-mountain languages) nor sufficient (given the lack of change in other mountain languages). In any case, the Alps were not the homeland of Proto-Germanic speakers. In another case, even from as distinguished a linguist as Henry Sweet (1900: 32) we read:

> The influence of climate may be seen in the frequency with which (a) is rounded in the direction of (o) in the northern languages of Europe – as in English *stone* from Old English *stān* – as compared with the southern languages, in which it is generally preserved; this rounding of (a) is doubtless the result of unwillingness to open the mouth widely in the chilly and foggy air of the North.

We now know that geographical determinism plays no significant role in language change.

Some spoke of '*racial*' and *anatomical determinism*. One example of this is the notion that Germanic tribes had a greater build-up of earwax (for reasons left unaddressed) which somehow impeded their hearing, resulting in the series of consonantal changes in Grimm's Law. Whatever else we might say of this theory, it at least has the advantage of being specific enough that it could perhaps be tested – we assume that the results of any such test would be a negative correlation, that earwax in those with Germanic genes is not a significant factor for bringing about change in the languages which they speak. More insidious are claims of language change due to physical attributes assumed to be associated with different races. A most obvious example attributes phonetic traits encountered in some African languages – such as implosives, clicks or labiovelar sounds – to changes that must have taken place to produce such sounds in the first place, which, according to those making these claims, are due to the anatomical structure of the lips of black Africans. Needless to say, this assumed correlation has proven totally devoid of foundation – change in African languages is in character just like that in languages elsewhere, and 'race' (i.e. human genetics) plays no role.

Etiquette, social conventions and *cultural traits*. Many have speculated concerning cultural motivations for certain linguistic changes. For example, Wilhelm Wundt (a famous psychologist and linguist, writing in 1900) believed that the reason why Iroquoian languages have no labial consonants is because according to Iroquoian etiquette, so he reported, it is improper to close the mouth while speaking. Apparently the only evidence for this principle of Iroquoian etiquette was the fact that the Iroquoian languages lack labials. The same absence of labial consonants from Aleut, Tlingit and some African languages has at times been attributed to labrets (plugs, discs inserted in holes cut into the lips, an important part of personal adornment and ornamentation in some societies). However plausible this idea might seem to some, it has the disadvantage of not being testable. If a group is found who lack labials, who also do not use labrets, it could be claimed that at some former time they did use the lip devices and this led to the loss of labial consonants and then sometime subsequently they just stopped utilizing labrets. Or, if a language possessing labial consonants were found among a group which did wear labrets, it might be claimed that the lip-ornament fashion must not yet have been in vogue long enough to lead to the loss of labials. That is, again, the proposed account for the loss of labials due to the wearing of labrets is neither a sufficient nor a necessary explanation.

Indolence. A particularly common assumption, especially among lay people, is that language change is the result of laziness – young people or particular social groups who are seen to be changing their speech in ways disapproved of are assumed to be just too slovenly to pronounce correctly, or to produce the full or distinct grammatical forms, and so on.

Ease and *simplification*. A common assumption has been that language speakers tend towards 'ease of articulation', which leads to language change. 'Simplification' became an important part of the generative linguists' approach to linguistic theory and consequently also to their views of linguistic change. We will need to look at this in more detail as we explore plausible explanations for why languages change.

Foreign influence (substratum) – borrowing. Languages do change through borrowing, indisputably, though often language contact has been exaggerated and abused in attempts to explain particular changes. Any change whose cause is otherwise not understood, or any exception to otherwise general accounts, was often attributed to influence from other languages, often in spite of no evidence in the neighbouring languages that might support such a view. For more practical views of the role of borrowing in linguistic change, see Chapters 3 and 12.

Desire to be distinct and *social climbing.* It is sometimes proposed that groups of people changed their language on purpose to distinguish themselves from other groups. Sociolinguistic study shows that group identity is a very important factor in many changes, but it is not achieved in quite such a simple-minded way as formerly conceived of. A more pervasive notion was that members of lower classes purposefully changed their speech by imitating the elite of society in order to improve their own social standing, and that as a consequence the upper class changed its language in order to maintain its distance from the masses – that is, the idea of the social-climbing masses in hot linguistic pursuit of society's fleeing elite. Sociolinguistic study of change, however, reveals that the more typical pattern is for the middle classes to initiate linguistic change and for the highest and lowest classes of society to change only later, if at all (see Labov 1994, 2001; see section 7.6 of Chapter 7).

External historical events. It is sometimes asserted that particular historical events are the cause of certain linguistic changes. A typical example is the proposed correlation between certain linguistic changes and the expansion of the Roman Empire. Jespersen correlates the Black Death and the wars and social disruption of the later Middle Ages which coincided in England and France with rapid linguistic change. Romance linguistics has had a tradition of more tolerance for explanations of linguistic changes involving external history; however, external history has not been accorded as much attention in the Germanic historical linguistics tradition, which has had the strongest influence on general historical linguistics of today. Perhaps there should be more tolerance for it, but also appeal to external historical factors should not be abused – there are many examples in past scholarship of assumed external causes presented without evidence of causal connections between the linguistic change and the external history asserted to be involved.

13.3   Internal and External Causes

Modern literature on linguistic change often distinguishes *internal* and *external* causes of change. The internal causes are based on what human speech production and perception is and is not capable of – that is, the internal causes are determined for the most part by the physical realities of human biology, by limitations on control of the speech organs and on what we humans are able to distinguish with our hearing or are able to process with our cognitive make-up. Thus, *internal* causes include physical and psychological factors. An example of a *physical* factor, involving the physiology of human speech organs, is seen in the typical sound change which voices stops between vowels (let us symbolize this as VpV > VbV). This change is in some sense explained by the limitations of human muscle control, which tends to maintain the vibration of the vocal cords (the voicing, which is inherent in vowels) across the intervening consonant. That is, it is much easier to allow the vocal cords to continue to vibrate right through the V-p-V sequence (resulting in *VbV*) than it is to have the vocal cords vibrating for the first vowel, then to break off the voicing for the stop, and then to start up the vibration of the vocal cords once again for the second vowel (to produce *VpV*). *Psychological* or *cognitive* explanations involve the perception, processing and learning of language. For example, the change in which nasalized vowels are lowered (let us symbolize this as ĩ > ɛ̃), found so frequently in languages with contrastive nasalized vowels, is explained by the fact that, with nasalization, vowel height tends to be perceived as lower. Thus [ɛ̃] tends to be perceived as [æ̃], for example, and this perception leads to changes in what speakers think the basic vowel is. This is illustrated, for example, by changes in French nasalized vowels:

ẽ > ã (in the eleventh century), as in *pendre* > [pãdr(e)] 'to hang'
ī > ẽ (in the thirteenth century), as in *voisin* > [vwaˈzẽ] 'neighbour'
ỹ > œ̃ (thirteenth century), as in [brỹ] (spelled *brun*) > [brœ̃] 'brown'.

External causes of change involve factors that are largely outside the structure of language itself and outside the human organism. They include such things as expressive uses of language, positive and negative social evaluations (prestige, stigma), the effects of literacy, prescriptive grammar, educational policies, political decree, language planning, language contact and so on. The following are a few examples of changes which illustrate external motivation.

(1) Finnish changed *ð* to *d* (for example, *veðen* > *veden* 'water (genitive singular)') due to spelling pronunciation based on the Swedish reading model which dominated in Finland and was imposed in Finnish schools.

(2) Teotepeque Pipil (of El Salvador) changed *š* to *r* (voiceless retroflex fricative became a trilled 'r') because local Spanish has *š* as a highly stigmatized variant of its *r*. In this case, Spanish is the dominant national language and sociolinguistic attitudes about variant pronunciations of its /r/ have been transferred to this variety of Pipil, the minority language, leading to a change in its native phoneme which originally in Pipil had nothing to do with different pronunciations of /r/–native Pipil has no 'r' sound of any sort.

13.4   Interaction of Causal Factors

Change in one part of a language may have consequences for other parts. There is a trade-off between the phonological needs and the semantic needs of a language. A change in sound may have deleterious effects on aspects of the meaning side of language, and a change in meaning/function can have consequences for the sound system. At the crux of much debate concerning the explanation of linguistic change is thinking about the outcome of cases where a change in one side of a language has consequences for another side of the language. To understand the sort of causal factors that have been proposed and the debate over explanation of linguistic change, it will be helpful to begin with some examples which illustrate what is debated, and then to return to the debated explanations themselves afterwards with the examples as a basis for understanding the claims. Let us begin with well-known (putative) examples of morphological conditioning of sound change. (See also section 10.11 in Chapter 10.)

13.4.1 Classical Greek loss of intervocalic *s*

In a well-known change in Classical Greek, *s* was lost between vowels (s > Ø /V__V) except in certain 'future' and 'aorist' forms. In this case, loss of *s* by regular sound change would have destroyed the phonological form of the 'future' morpheme. One view of this set of circumstances is that the sound change was blocked, prevented from happening in just those cases where the meaning distinction between 'future' and 'present' would have been lost, and that is why intervocalic *s* was not lost in those 'future' forms. Changes such as this are called *morphologically conditioned* sound changes. Note, however, that the *s* of the 'future' was freely lost in verbs ending in a nasal or a liquid, where the future/present distinction could be signalled formally by the *e* which these future stems take. Compare the following two sets of verbs, where Set I retains *s* in the 'future' and Set II–*l*-stem or *n*-stem verbs with *e* in the future stem –loses the *s*:

Set I:

| páu-ō | 'I stop, cease' | páu-s-ō | 'I will stop, cease' |
| lú-ō | 'I loosen' | lú-s-ō | 'I will loosen' |

Set II:

| stéllō | 'I send' | steléō [< *stele-s-ō] | 'I will send' |
| mén-ō | 'I remain' | mené-ō [< *mene-s-ō] | 'I will remain' |

It is said in this case that the need of the meaning side of language to be able to distinguish 'future' from 'present' prevented the sound change from occurring in Set I verbs where the 'future' would have been lost, but the sound change was allowed freely to delete intervocalic *s* even of the 'future' in Set II verbs where the contrast could be signalled by other means. With the verb stems ending in a nasal or a liquid, in Set II, where the distinction between 'present' and 'future' could still be signalled by the presence of the *e* of 'future' stems, the *s* of 'future' was freely lost (compare Anttila 1989: 99).

As noted in Chapter 10 section 10.11, some scholars believe Greek *s* was freely lost intevocalically, but that the *s* 'future' was later restored based on analogy with verbs such as *trép-s-ō* 'I will turn' in which *s* was not lost after a root ending in a consonant: *pausō* 'I will stop' > *pauō* (by regular sound change), then > *pausō* (by analogy to *trépsō*).

The first view, favouring morphological conditioning (the blocking of the sound change in just those cases where it would have had negative effects on important meaning distinctions), sees *prevention* for functional reasons (to maintain important meaning distinctions) as the explanation behind this example. Supporters of the second view, which favours analogical restoration after the initial loss by regular sound change, see post-operative *therapy* as the explanation, the fixing-up after the fact of the negative consequences of sound change for meaning distinctions by other means. Let us look at some additional examples that illustrate these notions.

13.4.2 Estonian loss of final -*n*

A change in Estonian, similar to that in Classical Greek, is also well known in the linguistic literature (Anttila 1989: 79, 100). The Northern Estonian and Southern Estonian dialects are quite different from one another. In all of Estonian, final *n* was lost; however, in Northern Estonian the -*n* of 'first person singular' verb forms was exempted from this otherwise regular sound change, while in Southern Estonian the change took place without restrictions, as illustrated in Table 13.1. Loss of both *ʔ* and *n* in Northern Estonian would have left the 'first person singular' and 'imperative' forms indistinct; prevention of loss of final *n* in the 'first person singular' forms maintained the distinction. In Southern Estonian, where *ʔ* was not lost, these verb forms remained distinct and so final *n* could also freely be lost in 'first person singular' verb forms without distress to the meaning difference.

TABLE 13.1: Estonian verb forms after certain sound changes

Northern Estonian	Southern Estonian	Proto-Balto-Finnic	
kannan	kanna	*kanna-n	'I carry'
kanna	kannaʔ	*kanna-ʔ	'Carry!'

Those who favour analogical restoration after the regular sound change must rely in this case on variation in an early stage of the change in which final *n* was lost when the next word began with a consonant or when there was no following word, but -*n* was not yet lost when the next word began with a vowel. They would say that, based on the instances of final *n* before a following vowel, -*n* was restored also before a following consonant (that is, in all instances) where it served to signal the 'first person' in Northern Estonian, but that -*n* was later lost completely in all contexts in Southern Estonian (including also before following vowel-initial words) and in non-first person contexts in Northern Estonian (that is, lost now also before an initial vowel of a following word).

13.4.3   Estonian compensation for lost final -*n*

The loss of final *n* in Estonian was not blocked in all instances where its loss would have resulted in the loss of meaning distinctions. For example, the 'accusative singular' suffix was also -*n*, but this was entirely lost in the sound change which deleted final -*n*. Rather than the sound change being 'prevented' from damaging the accusative's ability to be signalled, the change applied also to the final -*n* of the accusative singular; however, the damage to the meaning side of the language was *compensated* for by other means in the language. In many nouns, the nominative and accusative forms could still be distinguished by other means in the absence of the -*n* 'accusative singular'. Final vowels in certain contexts were deleted by an earlier sound change, and many roots underwent what is called consonant gradation, essentially a change in stops in closed syllables (syllables that terminate in a consonant). Thus, for example, the 'nominative' and 'accusative' for a noun such as *kand* [kant] 'heel' could still be signalled in spite of the lost *n*: *kand* (< *kanta*) 'nominative singular', *kanna* (< *kanna-n* < *kanta-n*) 'accusative singular' (where the difference between *nt* and *nn*, and the presence or absence of the root-final *a*, signal the distinction between nominative and accusative which formerly was indicated by Ø 'nominative singular' versus *-n* 'accusative singular'). However, in nouns such as *kala* 'fish', consonant gradation (which did not apply to *l*) and final-vowel loss (which applied in other contexts, but not this one) could not compensate for the lost *-n* of 'accusative' to signal the difference: *kala* (<*kala*) 'nominative', *kala* (<*kala-n*) 'accusative'. However, a different sort of therapy came to be called upon to fix up the negative consequences of the sound change, namely in instances such as *kala* 'nominative' / *kala* 'accusative', where nothing in the phonological form functions to distinguish the two, the particle *ära* 'up' could be used in partial compensation for the lost 'accusative', as in *söön kala ära* 'I eat the fish (up)'.

13.4.4 Compensation in Caribbean Spanish

Standard Spanish freely allows independent pronouns optionally to be absent, since the bound pronominal suffixes on verbs are sufficient to indicate the subject of the verb (for example, *ando* 'I walk', *andas* 'you walk', *andamos* 'we walk', and so on), and in connected discourse the independent pronouns are usually absent except when used for emphasis. However, in numerous studies of varieties of Caribbean Spanish, it has been observed that there is a much higher frequency of occurrence of the independent pronouns *tú* 'you (familiar)', *usted* 'you (formal)', *él* 'he' and *ella* 'she' than in other varieties of Spanish, and internally within these varieties these subject pronouns are much more frequent than the other subject pronouns (than *yo* 'I', *nosotros* 'we', *ustedes* 'you (plural)' and *ellos* 'they'). This is explained as therapeutic compensation in the wake of disruptive sound changes. In these varieties of Spanish, final *s* is changed to *h* and further to Ø with extreme frequency (approaching 100 per cent of occurrences for some speakers in colloquial contexts). This means that verb forms which are quite distinct in Standard Spanish, such as *andas* 'you walk' versus *anda* 'he/she walks', fail to be distinct if the final *s* is not realized. The loss of this distinction is compensated for through the more rigid use of the independent pronouns, especially *tú* 'you (familiar)', precisely where they are needed to help maintain the formal difference in verbs, now *tú anda* 'you walk' versus *él anda* 'he walks' in the colloquial language. This greater use of *tú* to compensate for the lost *-s* pronominal suffix parallels the change in French, where French once worked like modern Standard Spanish, with *vas* 'you go' versus *va* 'he/she goes', but as a result of sound changes which affected final consonants in French, the *-s* of the 'you' forms was completely lost and in French today the independent pronouns are obligatory, /ty va/ 'you go' (spelled *tu vas*) versus /il va/ 'he goes'. That is, the use of independent pronouns was made obligatory to compensate for the meaning contrast that would otherwise be lost with the loss of the final *-s* of second person.

13.4.5 Saami (Lapp) compensation for lost final *-n*

Saami (Finno-Ugric) also lost final *-n* in a change which was quite independent of Estonian's loss of final *-n*. However, as in Estonian, this Saami loss also affected certain grammatical cases – the 'genitive singular' suffix *-n* was lost.

As in Estonian, consonant gradation in closed syllables could compensate for the loss in some instances. Since the former *-n* 'genitive singular' constituted a consonant and therefore closed syllables, pairs formerly distinguished primarily by Ø 'nominative' versus *-n* 'genitive' could still be distinguished after the loss of final *-n* by non-gradated consonants in the stem in the nominative form and gradated consonants in the genitive form, as in Northern Saami *jokkâ* 'river (nominative singular)' : *jogâ* 'river (genitive singular)'. However, such compensation was not available for all nouns, since many contained no stops and so originally underwent no consonant gradation. In such cases, Saami underwent a therapeutic change whereby the consonant gradation pattern was extended to these consonants which earlier had not been subject to gradation, as seen here in the change from Proto-Saami to Northern Saami:

> *kōlē > guolle 'fish (nominative singular)'
> *kōlē-n > guole 'fish's (genitive singular)'.

Consonant gradation was extended to consonants, such as *l*, which formerly had not undergone gradation, to signal the difference between 'nominative' and 'accusative' (Korhonen 1981: 148).

13.4.6   Avoidance of pernicious homophony

Discussions of explanation of change in the linguistic literature often involve the concept of avoidance of homophony and refer to examples attributed to it. Therefore, *avoidance of homophony* will be the final example before we concentrate more directly on notions of how linguistic change may be explained.

While scholars opposed to functional explanations in linguistic changes have never been friends of avoidance of pernicious homophony as an explanation of certain changes, instances of such avoidance are nevertheless well documented. Avoidance of homophony can take several forms.

Lexical replacement and loss. The best-known cases involve lexical replacement or loss. A famous example comes from France, where in Gascony reflexes of Latin *gallus* 'rooster' (commonly *gal* in southern France) were replaced in exactly those dialects found within the area where a sound change took place in which original *ll* changed to *t*, where *gal* 'rooster' (from *gallus*) would have become *gat*, leaving *gat* 'rooster' homophonous with *gat* 'cat'. This homophony was avoided by the replacement of 'rooster' with other forms which formerly meant 'pheasant' or 'vicar', and this allowed 'cat' and 'rooster' to be signalled by phonetically distinct forms. Without appeal to avoidance of homophony, it would be difficult to explain why it is precisely and only in the area where the sound change would have left 'rooster' and 'cat' homophonous that this lexical replacement has taken place (Gilliéron 1921; Gilliéron and Roques 1912 as seen in Map 13.1). It will be helpful to look at a few other examples attributed to the avoidance of homophony.

(1) A much-cited example involves the fact that English had two words, *quean* 'low woman' and *queen*, but the former has disappeared nearly everywhere because of homophonic clash after Middle English [ɛ:] (of *quean*) and [e:] (of *queen*) merged, especially in East Midlands and Southeast English dialects.

MAP 13.1: Distribution of the names for 'rooster' in the southwest of France (Redrawn after Ilari 2001: 27)

Interestingly, in the south-western area, the two vowel sounds remained distinct and both words, *quean* and *queen*, still survive there, where there is no homophonic clash between them, but survive nowhere where they would have become homophonous (Menner 1936: 222–3).

(2) In Standard German, *Fliege* [fliːgə] 'fly' and *Flöhe* [fløːə] 'fleas' are phonetically distinct, but in certain German dialects the two would have become homophonous through regular sound changes (loss of intervocalic *g* and changes in the vowels). In this case, *Fliege* for 'fly' was replaced by *Mücke*, which had originally meant 'gnat, mosquito', as it still does in Standard German (Bach 1969: 168).

(3) In southern French dialects, reflexes of the Latin word *serrāre* 'to saw' survive today only in a few scattered areas. It has disappeared because it became homophonous with the French reflexes of Latin *serāre* 'to close'. In these areas where *ser(r)āre* 'to saw' disappeared, it has been replaced by words which come from Latin *sectāre* 'to cut', *secāre* 'to cut, divide', *resecāre* 'to cut back, curtail' (Palmer 1972: 331).

(4) Due to the sound change in which initial *h* was lost before other consonants, the Old English word *hrūm* 'soot', homophonous after the change with

rūm 'room', was simply dropped from the language, and *soot* now exclusively carries that meaning.

Prevention. Avoidance of homophony can also sometimes block otherwise regular sound changes from taking place in certain forms. For example, in some German dialects, regular sound changes (the loss of intervocalic *g* and the unrounding of *ü*) would have left *liegen* [li:gən] 'to lie (down)' and lügen [ly:gən] 'to lie (tell falsehoods)' homophonous, but these otherwise regular sound changes were blocked in these words to preserve the distinction between these two common words (Öhmann 1934). Not all linguists accept proposals which call upon prevention as a way of dealing with problems of impending homophony. In this German example, some would argue that it is not that the changes were blocked and prevented from taking place in these words so much as that the changes took place and the sounds were later restored to these words by analogy based on related verb forms in which these sounds appear. (See Anttila 1989: 182 for other examples.)

Deflection. Another way by which some languages have avoided certain uncomfortable homophonies is through irregular or spontaneous changes in one or more of the homophonous forms, the result of which maintains a distinction between the forms that clash. A simple example that illustrates how such deflection can come about is seen in the euphemistic *fudge!* as an expletive to avoid the stronger obscene expletive which begins with the same sounds but ends with a different consonant. A change of this sort involving the homophonous *quean* / *queen* pair of words took place in some locations. In some northern English dialects, an initial *wh* [ʍ] was substituted for the *qu* [kw] of *quean* (but not of *queen*), and both words survive; the homophonic conflict is avoided through this special, sporadic change. The Middle English form for 'rabbit', variously spelled as *cony*, *coney* or *cunny*, was considered too close in pronunciation to a phonetically similar obscenity for comfort and so was changed by deflection to *bunny*. If the ancestor of English *shut*, Old English *scyttan*, had not been deflected, by regular sound change it should have become *shit*, a homophony apparently too pernicious to abide – from **skuttjan* 'obstruct', *u > y* (umlaut because of /j/ in the next syllable), *sk > 'sh'* (/š/), *y > i* (unrounding of front rounded vowels), *skuttjan > skytt- > shyt*, deflected away from changing *shyt* to *shit* by avoidance of homophony.

13.4.7 Loss (neglect)

As is well known, many cases of homophony are not prevented, deflected or replaced; in these, the sound changes create homophonous forms that remain in the language – we see this in English in such sets of words as *sun/son*, *eye/I*, *rock* (stone)/*rock* (move back and forth), *to/too/two* and so on. An example from German, mentioned in section 10.6 of Chapter 10, illustrates a change in which neither blocking nor direct therapy was exercised. In it, the partitive construction was lost due to the phonological changes which resulted in the merger of neuter adjectives marked with *-es* 'genitive' and *-ez* 'nominative/accusative'. After the merger, the old *-es* ('genitive') with partitive interpretation was seen as 'accusative' and so was interpreted as full direct objects in these instances. The outcome was that the partitive object construction was simply lost from German as a result of the phonological merger which left the genitive and accusative undifferentiated – neither prevention nor compensation occurred to rescue it.

As the discussion of these examples (several of them well known in the literature) shows, a broad view of language will be required in order to explain linguistic change, a view which must include internal factors, external factors, the structure of the language as a whole and how different parts of the language interact with one another, the communicative and social functions of the language, the role of the individual, the role of society/the speech community, and more – that is, the complex interaction and competition among a large number of factors. Let us look at some views of what it means to 'explain' linguistic change, with the examples just considered as background for the discussion.

13.5   Explanation and Prediction

The recognition of a large number of interacting and competing causal factors in language change means that at present we are unable fully to predict linguistic change. Some scholars conclude from this that it is impossible to explain linguistic change, since they equate 'explain' with 'predict', as required in some approaches to the philosophy of science. These scholars believe that the need to postulate competing principles and multiple causes renders law-like explanations of the sort sought in physics and chemistry impossible in historical linguistics. Others are more optimistic, believing that the current unpredictability may ultimately be overcome through research to identify causal factors and to understand the complex ways in which these factors interact. This more optimistic approach hopes for prediction (for law-like explanations) in the future, to the extent that they may be possible. On the other hand, some scholars recognize that absolute predictability may not be an appropriate requirement, since evolution by natural selection in biology is almost universally recognized as scientifically legitimate explanation, though it does not 'predict' the evolutionary changes that it explains.

In the view held by many historical linguists, the overall outcome of changes is usually (though not always) in the direction of maintaining or achieving the language's functional needs (a loose but hopefully useful notion about languages being able to serve the communicative needs of speech communities). These functional needs may be served in some cases by preventing or deflecting certain changes in order to avoid their detrimental effects on the language, or by permitting the disruptive changes to take place but then following them with subsequent compensatory (therapeutic) changes which rectify the situation. Of course, not all historical linguists agree with all of this; some insist that 'languages do not practice prophylaxis [no prevention or blocking], only therapy' (first said by Hermann Paul in the late nineteenth century, and reasserted more recently by linguists such as Paul Kiparsky (1982: 190), William Labov (1994) and David Lightfoot (1979: 123)) – that is, they accept the compensatory changes, therapy after a change has had negative consequences, but reject the interpretations which involve prevention and deflection in the examples considered above.

From the point of view of scholars who insist on predictability for explanation, it might be objected that appeal to such things in the examples above as prevention (prophylaxis, to head off the ill effects of some changes) and compensation (therapy, to fix things up after deleterious changes) cannot predict when such changes will take place, what exact form they may take, or when they may fail to occur even though the appropriate condition may have been present. It is important to distinguish what is impossible to predict (for example, that a change will occur, which change will occur, when a change will occur, and so on) from what is possible to predict (the nature of the changes that do occur, the conditions under which they can occur, what changes cannot occur).

Certain predictions may in fact already be possible, though these are not necessarily the mechanistic causal or deterministic kind known from physics or astronomy which some scholars would insist on for any explanation in any field to be considered valid. For example, to use an analogy (from Wright 1976), given certain circumstances, we may be able to determine in an objective manner that a rabbit will flee from a pursuing dog and that the paths which the rabbit follows are indeed appropriate for attempting to escape the dog, but we may not be able to predict the particular escape route which it will follow. Similarly, given certain conditions, we may be able to predict that a language (or more accurately, its speakers) may resort to one of a variety of alternative means for resolving the conflicting consequences of changes, though we may not be able to predict the particular 'escape route' that will be taken, be it prevention of sound change (as claimed in the morphological-conditioning view of the Greek in 13.4.1 and the first Estonian example in 13.4.2 and for some of the cases of avoidance of homophony in 13.4.6), or compensation (as in the Saami example in 13.4.5, the second Estonian case in 13.4.3, and in Caribbean Spanish in 13.4.4 above), or deflection (as in some of the instances of homophony avoidance in 13.4.6). That is, there are different kinds or degrees of prediction: weak prediction (something is likely to happen), strong prediction (something will happen, though when and where is unclear), and absolute prediction (something will happen at a specifiable time and place) (Aitchison 1987:12). We may be able to obtain some degree of predictability without needing to insist on the strongest absolute sort of prediction.

That more than one cause is frequently involved in a particular change also makes prediction difficult. Change within complex systems (languages, living organisms, societies) involves many factors which are interrelated in complex ways. Given that multiple causes frequently operate simultaneously in complex ways to bring about particular linguistic changes, to explain linguistic change we must investigate the multiple causes and how they jointly operate in some cases and compete in others to determine the outcome of linguistic change.

Because we do not yet understand fully the complex interactions among the causal factors, we cannot predict all outcomes. The internal causal factors (mentioned above) rely on the limitations and resources of human speech production and perception, physical explanations of change stemming from the physiology of human speech organs, and cognitive explanations involving the perception, processing or learning of language. These internal explanations are largely responsible for the natural, regular, universal aspects of language and language change. However, even well-understood internal causal factors can compete in their interactions in ways which make prediction difficult and for the present out of reach. Consider another analogy, that of a car smashed against a tree, where the following conditions obtain: it is dark and foggy (poor visibility), the road is narrow and covered with ice (poor driving conditions), the driver is intoxicated and suffers from several physical disabilities (driver impaired), and the car was in poor operating condition (worn tyres, bad brakes, loose steering), the driver was exceeding the speed limit and not watching the road at the time of the accident (poor judgement), and finally, the tree happened to be situated at just the spot where the vehicle left the road (chance). In such a situation, it would not be possible to determine a unique cause (or even a joint interaction of causes) of the accident with sufficient precision to allow us to predict the crash. Linguistic changes are often like this crash, where competing or overlapping causal factors may be at play, but precise prediction of whether a change will take place (will the car in fact crash?) or when and how a change (a crash) will be realized is not fully possible. Still, it would be foolish to dismiss the probable or potential contributing causal factors as irrelevant to the event (a car crash, a linguistic change). From the study of many other crashes, we may be certain that each of these is capable of contributing to car accidents.

At this stage of our understanding, we cannot ignore any potential causal factor, such as prevention or therapy in the examples above, and thus cut off inquiry before we arrive at a fuller picture of how and why changes occur. It will only be through further extensive investigation of the interaction of the various overlapping and competing factors that are suspected of being involved in linguistic changes that we will come to be able to explain linguistic change more fully.

Moreover, even if mechanistic (internal) explanations were more readily available for linguistic change, that would not necessarily invalidate other sorts of explanations. There are different kinds of legitimate explanation. Consider one more analogy (from Wright 1976: 44). To answer the question 'why did the window break?' with 'because John slammed it' is a completely adequate answer/explanation, even if shock waves and molecular structure may lie behind the breaking at some other level of interpretation. There are contexts in which an answer of 'because of a certain causal factor *x*' is correct and adequate, even if there may be deeper, more mechanistic causal things which one could mention. For example, consider the constraint 'no language will assume a form in violation of such formal principles as are postulated to be universal in human languages' (Weinreich et al. 1968: 100) (mentioned in Chapter 7). That languages cannot undergo changes which would violate universals is an adequate explanation in certain contexts of inquiry even if we discover the aspects of human physiology and cognition (mechanistic, internal factors) which explain the universals themselves. The existence of the underlying internal explanation of universals at some level does not invalidate explanations such as 'because languages do not undergo changes which would violate universals' at some other level. Even if we may ultimately come to understand more fully the aspects of human cognition which underlie avoidance of homophony or therapeutic compensation in the wake of other disruptive changes, and the like, at another level these factors remain potentially valid in explanations for the changes which they deal with.

13.6   Myths and Misconceptions about Linguistic Change

Myths (misconceptions) abound about how and why languages change. Some are old, though echoes of them may still be heard, and others are fresher. Since these claims can be misleading, it will be helpful to set the record straight, to the extent possible, and therefore in this section several of the more prominent misconceptions are inspected.

13.6.1   Myths about the comparative method

A number of misconceptions, both old and new, involve the comparative method.

(1) *'Primitive' languages and the comparative method.* In the past, with weak echoes even today, misconceptions about so-called 'primitive' languages caused doubts about whether the comparative method was applicable to 'exotic' (little-known) and unwritten languages. Linguists today know that there are no primitive languages as once thought, but some of these misgivings linger on. They include the following.

(1a) *The myth of imprecise sounds.* Some scholars doubted that the comparative method could be applied to exotic languages, based on the nineteenth-century belief that such languages were imprecise, with vague or fluctuating articulations that defied description and transcription. For example, two famous scholars expressed the following opinions:

> In many languages, as is well known, there are elementary sounds of an indeterminate nature, which seem to float between two, and sometimes even three or four, diverse articulations. (Horacio Hale 1884: 233)

> In spite of the significance attached to the phonetic elements, they are, in many American [Indian] languages, singularly vague and fluctuating. (Daniel Brinton 1888: 8)

The imprecision they reported was not real and not a fault found in these languages, but rather lay in the inability of those recording the languages to hear and represent sounds unfamiliar to them accurately. Boas' (1889) article 'On alternating sounds' explained away once and for all this misconception about imprecise sounds in so-called 'primitive' languages.

(1b) *The myth of rapid change.* Another misconception associated with the idea of imprecise sounds, also with some rare echoes still today, is that 'primitive' languages 'change with a rapidity that soon renders reconstruction so tenuous as to be meaningless' (Haas 1969: 27). For example, Archibald Sayce (1874: 46–7) in his *The Principles of Comparative Philology* asserted:

> as a general rule, tribes in a low state of civilisation . . . are continually changing the character of their idioms, so that in the course of a single generation two neighbouring villages become mutually unintelligible.

In like fashion, Edward John Payne (1899: 92) insisted that 'from 20 to 40 years is probably a liberal allotment for the average life of a very low savage language'. Ernst Pulgram (1961: 32) thought the assumed rapidity of change compromised reconstruction by the comparative method by 'the third or fourth generation'. It is now clear that change is no faster nor slower in little-known or unwritten languages than in well-known languages with long written traditions.

(1c) *The myth that sound change is not regular in 'primitive' languages.* Though this myth is long disproven, doubt has notwithstanding lingered about the regularity of sound change in so-called 'exotic' languages. Meillet and Cohen (1924: 9) wrote in their influential *Les Langue du Monde*:

> One may well ask whether the languages of America (which are still for the most part poorly known and insufficiently studied from a comparative point of view) will ever lend themselves to exact, exhaustive comparative treatment; the samples offered so far hold scant promise . . . it is not even clear that the principle of genealogical classification applies. (See also Meillet 1925: vi–vii and Rivet 1925: 26)

Leonard Bloomfield (1925, 1928) conclusively demonstrated the regularity of sound change for so-called 'primitive' languages. Bloomfield (1925: 130) responded directly to Meillet's and others' doubts:

> I hope, also, to help dispose of the notion that the usual processes of linguistic change are suspended on the American continent. (Meillet and Cohen, *Les langues du monde*, Paris, 1924: 9). If there exists anywhere a language in which these processes do not occur (sound-change independent of meaning, analogic change, etc.), then they will not explain the history of Indo-European or any other language. A principle such as the regularity of phonetic change is not part of the specific tradition handed on to each new speaker of a given language, but is either a universal trait of human speech or nothing at all, an error.

Edward Sapir (1949 [1929]: 160–1), who had engaged in the comparative reconstruction of a number of American Indian language families, seconded Bloomfield:

> The methods developed by the Indo-Europeanists have been applied with marked success to other groups of languages. It is abundantly clear that they apply just as rigorously to the unwritten primitive languages of Africa and America as to the better known forms of speech of the more sophisticated peoples . . . The more we devote ourselves to the comparative study of the languages of a primitive linguistic stock, the more clearly we realize that phonetic law and analogical leveling are the only satisfactory key to the unravelling of the development of dialects and languages from a common base. Professor Leonard Bloomfield's experiences with Central Algonkian and my own with Athabaskan leave nothing to be desired in this respect and are a complete answer to those who find it difficult to accept the large-scale regularity of the operation of all those unconscious linguistic forces which in their totality give us regular phonetic change and morphological readjustment on the basis of such change. It is not merely theoretically possible to predict the correctness of specific forms among unlettered peoples on the basis of such phonetic laws as have been worked out for them – such predictions are already on record in considerable number. There can be no doubt that the methods first developed

in the field of Indo-European linguistics are destined to play a consistently important rôle in the study of all other groups of languages.

Sapir (1949 [1931]: 74) summarized the now almost universal attitude:

> Is there any reason to believe that the process of regular phonetic change is any less applicable to the languages of primitive peoples than to the languages of the more civilized nations? This question must be answered in the negative . . . If these laws are more difficult to discover in primitive languages, this is not due to any special characteristic which these languages possess but merely to the inadequate technique of some who have tried to study them.

Since Sapir and Bloomfield's work, the assumption that sound change is regular has proved itself useful and valid in case after case in comparative work on 'exotic' languages.

(1d) *The myth that the comparative method is not applicable to 'exotic' languages.* Related to doubts about the regularity of sound change in 'primitive' languages is the myth that the comparative method may not be applicable to some languages. Some doubts about the applicability of the comparative method to 'exotic' languages stem from a belief that change in 'exotic' languages is fundamentally different from change in better-known language families, such as Indo-European. Frequently, Australian languages have been implicated in these doubts, where extensive borrowing is cited as a confounding factor. Even if borrowing makes the task more complicated, it does not invalidate the comparative method or its applicability to these languages. In fact, it was through a demonstration of regular changes that Kenneth Hale (1964, 1976) was able to show that languages of northeastern Queensland with many short monosyllabic words, formerly thought to be quite aberrant, had developed regularly from Pama-Nyungan, a large language family of Australia. The comparative method has to contend with lexical borrowings everywhere, not just in Australia. (More on this below.) Modern research shows that change in languages of Australia is not fundamentally different from change in other languages (see for example Bowern and Koch 2004, Evans 2003). Abundant comparative research involving 'exotic' and unwritten languages from all over the world has demonstrated time and again the applicability of the comparative method to 'exotic' languages, and to unwritten as well as to written languages.

13.6.2 The myth of insurmountable convergence

Another misconception is that languages in contact may undergo so much convergence that it may become impossible to determine a single ancestor, and thus impossible to classify them or to apply the comparative method. R.M.W. Dixon's (1997) *The Rise and Fall of Languages* has been a major promoter of this view. At the heart of Dixon's approach is the notion of *punctuated equilibrium*, taken from biology. Dixon believes that extensive diffusion and language convergence can place languages beyond the reach of the comparative method and can challenge classification by the family tree model (Dixon 1997, 2002). He correlates states of equilibrium with extensive language contact and diffusion, and correlates punctuation events with diversification into language families. He imagines that during a period of equilibrium:

> languages in contact will diffuse features between each other, becoming more and more similar. These similarities will gradually *converge*, towards a *common prototype*. We can thus say that language families are rapidly made during a period of punctuation . . . and slowly blurred during the long period of equilibrium . . . that follows. (Dixon 1997: 70–1; see also Dixon 2002: 32–5)

Dixon assumes this makes classification in terms of language families difficult.

There are, however, problems with this conception.

The notion of punctuated equilibrium, inspired by Eldredge and Gould (1972), is challenged in biology. Evolution continues even without punctuated events disrupting equilibrium (Dennett 1995). Language change and differentiation into language families also continue in periods of equilibrium (in the absence of disruptive events). The problems with the concept detected in biology also hold for its application to languages – changes of both sorts, divergence and borrowing, take place both in states of equilibrium and of punctuation.

Dixon's assumptions about social structure are unrealistic. He says, 'the necessary scenario for a period of equilibrium is a number of groups living in relative harmony with one another' (Dixon 1997: 78), and adds:

> All groups would be roughly similar in terms of lifestyle and beliefs. That is, they would have a comparable level of sophistication in the tools and weapons they possess, the sorts of shelters they build, and the food resources they have available. They would have comparable types of (non-aggressive) religious beliefs. (Dixon 2002: 32)

Here, Dixon has fallen prey to the tendency to portray non-industrial societies as pristine and ideal. The ethnographic literature does not support a picture of small-scale traditional societies as egalitarian and living in harmony. It shows enormous variation in social structure and political organization, where harmony and equality are mostly absent. Many anthropologists today believe that all societies are systems of inequality. Anthropologists have made repeated attempts to come up with a list of peaceful societies, and on a world-wide basis they come up with at best four to seven possible examples (LeBlanc 2003). Moreover, it is not uncommon to find human groups in the same region who have different kinds of socio-cultural integration, markedly different sorts of social stratification and social organization, and different subsistence patterns. Dixon's view of human societies in the past does not stand up. Since his notion of punctuated equilibrium in language change depends on this view of society, this is a serious problem for the approach.

(1) *Equilibrium with diversification.* Dixon's scheme equates equilibrium with language convergence. Nevertheless, normal change leading to diversification into language families also takes place in times of equilibrium. We see cases with no evidence of punctuation where the languages have nevertheless diversified into language families: the Eastern Mayan (K'ichean, Mamean subgroups), Zapotecan, Eskimoan, Nakh-Daghestanian, Saami (a Finno-Ugric subfamily with ten distinct languages), etc. A number of language families have developed

in situ, in relative harmony, without punctuation events, in spite of the predictions of the model.

(2) *Equilibrium without diffusion.* Situations of equilibrium without diffusion also go contrary to the model. Dixon (1997: 70–1) believes that in periods of equilibrium, languages in contact diffuse features and gradually converge. But linguistic diffusion does not always happen in situations of harmonious equilibrium. Languages in the same area over a long time in equilibrium may exhibit little evidence of contact-induced change. Among numerous examples, the case of the Hano Tewa (Tanoan language) and Hopi (Uto-Aztecan) can be cited. The two groups harmoniously share the same tiny mesa top in Arizona, yet extremely little borrowing or diffusion has taken place in either language (Kroskrity 1993). Cases such as this constitute a problem for the model's expectation that equilibrium results in diffusion and convergence.

(3) *Diffusion in punctuation.* Dixon correlates punctuation with changes leading to diversification, not diffusion, which is associated with equilibrium. But diffusion can actually be caused by punctuation and does not take place just in equilibrium. Conquest and political inequality promote structural diffusion among languages. For example, the history of English is mostly that of punctuation, with the Scandinavian invasion and the Norman French conquest, but the outcome is more in tune with that envisaged for equilibrium states: English assimilated much vocabulary, borrowed sounds and some pronouns, and levelled morphosyntactic complexity. Similarly, the impact of Spanish on the grammar of many indigenous languages of Latin America is a direct reflection of the inequality in the status of the languages involved and the punctuation that Spanish domination brought (Brody 1989, 1995, Campbell 1987). Forced language contact (punctuation) and peaceful contact (equilibrium) can have similar outcomes with respect to diffusion and convergence. Linguistic areas and traits shared across languages of a geographical region can result from responses to punctuating factors.

The correlation which equates equilibrium with convergence, and punctuation with diffusion and divergence, is not supported – both kinds of change take place in both kinds of situations. Languages both diversify and spread in situations of both punctuation and equilibrium.

(4) *Excessive zeal for 'convergence'.* Some scholars have gone too far in assuming language convergence. They believe that so much convergence is possible that the comparative method is no longer valid and whole language families can disappear, converging with one another. However, it is known from the well-studied linguistic areas (see Chapter 12) that: (1) typically few diffused structural features are found, often less than a dozen main ones. (2) Cases of profound language mixture are mostly not found; clear cases of language mixture are truly rare and do not arise through normal language contact (see Chapter 12); rather, they can come about only in extreme social circumstances, for example with forced population removals and new ethnic allegiances, generally not found in pre-colonial settings. (3) Identity of family membership is needed to determine whether something is borrowed or inherited and to determine the extent of diffusion. In documented linguistic areas, cases of wholesale convergence are not known – diffused traits can make distinguishing inherited material from diffused

elements difficult in some instances, but cases of convergence of initially independent languages to the extent of obliterating family connections and making
the comparative method inapplicable are not known.

13.6.3   Temporal limitation to the comparative method

There are real limitations of the comparative method, which must be accepted
and dealt with, as seen in Chapter 5. There are also misconceptions associated
with these limitations. A principal one is the *temporal limitation*: the comparative method cannot see back in time forever. It is generally acknowledged that
there is a limit to how far into the past the comparative method can reach, said
by different scholars to be somewhere between 6,000 and 10,000 years ago. This
is because so much language change takes place in the passage of time that after
a very long time accompanied by much change, little that was original in the language may be preserved, and it becomes no longer possible to identify accurately
what may have been inherited. For example, vocabulary changes and is replaced.
According to glottochronology (see Chapter 17), after about 14,000 years, nearly
all of a language's basic vocabulary will have been replaced, meaning that if we
were to compare two related languages which had split up before, say, 15,000
years ago, it is unlikely, according to the method, that we would find any recognizable cognates. Nichols (1998: 128) reports that 'after 6,000 years of separation, two languages are expected to exhibit only 7% shared cognates, and 7%
represents the lowest number of resemblant items that can safely be considered
distinct from chance'. It matters not whether either of these views is correct –
certainly there is no reason to believe in the glottochronological date; however,
they do correctly note that over time vocabulary items are replaced and change.
We cannot expect unreplaced cognate vocabulary to survive in languages or to
persist in recognizable form for tens of thousands of years. Clearly, after nearly
all of the vocabulary of related languages has been replaced or changed so that
it is no longer possible to recognize connections, we cannot expect meaningful results from the application of the comparative method. While the temporal
threshold may vary from case to case, in the long run, after enough structural
change and vocabulary replacement, comparison of only very distantly related
languages by the comparative method ceases to be effective.

The amount of change over time is relevant to the many hypotheses of proposed distant genetic relationships. It is quite likely that, for many of these proposals, even if there had ever been a relationship among some of the languages
involved, it lies so far in the distant past that the amount of inherited material
in recognizable form is so vanishingly small that no effective case for a genetic
relationship among the languages compared can be made. In such cases it is
impossible to distinguish merely accidental similarities from evidence thought to
support a relationship. (See Chapter 14.)

13.6.4   Do kinds of societies determine linguistic change?

Is there a causal connection between the type of society speakers of a language
live in and the structure of the language they speak? Does the kind of society

cause the language to change to become simpler or more complex? There are various claims which attribute linguistic complexity or simplicity to the kinds of societies (or cultures) involved, particularly to the size in terms of numbers of speakers or their relative isolation. An often-repeated opinion is that language becomes more complex in isolated communities or in small-scale societies where most members interact with one another face to face (Andersen 1988, Hymes 1974, Nettle 1999a, Nettle and Romaine 2000, Ross 1996, 1997, Trudgill 1989, 2002, 2004a, 2004b). The assumed correlations between society type and language structure or kind of language change are misleading at best. The idea often expressed is that in such communities, isolated or characterized by face-to-face communication, where most speakers know each other, people tolerate eccentricities, and so complexity can develop and changes can make unusual linguistic traits become part of the structure of the language.

There are many counter-examples – simple but relatively isolated small languages and large, non-isolated but complex languages. For example, for phonological complexity, the topic most often cited with respect to complexity arguments, there are counter-examples in numerous relatively small and isolated languages such as Rotokas, Pirahã, Hawai'ian, Māori, etc. which have extremely limited phoneme inventories. Rotokas (a 'Papuan' language of Bougainville, 4,000 speakers) has only eleven segments, only six consonants; Pirahã (Muran family, Brazil, 150 speakers) also has only eleven segments, eight consonants and three vowels; Hawai'ian has only eight consonants. The small and isolated South Island Māori, instead of becoming more complex, reduced the already limited inventory of eleven consonants by merging /ŋ/ with /k/. There are also numerous large non-isolated languages which are complex and exhibit unusual traits, some of which became more complex over time. For example, varieties of Quechua, spoken by several million speakers in the Andes, have three series of stops and affricates (plain, glottalized, and aspirated), uvular consonants, and in some varieties retroflex obstruents, with very complex morphology. Zulu (6,000,000 speakers) is not isolated, but has thirty-five consonants, plus an elaborate system of clicks, which are due to contact with so-called 'Khoisan' languages. Georgian (4,000,000 speakers), not isolated or small, is complex, with twenty-nine consonants, with plain, voiced, and glottalized stops and affricates, uvular stops, and, complex morphology. Arabic, with many millions of speakers, a language of civilization and empire for centuries, has the dentals /θ/, /ð/, plain and pharyngealized coronal fricatives and stops, and pharyngeals (/ʕ/ and /ħ/).

Trudgill (2002, 2004a) elaborated his views; he holds that 'large phonological inventories, then, may be the result of borrowing'. But, he believes that when the kind of language contact involves adult language acquisition, because of adults' imperfect learning, simplification resulting in loss of phonological contrasts may take place. He concludes: 'long-term contact involving child bilingualism may produce large inventories, through borrowing, and adult language contact may produce smaller inventories through imperfect learning, pidginization [meaning three processes: reduction, admixture, simplification, but not necessarily the formation of new pidgins], and simplification' (Trudgill 2004a: 314). Trudgill (2004a: 318) concludes with what he believes are better generalizations:

1. Isolated languages 'will be more likely to have *either* very small inventories *or* very large ones'.
2. 'Non-isolated languages spoken in larger communities will ... tend to have medium-sized inventories'.
3. 'The factors of isolation and small community size can quite simply lead to the development of *unusual* phonological systems ... these systems may be either unusually small ... or unusually large'.

Commentators found no support for these claims; rather, they found numerous counter-examples. Rice (2004) notes very little variation in the phoneme inventories of Athabaskan languages, though they are involved in different contact situations, some with child bilingualism, others with adult learners, some in contact with languages with larger phoneme inventories, some with smaller inventories, and so on. Hajek (2004) found relatively small phonemic inventories in the New Guinea and Pacific region regardless of the kind of contact or isolation, number of speakers, or language family involved. Bakker (2004) examined numerous languages with large phoneme inventories, finding a large range of social situations where the languages were spoken, and no tendency towards the simplifications Trudgill predicts. Pericliev (2004) found a lack of correlation between the size of the community of speakers and the size of the phonological inventories. Moreover, language contact situations usually do not involve distinctly child bilingualism or adult learning contact, but can include both adult learners and childhood acquirers together, making the speculative correlations impossible to verify.

There is no clear correlation between amount of language contact, isolation, or community size and structural complexity of the languages involved. (See Campbell and Poser 2008: 457–62.)

Hay and Bauer (2007) argue that there is a positive correlation between the number of speakers of a language and how many phonemes that language has. They found evidence of smaller populations favouring smaller phoneme inventories. They also note that neither the number of speakers of a language nor its phoneme inventory remains constant over time, raising the question of how changes in population size could lead to changes in phoneme inventory size. Their tables show an overall statistical tendency but with reasonably large amounts of 'scatter', that is, exceptions that do not conform to the trend. They admit that language family membership has a significant influence on the size of the phoneme inventory, regardless of the number of speakers of the various languages in the family, though they argue that this, nevertheless, does not overpower the statistical tend for population size and phoneme inventory size to correlate. While theirs is a significant finding, it is unlikely to convince historical linguists that population size plays a significant factor in how languages change. There are so many exceptions that do not conform, and the proportion of languages that do conform is so small, that the observed tendency does not support strong predictions about change in language. The fact that language family membership also has an influence on phoneme inventory size, regardless of numbers of speakers, suggests that the population size is not a compellingly strong determining factor in how or why languages will change.

13.6.5   Is the family tree merely a metaphor?

As seen above, some scholars would challenge the validity of the family tree model and with it the applicability of the comparative method, based on beliefs about convergence and language contact. Their criticisms seem to blame the comparative method for contact phenomena or at least for not dealing with them. Critics misunderstand (1) that the comparative method was not designed to deal with diffusion – it focuses on what is inherited, on what can be reconstructed; (2) that historical linguists have other tools for dealing with diffusion; and (3) that in fact the comparative method actually performs well at identifying borrowing.

Some critics contrast linguistic areas and the comparative method, claiming the idea of areal linguistics came about because of the comparative method's inability to explain diffusion (see for example Dahl 2001). This is short-sighted. The goal of the historical linguist is to answer the question 'What happened?', whether the explanation be due to inheritance, diffusion, or both. Some critics, in their zeal, challenge the comparative method for an assumed failure to deal with diffusion and call for alternative models. For example, Dixon (1997: 28) asserts 'the family tree model . . . is not applicable everywhere and cannot explain every type of relationship between languages. We need a more inclusive model, which integrates together the ideas of the family tree and of diffusion area' (see also 2002: 31). Mainstream historical linguists respond that we do not need such a model; we already have in our arsenal not only the comparative method, but also tools for addressing diffusion which include the techniques for indentifying borrowing, the wave theory, and areal linguistics. Both inheritance and diffusion have always been of crucial importance to answering the historical linguist's primary question, 'What happened?', and historical linguistic accounts have always addressed borrowing and diffusion (see Chapters 3, 7, and 12). It was never thought that the comparative method was to tackle all of this on its own, or that it was the only tool available.

Moreover, the comparative method is not at odds with diffusion; it is often a major tool for detecting borrowing and thus for discriminating what is inherited from what is diffused. As Calvert Watkins (2001: 59) writes, 'the resilience and the power of the comparative method lies in its sensitivity to similarity due both to genetic filiation and areal diffusion alike. Both are historical models, and the goal of comparison is history.' The history of the classification of Armenian provides a telling example. Armenian contains a massive number of loans from Iranian, but it was Hübschmann's (1875) application of the comparative method which identified these loans and their source and proved that Armenian was a separate branch of Indo-European. His findings corrected the classification of Armenian, showing that it is not a member of the Iranian subfamily as previously thought (Watkins 2001: 59). The comparative method, by helping to sort out what is borrowed, also contributes to the definition of the linguistic areas, for example the linguistic areas that involve Indo-European languages: the Balkans, Baltic, South Asia (Indian subcontinent), and Anatolian linguistic areas (see Chapter 12). That both inheritance and diffusion can be tackled with the comparative method has been shown time and again (see Watkins 2001, Campbell and Poser 2008, for examples).

So, is the family tree merely a bad 'metaphor', as some think? There is a reality – not just a metaphor – that the family tree diagrams attempt to reflect: languages do diverge into separate languages which are related to one another by descent from the earlier common ancestor, sister languages belonging to language families, daughters of the original parent. If some scholars limit their vision to only that which is inherited, that is unfortunate, but that is not an accurate characterization of what historical linguists usually do or of all that the comparative method is capable of, as the Armenian case shows (one of many that could be cited).

What about cases where it is difficult or impossible to determine whether shared traits are due to inheritance, diffusion, independent parallel development, or accident? The difficulty of distinguishing what is inherited from what is diffused is often called forth by those who criticize the comparative method or the family tree model. All historical sciences face the same problem: we do our best to understand the past with the evidence on hand, and sometimes that evidence is insufficient to allow definitive answers. Fortunately for us, methods in historical linguistics have proven successful over and over in distinguishing instances of borrowing from inheritance. We do not abandon such successful methods just because the evidence at hand in some specific instance is insufficient to resolve uncertainty, just as we do not conclude that a car can never take us anywhere just because on some occasion the petrol ran out.

Challenges to the comparative method appear to be overstated and to have misunderstood fundamental matters in historical linguistics.

14

Distant Genetic Relationship

De Laet [1643], speaking of Hugo Grotius' methods: If you are willing to change letters, to transpose syllables, to add and subtract, you will nowhere find anything that cannot be forced into this or that similarity; but to consider this as evidence for the origin of peoples – this is truly not proved as far as I am concerned.

(Metcalf 1974: 241)

14.1 Introduction

A topic of great current interest in historical linguistics is that of distant genetic relationships, and both the methods and the hypothesized distant family relationships have been much debated. Postulated remote relationships such as Amerind, Nostratic and Proto-World have been featured in newspapers, magazines and television documentaries, and yet these same proposals have been rejected by most mainstream historical linguists. How is one to know what to believe? How can claims about very remote linguistic relationships be evaluated? This chapter addresses these questions by surveying the various methodological principles, criteria and rules of thumb that are considered important in proposals of distant genetic relationship. The goal is to prepare you to be able to see past the controversies by explaining the methods and their limitations. Armed with these, you should be able to evaluate proposals of remote linguistic affinity for yourself.

Two outlooks can be distinguished, or stages in research on potential distant genetic relationships, each with its own practices. The first is like a scouting expedition. In it, the intention is to call attention to a possible but as yet untested connection between languages not known to be related to one another. In this approach, a wide net is often cast in order to haul in as much potential evidence as possible. The second outlook comes into play typically when the intention is to test a proposal that has already been made. In it, those forms considered initially as possible evidence are submitted to more careful scrutiny. Unfortunately, the more laissez-faire setting-up type hypotheses of the first approach are not always distinguished from the more cautious hypothesis-testing type of the second. Both orientations are valid. Nevertheless, long-range proposals which have not been evaluated carefully are not considered acceptable or established. As Antoine Meillet, a famous Indo-Europeanist well known for his common-sense discussions of historical linguistic methods, cautioned, excessive zeal for long-range relationships can lead to methodological excesses: 'The difficulty of the task of trying to make every language fit into a genetic classification has led certain eminent linguists to deprive the principle of such classification of its precision and its rigour or to apply it in an imprecise manner' (1948 [1914]: 78). The comparative method has always been the basic tool for establishing genetic relationships, though it is necessary to discuss a number of particular aspects of how it is applied in work on distant genetic relationships and to address approaches which have sometimes been advocated as competitors of the comparative method.

In order to give an idea of what is at issue, the following is a list of some of the better-known hypotheses which would group together languages which are not yet known to be related. None of the proposed genetic relationships in this list has been demonstrated yet, even though some are repeated frequently, for example in encyclopaedias and textbooks. Many other unconfirmed proposals of distant genetic relationship (not listed here) have also been made.

Altaic (proposed grouping of Turkic, Tungusic, Manchu and Mongolian, to which some proposals also add Ainu, Japanese, Korean and others)

Amerind (Joseph Greenberg's proposal which would lump all the 180 or so Native American languages families except Eskimo-Aleut and so-called Na-Dene into one large group)

Austric (Austro-Asiatic with Austronesian)

Austro-Tai (Japanese-Austro-Thai)

Basque-Caucasian, Basque-SinoTibetan-Na-Dene

Dene-Sino-Tibetan (Athabaskan [or Na-Dene] and Sino-Tibetan

Dravidian-Japanese

Dravidian-Uralic

Eskimo and Indo-European

Eskimo-Uralic

Eurasiatic (Greenberg's (2000) grouping of Indo-European, Uralic, Eskimo-Aleut, Ainu and several other otherwise unaffiliated languages)

Hokan (in various versions which group many American Indian families and isolates)

Indo-European and Afroasiatic

Indo-European and Semitic

Indo-Pacific (Greenberg's (1971) grouping of all the non-Austronesian languages of the Pacific, including all Papuan families, Tasmanian, and the languages of the Andaman Islands)

Indo-Uralic (Indo-European and Uralic)

Japanese-Altaic

Japanese-Austronesian

Khoisan (the African families with clicks, except the Bantu languages which borrowed clicks; now considered more likely an areal grouping than a genetic one)

Macro-Siouan (Siouan, Iroquoian, Caddoan, sometimes also Yuchi)
  Maya-Chipayan (Mayan, Uru-Chipayan of Bolivia)
Na-Dene (Eyak-Athabaskan, Tlinglit, Haida – the position of Haida is highly
  disputed)
Niger-Kordofanian (Niger-Congo) (Africa, Greenberg's grouping which
  includes Mande, Kru, Kwa, Benue-Congo [of which Bantu is a branch],
  Gur, Adamawa-Ubangi, Kordofanian, and others)
Nilo-Saharan (large number of African families; Greenberg's grouping which
  contains most of the African languages not otherwise classified as belong-
  ing to one of the other three groupings)
Nostratic (various versions; the best-known groups Indo-European, Uralic,
  Altaic, Kartvelian, Dravidian and Afroasiatic, though some add also
  Chuckchi-Kamchatkan, Eskimo-Aleut, Sumerian and Gilyak (Nivkh))
Penutian (in various versions which group a number of American Indian
  families and isolates)
Proto-Australian (all twenty-six or so of the Australian families)
Proto-World (Global Etymologies)
Ural-Altaic (Uralic and 'Altaic')
Ural-Altaic and Eskimo-Aleut
Yukaghir-Uralic
(Compare the less controversial classifications in Table 6.2, Chapter 6.)

Let us look now at the methods and criteria that have been used in research
on distant genetic relationships. (These are treated in more detail in Campbell
1997a: 206–59, 2003c, and Campbell and Poser 2008.)

14.2   Lexical Comparison

Throughout history, word comparisons have been employed as evidence of
family relationship, but, given a small collection of likely-looking potential
cognates, how can we determine whether they are really the residue of common
origin and not the workings of pure chance or some other factor? It turns out that
lexical comparisons by themselves are seldom convincing without additional
support from other criteria. Because lexical comparisons have typically played
the major role in hypothesized distant genetic relationships, we begin by considering the role of basic vocabulary and lexically based approaches.

14.2.1   Basic vocabulary

Most scholars insist that basic vocabulary should be part of the supporting evidence presented in favour of any distant family relationship. Basic vocabulary is
usually not defined rigorously but is understood generally to include terms for
body parts, close kinship, frequently encountered aspects of the natural world
(mountain, river, cloud and the like) and low numbers. Basic vocabulary is in
general resistant to borrowing, and so, similarities found in comparisons involving basic vocabulary items are unlikely to be due to diffusion and hence stand a
better chance of being evidence of distant genetic relationships, of being inher-

ited from a common ancestor, than other kinds of vocabulary. Of course, basic vocabulary can also be borrowed – though less frequently – so that its role as a safeguard against borrowing is not foolproof (see examples below).

14.2.2 Glottochronology

Glottochronology, which depends on basic, relatively culture-free vocabulary, has been rejected by most linguists, since all its basic assumptions have been challenged. Therefore, it warrants little discussion here. Suffice it to repeat that it does not find or test distant genetic relationships, but rather it *assumes* that the languages compared are related and merely proceeds to attach a date based on the number of core-vocabulary words that are considered similar among the languages compared. This, then, is no method for determining whether languages are related. (See Chapter 17 for more details.)

Glottochronology's focus on vocabulary replacement does draw attention indirectly to a serious problem concerning lexical evidence in long-range relationships. Related languages which separated long ago may have undergone so much vocabulary replacement that insufficient shared original vocabulary will remain for an ancient shared linguistic kinship to be detected. This constitutes a serious problem for detecting really ancient relationships.

14.2.3 Multilateral (or mass) comparison

The best-known of the approaches which rely on inspectional resemblances among lexical items is that advocated by Joseph Greenberg, called 'multilateral (or mass) comparison'. It is based on 'looking at . . . many languages across a few words' rather than 'at a few languages across many words' (Greenberg 1987: 23). The lexical similarities determined by superficial visual inspection which are shared 'across many languages' alone are taken as evidence of genetic relationship. This approach stops where others begin, at the assembling of lexical similarities. These inspectional resemblances must be investigated to determine why they are similar, whether the similarity is due to inheritance from a common ancestor (the result of a distant genetic relationship) or to borrowing, accident, onomatopoeia, sound symbolism, nursery formations and the various things which we will consider in this chapter. Since multilateral comparison does not do this, its results are controversial and rejected by most mainstream historical linguists.

In short, no technique which relies on inspectional similarities in vocabulary alone has proven adequate for establishing distant family relationships.

14.3 Sound Correspondences

It is important to emphasize the value and utility of sound correspondences in the investigation of linguistic relationships. Nearly all scholars consider regular sound correspondences strong evidence of genetic affinity. While sound correspondences are fundamental to most approaches to determining language families, they can be misused, and it is important to understand how this can be.

First, it is systematic correspondences which are crucial, not mere similarities;

correspondences do not necessarily involve similar sounds. The sounds which are equated in proposals of remote relationship are typically very similar, often identical, although such identities are not so frequent among the daughter languages of well-established non-controversial older language families. The sound changes that lead to such non-identical correspondences often result in cognate words being so changed that their cognacy is not apparent. These true but non-obvious cognates are missed by methods, such as multilateral comparison, which seek only inspectional resemblances. They miss such well-known true cognates as French *cinq*/Russian *pʲatʲ*/Armenian *hing*/English *five* (all derived by straightforward changes from original Indo-European *penkʷe*- 'five'), French *bœuf*/ English *cow* (from Proto-Indo-European *gʷou*-), French /nu/ (spelled *nous*) 'we, us'/English *us* (both ultimately from Proto-Indo-European *nos*-; English from Germanic *uns* <*n̥s*); the words in these cognate sets are not visually similar to each other, but they exhibit regular correspondences among the cognates.

There are a number of ways in which the criterion of sound correspondences can be misapplied. Sometimes regularly corresponding sounds may also be found in loanwords. For example, it is known from Grimm's Law that real French–English cognates should exhibit the correspondence *p* : *f*, as in *père/father*, *pied/ foot*, *pour/for* (mentioned in Chapter 5). However, French and English appear to exhibit also the correspondence *p* : *p* in cases where English has borrowed from French or Latin, as in *paternel/paternal*, *piédestal/pedestal*, *per/per*. Since English has many such loans, examples illustrating this bogus *p* : *p* sound correspondence are not hard to find. In comparing languages not yet known to be related, we must use caution in interpreting sound correspondences to avoid the problem of apparent correspondences found in undetected loans. Generally, sound correspondences found in basic vocabulary warrant the confidence that the correspondences are probably legitimate, since, as mentioned above, terms for basic vocabulary are borrowed only infrequently. However, even here we have to be careful, since items of basic vocabulary can also be borrowed, though more rarely. For example, Finnish *äiti* 'mother' and *tytär* 'daughter' are borrowed from Indo-European languages; if these loans were not recognized, one would suspect a sound correspondence of *t* : *d* involving the medial consonant of *äiti* (compare Old High German *eidī*) and the initial consonant of *tytär* (compare Germanic *duhtēr*) based on these basic vocabulary items (found also in other loans).

Some non-genuine sound correspondences can also come from accidentally similar lexical items among languages. Languages share a certain amount of similar vocabulary by sheer accident. A few examples that show this are: Proto-Jê *niw* 'new'/English *new*; Kaqchikel dialects *mes* 'mess, disorder, garbage'/ English *mess*; Jaqaru *aska* 'ask'/English *ask*; Māori *kuri* 'dog'/English *cur*; Lake Miwok *hóllu* 'hollow'/English *hollow*; Gbaya *be* 'to be'/English *be*; Seri *kiʔ*/ French *qui* (/ki/) 'who?'; Yana *t'inii*- 'small'/English *tiny, teeny*; and the famous handbook examples of Persian *bad*/English *bad*, and Malay *mata* 'eye'/Modern Greek *mati* 'eye'.

Other cases of unreal sound correspondences may turn up if one permits wide semantic latitude in proposed cognates, so that phonetically similar but semantically disparate forms are equated. For example, if we were to compare Pipil (Uto-Aztecan) and Finnish (Uralic) words such as Pipil *teki* 'to cut' : Finnish *teki* 'made', *te:n* 'mouth' : *teen* 'of the tea', *tukat* 'spider' : *tukat* 'hairs', *tila:n* 'pulled' : *tilaan* 'into the space', *tu:lin* 'cattails, reeds' : *tuulin* 'by the wind', and so on, we note a recurrence of a *t* : *t* correspondence. However, the phonetic correspondence in these words is due to sheer accident, since it is always possible to find phonetically similar words among languages if their meanings are ignored. With too much semantic liberty among compared forms, it is easy to come up with spurious correspondences such as the Pipil–Finnish *t* : *t*. Unfortunately, wide semantic latitude is frequently a problem in proposals of remote relationship. Additional non-inherited phonetic similarities crop up when onomatopoeic, sound-symbolic and nursery forms are compared. A set of proposed cognates involving a combination of loans, chance enhanced by semantic latitude, onomatopoeia and such factors may exhibit false sound correspondences. For this reason, some proposed remote relationships which purportedly are based on regular sound correspondences nevertheless fail to be convincing.

Most linguists find sound correspondences strong evidence, but many neither insist on them solely nor trust them fully. Most are happier when additional evidence from comparative morphology and grammar also supports the hypothesis.

14.4   Grammatical Evidence

Scholars throughout linguistic history have considered morphological evidence important for establishing language families. Many favour 'shared aberrancy' (talked about sometimes as 'submerged features', 'morphological peculiarities', 'arbitrary associations'), as illustrated, for example, by the corresponding irregularities in forms of the verb 'to be' in branches of Indo-European in Table 14.1 (Pers = person, Pl = plural, Sg = singular; OCS = Old Church Slavonic).

TABLE 14.1: Forms of the verb 'to be' in some Indo-European languages

	3rd Pers Sg	*3rd Pers Pl*	*1st Pers Sg*
Hittite	estsi	asantsi	—
Sanskrit	ásti	sánti	asmi
Greek	estí	eisí	eimí
Latin	est	sunt	sum
OCS	jestɪ	sãntɪ	jesmɪ
Gothic	ist	sind	im

For example, the Algonquian–Ritwan hypothesis, which groups Wiyot and Yurok (two languages of California) with the Algonquian family, was controversial, but morphological evidence such as that in the following comparison of Proto-Central Algonquian (PCA) and Wiyot helped to prove the relationship to everyone's satisfaction:

PCA   *ne + *ehkw- = *netehkw 'my louse'
Wiyot   *du + híkw*   = *dutíkw* 'my louse' (Teeter 1964: 1029).

In Proto-Central Algonquian, a -*t*- is inserted between a possessive pronominal prefix and a vowel-initial root, while in Wiyot a -*t*- is inserted between possessive prefixes and a root beginning in *hV* (with the loss of the *h* in this process). Sapir (1913) had proposed that Wiyot (and also Yurok) of California were related to the Algonquian family; this proposed relationship was controversial, but evidence increased, including that presented here, which ultimately demonstrated the validity of the hypothesis to the satisfaction of all.

There is no phonetic (or other natural) reason for why a language would add a *t* in this environment (between vowels or between a vowel and *hV*), and this is so unusual that it is not likely to be shared by borrowing or by accident. Inheritance from a common ancestor which had this peculiarity is more likely, and this is confirmed by other evidence shared by these languages. Another often-repeated example is the agreement between English *good/better/best* and German *gut/besser/best*, said to be 'obviously of enormous probative value' for showing that languages are related (Greenberg 1987: 30).

Morphological correspondences of the 'shared aberrancy'/'submerged features' type, just like sound correspondences, are generally thought to be an important source of evidence for distant genetic relationships. Nevertheless, caution is necessary here as well. There are impressive cases of apparent idiosyncratic grammatical correspondences which in fact have non-genetic explanations. Since some languages do share some seemingly submerged features by accident, caution is necessary in the interpretation of morphological evidence. Clearly, then, the strongest hypotheses of relationship are those which have evidence of several sorts, recurrent sound correspondences in basic vocabulary and multiple examples of grammatical evidence of the sort just discussed.

14.5   Borrowing

Diffusion is a source of non-genetic similarity among languages. It can complicate evidence for remote relationships. Too often, scholars err in not eliminating loans from consideration as possible evidence of wider relationship. An example which was presented as evidence of the controversial 'Chibchan–Paezan' genetic grouping (involving several South American language families) illustrates this problem. For the proposed cognate set meaning 'axe', forms from only four of the many languages were cited, two of which are loanwords: Cuitlatec *navaxo* 'knife', borrowed from Spanish *navajo* 'knife, razor', and Tunebo *baxi-ta* 'machete', from Spanish *machete* (in Tunebo [x] alternates with [ʃ]; nasal consonants do not occur before oral vowels; the vowels of the Tunebo form are expected substitutes for Spanish *e*) (Greenberg (1987: 108). Clearly, because two of the four pieces of evidence are borrowings, the putative 'axe' cognate is not good evidence for the hypothesis. Among compared forms cited as support for the controversial Nostratic hypothesis (which would join Indo-European, Uralic, so-called Altaic, Kartvelian, and for some scholars also Dravidian and Afroasiatic into one large super-family; see Kaiser and Shevoroshkin 1988), some involve known loanwords (for example, those for 'practice witchcraft'), and others have been claimed to involve loans, for example those for 'vessel', 'honey', 'birch', 'bird-cherry', 'poplar', 'conifer' and so on (see Campbell 1998, 1999).

Since it is not always possible to recognize loanwords without extensive research, it is frequently suggested (as mentioned above) that the problem of borrowing can be made less severe by sticking to basic vocabulary and avoiding words with cultural content. By this rule of thumb, the Nostratic forms which have been questioned as possible loans would all be set aside. While this is good practice, it must be remembered (as mentioned above and shown in Chapter 3) that even basic vocabulary can sometimes be borrowed. Finnish borrowed from its Baltic and Germanic neighbours various terms for basic kinship and body parts, for example 'mother', 'daughter', 'sister', 'tooth', 'navel', 'neck', 'thigh', 'fur' and so on. English has borrowed from French or Latin the basic vocabulary items 'stomach', 'face', 'vein', 'artery', 'intestine', 'mountain', 'navel', 'pain', 'penis', 'person', 'river', 'round', 'saliva' and 'testicle'. The problem of loans and potential loans is very serious for distant genetic relationships.

14.6   Semantic Constraints

It is dangerous to present phonetically similar forms with different meanings as potential evidence of remote genetic relationship under the assumption that semantic shifts have taken place. Of course meaning can shift, as seen in Chapter 10 (for example, Albanian *motër* 'sister', from Indo-European 'mother'), but in hypotheses of remote relationship the assumed semantic shifts cannot be documented, and the greater the semantic latitude permitted in compared forms, the easier it is to find phonetically similar forms which have no historical connection (as in the Pipil–Finnish examples above). When semantically non-equivalent forms are compared, the possibility that chance accounts for the phonetic similarity is greatly increased (cf. Ringe 1992). Within families where the languages are known to be related, etymologies are still not accepted unless an explicit account of any assumed semantic changes can be provided. The advice often given is to count only exact semantic equivalences. The problem of excessive semantic permissiveness is one of the most common and most serious in long-range proposals. The following are a few of the many examples from various proposals of long-range relationships, presented just for illustration's sake (only the glosses of the various forms compared are cited). Among evidence cited for Nostratic, we find 'lip/mushroom/ soft outgrowth', 'grow up/become/tree/be', 'crust/rough/scab' (see Kaiser and Shevoroshkin 1988). In the proposed global etymology for 'finger, one' (in the Proto-World hypothesis, the claim that all the world's languages are related), we find all the following: 'one/five/ten/once/only/first/single/fingernail/finger/toe/ hand/palm of hand/arm/foot/paw/guy/thing/to show/to point/in hand/middle finger' (Ruhlen 1994: 322–3). In forms from the Amerind hypothesis (which proposes that most of the languages of the Americas are related), we find semantic equations such as the following:'excrement/night/grass','body/belly/heart/skin/ meat/be greasy/fat/deer', 'child/copulate/son/girl/boy/tender/bear/ small', 'field/ devil/bad/underneath/bottom' (Greenberg 1987). It is for reasons like this that each of these proposals of more remote linguistic relationship is highly disputed.

14.7   Onomatopoeia

Onomatopoeic words imitate the real-world sound associated with the meaning of the word, such as *bow-wow* for the noise that dogs make when barking, *cockadoodledoo* for roosters' crowing, and so on. Sometimes the connection to the sounds in nature is strong enough to inhibit onomatopoeic words from undergoing otherwise regular sound changes. For example, English *peep* /pip/, from earlier *pīpen*, would have become /paip/ by regular sound change (via the Great Vowel Shift; see Chapter 2) if not for the influence of onomatopoeia (Anttila 1989: 86). Onomatopoeic forms may be similar in different languages because they have independently approximated the sounds of nature, not because they share any common history. Examples involving onomatopoeia must be eliminated from proposals of distant genetic relationship. A way to reduce the sound-imitative factor is to omit from consideration words which cross-linguistically are often imitative in form, for example, words meaning 'blow', 'breathe', 'suck', 'laugh', 'cough', 'sneeze', 'break/cut/chop/split', 'cricket', 'crow' (and many bird names in general), 'frog/toad', 'lungs', 'baby/infant', 'beat/hit/pound', 'call/shout', 'choke', 'cry', 'drip/drop', 'hiccough', 'kiss', 'shoot', 'snore', 'spit' and 'whistle', among others. Unfortunately, examples of onomatopoeic words are found very frequently in proposals of distant genetic relationships.

14.8 Nursery Forms

It is generally recognized that nursery words (the 'mama–nana–papa–dada–caca' sort of words) should be avoided in considerations of potential linguistic relationships, since they typically share a high degree of cross-linguistic similarity which is not due to common ancestry. Nevertheless, examples of nursery words are frequent in evidence put forward for distant genetic relationship proposals. The forms involved are typically 'mother', 'father', 'grandmother', 'grandfather' and often 'brother', 'sister' (especially elder siblings), 'aunt' and 'uncle', and have shapes like *mama, nana, papa, baba, tata, dada*, where nasals are found more in terms for females, and stops for males, but not exclusively so. Jakobson explained the cross-linguistic non-genetic similarity among nursery forms which enter adult vocabulary. In his view, the sucking activities of a child are accompanied by a nasal sound, which can be made while nursing, then the nasal sound first associated with nursing is reproduced to show a desire to eat or impatience for missing food or the absent nurse/mother. Since the mother dispenses the food, most of the infant's longings are addressed to her, and the nasal form is turned into a parental term. Then comes a transitional period when *papa* means whichever parent is present while *mama* signals a request for need-fulfilment, and eventually the nasal–mother, oral–father association becomes established (1962 [1960]: 542–3). This helps to explain frequent spontaneous symbolic, affective developments, seen when inherited *mother* in English is juxtaposed to *ma, mama, mamma, mammy, mommy, mom, mummy, mum*, and *father* is compared with *pa, papa, pappy, pop, poppy, da, dad, dada, daddy*. Such nursery words do not provide reliable support for distant genetic proposals.

14.9 Short Forms and Unmatched Segments

How long proposed cognates are and the number of matched sounds (segments) within them are important, since the greater the number of matching segments in a proposed cognate set, the less likely it is that accident accounts for the similarity. Monosyllabic words composed of a single consonant and vowel may be true cognates, but they are so short that their similarity to forms in other languages could also easily be due to chance. Likewise, if only one or two sounds of longer forms are matched (and other sounds are left unmatched), then chance remains a strong candidate for the explanation of the similarity. Such comparisons will not be persuasive; the whole word must be accounted for. (See Ringe 1999.)

14.10   Chance Similarities

Chance (accident) is another possible explanation of similarities among compared languages, and it needs to be avoided in questions of deep family relationships. Conventional wisdom holds that 5–6 per cent of the vocabulary of any two compared languages may be accidentally similar. Also, phoneme frequency within a language plays a role in how often one should expect chance matchings involving particular sounds to come up in comparisons of words from that language with ones from other languages; for example, about 15 per cent of English basic vocabulary begins with *s*, while only about 7.5 per cent begins with *w*; thus, given the greater number of initial *s* words in English, one must expect a higher possible number of chance matchings for *s* than for *w* when English is compared with other languages. The potential for accidental matching increases dramatically when one leaves the realm of basic vocabulary, or when one increases the pool of words from which potential cognates are sought or when one permits the semantics of compared forms to vary even slightly (Ringe 1992: 5).

Cases of non-cognate words which are similar in related languages are well known, for example French *feu* 'fire' and German *Feuer* 'fire' (French *feu* < Latin *focus* 'hearth, fireplace' [-k- > -g- > -Ø-; o > ø]; German *Feuer* < Proto-Indo-European **pūr* 'fire', Proto-Germanic **fūr-i*; compare Old English *fȳr*). As is well known, these cannot be cognates, since French *f* comes from Proto-Indo-European **bh*, while German *f* comes from Proto-Indo-European **p* (by Grimm's Law). The phonetic similarity which these basic nouns share is due to the accidental convergence resulting from sound changes that they have undergone, not to inheritance from any common word in the proto-language. That originally distinct forms in different languages can become similar due to sound changes is not surprising, since even within a single language originally distinct forms can converge, for example, English *son/sun*, *eye/I* and *lie/lie* (Proto-Germanic **ligjan* 'to lie, lay'/**leugan* 'to tell a lie').

14.11   Sound–Meaning Isomorphism

A generally accepted principle (advocated by Meillet) permits only comparisons which involve both sound and meaning together. Similarities in sound alone (for example, the presence of tonal systems in compared languages) or in meaning alone (for example, grammatical gender in the languages compared) are not reliable, since they often develop independently of genetic relationship, due to diffusion, accident and typological tendencies (see Greenberg 1963).

14.12   Only Linguistic Evidence

Another valid principle permits only linguistic information, with no non-linguistic considerations, as evidence of distant genetic relationship. As Gabelentz (1891: 157) put it, 'the only sure means for recognizing a [genetic] relationship lies in the languages themselves.' (See also Greenberg 1963.) Shared cultural traits, mythology, folklore and gene pools must be eliminated from arguments for linguistic relationship. The wisdom of this principle becomes clear when we take into account the many strange proposals based on non-linguistic evidence. For example, some earlier African classifications proposed that Ari (Omotic) belongs to either Nilo-Saharan or Sudanic 'because the Ari people are Negroes', that Moru and Madi belong to Sudanic because they are located in central Africa, or that Fula is Hamitic because its speakers herd cattle, are Moslems, and are tall and Caucasoid (Fleming 1987: 207). Clearly, language affinities can be independent of cultural and biological connections.

14.13   Erroneous Morphological Analysis

Where compared words are analyzed as being composed of more than one morpheme, it is necessary to show that the segmented morphemes (roots and affixes) in fact exist in the grammatical system. Unfortunately, unmotivated morphological segmentation is found frequently in proposals of remote relationship. Often, a morpheme boundary is inserted in forms where none is justified, as for example the arbitrarily segmented Tunebo 'machete' as *baxi-ta* (a loanword from Spanish *machete*, as mentioned above, which contains no morpheme boundary but rather is a single morpheme). This false morphological segmentation makes the form appear more similar to the other forms cited as putative cognates, Cabecar *bak* and Andaqui *boxo-(ka)* 'axe' (Greenberg 1987: 108).

Undetected morpheme divisions are also a frequent problem. An example of this, taken from the Amerind hypothesis (which attempts to unite most of the language families and isolates of the Americas in one very large genetic grouping), compares Tzotzil *ti?il* 'hole' with Lake Miwok *talok^h* 'hole', Atakapa *tol* 'anus', Totonac *tan* 'buttocks' and Takelma *telkan* 'buttocks' (Greenberg 1987: 152); however, the Tzotzil form is *ti?-il*, from *ti?* 'mouth' + *-il* 'indefinite possessive suffix', meaning 'edge, border, outskirts, lips, mouth', but not 'hole'. The appropriate comparison *ti?* bears no particular resemblance to the other forms in this comparison set.

14.14   Non-cognates

Another problem is the frequent comparison of words which are not cognates within their own family with words from other languages as evidence of distant genetic relationship. Often, unrelated words from related languages are joined together in the belief that they might be cognates and then are compared further with forms from other language families as evidence for even more distant relationships. However, if the words are not even cognates within their own family, any further comparison with forms from languages outside the family is untrustworthy. Examples from the Maya–Chipayan hypothesis (Olson 1964, 1965) illustrate this difficulty. Tzotzil *ay(in)* 'to be born' (actually from Proto-Mayan **ar-* 'there is/are', Proto-Tzotzilan **ay-an* 'to live, to be born') is not cognate with the *ya?* (*yah*) 'pain' of the other Mayan languages listed in this set (< Proto-Mayan **yah* 'pain, hurt'), though its inclusion makes Mayan comparisons seem more like Chipaya *ay(in)* 'to hurt'. (*y* = [j] in these examples.) Yucatec Maya *čal(tun)* 'extended (rock)' is compared to non-cognate *č'en* 'rock, cave' in some other Mayan languages; the true Yucatec cognate is *č'e?en* 'well' (and 'cave of water') (< Proto-Mayan **k'e?n* 'rock, cave'). Yucatec *čal-tun* means 'cistern, deposit of water, porous cliff where there is water' (from *čal* 'sweat, liquid' + *tun* 'stone' compare Proto-Mayan **to:ŋ* 'stone'). The non-cognate *čaltun* suggests greater similarity to Chipaya *žara* 'rock (flat, long)' with which the set is compared than the **k'e?n* cognates do (Campbell 1993b). (*č* = [tʃ] in these examples; *ž* = retroflex affricate.)

14.14.1 Words of limited distribution

Often in proposals of distant genetic relationship, an isolated word from some language with no known cognates in other languages of its family is compared to forms in languages from other families. However, a word which has cognates in its own family stands a better chance of perhaps having an even more remote connection with words of languages that may be distantly related than an isolated word which has no known cognates in other languages in its family and hence offers no prima facie evidence of potential older age. Inspectionally resemblant lexical sets of this sort are not convincing. Meillet's principle for established families is just as important – even more so – when considering proposals of distant genetic relationship, where the languages are not yet known to be related:

> When an initial 'proto language' is to be reconstructed, the number of witnesses which a word has should be taken into account. An agreement of two languages . . . risks being fortuitous. But, if the agreement extends to three, four or five very distinct languages [of the same family], chance becomes less probable. (Meillet 1966: 38, Rankin's 1992: 331 translation)

14.14.2 Neglect of known history

It is not uncommon in proposals of distant genetic relationship to encounter forms from one language which exhibit similarities to forms in another language where the similarity is known to be due to recent changes in the individual history of one of the languages. In such cases, when the known history of the languages is brought back into the picture, the similarity disintegrates. An example of this sort is seen in the set of lexical comparisons labelled 'dance' in the Amerind hypothesis which compares Koasati (a Muskogean language) *bit* 'dance' with Mayan forms for 'dance' or 'sing': K'iche' *bis* (actually *b'i:ʃ* 'sing'), Huastec *bisom* and so on (Greenberg 1987: 148). However, Koasati *b* comes from Proto-Muskogean **kʷ*; the Muskogean root was **kʷit-* 'to press down', where 'dance' is a semantic shift in Koasati alone, apparently first applied to stomp dances

(Kimball 1992: 456). Only by neglecting the known history of Koasati (that $b <$ *k^w, and the original meaning was not 'dance') could the Koasati form be seen as similar to Mayan.

14.15   Spurious Forms

Another problem is that of non-existent 'data', that is, difficulties that have to do with the 'bookkeeping' and 'scribal' errors which result in spurious forms being compared. For example, among the forms presented as evidence for the Mayan–Mixe-Zoquean hypothesis (Brown and Witkowski 1979), Mixe-Zoquean words meaning 'shell' were compared with K'iche' (Mayan) *sak'*, said to mean 'lobster', but which actually means 'grasshopper' – a mistranslation of the Spanish gloss *langosta* found in a K'iche'–Spanish dictionary, which in Guatemala means 'grasshopper', though it means 'lobster' in other varieties of Spanish. While a 'shell'–'lobster' comparison is a semantic stretch, it is not as fully implausible as the comparison of 'shell'–'grasshopper', which makes no sense. Errors of this sort can be very serious. Such a case is that of the words given as Quapaw in the Amerind hypothesis (Greenberg 1987) where in fact none is from the Quapaw language, but rather all are from Biloxi and Ofo (other Siouan languages, not closely related to Quapaw; see Rankin 1992: 342). Skewed forms also often enter proposals due to philological mishandling of the sources. For example, in the Amerind evidence, the <v> and <e> of the Creek source of the data was systematically mistransliterated as *u* and *e*, although these represent /a/ and /i/ respectively. Thus <vne> 'I' is presented as *une* rather than the accurate *ani* (Kimball 1992: 448). Spurious forms skew the comparisons.

14.16   Methodological Wrap-up

Given the confusion that certain claims regarding proposed distant genetic relationships have caused, the methodological principles and procedures involved in the investigation of possible distant genetic relationships are extremely important. Principal among these are reliance on regular sound correspondences in basic vocabulary and patterned grammatical (morphological) evidence involving 'shared aberrancy' or 'submerged features', with careful attention to eliminating other possible explanations for similarities noted in compared material (for example, borrowing, onomatopoeia, accident, nursery forms and so on). Research on possible distant genetic relationships which does not heed the methodological recommendations and cautions of this chapter will probably remain inconclusive. On the other hand, investigations informed by and guided by the principles and criteria surveyed here stand a good chance of advancing understanding, by either further supporting or denying proposed family connections.

Many proposals of distant genetic relationship have not stood up well when the evidence presented for them has been subjected to the methodological considerations surveyed in this chapter. This fact might seem to cast a doubt on the likelihood of demonstrating new as yet unproven relationships. However, we can take encouragement from the number of success stories of previously unknown or disputed relationships which subsequently have come to be demonstrated since the beginning of the twentieth century which satisfy the methodological recommendations seen in this chapter. A few examples are: Hittite and the other Anatolian languages demonstrated to be Indo-European; the Uto-Aztecan family demonstrated to the satisfaction of all; the Otomanguean family proven, and then later the proof that Tlapanec belongs to Otomanguean (not to 'Hokan' as previously believed); Algic demonstrated to the satisfaction of all (that Yurok and Wiyot of California and the Algonquian family belong to a more inclusive family); Miwokan and Costanoan proven to be related, members of the more inclusive Miwok–Costanoan family; Rama shown to be Chibchan; Sino-Tibetan established. Indeed, in recent years numerous new families have been recognized and the membership of others has been extended to include additional languages in Papua New Guinea, southeast Asia, Australia and Latin America. Future demonstrations of linguistic relatedness can be expected if proper methodological procedures are followed.

14.17   Some Examples of Long-range Proposals

It will be helpful to look briefly at a few well-known but disputed proposals of distant genetic relationship to see why most mainstream historical linguists are sceptical about them.

14.17.1   Altaic

The Altaic hypothesis would group Turkic, Mongolian, and Tungusic, and some versions also include Korean and Japanese. While 'Altaic' continues to be repeated in encyclopadias and handbooks, most leading 'Altaicists' have abandoned the hypothesis. As mentioned in Chapter 12, the most serious problems for the Altaic proposal are the extensive lexical borrowings among the languages involved, lack of significant numbers of convincing cognates, extensive areal diffusion, and typologically commonplace traits presented as evidence of relationship. The shared 'Altaic' traits typically cited include vowel harmony, relatively simple phoneme inventories, agglutination, exclusively suffixing, (S) OV word order, postpositions, no verb 'to have' for possession, no articles, no grammatical gender, and non-finite verb forms for subordinate clause constructions. These shared features are not only commonplace traits which occur with frequency in unrelated languages of the world, they are also areal traits, shared by a number of languages in surrounding regions whose structural properties were not well known when the hypothesis was first framed (see Chapter 12). Proposed cognates for Altaic languages lack basic vocabulary; for example, most body-part terms and low numbers are lacking. Criticisms also involve problems with the putative sound correspondences that have been suggested among the 'Altaic' languages.

In short, the evidence for genetic relationship has not been persuasive, explaining why many are not convinced by the evidence that has been presented for the 'Altaic' hypothesis. (See Campbell and Poser 2008.)

14.17.2 Nostratic

The Nostratic hypothesis as advanced in the 1960s by Illich-Svitych groups Indo-European, Uralic, Altaic, Kartvelian, Dravidian, and Hamito-Semitic (later Afroasiatic), though other versions of the hypothesis would include various other languages. The sheer number of languages and the many proposed cognates might make it seem difficult to evaluate Nostratic. Nevertheless, assessment is possible. With respect to the many putative cognate sets, assessment can concentrate on those cases considered the strongest by proponents of Nostratic (see Dolgopolsky 1986, Kaiser and Shevoroshkin 1988). Campbell (1998) shows that these strongest cases do not hold up and that the weaker sets are not persuasive. It is relatively easy to determine to what extent the proposed reconstructions correspond to typological expectations, whether sounds in proposed cognate sets actually fit the proposed sound correspondences, whether the proposed cognates involve excessive semantic latitude, and when onomatopoeia, forms too short to deny chance, nursery forms, and the like are involved.

Illich-Svitych's (henceforth IS) version of Nostratic exhibits the following methodological problems (as seen, for example, in Illich-Svitych 1990).

(1) *'Descriptive' forms.* IS is forthright in labelling 26 of his 378 forms – that is, 7 per cent of the total – as 'descriptive', meaning onomatopoeic, affective, or sound-symbolic. There are 16 additional onomatopoeic, affective, or sound-symbolic forms, not so labelled, giving a total of about 11 per cent.

(2) *Questionable cognates.* IS himself indicates that 57 of the 378 sets (15 per cent) are questionable, signalling them with a question mark. However, this number should be much increased, since in numerous forms IS signals problems in other ways, with slanted lines (/ /) for things not conforming to expectations, with question marks, and with upper-case letters in reconstructions to indicate uncertainties or ambiguities.

(3) *Sets with only two families represented.* One of IS's criteria was that only cognate sets with representatives from at least three of the six 'Nostratic' families would be considered as supportive. Nevertheless, 134 of the 378 sets (35 per cent) involve forms from only two families, questionable by IS's own criteria.

(4) *Non-conforming sound correspondences.* Frequently the forms presented as evidence of Nostratic do not exhibit the proposed sound correspondences, that is, they have sounds at odds with those that would be required according to the claimed Nostratic correspondence sets. Campbell (1998), looking mostly only at stops and only at the Indo-European and Uralic data, found twenty-five sets that did not follow the proposed Nostratic correspondences. There is another way in which IS's putative sound correspondences are not consistent with the standard comparative method. Several of the putative reconstructed Nostratic sounds are not reflected by regular sound correspondences in the languages. For example, 'in Kartv[elian] and Indo-European, the reflexes of Nostratic [**]*p* are found to be unstable' (IS 1990: 168); Nostratic forms beginning in **p reveal that both the Indo-European and the Kartvelian forms arbitrarily begin with either *p or *b, but this is not regular and is not sanctioned by the comparative method. Similarly, glottalization in Afroasiatic is said to occur 'sporadically under other conditions still not clear' (IS 1990: 168). In the correspondence sets, several of

the languages are listed with multiple reflexes of a single Nostratic sound, but with no explanation of conditions under which the distinct reflexes might appear.

(5) *Short forms.* Of IS's 378 forms, 57 (15 per cent) involve short forms (CV, VC, C, or V), too short to deny chance as an alternative explanation.

(6) *Semantically non-equivalent forms.* Some 55 cases (14 per cent) involve comparisons of forms in the different languages that are fairly distinct semantically.

(7) *Diffused forms.* Given the history of central Eurasia, with much language contact, it is not at all surprising that some forms turn out to be borrowed. Several of the Nostratic cognates have words which have been identified by others as loans, including 'sister-in-law', 'water', 'do', 'give', 'carry', 'lead', 'to do'/'put', 'husband's sister', to which we can add the following as probable or possible loans: 'conifer, branch, point', 'thorn', 'poplar', 'practice witchcraft', 'deer', 'vessel', 'birch', 'bird cherry', 'honey', 'mead'.

(8) *Typological problems.* Nostratic as traditionally reconstructed is typologically problematic. Counter to expectations, few Nostratic roots contain two voiceless stops; glottalized stops are considerably more frequent than their plain counterparts; and Nostratic affricates change to a cluster of fricative + stop in Indo-European.

(9) *Evaluation of the strongest lexical sets.* An examination of the Nostratic sets held by proponents to be the strongest reveals serious problems with most. These include Dolgopolsky's (1986) fifteen most stable lexemes. Most are questionable in one way or another according to the standard criteria for assessing proposals of remote linguistic kinship. In the Nostratic sets representing Dolgopolsky's fifteen most stable glosses, four have problems with phonological correspondences; five involve excessive semantic difference among the putative cognates; four have representatives in only two of the putative Nostratic families; two involve problems of morphological analysis; IS himself listed one as doubtful; and finally, one reflects the tendency to rely too heavily on a form from Finnish when not supported by the historical evidence. All but two are challenged, and for these two the relevant forms needed for evaluation are not present. These 'strong' cases are not sufficiently robust to support the proposed genetic relationship.

Once again, it is for reasons such as these that most historical linguists reject the Nostratic hypothesis.

14.17.3 Amerind

Joseph Greenberg's Amerind hypothesis, represented principally in his book *Language in the Americas* (1987), contends that all Native American languages, except the 'Na-Dene' and Eskimo-Aleut languages, belong to a single macrofamily, 'Amerind', based on multilateral comparison. Amerind is rejected by virtually all specialists in Native American languages and by the vast majority of historical linguists. They maintain that valid methods do not at present permit reduction of Native American languages to fewer than about 180 independent language families and isolates. Amerind has been criticized, on various grounds. Specialists find extensive inaccuracies in Greenberg's data: 'the number of erroneous forms probably exceeds that of the correct forms' (Adelaar 1989: 253). Greenberg assembled forms which on superficial inspection are similar from among the languages which he compared and declared them to be evidence of common heritage. However, where Greenberg's method stops, after having assembled the similarities, is where other linguists start. Since similarities can be due to a number of factors – accident, borrowing, onomatopoeia, sound symbolism, nursery words, and universals – for a plausible proposal of remote relationship one must attempt to eliminate all other possible explanations, leaving a shared common heritage the most likely. Greenberg made no attempt to eliminate these other explanations, and the similarities he amassed appear to be due mostly to accident and a combination of these other factors. In various instances, Greenberg compared arbitrary segments of words, equated words with very different meanings (for example, 'excrement/night/grass'), misidentified numerous languages, failed to analyze the morphology of some words and falsely analyzed that of others, neglected regular sound correspondences, failed to eliminate loanwords, and misinterpreted well-established findings. The Amerind 'etymologies' proposed are often limited to a very few languages of the many involved. (For details and examples, see Adelaar 1989, Berman 1992, Campbell 1988b, 1997, Kimball 1992, McMahon and McMahon 1995, Poser 1992, Rankin 1992, Ringe 1992, 1996.) Finnish, Japanese, Basque and other randomly chosen languages fit Greenberg's Amerind data as well as or better than any of the American Indian languages do; Greenberg's method has proven incapable of distinguishing implausible relationships from Amerind generally.

Critics of the hypothesis point out problems of various sorts. Greenberg introduced some *language names* into his classification which are not languages at all – for example, *Membreño*, which Greenberg classified as a Lencan language, is a person's name, a reference (Membreño 1897). Greenberg gave town names where a certain language was spoken as names of distinct languages; for example, there are not six Lencan languages, only two, though Greenberg gives as distinct languages such town names as Guajiquero (*sic*, for Guajiquiro), Intibucat (*sic*, Intibucá), Opatoro, and Similatón. Terraba, Tiribí, and Tirub are also not separate languages, but rather refer to Tiribí; the Christianized Tiribí brought to Costa Rica after 1700 are called Terraba; Tirub is the native name of the Tiribí. There are numerous examples that involve *borrowing*, some examples mentioned above. Some examples of *excessive semantic latitude*, where only the meanings compared are listed here, include 'excrement/night/grass', 'ask/wish/ seek/pleasure', 'bitter/to rot/sour/sweet/ripe/spleen/gall', 'body/belly/heart/skin/ meat/be greasy/fat/deer', 'child/copulate/son/girl/boy/tender/bear/small', 'deer/ dog/animal/silver fox/lynx', 'earth/sand/sweepings/mud/dirty', 'field/devil/bad/ underneath/bottom', 'earth/island/forest/mud/village/town/dust/world/ground', 'feather/hair/wing/leaf', 'hole/mouth/ear/listen/chin/nose/smell/blow nose/sniff'. Such semantic permissiveness increases the probability that chance explains the compared forms. Numerous forms involved *onomatopoeia*; one example is the set with *pui, puhi, phu-* for 'blow'(Greenberg 1987: 196). Undetected *morpheme divisions* can make forms seem more similar than they actually are; Greenberg has a number of these, including Rama *mukuik* 'hand' as "cognate" with other American Indian languages with forms like *ma* or *makV*; however, 'hand' in

Rama is *kwi:k*; the *mu-* is the 'second person possessive' prefix; the root *kwi:k* bears no significant resemblance to Greenberg's **ma-ki*. Similarly, several examples involve insertion of *morpheme boundaries where none is justified.* Poser (1992) showed that of Greenberg's Salinan and Yurumanguí forms, 11 of 26 cited have specious morphological analyses. Berman (1992: 232) noted 'there is not a single Tualatin [Kalapuya] word in which Greenberg segments any of these prefixes correctly'. Other examples are mentioned above. There are numerous *spurious forms*, scribal errors, etc. For example, as mentioned, none of the Quapaw entries in Greenberg (1987) is from Quapaw; rather they are from Biloxi or Ofo (two other Siouan languages, not closely related to Quapaw). In short, it is with good reason Amerind has been rejected.

14.17.4 The Dene–Yeniseian hypothesis

Edward Vajda's (2010) proposal of a connection between the Yeniseian language family of central Siberia and 'Na-Dene' (Athabaskan-Eyak-Tlingit, minus Haida of the traditional Na-Dene hypothesis) has received considerable attention. Factors that scholars have thought support Vajda's hypothesis include the following: Vajda is a respected, serious linguist; he attempts to deploy appropriate methods judiciously, presenting as evidence proposed cognates, several from basic vocabulary; he presents regular recurring sound correspondences, not all of them nearly identical, and morphological matchings. Factors which have been thought to go against the hypothesis include geographical implausibility, with a great distance separating Yeniseian and Na-Dene territories; the long time depth separating the two; grammaticalizations which weaken seeming similarities in verb affix patterns; some typological mismatches; the limited overall amount of evidence; lack of non-linguistic corroborating evidence, with little or no support from archaeology and human genetics; lack for the most part of matchings in pronouns and in basic kinship terms; problems with phonological and semantic matches in the proposed cognates; and poor fit with areal neighbours.

Vajda presented lexical and morphological evidence. Several scholars have commented on the limited amount of lexical evidence, c. 100 proposed cognates between Yeniseian and Na-Dene – though others consider this a significant number. Many of the word comparisons would be questioned on the basis of the standard criteria (above): semantic latitude, onomatopoeia, shortness of compared forms, borrowing, etc.

Of Vajda's c. 100 proposed cognate sets, some 27 involve *permissive semantic differences*; for example (only the glosses are presented here, Na-Dene first, followed by Yeniseian) black / blue, green, grey, brown; cloud / dark, darkness; day / light; distributional plural proclitic / collective suffix; eat (animate object) / swallow; fire / day, daytime; fly / dragonfly; go in a herd / in a row, small fish, vee (of birds); handle / kettle; hem, hanging end of garment, breechcloth / sews; hill / cliff, concave edge of riverbank; hook-shaped, hook / back, return, half; hot / molten fat, summer; jump (also fire ignites, burns, blazes; shine) / by moonlight, moonlit night, flare up; king salmon / burbot; knee / waist seam of dress, up to the edge; lower leg, shin / thigh, base of tree; point, end / fishhook barb; poke / dig; rear, back end, rump, buttocks / under; ridge, hill / pile of small fragments, small pile; robin / colour, paint; sharp / claw, fingernail; shrub, plant / willow; stone / mountain; thorn / penis; undergo pangs / die. Admitting comparisons between non-synonyms does not make it easier to demonstrate the genetic relationship among compared languages; when semantically non-equivalent forms are compared, the possibility that chance accounts for the phonetic similarity is greatly increased.

A dozen of the sets involve *onomatopoeia*:

breast, teat, milk
breath, breathe, shadow, shade, safety, health, life / soul, vapour
cry
eagle
laugh
medicine song, cure by singing, shaman / shaman
merganser / common goldeneye (duck)
robin
spit
spruce hen
spruce grouse
wind blows / wind

Onomatopoeic forms are eliminated from proposals of distant genetic relationship because their similarity may be explained by mimicry of sounds in nature rather than inheritance from a common ancestor.

Some examples involve *borrowings*: Ket *quɯ'j* (Yugh *quɯ'j*) 'birch bark' is a loan from Selkup, a Uralic language of the Samoyedic branch, *k̦wā̃, k̦oä, qwä, küe köe, k̦öe, kä, k̦ā̃, qä* in different varieties of Selkup, from Proto-Uralic **koxji* 'birch'; 'wart' is also acknowledged as perhaps a Selkup loan; sets for 'name', 'shaman' (that is, 'medicine song, cure by singing, shaman' / 'shaman'), 'son-in-law', and 'canoe' involve terms identified as loans in some other Eurasian languages.

About thirty of the sets involve very *short forms*, of the shape V or CV. The length of proposed cognates is important, since the greater the number of matched segments in a proposed cognate set, the less likely it is that accident may account for the similarity; with short forms such as these, it is difficult to show that it is not accidental similarity rather than shared history which explains the similarity in the sets.

In some cases a single form in one family is assumed to be cognate to *multiple forms* in the other family. A single form/etymon in one language cannot be cognate to multiple forms in another language, unless the two or more from the language with multiple forms are derived from a single original linguistic element, meaning that in reality only one cognate set is involved. Here, one case involves three cognate sets, presented as independent: (1) Pre-Proto-Athabaskan (PPA) **gʷe'n* 'day' paired with Yeniseian Ket *di'n*, Yugh *dʲi'n*, *čin* 'daylight, light of day', to illustrate Proto-Yeniseian (PY) initial **ǯ*, and (2) also paired with Yeniseian Ket / Yugh *kʌ'n* 'light', Kott *kinix ~ knix* 'dawn' to illustrate PY initial **g*, while (3) Ket *di'n* is listed as a cognate not only of the first of these two sets, but also in the comparison of Proto-Athabaskan-Eyak (PAE) **de'ñ* 'emit light'

/ Ket *di·n* 'emit light, blink'. In another case 'hook-shaped' is matched with two different forms, with 'back, return' and with 'holding hook, cradle hook'.

Most of the sound correspondences occur in *few cognate sets*. Only one cognate set illustrates **ts*, **g* before front vowels, **ʎ* before front vowels, and **y* in onset position and in coda position; only two support 'glottalized nasals', **t'*, **ts'*, **gʸ*, **kʸ*, and **kʸ'* before front vowels, **g*, **k* and **k'*, **ɢʷ* and **qʷ*, **kʷ'*, **x*, and **q* or **χ*. When the proposed cognate sets which are questioned because of excessive semantic latitude, onomatopoeia, possible borrowing, etc. are eliminated, too few remain to support the sound correspondences proposed. Also, some proposed cognates do not fit Vajda's sound correspondences – Vajda points out some of these. The Proto-Yeniseien phonological inventory, with 20 consonants – Ket with only 13 – is considerably smaller than that of Proto-Na-Dene, with 43 consonants. There are multiple targets in Na-Dene from which to seek matchings in Yeniseian for individual consonants, increasing the possibility of chance rather than inheritance from a common ancestor as the explanation.

The majority of the proposed cognates are problematic, questioned on the basis of standard criteria for investigating proposals of distant genetic relationship. The remaining forms are not sufficient in number to support conclusions about sound correspondences. As for the *morphological evidence*, the organization of the verbal affixes appears similar in the two families. Since complex verb morphologies are constantly changing, it would be very surprising if both Yeniseian and Na-Dene had managed to retain so much of the original morphology from which the two families are assumed to have developed in such strikingly similar form over such a long time span. In older language families, the morphology has changed much, resulting in different typological profiles for related languages, as in branches of Algic, Indo-European, Niger-Congo, Uralic, Uto-Aztecan, etc., and Vajda points out considerable change in Yeniseian due to foreign influences, with possibly 'a steady effect on realigning Yeniseian morphological typology' (2010: 36). Modern Ket verbs have eight prefix slots (the first actually a clitic) and one suffix slot, in contrast to only four prefix slots for Proto-Yenisean, refined later to five prefix slots and a suffix slot. Many of these compared verbal affixes are very short, composed of mostly highly frequent consonants, some with very general meanings, others with functions or meanings that do not match that well.

The biggest problem in the morphological evidence is the recognition that a number of the affixes and their slots are not original, but came about through grammaticalization of formerly independent items. As Vajda (2010: 40) says, 'one must start by considering that the elaborate prefixal strings typical of the modern [Yeniseian and Na-Dene] languages developed out of a more analytic structure. Evidence suggests a bipartite phrasal verb consisting of an auxiliary followed by a lexical verb root, each of which hosted its own prefixes and suffixes.' He adds that at least some Athabaskan tense/mood prefixes originated as auxiliary verbs. Some of Vajda's examples pair suffixes with prefixes, or clitics with bound morphemes, which in order to be cognate would almost certainly have to be the results of grammaticalizations that attached formerly independent elements to verbs.

Na-Dene verbs have a morphological slot for 'classifiers', morphemes placed directly before the verb stem to signal changes in grammatical role. However, there is no comparable classifier morpheme slot in the Yeniseian verb complex. Given its adjacency to the verb root, we would assume it is older than other prefix slots that must have been added later. The mismatch between the absence of the immediately pre-root 'classifiers' affixes in one and their presence in the other raises issues for the argument based on the similarity of the affix patterns. If what is compared turns out to be only elements that originally were just very short independent lexical items of general meaning which then later grammaticalized, which have ordinary phonological shapes, with strained meaning/function associations, then the morphological evidence ceases to be impressive.

For these reasons, the proposed Dene–Yeniseian connection should not be embraced at present. Unfortunately, neither the lexical evidence with putative sound correspondences nor the morphological evidence adduced is sufficient to support a distant genetic relationship between Na-Dene and Yeniseian. (For details, see Campbell 2011.)

14.18   Exercises

Exercise 14.1   The Xinka-Lenca hypothesis

Handbooks and encyclopaedias continue to report that "Xinca" (Xinka) and Lenca are related to one another and belong in a single family group. Essentially all the evidence ever published for this hypothesis is presented below. Evaluate this proposed evidence based on the criteria and considerations discussed in this chapter. What do you conclude about the strength of the supporting evidence?

Background: Xinca is actually a family, now called Xinkan, of four languages in southeastern Guatemala, two extinct and the two with only a couple of semi-speakers surviving. Lenca is also a small family, Lencan, of two languages, Chilanga (Salvadoran Lenca) and Honduran Lenca, both recently extinct. Walter Lehmann (1920: 767) suggested the hypothesis that links the two families, though he also included other languages in his comparison, a fact now long forgotten. Lehmann's evidence for the proposed relationship is reproduced here (with the form from Guazacapán Xinka in parentheses). Observations that may be relevant in your deliberations are also included as notes below the forms.

Xinka		*Lenca*
1. 'one'	ical (ik'aɬ)	etta, ita
2. 'two'	bi-al, pi-ar, pi (piʔ)	pe
3. 'three'	vuaal-al, hual-ar (waɬ, waɬa)	laagua, lagua
4. 'four'	iri-ar ((h)irha)	heria, erio (also sa, aria, eslea)

[Note: words for numbers higher than 'two' are widely borrowed in languages of this part of Central America; these include forms similar to those for 'two', 'three', and 'four' in these languages.]

5. 'water'	uÿ (uːy)	cuy (invierno ['winter'])
6. 'night'	suma (sa-sɨ'ma 'in the dark')	ts'ub (Nacht ['night'])

7. 'dark,   ts'ama (sɨ'ma)   ts'ana-uamba (Morgen
    black'   (grauen) 'morning (to dawn)')
8. 'shade'   ti-tzuma (ti-sɨ'ma 'in   saba
               the dark')

[Note: The Xinkan forms in 5, 6, and 7 all involve the same root, /sɨ'ma/ 'dark, black'.]

9. 'dog'   xusu (<x> = [š] (IPA [ʃ])   shushu

[Note: these languages in effect have no alveopalatal affricate *č*; note also that the most common word for 'dog' in colloquial Spanish of the area is *chucho*.]

10. 'cough' ojo [<j> = [x]] (oho)   hoo, oiguin
11. 'maize' au, aima (ayma)   ama, aima

[Note: forms similar to *aima, ama, aima* for 'maize' are found widely in other languages of this region; they involve borrowings.]

12. 'bean'   xinak (ši'nak)   shinag

[Note: Mayan languages border Xinkan territory and are close to Lencan territory. Cf. Cholan-Tzeltalan (Mayan) **čenek'* 'bean', from Proto-Mayan **kinaq'* 'bean'. Terms for 'bean' are borrowed from Mayan in some other languages of this part of Central America.]

Exercise 14.2 *An 'Amerind' putative 'etymology'*

Greenberg and Ruhlen (1992) presented the forms given here as one of the strongest examples of a putative cognate set to support the 'Amerind' hypothesis. Evaluate these data on the basis of the criteria and considerations discussed in this chapter.

    Background: Joseph H. Greenberg's (1987) 'Amerind' hypothesis would group all the language families and isolates of the Americas except Eskimo-Aleut and Na-Dene. Most specialists in American Indian linguistics believe there are about 180 independent language families and isolates, not just one big family – that is, they believe the evidence available today is insufficient to reduce this number of families by much, though it may be possible that in the remote past they were related, just so long ago we can no longer demonstrate it.

Nootka	t'an'a	'child'
Yuchi	tane	'brother'
Totonac	t'ána-t	'grandchild'
Coahuilteco	t'an-pam	'child'
Proto-Uto-Aztecan	*tana	'daughter, son'
Miskito	tuk-tan	'child, boy'
Warrau [Warao]	dani-	'mother's sister'
Aymara	tayna	'firstborn child'
Masaca	tani-mai	'younger sister''

Urubu-Kaapor	ta'ïn	'child'
Pavishana	tane	'my son'
Lengua	tawin	'grandchild'
Tibagi	tog-tan	'girl'
Yurok	tˢin	'young man'
Mohawk	-'tˢin	'male, boy'
Molale	pēn-t'in	'my elder brother'
Yana	t'inī-si	'child, son, daughter'
Cuicatec	'díínó	'brother'
Changuenga	sin	'brother'
Millcayac	tzhœng	'son'
Tehuelche	den	'brother'
Tiquie	ten	'son'
Mocochi	tin-gwa	'son, boy'
Yagua	dēnu	'male child'
Tacana	u-tse-kwa	'grandchild'
Guato	china	'older brother'
Coeur d'Alene	tune	'niece'
Yuchi	tˢ'one	'daughter, son'
Central Sierra Miwok	tūne-	'daughter'
Salinan	a-t'on	'younger sister'
Taos	-t'út'ina	'older sister'
Cayapa	tˢuh-ki	'sister'
Tehuelche	thaun	'sister'
Tiquie	ton	'daughter'
Morotoko	a-tune-sas	'girl'
Nonuya	-tona	'sister'
Tacana	-tóna	'younger sister'
Pikobyé	a-ton-kä	'younger sister'

Exercise 14.3 *Macro-Panoan distant genetic relationship*

All of the evidence presented by Greenberg (1987: 74–8) for his proposed Macro-Panoan hypothesis (part of his larger Amerind proposal) is repeated here. Evaluate it based on the criteria and considerations in this chapter. What other possible explanations (other than that of cognates inherited from some common ancestor) do you see for some of the similarities among the lexical items compared from the different languages? What kinds of problems do you notice? List the problems involved in each lexical set. (Pay attention also to the number of languages from which potential evidence is cited in comparison to the total number of languages hypothesized to belong to this group.) After you have set aside forms that potentially have other, non-genetic explanations, what evidence (if any) do you find that might support a possible genetic relationship among the languages compared here?

Greenberg's Macro-Panoan hypothesis would group several South American language families and isolates: Panoan, Tacanan, Moseten [Mosetenan], Mataco[an]], Guaicuru[an], Charruan, Lule, Vilela (recognized as Lule-Vilela), and Mascoy[an]. Note that though separated by Greenberg, Panoan and Tacanan belong to the Pano-Tacanan family. Clarification of some of the names and some of the forms not included in Greenberg's data are given in brackets, as [. . .].

1. BE ABLE [Mascoyan:] Lengua *wan(-či)*, *wan(-kje)*. Mataco[an]: Chulupi [Nivaclé] *ha-wanaia* [no such form exists; *xa-* 'first person pronoun'].

2. ANIMAL Guaicuru[an]: Toba-Guazu *sigiak*. [Mascoyan:] Lengua *askok*. Mataco[an]: Vejoz [Wichí] *łokue* [no such word exists in Wichi; *łokwe* is 'jug'; *lo* is the classifier for possessed domestic animals].

3. ANSWER (v.) Mataco[an]: Choroti *kamtini* 'speak'. Panoan: Cazinaua *køma*. Cavineña *kiema*.

4. ANUS Guaicuru[an]: Caduveo *-auio* 'buttocks'. Mataco[an]: Choroti *i-we*, Vejoz [Wichí] *wex* ['tail, backside']. Moseten *jive* 'buttocks, anus'. Panoan [Pano-Tacanan]: Caripuna *wahaa* 'open'. Tacanan [Pano-Tacanan]: Huarayo *wexa* 'opening', Chama *wexa* 'hole'.

5. AWAKE Charruan: Chana *inambi*. Guaicuru[an]: Toba-Guazu *tom* 'awake, dawn'. Mataco[an]: Vejoz [Wichí]: *nom* (intransitive) [*n-om* 'come, arrive', *n-* 'directional']. Panoan: Proto-Panoan **nama* 'to dream'.

6. BACK [Mascoyan:] Lengua *ak-puk*, *(eja-)puk* 'behind'. Panoan: Shipibo *puika*. Tacanan: Cavineña *ebekakwa*, Chama *kiibaaxaxe* 'behind'.

7. BAD Guaicuru[an]: Guachi [Guachi is not a Guaicuruan language, though there is a hypothesis that it may be related] <oetcho> 'devil'. Mataco[an]: Nocten [Wichí], Vejoz [Wichí] *tsoi* 'devil'. Moseten *ači-tui* 'make dirty'. Tacanan: Tacana *ači*. Cf. Lule *ičelo* 'devil'.

8. BAT Guaicuru [?]: *kahit (h < s)*. Panoan: Proto-Panoan **kaši*.

9. BE Lengua [Mascoyan]: Mascoy *h-*. [Matacoan:] Mataco [Wichí] *ihi, hi* [*i-* 'to be', *i-hi* 'be-Locative'].

10. BEAR (v.) Guaicuru[an]: Mocovi *koo*, Toba-Guazu *koe*. Lule *kaa* 'born'. [Matacoan:] Mataco [Wichí] *ko*, Vejoz [Wichí] *ko*. Panoan: Proto-Panoan **kai* 'to bear, mother', Chacobo *ko* 'born'. Tacanan: Chama *kwaja* 'be born'.

11. BEFORE Lengua [Mascoyan]: Lengua, Mascoy *nanič*, Lengua *nahno, nahtu* 'mucho anteo' [*anteo* is unclear in Spanish]. Mataco[an]: Chulupi [Nivaclé] *naxeš* 'forward' [no such form exists; possibly from *nax-* 'to end, terminate'; probably a mixture of *nayiš* 'road' and the verb derived from it, *nayi-n* 'to anticipate, prepare, be first, go on ahead', where one translation in Spanish is *adelantarse* 'to go ahead, to go forward', which is similar to *adelante* 'ahead, forward, in front of, before'], Payagua [not Matacoan, sometimes hypothesized as belonging to Guaicuruan or to proposed Macro-Guaicuruan with Guaicuruan, Matacoan, Payaga, Guachi, but not demonstrated] *inahi*. Moseten <yno>, *xinoje*.

12. BLOOD Guaicuruan: Toba *t-auo*, Lule *ewe*. Mataco[an]: Chunupi [Nivaclé] *woi* [*woʔy*]. Tacanan: Chama *woʔo* 'red'.

13. BODY Lule *toip* [*-p* 'third person possessive pronoun']. Mataco[an:]

Mataco [Wichí]: *tape* [*t-* 'third person possessive pronoun']. Tacanan: Cavineña *etibo* 'trunk' [*e-tibu*: *e-* 'pronoun', *tibu* 'base'].

14. BREAK   Lengua [Mascoyan]: Mascoy *pok-* (intransitive). Mataco[an:] Mataco [Wichí] *puhʷoje* [*pux-u* 'break, explode'], Suhin [Nivaclé] *poktoče* (intransitive) [*pakxet-ši*: *pakxet* 'break' + *-ši* 'indefinite direction or location']. Moseten *fok.*

15. BREAST   Lengua [Mascoyan]: Lengua *namakuk*, Kaskiha *neme* 'nipple'. Lule *ineme* 'milk'.

16. BROTHER   Charruan: Charrua *inčala*. Lule *kani* 'younger brother'. Mataco[an:] Mataco [Wichí] *čila* 'older brother' *[kʸila]*, *činix* 'younger brother' [*kʸinix*], Choroti *kiili* 'older brother', *kiini* 'younger brother'. Vilela *ikelebepe*. (Perhaps two related roots for older and younger brother [definitely two different lexical items in the Matacoan languages cited].)

17. CLOSE (v.)   Mataco[an:] Choroti *pone*, *pione* 'close, cover', Vejoz [Wichí] *ponhi* 'imprison', Towothli [Maká] *aponik* 'cover'. Tacanan: Cavineña *pene* ['cover, protect'].

18. COLD₁ [Mascoyan]: Lengua *math(-kaiyi)* 'be cold'. Panoan: Proto-Panoan **matˢi* 'be cold'.

19. COLD₂   Lule *kei*. Mataco[an:] Enimaga [Maká] *koija*, Chunupi [Nivaclé] *kui* [k'uy].

20. CUT   Lengua   [Mascoyan]: Guana *čečet* 'cut up'. Mataco[an]: Suhin [Nivaclé] *siči* [note that Nivaclé has ten distinct verbs which translate 'to cut'; probably intended is *seʔx* 'to cut up', perhaps *seʔx-ši* 'cut up-indefinite location or direction'], Choroti *esita*, *ešita*. Panoan: Proto-Panoan **šaʔti̇.*

21. DARK   Guaicuru[an]: Toba, Mocovi *epe*, *pe* 'night'. Mataco[an]: Choroti *pe* 'shadow'. Tacanan: Chama *kea-apo* 'night', Tacana *apu-* 'dark'.

22. DIG   Mataco[an]: Vejoz [Wichí] *tih*, Mataco [Wichí] *tiho* [*tix-i* 'dig']. Tacanan: Chama *teo.*

23. DOG   Mataco[an]: Suhin [Nivaclé] *nuu*, Choropi [Nivaclé] *nuux*. Panoan: Proto-Panoan **ʔino, *ʔinaka.*

24. DOOR   Lule *atˢiki-* <aciqui-p> 'hole'. Panoan: Proto-Panoan **šikʷi̇* 'doorway'. Tacanan: Proto-Tacanan ** t͡sekʷe* 'door, doorway'. [Note that Panoan and Tacanan belong to Pano-Tacanan.]

25. DRESS (v.)   Lule *tala* 'clothing', *talaks*. Mataco[an:] Mataco [Wichí] *tula* 'clothing' [form unknown].

26. DRY   [Mascoyan:] Lengua *jima(-gjaji)* 'be dry'. Mataco[an:] Mataco [Wichí] *ji̇m* 'dry up' [Wichí has no *i̇*], Suhin, Chuluipi [Nivaclé] *jim*, Macca [Maká] *iim*. Moseten *jiñ* 'bone'.

27. EMPTY   Lule *em-p*. Mataco[an:] Mataco [Wichí] *jim*, Chulupi [Nivaclé] *jimši* [*yim-ši* 'to dry up, to end', *yim* 'dry' + *-ši* 'indefinite direction or location'. Same root as in 26].

28. FEAR₁ (v.)   Guaicuru[an]: Toba-Guazu *nahi*. Mataco[an]: Vejoz [Wichí] *nowai* [the root is *oway*, *n-* 'middle voice marker']. Moseten *nojii* 'frighten'. Panoan: Cashibo *noo* 'frighten', Nocaman *no* 'enemy', Panobo, Shipibo *nawa* 'enemy'.

29. FEAR₂ (v.)   Lule *lako* 'be ashamed'. Panoan: Proto-Panoan **rakʷi̇.*

30. FINISH   Lule *tum-p* 'be finished'. Mataco[an]: Choroti *temi*, Suhin [Nivaclé] *timš* [*im* 'to end, run out'; perhaps based on *xa-t-im-ši* '1stPers-Verb.Class-end-Indefinite.Direction/Location]. Cf. Tacanan: Cavineña *tupu* 'enough'.

31. FLY (v.)   Moseten *naj*. Panoan: Proto-Panoan *noja.*

32. GREEN   Lule <za>. Moseten <za>. Panoan: Proto-Panoan *šoo* 'green, not ripe'. Tacanan: Proto-Tacanan *zawa.* [Note that Panoan and Tacanan are members of the Pano-Tacanan family.]

33. HANG   Moseten *pina* 'hammock'. Panoan: Conibo *panea* 'be hung', *pani* 'hang up', Shipibo *panni* 'hang up'.

34. HATE   Guaicuru[an]: Abipone *n-paak* 'hated'. Moseten *fakoj, fakin* 'be angry'.

35. HORN   Lengua [Mascoyan]: Guana *taša*. Moseten *daš* <dasc>.

36. KNEAD   [Matacoan:] Mataco [Wichí] *pʔon*. Moseten *puñe* 'knead, mud'.

37. KNOW   Mataco[an]: Vejoz [Wichí] *hanex* [*han-* 'to know', *-ex* 'applicative'], Choroti *hane* 'know, be able'. Moseten *(am)-xeñ* ('no se puede' [it is not possible]). Panoan: Proto-Panoan *onā* 'know, be able', Shipibo *huna.*

38. LEAF   Guaicuru[an]: Toba: *l-awe*. [Mascoyan:] Lengua *wa*.

39. LEAVE   (ABANDON)   Guaicuru[an]:   Toba-Guazu *jane*.   Lengua [Mascoyan]: Mascoy *jiño*. Panoan: Proto-Panoan *ɨnɨ*. Vilela *jane*.

40. LOOK   Charruan: Chana *sola*. Guaicuru[an]: Pilaga *čelage*, Toba-Guazu *silaha.*

41. LOSE   Moseten *moñi* 'perish, lose, err'. Panoan: Cashibo *mano* 'forget', Cashinahua *manu* 'miss'. Tacanan: Proto-Tacanan *manu* 'die'.

42. MAKE   Guaicuru[an]: Toba-Guazu *uo*. Panoan: Proto-Panoan *wa, *ʔa.* Tacanan: Proto-Tacanan *a* 'make, say'.

43. MANY   Guaicuru[an]: Toba-Guazu *lamai*. [Mascoyan:] Lengua *lamo*. Mataco[an]: Payagua [not a Matacoan language] *lehmi* 'all'.

44. MEAT   Guaicuru[an]: Pilaga *niiak* 'fish.' [Mascoyan:] Lengua *nohak* 'wild animal'. Tacanan: Chama *noe,* Tiatinagua, Huarayo *noči*. Vilela *nuhu* 'fish'.

45. MOSQUITO   Lengua [Mascoyan]: Mascoy *p-aija*. Mataco[an]: Choroti *eji*, Suhin [Nivaclé] *iya* [*(y)iyaʔ*].

46. MOTHER   Mataco[an]: Macca [Maká] *nana*. Tacanan: Proto-Tacanan *nene* 'aunt'. Vilela *nane*.

47. MOUSE   Guaicuru[an]: Toba-Guazu *mekahi* 'bat'. Moseten *meče* 'rat'. Panoan: Proto-Panoan *maka* 'rat, mouse'. Cf. Mataco[an]: Mataco [Wichí], Suhin [Nivaclé], Chulupi [Nivaclé] *ama*, Vejoz [Wichí] *ma*.

48. NECK₁   Moseten *tetˢ* <tez>. Panoan: Proto-Panoan *tɨšo.*

49. NECK₂   Lule *u(-p)*. Mataco[an]: Mataco [Wichí], Choroti, etc. *wo*. Moseten <huh> 'throat'.

50. OLD   Guaicuru[an]: Guachi [Guachi is not a Guaicuruan language] *seera*. Mataco[an]: Payagua [Payagua is not a Matacoan language] *aheri* 'old woman'. Panoan: Proto-Panoan *šɨnɨ*. Tacanan: Proto-Tacanan *ziri.*

51. RED   Guaicuru[an]: Toba, Mocovi *tok*. [Mascoyan:] Lengua *eteig-ma*. Mataco[an]: Macca [Maká] *tek* 'blood' [no such form exists in Maká; see

-*athits* 'blood', -*atxuʔ* 'to bleed', *siyixiʔ* 'red']. Tacanan: Proto-Tacanan *čiaka*.

52. RIB   Guaicuru[an]: Mocovi <emeneh>. Moseten *mana*.

53. ROTTEN   [Mascoyan:] Lengua *abik*. Lule *poko* 'to rot'. Moseten *fokoi*.

54. SHOUT   Lule *se* 'cry'. Panoan: Shipibo *sei*, Conibo *sije*, Cashinahua *sa*. Tacanan: Proto-Tacanan *ʦea*.

55. SIDE   Guaicuru[an]: Toba-Guazu *ai, aji*, Mocovi *ai* 'side', Abipone *uii*. Lule *je*.

56. SMALL   Lengua [Mascoyan]: Mascoy *etkok*. Mataco[an]: Churupi [Nivaclé] *tikin* [*tik'in*], Suhin [Nivaclé] *tika* [no such form exists, perhaps a mistake for *tik'in*]. Towothli [Maká] *taake* 'short.' Panoan Culino *tukuča* 'short'.

57. SON   Charruan: Chana, Guenoa *ineu*. Guaicuru[an]: Guachi [Guachi is not a Guaicuruan language] *inna*. Vilela *ina-hmi* (Pelleschi [source]), *ina-ke* 'son, daughter' (Gilij [source]), *hina-kis* (Fontana [source]).

58. SOUR   Mataco[an]: Choroti *paši* <paxhi>. Moseten *pase*. Panoan: Proto-Panoan *paša* 'sour, raw, uncooked', Tacanan: Proto-Tacanan *paʦe*.

59. SWIM   Guaicuru[an]: Pilaga *ubogai*. Moseten <vigi>. Tacanan: Proto-Tacanan *beʦa*.

60. THIN   Lule *kam*. Moseten *kum*. Cf. Mataco[an]: Vejoz [Wichí] *čemsa-* 'small'.

61. URINE   [Mascoyan:] Lengua *jis(-weji)* 'urinate'. Lule <ys> 'urinate'. Mataco[an]: Suhn [Nivaclé] *yuł*, Churupi [Nivaclé] <yius, yiusl> 'urinate' (*sl* probably represents the voiceless lateral fricative *ł*) [both are from the root -*uł* 'urine, to urinate', *y-uł* 'he/she/it urinates', *y-* 'third person pronoun']. Panoan: Proto-Panoan *isõ, *istõ*.

62. WEAK   Lengua [Mascoyan]: Mascoy *jil, jel-k*. Mataco[an]: Mataco [Wichí] *jel* 'weak, tired' [*y-* 'third person pronoun', root -*eł* 'to tire'].

15

Writing and Philology:
The Role of Written Records

Philologists, who chase
A panting syllable through time and space
Start it at home, and hunt it in the dark,
To Gaul, to Greece, and into Noah's Ark.

(William Cowper [1731–1800], *Retirement*, 691)

15.1 Introduction

This chapter is about writing, writing systems, and philology. Philology has to
do primarily with the use of written attestations of earlier stages of languages,
and with how the information from written forms of a language can be used
to determine aspects of that language's history – with the methods for extract-
ing historical linguistic information from written sources. The investigation of
written records has always been important in historical linguistics. This chapter
treats the role of writing and philology.

15.2 Writing and the History of Writing Systems

We hardly need a definition of writing, since everybody reading these words
has some sense of what writing is. Still, a formal definition might be helpful
as we consider the development of writing systems and how written records
can contribute to historical linguistic interests. Therefore, writing, defined, is
visual (or tactile) signs used to represent language; it is a visual (or tactile) code
for recording and communicating information. We add 'tactile' to the ordinary
definition, which is usually limited to 'visual' signs, in order to allow for writing
for the blind, in particular Braille, devised by Louis Braille, a blind Frenchman,
in 1821. Each Braille character or cell is made up of six dot positions, arranged
in a rectangle containing two columns of three dots each. Its signs are distinct
from one another in form and are generally alphabetic, so that sighted persons
could also read the system if they knew what to look for. While the definition
offered here is intended to include writing for the blind, it is the visual signs we
concentrate on in this chapter.

It is useful to point out early in this chapter that the notation < . . . > is often used to enclose written attestations in order to symbolize that the material is presented precisely as found in the source.

15.2.1   Kinds of writing systems

Some writing systems are called *hieroglyphic* (from Greek *hieros* 'sacred' + *glyphein* 'to carve'). These are usually mixed systems with signs representing logograms (whole words) as well as some phonetic and other signs (see below). A number of early scripts were *cuneiform* ('wedge-shaped', from Latin *cuneus* 'wedge'; compare for example Spanish *cuña* 'wedge'). Some are *syllabaries*, and many are *alphabetic*. Some of these are described below as we consider how writing systems developed.

Some better-known writing systems include the following:

Akkadian cuneiform (2500 BC to AD 100)

Anatolian hieroglyphics (called 'Hittite' hieroglyphics, though representing the Luwian language, c. 1400 to 700 BC)

Aztec writing (c. AD 1400 to 1600, logographic with syllabic signs)

Brahmi script (syllabary, 400 BC to AD 300), ancestor of many South Asian and other scripts, for example those used for Burmese, Thai, and Tibetan, including Devanagari, used to write Sanskrit and numerous languages of India

Cherokee syllabary (AD 1821 to present)

Chinese (1500 BC to present, logographic) – Chinese Kanji was influential in the writing that developed for several other East Asian languages

Coptic (100 BC to present, adopted from Greek with five letters added from Egyptian hieroglyphics)

Cree 'syllabics' (syllabary, AD 1840 to present)

Cyrillic alphabet (AD 800 to present, based on the Greek alphabet)

Egyptian hieroglyphics (3100 BC to AD 400)

Elamite (c. 3300 to 500 BC)

Epi-Olmec script (hieroglyphic, c. 70 BC to AD 500)

Hittite cuneiform (1650 to 1200 BC)

Japanese writing (400 BC to present, first based on Chinese Kanji logographic characters, to which Hiragana and Katakana syllabaries were added, based on Chinese signs to represent sounds)

Korean Hangul (AD 1443 to present)

Linear A (Cretan, Minoan, 1800 to 1400 BC), remains undeciphered

Linear B (Greek) (1500 to 1200 BC)

Maya hieroglyphic writing (by 400 BC to AD 1600, logographic with syllabic signs)

Mixteca (Mixteca-Puebla, AD 1200 to 1600)

Ogham (AD 200 to 500), recording Old Irish

Runic writing (called 'Futhark', AD 150 to 1600, in two forms: Anglo-Frisian Futhork and earlier Continental Germanic Futhark)

Semitic family of scripts (Phoenician)

Sumerian (3300 to 100 BC, hieroglyphic), evolved into cuneiform

Tibetan (AD 600–700 to present; its ultimate ancestor was the Brahmi script)

Zapotecan script (hieroglyphic, c. 500 BC to AD 1000)

Several alphabets:

> Proto-Sinaitic (Proto-Canaanite) consonantal alphabet (1700 BC, perhaps as early as 1900 BC, which evolved into the Phoenician script)
>
> Phoenician consonantal alphabet (1100 to 300 BC)
>
> Greek (eighth century BC to present, adopted from Phoenician)
>
> Etruscan (700 BC to AD 100, adapted from the Greek)
>
> Latin (Roman) (seventh century BC to present, modified version of Etruscan alphabet), source of most European alphabets (though some are closer to Greek in origin).

Note that the Indus 'script' or Indus Valley 'writing' (c. 2600 to 1900 BC), which is often listed as an undeciphered writing system, is disputed and may not be writing at all. (Farmer et al. 2004.)

15.2.2 Origins of writing

It is often thought that the earliest writing systems evolved out of tally systems for economic purposes, to keep track of inventories and transactions, for example, the 'sheep' sign $\oplus$ in Sumerian writing associated with keeping track of transactions involving sheep. However, scholars of writing systems today believe that tally systems had origins which are distinct from true writing. It has also been proposed that some writing systems develop out of icono-graphic representations – sets of conventionally recognized symbols – often with religious motivations. However, there seems to be little reason to believe that the representations of linguistic features in true writing developed from earlier pictorial elements. The beginning of writing systems seems generally to be independent of numeral systems and art. In modern English, we use the Roman alphabet alongside Arabic numerals, two separate systems with independent origins. Also, letters of our alphabet can be traced back to signs that were more pictorial in origin; for example, the letter 'A' once looked like an ox head (rotated 180°), and its name referred to 'ox' – 'A' is from Latin *alpha*, taken from Greek *alpha*, itself a borrowing from Phoenecian *'aleph* 'ox'. However, there is no evidence that portraits of oxen predated the use of this sign to represent the associated sound. (See below for more on the origin of this alphabet.)

The bar and dot notation for numbers in Mesoamerican tally systems was used in conjunction with writing. A dot is for 'one', so two dots is 'two', three dots 'three', etc. A bar is for 'five'. A combination of four dots (1 × 4) and three bars (3 × 5), thus, is 'nineteen'. An example with 'four' in the Maya system is seen below in Figure 15.3a.

In the past some scholars supported the hypothesis of *monogenesis*, believ-ing that writing had a single origin, that it was invented only once in the world, and then spread. There are (or have been) many writing systems in the world, and some well-known writing systems that probably had independent origins include Chinese, Egyptian, and Sumerian, among others. For certain the writing systems of ancient Mesoamerica are completely independent of Old World writing, meaning that the notion of monogenesis for the origin of all writing is just incorrect, even if many Old World scripts developed from other scripts before them.

15.2.3   Generalizations about writing and its origins

An interesting question is: to what do we owe similarities among many ancient writing systems? Proposed explanations have been offered, to which we now turn.

(1) *Reading order* (direction of reading and writing). Top-to-bottom reading or writing order is often thought to have developed due to close association with the vertical axis of the dominant figures in the pictorial scenes that writing often accompanied. Since the associated depiction of a person or animal or scene from nature is typically scanned from the head or top downward, the direction of writing naturally followed the same direction. Left-to-right order is favoured in scripts that developed in the context of painting or recording in clay, that is, when the writing was on materials that smudge easily. A reason for this seems to be that, since most scribes are right-handed, if they write from left to right in the direction away from the symbols they write, they do not smear what they have just written. The etymological origin of the word 'to write' in a good number of languages is 'to paint', for example Proto-Mayan **ts'ihb'* 'paint', later 'write', Proto-Aztecan **(tla)hkʷilowa* 'to paint, to stripe', later 'to write'. In contrast, English *write* is form Germanic **wrītan* 'to cut, scratch, tear', calling to mind the carving of runes in wood or on stone; compare the German cognate *reissen* 'to tear', and Old English *wrītan* 'to score, outline, draw the figure of', and then later 'to write'. The earliest writing for Germanic peoples involved carving or cutting marks on wood, etc. When writing came to be done with pen and ink, the term carried over.

These terms for writing are sometimes connected with the material upon which these writing systems were typically written. For example, English *book* derives from *beech*, presumably reflecting a wooden surface used to scratch or carve the earliest runes; Old English *bōc* meant any written document. Similarly, in some Slavic languages, such as Russian and Bulgarian, the word for 'letter', *bukva*, is similar to English 'beech', reflecting the same medium for writing. Also, Latin *liber* 'book' originally meant the 'interior part of tree bark', used for writng; this is the origin of such words for 'book' as French *livre*, Italian and Spanish *libro*, and is ultimately behind English *library*. The Proto-Mayan word **huʔŋ* originally meant a kind of 'fig tree' but also came to mean 'bark paper' and 'book'; the word for a kind of 'fig tree' also means 'paper' and 'book' in several other Mesoamerican languages, for example Nahuatl *āmatl*, for the books and paper of the Aztecs – reflecting the fact that the earliest Mesoamerican writing was painted on perishable media, not carved in stone. In English, *paper* comes from Latin *papyrus*, which got it from Greek *pápuros*, a wetland reed once abundant in the Nile Delta of Egypt and used in ancient

Egypt and throughout the Mediterranean region as a writing material. A second Greek word for 'papyrus' was *búblos*, perhaps derived from Byblos, the name of a famous Phoenician city, used in a more restricted sense for certain products made of papyrus, including writing material. This is seen in the origin of such English words as *Bible*, *bibliography*, and *bibliophile*, and of French *bibliothèque*, German *Bibliotek*, Italian and Spanish *biblioteca* 'library', with similar forms in several other languages.

Though the left-to-right reading order may be very common, it is by no means universal. There are scripts which are written right-to-left, those used for writing Arabic, Hebrew, and Persian being well-known examples. In some situations, writing was in both directions, left-to-right and right-to-left, called *boustrophedon*, from Greek *boustrophēdon* 'ox-turning' (*bous* 'ox' + *strophē* 'turn'). The name suggests an ox drawing a plough across a field and turning at the end of each furrow to return in the opposite direction; this is because in boustrophedon every other line of writing reversed the direction of reading. For example, some archaic Greek stone inscriptions and scripts such as Safaitic and Sabaean used boustrophedon.

(2) *Orientation of signs or characters.* Signs or characters tend to face left, since most writing is from left to right, facing the direction from which the reader would read or from which the scribe would write. More precisely, in pictorially based scripts, figures universally face the direction in which one reads. Thus, consistency in sign orientation mostly amounts to consistency in reading order, where a consistent orientation of signs makes reading easier to process for the reader. Thus, where the direction of writing is left-to-right, characters face left. In boustrophedon writing, characters switch their orientation in alternate lines to face the direction in which the line is read.

(3) *Part-for-whole (Pars pro toto) principle.* This principle is often cited in discussions of origins of signs in writing systems, referring to the depiction of a part of something to represent the whole of what is indicated. This principle is not universally found in writing systems. In fact it is rare in Old World scripts, which tend to emphasize wholes not parts of what is depicted; however, it is common to the formation of all Mesoamerican scripts, where some part of animals or humans, particularly the head, is used to represent the entire object, as illustrated in Figure 15.1.

(4) *Columns.* Writing when it is in columns is read from top to bottom (see above), rather than in rows. This too is not universal. Column format is common in several early scripts, for example Sumerian, Chinese, and most Mesoamerican systems. When writing develops in a context of iconography, the vertical axis corresponds to the orientation of dominant figures in scenes.

15.2.4 Kinds of signs and their evolution in writing systems

The kinds of signs employed in different writing systems are not universal, of course, though there are often common patterns of how the signs in writing systems evolve over time. This can be illustrated with a brief look at Maya hieroglyphic writing. Egyptian writing evolved in parallel fashion, and also illustrates these stages in the development of signs in a writing system.

FIGURE 15.1a: Maya HIX (/hiš/) 'feline' head

FIGURE 15.1b: Maya HIX (/hiš/) 'feline' ear

FIGURE 15.1c: Maya *ka* syllable, fish body (from *kay* 'fish')

It is sometimes difficult to draw a sharp line between where artistic representation stops and true writing starts. *Iconography* is conventionalized symbolic representation, not language per se. For example, images of crosses, † ✝ ✞, have conventional meanings in Christian religions, though they are not considered writing. Any symbolic representation with direct connection to language is of interest for how writing develops, though writing systems appear not to have originated directly from iconography.

FIGURE 15.1d: Maya *ka* syllable, fish fin (from *kay* 'fish')

FIGURE 15.1e: Aztec TSINAKAN 'bat' body

FIGURE 15.1f: Aztec TSINAKAN 'bat' head

(1) *Pictograms*. It was thought that writing systems begin with pictographic symbols in their early stages – symbols which broadly represent ideas or concepts which could be interpreted relatively independently of any particular language. Some examples of pictograms in use today include road signs, danger signs, airport signs, a heart for 'love', smiley faces, and symbols of a man or woman on lavatory doors. Such signs may be used in combination with writing, but true writing is not divorced from the language of the writers and readers. Most scholars no longer believe that pictograms have any significant role in the development of writing. The notion of 'ideographic' writing, as systems such as Chinese writing are sometimes called, is also misleading, since no ideographic writing system has ever existed in the sense intended where the signs represent pure ideas rather than linguistic units of some sort.

(2) *Logograms*. Logographic signs represent whole words (or morphemes). Some examples of logographic signs in use today, which represent whole words not spelled out alphabetically, are: *$, %, &, +, @, 1, 2, Ø*, etc. These can be interpreted in various languages, so that the logogram *2* in an English text would be read as 'two', in a Spanish text as 'dos', and in German as 'Zwei', for example. Nevertheless, these signs are indeed intrepreted as representing those words in those languages.

Many Maya logographic signs are undoubtedly pictorial in origin. The sign B'AHLAM 'jaguar' is a portrait of a jaguar, for example (seen in Figure 15.4a–1, below); however, it serves no purpose to call this a 'pictogram' because it does not convey the concept JAGUAR independently of the word for jaguar itself in the language represented. Not all Maya logograms are pictorial in origin. Some are abstract or stylized signs for ritual products, foodstuffs, gods, etc. It is not their origin but their behaviour that defines logograms: logograms represent real words in the language that is written.

Some examples of logograms in the Maya and Aztec scripts were seen in Figure 15.1 (above), and other examples are illustrated in Figure 15.2. Figure 15.2a is the logogram for 'jaguar'. Similarly, Figure 15.2b is the Maya logogram for 'stone', Figure 15.2c for 'mountain', and Figure 15.2d for 'sun'. Figures 15.2e–h are the Aztec logograms for 'ocelot', 'stone', 'mountain', and 'sun', respectively. These can be compared with the Maya logograms in Figure 15.2a–d to see similarities but also considerable differences.

(3) *Rebus*. The name rebus comes from Latin *rebus* 'by means of objects' (the ablative plural of *res* 'thing, object'). Rebus signs are in effect logograms which have been pressed into phonetic service, sometimes seen as the first steps towards signs representing phonological aspects of the language of a writing system in a more direct fashion. Rebus signs involve morphemes which are not easy to depict graphically. In such cases, sometimes signs for words or morphemes that are easier to depict graphically can be used to represent other words or morphemes that are difficult to depict but which sound like the ones that are easier to draw – like a visual pun. These signs that exploit homophonic or nearly homophonic words are called rebus signs; for example, in English the picture of an 'eye' to represent 'I', as in rebus 'spelling' of 'eye' '(tin)can' C U for 'I can see you', or the more conventional rebus spelling of IOU for 'I owe you'. Another example is the series of pictures '2' 'bee' 'oar' 'knot' '2' 'bee' to represent 'To be or not to

FIGURE 15.2a: Maya B'AHLAM 'jaguar' logogram

FIGURE 15.2b: Maya TUN 'stone' logogram

FIGURE 15.2c: Maya WITS 'mountain' logogram

FIGURE 15.2d: Maya K'IN 'sun' logogram

FIGURE 15.2e: Aztec OSELO- 'ocelot' logogram

FIGURE 15.2f: Aztec TE- 'stone' logogram

FIGURE 15.2g: Aztec TEPE- 'mountain' logogram

be'. Many coats of arms (family crests) involved rebus symbols, called 'canting arms'. A famous example is the coat of arms of the English queen mother, born Elizabeth Bowes-Lyon. Her crest has depictions of bows and lions, a rebus representation of the Bowes and Lyon family names.

Some examples of rebus signs in Maya hieroglyphic writing include the interchange of several signs that represent words pronounced /čan/ in Cholan (a subgroup of Mayan): ČAN 'four', ČAN 'snake', and ČAN 'sky', seen in Figure 15.3a–c. Occasionally Mayan scribes utilized one of the logographic signs in Figure 15.3 to represent the meaning of one of the other words that sounded

FIGURE 15.2h: Aztec TONATIW- 'sun' logogram

like it, for instance writing the 'snake' sign to represent 'sky', or writing either 'snake' or 'sky' in calendrical contexts where 'four' was intended. The fact that these signs could be interchanged in this way is an indication that Cholan was the language in which they were written. The cognate words in Yucatec Maya, once thought by some to be the language of the hieroglyphic texts, are not homophonous: *kan* 'four', *kàan* 'snake', and *káʔan* 'sky'. The Maya codices, written much later, are in Yucatec Maya, but the glyphic texts from the earlier monuments are written in Cholan.

(4) *Phonetic complements.* Logograms can be ambiguous, where the thing depicted may correspond to more than one possible word in the language. Phonetic complements were used in some writing systems to help disambiguate the forms represented. It is sometimes thought that logograms with a particular pronunciation in the language could be used in association with other ambiguous logograms to specify some aspect of the pronunciation of the latter in order to make the intended referent clear and to distinguish between multiple possible interpretations of the logogram in question. However, this does not seem to be the role logograms play in most writing systems, and phonetic complements do not themselves need to be independent signs, but can serve the role played by signs in other scripts which have phonetic content, as in the case of the *nd* in *2nd* for 'second' in English. Several examples with phonetic complements to logograms are seen below in Figure 15.4.

Phonetic complements were used in other scripts which employed logograms, for example in Akkadian, Egyptian, Japanese, and Sumerian writing. In nearly all these scripts, the phonetic complements are selected from words with the phonetic shape CVC, where the final consonant is phonetically weak, for example in Mayan *h, ʔ,* and more rarely also *w* and *y*, as in Figures 15.1c–d, where the syllabic sign *ka* is derived from *kay* 'fish', with weak final *y*. In other writing systems, sometimes the final consonant that was considered weak also included liquids (*l* and *r*) and nasals.

(5) *Syllabic signs.* In Maya and Egyptian writing, and in other similar systems, a set of signs developed that could be employed as phonetic complements and could be used in combination to 'spell' out words or morphemes 'syllabically',

FIGURE 15.3a: Maya ČAN 'four'

FIGURE 15.3b: Maya ČAN 'snake'

FIGURE 15.3c: Maya ČAN 'sky'

using these signs for their constant phonetic values, independent of the meaning of words from which the symbol may have been derived originally. The phonetic complements, when they come to be able to represent phonetic content alone, are called 'syllabic' signs (or 'syllabograms'), and a writing system composed primarily of them is called a *syllabary*, as for example Japanese *hi*ragana and *k*atakana, the Cherokee and Cree syllabaries in North America, and Linear B (Mycenaean Greek). In syllabaries, some signs only approximate syllables but

FIGURE 15.4a-1: Maya B'AHLAM 'jaguar' logogram

FIGURE 15.4a-2: Maya B'AHLAM 'jaguar' logogram + *ma* complement

FIGURE 15.4a-3: Maya /b'ahlam/ 'jaguar' spelled out with phonetic signs
ba + *la* + *ma*

are not necessarily identical to syllables of the language they represent. In many writing systems that use syllabic signs, the signs are restricted mostly to those which phonetically are composed of only CV (a consonant and a vowel) or of CVC syllables ending in a weak C (as mentioned above).

Mayan root morphemes are mostly monosyllabic and of the shape CVC, and can be spelled syllabically by two syllabic signs together, where the V of the second is silent, that is, a spelling of <CV-CV> with two syllabic signs represents

FIGURE 15.4a-4: Maya /b'ahlam/ 'jaguar' spelled differently with
phonetic signs *ba* + *la* + *ma*

/CVC/. Typically when the vowel of the root is not complex – that is, when it
has neither a long vowel nor *h* or *ʔ* (not of the form V:C, VhC, nor VʔC) – and
is not followed by a grammatical affix, the two V's of the two syllabic signs are
the same (harmonic), though there are many exceptions.

In Maya writing, words could be and sometimes were spelled out entirely
using these syllabic signs, though the writing system remained a mixed one,
just as in Ancient Egyptian writing, where a form could be represented sometimes by only a logogram, sometimes by a logogram in combination with
a phonetic complement, sometimes by multiple phonetic complements, and
sometimes by only combinations of syllabic signs without a logogram at all.
This kind of variation of representation in Maya writing is exemplified in
Figures 15.4a and 15.4b. Figure 15.4a–1 is the Maya logogram for 'jaguar'
with no phonetic complements. Figure 15.4a–2 has the Maya 'jaguar' logogram plus the phonetic complement *ma* beneath it. In Figure 15.4a–3, the word
for 'jaguar', *b'ahlam*, is spelled out phonetically with a combination of the
syllabic signs *ba* + *la* + *ma*, where it has a large *ba* sign, with *la* following
ba to the right and with *ma* below the *la* sign. Figure 15.4a–4 also spells out
b'ahlam 'jaguar' with a combination of *ba* + *la* + *ma*, where the large main
sign on the left represents *ba*, the sign with two circles below the *ba* sign is
for *la*, and the sign to the right of *ba* is for *ma*.

Figure 15.4b presents different ways in which /pakal/ 'shield' was written in
Maya writing. Because *pakal* not only meant 'shield' but also was the name of
a very powerful ruler of Palenque, a prominent Maya archaeological site, representations of *pakal* show up prominently in the glyph texts. Figure 15.4b–1 is the
logogram PAKAL 'shield' by itself; it depicts a shield. Figure 15.4b–2 has the
logogram PAKAL 'shield' with the phonetic complement *la* below the logogram.
Figures 15.4b–3–5 represent alternative ways of spelling out *pakal* with syllabic
signs. In 15.4b–3, the first sign, to the left, with cross-hatching, is *pa*, the large
sign is *ka* (fish sign), and the sign below *ka* is *la*. In 15.4b–4, the large sign with
the cross-hatching is *pa*, the *ka* sign (representing the fish fin) is below, and the *la*

FIGURE 15.4b-1: Maya PAKAL 'shield' logogram

FIGURE 15.4b-2: Maya PAKAL 'shield' logogram with *la* phonetic complement

FIGURE 15.4b-3: Maya /pakal/'shield' spelled out with phonetic signs *pa* + *ka* + *la*

sign is to the right. In 15.4b–5, *pa* is at the top, *ka* is in the middle below *pa*, and *la* is at the bottom.

(6) *'Mixed' scripts.* Mixed scripts, such as Maya and Egyptian hieroglyphic writing – sometimes called 'logosyllabic' scripts – can use combinations of signs as seen above, mixtures of logograms, phonetic complements, and syllabic signs, and are thus able to represent the same words or morphemes in varying forms. The kinds of alternative representations available to Maya writing are seen above in examples in Figure 15.4.

FIGURE 15.4b-4: Maya /pakal/'shield' spelled differently with phonetic
signs pa + ka + la

FIGURE 15. 4b-5: Maya /pakal/'shield' spelled out again with phonetic
signs pa + ka + la

15.2.5   The organization of Maya writing

Maya writing is organized according to the following principles.

(1) *Columns.* Maya glyphic texts are read top-to-bottom usually in pairs, two columns at a time, rather than in rows, with the reading order beginning with the first two columns (on the left), read together left-to-right from top to bottom, then the next two columns together top to bottom, and then the next two after that. If there is a left-over single column at the end, it is read as a single unpaired column, top to bottom. Let us assume that Figure 15.5 represents abstractly a Maya hieroglyphic text, where each box corresponds to a glyph block, with columns under the letters and rows across corresponding to the numbers. Reading begins A1 then B1, then A2 and B2, then A3–B3, and so on to the bottom of the first pair of columns (ending in A5–B5 here). Then the reading proceeds to the next pair of columns, C and D, reading them from top to bottom, C1–D1, C2–D2, and so on to C5–D5. Then, since E is a single left-over column, it is read straight from top to bottom, E1, then E2, then E3, to the bottom at E5.

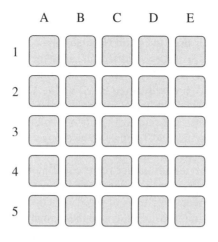

FIGURE 15.5: Illustration of reading order in Maya hieroglyphic texts

(2) *Glyph blocks*. Maya scribes used aesthetic principles to govern how they arranged signs within glyph blocks, with a preference for logograms, if present, to be dominant, represented as the largest sign in a group, what scholars called the main sign in earlier work. The glyph blocks can be composed of a larger sign in combination with smaller signs, called in earlier times affixes, before or above (formerly called prefixes) or after or below (postfixes in earlier terminology). J. Eric S. Thompson's (1962) catalogue of Maya glyphs has 842 glyphs, which reduces to about 750 when duplications are eliminated; Alan Gardner's (1957) Egyptian grammar has 603 signs, which expands to 734 when numbers and ligatures are added.

15.2.6 Alphabetic writing

As seen in the list of writing systems mentioned above, most Old World alphabets have a common ancestor, a much abbreviated pedigree of which is: the Proto-Sinaitic script begot the Phoenician alphabet, which begot the Greek alphabet, from whence the Etruscan alphabet, which lies behind the Latin (Roman) alphabet, from whence the alphabets of most western European languages, including English. The name of the 'alphabet' betrays some of this origin. It comes from a combination of the name of the first two letters of the Greek alphabet, *alpha* and *beta*. These letter names, however, are not Greek in origin, but reflect their Phoenecian origin, which represented consonants but not vowels. The first is from Phoenecian *'aleph* 'ox' and represented a glottal stop, the first sound in the word for 'ox' for which this letter was named; the sign represents an ox head – the <A> of modern alphabets now seemingly upside down, with the top originally depicting the ox's snout and the two lines at the bottom representing its horns. Since Greek had no phonemic glottal stop, it took the symbol to represent the first vowel of the word instead, <A> /a/, as in the English alphabet today. The second name is from the second letter of the Phoenecian alphabet, *beth* 'house'.

Anglo-Saxon scribes used the Latin (Roman) alphabet to write Old English, but added some letters: (1) <æ>, called 'ash' after the runic letter *æsc*, (2) the runic letter <þ> 'thorn' (for /θ/ and /ð/); (3) the runic letter <ƿ> 'wynn' (for /w/), and (4) <ð> 'edh', a modification based on the Latin letter *d*, also to represent a sound of 'thorn'. With the Norman conquest of 1066, Norman French scribes spelled English according to French orthographic practices. The non-Latin letters used to write Old English were dropped. Digraphs – the use of two letters to represent a single sound – came into use, <ch> for /č/ and <th> for both /θ/ and /ð/, the sounds earlier represented by the <þ> 'thorn' and <ð> 'edh' of Anglo-Saxon writers. The combinations <ph>, <th>, and <ch> were known in Latin and French spellings of words of Greek origin, and <h> came to be used in other digraphs to represent sounds unfamiliar to Latin or French, <gh> for /x/ (see below), <sh> for /ʃ/, and <wh> for /ʍ/ (so-called 'voiceless' or 'aspirated' *w*).

The letters <i> and <j> were not originally distinct; *j* was just the longer curved variant of *i* used for writing the last *i* in Latin words that ended in double *i*, as in <filij> for *filii* 'sons'. For English scribes <y> was the version of <j> used for the second *i* in these cases and for the last *i* of words generally, explaining such differences in spelling as *holy* but *holiest* and *holiday* (from *holy day*), *carry* but *carried*, *pretty* but *prettier*, *worry* but *worrier*, and so on. The dot over *i* and *j* was not originally used, and is still lacking from capital (upper-case) *I* and *J*. It owes its origin to a small sloping line that came to be placed above the very slim letter *i* to distinguish it from letters composed of more strokes such as *m*, *n*, and *u*, often difficult to distinguish in the handwriting of many scribes, and the dot was extended to *j* (thought to be a variant of *i*). The lack of distinction between <I> and <J> is illustrated well in the '*INRI*' caption on Roman Catholic representations of crucifixes and paintings of the crucifixion of Christ. It is an abbreviation of the title Pontius Pilate was reported to have had written on the cross of Jesus Christ, *Iesvs Nazarenvs Rex Ivdaeorvm*, or in more conventional modernized spelling, *Jesus Nazarenus Rex Judaeorum* 'Jesus of Nazerus, King of the Jews'. Association of <j> with an affricate [ǰ] (IPA [dʒ]) is due to later developments in French, where initial *j* (/y/, IPA [j]) inherited from Latin had become [dʒ] word-initially, due to sound change, though still spelled <j>, and this was the Norman French convention that was used to write English after the Norman conquest. Thus French loans in English from an earlier period reflect the earlier pronunciation with [dʒ] in words written with <j>, as for example, *jolly*, *journey*, *juice* and so on. Later, this [dʒ] of French changed further to [ʒ], but after the orthographic value of [dʒ] for <j> had been established for English spelling. Thus, these French words, the source of the English loans, in modern French are *joli* [ʒoli] 'pretty', *journée* [ʒuʁne] 'day's earnings, day's travel', and *jus* [ʒy] 'juice'.

The letters *u*, *v*, and *w* have a similar history. In Latin spelling, which persisted in earlier French spelling practice, *u* and *v* were interchangeable, used for either /u/ or /w/. Later, in the early Christian era, Latin /w/ changed to /v/, though the two letters continued in use essentially interchangeably for either the vowel /u/ or the consonant /v/. The letter *w* was originally formed from a double *u*, as the name suggests, or from a double *v* in shape, which was not distinct from *u* in its function, and later came to be considered a different letter for a different sound, no longer valid for the vowel /u/. The *u* shape of the letter came to be associated with vowels and the *v* shape with consonants, considered distinct letters.

Additionally, in some contexts, some cases that are today spelled in Enlish with *o* actually should have *u* according to expectations. In cases with the sequence /uv/ (or /ʊv/), the convention was to close the *u* in writing, making it into an *o*, in order to distinguish /uv/ from sequences of letters difficult to identify in squiggled handwriting involving *m, n, u, v, w*. Thus <love> 'love', from Old English *lufu*, never had the pronunciation usually associated with the *o* of the spelling, but rather was meant to represent /lʊv/.

15.3 Philology

Philology is understood in different ways. Sometimes it is taken to be merely the study of some classical or older language – in this sense we see university departments and professional journals dedicated to Classical philology, English philology, Germanic Philology, Nordic philology, Romance philology, and so on. Sometimes philology is understood to mean historical linguistics as practiced in the nineteenth century, since what today is called historical linguistics was earlier often referred to as 'philology', as in 'Indo-European philology'. In another sense of the word, philology is understood as the scholarly activity that attempts to get systematic information about a language from written records. Definitions of *philology* range across these varied notions: the intensive study of texts, especially old ones; the humanistic study of language and literature, considering both form and meaning in linguistic expression, combining linguistics and literary studies; the history of literature and words; the systematic study of the development and history of languages; and the study of written records to determine their authenticity, original form, and meaning. Definitions of *philologist* involve these notions, meaning a collector of words and their etymologies; a humanist specializing in classical scholarship; and a person who engages in philology (historical linguistics).

One aim of philology is to get historical information from documents in order to learn about the culture and history of the people behind the text; another aim is to examine and interpret older written attestations with the goal of obtaining information about the history of the language (or languages) in which the documents are written. This second aim is the most common in historical linguistics today, and it is in this sense that the term *philology* is used in this book.

In the use of philology for historical linguistic purposes, we are concerned with what linguistic information can be got from written documents, with how we can get it, and with what we can make of the information once we have it. The philological investigation of older written attestations can contribute in several ways, for example by documenting sound changes that have taken place, distinguishing inherited from borrowed material, dating changes and borrowings, and helping to understand the development and change in writing systems and orthographic conventions, among others. Results of these studies can have implications for claims about scribal practice, subgroup classification, causes of changes, the reconstruction of a proto-language, borrowed changes and rules, the identification of extinct languages, and the historical interpretation of many changes within the languages investigated in this way.

15.3.1 Examples of what philology can contribute

The following examples illustrate some of the kinds of information that can be retrieved through philological investigations and the implications such information can have for historical linguistic understanding of the languages involved. Examples abound from Indo-European and ancient Near Eastern languages. Here, cases from the history of English are presented because they are easier for English speakers to understand, and then, in order to illustrate the general applicability of philological notions, cases are selected from the rich written attestations in various Mayan languages since the 1500s and from Maya hieroglyphic writing. It is often believed, erroneously, that Native American languages lack older written sources and that therefore little can be gained from philological investigation of them. The examples presented here are interesting both for what they reveal and because they show the applicability of philology to American Indian languages.

(1) Proto-Mayan contrasted *x [velar fricative] and *h [glottal fricative], as several of the thirty-one Mayan languages still do; however, in Yucatec Maya these both merged to h (*x, *h > h). Nevertheless, colonial sources show that the contrast survived until after European contact. For example, in the Motul Dictionary from c. 1590 the two sounds were distinguished as 'loud H' (< *x) and 'simple H' (< *h), though both were written with <h>. (The orthography of this and following cases is based on that of Spanish at the time that the documents were written.) Some example dictionary entries which illustrate the contrast are seen in Table 15.1.

TABLE 15.1: Contrastive *h* and *x* in Classical Yucatec Maya

Under 'simple H' ([h])	Under 'loud H' ([x])
haa [Proto-Mayan *ha?] 'water'	haa [xa?] 'to scrape, file'
hel- [Proto-Mayan *hil] 'rest'	hel [Proto-Mayan *xel] 'succeed, exchange'
halab- [halaɓ-] 'thing said or sent'	halab- [Proto-Mayan *xal] 'weaving stick'

This example shows that through philological investigation we can sometimes recover information about sound changes in the language under investigation, in this case about a merger in Yucatec Maya, and information about the relative date when the change took place; in this case the merger of *x, h > h* took place sometime after the Motul Dictionary was written in c.1590.

(2) Huastec, another Mayan language, has contrastive k^w (labialized velar stop) and $k^{w'}$ (glottalized labialized velar stop), though no other Mayan language has these sounds. Based on the correspondence sets of Huastec k^w: others k, and Huastec $k^{w'}$: others k', some had thought Proto-Mayan must be reconstructed with $*k^w$ and $*k^{w'}$. However, written attestations from the eighteenth century show that the labialized velars in Huastec are the results of a recent change. In words which originally had a velar stop (k or k') followed by back rounded vowel (u or o) followed by a glide ($w, j, h,$ or $ʔ$) followed by a vowel, the velars were labialized and the rounded vowel together with the glide was lost:

$$\begin{Bmatrix} k \\ k' \end{Bmatrix} \begin{Bmatrix} u \\ o \end{Bmatrix} \begin{Bmatrix} w \\ j \\ h \\ ʔ \end{Bmatrix} V > \begin{Bmatrix} k^w \\ k^{w'} \end{Bmatrix} V$$

Some examples are seen in Table 15.2.

TABLE 15.2: The origin of Huastec labialized velars

Colonial Huastec	*Modern Huastec*
<cuyx> [kuwi(:)š] 'vulture'	kʷi:š 'vulture'
<coyen> [koyen] 'mass'	kʷen 'piled together'
<cohuych> [kowi(:)č] 'tamale'	kʷi:č 'tamale'

This philological evidence shows that Huastec k^w and $k^{w'}$ are the results of a later sound change and therefore do not belong in separate sound correspondences sets which would require that these sounds be reconstructed to Proto-Mayan. This case shows how philological information can be relevant to the reconstruction of proto-languages, as well as to determining the source of certain sounds and what sound changes brought them about. It also reveals something about when the change took place, in this case some time after these eighteenth-century sources were written.

(3) Poqoman, Poqomchi', and Q'eqchi', three neighbouring Mayan languages, have all undergone the sound change $*ts > s$. Some scholars had thought this shared innovation (see Chapter 6) was evidence that the three should be grouped together in a subgroup of languages more closely related to one another than to other languages of the family. Other evidence, however, shows that while Poqomam and Poqomchi' are very closely related, Q'eqchi' is considerably more distant. Philological evidence shows that the change $*ts > s$ is not in fact a shared innovation reflecting a change in some immediate ancestor of the three languages at a time before they split up. Rather, the earliest written attestations in these languages reveal that the change was under way but not completed after European contact and that the change diffused later through these three languages. For example, the Zúñiga Poqomchi' Dictionary (from c. 1608) has entries such

as: *vatz* [w-ats] *vaz* [w-as] 'older brother' [modern Poqomchi' *w-as* 'my older brother', Proto-Mayan **ats* 'elder brother'], *azeh* [as-ex], *atzeh* [ats-ex] 'to treat as a brother, to take an older brother' – 'some say it with *tz* atzeh, and others with only *z*, azeh; say it as you please. Most say azeh, with *z*, and some with *tz*.' Some other examples are:

tzeel, zeel	'laugh' (Proto-Mayan **tse?l*)
tzab, zab	'addition, balancing weight'
tzinuh, zinuh	'oak'
tzub, zub	'the profit from what is sold'

The Morán Poqomam Dictionary (c. 1720) has examples such as:

azvez, atzvez	'elder brother' (Proto-Mayan **ats*, modern Poqomam *as-w¹es*)
ah zeel, ah tzeel	'laughter' (Proto-Mayan **tse?l*)
alaz, alaatz	'descendants'
ah itz	'witch, sorcerer' (modern Poqomam *ax is*, Proto-Mayan **its* 'evil')

Other sources show that this change was complete in Poqomchi' and Poqomam shortly after these were written, but that it diffused to Q'eqchi' only later. For example, the Morales Q'eqchi' Grammar (1741) shows most forms with <tz> ([ts]):

tzum	'companion' (modern Q'eqchi' *sum*)
tzuc	'gnat' (modern Q'eqchi' *suq*)
tzimaj	'bow, arrow' (modern Q'eqchi' *simax*)

Only a very few of the words cited then show the beginnings of the change, for example:

tzununk, sununk	'smell' (modern Q'eqchi' *sunu:nk*)

The philological evidence in this example shows that the change **ts > s* in these three languages took place after European contact and spread later among these already independent languages. This means that this change is not support for subgrouping these languages together as more closely related. This case shows how philological evidence can be relevant for subgrouping, as well as for determining the date when changes took place.

(4) Philological information can also document grammatical changes. Modern Kaqchikel (Mayan) has affixes that mark tense, but Old Kaqchikel, recorded in numerous colonial documents from the late 1600s and 1700s, did not have tense markers; these are the result of rather recent change involving aspect markers. Colonial sources reveal an aspect system with:

<x-> (/š-/ [IPA /ʃ-/]) 'completive' (perfective)
<t-> (/t-/) 'incompletive' (imperfective) for transitive verbs
 <c-> or <qu-> (/k-/) 'incompletive' (imperfective) action for intransitive verbs (where, following Spanish orthographic conventions, <c-> occurred before *a, o, u*, and <qu-> before *i* and *e*).

The present tense developed from the verbs in incompletive aspect when they followed the adverb <tan> 'now'. The combination of <tan> and the incompletive aspect marker changed, where *tan + t-* was ultimately reduced to *nd-* or *n-* in modern dialects, for example <tan t-in-ban> 'I am doing' [now INCOMPLETIVE. TRANSITIVE-1st.Pers.ERGATIVE-do] > /n-in-b'an/. The verbs with *tan + k-* 'incompletive intransitive' > *ng-, ny-, y-* in different modern dialects. The 'completive' <x-> was reinterpreted as 'past' *š-*, since completive (completed) actions typically take place in the past. Earlier, these morphemes did not mark tense; 'completive' (perfective) could involve non-past events, as in English equivalents such as 'I did it', 'I have done it', 'I will have done it (by tomorrow)', and incompletive equivalents as in 'I am doing it', 'I was doing it', 'I will be doing it'.

The ample documentation in colonial texts attests the change from the former aspect system with no tense morphology to the modern tense system.

(5) Philological information which can be derived from Maya hieroglyphic writing helps to identify the language in which the hieroglyphic texts (c. 400 BC – AD 1600) were written and demonstrates that certain sound changes had already taken place by the date of writing. The language of the script is Cholan, and it had already undergone such distinctive Cholan sound changes as **k > č* (IPA [tʃ]) and *e: > i*. (Note, there is some difference of opinion among specialists about which Cholan language or languages may be involved, but no disagreement that the hieroglyphic texts on the earlier monuments represent some form of Cholan.) The change **k > č* is seen in Figure 15.3, where the forms interchanged as rebuses in that figure are all pronounced /čan/ in Cholan (ČAN 'four', ČAN 'snake', and ČAN 'sky'). As pointed out above, that these signs could be interchanged in this way shows that Cholan was the language of the writing, since in Yucatec Maya the cognate words are not homophonous: *kan* 'four', *kàan* 'snake', and *káʔan* 'sky'. Figure 15.6 shows not only that Cholan was the languages of the script, but also that two Cholan sound changes had already taken place by the time of the writing, **k > č* and *e: > i*. Figure 15.6 presents the syllabic spelling of 'deer',

FIGURE 15.6: Cholan 'deer' spelled syllabically či-xi /čix/

written <či-xi> for *čix* – the first syllabic sign is *či*, the second *xi*. 'Deer' in Proto-Mayan was **kehx*, and is *ké:h* in Yucatec. The syllabic spelling shows the results of the two Cholan sound changes **k > č* and *e: > i*, and is seen in Cholan *čix* (see modern Chol *čih*), not the form of cognates for 'deer' in Yucatecan or the other subgroups of Mayan.

These brief examples from Maya hieroglyphic writing show how the philological investigation of these written records contributes by showing which language the hieroglyphic script was written in, and that the changes **k > č* and *e: > i* took place at a time before the texts were written. (For other examples from Maya hieroglyphic writing, see Campbell 1984 and Justeson et al. 1985.)

The examples cited in this section show that findings from philological investigation can have implications for, among other things (1) documenting former contrasts now lost and sound changes that have taken place; (2) refining and clarifying the reconstructions of proto-phonology; (3) distinguishing borrowed changes from legitimate shared innovations, and clarifying evidence for subgrouping; (4) documenting grammatical changes; (5) identifying ancient, sometimes extinct, languages, and deciphering writing systems; and (6) establishing the relative age of changes. In effect, if the right kind of information is preserved in the written sources, the philological investigation of written records can contribute insight and understanding to most areas of linguistic change.

15.4   The Role of Writing

The relationship of writing to the comparative method has sometimes been misrepresented but needs to be understood. Since reliance on written languages had been important in the development of understanding of relationships among Indo-European languages and the changes they have undergone, some scholars came to believe that it was impossible to do reliable historical linguistic investigation without written records from earlier stages of the languages investigated. This belief continued to be repeated by some scholars in spite of the fact that the comparative study of unwritten, so-called 'exotic' languages has had a long and successful history. Leonard Bloomfield disproved once and for all the assertion that a proto-language could not be reconstructed successfully in the absence of written records from earlier stages of the languages. Bloomfield's (1925, 1928) famous proof of the applicability of the comparative method in unwritten languages (see Chapter 5) was based on the assumption that sound change is regular. This meant that different sound correspondence sets among Algonquian languages that could not be explained away required different proto-sounds to be reconstructed. Bloomfield's decision to reconstruct **çk* for one sound correspondence set, even though it contained sounds found in other correspondence sets but corresponding to different sounds in the different daughter languages, was confirmed by the discovery of Swampy Cree, which contained distinct sounds as the reflexes in each of the sound correspondences (see Chapter 5 for details). Bloomfield's proof of the applicability of the comparative method to unwritten languages is considered a major contribution to historical linguistics. It means that while we are happy to have the testimony of written records for earlier periods when we can get it, written attestations are by no means necessary to comparative reconstruction. Moreover, it must be recalled that written records have to be interpreted – one of the roles of philology – and they are only as valuable and reliable as our ability to determine the sound system underlying them.

Hittite illustrates this point. While Hittite has radically revised our understanding of Indo-European phonology, it was written in an imprecise cuneiform syllabary on clay tablets from 1650 to 1200 BC, and several aspects of its phonetic interpretation are still in dispute. For example, did Hittite have four or five vowels? Did it have an [o]? Did Hittite have contrastive vowel length, or, what does the doubling of vowels in the texts mean? What do the frequent double signs for stop consonants in the orthography represent? Clearly, then, Hittite writing provides much useful information, but it also has limitations for the historical interpretation of the language.

In part the prejudice in favour of old written traditions is a hold-over from a pre-Neogrammarian stage of comparative linguistics, when language change was thought to take place in discrete stages of first progress and then decay. The languages of so-called 'savage' people were thought to be 'primitive' relics which had not yet evolved – not progressed, through processes of compounding and amalgamation – to the state of greater perfection which older written Indo-European languages, in particular Sanskrit, had attained, in this view. Modern languages were typically viewed as just decayed reflections of their more perfect ancestors due to affects of analogy and sound changes, which were assumed to be operative only in this later phase. Thus, the older written languages, thought to be more perfect, were allotted a special status. In contrast, in the Neogrammarian movement, comparative linguistics adopted the position that language change did not take place in discrete stages of either progress or decay, but rather that languages undergo the same kinds of changes at all times throughout their histories. With this reorientation, written language was accorded less of a special status and attention turned more towards spoken language, in particular to dialects, and attention to dialectology promoted the development of phonetics, techniques for recording forms of spoken language (see Chapter 7). Thus, speaking of the principle that sound laws are without exception, Berthold Delbrück (1882 [1880]: 61) affirmed in his influential Neogrammarian introduction to linguistics:

> This natural constitution of language is not manifested in the cultivated tongues, but in the dialects of the people. The guiding principles for linguistic research should accordingly be deduced not from obsolete written languages of antiquity, but chiefly from the living popular dialects of the present day.

In short, the existence of an old written tradition with older texts is by no means necessary for the comparative method to be applicable, and in any case, the written records are only as valuable for historical linguistic interests as our ability to interpret them and to determine accurately the phonetic and structural properties of the language they represent.

15.4.1 Getting historical linguistic information for written sources

The techniques employed and the sort of information one can expect to obtain from written records vary greatly from case to case, depending on the circumstances. For example, how we investigate texts written in a logographic writing system (where signs represent whole words) will differ markedly from how we treat texts written in syllabaries (with symbols based on properties of syllables) or in alphabetic scripts. However, in general, we can use anything in philology which provides information helpful for interpreting the phonetic, phonemic, semantic, and grammatical contents of the language which the written records represent, so that this information can be put to use in unravelling further the history of the language involved.

Very often, what information we can derive for interpreting the structure of the language at the time when the texts were written and extrapolating from that for understanding the history of the language is a matter of luck, a matter of what happens to show up in the sources available. In the best cases, we may have descriptions of or commentaries about the pronunciation at the time the texts were written, and these can be immensely helpful. In most situations, however, we are not so fortunate as to have worthwhile, readily interpretable phonetic descriptions from the past. Other valuable sources of phonetic information include rhymes, metre, occasional spellings, transliterations of forms in other languages whose phonology is better known, aid from translations from texts known in other languages, and clues from related languages and dialects. Let us consider some of these briefly.

(1) *Rhymes and the testimony of poetry.* For example, the word 'night' was spelled variously <niht>, <nyʒt>, <nyght>, and <nicht> in Middle English texts. For various reasons it is assumed that the consonant before the final *t* represented in these various spellings (especially by <gh> and <ʒ>) of the word for 'night' and others like it was /x/, a voiceless velar fricative, even though that sound is gone from Modern English /nait/ 'night'. Some of the evidence for concluding that it represented /x/ in Middle English comes from the fact that in Middle English poetic texts, words with <gh> and <ʒ>, with the postulated /x/, rhyme only with other words spelled in this way and never with words which contain the same vowel but lack a spelling of the sound we believe to have been /x/. For example, Chaucer rhymes *knight* with *wight* 'strong' but not with *white* (Lass 1992: 30).

(2) *Occasional spellings.* An indirect source of knowledge about changing pronunciation is the variant spellings which sometime provide clues concerning what was changing and when the change took place. In the history of English, spelling conventions were starting to regularize in the 1600s, as printers more and more used uniform spelling, but standard spelling was far from fixed. Occasional spellings (not the more expected ones) from the period show change in pronunciation. For example variants such as *ceme/came*, *credyll/cradel* 'cradle', and *teke/take* show that former /a/ had changed to something closer to modern /e(i)/ in these words. Examples such as *symed/semed* 'seemed', *stypylle/stepel* 'steeple', reflect the /eː/ > /iː/ of the Great Vowel Shift. Spellings of *marcy/mercy* 'mercy', *sarten/certein* 'certain', *parson/persoun* 'person', and so on, show that /er/ changed to /ar/ in the pronunciation of the writer of these forms. (This change was fairly general, though sociolinguistically conditioned, and it was ultimately reversed, but left such doublets in English as *clerk/clark*, *person/parson*, *vermin/varmint*, and *university/varsity*.)

(3) *Interpretation from material from foreign languages.* For example, the principal source of information on Gothic is Bishop Wulfila's (311–382) translation of the Bible, part of which has survived, whose orthography was based on that of Greek at the time Wulfila wrote. The spellings with <ai> and <au> are interpreted as representing /ɛ:/ and /ɔ:/, respectively, based on the value of <ai> and <au> in Greek spelling at the time. This interpretation is supported by the Gothic spellings of foreign names and words known to have had *e(:)* and *o(:)* in the source languages, for example *Aílisabaíþ* 'Elizabeth', *Nazaraíþ* 'Nazareth', and *praúfetus* 'prophet', *Gaúmaúrra* 'Gomorrah', and *Naúbaímbaír* 'November'. This gives greater confidence in the interpretation of the phonetic value of Gothic <ai> and <au> (Krause 1968: 67).

(4) *Clues from related languages.* In the case of texts in languages which are less well known, sometimes clues to the interpretation of the writing can be obtained from related languages. For example, in the case of Middle English <gh> / <ʒ> (above), although 'night' in Modern English has no /x/, we can be more assured of our /x/ interpretation of the phonetic value based on the fact that English's closest relatives have /x/ in cognate words, as in German *Nacht* ([naxt]) 'night' and similar forms in Dutch and Frisian (Lass 1992: 30).

An example which shows how both translated texts and clues from related languages can help comes from Chicomuceltec, an extinct Mayan language, closely related to Huastec. Very little is known directly about Chicomuceltec, just limited wordlists (no more than 500 words) and one short text from before it became extinct. The text is a *Confesionario* from 1775 with about ten lines in Chicomuceltec corresponding to the adjacent Spanish text. The orthography is based on Spanish, and by referring to the Spanish translation of the text for possible meanings and to corresponding Huastec forms, it is possible to work out much of the contents of the text, as seen in the following line:

Chicomuceltec:	ixcataton tan Domingo?
Spanish:	Has trabajado los Domingos?,

The Spanish line means 'Have you worked on Sundays?' and leads us to believe the Chicomuceltec version has the same meaning. In the Spanish orthography at the time, <x> represented [š] (IPA [ʃ]); Spanish /š/ changed to a velar fricative [x] in the early 1700s, and is spelled today primarily with <j>. In comparing Huastec material, we postulate that the Chicomuceltec text contains *ixca-* [iška-] 'you-Past' (containing within it *-a-* 'you-Singular') + *-t'ohn-* 'work', *tan* 'in', and the Spanish loanword *Domingo* 'Sunday'. Without access to related Huastec forms and corresponding translation of the same text in Spanish, we would have no basis for segmenting the morphemes or guessing what this line meant. Without reference to Huastec forms, we would not be able to recover the word 'to work' or to postulate that it contained a glottalized *t'* as in the Huastec cognate, since the glottalized stops are not distinguished from plain ones in the Spanish-based orthography of the Chicomuceltec text. Together, the corresponding translation in a better-known language (Spanish in this case) and comparison with a closely related language (Huastec) provide for a fairly successful philological interpretation of this text in an otherwise very poorly known extinct language. (Campbell 1988a: 202–7.)

There are also many potential pitfalls and sources of error in attempts to interpret older written sources, and it is important to keep in mind the many ways in which well-meaning interpretations can go astray. Sometimes the writing system just underrepresents the contrasts that existed in the language at the time it was written, and so information is simply not available for a full interpretation. In the Chicomuceltec example, this is illustrated by the lack of distinction in the Spanish-based orthography between plain /t/ and glottalized /t'/ in the language. In early attestations of other Native American languages, contrastive tones, glottal stops, and long vowels, for example, are simply not represented in the documents. Other problems can come from the difficulty of interpreting variations in the writing, from cases where different dialects with different features are represented, and from the tendency for writing systems to preserve representations of features which have been lost in the spoken language, long after the language has changed – witness the <gh> in Modern English *night*. The needs of poetic form (especially metre) may distort the written language, for example in cases of poetic licence using word orders not normally found in the spoken language. Old texts which are translations of texts in other languages, such as the Bible in Gothic based on Greek, or in English based on translations from Latin, often lead to grammatical distortions, loan translations or calques, and so on, which were not actually part of the language.

(5) *Grammatical change*. The Kaqchikel example above shows how information about grammatical change in a language can be obtained. Many examples in other languages also illustrate this.

In summary, in many cases, exercising appropriate caution, we can obtain much information from older written attestations of value to the historical interpretation of languages. This is a very important source of historical linguistic information, useful in the arsenal of tools the historical linguist uses to recover the history of languages.

15.5   Exercises

Exercise 15.1   Philological analysis of Latin *Appendix Probi*

The *Appendix Probi* ('Appendix of Probus') was compiled in 3rd–4th century AD. It lists 227 Latin words in what the scribe considered both 'correct' and 'incorrect' form. It was devised to aid scribes with the orthography, but the forms listed also illustrate some phonological and analogical changes that were taking place or had already taken place in spoken Latin language at that time. Compare the following examples from the list and attempt to formulate the changes that they appear to reflect. These examples are of the form *X non Y*, that is *X not Y*, where the scribe considers the 'X' form 'correct' and the 'Y' form 'incorrect', as in *masculus non masclus*, meaning '*masculus* ['male'] not *masclus*', that is, more precisely, 'write *masculus*; do not write *masclus*'. For this exercise, assume that the forms on the left of *non* represent conservative and thus older pronunciations and that the forms on the right of *non* correspond to later pronunciations which result from changes in the language.

HINT: in instances where some forms seem to change in the opposite direction of others, consider the possible role of hypercorrection.

	Appendix Probi	*Conventional Classical Latin spelling and gloss*

Set 1

1. masculus non masclus — māsculus 'male, manly'
2. vetulus non veclus — vetulus 'little old, poor old'
3. vitulus non viclus — vitulus 'calf, foal'
4. vernaculus non vernaclus — vernāculus 'native, of home-born slaves'
5. articulus non articlus — articulus 'joint, knuckle, limb'
6. angulus non anglus — angulus 'angle, corner'
7. oculus non oclus — oculus 'eye'
8. tabula non tabla — tabula 'board, plank'
9. calida non calda — calida 'warm, hot'
10. frigida non fricda — frīgida 'cold'
11. viridis non virdis — viridis 'green'

Set II

12. vacua [vakua] non vaqua [vakwa] — vacua 'empty, void'
13. equs [ekwus] non ecus [ekus] — equus 'horse'
14. coqus [kokwus] non cocus [kokus] — coquus 'cook'
15. rivus [rīwus] non rius [rius] — rīvus 'stream, brook'
16. avus [awus] non aus — avus 'grandfather'
17. flavus [flāwus] non flaus [flaus] — flāvus 'yellow, golden'

Set III

18. passim non passi — passim 'here and there, at random'
19. pridem non pride — prīdem 'long ago, long'
20. olim non oli — ōlim 'once, at the time, at times'
21. idem non ide — īdem, idem 'the same, likewise'
22. numquam non numqua — numquam 'never'
23. triclinium non triclinu — trīclīnium 'dining-couch, dining room'

Set IVa (the more common direction of change)

24. ansa non asa — ānsa 'handle'
25. mensa non mesa — mēnsa 'table, meal'
26. Capsensis non Capsessis — Capsensis 'from Capsitanus'

Appendix Probi	*Conventional Classical Latin spelling and gloss*

Set IVb (occasional examples)

27.	Hercules non Herculens	Herculēs
28.	occasio non occansio	occāsiō 'opportunity, convenient time'

Set Va (the more common direction of change)

29.	vinea non vinia	vīnea 'vineyard'
30.	cavea non cavia	cavea 'cage, coop, hive'
31.	lancea non lancia	lancea 'lance, spear'
32.	balteus non baltius	balteus 'belt, girdle, sword-belt'
33.	cochlea non coclia	coclea, cochlea 'snail'

Set Vb (occasional examples)

34.	ostium non osteum	ōstium 'door, entrance'
35.	noxius non noxeus	noxius 'harmful'
36.	alium non aleum	ālium 'garlic'

Set VI

37.	vapulo non baplo	vāpulō 'be beaten, flogged'
38.	alveus non albeus	alveus 'hollow, trough, bathtub'
39.	tolerabilis non toleravilis	tolerābilis 'bearable, tolerable'

Set VII The more common direction of change was <x> [ks] becoming <s> [s]. In light of this, how would you explain the following:

40.	miles non milex	mīles 'soldier'
41.	aries non ariex	ariēs 'ram'
42.	poples non poplex	poples 'knee'
43.	locuples non locuplex	locuplēs 'rich, reliable'

(From Baehrens 1922.)

Exercise 15.2   Greek philological comparison

The short text in line (1) is from Mycenaean Greek (before 1200 BC), given in the conventional transliteration for the Linear B syllabary. Roots for the words in this text are compared in line (2) with Attic Greek (Classical Greek from Athens, end of the fifth century BC), and then in line (3) with Modern Greek. Each is given with its phonetic equivalents, well understood from a variety of sources of information. Compare the Greek from these three different times and attempt to specify sound changes that can be detected in these data. What other historical information can you draw from this example? Note that FOOTSTOOL is represented by an logogram, where the sign signals the whole word and it is not spelled out in the syllabary. Inst = Dative-Instrumental. 'Octopus' is literally 'many-foot' (*polu-/poly-* 'many' + *pod-* 'foot'). The word for 'griffin' (glossed as 'phoenix' in Modern Greek) also means 'palm tree'. This text means 'One footstool inlaid in ivory with a man and a horse and an octopus and a griffin/ palm tree.'

(1) Linear B (c. 1400 BC):

Ta-ra-nu	a-ja-me-no	e-re-pa-te-jo	a-to-ro-qo	i-qo-qe		po-ru-po-de-qe	po-ni-ke-qe FOOTSTOOL
[tʰrâ:nus	aia:ménos	elepʰanteío:i	antʰró:kʷo:i	híkkʷo:ti-kʷe		polupódei-kʷe	pʰoiní:kei-kʷe X]
stool.Nom	inlaid.Nom	ivory.Inst	man.Inst	horse.Inst-and	octopus.Inst-and	griffin.Inst-and X

(2) Attic Greek (c. 400 BC):

θρανίον	ελεφάντινο-	'άνθρωπο-	ίππο-	πολύποδ-	φοίνικ-
[tʰra:níon	elepʰántino-	ántʰro:po-	híppo-	polýpod-	pʰoíni:k-]

(3) Modern Greek (c. 2000 AD):

θρανίο	ελεφάντινο-	άνθρωπο-	ιππο-	πολύποδ-	φίνιξ
[θranío	elefá(n)dino-	ánθropo-	íppo-	polípod-	fínix]
'desk, form'	'made of ivory'	'man'	'horse'	'polyp, polypod'	'phoenix/ palm tree'

(From Horrocks 1997: 4–5.)

Exercise 15.3 Spanish philological interpretation

The epic poem, *Cantar de Mio Cid*, is one of the oldest texts in Spanish, from about 1140 AD. A fragment of the poem is given here and compared with the modern equivalent in Latin American Spanish (as, for example, spoken in Mexico or Central America). Each line is given with broad phonetic equivalents. Compare the two versions. What lexical changes do you note? What other changes have taken place in this variety of modern Spanish? Assume for present purposes that any non-lexical, non-grammatical phonetic difference between the two versions represents a general change even if only one example appears in these data. What conclusions can you draw about the history of some of these changes?

NOTE: ñ = palatal nasal, IPA [ɲ]; [s̪] = dental 's' (which in modern Peninsular Spanish became [θ]); [ş] = apical post-alveolar 's'. OBJ = marker of human specific object; REFL = reflexive.

Original from Cantar de Mio Cid:

(1)	Nós	çercamos	el	escaño	por	curiar	nuestro	señor,
	[nos̪	şerkamos	el	eşkaño	por	kuriar	nueştro	şeñor]
	We	surrounded	the	bench	for	to.guard	our	lord,

(2)	fasta	do	despertó	mio	Cid,	el	que	Valencia	ganó;
	[faşta	do	despertó	mio	şid	el	ke	valenşia	ganó]
	until	where	awoke	my	Cid	he	who	Valencia	won

(3) levantós   del   escaño   e   fos   poral león;
    [levantó-ş del   eşkaño   e   fo-ş   por-al león]
    got.up- refl from.the bench and went-REFL for. lion;
                                                    the

(4) el   león   premió   la   cabeça, a   mio Cid   esperó,
    [el   león   premió   la   kabeşa a   mio şid   eşperó]
    the   lion   lowered   the   head,   for my   Cid   waited

(5) dexósle   prender al   cuello, e   a   la   red le metió.
    [deʃó-ş-le   prender al   kuelʲo e   a   la   red le metió]
    allowed-REFL-him to.take   to.the neck   and to   the net it put

Modern equivalent:

(1) Nosotros rodeamos   el   escaño   para custodiar   a   nuestro señor,
    [nosotros rodeamos   el   eşkaño   para kustodiar   a   nuestro señor]
    We   surrounded the   bench   for   to.guard   obj our   lord,

(2) hasta   que   se   despertó mi   Cid,   el   que   ganó   Valencia;
    [asta   ke   se   despertó mi   sid   el   ke   ganó   balensia
    until   that   refl   awoke   my   Cid   he   who   won   Valencia;

(3) se levantó   del   escaño   y   se   fue   por el   león;
    [se lebantó   del   eşkaño   i   se   fue   por el   león]
    REFL got.up   from.the   bench   and   REFL   went for the   lion;

(4) el   león   bajó   la   cabeza,   esperó   a   mio   Cid,
    [el   león   baxó   la   kabesa,   esperó   a   mi   sid]
    the   lion   lowered the   head,   waited   for my   Cid

(5) se le   dejó   coger por   el   cuello y   meter-lo en   la jaula.
    [se le   dexó   koxer por   el   kueyo i   meterlo en   la xaula]
    REFL him   allowed   to.take by   the   neck   and put-it   in   thecage

'We surrounded the bench to guard our lord,
until my Cid awoke, he who conquered Valencia;
he got up from the bench and he went for the lion;
the lion lowered its head, waited for my Cid;
it allowed him to take it by the neck and put it in the cage.'
(Additional notes: *nosotros* < *nos* 'we' + *otros* 'others'; *do* = modern *donde*
'where'.)

16

Linguistic Prehistory

> Language, too, has marvels of her own, which she unveils to the inquiring
> glance of the patient student. There are chronicles below her surface, there are
> sermons in every word.
>
> (Max Müller 1866: 12–13)

16.1 Introduction

Linguistic prehistory has been associated with a number of names in the
literature: linguistic palaeontology, linguistic archaeology, applied historical
linguistics and so on. It has a long (and sometimes chequered) history, though
in recent years it has again come into focus. Broadly speaking, linguistic prehistory uses historical linguistic findings for cultural and historical inferences.
Linguistic prehistory correlates information from historical linguistics with
information from archaeology, ethnohistory, history, ethnographic analogy,
human biology and other sources of information on a people's past in order
to obtain a clearer, more complete picture of the past. Thus, the comparative
method, linguistic homeland and migration theory, cultural inventories from
reconstructed vocabularies of proto-languages, loanwords, place names, classification of languages, internal reconstruction, dialect distributions and the like
can all provide valuable historical information useful to linguistic prehistory.
How these methods can contribute to a fuller picture of prehistory is the focus
of this chapter. What linguistic prehistory is all about is illustrated by a few
well-known and informative cases. At the same time, it is also important to be
aware of the limitations of linguistic prehistory and of the possible pitfalls and
problems which can be encountered by attempts to correlate historical linguistic information with the findings in other fields. This is the subject of the last
section of this chapter.

16.2   Indo-European Linguistic Prehistory

To get started, it is helpful to look briefly at some of the findings and claims about the prehistory of Indo-European-speaking peoples as reflected in linguistic evidence. This is an instructive case study.

By the mid-1800s, comparative Indo-European linguistics had advanced sufficiently that it was possible to say how the Indo-European languages had diversified and to make reasonably informed hypotheses about the material culture and social structure of the Proto-Indo-Europeans (the speakers of Proto-Indo-European) and about their homeland – all based solely on linguistic findings and interpretations (see Kuhn 1845, Pictet 1859–1863 and Schrader 1883 [1890]). However, crucial archaeological and other information was not yet available at that time, and the first archaeological data that did become available seemed to clash with the most probable linguistic interpretations. For example, according to an early hypothesis based on linguistic evidence, the Indo-European homeland (the place where Proto-Indo-European was originally spoken, from where Indo-European languages diversified and spread out, ultimately to their current locations) was located in the steppes to the north of the Black Sea; however, it was objected that no likely archaeological culture was known from this area at that time. In fact, supportive archaeological evidence did not appear until some 100 years later, with Marija Gimbutas' (1963) work on the Kurgan culture of the Pontic and Volga steppes. The correlation between Proto-Indo-European and the Kurgan archaeological culture now has much support, though there is also much debate (see Mallory 1989). In Gimbutas' view, the expansion of Kurgan culture corresponds in time and area with the expansion of Indo-European languages outwards from this homeland, and correlates with the arrival in these areas of such typically Indo-European things as horses, wheeled vehicles, double-headed axes, small villages, pastoral economy and patriarchal society.

Reconstruction by the comparative method has provided a fairly clear view of important aspects of Proto-Indo-European culture, including valuable information on the original homeland, social structure, kinship, subsistence, economy, law, religion, environment, technology and ideology. As Calvert Watkins observed,

> When we have reconstructed a protolanguage, we have also necessarily established the existence of a prehistoric society . . . the contents of the Indo-European lexicon provide a remarkably clear view of the whole culture of an otherwise unknown prehistoric society . . . The evidence that archaeology can provide is limited to material remains. But human culture is not confined to material artifacts. The reconstruction of vocabulary can offer a fuller, more interesting view of a prehistoric people than archaeology precisely because it includes nonmaterial culture. (2000: xxii)

Aspects of Proto-Indo-European's cultural inventory can be recovered from the reconstructed vocabulary of Proto-Indo-European, as seen in the list below, which is based upon Mallory and Adams (1997) and Watkins (2000). The traditional Indo-Europeanist notation used here requires some explanation.

Most specialists in Indo-European recognize three sounds traditionally labelled laryngeals, but their phonetic values are disputed. They are represented conventionally as: *h_1* ('neutral, perhaps /h/ or /ʔ/); *h_2* ('*a*-colouring', perhaps /x/ or /ħ/); and *h_3* ('*o*-colouring', perhaps /ʕ/). Undisputed consonantal reflexes of these survive only in Hittite and the other Anatolian languages. The laryngeals are gone from all the other Indo-European languages, but not without a trace. The evidence of their earlier presence is seen primarily in their effect on vowels in these languages, changing the quality of both preceding and following vowels, and lengthening any vowel preceding them. In addition a number of languages provide other bits of evidence for the reconstruction of the Proto-Indo-European laryngeals. In Greek and Armenian initial laryngeals before consonants leave a trace in a prothetic vowel. In the earliest Indo-Iranian a hiatus (a break between vowels so they do not occur in the same syllable) is sometimes preserved which arises from the loss of an intervocalic laryngeal. In Balto-Slavic and Germanic certain accentual and intonational phenomena can point to the former presence of laryngeals.

Indo-Europeanists normally reconstruct three distinct series of velars: the palatovelars (*$\hat{k}$, $\hat{g}$, $\hat{g}^h$*), the plain velars (*k, g, g^h*) and the labiovelars (*k^w, g^w, g^{wh}*). This reconstruction has not gone unchallenged, for until recently, it was generally believed that no single language preserved distinct reflexes of all three series. However, it has now been shown that the Anatolian language Luvian has in fact kept the reflexes of all three series apart, requiring all three to be reconstructed for Proto-Indo-European.

The position of the accent in Proto-Indo-European is reconstructible for many lexical items. However, in many forms the accent could move depending on its morphology (its paradigm), and in many cases the crucial testimony from the limited number of branches which preserve direct or indirect traces of the Proto-Indo-European accent (Balto-Slavic, Indo-Iranian, Greek, Germanic and Anatolian) is missing. For these reasons no indication of the accent has been given in the following reconstructions.

Verbal roots are cited with an inserted *e* vowel (the so-called *e*-grade), which should in principle appear in certain morphological categories. Most nouns are cited in a stem-form without case endings. (The exceptions are neuter nouns, which are cited in the nominative–accusative form, and those nouns for which a stem cannot be reconstructed with certainty. These are cited as mere roots.)

(I thank Michael Weiss for his very extensive help with these Indo-European forms and for this section generally.) The reconstructed cultural lexicon of Proto-Indo-European includes the following:

16.2.1 Agriculture

'grain'
> **yewo-* 'a grain, particularly barley'
>
> **gr̥$h_x$nom* (younger than **yewo-*, perhaps meaning 'ripened grain', which replaced **yewo-* in most of the west and centre of the IE world and competes with it in Iranian)

CROP
  'fruit'
    seso- (occurred on the margins of IE world if derived from
      the root *seh_1-* 'sow'; the reconstruction could be *$sesh_1o$-* or
        sh_1eso-)
  'barley'
    $\hat{g}^hrV(s)d(h)$- (a very problematic reconstruction)
    b^haros (confined to the northwest of the IE world)
  'wheat'
    puh_xro-
    ga/ond^h- (southern and eastern peripheries of the IE world)
  'rye'
    rug^hi- (confined to the northwest of the IE world)
  'ear of grain, chaff'
    $h_2e\hat{k}os$ (from *$h_2e\hat{k}$-* 'point, sharp')
LAND
  'field'
    $h_2e\hat{g}ro$- (probably derived from *$h_2e\hat{g}$-* 'to drive', hence originally
      'pasture'; Vedic *ájra-* still just means 'plain')
    h_2erh_3ur ~ *h_2erh_3wo-* (derived from *h_2erh_3-* 'to plough', at least late
      PIE in the west and centre of the IE world)
  'piece of land/garden'
    $\hat{k}eh_2po$-/eh_2-
  'enclosure/garden'
    g^horto- (connection with the root *$\hat{g}^her$-* 'take' uncertain)
FIELD PREPARATION AND PLANTING
  'to plough'
    h_2erh_3-
  'plough'
    h_2erh_3trom (widespread derivative of *h_2erh_3-*)
  'ploughshare'
    $wog^{wh}ni$- (at least west and centre of the IE world)
  'furrow'
    le/oiseh$_2$- (west and centre of the IE world)
  'harrow'
    h_xokete_2-
  'hoe'
    mat- (root only)
  'sow'
    seh_1-
HARVESTING
  'harvest'
    (s)kerp-
  'mow'
    h_2meh_1-
  'sickle'
    $srpo$-/eh_2-

GRAIN PROCESSING

'thresh'

    peis- (earlier meaning 'stamp, crush')

    wers- (earlier meaning perhaps 'sweep')

'winnow'

    neik- (at least late PIE)

'grind'

    melh$_2$- (agreement in various European subgroups on the agricultural sense of 'grind')

    g^{h}rend(h)- 'grind' (a somewhat problematic reconstruction; younger than *melh$_2$-*; west and centre of the IE world)

'quern'

    g^{w}réh$_2$won- ~ *g^{w}erh$_2$nu-* 'quern' (from suffixed form of *g^{w}erh$_2$-* 'heavy')

16.2.2 Domestic animals and animal husbandry

'livestock'

    pek̂u ('moveable wealth' > 'wealth')

'herdsman'

    westor- (though not widely attested, the distribution (Anatolian and Iranian) suggests great antiquity in IE probably derived from the following)

'graze'

    wes-

'guard, protect'

    peh$_2$- (to describe the herdsman's activities)

'dog'

    k̂(u)won-

'horse'

    h$_2$ek̂wo-

'larger domestic animal'

    steuro-

'pig'

    sū- or *suh$_x$-*

'boar'

    h$_1$epero- (at least west and centrel of the IE world)

'piglet'

    pork̂o-

'sheep'

    h$_2$owi-

'ram/fleece'

    moiso-

'ewe'

    h$_2$owikeh$_2$-

'lamb/kid'

    h$_1$er- (root only)

'lamb'

    h_2eg^wno- (at least the west and centre of the IE world; some prefer the
        reconstruction $h_2eg^{wh}no$-)

    $wr(h_x)en$- (centre and east of the IE world)

'goat'

    $h_2eig̑$- (centre and east of the IE world)

    g^haido- (northwest region)

'he-goat'

    $b^hug̑o$- (also male animal of various kinds, stag, ram)

    kapro-

    $h_2eg̑o$- (centre and east of the IE world)

'bovine'

    g^wou-

'bull'

    uksen-

    tauro- (possibly also 'aurochs')

'cow'

    $wakeh_2$-

'cowherd'

    $g^wouk^wolh_1o$- (at least west and centre of the IE world, based on *g^wou-*
        'cow' + *k^wolh_1o-* 'one who turns, moves' from *k^welh_1-* 'turn, move
        around')

DAIRY PRODUCTION

'to milk'

    $h_1melg̑$-

'milk'

    g(a)lakt

'coagulated' milk'

    $d^hed^hh_1e$ (at least centre and east of the IE world)

'curds'

    tuh_xro/i- (at least centre and east of the IE world)

'whey'

    $ksih_xrom$ (centre and east of the IE world)

'buttermilk'

    tenklom ~ tn̥klom (from *temk-* 'congeal')

'butter'

    $h_3eng^wn̥$ (from *h_3eng^w-* 'anoint')

'rich in milk'

    $pipih_xusih_2$- (at least centre and east of the IE world; a feminine perf.
        ptc. of the root *$peih_x$-* 'swell')

16.2.3 Foods

'salt'

    sal-

'honey'

    melit (also *$melit-ih_2$-* 'honey bee')

'mead'

 med^hu

'beer'

 $*h_2elut$- or $*alut$- (northwest of the IE world with an outlier in eastern
  Iranian; at least late IE in date)

'wine'

 $*wih_xVno$- ~$*woih_xno$- ~ wih_xnom (related to words for wine in non-Indo-
  European Georgian and West Semitic; the ultimate relationship
  between these forms is unclear)

'apple'

 $*h_2ebVl$- (late PIE ?)

 $*meh_2lom$ (or any seed- or pit-bearing fruit)

'cherry'

 $krnes$- ~ $*krnom$ 'cornel cherry'

'fruit /berry'

 $*h_2ogeh_2$-

 $*h_xoiweh_2$- (at least west and centre of the IE world)

'blackberry, mulberry'

 $*morom$

'bean'

 $*b^hab^heh_2$- (at least west and centre of the IE world with variant $*b^ha\text{-}un$
  in Germanic)

'porridge'

 $*plt$- ~ $polto$- (late IE of the west and centre?)

'broth'

 $*yuh_x$- 'broth'

16.2.4 Economy and commerce

'exchange'

 $*mei$- (extended form $*meit$-'to change, go, move'; with derivatives
  referring to the exchange of goods and services within a society as
  regulated by custom or law)

'to sell'

 $*perh_2$- (at least of late IE status)

'to buy'

 $*wes$-

'purchase'

 $*wVs\text{-}no$- (derived from the above)

'payment, prize'

 $*h_2elg^{wh}o\text{-}/eh_2$- (derived from $*h_2elg^{wh}$- 'to earn, be worth')

'gift'

 $*deh_3rom$ (derived from $*deh_3$- 'give')

'apportion, get a share'

 $*b^hag$-

'wealth'

 $*h_3ep$-

16.2.5   Legal terms

'law'

d^heh_1ti- 'thing laid down or done, law, deed' (derived from *d^heh_1-* 'to set, put')

$yewos$ 'religious law, ritual, norm'

'plead a case'

$(h_1)arg^w$-

'guilty'

h_1sont- (literally 'being' the present participle of the verb *h_1es-* 'be')

'penalty'

k^woineh_2- (derived from *k^wei-* 'to pay, atone, compensate')

'make whole'

$serk$- (legal expression 'to pay for damages')

16.2.6   Transport

'yoke'

$yugom$ (derived from *$yeug$-* 'to yoke')

'wagon'

$we/oĝ^hno$- (derived from *$weĝ^h$-* 'to go, transport in a vehicle')

'wheel'

$h_2wr̥g$- (root only; reflexes in Hittite and Tocharian suggest antiquity derived from *h_2werg-* 'turn')

$roteh_2$- (derived from *ret-* 'to run, roll'; old PIE word for 'wheel', derivatives came to mean 'wagon' or 'war-chariot' in a number of eastern subgroups)

k^wek^wlom (probably from the root *k^welh_1-*)

'axle'

$h_2ek̂s$-

'shaft' (of a cart or wagon)

$h_{2/3}eih_1os$ ~ $h_{2/3}(e)ih_1so$-

'pole/peg'

d^hur- 'pivot of door or gate, axle of a chariot, harness, means of harnessing a horse to a cart, pole, yoke, peg of axle'

'reins'

$h_2ensiyo$-/eh_2- (the equivalence in form and meaning in Greek and Irish is evidence of PIE antiquity)

'boat'

neh_2us derived from the verb *neh_2-* 'float' *h_xold^hu-* '(dugout) canoe, trough' (probably late PIE)

'row'

h_1erh_1-

16.2.7   Technology (other tools and implements)

'craftsman'

d^hab^hro- (from *d^hab^h-* 'to fit together')

'metal'
'craft'
    *kerdos
'metal'
    *h₂ey(o)s (often specialized as 'copper' or 'bronze')
'gold'
    *h₂eusom
'silver'
    *h₂erĝntom 'white (metal), silver' (based on **h₂erĝ-* 'white')
TOOLS
'axe'
    *(h₁)adʰes- or **h₁odʰes-?*
'spit, spear'
    *gʰeru (presence in Avestan, Celtic and Italic strongly suggests it was once widespread in PIE)
'auger'
    *terh₁trom (derived from **terh₁-* 'to rub, turn')
'awl'
    *hₓoleh₂-
'whetstone'
    *ĥohₓno- ~ *ĥohₓini- (limited distribution, from PIE **ĥehₓ(i)* sharpen, hone', which is widespread)
'net'
    *h₁ekt-

16.2.8 House and building(s)

'to build'
    *demh₂-
'carpenter'
    *tetĥˀon- (derived from **teĥ-* 'create')
'house'
    *dom-
    *domh₂o- (both derived from **demh₂-* 'build')
'hearth'
    *h₂ehₓseh₂-
'door'
    *dʰwor-
'doorjamb'
    *h₂enhₓt(e)h₂
'roof'
    *(s)tegos (derived from **(s)teg-* 'cover')
    *h₁rebʰ- 'cover with a roof'
'room'
    *ket- (root only)
'beam/plank'
    *bhelh₂ĝ- (at least west and centre of the IE world)
    *kḷh₂ro- (late IE)

'dwelling, settlement'

    *wastu, *wāstu-* (not related to *h_2wes- 'spend the night')

    treb- (west and centre of the IE world)

HOUSEHOLD

'cualdron'

    k^weru-

'dish'

    potr̥

'plate'

    tek̂steh₂- (an Iranian-Italic match)

'cup'

    peh₃tlom (derived from *peh₃(i)-* 'to drink')

'bed'

    *legʰos ~ *logʰo-* (derived from *legʰ-* 'to lie, lay')

16.2.9 Clothing and textiles

'wool'

    h₂wl̥h₁neh₂-

'comb'

    kes- (early meaning probably 'put in order')

    kars- (the meaning 'comb (wool)' is found only in European languages)

'spin'

    sneh₁- 'twist fibres together to form thread; occupy oneself with thread'

    spenh₁- (earlier meaning 'stretch'; the specialization of 'working with thread' must be at least late IE)

'braid'

    plek̂-

'plait'

    resg-

'twist'

    weih$_x$-

'weave'

    h$_x$eu-

    webʰ- 'weave' (in later PIE)

    tek(s)-

'sew'

    syeuh$_x$-

'fasten'

    (s)ner- 'fasten with thread or cord' (a late PIE word at least)

'thread'

    dek̂- (root only; probably the oldest which can be reconstructed whose meaning subsumes 'thread')

'sinew'

    g^{wh}ih$_x$slo-

'wear'

    wes-

'skin bag'

    $*b^h ol\hat{g}^h i$- (derived from $*b^h el\hat{g}^h$- 'to swell')

16.2.10 Warfare and fortification

'war-band'

    $*koryo$- ~ $koro$- (at least from the west and centre of the IE world)

'hold/conquer'

    $*se\hat{g}^h$-

'citadel'

    $*pelh_x$- (of the centre and east of the IE world, at least)

'hillfort'

    $*b^h \underset{.}{r}\hat{g}^h$- (derived from $*b^h er\hat{g}^h$- 'high')

'fort'

    $*wriyo\text{-}/eh_2$-

'booty'

    $*soru$ (particularly men, cattle and sheep)

'sword'

    $*h_{2/3}\underset{.}{n}si$-

'spear'

    $*\hat{g}^h ais\text{-}o$-

'spear-point'

    $*\hat{k}el(hx)$- (root only)

16.2.11 Social structure and social interaction

'master'

    $*poti$-

'housemaster'

    $*dems\text{-}pot(i)$-

'household/village'

    $*\hat{k}oimo$- (west and centre of the IE world)

'member of a household'

    $*\hat{k}eiwo$-

'group'

    $*wi\hat{k}$- (a settlement unit composed of a number of extended fam- ilies which was later extended to the complex of buildings they occupied and, later still, to the socio-political unit) derived from PIE $*wei\hat{k}$- 'to settle')

'groupmaster'

    $*wi\hat{k}\text{-}pot(i)$- (at least of the centre and east of the IE world)

'family'

    $*\hat{g}enh_1 os$ (derived from $*\hat{g}enh_1$- 'to give birth, beget')

'people'

    $*teuteh_2$-

'member of one's group'

    $*(h_1)aro$- ~ $*(h_1)aryo$- 'self-designation of the Indo-Iranians' (perhaps derived from $*(h_1)ar$- 'to fit') 'dear'

    prih$_x$o- (in west of IE world 'free'; from *preih$_x$-* 'delight')

'king'

    h$_3$rēĝs (derived from *h$_3$reĝ-* 'to move in a straight line' with derivatives meaning 'to direct in a straight line, lead, rule')

'rule'

    welh$_x$- (earlier meaning 'be strong')

    med- 'to apply the appropriate measures' (sometimes special- ized in medical sense)

'free'

    h$_1$leud^{h}ero- 'free born' (derived from *h$_1$leud^h-* 'to mount up, grow')

'stranger, guest/host'

    g^{h}osti- 'someone with whom one has reciprocal duties of hospi- tality' (an outsider could be considered both guest and potential foe)

'servant'

    h$_2$entb^{h}i-k^{w}olh$_1$o- (compound, *h$_2$entb^{h}i-* 'on either side, around'+ *k^{w}olh$_1$o-*, from *k^{w}elh$_1$-* 'turn, move round in a circle')

'dowry'

    h$_2$wedmno- (west and centre of the IE world)

'one's own custom'

    swed^h- 'custom, characteristic, individuality' (connected in particular to reciprocal and contractual relationships, including poet–patron relations and other gift exchanges; from *swe-* 'third person pronoun and reflexive', appearing in various forms referring to the social group as an entity)

'fame'

    ĝlewos- (literally 'what is heard' derived from *ĝleu-* 'to hear')

'poet/seer'

    weh$_2$t- (as 'poet' confined to west of the IE world (Greek and Indo-Iranian provide evidence of a PIE *wekwos tetĝon-* 'fashion speech')

16.2.12 Religion and beliefs

'holy'

    ish$_1$ro-

    sakro- (derived from *sak-* 'to sanctify')

    ĝwen(to)-

    noib^{h}o-

DIVINITIES

'god'

    deiwo- (derivative of *dyeu-* 'daylight sky god of daylight sky' itself a derivative of a root *dei-* 'shine')

'sky-father' nom

    dyeusp$_2$tēr VOC., *dyeu-ph$_2$ter* 'o father Jove' (cf. Jupiter, Zeus) (compound of *dyeu-* 'Jove, god of the daylight sky, head of the Indo-European pantheon' + *ph$_2$ter* 'father')

PRAYER

  'pray'

    $pre\hat{k}$-

    $meld^h$-

    $g^{wh}ed^h$-

  'speak solemnly'

    h_1weg^{wh}-

  'call/invoke'

    $\hat{g}^heuh_x$- (perhaps English *god* < *$\hat{g}^hu$-to-* from 'that which is invoked', but derivation from *$\hat{g}^hu$-to-* 'libated' from *$\hat{g}^heu$-* 'libate, pour' is also possible)

  'priest, seer/poet'

    $kowh_xei$-

CULT PRACTICE

  'worship'

    $h_xia\hat{g}$-

  'consecrate'

    weik- (earlier meaning perhaps 'to separate')

  'handle reverently'

    sep-

  'libate'

    spend-

    $\hat{g}^heu$-, *$\hat{g}^heu$-mṇ* 'libation'

  'sacrificial meal'

    dapnom derived from *dap-* 'to apportion (in exchange)'

  'meal'

    $tolko/eh_2$- (at least late PIE)

  'sacred grove'

    nemos (west and center of the IE world)

  'sacred enclosure'

    $werb^h$- (attestation in Anatolian, Tocharian and probably Italic suggests antiquity)

SUPERNATURAL

  'magical glory'

    keudos

  'sorcery'

    $(h_1)alu$-

  'phantom'

    d^hroug^ho- (from *d^hreug^h-* 'deceive')

  'dragon'

    $dṛ\hat{k}ont$- (from *$der\hat{k}$-* 'see', from the dangerous, potentially lethal, gaze of dragons)

The implications of Indo-European linguistic research were seldom ignored by archaeologists working in the area; they frequently took linguistic hypotheses into account in framing their own research. Archaeology and linguistics have contributed reciprocally in famous cases of Old World ancient history where, for example, archaeology brought forth the tablets and documents of such places as Boğazköy (in modern Turkey), Knossos (on Crete), Tel El Amarna (in Egypt) and so on, and then scholars with linguistic skills deciphered and translated them, pushing back the recorded history of this part of the world by several millennia. Such decipherments also contributed to the picture of which languages were spoken, when and where they were spoken, and how they are classified. For example, the picture of the Indo-European family was radically revised by the addition of the languages of the Anatolian branch (in which Hittite is of major importance), which came to light through these discoveries and decipherments. Successful interaction to the mutual benefit of both archaeology and linguistics is perhaps not surprising for cultures with ancient writing systems, which provide written documentation of ancient history. However, linguistic prehistory is able to contribute significantly to cases which lack writing, and indeed it has contributed much to the interpretation of the prehistory of many other regions of the world.

16.3   The Methods of Linguistic Prehistory

Virtually any aspect of linguistics which renders information with historical content or implications for historical interpretations can be valuable in linguistic prehistory. Let's consider some of these and see how they work in specific examples.

16.3.1   The cultural inventory of reconstructed vocabulary

As we saw in the Indo-European case study (above), much information about the culture and society of the speakers of a proto-language can be recovered from the reconstructed vocabulary. Here we look at a few other cases, where the cultural inventory of the reconstructed vocabulary has been investigated. In these cases, only the glosses of the items that have been reconstructed in these proto-languages are given. (For the actual forms and details of the studies, see the references cited after each case.)

16.3.1.1   *Proto-Finno-Ugric and Proto-Uralic culture*
Uralic is a language family of about forty-five languages spoken across northern Eurasia. It includes the various Samoyed languages, Saamic (Lapp) languages, Finnish, Estonian, Hungarian and many others (see Map 16.1 and Figure 6.2: The Uralic Family tree, in Chapter 6). Studies have dealt with both older Proto-Uralic culture and younger Proto-Finno-Ugric culture based on the reconstructed vocabulary, though these are difficult (perhaps impossible) to separate based on the evidence. We look at each, in turn.

16.3.1.1.1   Proto-Uralic culture
Kaisa Häkkinen (2001) finds in the vocabulary reflecting Proto-Uralic culture thirty-one animal and animal-related terms, seventeen terms for transport, traffic

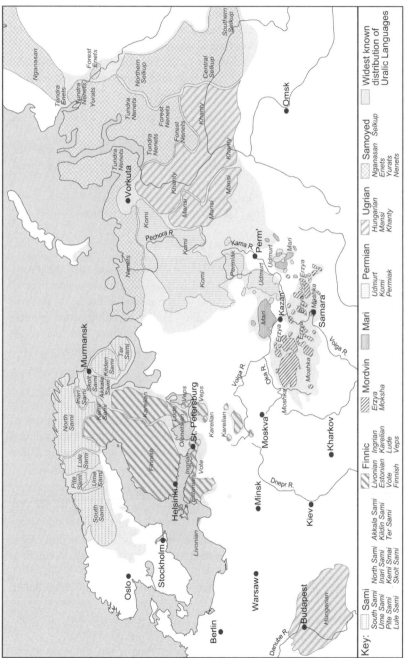

MAP 16.1: The Uralic languages (redrawn after Grünthal and Salminen 1993)

and motion, five for water and water systems, nine hunting and fishing terms, six for buildings, constructions and equipment, two for foodstuffs and four for dishes and food preparation, sixteen for family and personal relationships, twenty-two for tools, work and work implements, and two for clothing. Analysis of the cultural inventory of reconstructed Proto-Uralic vocabulary (based on Sammallahti's 1988 rigorously constrained reconstructions) reveals aspects of the life of a Stone Age hunting and gathering people. Bearers of Proto-Uralic culture knew and presumably utilized the following things which reflect their culture:

> *Hunting, fishing and food terms*: bow, arrow, bowstring, knife; egg, fish, berry, bird-cherry (?), hare, to pursue/hunt, track.
>
> *Other tools, implements, clothing and technology*: needle, belt, glue, birch-bark, drill, cord/rope, handle, (lodge)pole, bark/leather, enclosure/fence, metal, to braid, shaft, to cook.
>
> *Travel and transport*: ski, to row, fathom, cross-rail (in boat).
>
> *Climate and environment*: snow, lake, river, wave, summer/thaw, water.
>
> *Commerce*: to give/sell.
>
> (Cf. Sammallahti 1988, Janhunen 1981.)

From such evidence, Péter Hajdú (1975: 51–9) concluded that the Proto-Uralic people were engaged in hunting and fishing, with close connections to water. Their food was mostly fish and game. They travelled in boats, on skis and in sleighs. Hajdú doubts they were involved in reindeer breeding, since reindeer breeding is fairly recent, but believes, rather, that wild reindeer was 'one of the most important prizes for the hunter' (Hajdú 1975: 54; see also various papers in Fogelberg 1999; Campbell 1997b).

16.3.1.1.2 Proto-Finno-Ugric culture

The reconstructed Proto-Finno-Ugric vocabulary is more extensive than that of its parent, Proto-Uralic, and provides a somewhat better picture of the cultural inventory of the speakers of the proto-language. It inherited all that was in Proto-Uralic culture (listed above) plus it had the following:

> *Fishing*: spawn, net, to fish with a net, gill/mouth, raft/loft (?), netting needle, ide (fish species), tench (fish species), fish skin/scales, crossrail (in boat), loon, duck, wall/dam.
>
> *Hunting and animal foods*: spear, drive, track/trace, to skin/flay, horn, marrow, (domestic) animal (?), grouse, tallow, hunting party, to catch, to shoot/hit, to rut, goose/bird.
>
> *Plant and other foods*: broth/soup, two berry species, honey, bee, butter, mushroom.
>
> *Technology* (tools and implements): birch-bark vessel, knife, rope, to grind, pole, (soft) metal, gold (?), to sew, knife, pot, rope, needle, net.
>
> *Building and household items*: canopy, bed, house/hut, scoop, pot, shelter, hut/ house, board, to cook, pole.
>
> *Clothing*: sleeve, glove, to sew.
>
> *Climate amd environment*: ice crust, frost, ice, to melt, sleigh (sled), to snow,

ski, winter, summer, autumn, bog, to sink, lake/flood, flood soak, down-
river, stream.
Social structure and society: lord, orphan.
Religion and beliefs: soul, spirit, ghost, idol/village.
Commerce: to buy, value/price/worth, to give/sell.
(Cf. Sammallahti 1988)

There is no evidence of agriculture in Proto-Uralic and its existence in Proto-
Finno-Ugric culture is also generally doubted. Reasonably widespread terms for
'wheat' and 'grain' are encountered, though mostly as diffused loanwords. Hajdú
(1975: 57) believes that Proto-Finno-Ugric speakers did not know agriculture
based on the lack of reconstructible names for implements and processes connected with agriculture; for example, no word for 'sowing', 'reaping', 'scythe',
'hoe' and so on can be traced to Proto-Finno-Ugric (Fogelberg 1999; Campbell
1997b.) He believes that 'pig' and probably also 'sheep' were known through
contact with Indo-European neighbours, but that pig breeding began only later.
In the realm of religion, Hajdú thinks that ancestor worship and gods in natural
phenomena were typical (Hajdú 1975: 58). He finds animism suggested by cognates for: (1) 'evil spirit', 'lord (of underworld)', 'giant' (with compounds found
in disease names), and (2) 'spirit, fall into a trance', though not all of these are
fully accepted as cognates. (Cf. Campbell 1997b.)

16.3.1.2 *Proto-Mayan culture*
Mayan is a family of thirty-one languages, argued to have begun to separate at
around 2200 BC. Both the linguistic and the non-linguistic prehistory of Mayan-
speaking peoples has been intensively investigated, perhaps because of the
romantic appeal of Classical Maya civilization. The cultural inventory reflected
in the reconstructed vocabulary of Proto-Mayan includes the following:

Maize complex: maize, corncob, ear of corn, roasting ear, atole (a corn drink),
    to sow, to harvest, to grind, metate (grindstone for corn), to roast (grains),
    flour, lime (used to leach corn kernel).
Other cultivated plants/food plants: avocado, chili pepper, sapodilla, custard
    apple, sweet manioc, squash, sweet potato, bean, achiote (bixa, a food-
    colouring condiment), century plant, cotton, tobacco, cigar.
Animals: dog, jaguar, opossum, mouse, gopher, armadillo, cougar, squirrel,
    deer, weasel, coyote, skunk, fox, bird, crow, vulture, hummingbird, owl,
    bat, hawk, flea, bee, honey, fly, gnat, ant, louse, spider, tick, butterfly,
    bumblebee/wasp, scorpion, toad, fish, worm, snake, snail, crab, alligator,
    monkey, quetzal.
Trees and other plants: nettle, vine, willow, oak, cypress, pine, palm, silk-
    cotton tree (ceiba).
Religion and ritual: god/holy, writing, paper, evil spirit/witch, priest, sing/
    dance, drum/music, rattle, tobacco (used ritually).
Social structure: lord, slave/tribute.
Implements (and other technology): water gourd, trough/canoe, bench, cord,
    mat, road, house, home, whetstone, axe, toy, hammock, sandals, trousers,
    to sew, spindle.

Economy and commerce: to pay, to lose, to sell, poor, market, town (Campbell and Kaufman 1985; Kaufman 1976).

16.3.1.3 *Proto-Mixe-Zoquean culture*

Mixe-Zoquean is a family of some twenty languages spoken in southern Mexico in the region across the Isthmus of Tehuantepec. It is assumed to have been unified until about 1500 BC, and is considered to be of great cultural significance in the region, since it is argued that bearers of the Olmec archaeological culture (the earliest civilization in the region) were speakers of Mixe-Zoquean languages (see below). The reconstructed vocabulary reveals the following cultural inventory:

Maize complex: corn field, to clear land, to sow, to harvest, seed, maize, to grind corn, leached corn, corncob, corn gruel, to grind grains, to shell corn, lime (used to soften kernels of corn for grinding).

Other cultivated plants (and food plants): chili pepper, bean, tomato, sweet potato, manioc, a tuber (species); chokecherry, custard apple, avocado, sapote, coyol palm, guava, cacao.

Animals and procurement of animal resources: deer, rabbit, coati-mundi, honey, bee; fish, crab, to fish with a hook, to fish with a net, canoe.

Religion and ritual: holy, incense, knife-axe (used in sacrifice), to write, to count/divine/adore, to dance, to play music, ceremony, year, twenty, bundle of 400, tobacco, cigar, to smoke tobacco (tobacco was used ceremonially).

Commerce: to sell, to pay, to cost, to buy.

Technology: to spin thread, agave fibre, to twist rope/thread, hammock, cord, water gourd, gourd dish, ladder, house, house pole, adobe wall, rubber, ring, arrow, bed, to plane wood, sandals; remedy-liquor (Campbell and Kaufman 1976; Justeson et al. 1985).

16.3.1.4 *Cautions about reconstructed vocabulary*

Textbooks are fond of repeating warnings about anachronistic reconstructions, which can complicate cultural interpretation based on the reconstructed vocabulary. For example, Bloomfield, in his reconstruction of Proto-Central Algonquian, found cognates which seemed to support reconstructions for a couple of items which were unknown before contact with Europeans, for example 'whisky'. It turns out that the different languages had created names based on the same compound, 'fire'+ 'water' (for example, Cree *iskote:w-a:poy*, composed of *iskote:w* 'fire' + *a:poy* 'water, liquid'), and this 'firewater' compound found in each of the languages looked like a valid cognate set to support the reconstruction, though it is due either to independent parallel development or to diffusion of a loan translation (calque) among these languages. We have no secure guarantees against such anachronisms entering our cultural interpretations of the past based on reconstructed vocabulary, although we rely on clues from our knowledge of what things were introduced by Europeans and on the criterion which we will see directly (below) that the age of analyzable terms (ones with multiple morphemes) is not as secure as that of unanalyzable terms (those composed of but a single morpheme). In actual cases, this problem comes up rarely; that is, it is not as serious as it might at first appear to be.

16.3.2 Linguistic homeland and linguistic migration theory

A question which has been of great interest in the study of many language families, and especially of Indo-European, is that of the geographical location of the speakers of the proto-language. Two different techniques have been utilized in attempts to determine where speakers of proto-languages lived, that is, where the linguistic 'homeland' (*Urheimat*) of the family was located. We consider each in turn.

16.3.2.1 Homeland clues in the reconstructed vocabulary

The first technique seeks geographical and ecological clues from the reconstructed vocabulary which are relevant to the location of where the proto-language was spoken, especially clues from reconstructed terms for plants and animals. In this approach, attempts are made to find out what the prehistoric geographical distributions were of plants and animals for which we can successfully reconstruct terms in the proto-language, and then these are plotted on a map. The area where the greatest number of these reconstructible plants' and animals' ranges intersect is taken to be the probable homeland of the language family. We will see how this works in the examples considered below.

For the prehistoric geographical distributions of the plants and animals involved, the information which palaeobotany, biology or other fields can provide is relied on. Due to climatic changes and other factors during the last few thousand years, the range of plants and animals is often not the same today as it was in former times. For example, earlier it was argued, based on the reconstruction of **bherəĝ-* (**bherh₁ĝ-*) 'birch', that the Proto-Indo-European homeland lay north of the 'birch line' (where birches grow) which today runs roughly from Bordeaux (France) to Bucharest (Romania). However, this interpretation failed; the birch has shifted its habitat significantly over time and formerly extended considerably to the south, and furthermore it has always been present in the Caucasus region (Friedrich 1970: 30). That is, to locate the birch's distribution during Proto-Indo-European times, we must rely on the results of palynology (the study of ancient pollens). While the case of the birch's earlier distribution is clear, this can make matters difficult, since palynological information may not yet be available for some of the regions in question. Also, in many cases we may have only the roughest of estimates concerning the time when the proto-language was spoken. It is difficult to correlate the distribution of ancient plants based on palynology and of languages without some idea of the period of time at which their respective distributions are being correlated (Friedrich 1970).

16.3.2.2 Linguistic migration theory

The other technique for getting at linguistic homelands – called *linguistic migration theory* – looks at the classification (subgrouping) of the family and the geographical distribution of the languages, and, relying on a model of maximum diversity and minimal moves, hypothesizes the most likely location of the original homeland. The underlying assumption is that when a language family splits up, it is more likely for the various daughter languages to stay close to where they started out and it is less likely for them to move very far or very frequently. Therefore, turning this process around, if we look at today's geographical distribution of related languages, we can hypothesize how they got to where they are now and where they came from. This procedure deals not with just the geographical spread of the languages of the family, but rather with the distribution of members of subgroups within the family. The highest branches on a family tree (the earliest splits in the family) reflect the greatest age, and therefore the area with the greatest linguistic diversity – that is, with the most representatives of the higher-order subgroups – is likely to be the homeland. This is sometimes called the *centre of gravity* model (after Sapir 1949 [1916]: 455). Lower-level branches (those which break up later) are also important, because they may allow us to postulate the direction of later migration or spread of members of the family. In this model, we attempt to determine the minimum number of moves which would be required to reverse these migrations or spreads to bring the languages back to the centre of gravity of their closest relatives within their individual subgroups, and then to move the various different subgroups back to the location from which their later distribution can be accounted for with the fewest moves. In this way, by combining the location of maximum diversity and the minimum moves to get languages back to the location of the greatest diversity of their nearest relatives, we hypothesize the location of the homeland.

Let's consider some of the better-known cases in which these two techniques have been employed in order to get a feel for how they work.

16.3.2.3 *Proto-Indo-European homeland*

There is a very large literature on the question of the Proto-Indo-European homeland (see Mallory 1989, Mallory and Adams 1997: 290–9, 2006: 442–63). While there are a number of competing hypotheses, most mainstream historical linguists favour the view which places the Proto-Indo-European homeland somewhere in the Pontic steppes-Caspian region. The evidence for this comes from linguistic migration theory, interpretation of geographical and ecological clues in the reconstructed vocabulary of the proto-language, loans and the location of their neighbours from whom they borrowed, and attempted correlations with archaeology (though the archaeological interpretations are subject to dispute).

Proto-Indo-European tree names have been at the centre of some homeland considerations, and Proto-Indo-European *bhāǵo (*bheh₂ǵo) 'beech' has been given much weight. It was thought that beech did not grow to the east of a line running from Königsberg (in East Prussia) to Odessa (in the Crimea). This would seem to place constraints on the location of the Proto-Indo-European homeland, locating it essentially in Europe. However, there are various difficulties with this. There are doubts about the original meaning of the word; the cognates do not all refer to the same tree; Greek *phēgós* means 'oak' and the Slavic forms mean some sort of 'elder', as for example Russian *buziná* 'elder(berry)'; and no reflexes are known from Asiatic Indo-European languages. If *bhāǵo-* did not originally mean 'beech', then arguments based on the distribution of beeches in Proto-Indo-European times would not be relevant. There are phonological problems in that the sounds in the putative cognates for 'beech' in some branches of the family do not correspond as they should. Finally, two species of beech are involved and the eastern or Caucasian beech was (and still is) present in the Caucasus and extended to the east. Therefore, many Indo-European groups would have been familiar with it, not just those of Europe west of the infamous Königsberg–Odessa line (Friedrich 1970: 106–15). The problem with the arguments for the homeland based on this distribution of 'birch' was mentioned already above (16.3.2.1); the current distribution of birches is not the same as it was in Proto-Indo-European times, and this nullifies the original argument.

Another important participant in the discussion has been Proto-Indo-European *loks-* 'salmon', which was formerly thought to have a limited distribution, involving rivers which flowed into the Baltic Sea – this was seen as indicating a Northern European homeland. However, the original meaning of the word appears to include not only 'salmon' but species of salmon-like trout which are found in a very wide distribution which also includes the Pontic steppes and Caspian region, the current best candidate for the homeland (Mallory 1989: 160–1).

The centre of gravity model, when applied to Indo-European, also suggests this area. (For details of other hypotheses for the Indo-European homeland, see Mallory and Adams 1997: 290–9, 2006: 442–63.)

16.3.2.4 *Proto-Algonquian homeland*

Frank Siebert (1967) found some twenty Proto-Algonquian terms for plants and animals whose distributions overlap in southern Ontario; these animal terms are included among the various ones reconstructed for Proto-Algonquian: golden eagle, pileated woodpecker, oldsquaw, common raven, quail, ruffed grouse, kingfisher, common loon, nighthawk, sawbill duck, seal, raccoon, lynx, squirrel, flying squirrel, moose, porcupine, skunk, fox, bear, woodchuck (groundhog), buffalo (bison), caribou, buck, fawn, beaver, muskrat, weasel, mink, white spruce, tamarack (larch), white ash, conifer–evergreen tree, elm, alder, basswood (linden), sugar maple, beech, willow, quaking aspen; black bass, lake trout, northern pike and brown bullhead. From this he concluded that the original homeland lay between Lake Huron and Georgian Bay and the middle course of the Ottawa River, bounded by Lake Nipissing and the northern shore of Lake Ontario. Dean Snow (1976) reconsidered the Proto-Algonquian homeland focusing on only the names of species whose ranges were most sharply defined; these included five tree names and six animal terms. This resulted in a broader homeland than Siebert had defined, a homeland defined most clearly by the overlap in the territories of the 'beech' and 'tamarack' – the Great Lakes lowlands east of Lake Superior, the St Lawrence valley, New England and Maritime Canada. This was bounded on the west by the Niagara Falls in order to accommodate the reconstructed word for 'harbour seal'. This constitutes a large hunting and trapping zone for nomadic bands. (Considerations mentioned below give a different picture of the Proto-Algonquian homeland.)

16.3.2.5 *Proto-Uto-Aztecan homeland*

For the Uto-Aztecan family, the results are interesting but not so definitive. Early work on the Proto-Uto-Aztecan homeland had suggested the region between the Gila River and the northern mountains of north-west Mexico, though later work showed that not all the items upon which this conclusion was based could actually be reconstructed in Proto-Uto-Aztecan. Terms which can be reliably reconstructed include, among others, 'pine', 'reed/cane' and 'prickly pear cactus', upon which considerable attention has been focused. Based on nine certain reconstructions and eighteen less secure but likely reconstructed terms, the Proto-Uto-Aztecan homeland was interpreted to be in 'a mixed woodland/grassland setting, in proximity to montane forests', and this fits a region across south-eastern California, Arizona and north-western Mexico (see Map 16.2) (Fowler 1983).

MAP 16.2: The Uto-Aztecan homeland (redrawn after Fowler 1983: 233)

The results for the Proto-Numic homeland, however, are much more precise. Numic is a subgroup of Uto-Aztecan (to which Shoshone, Ute and Comanche belong, as well as several others from southern California to Oregon and across the Great Basin into the Great Plains). Catherine Fowler (1972: 119) found that

The homeland area for Proto-Numic . . . must have been diverse in elevation, allowing for stands of pine and pinyon, but also for such mid- to low-altitude forms as cottonwood, oaks, chia, cholla and tortoises; two, the homeland area was probably in or near desert zones capable of supporting prickly pear, chia, lycium, ephedra, cholla, tortoise, . . . three, based on the presence of proto-forms for cane, crane, heron, mud-hen, tule [reeds], cattail and fish, the area probably contained marshes or some other substantial water sources.

She concludes that the Proto-Numic homeland was in Southern California slightly west of Death Valley.

16.3.2.6 *Proto-Salishan homeland*

Salishan is a family of twenty-three languages spoken on the north-west coast of North America and into the interior as far as Montana and Idaho. From more than 140 reconstructed plant and animal terms in Proto-Salishan, most of which occur throughout the area and thus are of less value in localizing the homeland, M. Dale Kinkade (1991: 143) determined that some 'two dozen represent species found only on the coast, and hence suggest a coastal, rather than an interior, homeland for the Salish'. These terms include 'harbour seal', 'whale', 'cormorant', 'band-tailed pigeon', 'seagull' (two terms), 'flounder', 'perch', 'smelt' (two terms), 'barnacle', 'horse clam', 'littleneck clam', 'cockle', 'oyster', 'sea cucumber', 'sea urchin', 'red elderberry', 'bracken fern', 'bracken root', 'sword fern', 'wood fern', 'red huckleberry' (two terms), 'salal' (a plant), 'salmonberry' (two terms), 'seaweed', 'red cedar' and 'yew' (Kinkade 1991: 144). Several of these strongly suggest a coastal origin, but not all are equally good as evidence. The terms for 'band-tailed pigeon', 'oyster', 'barnacle', 'sea urchin' and 'flounder' would be supportive, but 'similar forms occur widely throughout the area in several non-Salishan languages and may in the long run turn out to be loanwords; for example, "sea cucumber" and "seaweed" were probably borrowed from neighbouring Wakashan languages' (Kinkade 1991: 147). Proto-Salishan speakers, with their coastal homeland, 'must also have had access to mountains, in particular the Cascade Mountains, because they had names for mountain goats and hoary marmots, both of which are found only at higher elevations' (Kinkade 1991: 147). Based on the distribution of 'bobcats' (not far up the Fraser River) and 'porcupines' and 'lynx' (which did not extend past southern Puget Sound) – for which Proto-Salishan terms are reconstructible – the homeland is further pinpointed:

> extend[ing] from the Fraser River southward at least to the Skagit River and possibly as far south as the Stillaguamish or Skykomish rivers . . . From west to east, their territory would have extended from the Strait of Georgia and Admiralty Inlet to the Cascade Mountains. An arm of the family probably extended up the Fraser River through the Fraser Canyon. (Kinkade 1991: 148)

16.3.2.7 *Uralic and Finno-Ugric homeland*

Much research has been done on the Proto-Uralic and the Proto-Finno-Ugric homelands. and their identification is on firmer footing than that of Proto-Indo-European (Mallory 2001: 345). These homeland studies often did not distinguish between Proto-Uralic and Proto-Finno-Ugric (a daughter of Proto-Uralic), and many scholars place the homeland of both in the same location. Information from linguistics, archaeology, human genetics and other areas of knowledge has been correlated, generally interpreted in more or less consistent ways, but in hypotheses that differ in their details. For example, the Uralic peoples today have no common culture and are genetically diverse – all Uralic-speaking peoples have received cultural and genetic traits from several directions, in several cases sharing more with non-Uralic neighbours than with other Uralic groups.

Study of the Finno-Ugric homeland has an ample history, though earlier proposals assigning the homeland to central Asia, southern Europe and the like, now have few supporters. The main candidates differ from one another mainly according to the size assumed for the area of the original homeland. They include: (1) the region of the middle course of the Volga River and its tributaries; (2) the region of the northern Urals on both sides of the mountains; (3) the central and southern Urals on both sides; (4) rather eastward on the Asian side of the Urals; (5) rather westward on the European side; (6) the broad area between the Urals and the Baltic Sea. There is actually considerable agreement in these views, since the areas represented are near one another and partially overlapping (Korhonen 1984 and Suhonen 1999; see Map 16.1).

Plant and animal terms have been presented as supporting evidence for hypothesis (1), which is widely held, that the homeland was in the region of the Middle Volga. In view (4), also widely held, the homeland would have been further east and north, between the Urals and the Volga-Kama-Pechora area or on both sides of the Ural Mountains. Supporters of candidate (6) believe that the Proto-Uralic population, at least in its final phases and perhaps also the Proto-Finno-Ugric population, may have occupied a wide area from the Urals to the Baltic Sea, based on the notion that hunting and fishing groups need to exploit wide territories for their subsistence. Ethnographic analogies from subarctic peoples of both the Old and New Worlds have been called upon for supporting evidence, with examples of some reindeer and caribou hunters who travel over 1,000 kilometres twice yearly as they follow the migrating herds of deer (Sammallahti 1984, Mallory 2001). Mikko Korhonen (1984: 63) was of the opinion that while hunting societies typically exploit wide ranges, the proto-language could not have remained unified for long if the speakers were spread from the Ural Mountains to the Baltic. For Korhonen, such a picture could be true, if at all, only briefly at the very end of the unified Finno-Ugric period – the earlier homeland would need to be sought in a smaller area. Pekka Sammallahti (1984: 153), on the other hand, points out that a journey from Lake Ladoga (in the Baltic region) to the Urals (c. 1,200 km) is no longer than from one extreme of Saami territory to the other (c. 1,500 km), and he therefore supposes that a Proto-Uralic or Proto-Finno-Ugric population could have lived in the area between Finland and the Urals and still have maintained a relative linguistic unity (see also Mallory 2001). Hajdú argues that fishing kept the Finno-Ugric people to relatively fixed bases, that 'their manner of life offers no reason for extending their homeland as far as the Baltic' (1975: 38). In any event, most scholars assume that the relative homogeneity of the family was broken up by the introduction of Neolithic techniques and agriculture from areas south of the Proto-Uralic and Proto-Finno-Ugric homeland, and that the onset of farming and cattle herding – factors contributing to sedentarism – probably contributed to diversification of the family. Sammallahti points to the uniformity of practically all the paleolithic cultures between the Baltic Sea and the Ural Mountains, which might suggest a linguistic unity, with all the languages of the area perhaps members of a single language family. As long as there were no surplus-producing cultures anywhere nearby, communication among groups was confined to a common ecological (and perhaps cultural) zone, and unity may have been maintained over wide areas by marriage patterns in which spouses as well as linguistic innovations moved from one community to another. However, with the emergence of surplus-producing cultures to the south of the Uralic area, communication was reoriented from latitudinal change to longitudinal change. Longitudinal communication (and weaker latitudinal exchange) caused the ultimate disintegration of the Proto-Uralic area into a series of areas with their own identity and with relatively little interaction, genetic or linguistic, with others. (See also Carpelan 2001.)

Paavo Ravila (1949), employing the techniques of linguistic migration theory, noticed that the Finno-Ugric-speaking groups are spread geographically today in a way that reflects their linguistic relationships (degree of relatedness), as though the modern situation was created by movements of these groups to settle in the economically most favourable sections of their former overall territory. Indeed, the region around the middle course of the Volga River with its Oka and Kama tributaries appears to be a Finno-Ugric centre of gravity; speakers of Mordvin, Mari (Cheremis) and Udmurt (Votyak) live in this region as neighbours, though they represent diverse branches of the family.

Proto-Finno-Ugric vocabulary offers clues for delimiting the homeland; some plant and animal names and some culture words have been considered relevant. The words for 'honeybee' (*mekſi) and 'honey' (*meti) have been emphasized. These were borrowed into Proto-Finno-Ugric from Indo-European. The area where such contact could have taken place is thought to be the region of the middle course of the Volga River, where apiculture was practiced from early times. The honeybee was unknown in Siberia, Turkestan, Central Asia, Mongolia and most of the rest of Asia, but was found in eastern Europe west of the Urals. This area of bee-keeping is often considered one of the clues to the Proto-Finno-Ugric homeland, though this is not without controversy. That the terms refer to wild bees and honey collecting are not ruled out as possibilities (Häkkinen 2001: 176).

There are a sizeable number of reconstructed Proto-Finno-Ugric plant names, but most of these are found in a wide area and are thus not very helpful in limiting the homeland. However, reconstructed tree names have been vigorously discussed in this regard along with five principal trees that have played a role: 'spruce' [Picea obovata], 'Siberian pine' [Pinus sibirica], 'Siberian fir' [Abies sibirica], 'Siberian larch' [Larix sibirica] and 'brittle willow' [Salix fragilis]/'elm' [Ulmus] (outside the Balto-Finnic subgroup the cognates mean 'elm' [Ulmus], compare Finnish *salava* 'willow' and Hungarian *szil* 'elm'). According to Hajdú (1969, 1975), the Finno-Ugric homeland could be located only in an area where all these trees were found at the appropriate time. The only place which fits temporally and geographically is from the Middle Urals towards the north, including the lower and middle course of the Ob and the headwaters of the Pechora river in the area of the northern Urals. Not everyone, however, accepts this interpretation.

Other sorts of vocabulary have also been part of the picture. Cognates for 'hedgehog' have also been taken as evidence for the Finno-Ugric homeland (compare Estonian *siil*, archaic Hungarian *szül-* [syl-] (cf. *sün-* (ʃyn-]); hedgehogs are not found east of the Urals, but do extend as far north as 61° latitude. A word that has given rise to much speculation is 'metal', with cognates in nearly all Uralic languages meaning 'copper, iron, ore, metal' (reconstructed as *wäśkä for Proto-Uralic, seen in Finnish *vaski* 'copper', Hungarian *vas* 'iron', Nenets *veś* 'iron, money', etc.). Since Uralic dates to the Stone Age, such an ancient term for metal is interesting; some suggest the presence of copper trading or cold working of crude copper, but not metallurgy. A metal term of similar shape is also found in various Indo-European (for example, Tocharian A *wäs* 'gold'), and other languages, so that it may be an old widely borrowed word (Joki 1973: 339–40). It has also been argued that the lack of old terms for 'sea' ('ocean') in Finno-Ugric languages points to a landlocked original homeland (for example, Finnish *meri* 'sea' is a loanword from Baltic (Indo-European)). There are, however, abundant freshwater terms in the Finno-Ugric vocabulary. Of course, arguments from negative evidence can never be fully persuasive, although this one has been popular.

Salminen (2001) believes the reconstructed plant and animal names are not specific enough in their distribution to warrant a conclusion of anything more than that the homeland was far from the sea, in the deep forests rather than in a tundra or steppe environment, though he sees the distribution of the languages as better support for locating the homeland, in the traditional area between the Volga River and the Ural Mountains.

Evidence for the original homeland has also been sought in contacts with other languages. Finno-Ugric has a significant layer of loans from Proto-Indo-European, and also from Indo-Iranian. If we knew the location of Proto-Iranian, perhaps it would help us locate more precisely the Proto-Finno-Ugric homeland. Some scholars argue for even older Indo-European loans in Uralic, though this is controversial, and some others imagine that the loans were all younger but spread across the Finno-Ugric area by diffusion. That is, the testimony of loans is helpful, but apparently not concousive. Nevertheless, on strong evidence, most scholars believe Proto-Finno-Ugric and Proto-Indo-European were neighbours. (See Joki 1973, Campbell 1997b, Häkkinen 2001, Koivulehto 2001, Sammallahti 2001.)

16.3.2.8 *Cautions concerning linguistic homelands migration theory*

In linguistic migration theory, the homeland of a language family is inferred to be in the area represented by the greatest diversity (largest number of subgroups) for which the minimum number of moves (migrations) would be required to bring the speakers of the diverse languages back to one place. On the whole, the inferences afforded by this method are strong, and few documented cases fail to conform. In principle, however, it is not difficult to imagine rather straightforward situations in which linguistic migration theory would fail to produce reliable results. For example, suppose a language family with a number of subgroups had once been found in one particular geographical area, but something forced all their speakers to abandon that area, say a volcanic eruption, a drought, an epidemic or the onslaught of powerful aggressors. In such a case, it is possible that many of the migrating speakers of the different subgroups could end up bunched relatively closely together in a new area, particularly if driven until they encountered some serious obstacle such as insurmountable mountains, an ocean, inhospitable lands without sufficient subsistence resources, or other peoples who prevented entry into their territory. It is also possible that, rather than being driven, several groups speaking languages of the same family might independently be attracted to the same area (or nearby areas), for example to take advantage of better resources available there, to forge alliances with other groups of the area, and so on. In such scenarios, it is in principle possible that we might find that the greatest linguistic diversity would in fact not be in the original homeland, but in the new area where the groups come to be concentrated. Another problem for linguistic migration theory would be the possible situation in which all the languages of a family in the former area of greatest diversity were lost with no trace (where the speakers were annihilated by war or pestilence or whatever), or where the inhabitants remained but their languages were replaced by some other unrelated language or languages. In such a situation, what may appear to be a language family's area of greatest diversity today may not have been that in former times.

The fact that such counter-examples could exist means that the conclusions which we draw from linguistic migration theory can never be absolute, but rather remain inferences, warranted by the evidence but not proven. In our attempts to understand the past, we accept that migration theory has a stronger probability of being correct than any random guess we might make which is not based on these principles. That is, all else being equal, in the absence of other information to help us answer the question, our inference about original homeland based on linguistic migration theory has a better chance of being right than anything else we have to go on.

There are similar problems in relying on clues from reconstructed vocabulary for determining the most likely location of the homeland. One is that groups may migrate to geographical zones where certain flora or fauna of the homeland area are no longer found and as a result lose the words which refer to those items. In such a case, those languages lack the sort of evidence upon which we typically rely to infer the homeland. It is possible that in some cases so many languages have left and as a result lost the relevant vocabulary that these items could not be reconstructed in the proto-language and therefore the evidence for inferring the homeland would be inadequate. To take a specific example, Goddard (1994: 207) finds the terms which Siebert reconstructed 'consistent with the homeland of Proto-Algonquians being somewhere immediately west of Lake Superior' (see above), but points out the circularity of the method. Words for 'harbour seal' would typically only survive in languages in areas where harbour seals are found, leaving out languages (and hence regions) to the west which lacked a cognate for this word. In fact, Goddard concluded that the Proto-Algonquians were located more to the west based on other information, especially the distribution of the languages and the nature of the innovations which they share.

Another problem has to do with instances where the original word is not lost, but its meaning has shifted. Sometimes in such cases it is not sufficiently clear what the proto-meaning may have been to be able to make inferences about the geographical location of its speakers. For example, as mentioned, tree names have played an extremely important role in identifying the Proto-Indo-European and the Proto-Finno-Ugric homelands. If we know what tree names the proto-language had and if we can figure out the geographical distribution of these trees during the time when the proto-language was spoken, we can narrow the homeland down to an area where the distributions of all the trees known in the proto-language intersect. However, semantic shift in some of the tree names to accommodate the fact that the original tree is not found in the new areas to which some groups have migrated, or a shift in the name to accommodate new kinds of trees found in the new areas, severely complicates this sort of research. For example, in Proto-Finno-Ugric, the tree name *sala-* is reconstructed on very solid evidence from across the family; however, as mentioned earlier, this means 'willow' in Finnish and its closer relatives but 'elm' in Hungarian and its closer relatives. That is, we cannot be certain what the testimony of *sala-* is for the location of the homeland of Proto-Finno-Ugric, since the distribution of 'elms' and of 'willows' is quite distinct, but presumably one of these is not the original sense, but rather was acquired as the languages moved out of the territory where the original tree name was known. To take an Indo-European example, even *bherəĝ-* (*bherh₁ĝ-*) 'birch', which is one of the best supported of Proto-Indo-European tree names, shifted its meaning to 'ash' in Latin and to 'fir, pine, larch' in Albanian, and is absent in Greek (Friedrich 1970: 29–30; Mallory 1989: 161).

Semantic shifts need not always be a serious problem; in fact, in some cases they can provide us with additional evidence of homeland and migrations away from it. For Proto-Algonquian, a term for 'woodland caribou' is reconstructed based on abundant evidence across many of the branches of the family. This term has shifted its meaning in a few of the languages whose speakers have moved south of the caribou's range. It has come to mean 'bighorn sheep' in the Arapahoan branch and 'deer' in some Eastern Algonquian languages. Because the reconstruction with the meaning 'caribou' is secure on other grounds (distribution across branches of the family), the instances where it has shifted meaning to something else are additional evidence that Arapahoan and those Eastern Algonquian languages involved have moved away from the homeland area where the woodland caribou was found (Goddard 1994).

A problem of a different sort with linguistic homeland models is that they typically imagine a proto-language spoken in a rather restricted region from where groups spread out or migrated to fill up more territory later on. When we go through the exercise of reversing these movements or spreads to the assumed homelands of the various proto-languages, we often find that huge blank areas are left between homelands. The linguistic models seem to imply that these areas were simply not occupied at the time, but typically archaeology finds evidence of human occupation both in the homeland areas and throughout the zones left blank in the linguistic homeland interpretations. These conflicting results need to be accounted for. One possibility is that we have fully misunderstood the nature of how the languages expanded and the territory of the homelands in some cases, though we would like to be able to maintain some faith in these methods. Another possibility is that we do correctly recover the homelands for the most part with our techniques, and that the evidence of human presence in the areas left blank represents languages which have become extinct or been replaced.

16.3.3 Borrowing

Loanwords by their very definition provide evidence of contacts among peoples speaking different languages. The semantic content of loanwords often reveals a great deal about the kinds of contacts that took place and thus about the social relationships among different peoples. The following examples reveal something of the nature and range of historical information that can be retrieved from loanwords in different situations.

A rather straightforward example which illustrates the point about loanwords contributing historical information involves wine-making terms in German, most of which are borrowed from Latin, for example German *Wein* 'wine'< Latin *vīnum, Most* 'new wine, must' < *mustum, Kelter* 'wine-press' < *calcātūra* 'stamping with the feet' and so on. On the basis of these loans, the inference is drawn that very probably German-speaking people acquired knowledge of viticulture and wine production from the Romans (compare Polenz 1977: 23).

Another similar example comes from Xinkan (in south-eastern Guatemala) which borrowed most of its terms for cultivated plants from Mayan languages, leading to the inference that Xinkan speakers were not agriculturalists until their contact with Mayan groups and that they acquired knowledge of agriculture from their Mayan neighbours. Xinkan also borrowed several terms of a commercial nature from Cholan-Tzeltalan (a subgroup of Mayan), including 'to buy', 'to sell' and 'market', which suggests commercial contact between the two groups.

16.3.3.1   Turkic loans in Hungarian

Hungarian contains many loans, perhaps up to 35 per cent of the vocabulary, and the earliest stratum of these is from Turkic ('Chuvash-type'), many of them borrowed before the arrival of the Hungarians in present-day Hungary. The Turkic loans in Hungarian involve chiefly cattle breeding, agriculture, social organization, technology and implements, dress and religion. These demonstrate that there was extensive contact with Chuvash-type Turkic and that this led to important economic and social changes. Even the name of 'Hungary' appears to be a Turkish loan (see below) (Róna-Tas 1988; Hajdú 1975).

16.3.3.2   The Olmec–Mixe-Zoquean hypothesis

The Olmec civilization was the earliest in Mesoamerica (c. 1200–400 BC) and it had a huge impact on the languages and cultures of the region. Based primarily on loanwords, the Olmecs have been identified as a Mixe-Zoquean-speaking people. The geographical distribution of Olmec archaeological sites and the Mixe-Zoquean languages (spoken across the narrowest part of Mexico and in adjacent areas) coincides to a large degree, which initially suggested the hypothesis that if speakers of Mixe-Zoquean were there during Olmec times, perhaps the Olmecs spoke a Mixe-Zoquean language. This hypothesis is strongly supported by the many loanwords from Mixe-Zoquean languages found far and wide among other languages of the Mesoamerican area. Several of these loans are of significant cultural content, including many terms for things which are diagnostic of the Mesoamerican culture area. Therefore, Mixe-Zoquean speakers had to be involved in a culture important enough to contribute on an extensive scale to others during Olmec times when the culture area was being formed. Examples of Mixe-Zoquean borrowings into the various other languages of the area include the following.

Cultivated plants: 'cacao', 'gourd', 'small squash', 'pumpkin', 'tomato', 'bean', 'sweet potato', as well as 'guava', 'papaya', 'sweet manioc' and others.

Terms in the maize complex (maize was at the centre of Mesoamerican cultures): 'to grind corn', 'nixtamal (leached corn for grinding)', 'tortilla', 'corn dough' and others.

Ritual and calendric terms: 'incense', 'to count, divine' (into Q'eqchi and Poqomchi' 'twenty-year period', 'twenty', into Yucatec 'calendar priest', into K'iche' and Kaqchikel 'calendar'), 'day names in various calendars of the region', 'sacrifice/axe', 'woven mat' (which functioned as 'throne' for rulers), 'paper' and so on.

Other terms: 'turkey', 'salt', 'pot', 'tortilla griddle', 'ripe', 'fog/cloud', 'child/infant' (a central motif in Olmec art), 'iguana', 'rabbit', 'opossum' among others. Based on these loans, it is concluded that the Olmecs spoke a Mixe-Zoquean language.
(Campbell and Kaufman 1976.)

This example shows how loanwords can contribute to hypotheses about the ethnolinguistic identity of past cultures. (See also the impressive case of Romani ("Gypsy") migrations in Chapter 3 section 3.8).

16.3.3.3   *Cautions about interpreting loans*

Some cautions are necessary, too, in the cultural interpretation of loanwords, since some loans may not come immediately from the original donor language but via some intermediate language which borrowed the form first. For example, in the case of English *coyote*, which is borrowed from Spanish *coyote*, which originally borrowed the word from Nahuatl *koyō-tl* 'coyote', it would be wrong to propose a direct cultural contact between English and Nahuatl based on the fact that English has a word which is ultimately Nahuatl in origin. (English has several other loans which have this history, borrowed from Spanish, but being originally from Nahuatl, for example *avocado, chilli, chocolate, tomato* and so on.) Also, some loans come about in spite of limited contact between speakers of the respective languages, for instance English *yak* from Tibetan *gyag* 'yak'.

16.3.4   'Wörter und Sachen'

Wörter und Sachen means 'words and things' in German and has to do with historical cultural inferences that can be made from the investigation of words. (Mentioned earlier in Chapter 6, section 6.2.2). For example, one *Wörter und Sachen* technique is based on the 'analyzability of words'. It is assumed that words which can be analyzed into transparent parts (multiple morphemes) tend to be more recently created in their language than words which have no internal analysis. This technique gives a rough relative chronology for different sorts of vocabulary, but more importantly, it is assumed that cultural items named by analyzable terms were also acquired more recently by the speakers of the language and those expressed by unanalyzable words represent older items and institutions. For example, by this technique, we would reason that *skyscraper* – analyzable into the pieces *sky* and *scraper* – is a newer term in the language and hence a more recent acquisition in the culture than *house* or *barn*, which, since they are unanalyzable today, must be older in the language and in the associated culture. As Edward Sapir said, 'we know, for instance, that the objects and offices denoted in English by the words *bow*, *arrow*, *spear*, *wheel*, *plough*, *king*, and *knight*, belong to a far more remote past than those indicated by such words as *railroad*, *insulator*, *battleship*, *submarine*, *percolator*, *capitalist*, and *attorney-general*' (1949[1916]: 434–5).

Of course, this kind of inference does not always work out. Sometimes languages borrow names from other languages which result in unanalyzable terms coming into the language to represent newly acquired cultural items. For example, in English, *palace* is unanalyzable (monomorphemic), but is a loan (from Old French *palais*) and yet is younger than *house* and *barn* (compare their Old English sources, *hūs* 'house' and *bere-ern* 'barley-storeroom'). Sometimes older unanalyzable names for things are replaced for various reasons by later names which are analyzable. For example, replacement of names of things due to taboo and euphemism can result in older items and institutions coming to have analyzable names, for example, older *toilet* which is replaced later by analyzable *restroom*, or *bathroom* in North America.

Another *Wörter und Sachen* technique involves deriving historical information from cultural items whose names have visibly undergone a change in meaning. Sapir (1949[1916]: 439) cites *spinster* 'unmarried female of somewhat advanced age' as an example, since it comes originally from 'one who spins', which suggests that the specialized meaning of 'spinster' is the result of a change and that 'the art of spinning was known at an early time and that it was in the hands of the women'. The age of the form is further suggested by the fact that the suffix -*ster* for someone who does something is no longer a productive one (seen frozen in such names as *Baxter*, originally 'baker' *Webster*, 'weaver'). To be completely reliable, this technique requires fairly explicit comparative evidence from related languages.

As in the *spinster* example, another technique infers that vocabulary items which have morphological forms which are no longer productive refer to things that are older in the culture. Thus, *ox* and *calf* must be reasonably old cultural items in English, since they both have non-productive plural forms which new nouns entering the language today would not have, *oxen* with the archaic -*en* plural and *calves* with the *f*/*v* alternation. Such irregularities 'are practically always indicative of the great age of the words that illustrate them and, generally speaking, of the associated concepts'. Sapir cites the example in Nootka (Northwest Coast of North America) of *ħaʔwiḷ* 'chief' and *qoːḷ* 'slave' having the irregular, non-productive plural forms *ħaʔwiːħ* 'chiefs' and *qaqoːḷ* 'slaves', from which we infer a relatively remote antiquity for an office of chief, the institution of slavery, and some degree of social stratification (Sapir 1949[1916]: 441).

Another *Wörter und Sachen* strategy has already been encountered in the investigation of the cultural inventory revealed in the reconstructed vocabulary of a proto-language. Related to this is the assumption that cultural items which are represented by terms which have cognates widely spread across the languages in the language family are older in the associated cultures than terms which lack such a wider distribution among the related languages.

16.3.5   Toponyms (place names)

Linguistic aspects of place names very often permit historical inferences about languages and the people who spoke them. A much-cited example is that of place names in England whose distribution and linguistic content reflect aspects of history. For example, English place names which end in *-caster*, *-cester* and *-chester* reflect Latin *castra* 'camp' (originally 'military posts') borrowed into Old English as *ceaster*, as in *Lancaster, Gloucester, Chester, Dorchester, Winchester* and so on. These provide information on the history of Roman occupation in England. The area with heavy settlement from Scandinavia during Old English times (called the 'Danelaw', north and east of a line running roughly from Chester to London) has over 2,000 place names of Scandinavian origin (see Map 16.3), and these reflect the invasion and impact of Scandinavians in the history of England. The names of Scandinavian origin are recognized from linguistic elements of Scandinavian origin such as *-by*, from Old Norse *by* 'settlement' ('village, town'), as in *Busby, Derby, Grimsby, Kirby, Rugby*; *-thorp*,

. Parish names of Scandinavian origin
— Southern limit of the Danelaw

MAP 16.3: Distribution of place names of Scandinavian origin in England (redrawn after Wakelin 1988: 24)

from Old Norse *þorp* 'village', as in *Gunthorpe, Scunthorpe,Winthorp*; and *-waite/-thwaite*, from Old Norse *þveit* 'clearing', as in *Curthwaite, Linthwaite, Micklethwaite, Seathwaite.* This distribution is seen in Map 16.3. In the region south of the Danelaw, names with analyzable Anglo-Saxon (Old English) elements predominate, for example Old English *-hām* 'home' (used also in the sense of 'town, village', as in *hamlet*), seen in places with *-ham*, as in *Birmingham, Buckingham, Chatham, Durham, Nottingham,* etc.; and *tūn* 'enclosure, village, farmstead', seen in the *-ton* of *Arlington, Burton, Kensington, Southampton* and so on.

The evidence from place-name etymology shows that although today Xinkan speakers are relegated to a very small area near the coast in southeastern Guatemala, in former times Xinkan territory was much larger. This is demonstrated by place names found in the region which have an etymology in Xinkan but not in any other language. A few examples, with their probably Xinkan sources, are:

Ayampuc: *ay-* 'place of' + *ampuk* 'snake' (Ayampuc is on a snake-like ridge)
Ipala: *ipal'a* 'bath' (the volcano of Ipala has a crater lake)
Sanarate: *šan-* 'in, at' + *aratak* 'century plant'
Sansare and *Sansur*: *šan-* 'in, at' + *šar-* 'flats, coast'.

It is interesting in this case that J. Eric S. Thompson, the famous Mayan archaeologist and explorer, concluded from place names ending in *-agua, -ahua, -gua* and *-hua* that there had been what he called an '*Agua* people' in the region, a non-Mayan people who were displaced by invading lowland Maya (Chortí speakers) (1970: 98–9). On closer inspection, however, many of Thompson's *-agua* place names appear to be based on Xinkan *šawɨ* 'town, to dwell'. Some of the place names involved are: Xagua, Jagua, Anchagua, Sasagua, Eraxagua (*ɨra-* 'big'), Conchagua, Comasahua and Manzaragua. When Spanish speakers began to record these names, since Spanish had no equivalent of the Xinkan retroflex laminal fricative /ʂ/ (which varies with /ʃ/ in some varieties), Spanish speakers rendered it as <s>, <x> (/ʃ/ in Guatemalan Spanish) or <r>. Later, Spanish *ʃ* changed to /x/ (velar fricative), spelled <j> in Standard Spanish. Thus, these place names appear to contain reasonable renditions of Xinkan *šawɨ* 'town'; Thompson's *Agua* people appear to have been Xinkan speakers.

An often-mentioned but less reliable approach to obtaining information from place names is the same as the *Wörter und Sachen* technique involving the analyzability of vocabulary terms, where it is assumed that names which are not analyzable are older and that toponyms which can be analyzed into component morphemes are younger. Sapir (1949[1916]: 436) explains the logic of this: 'the longer a country has been occupied, the more do the names of its topographical features and villages tend to become purely conventional and to lose what descriptive meaning they originally possessed'. From this we infer that the place names *London, Paris* and *York*, which are otherwise meaningless today, are older than those with more transparent analyses such as *New York, St Louis, New Orleans* and *Buffalo*. Though these older place names are unanalyzable, they may once have exhibited a more descriptive meaning or clearer linguistic analysis which was obscured by changes over time (which confirm Sapir's point), as in the case of *London* < Latin *Londinium*, based on a Celtic root *lond-* 'wild, bold'; *Paris* < *Parisii* (the name of a Gallic tribe); *York* < *Jor-vik* (a Scandinavian name containing *vik* 'small bay').

16.3.6 Onomastics (peoples' names)

Often, valuable information for linguistic prehistory can be recovered from names for peoples. For instance, there is evidence of early cultural contact in the ethnonyms for 'Russia' and 'Russian'. As is well known, English *Russian*, German *Russe* and similar names in other European languages derive from the early Scandinavians, a dominant force, in the Novgorod region of Russia, as is reflected in the Finnish word *Ruotsi* 'Sweden, Swedish', a loan from Old Swedish **rōþ(r)s-* 'inhabitant of Roslagen', which was also borrowed into Old Russian as *rusī* 'Russia' – the Viking source for these terms for 'Russia' and 'Russian' in these European languages. Finnish *Venäjä* 'Russia', *Venä-läinen* 'Russian' (*-läinen* '-ite'; compare dialectal *Venät*) and Estonian *vene* (dialectal *vend*) 'Russian' tell a different story. The source of these names is actually an old loan from Germanic **veneð*, reflected by Old English *Winedas*, Old High German *Winidā* and Old Norse *Vindr*, names which refer to the 'Wendish' (also called 'Sorbians'), speakers of a Slavic language who lived on the south coast of the Baltic sea. The Hungarian ethnonym is revealing, reflected in German *Ungarn*, Russian *venger-*, English *Hungarian/Hungary* and Hungarian *Ugry* (< *Ogry*). These apparently reflect the tribal confederation of the *Onogurs* and the close contact between Hungarians and the Onogur-Bulgar Turks. It is by this Turkic tribal name, *on-ogur*, which means 'ten-arrows', that the Hungarians came to be known.

16.4 Limitations and Cautions

So far, we have considered only the various historical linguistic sources of information and how they might be applied to contribute to greater understanding of prehistory. All these things reflect historical events and connections. However, we need also to consider potential problems and limitations that we may encounter in attempting to recover the past of a people through historical linguistic evidence.

Very often, a principal criterion for determining ethnic identity is the language which a group speaks, and anthropologists and linguists often use language as the most important marker of ethnicity. However, it is well understood that language, culture and human genetics need not coincide and frequently do not. There are many cases where a single culture involves speakers of various languages, where a single language involves diverse cultures, and where human population genetics does not correspond in a straightforward fashion to either cultural identity or linguistic identity. The genetic make-up of speakers of Indo-European languages varies considerably; there is a large difference between speakers of the Indo-European languages in northern India and those of Iceland. Similarly, Finno-Ugric languages are spoken by the western Caucasian Finns and the eastern mongoloid Khanty (Ostyaks) and Mansi (Voguls). Multicultural language groups and multilingual cultural groups (societies) exist, both with or without a relatively fluid gene pool. Language is often a symbol of identity, but it is not the only such symbol, and difference in language does not necessarily mean difference in ethnicity. Ethnic identity can be based on various things other than language, for example shared cultural tradition (heritage), kinship or perceived genealogy, religion, territory, national origin, even ideology, values and social class.

All this notwithstanding, most of the correlations between linguistics and other sources of information in linguistic prehistory assume a more or less clearly identifiable correlation between language and culture, and between language and human biology, through time. This raises important questions which call for caution in research in linguistic prehistory. To what extent do groups with a shared cultural tradition and a common language tend to coincide? To what extent does the correlation, when it does exist, tend to last? Unfortunately, on the whole, cultural change and linguistic change are very different in nature. In particular, it is much easier for a group to change its material culture substantially in a relatively short period of time, but a language's structure changes much more slowly. This means that a lack of correlation between language and non-linguistic culture can develop relatively easily.

Similarly, it is too frequently assumed in work seeking correlations between languages and genes that the genetic classification of human groups may help answer questions about the classification of the languages. However, the frequent expectation of a direct association between language and genes (the assumption of parallel descent) is incorrect. Work comparing findings in linguistics and in human genetics needs to take seriously into account (1) that while a person has only one set of genes (for life), a person can be multilingual, representing multiple languages, and (2) that individuals (and communities) can abandon one language and adopt another, but people do not abandon their genes or adopt new ones – language shift (language replacement) is a common fact of linguistic life; there is no deterministic connection between languages and gene pools. Languages become extinct in populations which survive genetically, language replacement and extinction being frequent. We cannot assume, a priori, that linguistic history and human biological history will correlate well. Since human genetic and linguistic lines of descent very often do not match, it cannot be assumed the non-linguistic facts from human biology can be either reliable evidence of distant genetic relationships among languages or directly relevant to determining the historical trajectory that the language may have followed.

It is important to acknowledge these problems, but it does not defeat the overall enterprise of linguistic prehistory. Some scholars seem to fear that, if linguistic identity and ethnic identity do not coincide through history, then we can say nothing about prehistory from linguistic data. However, this is short-sighted. We have many sorts of information from 'language history' that tell us about the past: place names, information on contacts from borrowings, cultural inventory from reconstructed proto-languages, and evidence of language spread or migration. This remains historical information regardless of whether there was continuity in the linguistic-ethnic identity. This could be turned around. We cannot always know from material culture whether the language remained constant, whether new genes filtered into the population, whether a trait of material culture spread across ethnic and language boundaries or spread with the expansion of its bearers into territory formerly associated with other cultural and linguistic groups. The whole point of research in prehistory is to take as much evidence from as many lines as possible to try to answer questions such as these. Knowing that speakers of Proto-Indo-European had horses, cows, wagons, tribal kings and so on is historical information regardless of whether we know their precise ethnic and genetic identity, who their present-day lineal descendants are, and so on, and it would be foolish to ignore such information when trying to come to grips with a fuller picture of prehistory.

Attempts to correlate language with material culture may be complicated by the fact that a single cultural tradition may not be continuous in time, since it may change radically through contact with other cultures. Language, too, can change and even be replaced due to contact with other languages. Thus, how successful can we be when we look at the cultures and languages which we know about today and attempt to project back in time to the human groups with whom each may have been associated in the past? We cannot always know, and for that reason it is very important that the lines of evidence be investigated independently before correlations are attempted. However, when independently established sources of evidence point to the same sorts of conclusions, we can be happier about the plausibility of the conclusions which we reach about prehistory. Linguistic prehistory has an important role to play in prehistory in general.

16.5 Farming Language Dispersal Model

It is also worthwhile to be aware of other approaches to particular aspects of linguistic prehistory. One is the *farming/language dispersal model*, an approach to explaining the dispersals and spreads of many language families, advocated by Colin Renfrew and Peter Bellwood. It emphasizes agriculture as the primary agent of language dispersal. As Renfrew (1996: 70), puts it, 'farming dispersals, generally through the expansion of populations of farmers by a process of colonization or demic diffusion, are responsible for the distribution and areal extent of many of the world's language families'. Linguists have criticized the model for being too single-minded, leaving out of the picture the many other factors known to be involved in the dispersal of various languages and language families.

Agriculture can provide a people with the stability just to stay put, in relative self-sufficiency, so that they do not need to expand, as predicted by the model. Agriculture does not always lead to population pressure which exceeds the carrying capacity of the land. Some examples of such stay-at-home agricultural language families are seen below in the list of non-spread agricultural languages in Table 16.1. The existence of non-expansionist agricultural languages goes against the farming/language dispersal model.

To test the hypothesis, it is important to survey language families to see if they have spread significantly or not and whether they have agriculture. Table 16.1 presents some language families that have agriculture and others that do

TABLE 16.1: Spread and non-spread language families with and without agriculture

	Agricultural	*Lacked agriculture*
Spread families	Austronesian	Athabaskan
	Bantu (Niger-Congo)	Chonan (Tehuelche, Ona)
	Cariban	Eskimo-Aleut
	Chibchan	Pama-Nyungan
	Dravidian	Salishan
	Indo-European	Siouan
	Otomanguean	Tungusic
	Semitic	Uralic
	Sino-Tibetan	Uto-Aztecan
	Tai	Yuman
	Tupían	
Relatively non-spread families	Kartvelian	Australian families (26)
	Keresan	Chinookan
	Mayan	Chumashan
	Mixe-Zoquean	Pomoan
	Munda	Tsimshian
	Nakh-Daghestanian	Wakashan
	Papuan families	Wintuan
	Tanoan (Kiowa-Tanoan)	Yukian
	Totonacan	Isolates: Alsea, Beothuk,
	Isolates: Basque,	Cuitlatec, Esselen,
	Burushaski, Chitimacha,	Haida, Kutenai, Siuslaw,
	Japanese, Korean,	Takelman, Washo, Yana
	Natchez, Sumerian,	
	Tarascan, Tunica, Zuni	

Note that the presence of agriculture is clear in the reconstructed vocabulary of the proto-language of several of these families, for example for Proto-Austronesian, Proto-Bantu, Proto-Indo-European, Proto-Mayan, Proto-Mixe-Zoquean, Proto-Munda, Proto-Otomanguean, Proto-Semitic, Proto-Tai, and others.

not, distinguished according to those which have spread significantly and those which have not. The language families listed under the category of 'lacked agriculture' are assumed not to have had agriculture at the time of their initial break-up and main dispersal.

Note that the presence of agriculture is clear in the reconstructed vocabulary of the proto-language of several of these families, for example for Proto-Austronesian, Proto-Bantu, Proto-Indo-European, Proto-Mayan, Proto-Mixe-Zoquean, Proto-Munda, Proto-Otomanguean, Proto-Semitic, Proto-Tai, and others.

What we see in Table 16.1 is a significant number of spread and non-spread language families both with and without agriculture. Clearly this means that the farming/language dispersal model alone is neither necessary nor sufficient to explain these distributions. It is not necessary, since there are widespread non-agricultural language families; it is not sufficient, since there are non-spread agricultural families. Therefore, other processes of spread must also be called upon.

Moreover, the farming/language dispersal notion that farmers spread with their languages at the expense of of non-farmers speaking neighbouring languages clashes with the evidence of loanwords in a number of regions. Loanwords, a powerful tool in linguistic prehistory as we have seen, often provide strong evidence of agricultural acculturation rather than of language replacement. This is seen in the case of Xinkan, a small family of four languages in southeastern Guatemala, where nearly all terms for cultivated plants are borrowed from neighbouring Mayan languages. This strongly suggests that the Xinkan speakers were not agriculturalists until the contact with Mayan groups gave them agriculture. That is, Mayan languages did not spread and wipe out non-agricultural Xinkan; rather agriculture spread but the languages stayed put. Another well-known example is the borrowing of Proto-Indo-Iranian *porǩo-s 'pig, piglet' into Proto-Finno-Ugric (cf. Finnish *porsas* 'pig'), a case of acculturation of aspects of farming from one language community to another without language replacement – numerous plant and animal terms having to do with farming are borrowings from Indo-European languages in Finno-Ugric without these languages being replaced by Indo-European ones.

Another difficulty for the agricultural dispersal model is that it provides no account for the coexistence of small languages (with few speakers or confined to a small geographical area) surrounded by large languages (widespread geographically, or with many speakers). Many such cases exist, for example various Munda languages surrounded by Indo-European languages, several Dravidian languages surrounded by Indo-European, Sorbian surrounded by German, Tulu surrounded by Malayalam, several Berber languages surrounded by Arabic, Sandawe surrounded by Cushitic languages, Uspanteko and Sakapulteko surrounded by K'iche' (Mayan languages), Natchez and Chitimacha (two isolates) surrounded by Muskogean languages, etc. Such cases go against the assumptions of the model as Bellwood (2002: 21) believes it should be: 'agriculturalist language families spread over vast areas leaving virtually no enclaves'. The model predicts that the small languages in the geographical domain of larger languages should be swallowed up and eliminated by the expanding larger agricultural languages. The coexistence of such smaller languages with larger ones is a difficulty for the model. Moreover, many of the small surviving agricultural languages were not agricultural in the past when agricultural languages came into contact with them, as seen in the Xinkan case just mentioned.

With respect to distribution difficulties, in short, widespread non-agricultural cases such as Pama-Nyungan and Athabaskan and non-spread agricultural cases such as the 'Papuan' language families and Mixe-Zoquean, which go against the predictions of the model, are serious problems for the farming/language dispersal hypothesis.

The independence of language and agriculture is highlighted by examples that show that language and agriculture can follow separate paths. (1) People speaking the same language can have radically different subsistence patterns, for example the highly modern industrialized Tamil speakers and the Paliyans, who live in forest-dwelling, food-gathering, moving bands (Gardner 2000), all speakers of Tamil; or the forest-dwelling hunter-gatherer pygmies and their farming neighbours, all now speakers of Bantu languages. Speaking the same language does not necessarily impose the same subsistence strategies. That is, agriculture not only does not always swallow up little languages in its expansionist wake, it does not even always impose itself on all the speakers of a particular language. Subsistence diversity is what gives many non-industrial societies an edge for survival, should one of the modes of procuring food suffer shortfalls. (2) People speaking different languages can share the same culture, including the same subsistence strategies.

Even in some cases that might appear to fit the model there are problems of interpretation. For example, if the Indo-Europeanization of Europe and northern India took several millennia, is it appropriate to consider it as representing a single expansion or dispersal with a single motivation? Most Indo-European linguists would insist on a number of independent movements scattered over scores of centuries to account for the distribution of Indo-European languages. Greece already had agriculture when the Indo-European Greeks entered, meaning agricultural dispersal could not have been the cause of this expansion. Vansina (1995: 191) shows that Bantu 'expansion' actually involved 'a minimum of nine diffusions, at least, before communities speaking Bantu languages could be found here and there over most of the area now occupied by Bantu speakers, and those nine diffusions together may have taken up to two millennia to spread'. This telescoping of the events which resulted in the distribution of the languages of a family into a single spread with a single cause does disservice to the prehistory we are attempting to understand. (See Campbell 2003b, and see Hammarström 2010 for a more thorough examination of the farming/language dispersal hypothesis.)

In short, we want to know what causes linguistic diversity in general (and what impedes it), and spread due to agriculture is only one factor.

16.6 Exercises

Exercise 16.1 Proto-Chibchan cultural inventory

Chibchan is a language family of more than twenty languages spoken in southern Central America and northern South America. What do the following reconstructed Proto-Chibchan vocabulary items reveal about the culture of Proto-Chibchan speakers?

1. **dihke* 'to sow'
2. **taˡ* 'cultivated clearing'
3. **ike* 'manioc'
4. **tuʔ* 'tuber, yam'
5. **apì* 'pumpkin, squash'
6. **e, *ebe* 'maize'
7. **du, *duaˡ* 'tobacco'
8. **tãˡ* 'gourd rattle'
9. **toka* 'gourd cup'

(Data from Constenla Umaña 2012)

Exercise 16.2   Proto-Tupían cultural inventory

Tupían is a large language family of South America with about seventy languages, spoken in Argentina, Bolivia, Brazil, Colombia, French Guiana, Paraguay, Peru, and Venezuela. (Tupí-Guaraníán is a large subgroup of this family.) Examine the following reconstructed Proto-Tupían vocabulary items; what are you able to say about the culture of the speakers of Proto-Tupían based on these?

1.	*awai 'yam (*Dioscorea sp.*)'	15.	*mani 'manioc'
2.	*čekʷ 'to pound'	16.	*mõj 'to cook'
3.	*ǎt 'to bake'	17.	*ŋo/ŋe 'cultivated field'
4.	*čʔam 'rope'	18.	*pe 'tobacco'
5.	*čét 'digging stick'	19.	*rʲuku 'achiote (*Bixa orellana*)'
6.	*ekʷ 'house'	20.	*t'ap 'thatch'
7.	*ekʷat 'village patio'	21.	*upap 'bed, lying place'
8.	*ekʷen 'door'	22.	*wamu/wamuã 'shaman'
9.	*ekʷʔip 'arrow'	23.	*waʔẽ 'ceramic pot'
10.	*ẽri 'hammock'	24.	*wekẽʔa 'fish trap'
11.	*eʔe 'to grate'	25.	*wetʲɨk 'sweet potato'
12.	*irʲu 'basket'	26.	*wɨ 'ax'
13.	*iʔa 'calabash (gourd)'	27.	*wɨp 'to cook, bake'
14.	*kuɾua 'pumpkin'		

(From Rodrigues and Cabral 2012)

Exercise 16.3   Proto-Muskogean environment

Languages of the Muskogean family include Choctaw, Chicasaw, Creek, Mikasuki, and others, once spoken widely in the southeastern USA. What can you say about the Proto-Muskogean speakers' knowledge of their environment and possibly about the Proto-Muskogean homeland based on the fact that terms for the following can be reconstructed to Proto-Muskogean? (Only the glosses of the reconstructed items are given.)

1.	apple (crab-apple or persimmon)	13.	chigger
2.	bat	14.	chipmunk
3.	bee	15.	clam/spoon
4.	beetle	16.	copperhead
5.	bluejay	17.	corn (maize)
6.	briar	18.	cotton
7.	briar (blackberry)	19.	crane (whooping crane)
8.	buckeye	20.	crawfish
9.	buffalo	21.	cricket
10.	chestnut	22.	deer
11.	chicken snake	23.	dove
12.	chickenhawk	24.	duck

25. falcon
26. flea
27. frog
28. goose
29. grape
30. grasshopper
31. hackberry
32. haw
33. heron
34. hickory
35. hoe/plough
36. honey locust
37. hoot owl
38. horned owl
39. hornet/wasp
40. horsefly
41. hummingbird
42. katydid
43. lamb's quarters (*chenopodium*)
44. leech
45. lightning bug
46. lizard
47. locust/cicada
48. louse
49. martin
50. milkweed
51. mole
52. moss
53. mountain lion
54. muddauber
55. mulberry
56. muscadine grape
57. mushroom
58. oak (three kinds)
(From Broadwell 1992)

59. onion
60. opossum
61. palmetto
62. pear
63. perch
64. pigeon
65. pokeweed
66. potato
67. prickly
68. pumpkin
69. quail
70. rabbit
71. redbud
72. redheaded woodpecker
73. screech owl
74. skunk
75. slippery elm
76. snake
77. spider
78. squirrel
79. stinging plant (poison ivy?)
80. tadpole
81. thrush
82. trout
83. turtle
84. turtle (soft-shelled)
85. walnut
86. water lily
87. whippoorwill
88. wildcat
89. woodpecker
90. worm
91. wren
92. yellowhammer

Exercise 16.4   *Proto-Uto-Aztecan cultural inventory*

Uto-Aztecan is a large language family with languages stretching from Oregon to Nicaragua. Examine the following reconstructed Proto-Uto-Aztecan terms. What can you say about the culture of the speakers of Proto-Uto-Aztecan? What might you be able to say about the probable homeland of Proto-Uto-Aztecan?

1.	*aCta	'bow, atlatl'	26.	*pɨtsɨN	'duck'
2.	*amu	'agave (yucca plant)'	27.	*piʔa	'gather, pick'
3.	*amu	'hunt'	28.	*pona	'play music, play drum'
4.	*ayaw	'gourd, squash'			
5.	*ayo	'turtle'	29.	*pota	'cottonwood tree'
6.	*hulapɨ	'badger'	30.	*putsi	'seed, pit'
7.	*huma	'flour, meal'	31.	*sayo	'enemy'
8.	*hutsa	'arrow'	32.	*sikuli	'peyote'
9.	*kakV	'crow'	33.	*taka	'fruit'
10.	*kɨmal	'blanket'	34.	*tapi	'hawk'
11.	*koloka	'beads, necklace'	35.	*tɨkpa	'cutting tool, obsidian, knife'
12.	*kuma	'tool (for poking, cutting), knife'			
			36.	*tɨsoli	'quail'
13.	*kuna	'sack, bag'	37.	*topi	'cottontail rabbit'
14.	*kusa	'bag, sack'	38.	*toptu	'dance'
15.	*kwika	'sing'	39.	*tsal	'loincloth'
16.	*kwisa	'eagle'	40.	*tsik	'basket'
17.	*maCta	'grinding stone (for seeds, grains), mortar'	41.	*tsɨka	'duck'
			42.	*tuʔi	'grind, flour'
18.	*motoʔo	'squirrel'	43.	*tuʔtsa	'hummingbird'
19.	*muCta	'cholla cactus'	44.	*wa(s)sa	'crane'
20.	*naka	'mountain sheep (meat)'	45.	*wi-talo	'roadrunner'
21.	*osa	'paint, draw'	46.	*wika	'digging stick'
22.	*pakaN	'read'	47.	*wiki	'rope, string'
23.	*paʔtsi	'seed'	48.	*wipula	'belt, sash'
24.	*piŋa	'grind'	49.	*wokoN	'pine, pine tree'
25.	*pipa	'tobacco'	50.	*yawa	'dance'

(From Stubbs 2011)

17

⎯

Quantitative Approaches to Historical Linguistics

⎯

In the end, the things that count are the things that you can't count.

(Proverb)

17.1 Introduction

The topic of this chapter is the use of quantitative methods in historical linguistics. Quantitative approaches have not traditionally played a large role in historical linguistics, and those that were proposed in the past have been controversial. Thus the topic does not receive much attention in most introductory textbooks on historical linguistics. However, quantitative approaches addressed to historical linguistic questions have gained prominence in recent years, and therefore it is important to consider them here. There were earlier attempts to apply quantitative tools to historical linguistic questions. Some were better and some were worse, now mostly discredited, but all have in common that they have had little enduring impact. (See Embleton 1986 for a good survey of this work.) Glottochronology is the best-known of these, and we begin this chapter with a scrutiny of it. Following this, we turn to more recent and more promising approaches, many of them based on models, statistical methods, and software packages that were originally developed for evolutionary biology.

Although historical linguistics has no generally accepted quantitative or statistical methodology, it is clear that appropriate computer applications could increase the ability to investigate historical linguistic data, providing the possibility for research on large datasets in ways that would be impossible for humans without computer assistance. In recent years, quantitative methods have been applied to a number of historical linguistic topics, to subgrouping (the internal classification of languages of a language family), to issues of detecting relationships among languages or to evaluating proposals of distant genetic relationship, to dating the split-up of related languages, to finding or quantifying similarities among languages, to detecting cognates, to finding sound correspondences, to determining which lexical items are more resistant to replacement based on their meanings, and to questions of linguistic prehistory such as probable homelands and migrations, among others. The principal quantitative applications to historical linguistics are considered in this chapter.

It has been asserted that adoption of these new quantitative methods, particularly those derived from evolutionary biology, would have many advantages for historical linguistics. It is claimed that modern phylogenetic methods which utilize statistical, computational, and algorithmic tools allow a wider range of different aspects of language to be modelled. It is also often repeated that the new quantitative methods are not seen as alternatives to traditional historical linguistic methods, especially the comparative method, but rather are intended to supplement the traditional methods – although some scholars do argue that their models have the potential to replace traditional historical linguistic methods. Cautions are also called for. For the task of working out family trees (phylogeny), no matter how sophisticated the numerical processing tools, if the task of turning language data into numbers is not done meaningfully and representatively, the outcomes will be neither useful nor convincing. Major problems which leave the analyses unconvincing lie in this first stage of converting considerations of linguistic data into numbers (Heggarty 2006: 186).

We turn first to glottochronology, which has had a more prominent history in linguistics, and we will see why most linguists reject it.

17.2   Glottochronology

Glottochronology is a well-known method which is still sometimes used but which has been rejected by most historical linguists. It is sometimes likened to ^{14}C ('carbon14') dating in archaeology. It turned out to be particularly misleading and it is important to understand why. (Models employing similar methods have also been rejected in biology.)

The names *glottochronology* and *lexicostatistics* are often used interchangeably, though there is a difference and in more recent times scholars have called for the two to be distinguished. Glottochronology is defined as a method with the goal of assigning a date to the split-up of some language into daughter languages, whereas lexicostatistics is defined as the statistical manipulation of lexical material for historical inferences (not necessarily associated with dates). McMahon and McMahon (2005: 33) define lexicostatistics as 'the use of standard meaning lists to assess degrees of relatedness among languages'. In this view, lexicostatistics is a prerequisite to glottochronology.

17.2.1 Basic assumptions

There are four basic assumptions of glottochronology, all of which have been challenged. We look at each in turn and consider some of the criticisms that have been raised concerning them.

(1) *Basic vocabulary*. The first assumption is that there exists a basic or core vocabulary which is universal and relatively culture free, and thus is less subject to replacement than other kinds of vocabulary. The *Swadesh 100-word list* of basic vocabulary is:

1.	I	35.	tail	69.	stand
2.	you	36.	feather	70.	give
3.	we	37.	hair	71.	say
4.	this	38.	head	72.	sun
5.	that	39.	ear	73.	moon
6.	who?	40.	eye	74.	star
7.	what?	41.	nose	75.	water
8.	not	42.	mouth	76.	rain
9.	all (of a number)	43.	tooth	77.	stone
10.	many	44.	tongue	78.	sand
11.	one	45.	claw	79.	earth (soil)
12.	two	46.	foot	80.	cloud
13.	big	47.	knee	81.	smoke
14.	long	48.	hand	82.	fire
15.	small	49.	belly	83.	ash(es)
16.	woman	50.	neck	84.	burn
17.	man	51.	breast (female)	85.	path (road)
18.	person	52.	heart	86.	mountain
19.	fish (noun)	53.	liver	87.	red
20.	bird	54.	drink	88.	green
21.	dog	55.	eat	89.	yellow
22.	louse	56.	bite	90.	white
23.	tree	57.	see	91.	black
24.	seed	58.	hear	92.	night
25.	leaf	59.	know	93.	hot
26.	root	60.	sleep	94.	cold
27.	bark (of tree)	61.	die	95.	full
28.	skin	62.	kill	96.	new
29.	flesh (meat)	63.	swim	97.	good
30.	blood	64.	fly	98.	round
31.	bone	65.	walk	99.	dry
32.	grease (fat)	66.	come	100.	name
33.	egg	67.	lie (down)		
34.	horn	68.	sit		

The *Swadesh 200-word list* is:

1.	all	10.	belly	19.	to burn (intransitive)
2.	and	11.	big	20.	child (young)
3.	animal	12.	bird	21.	cloud
4.	ashes	13.	to bite	22.	cold (weather)
5.	at	14.	black	23.	to come
6.	back	15.	blood	24.	to count
7.	bad	16.	to blow (wind)	25.	to cut
8.	bark (of a tree)	17.	bone	26.	day (not night)
9.	because	18.	to breathe	27.	to die

28. to dig	70. heart	112. to play
29. dirty	71. heavy	113. to pull
30. dog	72. here	114. to push
31. to drink	73. to hit	115. to rain
32. dry (substance)	74. hold (in hand)	116. red
33. dull (knife)	75. how	117. right (correct)
34. dust	76. to hunt (game)	118. right (hand)
35. ear	77. husband	119. river
36. earth (soil)	78. I	120. road
37. to eat	79. ice	121. root
38. egg	80. if	122. rope
39. eye	81. in	123. rotten (log)
40. to fall (drop)	82. to kill	124. rub
41. far	83. know (facts)	125. salt
42. fat (substance)	84. lake	126. sand
43. father	85. to laugh	127. to say
44. to fear	86. leaf	128. scratch (itch)
45. feather (large)	87. left (hand)	129. sea (ocean)
46. few	88. leg	130. to see
47. to fight	89. to lie (on side)	131. seed
48. fire	90. to live	132. to sew
49. fish	91. liver	133. sharp (knife)
50. five	92. long	134. short
51. to float	93. louse	135. to sing
52. to flow	94. man (male)	136. to sit
53. flower	95. many	137. skin (of person)
54. to fly	96. moon	138. sky
55. fog	97. mother	139. to sleep
56. foot	98. mountain	140. small
57. four	99. mouth	141. to smell (perceive odour)
58. to freeze	100. name	142. smoke
59. fruit	101. narrow	143. smooth
60. to give	102. near	144. snake
61. good	103. neck	145. snow
62. grass	104. new	146. some
63. green	105. night	147. to spit
64. guts	106. nose	148. to split
65. hair	107. not	149. to squeeze
66. hand	108. old	150. to stab (stick)
67. he	109. one	151. to stand
68. head	110. other	152. star
69. to hear	111. person	153. stick (of wood)

154. stone	170. to throw	186. where
155. straight	171. to tie	187. white
156. to suck	172. tongue	188. who
157. sun	173. tooth (front)	189. wide
158. to swell	174. tree	190. wife
159. to swim	175. to turn (veer)	191. wind (breeze)
160. tail	176. two	192. wing
161. that	177. to vomit	193. wipe
162. there	178. to walk	194. with (accompanying)
163. they	179. warm (weather)	195. woman
164. thick	180. to wash	196. woods
165. thin	181. water	197. worm
166. to think	182. we	198. ye
167. this	183. wet	199. year
168. thou/you singular	184. what	200. yellow
169. three	185. when	

(Actually, different versions of these lists exist, with small variations, especially versions of the 200-word list, because one or another word on the list was considered problematic by different linguists at different times. The list given here is representative.) These are not actually lists of 'words' per se, but rather of meanings for which relevant words with the corresponding meanings are sought in the languages investigated.

Swadesh refined his list of basic vocabulary several times in attempts to arrive at a list of words that were universally found in all languages and relatively culture-free. An earlier version had 200 words, but it was discovered that some of these were not universal or culture-free, and eventually Swadesh arrived at his basic 100-word list. It was thought the 100-word list would be more reliable; however, the 200-word list has had something of a revival, since some who utilize quantitative techniques find the 100-word list too small for their methods to work effectively.

To apply glottochronology, lists of the most natural, most neutral translation of each of the basic semantic concepts from the word list are assembled and compared in two or more related languages – or at least languages thought to be related. In one common version, the forms which are deemed phonetically similar in the compared lists receive a check mark (tick) to indicate probable cognates and, as will be seen below, the date when these languages separated from one another is calculated based on the number of the checked/ticked items that they share. In a different version, scholars argue that the method should be constrained to require that only forms known to be real cognates from historical linguistic research be counted, rather than mere 'look-alikes', as in the more common approach. The two practices differ in that the second, which requires actual cognates, depends on the prior application of the comparative method to determine the cognates, whereas the first does not, requiring only a judgement

of phonetic similarity. This lexical inspection approach to glottochronology has
been criticized:

> All that these pretty numbers represent is the proportion of arbitrary resem-
> blances between the languages by which the authors are prepared to be
> impressed. Such work constitutes an abuse of lexicostatistics: guesswork
> wrapped up in numbers expressed to any number of decimal places is still
> guesswork. (Trask 1996: 362)

(See Chapter 14 for additional criticism of approaches based on superficial
lexical similarity alone.)

(2) *Constant rate of retention through time*. The second assumption is that the
rate of retention of items of core vocabulary is relatively constant through time,
that a language will retain about 86 per cent of the words of the 100-word list
each 1,000 years (for the 200-word list the figure is 80.5 per cent, rounded to 81
per cent retention).

(3) *Constant rate of loss cross-linguistically*. The third assumption is related
to the second; it claims that the rate of loss of basic vocabulary is approximately
the same for all languages. It is assumed that languages everywhere lose about 14
per cent of the 100-word list, that is, that some 14 words from the 100-word list
will be lost (and thus some 86 of the basic 100 words will be retained) in each
1,000-year period throughout their history.

(4) *Calculation of the date of divergence*. The fourth assumption is that when
the number of 'cognates' in the basic vocabulary list shared by related languages is
known, the number of centuries since the languages split from an earlier ancestor
can be computed. This is perhaps less of an 'assumption' and more a formula following from assumptions (3) and (4). The time depth is computed with the formula:

$$t = \frac{\log C}{2 \mathrm{Log} r}$$

where *t* is 'time depth' in millennia (1,000-year periods); *C* is 'percentage of cognates'; and *r* is 'retention rate' (the percentage of cognates assumed to remain after
1,000 years, that is, 86 per cent for the 100-word list). *Log* means 'logarithm of'.

17.2.2   Historical background of glottochronology

Glottochronology was invented by the American linguist Morris Swadesh in the
1950s. Swadesh began by trying to determine whether there were broad trends
involving vocabulary change within particular language families. He was sur-
prised to discover, so he reported, that not only were there constant trends within
particular language families, but the rate of change turned out to be the same
across languages, regardless of their family affiliations. This claim constitutes
one of the basic assumptions of the method, and it has been vigorously criticized
(see below). Development of glottochronology was based on the examination
of thirteen test cases – languages with long attested histories where vocabulary
change could be checked against written evidence. In these 'test cases' modern
versions of English, German, and Swedish (Germanic languages) were com-

pared with older attested stages of each language (for example, Modern English with Old English). Catalan, French, Italian, Portuguese, Romanian, and Spanish (Romance languages) were compared with Latin. Athenian Greek and Cypriotic Greek were compared with Classical Greek; Coptic was compared with Middle Egyptian (its ancestor); and modern Mandarin Chinese was compared with Ancient Chinese. (See Lees 1953.) However, only two of these thirteen (Coptic and Mandarin) are non-Indo-European languages, and this has raised doubts about the method. The strong geographical bias also raises questions, with only Mandarin and Coptic from outside Europe. From later tests with control cases involving Kannada, Japanese, Arabic, Georgian, Armenian, and Sardinian, the claim of a constant rate of retention has been challenged (see below).

17.2.3   Criticisms of glottochronology

17.2.3.1   *Problems with the assumption of basic vocabulary*

There are serious problems with the assumption of a universal, culture-free basic vocabulary. One is that many of the items on the lists are not culture-free, but rather are borrowed for cultural reasons in numerous languages. Examples of borrowed terms for items on the list are found for each item of the 100-word list in some language somewhere. Only a few revealing examples of such loans are mentioned here to illustrate the problem. In several Mayan languages *winaq* 'person' was replaced by a loanword, *krištian* (or something similar), from Spanish *cristiano* 'Christian', colloquially 'person, living being'. In the early colonial period, Spanish contrasted Christianized Indians (the *cristianos*) with pagans. When ultimately all had been 'pacified' (converted), by default all were then called *krištian* 'person', resulting in the elimination from the vocabulary of former *winaq* 'person'. In the case of 'dog', while native peoples of Central America had dogs before the coming of the Spanish, their dog was small, hairless, barkless, and served as a food item. The big, hairy, noisy dogs which arrived with Europeans were sufficiently different from these native dogs for a number of groups (Pipil, Lencan, Xinkan, etc.) to borrow the foreign name for 'dog' and eventually come to have a native term for 'dog' no longer. Thus, for example, 'dog' in Pipil (Uto-Aztecan) is *pe:lu*, borrowed from Spanish *perro* 'dog' (Pipil has no *r*). The word for 'heart' is borrowed in a number of Mayan languages from Totonac (a non-Mayan language of Mexico); this presumably has to do with the importance of 'heart' in native religion (for example, human sacrifice by cutting out the heart was practiced). Forms for 'sun' and 'moon' are widely borrowed among many languages of Southeast Asia and the Andes, due to their central role in religion and cosmology. Words for 'name' are also often borrowed. In fact, if we just look at the English glosses among the items of the 100-word list, we see that the following are borrowings: *die, egg, give, skin* (Scandinavian loanwords), *grease, mountain,* and *person* (from French), among others. From the 200-word list, we see a considerable number of additional borrowings in English: *animal, vomit* (Latin loans), *count, flower, fruit, lake, river* (French loans), and *sky* (Scandinavian loan). 'Fish' is borrowed in several South American languages from Quechua, and the term for 'fish' is diffused among some highland Guatemalan Mayan languages. 'Tooth' is borrowed in Finnish from Baltic (Indo-European). Borrowing is a serious problem for the assumption that there is a relatively culture-free basic vocabulary. On the other hand, it is certainly true that the Swadesh lists are, broadly speaking, more universal and culture-free than any randomly selected list of words, more resistant to borrowing than much non-basic vocabulary. Bowern et al. (2011) find in their survey of hunter-gatherer and small-scale cultivator languages that few languages had borrowed more than 10 per cent of their 204-word list of basic vocabulary. (See Haspelmath and Tadmor 2009 for details and discussion of borrowability.)

Another problem is that glottochronology assumes there will be a direct, one-to-one matching between each word (actually meaning) on the Swadesh list and a word of each language. However, this is very often not the case. For many of the items on the list, languages often have more than one neutral equivalent. For example, for 'I', many languages of Southeast Asia have several forms all meaning 'I' whose use depends on the relative social status of the person spoken to. Similarly, 'you' even more frequently than 'I' has multiple forms, depending on social status and degree of intimacy, for example the familiar versus polite pronouns, Spanish *tu* and *usted*, German *du* and *Sie*, French *tu* and *vous*, Finnish *sinä* and *te*, K'iche' *at* and *la:l*, and earlier English *thou* and *ye* (*you*), to mention just a few, where one form is not more basic than the other. For 'we', many languages have distinct forms for 'inclusive' (includes the addressee) versus 'exclusive' (excludes the addressee) first person plural pronouns. For 'not', some languages have no single form, but rather have conjugated negative verbs with several forms; compare Finnish *en* 'I.Negative' (first person singular negative [like 'I don't']), *et* 'you.Negative', *ei* 'he/she/it.Negative', *emme* 'we.Negative', *ette* 'you-Plural. Negative', *eivät* 'they.Negative'. For 'all', some languages have different terms depending on whether the meaning is 'all' = 'each member of a group', or 'all' = 'the entire amount'. Navajo and its close sister languages have no unique word for 'water'; rather they have several different words for 'stagnant water in a pool', 'rain water', 'drinking water', etc. Some Slavic languages have no unique word for 'cloud', but rather one word for 'dark storm cloud' (as Russian *tuča*) and a separate word for 'light cloud' (as Russian *oblako*). For 'burn', many languages have more than one equivalent; for example, Spanish *arder* 'burn' (intransitive) and *quemar* 'burn' (transitive), or several K'ichean (Mayan) languages *-k'at* 'burn' (accidental) and *-por* 'burn' (purposeful). For 'hot' several K'ichean languages have two equally common forms: *k'atan* 'hot' (of weather, water, a room, etc.) and *meq'en* 'hot' (of food, drinks, fire, etc.). The same is true for 'cold': *te:w* 'cold' (of weather, wind, people, ice, etc.) and *xoron* 'cold' (of food, water, etc.). K'ichean languages often have as many as seven different terms for 'to eat'; for example, K'iche' *-waʔ* 'eat (bread-like things)', *-tix* 'eat (meat)', and *-loʔ* 'eat (fruit-like things)' are equally common and none of them is more neutral or basic than the others. Similar examples can be cited for many of the other words in the list.

Not only do many of the items from the 100-word list have more than one natural, neutral equivalent in many languages, some have no equivalent at all – or better said, in a number of cases, some languages make no distinction between two separate items on the list. For example, 'man' and 'person' are homonymous in many languages. Many languages do not distinguish 'bark' from 'skin' or 'feather' from 'hair', where 'bark' is just '(tree) skin', and 'feather' is just '(bird) hair'. Some Latin American Indian languages do not distinguish 'root' from 'hair', where 'root' is equivalent to '(tree) hair'. Work on colour universals has shown that, while all languages have an equivalent (more or less) for 'white' (or light) and 'black' (or dark) and most have a term for 'red', it is not at all uncommon for languages to lack basic colour terms for 'green' and 'yellow' (Berlin and Kay 1969).

In instances where a language has more than one word which is equivalent to a single item on the basic vocabulary list or where a single term in a language covers more than one item on the list, the results can be skewed. For example, two languages will appear less closely related than in fact they are if both have, for example, two equivalents for 'hot', but the one meaning 'hot of weather' turns up checked/ticked on one language's list and the one meaning 'hot of food' gets checked/ticked on a related language's list. Similarly, if related languages make no distinction between 'feather' and 'hair', then the same word will turn up twice, as the equivalent to these two separate items in the list, making the languages seem to share more and therefore appearing to be more closely related than would be the case if only distinct items were compared. Such skewing is a problem for the method.

Some 'basic vocabulary' appears to change rather easily for cultural reasons in addition to just borrowing, for example terms for 'head' in various languages. Proto-Indo-European *kaput 'head' gave Proto-Germanic *haubidam / *haubudam (hence Old English hēafod > head) and Proto-Romance *kaput. However, several Germanic and Romance languages no longer have cognates of these terms as their basic form referring to the human head. For example, German Kopf 'head' originally meant 'bowl'; the cognate from *kaput is haupt, which now means basically only 'main', 'chief', as in Hauptbahnhof 'main/ central train station' (haupt 'main' + Bahnhof 'train station'). French tête and Italian testa both meant originally 'pot'; the French cognate from Latin *kaput is chef, but this means now 'main, principal, chief', not a human head. The Italian cognate capo now means 'top, chief, leader'. Pipil (Uto-Aztecan) tsuntekumat 'head' comes from tsun - 'top, hair (in compound words only)' + tekumat 'bottle gourd', and has replaced Proto-Nahua *kʷāyi- for 'head' (though kwa(h)- is still seen in some compounds, for example nu-kwah-tetun 'my pillow' < nu- 'my' + -kwah- 'head' + -tetun 'wedge'). It is a problem for the method that some items on the list seem to be replaced more frequently and more easily than others (more on this below).

Finally, it has been pointed out that taboo has resulted in the replacement of considerable vocabulary, particularly in some languages in Australia, New Guinea, and the Americas, where words similar to the names of recently deceased relatives are avoided and substitutions or circumlocutions are used instead. Some of these result in permanent vocabulary replacement. It is important, however, not to overestimate the impact of this kind of taboo avoidance, since often the taboo does not extend across all the communities of speakers of the language and the taboo avoidance does not persist too long. Other kinds of taboo replacement of items in the basic vocabulary list are also frequent. For example, as mentioned in Chapter 9, section 9.2.9, in dialects of K'iche' and

Tz'utujil (Mayan languages), *ts'ikin* 'bird' has been replaced by *čikop* (origi-nally 'small animal') due to taboo. In Latin American Spanish, *pájaro* 'bird' has come to mean also 'male genitals' and is obscene; for that reason many Spanish speakers avoid it and substitute *pajarito* 'small bird' or something else instead. Because Spanish is the dominant language where Mayan languages are spoken, speakers of some Mayan languages have transferred the obscenity associated with 'bird' in Spanish to the term for 'bird' in their native language and for that reason replaced the vocabulary item. Another example is 'egg'; Spanish *huevo* 'egg' also means 'testicle' and is obscene, and for that reason in parts of Mexico and Central America, *blanquillo* (literally 'little white thing') is substituted for 'egg', replacing *huevo* in this meaning. In Nivaclé (a Matacoan language spoken in Argentina and Paraguay), native *puta* 'hare, jackrabbit' is replaced by *nanxa-tetax*, derived from *nanxate* 'rabbit' + *-tax* 'similar to', to avoid sounding like the obscene Spanish *puta* 'whore'.

Facts such as these show that there is no universal, culture-free vocabulary for which a one-to-one translation equivalent exists in all languages. Still, pro-ponents of glottochronology would respond to this criticism that something must account for the portion of the vocabulary which is lost, and it may be borrowing, taboo, and so on which bring about that loss.

17.2.3.2 Problems with assumptions (2) and (3)

Since the assumption of a constant rate of retention through time and of a con-stant rate of loss cross-linguistically are related, criticisms of these two assump-tions are considered together.

To begin with, common sense would call these assumptions into question. There are good reasons why sound change might be regular, based on what is known about the structure and limitations of human speech-organ physiology and auditory capacity; however, there is nothing inherent in the nature of vocabulary (or in the organization of the lexicon) which would lead us to suspect any sort of regular pattern to lexical change, certainly not that basic vocabulary should be replaced everywhere at the same rate – vocabulary changes for many reasons, including social and cultural ones (as seen in Chapter 9), and there is no reason to expect the rate of change to behave in a law-like fashion. Additional control cases published after Swadesh's work show that this is indeed the case, that there really is no constant rate of loss or retention across languages or through time. Icelandic has retained 97.3 per cent, English 67.8 per cent, Faeroese over 90 per cent, Georgian and Armenian about 95 per cent each during the time that these languages have had written attestations. The large difference between Icelandic's 97.3 per cent and English's 67.8 per cent gives little confidence in the claim of an expected 86 per cent retention, regardless of what the range of error (standard deviation) permitted by the statistical calculation may be. That is, these control cases show that the rate is neither constant across time nor the same for all lan-guages.

Proponents might respond to this that there must be some temporal informa-tion in the data, since we do not see the basic vocabularies of languages changing in wildly different ways. They would ask: how much information is there and how variable are the rates of change? To address this question they would say that good models are needed that allow us to quantify rates, their variation, and uncertainties. So how much optimism or pessimism is warranted? Proponents hope, while sceptics doubt, that meaningful results can be obtained from such models.

With respect to the claim of a constant loss through time of 14 per cent for each 1,000-year period from the Swadesh 100-word list, written documentation exists for more than one 1,000-year period for extremely few languages. In the thirteen test-case languages, attestation for more than one or two 1,000-year chunks of time is available only for the Coptic and Mandarin cases (the interpretation of which is much less secure). Some scholars argue that it is possible that circumstances were so different in the more remote past that vocabulary loss and retention may have behaved differently in earlier 1,000-year chunks of time than in later ones, though most think this is unlikely and so not a serious objection. Still, it is jarring to some for a constant rate to be asserted for far into the past without more compelling evidence.

17.2.3.3 Problems in calculating dates of separation

Since the split-up of language families (or subgroups) is usually not sudden, in principle the notion of attaching a precise date to such gradual diversifications seems unrealistic – it is difficult to date a language split. Also, subsequent contact among the sister languages after a split is common, but as most commonly applied, the method makes no effort to distinguish loans that are the result of such contact from directly inherited cognates. For example, English *skin* and Norwegian *skinn* 'animal skin' are similar because English borrowed this word under the influence of Scandinavia. This means that in calculating how long ago English and Norwegian separated from one another, the date is skewed towards a more recent break-up because of this basic vocabulary item, which is shared due to contact after they split up.

It is also telling that this basic assumption about being able to calculate the date of separation has been vigorously challenged, or better said, the statistical model upon which glottochronology is based has been severely criticized, although others defend it or try to refine it.

In short, the underlying assumptions are controversial.

17.2.4 Purported uses of glottochronology

The principal use to which glottochronology has been put, besides dating when languages split up, is that of subgrouping language families. It is sometimes thought that glottochronological calculations of splits provide a fast and easy means for arriving at the internal classification of a language family, with no need to undertake the more difficult and time-consuming determination of subgrouping based on shared innovations (see Chapter 6). However, since glottochronology is unreliable and is rejected by most historical linguists, it should not be thought of as a substitute for the traditional means of subgrouping. It is simply not reliable for this purpose.

On the other hand, some have found glottochronology a useful starting point in beginning to classify large families, such as Austronesian, with a great number of languages (c. 1,200). Since it would be difficult at the outset to compare all the languages of large families with each other to determine shared innovations among them all, some suggest that a preliminary application of glottochronology may give an idea of the more promising hypotheses, which can then later be checked by traditional means. Even so, Dyen's (1965) work of this sort on Austronesian got numerous things about the classification wrong. More importantly, it should be recalled that glottochronology used in this way does not find or demonstrate subgrouping relationships, but merely points in directions where other sorts of research prove more fruitful. The other research is still necessary before the true groupings can be determined, and such preliminary classifications based on glottochronology may well have to be seriously revised or abandoned.

Some suggest that while the dates offered by glottochronology are not reliable, they nonetheless provide a relative chronology which more or less corresponds with what we know in many actual cases. That is, some scholars who reject glottochronology are still willing to entertain the results as a rough guide to the relative age of relationships. In the absence of other information which can help establish linguistic dates, this might seem helpful to some. Still, it must be remembered that many glottochronologically calculated dates are known often to be inaccurate.

Finally, some have thought that glottochronology might help to establish distant genetic relationships among languages. However, glottochronology cannot find or demonstrate remote relationships; rather, in the most common kind of application of the method for this purpose, forms which are phonetically similar in the languages being compared are checked/ticked as possible cognates and then, based on the number of checked/ticket words, a date is calculated for when the languages split up. That is, the method does not find or test distant genetic relationships, but rather just assumes a relationship and proceeds to attach a date. This is illegitimate for research on possible remote linguistic relationships (see Chapter 14).

Glottochronology has given linguistics a bad reputation with some other prehistorians. For example, many archaeologists initially were happy to embrace its dates, and frequently they proposed interpretations of the prehistory of different peoples and areas which relied on glottochronological dates, and attempted to correlate them with other sources of information on prehistory. However, as archaeologists came to find out about the problems of the method and the unreliability of the dates, some felt deceived and came to believe that linguistics had nothing to offer them. This is unfortunate, for though glottochronology proved misleading, historical linguistics has an important role to play in the study of prehistory in general and much to offer (as shown in Chapter 16).

In summary, glottochronology is not accurate; all its basic assumptions have been severely criticized. Most linguists have rejected it for good reasons. (For references and discussion, see Campbell 1977: 62–5, Embleton 1986, and McMahon and McMahon 2005.)

17.3 Word Lists, Stability, and Replacement Rates

An area which has received considerable attention recently is the nature of words in word lists (actually, lists of meanings) – how retentive or how subject to replacement individual words might be. Lohr (1999), for example, attempted to measure the relative reconstructability and retentiveness of words representing particular meanings. She reached her conclusions based on reconstructions from four proto-languages – Proto-Indo-European, Proto-Afroasiatic, Proto-Austronesian, and Proto-Sino-Tibetan – examining the meanings that could be reconstructed for all these proto-languages and could therefore be considered less likely to be culture-specific. On this basis she created her measure of reconstructability. Her measure of retentiveness was computed differently, much as others had computed it. (See below for other work based on Lohr.)

Questions arise about how applicable this approach might be to language families generally. It is based on the lexical reconstruction of only four language families. There is little agreement about the identity of cognates in one of these, in Afroasiatic, as seen, for example, in the great differences between Orel and Stolbova's (1995) and Ehret's (1995) proposed cognate lists and reconstructions. Reconstructions in Sino-Tibetan are certainly not on a par with those of better-established language families. All four cases involve widespread families where speakers of most of the languages are agriculturalists or pastoralists. Would the same result be expected for the vocabulary from other families, say those that are less widespread, with fewer languages, or whose speakers may not be sedentary?

There are several problems with respect to Lohr's most retentive words. Words for 'to spit', 'tongue', and 'wind' are onomatopoeic in many languages, and thus are not good evidence of genetic relationship, since similarities among forms with these meanings are too often explained by imitation of sounds in nature, not by inheritance from a common ancestor. Words for 'mother' typically involve nursery formations of the *mama, nana* type, and while they may be similar cross-linguistically, the similarity often is not the result of shared history. As seen earlier, a number of these terms involve borrowings in various languages (*give, moon, name, salt, sun, tooth*). For the numbers, for example, numerous languages of South America have no numbers for 'four' and 'five' (unless borrowed). Even 'three' is borrowed in a good number of cases. The list is too short to provide enough forms for recurrent systematic sound correspondences to be found, a requirement insisted upon by many linguists for showing linguistic relationships (see Chapter 14).

Several other lists of putatively stable words have also been proposed. One example is from Sergei Yakhontov, who presented a subset from the Swadesh 200-word list of thirty-five words posited as especially stable (see Starostin 1991). It contains:

1.	I	5.	what	9.	dog
2.	you (singular)	6.	one	10.	louse
3.	this	7.	two	11.	blood
4.	who	8.	fish	12.	bone

13.	egg	21.	hand	29.	stone
14.	horn	22.	know	30.	wind
15.	tail	23.	die	31.	fire
16.	ear	24.	give	32.	year
17.	eye	25.	sun	33.	full
18.	nose	26.	moon	34.	new
19.	tooth	27.	water	35.	name
20.	tongue	28.	salt		

As with Lohr's highly reconstructable list, several of these forms are really not that stable cross-linguistically.

Rather than attempting to identify a list of the most extremely retentive meanings and rejecting the rest, McMahon and McMahon (2005) constructed 'hihi' and 'lolo' contrasting sublists. The *lolo* sublist is of items that scored conspicuously low on Lohr's (1999) retentiveness and reconstructability counts, or are less universally found across languages. It consists of twenty-three meanings used in the Dyen, Kruskal, and Black (1992) database of Indo-European which could be reconstructed for only two proto-languages and had eight or more replacements in the sample. The *hihi* list consists of meanings high in reconstructability and retentiveness, or more universally found across languages, and reconstructable for at least three proto-languages and with no more than three replacements. Their lists are:

hihi (30 meanings)

1.	four	9.	sun	17.	five	25.	star
2.	name	10.	other	18.	mother	26.	to stand
3.	three	11.	sleep	19.	ear	27.	thou
4.	two	12.	to come	20.	I	28.	tongue
5.	foot	13.	day	21.	new	29.	tooth
6.	give	14.	to eat	22.	night	30.	wind
7.	long	15.	not	23.	one		
8.	salt	16.	thin	24.	to spit		

lolo (23 meanings)

1.	grass	7.	near	13.	to walk	19.	river
2.	mouth	8.	smooth	14.	back	20.	rope
3.	stone	9.	wing	15.	to flow	21.	straight
4.	heavy	10.	man	16.	left (hand)	22.	to think
5.	year	11.	neck	17.	to pull	23.	to throw
6.	bird	12.	tail	18.	to push		

McMahon and McMahon's hypothesis was that by isolating the top and bottom ends of the 200-word (meanings) list, the difference between trees determined on the basis of these lists could be made clearer. These authors hypothesize that the different family tree classifications that result from the different lists arise from borrowing among items on the lolo list. This approach also helps identify true cognates and distinguish them from items shared due to borrowing, and suggests a means of getting a perspective on degree of relatedness, since related languages are expected to seem closer to one another on the hihi list than on the lolo list.

However, even for the putatively retentive *hihi* sublist, there are several problems for its applicability across language families, as seen above in discussion of the words *to spit, tongue, wind* (often onomatopoeic), *mother* (nursery formations), *name, salt, star, sun* (often borrowed), *give* (loan in English), *tooth* (borrowed in some languages), and *three, four, five* (missing from some languages, borrowed in others).

Pagel (2000) applied an explicit maximum likelihood model (see below) to the question of lexical replacement and believes that the results allow inferences to be made about different rates of change for different words. He argues that his results indicate a correlation between the frequency with which words are used today and their stability over time, that the more a word is used, the slower it changes. Pagel, Atkinson, and Meade (2007) used phylogenetic methods to attempt to estimate the rates of lexical replacement in Indo-European languages. They compared the rates of change for each meaning in the list to the frequency of use in four modern Indo-European languages: English, Spanish, Russian and Greek. Pagel et al. built a tree of eighty-seven Indo-European languages and then estimated the instantaneous rate of change of each of the cognates on that tree. These authors draw the conclusion that the more frequently a word is used, the less likely it is to change: that the frequency with which specific words are used in everyday language exerts a general and law-like influence on their rates of change. Pagel and Meade (2006) applied similar methods to Bantu languages. Pagel and his associates report that across the meanings in the whole Swadesh 200-word list, frequently used words were replaced at slower rates while infrequently used words were replaced more rapidly.

Pagel et al. argue that frequency and the part of speech involved account for approximately 50 per cent of the variation in rates of lexical replacement. It may need to be kept in mind, however, that many other factors also influence vocabulary change in addition to frequency (see Chapter 9). Linguists have tended to be unimpressed with the putative findings, since linguists have generally assumed that frequency plays a role in language change, and the percentages themselves do not seem compelling.

The study involves four languages from a single language family, Indo-European, all quite similar in terms of the speakers' social structure, subsistence patterns, etc. What might the finding be if extended to other languages of other families, not sharing these languages' social and cultural contexts, with far more language contact or far less contact, for example? What about the numerous environmental and cultural factors which must result in different frequency of use for many of these words in different languages? We might ask: what is behind word-use frequency? Is the word for 'dog' more frequent in those languages whose speakers eat dogs than in languages whose speakers do not consider dogs to be food? Is 'dog' more frequent and so more stable in languages where speakers use dogs for towing sleds or for hunting in a hunting-and-gathering society? We should ask: what could there be about frequency which could retard loss or change? Environmental differences must contribute to different frequencies in different regions for words such as 'freeze' and 'snow/ice', and 'snake' (likely to be infrequent in Ireland and New Zealand, which do not have snakes). As already seen, several of the meanings on the list are known to involve loanwords in a number of languages, such as *salt, name, sun, moon*. Are all these things just part of the other 50 per cent not explained by frequency and so irrelevant for Pagel and Meade's results? Even if the other 50 per cent are declared irrelevant to the role that frequency plays, they certainly need to be part of the broader picture of lexical change. Also, even if frequent use of words may slow replacement, nevertheless over a long time, even resistant words will change.

Another approach, or set of approaches, relies on *Levenshtein distance*. Levenshtein distance methods have been applied in attempts to classify and subgroup languages, to explore the relationship between population size and the rates of language change (Wichmann and Holman 2009), to date human population expansions (Wichmann and Holman 2009, Serva and Petroni 2008, Wichmann et al. 2010), to determine whether languages emerge and go extinct at a constant rate (Holman 2010), and to find the homelands of language families (Wichmann, Müller, and Velupillai 2010). Advocates of Levenshtein classification have claimed that the results are similar to those from the comparative method, but that Levenshtein distance can be used to subgroup languages without the intensive time required for applying the comparative method (Brown et al. 2007) and without the potential subjectivity involved in identifying sound correspondences. However, as Greenhill (2011) shows, there are serious incongruities between Levenshtein classifications and classifications based on the comparative method. Greenhill demonstrated that the performance of the Levenshtein distance in classifying the Austronesian languages arrived at correct subgroups as established by linguists using the comparative method and the criterion of shared innovations only 41.3 per cent of the time. The Levenshtein method's performance is so poor because the Levenshtein distance does not distinguish between true cognates and non-cognate forms. The Levenshtein distance identifies only superficial similarity among words, though, as seen in several chapters of this book (for example Chapter 14), similarity among compared words can be due to several things – to borrowing, sheer accident, sound symbolism, onomatopoeia, and nursery forms – not just to inheritance from a common ancestor (to a phylogenetic relationship), as assumed by this method.

A number of recent papers involve the Automated Dating of the World's Language Families based on Lexical Similarity (ASJP) (see for example Holman et al. 2008, 2011). This approach is presented as a computerized alternative to glottochronology for estimating the time elapsed since parent languages diverged into daughter languages. It is based on the purportedly forty most stable items from the Swadesh 100-word list. Holman and associates attempted to calculate the relative stability of the words by comparing retentions from languages in established language families, and argued for a different 40-word list of the most stable lexical items:

1.	blood	15.	horn	29.	see
2.	bone	16.	I	30.	skin
3.	breasts	17.	knee	31.	star
4.	come	18.	leaf	32.	stone
5.	die	19.	liver	33.	sun
6.	dog	20.	louse	34.	tongue
7.	drink	21.	mountain	35.	tooth
8.	ear	22.	name	36.	tree
9.	eye	23.	new	37.	two
10.	fire	24.	night	38.	water
11.	fish	25.	nose	39.	we
12.	full	26.	one	40.	you
13.	hand	27.	path		
14.	hear	28.	person		

As mentioned, there is nothing in the structure of the lexicon or in how words are replaced or change their meanings that suggests that anything constant or law-like should be expected. For that reason, many doubt the claim of a 'constant rate of decrease for lexical similarity' and the dates derived from ASJP. The approach involves automated judgements of lexical similarity that rely on Levenshtein distances, and thus is subject to the limitations of Levenshtein distances just mentioned. As indicated already, unfortunately application of the method does not require real cognates, and complications can enter due to borrowing and even from the comparison of unrelated languages.

Levenshtein distance is defined as the minimum number of successive 'changes' (that is, substitutions) necessary to convert one word into another (that is, it is one of a class of 'edit' distances). How Holman et al. (2011) count 'changes' using ASJP orthographic symbols for Levenshtein distances raises questions. Why is the distance between Spanish <weso> and Italian <osso> 'bone' 3 (for Spanish to Italian: 1 *s* added, 2 *w* deleted, 3 *e* to *o*)? Many see Spanish <we> as a diphthong, a single unit, with *we* to *o* as 1 not 2 changes, with then a distance for the word pair of 2, not 3.

The claimed stability of items on the 40-word list is challenged, as seen above in the cases of loans involving *dog, fish, name, star, sun, tongue, tooth* in various languages, and in the borrowings *die, mountain, person,* and *skin* in English. Words for *breasts* and for *dog* are similar across numerous languages due to ono-matopoeia (*breasts* reflecting nursing or suckling sounds, *dog* reflecting barking and howling noises).

Dating by this method is based on calibration points from a number of languages around the world whose vocabulary change can be checked over known periods of time. However, there are calibration points from only seventeen language families, and some of the calibration points are unclear or disputed. This is not sufficient to warrant confidence in the method and its dates to represent the c. 420 language families (including isolates) of the world. For example, only five languages from the Americas (from c. 180 language families found in the Americas; see Chapter 6) are represented. This raises doubts about how the assumed stability of items on the list was determined. Choices for calibration were subjective. For example, identifying languages with archaeological materials is known to be fraught with difficulty, but nevertheless, Holman et al. (2011) use archaeological calibrations; they say these are the only ones available for chronologically deep families. For example, they date Benue-Congo at 6500 BP (before present) based on the arrival of macrolithic tools and pottery; they correlate Mississippi Valley Siouan with squash cultivation, and Tupí-Guaranían with ceramics and other archaeological materials. These are hardly satisfying, since technological innovation and agriculture often diffuse across linguistic as well as cultural boundaries, and sometimes take considerable time to take root, making the determination of a specific point in time difficult and misleading.

The calibration dates and ASJP-calculated dates differ greatly in numerous cases, ranging from −90 to +119. In several cases, higher-order groupings are estimated to be younger than some of the branches that are supposed to be their daughters, for example, Pama-Nyungan at 4295 BP, but the Paman branch 4918; Austronesian 3633, but its Eastern Malayo-Polynesian branch 3803; Algonquian 3343, but Plains Algonquian 5002; 'Hokan' 4915, but 'Northern Hokan' 5666, and Karok-Shasta (given as a branch of Northern Hokan) 5246; 'Penutian' 5522, but 'Oregon Penutian' a whopping 11,886!; and Chibchan 4400, but Rama (a branch of Chibchan) 5117.

ASJP and its dates are extremely problematic; it is no cure for glottochronology's failings. In fact, some quantitatively oriented scholars consider it worse than glottochronology, because glottochronology can be applied to counts of cognates, but ASJP does not deal with cognates. (See Heggarty 2010 for other considerations and arguments for not going along with the trend to jettison from word lists the meanings thought to be less stable over time.)

17.4 Other Recent Quantitative Approaches

In recent years, there has been something of an explosion of quantitative work aimed at historical linguistic questions. These methods have been claimed to have the following potential value for historical linguistics:

(1) Objectivity and replicability: helping avoid possible research bias in the kind of data dealt with (however, see below for accusations of biases in the selection and weighting of characters, the elements compared).

(2) Speed, and ability to handle large volumes of data.

(3) Seeking patterns in the data, in particular detecting patterns of diffusion.

(4) Giving historical linguistics a greater feel of respectability to scholars in other fields who rely on quantitative approaches in their own disciplines.

(5) Providing alternative models for representing relationships among languages – for example, not only family trees but also networks are useful for representing dialect continua and the outcomes of language contact; bringing new ways to visualize and quantify relations among languages.

(6) Comparing and quantifying evidence for possible alternative family tree classifications (subgroupings).

17.4.1 Some terminological prerequisites and preliminaries

It is important to clarify some terminology commonly encountered in works that take inspiration from evolutionary biology. It is helpful to know the following terms, together with their linguistic equivalences, though their full significance may become clear only when seen in actual contexts. The terms are listed alphabetically, though some make reference to other terms defined only later in the list; terms which are defined later in the list are underlined.

Autapomorphy (from Greek *auto-apo-morph-* 'self-away-form'): a derived trait possessed by a species or <u>clade</u> (a particular <u>taxon</u>) that is shared with no other species or clade; a unique innovation not shared by others.

Character: a feature or trait selected for comparison. With respect to language, a character is a linguistic attribute on which languages that are compared can agree or differ; languages are assigned the same character <u>state</u> if they agree, a different <u>state</u> if they differ. Languages are thus said to share the same <u>state</u> of the character or to exhibit different <u>states</u>. Many characters in language are scalar, and can be coded as scalar, though computational interests often force them to be treated as binary, sometimes misrepresenting their true nature in the process. (Characters are equivalent in a broad sense to how the term *comparanda* – the things compared – is used in some linguistic literature.)

Character set: the set of items that are compared; a collection of characters grouped together for a specific purpose, for example for grouping languages.

Clade (from Greek *klados* 'branch'): signifies a single 'branch' on the genealogical tree, a group composed of a single ancestor and all its descendants; a set of species or languages derived from a common ancestral species or language, a group of species or languages that share features inherited from a common ancestor.

Cladistics: evolutionary genealogy; a system of classification based on historical (chronological) sequences of divergence from a common ancestor.

Homology (from Greek *homologia* 'agreement'): defined in biology originally as 'the same organ in different animals under every variety of form and function' (for example, the human hand, a cat's paw, a seal's flipper, and a bat's wing), and having a common underlying structure and an assumed common origin. *Homologous* traits are assumed to be inherited, to be due to the sharing of a common ancestor. (*Homologous* is comparable to *cognate* in linguistics.) This contrasts with *analogous* traits, which involve similarities among organisms that were not present in the last common ancestor of the organisms being compared, but rather evolved independently, for example bat wings and bird wings.

Homoplasy (from Greek *homo-plasis* 'same mould'): a similarity not thought to be due to inheritance from a common ancestor; parallel, independent development (convergent evolution), the acquisition of the same trait in unrelated lineages. Homoplasy is a correspondence between the parts of different species acquired as the result of parallel evolution or convergence, not common origin. (It includes *'look-alike'* or *accidental similarity* in linguistics, but also other sorts of non-inherited similarities, for example due to borrowing, onomatopoeia, nursery forms, etc.)

Horizontal transfer (horizontal transmission, lateral gene transmission): the process in which an organism incorporates genetic material from another organism without being the offspring of that organism (not uncommon in bacteria). Horizontal transfer contrasts with *vertical transfer*, the transfer of genetic material down a lineage, that is, by inheritance. (It is equivalent to *diffusion, borrowing, contact-induced language change* in linguistics.)

Network: a representation of how tree-like or net-like the relationships among a given set of languages is. Network methods deal with cases where more than one genetic history may be possible. For parts of the genetic history where only one history is possible, the graphic representation looks tree-like; however, in cases where multiple historical sequences are possible (or where there may not be a true tree because language lineages do not necessarily diverge uniquely in all cases), network analysis draws a box shape, a reticulation or cell within a web, which shows that the data are compatible with more than one tree, if they are tree-like. (See below.)

Phylogenetic: the study of evolutionary relatedness among various groups of organisms or languages. (See phylogeny.) (It is equivalent to the use of *genetic* in linguistics, as in *genetic relationship*; as confusion with biological *genetics* has become more possible, linguists have been tending to substitute *phylogenetic* or *genealogical* for *genetic* in reference to relationships among languages.)

Phylogeny (or *phylogenesis*) (from Greek *phulon* 'tribe, race' + *geneia* 'producing, origin' < *genes* 'birth'): describes how species or languages are related, the evolutionary history of an organism or a language; the sequence of events involved in the development of a species, language, or taxonomic group of organisms, languages, etc. The taxa are often illustrated in a family tree.

Rooted tree: involves a root, descendants, and the time dimension – a root in the case of related languages is usually a proto-language, the ancestral language from which daughter languages descend. In a rooted tree one of the taxa is specified as the (assumed) common ancestor of all the others.

State, character state: the specific value taken by a character in a specific taxon or sequence (for example blue eyes as a specific state in the character set 'eye colour').

Symplesiomorphy (from Greek *sun-plesio-morph-* 'together-origin-form'): a shared ancestral character, a trait shared between two or more <u>taxa</u> due to inheritance from a common ancestor. (It is equivalent to *shared retention* in linguistics.)

Synapomorphy (from Greek *sun-apo-morph-* 'together-away-form'): a character or trait that is shared by two or more <u>taxonomic</u> groups and is derived by change from the original ancestral form. (It is equivalent to *shared innovation* in linguistics.)

Taxon (plural *taxa*): a classificatory group of (one or more) organisms or items, judged to be a unit. Usually the taxon is given a name and a rank, so, a taxon is any named group of items or organisms, any named unit of comparison, a category used in classification, for example phylum, species, genus, family, etc. While in principle taxa could be based on various criteria, usually in works about phylogenetics, the taxa refer to groups established specifically in terms of shared ancestry. In this context, the terms *taxon* and *taxa* are typically taken to refer to groupings in this sense, thus effectively equivalent to clades, groups whose members have a closer shared ancestry than other groups. It is common for *taxa* to be used to refer to the individual species or languages being compared to one other.

Taxonomy: a classification of organisms or items into groups based on similarities of structure or origin, etc.

Unrooted tree: a phylogenetic tree that shows which entities that are classified (languages in our case) are closer to one another, without, however, selecting a single root as the source from which all the other compared entities later descend. That is, in our case, it does not select a single proto-language from which all the other later languages descend. Thus, an unrooted tree is said not to be directed with respect to time.

Many approaches are concerned with investigating family trees (genetic relationships, phylogenetics, cladistics) computationally, and several of the approaches utilize methods adopted from biology and applied to language. Each of the algorithms relies on a different model of how phylogenetic divergence can best be handled. We turn to these shortly.

17.4.2 Probability approaches

Several other approaches, not just glottochronology, have also involved probability calculations applied to language comparison. Oswalt's (1970) shift (or permutation) test is considered excellent for detecting chance similarities. It has been applied by, for example, Lohr (1999), Baxter and Manaster Ramer (2000), and Kessler (2001). In it, languages are compared for similarities on a standard word list, for example the word for 'person' in Language₁ is compared with the word for 'person' in Language₂, the word for 'fish' with the word for 'fish' in the two languages, and so on. Then the comparison of lists is undertaken again, this time with the meaning slots shifted by one word in one of the languages but not the other, so, for example, the word for 'person' in Language₁ this time is compared with the word for 'fish' in Language₂, and the word for 'fish' in

Language$_1$ is compared with 'bird' (next item on the list) in Language$_2$, and so on. In languages that are not related, we expect the results for the first comparison of the forms with equivalent meanings not to be significantly different from the comparisons with shifted, non-equivalent meanings, and for related languages we expect a clear difference between the comparisons among items of equivalent meaning and the shifted comparisons. Kessler (2001) shows that this approach may distinguish historical connections from sheer chance, but may not distinguish a relationship due to common ancestry from connections due to borrowing.

In another approach, Ringe (1992, 1996, 1998, 1999) calculated the probability of chance resemblances and challenged the method of multilateral comparison because of its inability to deal appropriately with chance similarities (see Chapter 14). He showed that statistical tests are needed to indicate the degree of confidence warranted and whether the result is significant, that is, whether it is greater than expected by sheer chance. He concluded that the distant genetic hypotheses of Amerind and Nostratic, among others, did not hold up.

17.4.3   Methods inspired by evolutionary biology

Historical linguistics and evolutionary biology share a number of interests (see Atkinson and Gray 2005). Since language diversification and linguistic change are seen as similar to speciation and biological evolution, respectively, methods developed in biology to address historical questions may potentially be relevant for language change. Biology and linguistics are both interested in answering such questions as: how are similarities among languages or among species explained? How do species or languages arise and diverge? How are languages related to one another and how can species be related to each other? In both, it is asked, are similarities among languages or among species found because they share common ancestry, or are they similar due to diffusion (horizontal transmission), to parallel but independent development, to sheer accident, or to other reasons? Both linguists and biologists have a variety of techniques and tools with which to attempt to answer these questions. In recent years methods used in biology to address these matters have been applied to linguistic issues. Nevertheless, language change and biological evolution are also different in fundamental ways, as will be seen below, and it is from these differences that some significant problems for these methods arise.

The extensive amount of attention some of this work has received shows that these methods and their application to historical linguistic issues are considered significant. However, reactions from historical linguists to the methods imported from biology have been mixed, and we will see why. It is important to understand how these methods may contrast with or complement the traditional tried-and-true methods of historical linguistics, which typically draw on a broader range of kinds of linguistic data than those used in the quantitative approaches, several of which use lexical data alone. Most historical linguists will be unwilling to get behind an approach which seems to suggest to them that the lexicon can substitute for the whole of the language, for a language's entire structure, when it comes to working out questions of relatedness and language history. Traditionally linguists' decisions about language relatedness have been made based on sound correspondences, shared innovations, morphological agreements, etc. Scholars who apply modern quantitative approaches to questions of language change may view this differently. They might be well aware of the rest of the structure of language and of linguists' preference for using structural traits to arrive at family trees, but they wish to explore to what extent some restricted questions about language change might be answered based on basic vocabulary. The opinions, then, are very different. Linguists distrust lexical evidence alone and employ other kinds of data and methods to explain them, while the quantitatively oriented scholars have faith that lexical evidence will be sufficient to answer some questions, or that their quantitative methods will be adequate eventually for moving beyond lexical evidence alone to dealing with other sorts of linguistic data.

17.4.3.1 Background

The beginning of the relevant biological methods is often attributed to Watson and Crick's announcement of the structure of DNA in 1953, soon followed by work on protein sequences. This produced much more data than could be analyzed by hand, and biologists began working on algorithms for inferring phylogenies – family trees. The family tree model plays an extremely important role in historical linguistics, just as in evolutionary biology. The idea of constructing trees for linguistic groupings and for biological taxa was not new, though the application of computer-assisted tree-building algorithms for generating a range of trees compatible with the data, and for choosing one tree over another, was new (McMahon and McMahon 2003). Many scholars believe that these computational phylogenetic methods have revolutionized evolutionary biology (see for example Levinson and Gray 2012: 167), and indeed there has been an exponential growth in the use of these methods. In the inference of evolutionary histories from molecular data in biology, effort has focused on the development of software tools and algorithms for reconstructing phylogenies by means of these models. The result has been a whopping amount of software for reconstructing phylogenies from such data. Some of these phylogenetic approaches have been applied to linguistic data – mostly to lexical information, though nothing in the methods limits their application to lexical items – in order to investigate subgrouping relationships among languages already known to be members of a particular language family.

The notion of evolution in biology, the Darwinian idea of descent with modification, corresponds reasonably well to aspects of linguistic change, so that it is not surprising that methods established to deal with biological evolution might be thought applicable to language change. Of course, this concept of evolution was understood in linguistics long before Darwin, and methods were developed to deal with it. Scholars attempting to adapt methods developed in biology to linguistics initially believed that it would be relatively easy to identify homologous characters in languages (that is, cognates and correspondences among linguistic elements), which, like homologous biological structures, would serve as evidence for inheritance from a common ancestor. These scholars imagined that languages contain heritable units comparable to DNA sequences, though what the linguistic counterparts of DNA molecules might be was not clear, and most of the work employing these methods has been limited to lexical data, although some deal with structural or typological traits. The thought was that processes of mutation (change) operate on linguistic characters (traits, features, elements) just as they do on genes. The diversification of languages into language families and subgroups matches biological cladogenesis, where a single lineage splits into two or more new species. Often, in both linguistics and biology, such splits are due to geographic isolation or migration. There is also horizontal gene transfer in some bacteria, some plants, and a few amphibians, comparable to linguistic borrowing and change due to language contact. At first, the biology-inspired methods ignored horizontal transfer, and then later admitted the lateral transfer (borrowing) of words, though they continued to ignore change in other aspects of linguistic structure due to language contact. Still, horizontal transfer (diffusion) has generally been given little attention in most quantitative approaches, though it has a more prominent position in others (see below).

Several conceptual parallels between biological evolution and linguistic change are listed in Table 17.1, though different scholars have at times taken some of the particular linguistic concepts as matching other biology terms, different from those listed here. Also, it is important not to overemphasize the seeming analogies between the two. Some linguists feel that neglecting the differences and overstating the commonalities has given non-linguistic scholars unwarranted confidence that their methods can be applied directly to languages and the results should necessarily be trusted.

TABLE 17.1: Parallels between biological evolution and linguistic change

Biological evolution	Linguistic change
Discrete character	Lexical item (sometimes phonological or morphosyntactic trait)
Homology	Cognate
Mutation	Innovation, change
Natural selection	Social evaluation of forms, causes of change generally
Cladogenesis	Diversification (subgrouping)
Horizontal gene transfer	Borrowing, language contact
Hybrid (plants)	Mixed language (very rare)
Geographic cline, ring species	Dialects, dialect chain/continuum
Fossil	Relic, archaism
Extinction	Language death, extinction

Various approaches are involved (see below). Some assumptions shared by a number of the approaches are:

There are significant similarities between linguistic change and biological evolution which allow the same methods to be applied for determining phylogenetic arrangements.
Borrowing is rare (particularly in basic vocabulary).

The distribution of cognate sets among the languages compared can be used to model linguistic evolution in a phylogenetic tree.

Linguistic characters generally develop without homoplasy, that is, without independent parallel development (convergent evolution) and without acquisition of the same trait in unrelated lineages (branches) (counterfactual in that such cases in language change are not that infrequent and constitute significant problems in language classification).

17.4.3.2 Reactions

The application of new techniques from biology to historical linguistics has met with mixed reactions, ranging from excitement on the part of some non-linguists and journalists to outright hostility from a number of linguists (see Heggarty 2006). Some non-linguists have thought that the value of these phylogenetic methods for investigating the history of languages should be obvious, and so were shocked by the reticence and negative reactions from a number of linguists. To many historical linguists, on the other hand, it seemed that those applying these new methods were unaware of how complex languages and language change truly are and of how much was being missed as non-linguists applied their tools to linguistic questions (on this point, see also Heggarty 2006). On the other hand, those involved in constructing the models and applying the new methods see it differently. They do not deny the complexity of language and language change, but, as in other fields, they attempt to construct models to deal with limited aspects of the whole. It is standard behaviour in modelling to make simplifying assumptions in order to attack some of the complexity without having to take on everything all at once, and then hopefully to move on later to deal with more complexity as progress is made.

Some researchers, inspired by phylogenetic methods from biology, began with the simplistic view that equates replacement of words with replacement of molecular material in species. Rather than being simple and straightforward, as assumed in much of the earlier quantitative work, the language data relevant for addressing historical linguistic questions are vastly more complex than they initially assumed. It was clear to the linguists that unless these complications and complexities were taken into account in the application of quantitative methods, the results would not be useful for the purposes intended. Many linguists, aware of the inadequacies of glottochronology and multilateral comparison (see above, and see Chapter14), are understandably cautious. They want to know that the benefits of using these new techniques outweigh the shortcomings and risks. Some say that if a solution to a particular problem cannot be reach by tried-and-true historical linguistic methods, then they cannot trust a proposed mathematical solution, but at the same time they ask: if a solution is provided by standard linguistic methods, then what is the need for the mathematical solution in the first place?

Moreover, different encoding procedures and algorithms at first were contested among biologists. The debate in biology did nothing to give linguists confidence in the biologists' quantitative methods. It seemed that the biologists could not agree on ways to resolve questions of the relationships among related organisms and were confronted with results often contradictory to the phylogenies established by more traditional means, as well as being at odds with other studies that rely on other recent computational tools and phylogenetic approaches. However, in more recent times there has come to be much more agreement on the value of likelihood and Bayesian methods in evolutionary biology. Disagreements about molecular clocks and dating seemed especially intense, though relaxed clock methods are currently being explored (cf. Gray, Atkinson, and Greenhill 2011).

Linguists got the impression that scholars outside their field assumed that there is little to knowing about human language and how languages change, so that untrained outsiders could jump in and tell the linguists how to do their job properly. This was taken as naive arrogance. The linguists' doubts were made worse by publications which ignored linguistic facts or which got the linguistic facts wrong in well-understood cases. Linguists viewed the way the language data were handled in some publications as a tacit if not deliberate rejection of tried-and-true historical linguistic methods. In particular, because of the well-known failure of glottochronology, newly proposed dating methods were met with severe scepticism.

The application of techniques developed in evolutionary biology to language classification is almost certainly inadequate in some ways, since, despite the parallels mentioned above, there are significant differences between languages and biological species and how each changes (evolves). Language is not inherited biologically, but learned. Languages are subject to many kinds of changes that do not affect biological species. Textbooks such as this one list many kinds of language change and the explanations behind them that have no biological basis and no obvious counterpart in biology, but rather are motivated by a range of social, cognitive, and other factors. Biological and linguistic diversification happen on very different timescales. The genetic (phylogenetic) classification of languages reaches back in time reliably only as far as the oldest confirmed language families, less than 10,000 years, barely a beginning for most phylogenies (family trees) in biology.

Thus, considerable care is necessary when methods from biology are applied to linguistic questions. We need to ask: to what extent may things in linguistic data actually match things in biological data? The models adopted from biology do not fit or do not take into account many aspects of language change known to be significant, for example analogical change, chain shifts, directionality of many changes, how entities are constrained by and dependent upon other elements in particular language subsystems, sociolinguistic conditioning of change, impacts of language contact, reanalysis, grammaticalization, avoidance of homophony, aspects of semantic change and neologisms, taboo, etc. Clearly, say many linguists, if those employing methods inspired by evolutionary biology hope to find approbation of their efforts from linguists, then attention to the various other things linguists know to be important for explaining linguistic change is called for. Those modelling aspects of change using quantitative approaches, however, would say it is not necessary to attack all of this at once to get some positive outcomes. Biological evolution is very complex, too, but such approaches are employed there to address specific questions without needing to contend with the entirety of the complexity all at once.

17.4.4 Phylogenetic methods

The quantitative phylogenetic methods attempt to determine the classification and aspects of the history of languages using certain kinds of language data. This information is generally coded in a database, based on distance or on characters, and the methods are grouped as *distance-based methods* or *character-based methods*. Distance-based methods start with a set of characters, calculating from the character data a matrix of pairwise distances between all pairs of taxa. The resulting matrix of distances is the input to computer programs. In the distance methods, the initial character matrix is used to estimate (propose a hypothesis of) a phylogenetic tree. Other methods proceed character by character. As mentioned, these calculations usually involve lexical evidence alone, considered by linguists to be the least reliable data for determining phylogenetic affiliation.

Phylogenetic trees are called *unrooted* when they represent only relationships among languages but not the ancestor behind the relationships (for examples of unrooted trees, see Figures 17.1, 17.4, 17.5, 17.6, below). They are *rooted* when a common ancestor is identified for them (for examples of rooted trees, see Figures 17.3, 17.7). To oversimplify: when a method gives more than one tree having the same best score, a *consensus tree* has to be calculated. Put more specifically, the method may produce many hundreds of trees not all with the same score, but all are taken into account to combine into the single consensus tree.

Although tree diagrams are standard for representing language taxonomies (internal relationships among the languages of a language family, that is, subgrouping), those resulting from the biologically inspired methods do not represent the full story of language affinity that may emerge when phonological and morphosyntactic traits are taken into account, and when the causes of linguistic change are understood. This raises the question, then: how far can the imported models be trusted? Since models only approximate natural phenomena, they are inherently inexact. The question is: are the models imported from biological phylogenetics overly unrealistic with respect to the aspects of linguistic change they attempt to model or can they contribute to answering questions about linguistic history?

Several studies have relied on large databases that have been established. The Dyen, Kruskal, and Black (1992) database of Swadesh 200-word lists for 95 Indo-European languages has been widely used. Ringe, Warnow, and Taylor's (2002) database is similar to the one by Dyen et al. (1992); it has information on 24 Indo-European languages including, in addition to the lexical informaton, 22 phonological characters (traits) and 15 morphological characters. Gray and Atkinson's (2003) database of Indo-European, modified from Dyen et al. (1992), has 87 languages. Other databases have been created for Austronesian (see Greenhill, Blust, and Gray 2008, the Austronesian Basic Vocabulary Database, http://language.psy.auckland.ac.nz/austronesian), Bantu, Mayan (Mayan Basic Vocabulary Database, http://language.psy.auckland.ac.nz/mayan), Paul Heggarty's database of Andean languages (http://www.arch.cam.ac.uk/~pah1003/quechua/Eng/Cpv/DataSamples.htm), and the Automated Dating of the World's Language Families based on Lexical Similarity (ASJP) database (http://email.eva.mpg.de/~wichmann/ASJPHomePage.htm#), among others. A large database of a different sort is the World Loanword Database (WOLD) (http://wold.livingsources.org). It provides vocabularies of 1,000–2,000 entries for 41 languages from around the world, with information about the loanword status of each word, about source words and about donor languages, and also makes it possible to compare loanwords across these languages.

Application of the phylogenetic methods typically involves the following procedures (explained in Heggarty 2006: 184).

(1)   *Encoding*: coding linguistic data in the form of feature-based numerical or 'state' data, so that they can then be used as input to computational methods.

(2)   *Representation*: applying methods of analysis to these numerical or state data and converting the results into some form of representation, usually as trees or networks.

(3)   *Interpretation*: assessing the representations (trees or networks) for what they mean for languages and their relationships.

For *encoding*, the relations among languages are expressed in a numerical form usable for further analysis. This usually involves 'characters', which stand for specific observable characteristics of the species or the languages under study. A character is a partition of the taxa (species or languages) being investigated into distinct states. For example, in biology, a character could be defined based upon the number of legs the species under comparison have, with as many states to the character as there are different numbers of legs for the various species involved. In most applications involving languages, lexical items are the only characters coded (though not always).

Let us take a look at several of the specific approaches. Both the choice of the method for inferring phylogenetic trees and the selection of the data to be investigated significantly impact the result.

17.4.5   Distance methods

A common class of distance-based methods consists of *clustering algorithms* that apply an algorithm to a distance matrix in order to produce a phylogenetic tree. The distance matrix simply denotes the total *distance* between each pair of languages, usually by some method such as summing the total number of cognates shared. These methods are fast but their value is disputed. Two standard clustering algorithms extensively used in computational biology are the Unweighted Pair Group Method with Arithmetic Mean and neighbour joining.

The *Unweighted Pair Group Method with Arithmetic Mean* (*UPGMA*) algorithm is a distance-based method which is designed to work when changes obey the assumption of a *lexical clock* – of constant rates of change. This is the method used in lexicostatistical analyses. Phylogenies (family trees) constructed using these methods have often been challenged by linguists, and phylogenies from distance-based methods, for example the UPGMA used in lexicostatistics (glottochronology) and neighbour joining, are much less accurate than phylogenies based on character-based methods (such as maximum parsimony, weighted maximum parsimony, weighted maximum compatibility, etc.).

Neighbour joining (in several variants) is widely used for tree-like representation of language classifications (phylogenies). Neighbour joining is fast and useful for dealing with a large number of species or languages (taxa); it is, however, considered crude, finding but one tree even if alternatives might be possible, and the tree it finds is unrooted. Like other clustering algorithms, it produces a distance matrix from the data and builds up the tree starting by uniting the two closest taxa under a node. It then computes new distances where the node just added is treated as a single taxon replacing the two original taxa. This process is repeated until a whole tree is produced. The resultant tree has branch lengths which indicate relative distances. It minimizes the branch length to the nearest neighbour, while maximizing the length to the next neighbour – this distinguishes it from UPGMA and other agglomerative algorithms. McMahon and McMahon (2005) applied neighbour joining to 95 Indo-European languages based on 200 lexical items. The unrooted tree they obtained shows the ten branches generally recognized for Indo-European languages (see Chapter 6), but no clear relationship appears among the branches.

Neighbour joining is illustrated in Figure 17.1 for the K'ichean subfamily of Mayan languages (prepared by Simon J. Greenhill based on the Mayan Basic Vocabulary Database).

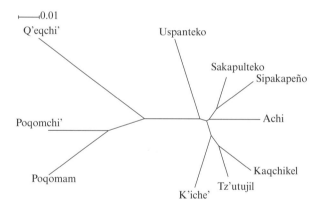

FIGURE 17.1: Neighbour joining for K'ichean languages

17.4.6 Character-based methods

Character-based methods include maximum parsimony, maximum compatibility (with 'perfect' phylogenies, outgrowths of maximum parsimony), and model-based methods. Character-based methods use the character data to evaluate a phylogeny (family tree). Multi-state characters are coded not as necessarily binary, but as potentially having representatives of multiple values for each of the alternative states in the character. For example, the set of words with the basic meaning 'hand' can be chosen as a character. Among Indo-European languages, those with cognates of English *hand* (Dutch *hand*, English *hand*, German *hand*, Swedish *hand*, Gothic *handus*, Old Norse *hönd*) are all assigned a single state of the 'hand' character, while languages that exhibit cognates of

Spanish *mano* 'hand' (Spanish *mano*, Portuguese *mão*, French *main*, Italian *mano*) are given a second state, and so on for each different cognate set with the meaning 'hand'.

Once the characters are selected and the dataset is encoded, the next step is analysis of the data. For this, the approach taken needs to specify how the changes between the character states should be counted.

A matrix with binary coding is illustrated in Figure 17.2, of the cognates of 'father' in a selection of Austronesian languages (prepared by Simon J. Greenhill, based on the Austronesian Basic Vocabulary Database).

Language	'father'	Cognate set (multi-state value)	Equivalent binary value for cognate set 1	Equivalent binary value for cognate set 2
Paiwan	tjama	A	1	0
Itbayaten	qamaq	A	1	0
Mangarrai	ema	A	1	0
Motu	tama-na	A	1	0
Fijian (Bau)	tama-na	A	1	0
Tongan	tama i	A	1	0
Rarotongan	*metua*	B	0	1
Maori	*matua*	B	0	1

FIGURE 17.2: Binary coded matrix of Austronesian languages

Determining which characters to select is an important part of the procedure. The characters selected should reflect language change, but judgements about what linguistic information to select for this purpose and about how to interpret that information have been subject to debate. (More on this below.)

For *encoding* and *representation*, many of these models rely exclusively on lexical data and involve the following:

1. Compiling a list of basic vocabulary items (most often a Swadesh 200-word list, since the 100-word list is sometimes thought to be too short to give good results).
2. Finding the equivalents of the items on the word list in the languages to be investigated.
3. Searching the language entries for cognates. Some approaches search just for similarities among the words compared. Many others rely on true cognates as already identified by linguists. (See below.)
4. Converting the data from cognate judgements into multi-state or binary form representations. They are converted into a binary matrix where each cognate set is coded for presence (1) or absence (0) of the cognate (a character) in the languages; or, alternatively, cognates are coded as multi-state characters, with as many possible values being coded as there are alternative states available to the character.

5.   Using the software to construct a phylogenetic tree (subgrouping) which explains the distribution of cognate sets.

For *interpretation*, much depends on which linguistic traits are chosen to be encoded, and also on how well the model embodied in the algorithm actually reflects the processes by which real languages diverge. Judgements about what linguistic information to select for this purpose and about how to interpret it have been subject to much debate. These approaches convert patterns involving correspondences in a dataset into a tree or network diagram that best fits those patterns. How representative of real history these diagrams may be depends heavily on the kind of data selected for coding, and on the model of divergence inherent in the algorithm. Eventually, in the interpretation stage, the significance of the identified components has to be assessed.

17.4.6.1   Maximum parsimony

Maximum parsimony is a statistical method whose target is to find an unrooted tree that requires the minimum number of changes to describe the observed data; its goal is to find the tree or set of trees with the minimal number of character state changes. Maximum parsimony methods were among the first used in modern phylogenetics and are still in use, though most scholars have moved beyond these to likelihood methods, which have been found to outperform parsimony methods. Parsimony methods allow the possibility of constraining an algorithm so that it can reflect tendencies for changes among individual characters, though maximum likelihood and Bayesian methods (below) do this much better.

Parsimony involves a calculation of cost in terms of the changes (or steps), and this makes it possible to specify that some changes cost more than others, forcing the process of tree construction to fit known facts about language change. Parsimony analyses are valuable for assessing assumptions about assigning different weighting to different characters or about directionality of change. (See likelihood frameworks and in particular Bayesian approaches, below, where attributing weights is easier and more flexible because the values are estimated from the data rather than manipulated subjectively.) However, assigning more weight to some characters than to others is tricky, because it opens the calculation up to the charge of bias, that the researchers' choice of particular traits to be characters and the differential weighting given to these traits/characters may bring into the picture preconceived ideas of what the researchers expect to find, biasing the results.

Gray and Jordan (2000) did a parsimony analysis of lexical characters to find an optimal tree for 77 Austronesian languages. Holden (2002) applied maximum parsimony to 75 Bantu and Bantoid languages, arguing that the most parsimonious tree follows the expansion of farming in sub-Saharan Africa. Rexova, Frynta, and Zrzavy (2003) performed a maximum parsimony analysis of Indo-European lexical items. Their results match all the known major branches of the Indo-European family, but with much uncertainty with regard to higher-order branches. These authors note that the basic vocabulary of Indo-European is strikingly tree-like, but this is hardly surprising, since their dataset was a predetermined set of cognates among Indo-European languages, thus with all the borrowings that could be identified by standard linguistic methods already removed. Dunn et al. (2005) applied a maximum parsimony analysis to a set of structural (morphosyntactic and phonological) features in a set of Oceanic languages which are known to be related.

In biological phylogenetics since the late 1990s or so, there has been a gradual shift away from parsimony analysis to likelihood models and Bayesian inference of phylogeny. The reason for this is that there are several problems with maximum parsimony. It can be misleading when there are large numbers of changes (a problem called 'long branch attraction'), and it does not take advantage of all the information, since unique (*autapomorphic*) characters, for example, do not qualify under parsimony because they would not tell the method anything about the tree; maximum likelihood and Bayesian approaches could use this information to get a better estimate of the length of branches, which they use to estimate (hypothesize) rates and amount of change. Maximum parsimony also does not give good estimates about the uncertainty in the data, as maximum likelihood and Bayesian approaches do (below).

17.4.6.2 Compatibility methods

The computational cladistics project at the University of Pennsylvania (Ringe, Warnow, and Taylor 2002) attempted to computerize aspects of the comparative method, based on computational mathematics. They used compatibility methods to infer an Indo-European language tree. Ringe et al. did not rely exclusively on lexical characters, as many others do, but included, in addition to 333 lexical characters, 22 phonological and 15 morphological characters among Indo-European languages. The University of Pennsylvania project scholars proposed to construct perfect phylogenetic networks by transforming a maximum parsimony tree into a network. (See also Nakhleh, Ringe, and Warnow 2005, Nakhleh et al. 2005).

Maximum compatibility is a non-parametric method (that is, it cannot be described using a finite number of parameters) which aims at finding an unrooted tree that presents the maximum number of compatible characters to illustrate the observed data. Being compatible here means evolving without any homoplasy, that is, without back mutation or parallel evolution. When all the characters are compatible, the tree is called a 'perfect phylogeny'. This method has been used by Ringe and colleagues in the computational cladistics project at the University of Pennsylvania.

A *perfect phylogeny* is a phylogenetic tree that is fully compatible with all of the data. Techniques for using multi-state characters have been devised which suggest that the majority of linguistic characters, if chosen and coded correctly, should be compatible on the true tree. The goal of recovering the evolutionary history of a set of languages becomes the search for a tree on which all of the characters in the dataset are compatible; such a tree, if it exists, is called a perfect phylogeny. Much earlier work was focused on developing the model of perfect phylogenies. In this approach, all (or at least the great majority) of the characters selected are compatible with a single phylogenetic tree. This means cases of borrowing, parallel but independent change, and changes back to an earlier state (back mutation) are excluded. A character is compatible with a particular tree if all the languages that form a single group (branch) share a particular state for that character. If a single state is shared by languages that fall on different branches of the tree, then the character is not compatible with that tree. If there is not a perfect phylogeny, the best trees will be the ones consistent with most of the data.

One possible explanation for situations where it is not possible to find perfect phylogenies is that the changes involved are not tree-like, that is, that some contact between lineages (languages, branches) must be inferred in order to explain the data that do not fit well. Non-tree-like development can definitely happen, since words can be borrowed across languages and branches of a family tree. This approach is not reliable for understanding the history of language families where there has been much diffusion across branches or where dialect continua are involved. In those cases, a tree model may be less appropriate, and the developments may be represented better in a network model.

17.4.6.3 *Model-based methods*

Maximum likelihood (ML) methods are based on explicit parametric models (that is, ones which can be described using a finite number of parameters) of character evolution, and they aim to estimate (hypothesize, propose) the tree and the parameters of that model which maximize the likelihood of producing the observed data. That is, ML methods aim to find the tree that best explains the data, under a given model. ML is thought generally to produce good estimates of the tree phylogeny in a robust statistical framework.

Figure 17.3 shows an ML tree for the K'ichean subgroup of Mayan languages (prepared by Simon J. Greenhill based on the Mayan Basic Vocabulary Database).

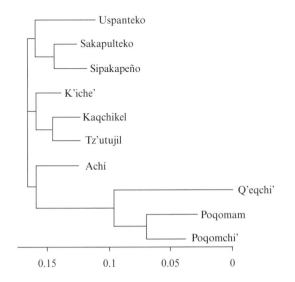

FIGURE 17.3: Maximum likelihood tree for K'ichean

Automated distance measures, originally introduced by dialectologists, have recently become popular among some scholars who classify forms of speech that are not considered dialects of one another, but rather are distinct languages. This operates with automated pairwise comparison of words for the same concept from a standardized list of basic meanings, such as the Swadesh list (see sections on glottochronology and on ASJP, above).

17.4.7 Network methods

Most scholars involved in the phylogenetic analysis of language data agree that a *network* or a *web* rather than trees alone can provide a more appropriate representation of what is seen in the data. Network methods shows how much support or lack of support there is for particular branchings in the data that are compared. A network that looks tree-like shows that many of the data compared support tree-like splits or branching. For a network that is not tree-like but instead looks like a web, there are multiple possible hypotheses to represent the relationships among the languages or species compared (the taxa). Networks address the problem of how characters change when distinct but related languages remain in contact with one another. Trees do not represent this kind of change well; networks help to reveal contact and diffusion (horizontal transmission) across branches and across languages. The network is, however, an analysis of trees (cladistic analysis), so that only changes relevant to constructing trees are applicable, equivalent to shared innovations in standard linguistic subgrouping (see Chapter 6). Characters that do not change are ignored. Network approaches have involved both character-based and distance-based methods. (See McMahon and McMahon 2005: 141.) Some scholars think that network approaches are more flexible and revealing than approaches based on trees alone, dealing with both divergence from a common ancestor and change due to language contact (McMahon and McMahon 2005: 174, 178). Others point out the difficulty of interpreting the results, the temptation to see in the networks what one wants to see, and the absence of tools to make inferences from them about processes of language change.

17.4.7.1 Neighbour-Net

Neighbour-Net uses an algorithm similar to neighbour joining that decomposes the data into a set of 'splits' (that is, groups of languages supported by some subset of the data). It is particularly useful for visual representation of the results, whether they are more tree-like or less tree-like. The network is not concerned with finding an optimal tree. Instead, alternative trees are suggested. The visual layout and interpretation of a neighbour net show how the relationships between different languages in a language family can be represented geometrically.

The Neighbour-Net program calculates the possible ways of splitting the data and scores them with confidence levels. In the networks, the lengths of the branches are proportional to the amount of divergence between languages. Box-like structures represent the conflicting signals when features support incompatible language groupings. If the languages split rather cleanly without a lot of subsequent interaction after the splits, we would expect the groupings in the network to reflect this and contain few boxes reflecting conflicting signals. In contrast, if the characters (linguistic elements) involve diffusion among adjacent languages, we would expect to see a network with more boxes and clusters reflecting the results of language contact. The extent to which the data are tree-like can be quantified by these methods.

Neighbour-Net trees are illustrated in Figures 17.4–6. The tree in Figure 17.4 is of the K'ichean subfamily of Mayan languages (prepared by Simon J. Greenhill based on the Mayan Basic Vocabulary Database). Figure 17.5 is based on 200 items of basic vocabulary from 20 Indo-European languages, and Figure 17.6 on 200 items of basic vocabulary from 20 Austronesian languages (both figures from Greenhill et al. 2010).

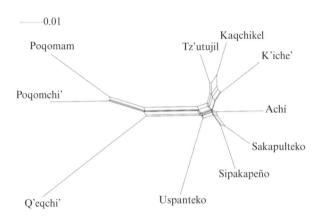

FIGURE 17.4: Neighbour-Net of the K'ichean subfamily of Mayan languages

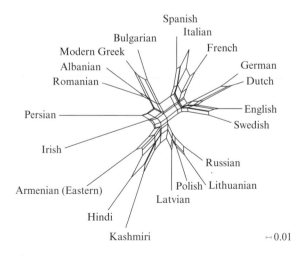

FIGURE 17.5: Neighbour-Net tree of Indo-European

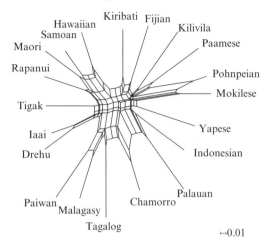

FIGURE 17.6: Neighbour-Net tree of Austronesian

17.4.7.2 Bayesian methods

Bayesian methods are based on explicit parametric models of character evolution (change), and are generally held to produce good estimates (hypotheses) of the phylogeny (genealogical tree classification). This set of approaches is largely an extension of the maximum likelihood approach within a Bayesian statistical framework. Bayesian analysis involves dataset construction, maximum likelihood modelling, and the search for the most probable evolutionary trees. Bayesian analysis is now at the forefront of phylogenetic algorithm development, and many think it is superior to other methods. Bayesian methods are thought to be valuable whenever there is a need to extract information from data that are uncertain or subject to error or noise. Bayesian inference allows uncertainties to be estimated in a natural way, and prior beliefs about parameters to be made explicit. It permits both quantification of uncertainty and the investigation of conflicting phylogenetic signals. It is difficult to evaluate its results because the history of most language families is not known.

Gray and Atkinson's (2003) well-known study combined a likelihood model of lexical change with Bayesian inference of phylogeny to determine the most probable trees for the Indo-European language family. Greenhill, Drummond, and Gray (2010) find their phylogeny of 400 Austronesian languages matches well the classification by historical linguists based on the comparative method. They believe this argues for the reliability of the method. Algorithm and software development in computational phylogenetics using Bayesian inference has been applied to a number of other linguistic topics. Greenhill, Currie, and Gray (2009) performed computer simulations to quantify the effect of undetected borrowing, concluding that Bayesian phylogenetic methods are good at getting revealing results even with high levels of borrowing. These authors see this as a test of the approach because Austronesian is known for its variation and complexity, which resulted in Dyen's (1965) unreliable classification of the family based on lexicostatistics.

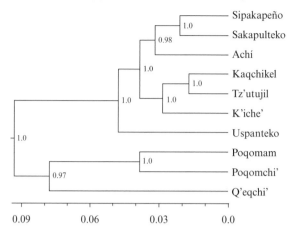

FIGURE 17.7: Bayesian phylogenetic analysis for K'ichean languages

Figure 17.7 illustrates Bayesian analysis; it is a maximum-clade credibility tree summary of a Bayesian phylogenetic analysis of the K'ichean languages, a subgroup of Mayan. The values on the nodes represent the posterior probability of the subgrouping. (It was prepared by Simon J. Greenhill based on the Mayan Basic Vocabulary Database.)

17.4.8 What counts as data, how is it dealt with?

As mentioned, many of the studies which apply quantitative methods to linguistics rely exclusively on lexical data. Historical linguists generally consider lexical items the least reliable kind of evidence of linguistic relationship, easily replaced or borrowed. Several of the quantitative techniques rely on mere observed similarity among lexical items, that is, they are essentially phenetic. Phenetics in biology is the attempt to classify organisms based on overall similarity, regardless of the traits' phylogeny or evolutionary status. Such techniques are used with the hope that the simpler and faster phenetic analyses will correlate sufficiently with true phylogenetic history. However, methods that investigate only superficial similarity among compared lexical items are known to be very unreliable, multilateral comparison being a notable example (see Chapter 14). For example, Forster and Toth (2003) did not use cognates in coding their data, but instead coded their data according to judgements of superficial similarity among the forms compared. They attempted to investigate Celtic and Romance languages, grouping together words which look similar even if they are known by linguists to have different origins, and treated as separate other words which are known to be cognates. ASJP attempts to calculate similarity automatically, without regard for whether true cognates are involved (Holman et al. 2011, and see above).

Similarity, as we have seen, can be due to several things – borrowing, accident, onomatopoeia, sound symbolism, nursery formation, etc. – and inheritance from a common ancestor (phylogenetic relationship) is only one of the possibilities. A straight coding of similarity among lexical items – 'characters' that are words – is not adequate. One familiar problem is that lexical items (as characters) are known to be particularly vulnerable to borrowing. Careful application of the comparative method and techniques for finding loanwords can detect much borrowing and thus can significantly reduce this problem for approaches that rely on lexical characters, but it may not eliminate all cases of borrowing. To get true cognate sets without the complications of borrowing requires application of tried-and-true historical linguistic techniques, especially the comparative method. It has also been assumed that word lists based on basic vocabulary will have the borrowings filtered out, since basic vocabulary tends to be resistant to borrowing. However, borrowing of basic vocabulary, while less frequent, is still quite common, as seen above in the loans in English from the Swadesh 100-word list (*die*, *egg*, *grease*, *mountain*, *person*, and *skin*). Most of the phylogenetic tools from biology were unconcerned with the problem of borrowing because they worked only with pre-established cognate sets, which presuppose that the loanwords have already been removed. However, Greenhill, Currie, and Gray (2009) and Nelson-Sathi et al. (2010) show that Bayesian methods deal well with undetected borrowing. Also, it is often difficult to determine whether compared lexical items are true cognates if they have undergone a significant amount of sound change which leaves them so different in the different languages as to be unrecognizable. These cases require careful application of the comparative method with attention to recurrent sound correspondences.

To the linguist, methods that depend on linguists identifying cognates in advance make it appear that standard linguistic methods are required to do the heavy lifting, to find the cognates, to eliminate the loanwords, and to deal with the many other complicating factors, just to get the data to a point where they are usable by the quantitative methods. As mentioned, character choices can also raise questions about the adequacy of the sample as well as of the analysis of the data, because of both what is included and what is left out. For example, if only lexical items are chosen as characters, then crucial information is neglected. This appears to linguists just to involve methods that depend on the results of the prior application of linguistic methods, made to masquerade as numbers and algorithms. Practitioners of the quantitative methods would see this differently, as ways to quantify uncertainty in hypotheses, putting numbers hopefully to help end or clarify debates.

Dealing with datasets based on cognates that require expert linguistic input fails to take into account the whole backdrop of what historical linguists have to do to determine cognacy: find sound changes, be aware of the directionality of change, sort shared innovations, ascertain semantic change and determine plausible semantic shifts, recognize recurrent sound correspondences, identify borrowings and contact-induced changes, eliminate forms which are similar due to analogical changes, etc. In short, very complex information and procedures go into the decisions about what forms are cognates. To do it right, it would seem that the techniques brought in from evolutionary biology must build into their procedures these various things that linguists know and do. As McMahon and McMahon (2005: 36) say, 'mathematical models and methods are not a substitute for careful and reasoned linguistic investigations, though that has not prevented attempts to use them in this way'. Methods that include more realistic views of language change must form the basis for worthwhile inferences about linguistic history. (See Kessler 2001 on the limits of statistical techniques applied to lexical items.)

Some have also included characters based on sound changes, morphology, and typological traits. Linguists have recommended that these approaches take phonological and morphosyntactic data into account, as well as contact-induced language change and the various other things necessary for fuller understanding of language change. When phonological and morphological characters are included, the results may improve significantly, but, as mentioned, this can introduce new problems, such as the charge of bias in character selection that might influence the results towards expected or desired outcomes. Linguists have also asked that more standard linguistic criteria for subgrouping be taken into account, for example shared innovations involving sound changes, shared morphological traits, etc. However, these are the things that historical linguists do anyway, so that models taken from biology and applied to the results of historical linguistic methods seem secondary, perhaps risking more than is gained because they deal with these crucial aspects of language beyond the lexicon less fully and less successfully than linguists already do.

Although the focus has primarily been on lexical items alone, the application of computational methods has not been restricted exclusively to lexical data. Some approaches also incorporate other characters. As mentioned, Ringe, Warnow, and associates use not only lexical characters but also phonological and some morphological ones for Indo-European subgrouping via computational algorithms (Ringe, Warnow, and Taylor 2002, Nakhleh, Ringe, and Warnow 2005, Nakhleh et al. 2005).

To most traditional historical linguists, the scholars who have invested in quantitative approaches to historical linguistic questions have appeared to progress by gradually reinventing the wheel. That is, they (re)discover complicating factors that force them to revise and refine their approaches, complications that linguists always knew about, such as that raw similarities among lexical items do not provide a reliable basis for classifying languages, that often lexical items alone are not sufficient, that phonological and morphological characters are important for determining phylogenetic status, that borrowing exists (that we are not dealing with perfect phylogenies), that homoplasy exists (both independent parallel evolution and back mutation), and so on. It seems these scholars have had to 'discover' aspects of the complexity of language and the unaddressed challenges of language change by being dragged through problems as they arose in their analyses, though even now many have not taken into account the full weight of the problems, and those who do acknowledge them have typically not dealt with them well. For example, the value of shared innovation as a diagnostic of subgrouping – the gold standard in linguistic phylogenetic classification – is not implemented in any significant way in most of the quantitative approaches. Some believe that the level to which cognates reconstruct on branches of phylogenetic trees reveals shared innovations, but shared innovation among lexical items is not accorded much weight by linguists, since lexical items can change in volatile ways and can be shared for many reasons in addition to inheritance from a common ancestor. This, then, is why many linguists have been and remain sceptical, some even disdainful, of much of the quantitative work in this area. This is, however, not a fair view of those applying quantitative methods to historical linguistic questions, or at least not of all of them. It is of course a common practice in mathematics and numerous sciences to make simplifying assumptions about some complex phenomenon in order to model it, and then, with progress, gradually to add complications as needed. A problem is that many scholars do not make their simplifying assumptions explicit, and what would be needed to test the models is usually not made sufficiently rigorous and plainly clear. It is also important to ask whether the simplifying idealizations called for in the models are too unrealistic to yield useful results.

Those interested in exploring the possibilities of dating might respond that they are definitely not reinventing linguistic wheels, since linguists have just given up on dating. Here, opinions from the two camps diverge. The traditional linguists' response is, predictably, not of optimism, rather of scepticism – the dating methods, though more sophisticated than glottochronology, are subject to the limitations and liabilities resulting from relying on lexical lists, which the linguists believe incapable of revealing a sufficient range of linguistic change, of how, why, and when language change happens.

Though a very positive development, incorporation of other sorts of characters beyond just lexical ones can bring with it additional complications. Borrowing can make phylogenetic classification difficult, except when the amount of borrowing is low. So characters that are resistant to borrowing are more useful in a phylogenetic analysis. Structural characters are valuable because they are more resistant to borrowing than lexical items – though structural borrowing is also not uncommon (see Chapters 11 and 12). Heggarty, Maguire, and McMahon (2010) used divergence in phonetics, advocating network-type phylogenetic methods. Some studies have attempted to use typological features, but their use is controversial (Dunn et al. 2005, Dunn, Levinson, and Lindström 2008, Wichmann and Saunders 2007). Typological traits have been employed not only for internal classification (subgrouping) of languages already known to be related, but also in attempts to address possible remote relationships among languages. It is claimed that the inclusion of typological features may help resolve issues about higher-order relationships where the available lexical data are relatively uninformative.

Dunn et al. (2005), based on typological traits, claimed to be able to detect historical signals among some Papuan languages (not known to be related to one another) that reach beyond the limits of the comparative method, to around 10,000 years ago. These authors ask whether a phylogenetic signal can be identified in the absence of identifiable lexical cognates. They based their study on a broad selection of abstract typological categories as characters which languages of the region might be expected to have, without regard for their form (the sounds that signal them), but rather with concern only for the presence of particular grammatical categories (shared functions or meanings only). This, however, violates one of the fundamental principles of comparative linguistics, the principle that permits as evidence of relatedness only comparisons which involve both sound and meaning together (see Chapter 14). Similarities in sound alone (for example, presence of tonal contrasts or of glottalized consonants in compared languages) or in meaning alone (for example, grammatical gender in the languages compared) are not sufficient, since such shared similarities can be due to diffusion, accident, or general typological tendencies, and thus are not strong evidence of genetic relationship among the compared languages (see Campbell and Poser 2008). Since Dunn et al. compare only similarities in the functions of the typological traits selected for characters, independent of the form (sounds) that signal them, their conclusions would be ruled out by many historical linguists on the basis of this standard principle. (See Donohue and Musgrave 2007 for criticism of the Dunn et al. 2005 paper on a number of grounds.)

Typological traits selected as characters can also reflect language contact and geographical distribution of traits rather than genetic (phylogenetic) relationships among the languages compared. For example, in a comparison of French, Spanish, and German, many characters shared by French and Spanish may actually be inherited and reflect the fact that they belong to the Romance languages. However, traits shared by French and German (the latter a member of the Germanic branch) may reflect traits shared only because of language contact among these two neighbouring languages. Thus, French and German share several traits which Spanish lacks: uvular *r*, front rounded vowels (/y, ø/), and requirement of an overt subject – French is not a null subject (pro-drop) language as Spanish is, where verbs in independent clauses can lack an explicit subject. For example, in Spanish, a null subject language, it is possible to say *viene mañana* (literally, 'comes tomorrow') meaning 'he is coming tomorrow', but in French and German an overt subject is required, French *il vient demain*, German *Er kommt morgen* '<u>he</u> is coming tomorrow'. On the other hand, French and Spanish share other traits not found in German, for example the order noun–adjective (French *maison blanche*, Spanish *casa blanca* 'white house' [literally, 'house white']) as opposed to German *weißes Haus* (literally, 'white house'). Since Dunn et al. are not able to distinguish typological traits that are shared due to language contact (such as the French–German shared traits here) from those that may be inherited and thus reflect a phylogenetic relationship among languages (such as the French–Spanish shared traits in this example), many linguists do not see Dunn et al.'s method of comparing raw typological traits to attempt to see into the distant linguistic past as able to offer reliable results.

Wichmann and Saunders (2007) also used typological features as characters. These authors attempted to identify features least likely to involve diffusion, parallel changes and back mutation, which can frustrate attempts to get accurate phylogenetic results. Wichmann and Saunders tried to choose the features which tend to be more stable diachronically and which are least amenable to change as the result of areal convergence. However, the complicating factors mentioned above are not eliminated directly from their typological features. These authors see their approach (based on the methods adapted from biology) as a new alternative to linguistic methods, not as complementary to the comparative method, as many others do. A serious problem for this approach is the difficulty of identifying stable typological features. Also, typological features exhibit relatively high rates of homoplasy (parallel but independent evolution). Similarly, there is the problem of limited possible typological states. For example, the choice of noun–adjective versus adjective–noun word order as a character is of little value for showing phylogenetic relationships, since even by chance alone, one would expect a 50 per cent match between languages' sharing of one or the other particular order. Some studies find substantial non-tree-like signals in typological data and a poor fit among some languages known to belong to particular language families.

17.4.9 Applications

The various quantitative methods have been applied to a variety of historical linguistic questions, some of which are described briefly in what follows.

17.4.9.1 *Subgrouping*

Most of the quantitative work in historical linguistics is not aimed at establishing new phylogenetic relationships among languages, but rather deals with internal classification (subgrouping) of the languages that belong to already established families. Applications to the Indo-European family of languages are especially well represented. Traditionally, subgrouping of languages that belong to a family of languages relies on the comparative method and on shared innovations (see Chapter 6). Methods designed to create phylogenetic trees should be good at providing subgroup classification of languages; however, as seen above, much depends on the kind of data involved. In the studies that rely on only lexical similarities, no distinction is made between shared innovations and shared retentions. Where this is not done, these approaches are typically less accurate than the traditional method of linguistic subgrouping.

17.4.9.2 *Distant genetic relationships*

Some scholars have attempted to evaluate particular proposals of distant genetic relationship, and some have used related techniques to propose even more wide-reaching groupings (see Chapter 14). As seen above, these proposals have not been found persuasive. On the other hand, Paul Heggarty, in several papers (see Heggarty 2010, for example), uses computational tools to argue against the Quechumaran hypothesis that proposes a distant relationship between Quechuan and Aimaran.

17.4.9.3 *Dating*

In addition to methods to build more accurate trees, new quantitative approaches have been developed to try to provide estimates for the dates of language divergence, and one of the earliest applications of new phylogenetic methods from biology to linguistics was to dating (Gray and Atkinson 2003, Atkinson and Gray 2006). These approaches do not assume that there is a single rate of lexical change, as was assumed in glottochronology. Sanderson (2002) developed the rate-smoothing approach to allow biologists to infer divergence times without having to assume a constant molecular clock. In maximum likelihood and Bayesian phylogenetic analyses of molecular evolution, the length of branches is proportional to the number of substitutions along a branch (changes in the data, that is, changes in cognate sets). The relative branch lengths can be converted into representations of time. This involves calibration points – places where nodes (branching points) on the trees can be matched to known historical dates. These known ages of nodes are combined with information about branch length to estimate rates of change across the whole tree.

The penalized likelihood rate-smoothing approach (Gray and Atkinson 2003), as well as newer dating methods which can relax the clock, have been employed. Drummond et al. (2006) have developed an alternative dating approach, based on 'relaxed phylogenetics', where the tree and the dates are simultaneously estimated, which was utilized, for example by Gray, Atkinson, and Greenhill (2011). The penalized likelihood model allows rates to vary across the tree. Gray and Atkinson (2003) and Atkinson and Gray (2006) attempted to date the divergence among branches of Indo-European. Gray and Atkinson (2003), relying on the Dyen, Kruskal, and Black (1992) Indo-European database, used a Bayesian Markov chain Monte-Carlo simulation method to estimate uncertainty in the trees obtained by sampling across a range of trees with different probabilities. These authors dated fourteen nodes of their Indo-European trees based on external historical information for calibration points, and applied the rate-smoothing algorithm. Their consensus tree is compatible with the trees linguists produce with conventional subgrouping procedures. Gray and Atkinson arrived at a date for the initial break-up of the Indo-European family at around 8700 BP. Most historical linguists disagree, finding this date too early, where the reconstructed vocabulary appears to reflect a date of c. 6500–4500 BP (Mallory and Adams 1997: 296; see also Clackson 2007: 18–19).

Other approaches have been far less sophisticated than the methods employed by Gray, Atkinson, and their colleagues. Forster and Toth (2003), for example, applied a median-joining network to Insular and Continental Celtic languages, calculating dates of split and the order of branching. Their analysis is based on 35 characters (both lexical and grammatical), reduced to 28 useful ones, in 13 Indo-European languages, though for dating only 21 lexical items were counted. Their dates rely on calibrating from known dates of language splits, from which they derive an average of one lexical mutation (change) per 1,350 years, and apply this figure to date the various branches of the tree, for example dating the split of Continental and Insular Celtic to 3200 BC and the break-up of Proto-Indo-European to 8100 BC, dates considered too early by most linguists. Their approach has received severe criticism. It is based on an extremely small number of data; the range of error is very high, ±1,900 years for Indo-European and ±1,500 for Celtic. They rely on superficial similarities rather than on true cognates and fail to take into account the impact of borrowing. This type of network is not used much any more.

As seen above, Holman et al. (2011) propose an automated dating of the world's language families based on lexical similarity (ASJP). They attempt to do a global survey of linguistic divergence, but their method of measuring divergence is not grounded in any reasonable model of linguistic change. The results gave many wrong or unlikely ages. As seen above, there is nothing in how words change or how they are organized in the lexicon that would suggest anything constant in how they change.

17.4.9.4   Contributions to prehistory

Various studies claim their outcomes have relevance for resolving issues in prehistory. For example, Gray and Atkinson (Gray and Atkinson 2003, Atkinson and Gray 2006) believe their results test the so-called Kurgan and the Anatolian hypotheses for the homeland or origin of the Indo-European languages (see Chapter 16), and they argue that the latter view is supported. This hypothesis holds that the original homeland of Proto-Indo-European was in Anatolia, and it links the dispersal of Indo-European languages with the Neolithic spread of agriculture from Anatolia to Europe c. 9000 BP. Gray and Atkinson date the start of the spread of the Indo-European family to around 8700 BP, as stated above. Their analysis does not, they say, agree with the Kurgan (or Steppe) hypothesis, which holds that the spread started around 6000 BP from the steppes of the Ukraine or southern Russian. One difficulty is that even if Gray and Atkinson's dates were accurate, it still does not follow that Anatolian farmers win out over Kurgan horsemen for locating the homeland. (For discussion of alternative hypotheses of the Indo-European homeland, see Mallory and Adams 2006: 460–3.) This is because Gray and Atkinson's study results in a date, not a location, so that Proto-Indo-European could have been spoken anywhere at the time indicated, and not necessarily in Anatolia. Also, as mentioned, most linguists think their date is too early and that the location is unlikely, based on the geographical and lexical evidence.

Phylogenetic methods have also been applied to the question of the settlement of the Pacific (Gray and Jordan 2000, Greenhill and Gray 2005, Gray, Drummond, and Greenhill 2009). Gray and associates argue that their results support the 'Out of Taiwan' hypothesis, with Taiwan as the homeland of Proto-Austronesian, reflecting a settlement pattern through Island Southeast Asia, New Guinea, and Oceania consistent with that postulated by linguists based on other kinds of evidence and considerations. Several other studies could be mentioned. Gray and colleagues believe their Austronesian work is vindication of their methods for a case where lexicostatistics failed. They report that their phylogenetic classification of the family matches that of the comparative method well and that the dates from their methods match the archaeology. (See, for example, Gray, Drummond, and Greenhill 2009, Gray and Jordan 2000, Greenhill, Blust, and Gray 2008, Greenhill, Drummond, and Gray 2010, and Greenhill and Gray 2005.)

17.4.9.5   Probability of cognacy

Work has been done to develop algorithms to determine the probability that lexical characters are cognate (Heeringa, Nerbonne, and Kleiweg 2002, Kondrak 2001, Covington 1996).

Kessler (2001) estimates the likelihood of chance phonemic correspondences using permutation statistics. Kondrak (2002) develops algorithms to detect cognates and sound correspondences. He proposed computer program methods for detecting and quantifying three attributes of cognates important for historical linguistics: phonetic similarity, recurrent sound correspondences, and semantic affinity. This approach combines novel algorithms developed for these tasks with algorithms adapted from biology and natural language processing. These algorithms can process large amounts of data very rapidly that would otherwise take weeks to do by hand. Kondrak, Beck, and Dilts (2007) apply these techniques to identifying cognate sets and sound correspondences, with the object of providing tools for the rapid construction of comparative dictionaries. There have also been some efforts to detect cognates automatically rather than needing to rely on the judgements of expert linguists (Mackay and Kondrak 2005). Ben Hamed, Darlu, and Vallée (2005) and Bouchard-Côté et al. (2007) developed models for phonological data and use them to attempt to identify language families.

McMahon and McMahon (2005) and Nakhleh, Ringe, and Warnow (2005) apply phylogenetic techniques to comparative reconstruction. Ellison and Kirby (2006) suggest means of detecting relationships which do not depend on word-by-word comparisons. Ellison (2007) combines Bayes' theorem with gradient descent in a method for finding cognates and correspondences. Michael Cysouw and Hagen Jung (2007) use an iterative process of alignment between words in different languages in an attempt to identify cognates.

17.4.9.6   Dialectology

Several quantitative publications examine language change from the point of view of dialectology. Hans Goebl, with quantitative analysis of linguistic varieties, also applies his dialectometric techniques to comparisons across related languages (see for example Goebl 2006, Heeringa, Nerbonne, and Kleiweg 2002, Nerbonne and Heeringa 2009). Some dialectometrical techniques have been used for subgrouping of related languages. Quite different quantitative approaches to dialects are found in McMahon et al. 2007 and Maguire et al. 2010, for example.

17.5   Conclusions

As seen here, the quantitative approaches that have been applied to historical linguistics have generated both much enthusiasm and considerable debate. New tools and techniques would clearly be welcome, if they can help resolve continuing uncertainties, contribute with more efficient means of achieving results, provide new insights or discoveries, help correlate findings from other fields, or give linguistics more credibility with scholars in other disciplines – though this should not be needed. Clearly computational methods and algorithms can make it possible to process and analyze quantities of data not imaginable by traditional means. And new approaches can perhaps provide us with more illuminating visual means of representing language relationships and changes, for example as Neighbour-Net and Bayesian analyses promise. However, as we have seen, approaches that do not move beyond lexical data alone, or that do not provide for the various ways that characters (traits) can be similar beyond just inheritance from a common ancestor (phylogenetic explanation), tend to find less favour among historical linguists. Glottochronology is rejected for good reasons. On the other hand, quantitative investigations have discovered or at least hold out promise for ways of investigating the possible significance of frequency of usage of particular words, which basic lexical items (meanings) tend to be replaced more often and which retained more. Many historical linguists are likely, however, to remain sceptical or to maintain a wait-and-see attitude about attempts to find and evaluate phylogenetic trees, to establish subgrouping, to date changes and the diversification of language families, to see into the distant past beyond the scope of the comparative method, or to detect distant genetic relationships.

Bibliography

Abondolo, Daniel, 'Introduction', in Daniel Abondolo (ed.), *The Uralic Languages* (London: Blackwell, 1998), pp. 1–42.

Adelaar, Willem F. H., 'Review of *Language in the Americas* by Joseph H. Greenberg', *Lingua* 78 (1989), 249–55.

Aitchison, Jean, 'The language lifegame: prediction, explanation and linguistic change', in Willem Koopman, Frederike van der Leek, Olga Fischer and Roger Eaton (eds), *Explanation and Linguistic Change* (Amsterdam: John Benjamins, 1987), pp. 11–32.

Aitchison, Jean, *Language Change: Progress or Decay?*, 3rd edn, Cambridge Approaches to Linguistics Series (Cambridge: Cambridge University Press, 2001 [1st edn London: Fortuna, 1981]).

Alvar, Manuel, *Lingüística románica*, reworked and heavily annotated; originally by Iorgu Iordan (Madrid: Ediciones Alcalá, 1967).

Andersen, Henning, 'Center and periphery: adoption, diffusion and spread', in Jacek Fisiak (ed.), *Historical Dialectology* (Berlin: Mouton de Gruyter, 1988), pp. 39–83.

Anderson, James M., *Structural Aspects of Language Change* (London: Longman, 1973).

Anttila, Raimo, 'The relation between internal reconstruction and the comparative method', *Ural-Altaischer Jahrbücher* 40 (1968), 159–73.

Anttila, Raimo, *An Introduction to Historical and Comparative Linguistics* (New York: Macmillan, 1972 [2nd edn: Current Issues in Linguistic Theory, 4, Amsterdam: John Benjamins, 1989]).

Arlotto, Anthony, *Introduction to Historical Linguistics* (Boston: Houghton Mifflin, 1972 [reprinted: Washington, DC: University Press of America, 1981]).

Atkinson, Quentin D. and Russell D. Gray, 'Curious parallels and curious connections? Phylogenetic thinking in biology and historical linguistics', *Systematic Biology* 54 (2005), 513–26.

Atkinson, Quentin D. and Russell D. Gray, 'Are accurate dates an intractable problem for historical linguistics?', in C. P. Lipo, M. J. O'Brien, M. Collard and S. J. Shennan (eds), *Mapping our Ancestors: Phylogenetic Approaches in Anthropology and Prehistory* (New Brunswick: Aldine, 2006), pp. 269–98.

Atkinson, Quentin, Geoff Nicholls, David Welch and Russell Gray, 'From words to dates: water into wine, mathemagic or phylogenetic inference?', *Transactions of the Philological Society* 10 (2005), 193–219.

Bach, Adolph, *Deutsche Mundartforschung*, 3rd edn (Heidelberg: Carl Winter, 1969).

Baehrens, W. A., *Sprachlicher Kommentar zur vulgärlateinischen Appendix Probi* (Halle an der Saale: Max Niemeyer, 1922). (Reprinted, Groningen: Bouma's Boekhuis, 1967.)

Bakker, Peter, 'Phoneme inventories, language contact, and grammatical complexity: a critique of Trudgill', *Linguistic Typology* 8 (2004), 368–75.

Baxter, William H. and Alexis Manaster Ramer, 'Beyond lumping and splitting: probabilistic issues in historical linguistics', in Colin Renfrew, April McMahon and Larry Trask (eds), *Time Depth in Historical Linguistics* (Cambridge: McDonald Institute for Archaeological Research, 2000), pp. 167–88.

Beekes, Robert S. P., *Comparative Indo-European Linguistics: An Introduction* (Amsterdam: John Benjamins, 1995).

Bellwood, Peter, 'Early agriculturalist population diasporas? Farming, languages and genes', *Annual Review of Anthropology* 30 (2001), 181–207.

Bellwood, Peter, 'Farmers, foragers, languages, genes: the genesis of agricultural societies', in Peter Bellwood and Colin Renfrew (eds), *Examining the Farming/Language Dispersal Hypothesis* (Cambridge: McDonald Institute for Archaeological Research, 2002), pp. 17–28.

Ben Hamed, M., P. Darlu and N. Vallée, 'On cladistic reconstruction of linguistic trees through vowel data', *Journal of Quantitative Linguistics* 12 (2005), 79–109.

Berlin, Brent and Paul Kay, *Basic Color Terms: Their Universality and Evolution* (Berkeley: University of California Press, 1969).

Berman, Howard, 'A comment on the Yurok and Kalapuya data in Greenberg's *Language in the Americas*', *International Journal of American Linguistics* 58 (1992), 320–48.

Bhat, D. N. S., *Sound Change* (Delhi: Motilal Banarsidass Publishers, 2001).

Bloch, Oscar and Walther von Wartburg, *Dictionnaire étymologique de la langue française*, 5th edn (Paris: Presses Universitaires de France, 1968).

Bloomfield, Leonard, 'On the sound system of Central Algonquian', *Language* 1 (1925), 130–56.

Bloomfield, Leonard, 'A note on sound-change', *Language* 4 (1928), 99–100.

Bloomfield, Leonard, *Language* (New York: Holt, Rinehart and Winston, 1933).

Blount, Ben G., 'Comments on *Speaking of forked Tongues: The Feasibility of Reconciling Human Phylogeny and the History of Language*', *Current Anthropology* 31 (1990), 15.

Boas, Franz, 'On alternating sounds', *American Anthropologist* 2 (1889), 47–53 (old series).

Bolnick, Deborah A. (Weiss), Beth A. (Schultz) Shook, Lyle Campbell and

Ives Goddard, 'Problematic use of Greenberg's linguistic classification of the Americas in studies of Native American genetic variation', *American Journal of Human Genetics* 75 (2004), 519–23. Also at: www.journals.uchicago.edu/AJHG/journal/issues/v75n3/41367/41367.web.pdf.

Börjars, Kersti and Nigel Vincent, 'The pre-conditions for suppletion', in Alexandra Galani, Glyn Hicks and George Tsoulas (eds), *Morphology and its Interfaces* (Amsterdam: John Benjamins, 2011), pp. 21–48.

Bouchard-Côté, Alexandre., Percy Liang, Thomas L. Griffiths and Dan Klein, 'A probabilistic approach to diachronic phonology', in *Proceedings of the 2007 Joint Conference on Empirical Methods in Natural Language Processing and Computational Natural Language Learning (EMNLP/CoNLL)* (Prague: Association for Computational Linguistics, 2007), pp. 887–96.

Bowern, Claire, Patience Epps, Russell Gray, Jane Hill, Keith Hunley, Patrick McConvell and Jason Zentz, 'Does lateral transmission obscure inheritance in hunter-gatherer languages?', *PLoS ONE* 6.e25195 (2011). www.plosone.org/article/info%3Adoi%2F10.1371%2Fjournal.pone.00251.

Bowern, Claire and Harold Koch (eds), *Australian Languages: Classification and the Comparative Method* (Amsterdam: John Benjamins, 2004).

Brinton, Daniel G., 'The language of palæolithic man', *Proceedings of the American Philosophical Society* (1888), 3–16. (Reprinted: 'The earliest form of human speech, as revealed by American tongues', in *Essays of an Americanist* by Daniel G. Brinton (Philadelphia: Porter & Coates, 1890), pp. 390–409.)

Broadwell, George Aaron, 'Reconstructing Proto-Muskogean language and prehistory: preliminary results', paper presented at the Southern Anthropological Society, St. Augustine, FL (1992). http://albany.academia.edu/GeorgeAaronBroadwell/Papers/540546/Reconstructing_Proto-Muskogean_Language_and_Prehistory_Preliminary_results.

Brody, Jill M., 'Particles borrowed from Spanish as discourse markers in Mayan languages', *Anthropological Linguistics* 29 (1989), 507–21.

Brody, Jill M., 'Lending the "unborrowable": Spanish discourse markers in indigenous American languages', in Carmen Silva-Corvalan (ed.), *Spanish in Four Continents: Studies in Language Contact and Bilingualism* (Washington, DC: Georgetown University Press, 1995), pp. 132–47.

Brown, Cecil H., Eric W. Holman, Søren Wichmann and Viveka Velupillai, 'Automated classification of the world's languages: a description of the method and preliminary results', *STUF-Language Typology and Universals* 61 (2007), 285–308.

Brown, Cecil H. and Stanley R. Witkowski, 'Aspects of the phonological history of Mayan-Zoquean', *International Journal of American Linguistics* 45 (1979), 34–47.

Brown, Herbert A., *A Comparative Dictionary of Orokolo Gulf of Papua*, Pacific Linguistics, C-84 (Canberra: Pacific Linguistics, 1986).

Bybee, Joan L., Revere D. Perkins and William Pagliuca, *The Evolution of Grammar: Tense, Aspect, and Modality in the Languages of the World* (Chicago: University of Chicago Press, 1994).

Bynon, Theodora, *Historical Linguistics* (Cambridge: Cambridge University Press, 1977).

Callaghan, Catherine A. and Geoffrey Gamble, 'Borrowing', in Ives Goddard (ed.), *Handbook of North American Indians*, vol. 17 (Washington, DC: Smithsonian Institution, 1997), pp. 111–16.

Campbell, Lyle, 'Distant genetic relationships and the Maya-Chipaya hypothesis', *Anthropological Linguistics* 15:3 (1973), 113–35. (Reprinted: *Special Issue: A Retrospective of the Journal of Anthropological Linguistics: Selected Papers, 1959–1985. Anthropological Linguistics* 35:1–4 (1993), 66–89.)

Campbell, Lyle, 'Language contact and sound change', in William M. Christie Jr (ed.), *Current Progress on Historical Linguistics: Proceedings of the Second International Conference on Historical Linguistics* (Amsterdam: North Holland, 1976), pp. 111–94.

Campbell, Lyle, *Quichean Linguistic Prehistory*, University of California Publications in Linguistics, 81 (Berkeley and Los Angeles: University of California Press, 1977).

Campbell, Lyle, 'The implications of Mayan historical linguistics for glyphic research', in John Justeson and Lyle Campbell (eds), *Phoneticism in Mayan Hieroglyphic Writing*, Institute for Mesoamerican Studies, Pub. 9 (Albany: State University of New York, Institute for Mesoamerican Studies, 1984), pp. 1–16.

Campbell, Lyle, 'Areal linguistics and its implications for historical linguistic theory', in Jacek Fisiak (ed.), *Proceedings of the Sixth International Conference of Historical Linguistics* (Amsterdam: John Benjamins, 1985), pp. 25–48.

Campbell, Lyle, 'Syntactic change in Pipil', *International Journal of American Linguistics* 53 (1987), 253–80.

Campbell, Lyle, *The Linguistics of Southeast Chiapas*, Papers of the New World Archaeological Foundation, 51 (Provo, UT: The New World Archaeological Foundation, 1988a).

Campbell, Lyle, 'Review article on *Language in the Americas*', *Language* 64 (1988b), 591–615.

Campbell, Lyle, 'Syntactic reconstruction and Finno-Ugric', in Henning Andersen and Konrad Koerner (eds), *Historical Linguistics 1987* (Amsterdam: John Benjamins, 1990), pp. 51–94.

Campbell, Lyle, 'Some grammaticalization changes in Estonian', in Elizabeth C. Traugott and Bernd Heine (eds), *Approaches to Grammaticalization, vol. I: Theoretical and Methodological Issues* (Amsterdam: John Benjamins, 1991), pp. 285–99.

Campbell, Lyle, 'On proposed universals of grammatical borrowing', in Henk Aertsen and Robert Jeffers (eds), *Historical Linguistics 1989: Papers from the 9th International Conference on Historical Linguistics* (Amsterdam: John Benjamins, 1993), pp. 91–109.

Campbell, Lyle, 'Linguistic reconstruction and unwritten languages', in R. E. Asher and J. M. Y. Simpson (eds), *Encyclopedia of Language and Linguistics* (London: Pergamon Press, 1994), pp. 3,475–80.

Campbell, Lyle, 'On sound change and challenges to regularity', in Mark Durie and Malcolm Ross (eds), *The Comparative Method Reviewed: Regularity and Irregularity in Language Change* (Oxford: Oxford University Press, 1996), pp. 72–89.

Campbell, Lyle, *American Indian Languages: The Historical Linguistics of Native America* (Oxford: Oxford University Press, 1997a).

Campbell, Lyle, 'On the linguistic prehistory of Finno-Ugric', in Raymond Hickey and Stanislaw Puppel (eds), *Language History and Linguistic Modelling: A Festschrift for Jacek Fisiak on his 60th Birthday* (Berlin: Mouton de Gruyter, 1997b), pp. 829–61.

Campbell, Lyle, 'Nostratic: a personal assessment', in Brian Joseph and Joe Salmons (eds), *Nostratic: Sifting the Evidence* (Amsterdam: John Benjamins, 1998), pp. 107–52.

Campbell, Lyle, 'Nostratic and linguistic palaeontology in methodological perspective', in Colin Renfrew and Daniel Nettle (eds), *Nostratic: Evaluating a Linguistic Macrofamily* (Cambridge: The McDonald Institute for Archaeological Research, 1999), pp. 179–230.

Campbell, Lyle (ed.), *Grammaticalization: a critical assessment*. Special issue of *Language Sciences*, vol. 23, 2–3 (2001).

Campbell, Lyle, 'Beyond the comparative method?', in Barry Blake and Kate Burridge (eds), *Historical Linguistics 2003* (Amsterdam: John Benjamins, 2003a), pp. 33–58.

Campbell, Lyle, 'What drives linguistic diversity and language spread?', in Peter Bellwood and Colin Renfrew (eds), *Examining the Farming/Language Dispersal Hypothesis* (Cambridge: McDonald Institute for Archaeological Research, 2003b), pp. 49–63.

Campbell, Lyle, 'How to show languages are related: methods for distant genetic relationship', in Brian D. Joseph and Richard D. Janda (eds), *Handbook of Historical Linguistics* (Oxford: Blackwell, 2003c), pp. 262–82.

Campbell, Lyle, 'What can we learn about the earliest human language by comparing languages known today?', in Bernard Laks with Serge Cleuziou, Jean-Paul Demoule and Pierre Encrevé (eds), *Origins and Evolution of Language: Approaches, Models, Paradigms* (London: Equinox, 2008), pp. 79–111.

Campbell, Lyle, 'Review of *The Dene–Yeniseian Connection* ed. by Kari, James and Ben A. Potter', *International Journal of American Linguistics* 77 (2011), 445–51.

Campbell, Lyle, 'The classification of South American indigenous languages', in Lyle Campbell and Verónica Grondona (eds), *The Indigenous Languages of South America: A Comprehensive Guide* (Berlin: Mouton de Gruyter, 2012), pp. 59–166.

Campbell, Lyle and Verónica Grondona, 'Who speaks what to whom? Multilingualism and language choice in Misión La Paz – a unique case', *Language in Society* 39 (2010), 1–30.

Campbell, Lyle and Terrence Kaufman, 'A linguistic look at the Olmecs', *American Antiquity* 41 (1976), 80–9.

Campbell, Lyle and Terrence Kaufman, 'Mayan linguistics: where are we now?', *Annual Review of Anthropology* 14 (1985), 187–98.

Campbell, Lyle, Terrence Kaufman and Thomas Smith-Stark, 'Mesoamerica as a linguistic area', *Language* 62 (1986), 530–70.

Campbell, Lyle and Ronald Langacker, 'Proto-Aztecan vowels' parts 1–3, *International Journal of American Linguistics* 44:2 (1978), 85–102, 44:3 (1978), 197–210, 44:4 (1978), 262–79.

Campbell, Lyle and Martha Muntzel, 'The structural consequences of language death', in Nancy Dorian (ed.), *Investigating Obsolescence: Studies in Language Death*, Studies in the Social and Cultural Foundations of Language 7 (Cambridge: Cambridge University Press, 1989), pp. 181–96.

Campbell, Lyle and David Oltrogge, 'Proto-Tol (Jicaque)', *International Journal of American Linguistics* 46 (1980), 205–23.

Campbell, Lyle and William J. Poser, *Language Classification: History and Method* (Cambridge: Cambridge University Press, 2008).

Campbell, Lyle and Jon Ringen, 'Teleology and the explanation of sound change', in Wolfgang U. Dressler, Oskar E. Pfeiffer and John R. Rennison (eds), *Phonologica* (Innsbruck: Innsbrucker Beiträge zur Sprachwissenschaft, 1981), pp. 57–68.

Canfield, Lincoln D., *Spanish Pronunciation in the Americas* (Chicago: University of Chicago Press, 1982).

Carpelan, Christian, 'Late palaeolithic and Mesolithic settlement of the European north – possible linguistic implications', in Christian Carpelan, Asko Parpola and Petteri Koskikallio (eds), *Early Contacts between Uralic and Indo-European: Linguistics and Archaeological Considerations* (Mémoires de la Société Finno-Ougrienne, 242) (Helsinki: Finno-Ugrian Society, 2001), pp. 37–53.

Cerrón-Palomino, Rodolfo, *Lingüística quechua*, Biblioteca de la tradición oral andina, 8 (Cuzco: Centro de Estudios Rurales Andinos 'Bartolomé de las Casas', 1987).

Cerrón-Palomino, Rodolfo, *Lingüística aimara* (Cuzco: Centro de Estudios Regionales Aninos 'Bartolomé de Las Casas', 2000).

Clackson, James, *Indo-European Linguistics: An Introduction* (Cambridge: Cambridge University Press, 2007).

Collinge, N. E., *The Laws of Indo-European* (Amsterdam: John Benjamins, 1985).

Constenla Umaña, Adolfo, 'Chibchan languages', in Lyle Campbell and Verónica Grondona (eds), *The Indigenous Languages of South America: A Comprehensive Guide* (Berlin: Mouton de Gruyter, 2012), pp. 391–440.

Cook, Eung-Do, 'Is phonology going haywire in dying languages? Phonological variations in Chipewyan and Sarcee', *Language in Society* 18 (1989), 235–55.

Corominas, Joan and José Pascual, *Diccionario crítico etimológico castellano e hispanico*, 6 vols (Madrid: Gredos, 1980).

Cortelazzo, Manlio and Paolo Zolli, *Dizionario etimologico della lingua italiana* (Bologna: Zanichelli, 1979–88).

Covington, Michael A., 'An algorithm to align words for historical comparison', *Computational Linguistics* 22 (1996), 481–96.

Croft, William, *Explaining Language Change: An Evolutionary Approach* (Harlow: Longman, 2000).

Crowley, Terry, 'Review of *The Rise and Fall of Languages* by R. M. W. Dixon', *Australian Journal of Linguistics* 19 (1999), 109–15.

Crowley, Terry and Claire Bowern, *An Introduction to Historical Linguistics*, 4th edn (Auckland: Oxford University Press, 2010).

Curnow, Timothy J. and Anthony J. Liddicoat, 'The Barbacoan languages of Colombia and Ecuador', *Anthropological Linguistics* 40 (1998), 384–408.

Cysouw, Michael and Hagen Jung, 'Cognate identification and alignment using practical orthographies', *Proceedings of Ninth Meeting of the ACL Special Interest Group in Computational Morphology and Phonology* (Prague: Association for Computational Linguistics, 2007), pp. 109–16.

Dahl, Östen, 'Principles of areal typology', in Martin Haspelmath, E. König, W. Oesterreicher and W. Raible (eds), *Language Universals and Language Typology: An International Handbook* (Berlin: Mouton de Gruyter, 2001), pp. 1456–70.

Dahl, Östen and Maria Koptjevskaja-Tamm (eds), *The Circum-Baltic Languages: Typology and Contact* (Amsterdam: John Benjamins, 2001).

Darmesteter, Arsène, *A Historical French Grammar* (London: Macmillan, 1922).

Dauzat, Albert, *La Géographie linguistique*, 9 cartes (Paris: Flammarion, 1822).

de Saussure, Ferdinand, *see* Saussure, Ferdinand de.

DeCamp, David, 'The development of pidgin and creole studies', in Albert Valdman (ed.), *Pidgin and Creole Linguistics* (Bloomington: Indiana University Press, 1977), pp. 3–20.

Delbrück, Berthold, *Introduction to the Study of Language: A Critical Survey of the History and Methods of Comparative Philology of the Indo-European Languages* (1882), English trans. of *Einleitung in das Sprachstudium: Ein Beitrag zur Methodik der vergleichenden Sprachforschung* (Leipzig: Breitkopf & Härtel, 1880).

Dennett, Daniel C., *Darwin's Dangerous Idea: Evolution and the Meanings of Life.* (London: Penguin, 1995).

Dixon, R. M. W., *The Rise and Fall of Languages* (Cambridge: Cambridge University Press, 1997).

Dixon, R. M. W., *Australian Languages* (Cambridge: Cambridge University Press, 2002).

Dolgopolsky, Aaron, 'A probabilistic hypothesis concerning the oldest relationships among the language families', in Vitaly V. Shevoroshkin and Thomas L. Markey (eds), *Typology Relationship and Time: A Collection of Papers on Language Change and Relationship by Soviet Linguists* (Ann Arbor: Karoma, 1986), pp. 27–50. (Translation of Aaron Dolgopolsky, 'Gipoteza drevnejsego rodstva jazykovyx semej Severnoj Evraziji s verojatnostnoj tochki zrenija', *Voprosy Jazykoznanija* 2 (1964), 53–63.)

Donohue, Mark and Simon Musgrave, 'Typology and the linguistic macrohistory of Island Melanesia', *Oceanic Linguistics* 46 (2007), 348–87.

Dorian, Nancy C., *Language Death: The Life Cycle of a Scottish Gaelic Dialect* (Philadelphia: University of Pennsylvania Press, 1981).

Drummond, A. J., S. Y. W. Ho, M. J. Phillips and A. Rambaut, 'Relaxed phylogenetics and dating with confidence', *PLoS Biology* 4:e88 (2006).

Dunn, Michael, Stephen C. Levinson and Eva Lindström, 'Structural phylogeny in historical linguistics: methodological explorations applied in island Melanesia', *Language* 84 (2008), 710–59.

Dunn, Michael, Angela Terrrill, Ger Reesink, Robert A. Foley and Stephen C. Levinson, 'Structural phylogenetics and the reconstruction of ancient language history', *Science* 309 (2005), 2072–5.

Dyen, Isidore, *The Lexicostatistical Classification of Austronesian Languages*, International Journal of American Linguistics Memoir 19 (Bloomington: University of Indiana, 1965).

Dyen, Isidore, Joseph B. Kruskal and Paul Black, *An Indo-European Classification: A Lexicostatistical Experiment*, Transactions of the American Philosophical Society vol. 82, part 5 (Philadelphia: American Philosophical Society, 1992).

Ebert, Robert Peter, *Historische Syntax des Deutschen* (Stuttgart: Sammlung Metzler, 1978).

Ehret, Christopher, *Reconstructing Proto-Afroasiatic (Proto-Afrasian): Vowels, Tone, Consonants, and Vocabulary* (Berkeley and Los Angeles: University of California Press, 1995).

Eldredge, Niles and Stephen Jay Gould, 'Punctuated equilibria: an alternative to phyletic gradualism', in T. J. M. Schopf (ed.), *Methods in Paleobiology* (San Francisco: Freeman, Cooper, 1972), pp. 82–115.

Ellison, T. Mark, 'Bayesian identification of cognates and correspondences', *Proceedings of Ninth Meeting of the ACL Special Interest Group in Computational Morphology and Phonology* (Stroudsburg, PA: Association for Computational Linguistics, 2007), 15–22.

Ellison, T. Mark and Simon Kirby, 'Measuring language divergence by intra-lexical comparison', *Proceedings of the 21st International Conference on Computational Linguistics and the 44th Annual Meeting of the Association for Computational Linguistics, Sydney, Australia* (Stroudsburg, PA: Association for Computational Linguistics, 2006), pp. 273–80.

Embleton, Sheila, *Statistics in Historical Linguistics* (Bochum: Brockmeyer, 1986).

Emeneau, Murray B., *Language and Linguistic Area: Essays by Murray B. Emeneau*, selected and introduced by Anwar S. Dil (Stanford: Stanford University Press, 1980).

Evans, Nicolas (ed.), *The Non-Pama-Nyungan Languages of Northern Australia: Comparative Studies of the Continent's Most Linguistically Complex Region* (Canberra: Pacific Linguistics, Research School of Pacific and Asian Studies, Australian National University, 2003).

Farmer, Steve, Richard Sproat and Michael Witzel, 'The collapse of the Indus-script thesis: the myth of a literate Harappan civilization', *Electronic Journal of Vedic Studies* 11 (2004), 19–57.

Ferguson, Charles, 'The Ethiopian language area', in M. L. Bender, J. D. Bowen, R. L. Cooper and C. A. Ferguson (eds), *Language in Ethiopia* (Oxford: Oxford University Press, 1976), pp. 63–76.

Fisher, John H. and Diane Bornstein, *In form of speche is chaunge: Readings in the History of the English Language* (Englewood Cliffs, NJ: Prentice-Hall, 1974).

Fleischman, Suzanne, 'The Romance languages', in William Bright (ed.), *International Encyclopedia of Linguistics*, 4 vols (Oxford: Oxford University Press, 1992), vol. 3, pp. 337–43.

Fleming, Harold C., 'Towards a definitive classification of the world's languages' (Review of *A Guide to the World's Languages* by Merritt Ruhlen), *Diachronica* 4 (1987), 159–223.

Fogelberg, Paul (ed.), *Pohjan poluilla: Suomalaisten juuret nykytutkimuksen mukaan* [On paths of the north: the roots of the Finns according to current research], Bildrag till kännedom av Finlands natur och folk, 153 (Helsinki: Finnish Society of Science and Letters, 1999).

Forster, Peter and Alfred Toth, 'Toward a phylogenetic chronology of ancient Gaulish, Celtic, and Indo-European', *Proceedings of the National Academy of Sciences* 100 (2003), 9079–84.

Fortson, Benjamin W., IV., *Indo-European Language and Culture: An Introduction* (Oxford: Wiley-Blackwell, 2011).

Fowler, Catherine S., 'Some ecological clues to Proto-Numic homelands', in D. D. Fowler (ed.), *Great Basin Cultural Ecology: A Symposium*, Desert Research Institute publications in the social sciences, 8 (Reno: University of Nevada, 1972), pp. 105–21.

Fowler, Catherine S., 'Some lexical clues to Uto-Aztecan prehistory', *International Journal of American Linguistics* 49 (1983), 224–57.

Friedrich, Paul, *Proto-Indo-European Trees: The Arboreal System of a Prehistoric People* (Chicago: University of Chicago Press, 1970).

Friedrich, Paul, 'Dialectal variation in Tarascan phonology', *International Journal of American Linguistics* 37 (1971), 164–87.

Gabelentz, Georg von der, *Die Sprachwissenschaft: ihre Aufgaben, Methoden, und bisherigen Ergebnisse* (Leipzig: T. O. Weigel Nachfolger, 1891).

Gardner, Alan, *Egyptian Grammar: Being an Introduction to the Study of Hieroglyphs*, 3rd edn (Oxford: Griffith Institute, 1957).

Gardner, Peter M., *Bicultural Versatility as a Frontier Adaptation among Paliyan Foragers of South India* (Lewiston, NY: Edwin Mellen Press, 2000).

Garrett, Andrew, 'A new model of Indo-European subgrouping and dispersal', in Steve S. Chang, Lily Liaw and Josef Ruppenhofer (eds), *Proceedings of the Twenty-fifth Annual Meeting of the Berkeley Linguistics Society* (Berkeley: Berkeley Linguistics Society, 1999), pp. 146–56.

Giacalone Ramat, Anna, 'Testing the boundaries of grammaticalization', in Anna Giacalone Ramat and Paul J. Hopper (eds), *The Limits of Grammaticalization* (Amsterdam: John Benjamins, 1998), pp. 227–70.

Gildea, Spike, 'The development of tense markers from demonstrative pronouns in Panare (Cariban)', *Studies in Language* 17 (1993), 53–73.

Gilliéron, Jules, *Pathologie et thérapeutique verbales* (Paris: Champion, 1921).

Gilliéron, Jules and Mario Roques, *Étude de géographie linguistique* (Paris: Champion, 1912).

Gimbutas, Marija, 'The Indo-Europeans: archaeological problems', *American Anthropologist* 65 (1963), 815–36.

Givón, Talmi, 'Historical syntax and synchronic morphology: an archaeologist's field trip', *Chicago Linguistic Society* 7 (1971), 394–415.

Goddard, Ives, 'Review of *Language in the Americas* by Joseph H. Greenberg', *Current Anthropology* 28 (1987), 656–7.

Goddard, Ives, 'The West-to-East cline in Algonquian dialectology', in William Cowan (ed.), *Actes du vingt-cinquième congrès des algonquinistes* (Ottawa: Carleton University, 1994), pp. 187–211.

Goebl, Hans, 'Recent advances in Salzburg dialectometry', *Literary and Linguistics Computing* 21 (2006), 411–35.

Gordon, Elizabeth, Lyle Campbell, Jennifer Hay, Margaret Maclagan, Andrea Sudbury and Peter Trudgill, *New Zealand English: Its Origins and Evolution* (Cambridge: Cambridge University Press, 2004).

Gorrochategui, Joaquín and Joseba Lakara, 'Nuevas aportaciones a la reconstruccíon del protovasco', in Francisco Villar and José d'Encarnação (eds), *La Hispania prerromana: Actas del VI Coloquio sobre lenguas y culturas de la Penísula Ibérica* (Salamanca: Ediciones Universidad de Salamanca, 1996), pp. 101–45.

Gorrochategui, Joaquín and Joseba Lakara, 'Comparación lingüística, filología y reconstrucción del protovasco', in Francisco Villar and José d'Encarnação (eds) *Religión, lengua y cultura prerromanas de Hispania: Actas del VIII Coloquio sobre lenguas y culturas de la Penísula Ibérica* (Salamanca: Ediciones Universidad de Salamanca, 2001), 407–38.

Gould, Stephen Jay and Elisabeth S. Vrba, 'Exaptation: a missing term in the science of form', *Paleobiology* 8 (1982), 4–15.

Gray, Russell D. and Quentin D. Atkinson, 'Language-tree divergence times support the Anatolian theory of Indo-European origin', *Nature* 426 (2003), 435–9.

Gray, Russell D., Quentin D. Atkinson and Simon J. Greenhill, 'Language evolution and human history: what a difference a date makes', *Philosophical Transactions of the Royal Society, B*, 366 (2011), 1090–100.

Gray, Russell D., A. J. Drummond and Simon J. Greenhill, 'Language phylogenies reveal expansion pulses and pauses in Pacific settlement', *Science* 323 (2009), 479–83.

Gray, Russell D. and F. M. Jordan, 'Language trees support the express-train sequence of Austronesian expansion', *Nature* 405 (2000), 1052–5.

Greenberg, Joseph H., *Languages of Africa*, Publications of the Research Center in Anthropology, Folklore, and Linguistics, no. 25 (Bloomington: Indiana University Press, 1963).

Greenberg, Joseph H., 'The Indo-Pacific hypothesis', in Thomas A. Sebeok (ed.), *Current Trends in Linguistics 8: Linguistics in Oceania* (The Hague: Mouton, 1971), pp. 807–71.

Greenberg, Joseph H., *Language in the Americas* (Stanford: Stanford University Press, 1987).

Greenberg, Joseph H., *Indo-European and its Closest Relatives: The Eurasiatic Language Family* (Stanford: Stanford University Press, 2000).

Greenberg, Joseph H. and Merritt Ruhlen, 'Linguistic origins of Native Americans', *Scientific American* 1992 (1992), 60–5.

Greenhill, Simon J., 'Levenshtein distances fail to identify language relationships accurately', *Computational Linguistics* 37 (2011), 689–98.

Greenhill Simon J., Quentin D. Atkinson, Andrew Meade and Russell D. Gray, 'The shape and tempo of language evolution', *Proceedings of the Royal Society B* 277 (2010), 2443–50.

Greenhill, Simon J., Robert Blust and Russell Gray, 'The Austronesian basic vocabulary database: from bioinformatics to lexomics', *Evolutionary Bioinformatics* 4 (2008), 271–83.

Greenhill, Simon J., T. E. Currie and Russell Gray, 'Does horizontal transmission invalidate cultural phylogenies?', *Proceedings of the Royal Society B* 276 (2009), 2299–306.

Greenhill, Simon J., A. J. Drummond and Russell D. Gray, 'How accurate and robust are the phylogenetic estimates of Austronesian language relationships?', *PLoS ONE*, 5.3:e9573 (2010).

Greenhill, Simon J. and Russell D. Gray, 'Testing population dispersal hypotheses: Pacific settlement, phylogenetic trees and Austronesian languages', in R. Mace, C. J. Holden and S. Shennan (eds), *The Evolution of Cultural Diversity: Phylogenetic Approaches* (London: University College London Press, 2005), pp. 31–52.

Grimm, Jakob and Wilhelm Grimm, *Deutsches Wörterbuch* (Leipzig: Hirzel, 1854).

Grünthal, Riho and Tapani Salminen (eds), *Geographical Distribution of the Uralic Languages* [map] (Helsinki: Finno-Ugrian Society, 1993).

Haas, Mary R., *The Prehistory of Languages* (The Hague: Mouton, 1969a).

Haas, Mary R., 'Internal reconstruction of the Nootka-Nitinat pronominal suffixes', *International Journal of American Linguistics* 35 (1969b), 108–24.

Hajdú, Péter, 'Finnougrische Urheimatforschung', *Ural-Altaische Jahrbücher* 41 (1969), 252–64.

Hajdú, Péter, *Finno-Ugric Languages and Peoples* (London: André Deutsch, 1975).

Hajek, John, 'Consonant inventories as an areal feature of the New Guinea-Pacific region: testing Trudgill's hypothesis', *Linguistic Typology* 8 (2004), 384–8.

Häkkinen, Kaisa, 'Wäre es schon an der Zeit, den Stammbaum zu fallen? Theorien über die gegenseitigen Verwandtschaftsbeziehungen der finnisch-ugrischen Sprachen', *Ural-Altaische Jahrbücher* 4 (1984), 1–4.

Häkkinen, Kaisa, 'Prehistoric Finno-Ugric culture in the light of historical lexicology', in Christian Carpelan, Asko Parpola and Petteri Koskikallio (eds), *Early Contacts between Uralic and Indo-European: Linguistics and Archaeological Considerations* (Mémoires de la Société Finno-Ougrienne, 242) (Helsinki: Finno-Ugrian Society 2001), pp. 169–86.

Hakulinen, Lauri, *Suomen kielen rakenne ja kehitys* [The structure and history of the Finnish language] (Helsinki: Otava, 1968).

Hale, Horatio, 'On some doubtful or intermediate articulations: an experiment in phonetics', *Journal of the Royal Anthropological Institute* 14 (1884), 233–43.

Hale, Kenneth, 'Classification of Northern Paman languages, Cape York Peninsula, Australia: a research report', *Oceanic Linguistics* 3 (1964), 248–64.

Hale, Kenneth, 'Phonological developments in particular Northern Paman languages', in Peter Sutton (ed.), *Languages of Cape York*, Research and Regional Studies 6 (Canberra: Australian Institute of Aboriginal Studies, 1976), pp. 7–40.

Hammarström, Harald, 'A full-scale test of the language farming dispersal hypothesis', *Diachronica* 27 (2010), 197–213.

Hancock, Ian, 'On Romani origins and identity', Romani Archives and Documentation Center, University of Texas, Austin (2006). www.radoc.net/radoc.php?doc=art_b_history_origins&lang=en&articles=true.

Harris, Alice C. and Lyle Campbell, *Historical Syntax in Cross-linguistic Perspective* (Cambridge: Cambridge University Press, 1995).

Harrison, S. P., 'On the limits of the comparative method', in Brian Joseph and Richard Janda (eds), *The Handbook of Historical Linguistics* (Oxford: Blackwell, 2004), pp. 213–43.

Haspelmath, Martin and Uri Tadmor, *Loanwords in the World's Languages: a Comparative Handbook* (Berlin: Mouton de Gruyter, 2009). Also at: http://wold.livingsources.org.

Hay, Jennifer and Laurie Bauer, 'Phoneme inventory size and population size', *Language* 83 (2007), 388–400.

Heath, Jeffrey, *Linguistic Diffusion in Arnhem Land*, Australian aboriginal studies research and regional studies, no. 13 (Canberra: Australian Institute of Aboriginal Studies, 1978).

Heeringa, Wilbert, John Nerbonne and Peter Kleiweg, 'Validating dialect comparison methods', in W. Gaul and G. Ritter (eds), *Classification, Automation, and New Media* (Berlin, Heidelberg and New York: Springer, 2002), pp. 445–52.

Heggarty, Paul, 'Interdisciplinary indiscipline? Can phylogenetic methods meaningfully be applied to language data – and to dating language?', in Peter Forster and Colin Renfrew (eds), *Phylogenetic Methods and the Prehistory of Languages* (Cambridge: McDonald Institute for Archaeological Research, 2006), pp. 183–94.

Heggarty, Paul, 'Beyond lexicostatistics: how to get more out of "word list" comparisons', *Diachronica* 7 (2010), 301–24.

Heggarty, Paul, Warren Maguire and April McMahon, 'Splits or waves? Trees or webs? How divergent measures and network analysis can unravel language histories', *Philosphical Transactions of the Royal Society B* 365 (2010), 3829–43.

Heine, Bernd and Tania Kuteva, *World Lexicon of Grammaticalization* (Cambridge: Cambridge University Press, 2002).

Heine, Bernd and Mechthild Reh, *Grammaticalization and Reanalysis in African Languages* (Hamburg: Buske, 1984).

Hock, Hans Henrich, *Principles of Historical Linguistics* (Berlin: Mouton de Gruyter, 1986).

Hock, Hans Henrich and Brian D. Joseph, *Language History, Language Change, and Language Relationship: An Introduction to Historical and Comparative Linguistics* (Berlin: Walter de Gruyter, 1996).

Hogg, Richard M., 'Phonology and morphology', in Richard M. Hogg (ed.), *The Cambridge History of the English Language*, vol. 1, *The Beginnings to 1066* (Cambridge: Cambridge University Press, 1992), pp. 67–167.

Hoijer, Harry, 'Tonkawa: an Indian language of Texas', in Franz Boas (ed.), *Handbook of American Indian Languages*, vol. 3 (New York: Columbia University Press, 1933), pp. i–x, 1–148.

Hoijer, Harry, 'Tonkawa', in Harry Hoijer (ed.), *Linguistic Structures of Native America*, Viking Fund Publications in Anthropology 6 (New York: Viking Fund, 1946), pp. 289–311.

Holden, Clare J., 'Bantu language trees reflect the spread of farming across sub-Saharan Africa: a maximum-parsimony analysis', *Proceedings of the Royal Society of London B* 269 (2002), 793–9.

Holman, Eric W., 'Do languages originate and become extinct at constant rates?', *Diachronica* 27 (2010), 214–25.

Holman, Eric W., Cecil H. Brown, Søren Wichmann, André Müller, Viveka Velupillai, Harald Hammarström, Sebastian Sauppe, Hagen Jung, Dik Bakker, Pamela Brown, Oleg Belyaev, Matthias Urban, Robert Mailhammer, Johann-Mattis List and Dmitry Egorov, 'Automated dating of the world's language families based on lexical similarity', *Current Anthropology* 52 (2011), 841–75.

Holman, Eric W., Søren Wichmann, Cecil H. Brown, Viveka Velupillai, André Müller and Dik Bakker, 'Explorations in automated lexicostatistics', *Folia Linguistica* 42 (2008), 331–54.

Hopper, Paul J. and Elizabeth Closs Traugott, *Grammaticalization*, 2nd edn (Cambridge: Cambridge University Press, 2003).

Horrocks, Geoffrey, *Greek: A History of the Language and its Speakers* (London: Longman, 1997).

Hübschmann, Heinrich, 'Über die Stellung des armenischen im Kreise der indogermanischen Sprachen', *Zeitschrift für Vergleichende Sprachforschung* 23 (1875), 5–42.

Hymes, Dell H., 'Speech and language: on the origins and foundations of inequality among speakers', in Morton Bloomfield and Einar Haugen (eds), *Language as a Human Problem* (New York: W. W. Norton & Co., 1974), pp. 45–71.

Igla, Birgit, 'Romani', in Hans Goebl, Peter H. Nelde, Zdenek Stary and Wolfgang Wölck (eds), *Contact Linguistics: An International Handbook of Contemporary Research* 14 (Berlin: Mouton de Gruyter, 1997), pp. 1961–71.

Ihalainen, Ossi, 'The dialects of England since 1776', in Robert Burchfield (ed.), *The Cambridge History of the English Language*, vol. 5: *English in Britain and Overseas: Origins and Development* (Cambridge: Cambridge University Press, 1994), pp. 197–274.

Ilari, Rodolfo, *Lingüística Românica*, 3rd edn (São Paulo:Editora Ática, 2001).

Illich-Svitych, Vladislav M., 'The Nostratic reconstructions of V. Illich-Svitych, translated and arranged by Mark Kaiser', in Vitaly Shevoroshkin (ed.), *Proto-Languages and Proto-Cultures: Materials from the first*

International Interdisciplinary Symposium on Language and Prehistory (Bochum: Brockmeyer, 1990), pp. 138–67.

Jakobson, Roman, 'Why "mama" and "papa"?', in Bernard Kaplan and Seymour Wapner (eds), *Perspectives in Psychological Theory* (New York: International Universities Press, 1960), pp. 21–9. (Reprinted: *Roman Jakobson: Selected Writings*, vol. 1, *Phonological Studies* (The Hague: Mouton, 1962), pp. 538–45.)

Janhunen, Juha, 'Uralilaisen kantakielen sanastosta' [On the vocabulary of the Uralic proto-language], *Journal de la Société Finno-Ougrienne* 77 (1981), 219–74.

Janhunen, Juha, 'On the structure of Proto-Uralic', *Finno-Ugrische Forschungen* 44 (1982), 23–42.

Janhunen, Juha, 'On the paradigms of Uralic comparative studies', *Finno-Ugrische Forschungen* 56 (2001), 29–41.

Janson, Tore, *Speak: A Short History of Languages* (Oxford: Oxford University Press, 2002).

Jasanoff, Jay H., *Hittite and the Indo-European Verb* (Oxford: Oxford University Press, 2003).

Jeffers, Robert J. and Ilse Lehiste, *Principles and Methods for Historical Linguistics* (Cambridge, MA: MIT Press, 1979).

Jespersen, Otto, *Progress in Language, with Special Reference to English* (London: S. Sonnenschein, 1894).

Jespersen, Otto, *Language, its Nature, Development, and Origin* (New York: W. W. Norton & Co., 1964).

Joki, Aulis J., *Uralier und Indogermanen*, Suomalais-ugrilaisen Seuran toimituksia, 151 (Helsinki: Suomalais-ugrilaisen Seura, 1973).

Joos, Martin, 'Preface', in idem (ed.), *Readings in Linguistics: The Development of Descriptive Linguistics in America since 1925*, 2nd edn (New York: American Council of Learned Societies, 1958), pp. v–vii.

Joseph, Brian, *Morphology and Universals in Syntactic Change: Evidence from Medieval and Modern Greek* (New York: Garland Publishers, 1990).

Joseph, Brian, 'Balkan languages', in William Bright (ed.), *International Encyclopedia of Linguistics*, 4 vols (Oxford: Oxford University Press, 1992), vol. 1, pp. 153–5.

Joseph, Brian D. and Richard D. Janda (eds), *The Handbook of Historical Linguistics* (Oxford: Blackwell, 2003).

Justeson, John and Lyle Campbell (eds), *Phoneticism in Mayan Hieroglyphic Writing*, Institute for Mesoamerican Studies Publication 9 (Albany/Austin: SUNY/University of Texas Press, 1984).

Justeson, John S. and Terrence Kaufman, 'A decipherment of epi-Olmec hieroglyphic writing', *Science* 259 (1993), 1703–11.

Justeson, John S., William Norman, Lyle Campbell and Terrence Kaufman, *The Foreign Impact on Lowland Mayan Languages and Script*, Middle American Research Institute, publication 53 (New Orleans: Tulane University, 1985).

Kaiser, Mark and Vitaly Shevoroshkin, 'Nostratic', *Annual Review of Anthropology* 17 (1988), 309–30.

Kaufman, Terrence, 'Gypsy wanderings and linguistic borrowing', unpublished paper (University of Pittsburgh, 1973).

Kaufman, Terrence, 'Archaeological and linguistic correlations in Mayaland and associated areas of Meso-America', *World Archaeology* 8 (1976), 101–18.

Kessler, Brent, *The Significance of Word Lists* (Stanford: CSLI Publications, 2001).

Kettunen, Lauri, *Suomen murteet II: Murrealueet* [Finnish dialects II: dialect areas] (Helsinki: Suomalaisen Kirjallisuuden Seura, 1930).

Kettunen, Lauri, *Suomen murteet III: Murrekartasto* [Finnish dialects III: dialect atlas], 3rd 'abridged' edn, (Helsinki: Suomalaisen Kirjallisuuden Seura, 1969).

Kimball, Geoffrey, 'A critique of Muskogean, "Gulf", and Yukian material in *Language in the Americas*', *International Journal of American Linguistics* 58 (1992), 447–501.

King, Robert, *Generative Grammar and Historical Linguistics* (Englewood Cliffs, NJ: Prentice-Hall, 1969).

Kinkade, M. Dale, 'Prehistory of the native languages of the Northwest Coast', in *The North Pacific to 1600*, 2 vols (Portland: The Oregon Historical Society Press, 1991), vol. 1, pp. 137–58.

Kiparsky, Paul, *Explanation in Phonology* (Dordrecht: Foris, 1982).

Klima, Edward, 'Relatedness between grammatical systems', *Language* 40 (1964), 1–20.

Kluge, Friedrich, *Etymologisches Wörterbuch der deutschen Sprache*, 24th edn [1st edn 1883] (Berlin: de Gruyter, 2002).

Koch, Harold, 'Pama-Nyungan reflexes in the Arandic languages', in Darrell Tryon and Michael Walsh (eds), *Boundary Rider: Essays in Honour of Geoffrey O'Grady*, Pacific Linguistics C-136 (Canberra: Research School of Pacific Studies, Australian National University, 1997), pp. 271–301.

Koivulehto, Jorma, 'The earliest contacts between Indo-European and Uralic speakers in the light of lexical loans', in Christian Carpelan, Asko Parpola and Petteri Koskikallio (eds), *Early Contacts between Uralic and Indo-European: Linguistics and Archaeological Considerations* (Mémoires de la Société Finno-Ougrienne, 242) (Helsinki: Finno-Ugrian Society, 2001), pp. 235–63.

Kondrak, Grzegorz, 'Identifying cognates by phonetic and semantic similarity', *Proceedings of the Second Meeting of the North American Chapter of the Association for Computational Linguistics (NAACL-2001)* (Pittsburgh, 2001), pp. 103–10.

Kondrak, Grzegorz, *Algorithms for Language Reconstruction* (University of Toronto, PhD dissertation, 2002).

Kondrak, Grzegorz, David Beck and Philip Dilts, 'Creating a comparative dictionary of Totonac-Tepehua', *Proceedings of Ninth Meeting of the ACL Special Interest Group in Computational Morphology and Phonology* (Prague: Association for Computational Linguistics, 2007), pp. 134–41.

Koptjevskaja-Tamm, Maria and Bernhard Wälchli, 'The Circum-Baltic languages: an areal-typological approach', in Östen Dahl and Maria

Koptjevskaja-Tamm (eds), *The Circum-Baltic Languages: Typology and Contact* (Amsterdam: John Benjamins, 2001), pp. 615–761.

Korhonen, Mikko, *Johdatus Lapin kielen historiaan* [Introduction to the history of the Lapp language] (Helsinki: Suomalaisen Kirjallisuuden Seura, 1981).

Korhonen, Mikko, 'Suomalaisten suomalais-ugrilainen tausta historiallisvertailevan kielitieteen valossa' [The Finno-Ugric background of the Finns in the light of comparative-historical linguistics], in Jarl Gallén (ed.), *Suomen väestön esihistorialliset juuret*, Bidrag till kännedom av Finlands natur och folk, Utgivna av Finska Vetenskaps-Societeten, 131 (Helsinki: Finska Vetenskaps-Societeten, 1984), pp. 55–71.

Krause, Wolfgang, *Handbuch des Gotischen*, 3rd edn (Munich: Beck, 1968).

Kroskrity, Paul V., *Language, History, and Identity: Ethnolinguistic Studies of the Arizona Tewa* (Tucson: University of Arizona Press, 1993).

Kuhn, Franz Felix Adalbert, *Zur ältesten Geschichte der indogermanischen Völker* (Berlin: Berliner Real-Gymnasium, 1845).

Kuryłowicz, Jerzy, 'La nature des procès dits "analogiques"', *Acta Linguistica* 5 (1947), 121–38.

Kuryłowicz, Jerzy, 'Zur Vorgeschichte des germanischen Verbalsystems', in *Beiträge zur Sprachwissenschaft, Volkskunde und Literaturforschung: Wolfgang Steinitz zum 60. Geburtstag* (Berlin: Akademie-Verlag, 1965), pp. 242–7.

Laalo, Klaus, *Imperfektimuotojen ti~si -vaihtelu suomen kielessä* [The past tense ti~si alternation in Finnish] (Helsinki: Suomalaisen Kirjallisuuden Seura, 1988).

Laanest, Arvo, *Einführung in die ostseefinnischen Sprachen* (Hamburg: Buske, 1982).

Labov, William (ed.), *Locating Language in Time and Space* (New York: Academic Press, 1980).

Labov, William, *Principles of Linguistic Change: Internal Factors* (Oxford: Blackwell, 1994, 2001).

Labov, William, *Principles of Linguistic Change: Cognitive and Cultural Factors* (Oxford: Wiley-Blackwell, 2010).

Labov, William, Sharon Ash and Charles Boberg, *The Atlas of North American English* (Berlin: Mouton de Gruyter, 2006).

Lakarra, Joseba A., 'Reconstructing the pre-Proto-Basque root', in José Ignacio Hualde, Joseba A. Lakarra and R. L. Trask (eds), *Towards a History of the Basque Language* (Amsterdam: John Benjamins, 1995), pp. 189–206.

Lapesa, Rafael, *Historia de la lengua española*, 9th edn (Madrid: Gredos, 1981).

LaPolla, Randy, 'The role of migration and language contact in the development of the Sino-Tibetan language family', in Alexandra Y. Aikhenvald and R. M. W. Dixon (eds), *Areal Diffusion and Genetic Inheritance: Problems in Comparative Linguistics* (Oxford: Oxford University Press, 2001), pp. 225–54.

Lass, Roger, *On Explaining Language Change* (Cambridge: Cambridge University Press, 1980).

Lass, Roger, 'Phonology and morphology', in Norman Blake (ed.), *The*

Cambridge History of the English Language, vol. 2, *1066–1476* (Cambridge: Cambridge University Press, 1992), pp. 23–155.

Lass, Roger, *Historical Linguistics and Language Change* (Cambridge: Cambridge University Press, 1997).

LeBlanc, Steven A., 'Conflict and language dispersal: issues and a New World example', in Colin Renfrew and Peter Bellwood (eds), *Examining the Farming/Language Dispersal Hypothesis* (Cambridge: McDonald Institute for Archaeological Research, 2003), pp. 357–65.

Lees, Robert B., 'The basis of glottochronology', *Language* 29 (1953), 113–27.

Lehiste, Ilse, *Lectures on Language Contact* (Cambridge, MA: MIT Press, 1988).

Lehmann, Christian, *Thoughts on Grammaticalization* (Munich: Lincom Europa, 1995).

Lehmann, Walter, *Zentral-Amerika* (Berlin: Museum für Völkerkunde zu Berlin, 1920).

Lehmann, Winfred P., *Historical Linguistics: An Introduction* (New York: Holt, 1962).

Levinson, Stephen C. and Russell D. Gray, 'Tools from evolutionary biology shed new light on the diversification of languages', *Trends in Cognitive Sciences* 16 (2012), 167–73.

Lightfoot, David, *Principles of Diachronic Syntax* (Cambridge: Cambridge University Press, 1979).

Lightfoot, David, *How to Set Parameters: Arguments from Language Change* (Cambridge, MA: MIT Press, 1991).

Lohr, Marisa, *Methods for the Genetic Classification of Languages* (University of Cambridge, PhD dissertation, 1999).

Lord, Robert, *Comparative Linguistics*, 2nd edn (London: English Universities Press, 1974).

Mackay, Wesley and Grzegorz Kondrak, 'Computing word similarity and identifying cognates with Pair Hidden Markov Models', *Proceedings of the 9th Conference on Computational Natural Language Learning (CoNLL)* (Morristown, NJ: Association for Computational Linguistics, 2005), pp. 40–7.

Maclagan, Margaret A. and Elizabeth Gordon, 'Out of the AIR and into the EAR: another view of the New Zealand diphthong merger', *Language Variation and Change* 8 (1996), 125–47.

Maguire, Warren, Paul Heggarty, April McMahon and Dan Dediu, 'The past, present and future of English dialects: quantifying convergence, divergence and dynamic equilibrium', *Language Variation and Change* 22 (2010), 69–104.

Maiden, Martin, *A Linguistic History of Italian* (London and New York: Longman, 1995).

Mallory, J. P., *In Search of the Indo-Europeans: Language, Archaeology, and Myth* (London: Thames and Hudson, 1989).

Mallory, J. P., 'Uralics and Indo-Europeans: problems of time and space', in Christian Carpelan, Asko Parpola and Petteri Koskikallio (eds), *Early Contacts Between Uralic and Indo-European: Linguistics and Archaeological*

Considerations (Mémoires de la Société Finno-Ougrienne, 242) (Helsinki: Finno-Ugrian Society, 2001), pp. 345–66.

Mallory, J. P. and D. Q. Adams, *Encyclopedia of Indo-European Culture* (London: Fitzroy Dearborn, 1997).

Mallory, J. P. and D. Q. Adams, *The Oxford Introduction to Proto-Indo-European and the Proto-Indo-European World* (Oxford: Oxford University Press, 2006).

Mańczak, Witold, 'Tendences générales des changements analogiques', *Lingua* 7 (1958), 298–325, 387–420

Martinet, André, *Économie des changements phonétiques: traité de phonologie diachronique*, 3rd edn [1st edn 1955] (Berne: A. Francke, 1970).

Masica, Colin P., *The Indo-Aryan Languages* (Cambridge: Cambridge University Press, 1991).

Matras, Yaron, *Romani: A Linguistic Introduction* (Cambridge: Cambridge University Press, 2002).

McMahon, April, 'Language, time and human histories', in Frank Brisard, Sigurd d'Hondt and Tanja Mortelmans (eds), *Language and Revolution/ Language and Time*, Antwerp Papers in Linguistics 106 (Antwerp: University of Antwerp, 2004), pp. 155–70.

McMahon, April, Paul Heggarty, Robert McMahon and Warren Maguire, 'The sound patterns of Englishes: representing phonetic similarity', *English Language and Linguistics* 11 (2007), 113–42.

McMahon, April and Robert McMahon, 'Linguistics, genetics and archaeology: internal and external evidence in the Amerind controversy', *Transactions of the Philological Society* 93 (1995), 125–225.

McMahon, April and Robert McMahon, 'Finding families: quantitative methods in language classification', *Transactions of the Philological Society* 101 (2003), 7–55.

McMahon, April and Robert McMahon, *Language Classification by Numbers* (Oxford: Oxford University Press, 2005).

Meillet, Antoine, 'L'évolution des formes grammaticales', *Scientia* 12:26 (Milan, 1912). (Reprinted: *Linguistique historique et linguistique générale* (Paris: Champion, 1948), pp. 130–48.)

Meillet, Antoine, 'Le problème de la parenté des langues', *Scientia* 15:35 (1914). (Reprinted: *Linguistique historique et linguistique générale* (Paris: Champion, 1948), pp. 76–102.)

Meillet, Antoine, *La Méthode comparative en linguistique historique* (Oslo: H. Aschehoug, 1925).

Meillet, Antoine, *The Comparative Method in Historical Linguistics* (trans. of *La Méthode comparative en linguistique historique*, 1925, reissued 1966) (Paris: Champion, 1967).

Meillet, Antoine, *Linguistique historique et linguistique générale*, Société Linguistique de Paris, Collection Linguistique, 8 (Paris: Champion, 1948).

Meillet, Antoine and Marcel Cohen, *Les Langues du monde* (Paris: Champion, 1924).

Membreño, Alberto, *Hondureñismos: vocabulario de los provincialismos de Honduras*, 2nd edn (Tegucigalpa: Tipografía Nacional, 1897).

Menner, Robert,'The conflict of homonyms in English', *Language* 12 (1936), 229–44.

Metcalf, George J., 'The Indo-European hypothesis in the sixteenth and seventeenth centuries', in Dell Hymes (ed.), *Studies in the History of Linguistics: Traditions and Paradigms* (Bloomington: Indiana University Press, 1974), pp. 233–57.

Meyer-Lübke, Wilhelm, *Romanisches Etymologisches Wörterbuch*, 5th edn (Heidelberg: Winter, 1972).

Michelena [Mitxelena], Luis [Koldo], *Sobre historia de la lengua vasca*, ed. Joseba A. Lakarra, Suplementos del *Anuario de Filología Vasca 'Julio de Urquijo'* 10, 2 vols (Donastia and San Sebastian: Diputación Foral de Guipúzcoa, 1988).

Michelena [Mitxelena], Luis [Koldo], 'The ancient Basque consonants', in José Ignacio Hualde, Joseba A. Lakarra and R. L. Trask (eds), *Towards a History of the Basque Language* (Amsterdam: John Benjamins, 1995), pp. 101–35.

Milroy, James, *Linguistic Variation and Change: On the Historical Sociolinguistics of English* (Oxford: Blackwell, 1992).

Müller, Max, *Lectures on the Science of Language* (New York: Charles Scribner and Company, 1866).

Mutaka, Ngessimo N., *An Introduction to African Linguistics* (Munich: Lincom Europa, 2000).

Nakhleh, Luay, Don Ringe and Tandy Warnow, 'Perfect phylogenetic networks: a new methodologyfor reconstructing the evolutionary history of natural languages', *Language* 81 (2005), 382–420.

Nakhleh, Luay, Tandy Warnow, Donald Ringe and S. N. Evans, 'A comparison of phylogenetic reconstruction methods on an Indo-European dataset', *Transactions of the Philological Society* 103 (2005), 171–92.

Nelson-Sathi, Shijulal, Johann-Mattis List, Hans Geisler, Heiner Fangerau, Russell D. Gray, William Marti and Tal Dagan, 'Networks uncover hidden lexical borrowing in Indo-European language evolution', *Proceedings of the Royal Society B Biological Sciences* 278 (2010), 1794–803.

Nerbonne, John and Wilbert Heeringa, 'Measuring dialect differences', in J. E. Schmidt and P. Auer (eds), *Language and Space: Theories and Methods* (Berlin: Mouton de Gruyter, 2009), pp. 550–67.

Nettle, Daniel, *Linguistic Diversity* (Oxford: Oxford University Press, 1999).

Nettle, Daniel and Suzanne Romaine, *Vanishing Voices: The Extinction of the World's Languages* (Oxford: Oxford University Press, 2000).

Nevis, Joel A., 'Language-external evidence for clitics as words: Lappish particle clitics', *Chicago Linguistic Society* 21 (1985), 289–305.

Newman, Paul, 'Comparative linguistics', in Bernd Heine and Derek Nurse, *African Languages: An Introduction* (Cambridge: Cambridge University Press, 2000), pp. 259–71.

Nichols, Johanna, 'The origins and dispersal of languages: linguistic evidence', in Nina Jablonski and Leslie Aiello (eds), *The Origin and Diversification of Language* (San Francisco: California Academy of Sciences, 1998), pp. 127–70.

Öhmann, Emil, 'Über Homonymie und Homonyme im Deutschen', *Suomalaisen Tiedeakatemian Toimituksia*, series B, 32 (1934), 1–143.

Oinas, Felix J., *The development of Some Postpositional Cases in Balto-Finnic Languages,* Mémoires de la Société Finno-Ougrienne 123 (Helsinki: Suomalais-Ugrilaisen Seura, 1961).

Olson, Ronald D., 'Mayan affinities with Chipaya of Bolivia I: Correspondences', *International Journal of American Linguistics* 30 (1964), 313–24.

Olson, Ronald D., 'Mayan affinities with Chipaya of Bolivia II: Cognates', *International Journal of American Linguistics* 31 (1965), 29–38.

Orel, Vladimir and Olga V. Stolbova, *Hamito-Semitic Etymological Dictionary: Materials for a Reconstruction* (Leiden: Brill, 1995).

Orton, Harold, Eugen Dieth, P. M. Tilling and Wilfrid J. Halliday, *Survey of English Dialects*, 4 vols (Leeds: Arnold, 1962–71).

Osthoff, Hermann and Karl Brugmann, *Morphologische Untersuchungen auf dem Gebiete der indogermanischen Sprachen* (Leipzig: S. Hirzel, 1878).

Oswalt, Robert L., 'The detection of remote linguistic relationships', *Computer Studies in the Humanities and Verbal Behavior* 3 (1970), 117–29.

Otsuka, Yuko, 'History of the Polynesian languages'. www2.hawaii.edu/~yotsuka/course/PN_history.pdf (2005).

Oxford English Dictionary, 2nd edn [1st edn 1971] (Oxford: Oxford University Press, 1989).

Pagel, Mark, 'Maximum-likelihood models for glottochronology and for constructing linguistic phylogenies', in Colin Renfrew, April McMahon and Larry Trask (eds), *Time Depth in Historical Linguistics* (Cambridge: McDonald Institute for Archaeological Research, 2000), pp. 189–207.

Pagel, Mark, Quentin D. Atkinson and Andrew Meade, 'Frequency of word-use predicts rates of lexical evolution throughout Indo-European history', *Nature* 449 (2007), 717–20.

Pagel, Mark and A. Meade, 'Estimating rates of lexical replacement on phylogenetic trees of languages', in Colin Renfrew and P. Forster (eds), *Phylogenetic Methods and the Prehistory of Languages* (Cambridge: McDonald Institute for Archaeological Research, 2006), pp. 173–82.

Palmer, Leonard R., *Descriptive and Comparative Linguistics: A Critical Introduction* (London: Faber & Faber, 1972).

Palosaari, Naomi and Lyle Campbell, 'Structural aspects of language endangerment', in Peter K. Austin and Julia Sallabank (eds), *The Cambridge Handbook of Endangered Languages* (Cambridge: Cambridge University Press, 2011), pp. 100–19.

Paul, Hermann, *Prinzipien der Sprachgeschichte*, 5th edn [1st edn 1880] (Tübingen: Max Niemeyer, 1920).

Payne, Edward J., *History of the New World called America* (Oxford: Clarendon Press, 1899).

Penny, Ralph, *A History of the Spanish Language* (Cambridge: Cambridge University Press, 1991).

Pericliev, Vladimir, 'There is no correlation between the size of a community speaking a language and the size of the phonological inventory of that language', *Linguistic Typology* 8 (2004), 376–83.

Pictet, Adolphe, *Les Origines indo-européennes, ou, les Aryas primitifs: Essai de paléontologie linguistique* (Paris: J. Cherbuliez, 1859–63).

Pinker, Steven, *The Language Instinct* (New York: W. Morrow & Co., 1994).

Polenz, Peter von, *Geschichte der deutschen Sprache* (Berlin: Walter de Gruyter, 1977).

Poser, William J., 'The Salinan and Yurumangui data in *Language in the Americas*', *International Journal of American Linguistics* 58 (1992), 202–9.

Pulgram, Ernst, 'The nature and use of proto-languages', *Lingua* 10 (1961), 18–37.

Rankin, Robert L., 'Review of *Language in the Americas*, by Joseph H. Greenberg', *International Journal of American Linguistics* 58 (1992), 324–51.

Ravila, Paavo, 'Suomen suku ja suomen kansa' [The Finnish stock and the Finnish people], *Suomen historian käsikirja I* [Handbook of the history of Finnish I] (Porvoo: Werner Söderström, 1949).

Ravila, Paavo, *Johtadus kielihistoriaan* [Introduction to language history] (Helsinki: Suomalaisen Kirjallisuuden Seura, 1966).

Ravila, Paavo, *Johdatus kielihistoriaan* [Introduction to language history], 4th edn, Tietolipas 3 (Helsinki: Suomalaisen Kirjallisuuden Seura, 1975).

Rédei, Károly, *Uralisches etymologisches Wörterbuch* (7 fascicles) (Budapést: Akadémiai Kiadó, 1986–8).

Renfrew, Colin, 'Language families and the spread of farming', in D. R. Harris (ed.), *The Origins and Spread of Agriculture and Pastoralism in Eurasia* (London: University College London Press, 1996), pp. 70–92.

Resnik, Melvyn C., *Introducción a la historia de la lengua española* (Washington, DC: Georgetown University Press, 1981).

Rexova, K., D. Frynta and J. Zrzavy, 'Cladistic analysis of languages: Indo-European classification based on lexicostatistical data', *Cladistics* 19 (2003), 120–7.

Rice, Keren, 'Language contact, phonemic inventories, and the Athapaskan language family', *Linguistic Typology* 8 (2004), 321–43.

Ringe, Donald A. Jr, 'On calculating the factor of chance in language comparison', *Transactions of the American Philosophical Society* 82 (1992), 1–110.

Ringe, Donald A., Jr, 'The mathematics of "Amerind"', *Diachronica* 13 (1996), 135–54.

Ringe, Donald A., Jr, 'Probabilistic evidence for Indo-Uralic', in Brian Joseph and Joe Salmons (eds), *Nostratic: Sifting the Evidence* (Amsterdam: John Benjamins, 1998), pp. 153–97.

Ringe, Donald A. Jr, 'How hard is it to match CVC-roots?', *Transactions of the Philological Society* 97 (1999), 213–44.

Ringe, Donald Jr, Tandy Warnow and Ann Taylor, 'Indo-European computational cladistics', *Transactions of the Philological Society* 100 (2002), 59–129.

Rivet, Paul, 'Les Australiens en Amérique', *Bulletin de la Société Linguistique de Paris* 26 (1925), 23–63.

Rodrigues, Aryon Dall'Igna and Ana Suelly Arruda Câmara Cabral, 'Tupían', in Lyle Campbell and Verónica Grondona (eds), *The Indigenous Languages of South America: A Comprehensive Guide* (Berlin: Mouton de Gruyter, 2012), pp. 59–166.

Róna-Tas, András, 'Turkic influence on the Uralic languages', in Denis Sinor (ed.), *The Uralic Languages: Description, History, and Foreign Influences* (Leiden: Brill, 1988), pp. 742–80.

Ross, Malcolm D., 'Contact-induced change and the comparative method: cases from Papua New Guinea', in Mark Durie and Malcolm Ross (eds), *The Comparative Method Reviewed: Regularity and Irregularity in Language Change* (Oxford: Oxford University Press, 1996), pp. 180–217.

Ross, Malcolm D., 'Social networks and kinds of speech community events', in R. M. Blench and Matthew Spriggs (eds), *Archaeology and Language 1: Theoretical and Methodological Orientations* (London: Routledge, 1997), pp. 209–61.

Ross, Malcolm D., Andrew Pawley and Meredith Osmond (eds), *The Lexicon of Proto Oceanic: The Culture and Environment of Ancestral Oceanic Society*, 1: *Material Culture* (Pacific Linguistics, C-152) (Canberra: Pacific Linguistics, 1998b).

Ruhlen, Merritt, *On the Origin of Languages: Studies in Linguistic Taxonomy* (Stanford: Stanford University Press, 1994).

Salminen, Tapani, 'The rise of the Finno-Ugric language family', in Christian Carpelan, Asko Parpola and Petteri Koskikallio (eds), *Early Contacts between Uralic and Indo-European: Linguistic and Archaeological Considerations* (Mémoires de la Société Finno-Ougrienne, 242) (Helsinki: Finno-Ugrian Society, 2001), pp. 385–96.

Sammallahti, Pekka, 'Saamelaisten esihistoriallinen tausta kielitieteen valossa' [The prehistorical background of the Saami in the light of linguistics], in Jarl Gallén (ed.), *Suomen väestön esihistorialliset juuret*, Bidrag till kännedom av Finlands natur och folk, Utgivna av Finska Vetenskaps-Societeten, 131 (Helsinki: Finska Vetenskaps-Societeten, 1984), pp. 137–56.

Sammallahti, Pekka, 'Historical phonology of the Uralic languages: with special reference to Samoyed, Ugric, and Permic', in Denis Sinor (ed.), *The Uralic Languages: Description, History, and Foreign Influences* (Leiden: Brill, 1988), pp. 478–554.

Sammallahti, Pekka, 'The Indo-European loanwords in Saami', in Christian Carpelan, Asko Parpola and Petteri Koskikallio (eds), *Early Contacts between Uralic and Indo-European: Linguistic and Archaeological Considerations* (Mémoires de la Société Finno-Ougrienne, 242) (Helsinki: Finno-Ugrian Society, 2001), pp. 397–415.

Sanderson, M. J., 'Estimating absolute rates of molecular evolution and divergence times: a penalized likelihood approach', *Molecular Biology and Evolution* 19 (2002), 101–9.

Sandfeld, Kristian, *Linguistique balkanique: problèmes et résultats* (Paris: Champion, 1930).

Sapir, Edward, 'Wiyot and Yurok, Algonkin languages of California', *American Anthropologist* 15 (1913), 617–46.

Sapir, Edward, 'The status of linguistics as a science', *Language* 5 (1929),

207–14. (Reprinted: David Mandelbaum (ed.), *Selected Writings of Edward Sapir in Language, Culture, and Personality* (Berkeley and Los Angeles: University of California Press, 1949), pp. 160–6.)

Sapir, Edward, 'The concept of phonetic law as tested in primitive languages by Leonard Bloomfield', in S. Rice (ed.), *Methods in Social Science: A Case Book* (Chicago: University of Chicago Press, 1931), pp. 297–306. (Reprinted: David Mandelbaum (ed.), *Selected Writings of Edward Sapir in Language, Culture, and Personality* (Berkeley and Los Angeles: University of California Press, 1949), pp. 73–82.)

Sapir, Edward, 'Time perspective in aboriginal American culture: a study in method', in David Mandelbaum (ed.), *Selected Writings of Edward Sapir in Language, Culture, and Personality* (Berkeley: University of California Press, 1949), pp. 389–467. (Original edn: Department of Mines, Geological survey, Memoir no. 90 (Ottawa: Government Printing Bureau, 1916).)

Saussure, Ferdinand de, *Cours de linguistique générale* (Paris: Payot, 1916).

Sayce, Archibald Henry, *The Principles of Comparative Philology* (London: Trübner, 1874).

Schleicher, August, *Compendium der vergleichenden Grammatik der indogermanischen Sprachen: Kurzer Abriss einer Laut- und Formenlehre der indogermanischen Ursprache* (Weimar: Hermann Böhlau, 1861–2).

Schmidt, Johannes, *Die Verwandtschaftsverhältnisse der indogermanischen Sprachen* (Weimar: Böhlau, 1872).

Schrader, Otto, *Sprachvergleichung und Urgeschichte: Linguistisch-historische Beiträge zur Erforschung des indogermanischen Altertums* (Jena: Costenoble, 1883). (English translation: *Prehistoric Antiquities of the Aryan peoples: A Manual of Comparative Philology and the Earliest Culture* (London: C. Griffin and Company, 1890).

Schuchardt, Hugo, *Vokalismus*, vol. 3 (Leipzig: Teubner, 1868).

Serva, Maurizio and Filippo Petroni, 'Indo-European languages tree by Levenshtein distance', *EPL (Europhysics Letters)* 81.6: paper 68005 (2008).

Siebert, Frank T. Jr, 'The original home of the Proto-Algonquian people', Contributions to Anthropology: Linguistics 1, *National Museum of Canada Bulletin* 214 (1967), 13–47.

Snow, Dean R., 'The archaeological implications of the Proto-Algonquian Urheimat', in William Cowan (ed.), *Papers of the Seventh Algonquian Conference* (Ottawa: Carleton University, 1976), pp. 339–46.

Spaulding, Robert K., *How Spanish Grew* (Berkeley: University of California Press, 1965).

Starostin, Sergei, *Altajskaja Problema i Proisxozhdenie Japonskogo Jazyka* [The Altaic problem and the origin of the Japanese language] (Moscow: Nauka, 1991).

Stubbs, Brian, *Uto-Aztecan: A Comparative Vocabulary* (Blanding, UT: Shumway Family History Services and Rocky Mountain Books and Productions, 2011).

Suárez, Jorge, *Estudios Huaves*, Colección Científica, Lingüística, 22 (México: Departamento de Lingüística, Instituto Nacional de Antropología e Historia, 1975).

Suhonen, Seppo, 'Uralilainen alkukoti' [The Uralic homeland], in Paul Fogelberg (ed.), *Pohjan poluilla: Suomalaisten juuret nykytutkimuksen mukaan* [On paths of the north: the roots of the Finns according to current research], Bildrag till kännedom av Finlands natur och folk, 153 (Helsinki: Finnish Society of Science and Letters, 1999), pp. 240–4.

Swadesh, Morris, 'The phonetics of Chitimacha', *Language* 10 (1934), 345–62.

Swadesh, Morris, 'Chitimacha', in Harry Hoijer (ed.), *Linguistic Structures of Native America*, Publications in Anthropology 6 (New York: Viking Fund, 1946), pp. 312–36.

Swadesh, Morris, 'Mosan I: a problem of remote common origin', *International Journal of American Linguistics* 19 (1953), 26–44.

Sweet, Henry, *The History of Language* (London: J. M. Dent & Co., 1900).

Sweetser, Eve, *From Etymology to Pragmatics: Metaphorical and Cultural Aspects of Semantic Structure* (Cambridge: Cambridge University Press, 1990).

Teeter, Karl V., 'Algonquian languages and genetic relationship', in Horace G. Lunt (ed.), *Proceedings of the 9th International Congress of Linguists* (The Hague: Mouton, 1964), pp. 1026–33.

Thomason, Sarah G., *Language Contact: An Introduction* (Edinburgh: Edinburgh University Press, 2001).

Thomason, Sarah Grey and Terrence Kaufman, *Language Contact, Creolization, and Genetic Linguistics* (Berkeley: University of California Press, 1988).

Thompson, J. Eric S., *A Catalogue of Maya Hieroglyphics* (Norman: University of Oklahoma Press, 1962).

Thompson, J. Eric S., *Maya History and Religion* (Norman: University of Oklahoma Press, 1970).

Todd, Loreto, *Pidgins and Creoles* (London: Routledge and Kegan Paul, 1974).

Tosco, Mauro, 'Is there an "Ethiopian Language Area"?' *Anthropological Linguistics* 42 (2000), 329–65.

Trask, R[ichard] L[arry], *Historical Linguistics* (London: Arnold, 1996).

Trask, R[ichard] L[arry], *History of Basque* (London: Routledge, 1997).

Traugott, Elizabeth Closs, 'On the rise of epistemic meanings in English: an example of subjectification in semantic change', *Language* 65 (1989), 31–55.

Traugott, Elizabeth Closs and Richard B. Dasher, *Regularity in Semantic Change* (Cambridge: Cambridge University Press, 2002).

Traugott, Elizabeth Closs and Bernd Heine, 'Introduction', in Elizabeth Closs Traugott and Bernd Heine (eds), *Approaches to Grammaticalization*, Typological studies in language, 19 (Amsterdam: John Benjamins, 1991), pp. 1–14.

Traugott, Elizabeth Closs and Ekkehard König, 'The semantics-pragmatics of grammaticalization revisited', in Elizabeth Closs Traugott and Bernd Heine (eds), *Approaches to Grammaticalization* (Amsterdam: John Benjamins, 1991), vol. 1, pp. 189–218.

Trudgill, Peter, 'Contact and isolation in linguistic change', in Leiv Egil Breivik and Ernst Håkon Jahr (eds), *Language Change: Contributions to the Study of its Causes* (Berlin: Mouton de Gruyter, 1989), pp. 227–38.

Trudgill, Peter, 'Linguistic and social typology', in J. K. Chambers, Peter Trudgill and Natalie Schilling-Estes (eds), *Handbook of Language Variation and Change* (Oxford: Blackwell, 2002), pp. 707–28.

Trudgill, Peter, 'Linguistic and social typology: Austronesian migrations and phoneme inventories', *Linguistic Typology* 8 (2004a), 305–20.

Trudgill, Peter, 'On the complexity of simplification', *Linguistic Typology* 8 (2004b), 384–8.

Vajda, Edward, *Yeniseian Peoples and Languages: A History of Yeniseian Studies* (London: Curzon, 2001).

Vajda, Edward, 'A Siberian link with Na-Dene languages', in James Kari and Ben A. Potter (eds), *The Dene–Yeniseian Connection*, Anthropological Papers of the University of Alaska, New Series, 5 (1-2), A special joint publication of the UAF (Fairbanks: Department of Anthropology and the Alaska Native Languages Center, 2010), pp. 33–99.

Vansina, J., 'New linguistic evidence and 'the Bantu expansion', *Journal of African History* 36 (1995), 173–95.

Vendryes, Joseph, *Le langage: introduction linguistique à l'histoire* (Paris: La Renaissance du Livre [re-edn 1968]).

Vovin, Alexander, *A Reconstruction of Proto-Ainu* (Leiden: Brill, 1993).

Wakelin, Martyn, *The Archaeology of English* (Totowa, NJ: Barnes & Noble, 1988).

Wang, William, 'Competing sound changes as a cause of residue', *Language* 45 (1969), 9–25.

Watkins, Calvert, 'Etymologies, equations, and comparanda: types and values, and criteria for judgement', in Philip Baldi (ed.), *Linguistic Change and Reconstruction Methodology* (Berlin: Mouton de Gruyter, 1990), pp. 289–303.

Watkins, Calvert, *The American Heritage Dictionary of Indo-European Roots* (Boston, MA: Houghton Mifflin Co., 1985, 2nd edn, 2000).

Watkins, Calvert, 'An Indo-European linguistic area and its characteristics: ancient Anatolia – areal diffusion as a challenge to the comparative method?', in Alexandra Y. Aikhenvald and R. M. W. Dixon (eds), *Areal Diffusion and Genetic Inheritance: Problems in Comparative Linguistics* (Oxford: Oxford University Press, 2001), pp. 44–63.

Weinreich, Uriel, *Languages in Contact: Findings and Problems*, Publications of the Linguistic Circle of New York, 1 (New York, 1953). (9th printing, The Hague: Mouton.)

Weinreich, Uriel, William Labov and Marvin Herzog, 'Empirical foundations for a theory of language change', in Winfred P. Lehmann and Yakov Malkiel (eds), *Directions for Historical Linguistics* (Austin: University of Texas Press, 1968), pp. 95–195.

Wells, John C., *Accents of English*, 3 vols (Cambridge: Cambridge University Press, 1982).

Wessén, Elias, *Språkhistoria I: ljudlära och ordböjningslära* (Stockholm: Almqvist & Wiksell, 1969).

Wichmann, Søren and Eric W. Holman, 'Population size and rates of language change', *Human Biology* 81 (2009), 259–74.

Wichmann, S., Eric W. Holman, André Müller, Viveka Velupillai, Johann-Mattis List, Oleg Belyaev, M. Urban and Dik Bakker, 'Glottochronology as a heuristic for genealogical language relationships', *Journal of Quantitative Linguistics* 17 (2010), 303–16.

Wichmann, Søren, André Müller and Viveka Velupillai, 'Homelands of the world's language families: a quantitative approach', *Diachronica* 27 (2010), 247–76.

Wichmann, Søren and Arpiar Saunders, 'How to use typological databases in historical linguistic research', *Diachronica* 24 (2007), 373–404.

Winteler, J., *Die Kerenzer Mundart des Kantons Glarus in ihren Grundzügen dargestellt* (Leipzig: Winter, 1876).

Winters, Margaret E., 'Jerzy Kuryłowicz: the so-called laws of analogy', *Diachronica* 12 (1995), 113–45.

Wright, Larry, *Teleological Explanation* (Berkeley: University of California Press, 1976).

Wundt, Wilhelm, *Völkerpsychologie. Eine Untersuchung der Entwicklungsgesetze von Sprache, Mythus und Sitte*, vol. 1, *Die Sprache* (Leipzig: W. Engelmann, 1900).

Zeps, Valdis, *Latvian and Finnic Linguistic Convergence*, Uralic and Altaic Series, 9 (Bloomington: Indiana University Press, 1962).

Zvelebil, Kamil V., *Dravidian Linguistics: An Introduction* (Pondicherry: Pondicherry Institute of Linguistics, 1990).

Name Index

Subject Index

accident *see* chance, chance similarities
accommodation (accommodate), 59, 61
acronyms, 240–1
acts of reception, 319
actuation problem, 193, 195
adaptation (adapted), 59, 61
adstratum *see* linguistic area
affix, 101, 242–3, 247, 251, 257–9, 266, 271,
    278, 281, 284, 301–2, 305, 356, 363, 365–6,
    386, 389, 394
affrication, 38
agglutinative, agglutination, 266, 309, 359
Akkadian cuneiform, 374
allomorph, allomorphy, 93, 96–7, 141, 198–200,
    202–4, 206, 214–15, 217–18, 248–50,
    252–3, 256, 260, 267
allomorphic change, 248
allophonic changes *see* non-phonemic changes
alphabet, 6, 8, 374–5, 389–90
alphabetic (scripts, writing), 374, 389–91, 398
amalgamation, 5, 102, 242–3, 397
amelioration *see* elevation
analytic language, 266
analogical extension, 95, 254, 265, 268
analogical levelling, 93–6, 248, 253, 265, 267,
    337
analogical models, 97–9
analogical restoration, 327–8
analogous (trait) *see* homologous
analogy, analogical (change), 5, 33, 64, 91–106,
    144, 195–7, 222, 224, 232, 238, 242–3,
    247–9, 251–4, 257, 262–5, 267, 268, 270,
    272, 285, 290, 292, 322, 327–8, 332, 337,
    397, 400, 405, 472, 484
anaptyxis, 30
Anatolian hieroglyphics, 'Hittite' hieroglyphics,
    374
Anglo-Frisian Futhork, 374; *see also* Futhark;
    runic writing
aphaeresis, 29–30
apocope, 29
apparent-time studies, 194
Appendix Probi, 101, 400–2
archaeology, archaeological, 363, 386, 405–6,

417–18, 422, 424, 427, 432–3, 437, 448,
    458, 464, 490
archaism, 289–92, 470
areal linguistics, xv, 56, 171, 298–9, 306–9, 344
ASJP *see* Automated Dating of the World's
    Language Families
assimilation, 24–26, 35
autapomorphy, autamorphic, 465, 478
automated distance measures, 480
Automated Dating of the World's Language
    Families (ASJP), 462–4, 473, 480, 483,
    489
avoidance of homophony, avoidance of
    pernicious homophony, 231, 330, 332,
    334–5, 472
Aztec script, Aztec writing, 374, 380

back formation, 101–2, 251, 290
Balkans linguistic area, 299–300
Baltic linguistic area, 69, 304
basic vocabulary, 111–12, 341, 348–50, 352–3,
    355, 358–9, 363, 448, 451–7, 469–70, 473,
    475–7, 479, 481, 483–4
Bayesian analysis, Bayesian methods, 472, 477,
    482–4, 491
bilingualism, 56, 60, 342–3
bioprogramme, 314
Black Death, 74, 325
blending, 103, 242–4, 282: blend/s, 103–4, 238,
    242; blended, 105
Boğazköy, 418
borrowing, 5–7, 30, 34, 56–68, 70–2, 74–6, 79,
    81, 88, 91, 94, 101, 104, 111–12, 136, 143,
    184, 188, 195–7, 209–10, 222, 228, 230,
    232, 238, 273, 277–8, 284, 286–8, 292,
    298–9, 306, 309, 313, 316, 324, 338–40,
    342, 344–5, 348–9, 352–3, 358–9, 362–5,
    367, 375, 392, 432–3, 439, 442, 453–6, 459,
    461–3, 466, 468, 470, 478, 482–6, 489
boundary change, 250–3, 256
boundary loss, 250
bound morpheme, 249, 251–3, 256–8, 266,
    270–1, 312, 365
Bounty, 311

Languages, language families, and proposed genetic relationships Index